Proceedings of the
11ᵗʰ European Conference on
Social Media

ECSM 2024

30-31 May 2024

Hosted By

University of Brighton
United Kingdom

Edited by

Dr Panagiotis Fotaris

Review Process
Papers submitted to this conference have been double-blind peer reviewed before final acceptance to the conference. Initially, abstracts were reviewed for relevance and accessibility and successful authors were invited to submit full papers. Many thanks to the reviewers who helped ensure the quality of all the submissions.

Ethics and Publication Malpractice Policy
ACIL adheres to a strict ethics and publication malpractice policy for all publications – details of which can be found here:
http://www.academic-conferences.org/policies/ethics-policy-for-publishing-in-the-conference-proceedings-of-academic-conferences-and-publishing-international-limited/

Self-Archiving and Paper Repositories
We actively encourage authors of papers in ACIL conference proceedings and journals to upload their published papers to university repositories and research bodies such as ResearchGate and Academic.edu. Full reference to the original publication should be provided.

Conference Proceedings
The Conference Proceedings is a book published with an ISBN and ISSN. The proceedings have been submitted to a number of accreditation, citation and indexing bodies including Web of Science and Scopus. Author affiliation details in these proceedings have been reproduced as supplied by the authors themselves.

From 2022 these proceedings are open access and freely available for all to read from https://papers.academic-conferences.org/index.php/ecsm . The Conference Proceedings for previous years can be purchased from http://academic-bookshop.com

The Electronic version of the Conference Proceedings is available to download from https://papers.academic-conferences.org/.

E-Book ISBN: 978-1-917204-01-9
E-Book ISSN: 2055-7221
Book version ISBN: 978-1-917204-00-2
Book Version ISSN: 2055-7213

Published by Academic Conferences International Limited
Reading, UK
www.academic-conferences.org
info@academic-conferences.org

Contents

The papers in these proceedings were presented at the conference in sessions organised by topics but are presented here by type of paper and then alphabetically by lead author surname.

PhD Papers

About the 11th European Conference on Social Media, 2024

The European Conference on Social Media (ECSM) is a well-established academic conference, held annually for over a decade, with a focus on advancing research and dialogue around social media. The primary aim of ECSM is to provide a platform for scholars, researchers, practitioners, and industry professionals to share and discuss their findings on the multifaceted impacts of social media. The conference emphasises the importance of understanding how social media influences various sectors, including society, education, business, and governance.

Aims and Scope

The primary aim of the ECSM is to encourage academic and professional dialogue on the diverse aspects of social media, promoting research that contributes to the better understanding of how social media impacts our lives. The conference seeks to bridge the gap between theory and practice by encouraging contributions that offer both theoretical insights and practical implications. It also provides a collaborative environment where participants can engage in knowledge exchange, interact with peers, and explore emerging trends and issues in social media.

The scope of ECSM is deliberately broad and interdisciplinary, encompassing research that explores the societal implications of social media, its role in communication and community building, and its integration into business and educational practices. Additionally, the conference addresses the analytical and technical aspects of social media, such as data mining, analytics, and the ethical and policy-related challenges that arise from its use. The Proceedings of the 11th European Conference on Social Media 2024 includes academic research papers, PhD research papers, Masters Research papers and work-in-progress papers, which have been presented and discussed at the conference. The proceedings are of an academic level appropriate to a professional research audience, including graduates, postgraduates, doctoral and post-doctoral researchers. All papers have been double-blind peer reviewed by members of the Review Committee.

Topics Covered

The call for papers for the ECSM conference asked for contributions that considered the following topics. In addition the committee welcomed papers on a number of specialist mini-tracks which can be seen at the end of this list.

Social Media and Society:
- how social media affects social behaviour
- cultural dynamics
- community building.

Social Media in Business:
- social media as part of business strategy,
- marketing,
- customer engagement
- brand management.

Educational Uses of Social Media:
- the integration of social media into educational settings,
- the impact of social media on learning, teaching methods, and academic engagement.
- Social media as a research tool.

Social Media Analytics and Data Mining:
- methodologies and tools for analysing social media data
- sentiment analysis

- network analysis
- big data challenges.

Policy and Ethical Issues:
- regulatory, legal, and ethical implications of social media use,
- privacy concerns,
- misinformation
- the digital divide.

Emerging Technologies:
- the intersection between social media and emerging technologies
- artificial intelligence
- virtual reality
- blockchain.

Experts in the field proposed mini tracks on the following topics. Papers accepted on these topics after the double-blind peer review process were presented as mini tracks at the conference and are also published in these proceedings.

- Social Media Challenges and Security
- E-Commerce and Digital Marketing with Social Media

The programme from the 2024 conference can be downloaded from here and full details about the conference can be seen from the conference website:
https://www.academic-conferences.org/conferences/ecsm/

ECSM Preface

These proceedings represent the work of contributors to the 11th European Conference on Social Media (ECSM 2024), hosted by the University of Brighton, UK on 30-31 May 2024. The Conference Chair was Dr Panagiotis Fotaris from the University of Brighton.

ECSM is a well-established event on the academic research calendar and in its 11th year the key aim remains the opportunity for participants from around the world to share ideas and meet the people who hold them. The scope of papers ensured an interesting two days. The broad and multidisciplinary range of subjects covered illustrate the diversity of topics that fall into this important and ever-growing area of research.

The opening keynote presentation was given by Dr Martin De Saulles, Principal Lecturer at The University of Brighton on *Establishing Trust in an AI-driven Economy.* On the second day, Dr Tony Sampson from The University of Essex, gave a talk on the subject: *Return to Virality: Contagion Theory in the Age of Social Media.*

With an initial submission of 138 abstracts, after the double blind, peer review process there are 37 Academic research papers, 7 PhD research papers, 2 Master's Research papers and 2 work-in-progress papers published in these Conference Proceedings. These papers represent research from Canada, China, Colombia, Czech Republic, Finland, Germany, Ghana, Greece, Hungary, India, Iraq, Israel, Japan, Kuwait, Lithuania, New Zealand, Nigeria, Norway, Philippines, Portugal, Romania, Saudi Arabia, Slovak Republic, Slovakia, South Africa, Spain, Sweden, The Netherlands, Türkiye, UAE, UK, USA and Vietnam.

We would like to thank everyone who participated in this conference.

Dr Panagiotis Fotaris
University of Brighton
May 2024

Biographies of Chairs and Keynote Speakers

Conference Chair

Dr Panagiotis Fotaris is Senior Lecturer and Course Leader for the BSc in Digital Games Development and BSc in Computer Science for Games at the University of Brighton, UK. He has previously held posts at the University of East London, University of West London, King's College London, and Abertay University. Before entering academia, he spent a decade in the Creative Industries in a variety of roles including mashup artist, radio producer, DJ, graphic designer, web developer, and music journalist. When not playing adventure games, Panagiotis focuses his research on the pedagogical potential of escape rooms, games, and immersive technology in the context of computing and design education.

Keynote Speakers

Dr Tony D. Sampson is reader in digital communication at the University of Essex. His publications include The Spam Book (Hampton Press, 2009), Virality: Contagion Theory in the Age of Networks (University of Minnesota Press, 2012), The Assemblage Brain: Sense Making in Neuroculture (University of Minnesota Press, 2017) and Affect and Social Media (Rowman and Littlefield, 2018). His latest book, A Sleepwalker's Guide to Social Media, was published by Polity in 2020. He is currently writing a critical theory book on the pervasive influence of UX design principles on contemporary life from cradle to grave. The book is provisionally titled Ubiquitous UX: The Struggle for [USER] Experience. Tony is a co-founder of the Cultural Engine Research Group (CERG) and organizer of the Affect and Social Media conferences in East London.

Dr Martin De Saulles is a Principal Lecturer at the University of Brighton where he teaches and carries out research in the areas of innovation and marketing. Martin has authored research papers and several books on these topics and is currently writing a book on the emerging data-driven AI revolution due for publication at the end of 2024. As well as his academic work, Martin helps B2B technology-based businesses with their marketing strategies.

Mini Track Chairs

Prof. Dr. Abbas Fadhil Aljuboori is Deputy Dean for Scientific Affairs at Alshaab University, Baghdad Iraq. He has a Ph.D. in Computer Science from Dongguk University, South Korea. He was a Fulbright Visiting scholar at the University of Central Oklahoma, Edmond, USA in 2017. His field of Interest are in Data Mining, Web Applications, Big Data, Data Security, Information Systems, Social Media Analysis, and Smart Applications. He is a Member of several of Academic and Professional Societies. He is an Editor-in-Chief, Editorial Board Member and Reviewer of many eminent International Journals and Conferences worldwide.

Dr habil. Maria-Magdalena Popescu is a Full Professor and a doctoral coordinator at Carol I National Defence University in Bucharest, Romania. With a background in humanities and social sciences and extensive teaching and research experience in the realm of security and defence issues, she has also authored/co-authored many research papers and scientific publications. Dr Popescu has given international lectures as a guest at universities in Switzerland, Italy and Belgium.

ECSM Review Committee

ECSM is fortunate to have a significant number of international experts in the field willing to review papers. Care is taken to ensure that a fully double-blind peer review process is followed, and reviewers are not selected if they have any research or organisational connection to the author/s.

TikTok as an Educational Platform: Teenagers' Experiences

Zinaida Adelhardt and Thomas Eberle

Friedrich-Alexander University Erlangen-Nürnberg, Germany

zinaida.adelhardt@fau.de
office@thomaseberle.de

Abstract: TikTok as social media in general has a controversial reputation and its academic potential is not much explored. Nowadays TikTok is extremely popular among teenagers for entertainment purposes and its popularity is constantly growing. The platform's short-length videos are delivering small and easily digestible pieces of information that are potentially suitable for attracting and capturing student attention. They deliver information in a concise manner, which could be useful for various school subjects. The aim of our study is to find out whether teenagers use the platform for education and how they evaluate the platform's academic potential. We asked 34 teenagers (M=15.59, SD=1.76, 59% female), who attend various grammar schools in Germany, about their use of TikTok and their perception of the platform's educational potential. The results show that those teenagers who use TikTok also consume school-relevant content from the platform, such as learning methods, physical explanations, mathematical tricks, astronomy and biology facts. Those who consider the platform helpful for learning highlight two main reasons: the speed and ease of access to information and the brief and easy-to-understand content. However, the teenagers also point out two main problems regarding the use of TikTok for learning: its high level of distraction and the absence of information about sources. Though the majority consider the platform as a purely entertaining medium, 44% of teenagers think that it can be used both for entertainment and education. 29% of teenagers consider TikTok to have a potential to be a supplementary educational medium. Teenagers suggested the following improvements for TikTok to make it more effective as an educational tool: mark credible sources and reliable information, create separate space for learning for instance through filters or special settings, create more reliable educational content, make the platform safer and less distractive. The captivating nature of TikTok is a double-edged sword: it can spark interest in complicated topics, but it also tends to draw attention to irrelevant content. The results and limitations of the study are presented in the article.

Keywords: TikTok use, Academic potential of TikTok, Teenagers' use of social media, Educational platform, Addictive behaviour

1. Introduction

TikTok is one of the most popular social media platforms nowadays. Since its market entry in 2016, TikTok has gained global popularity and, according to Statista (Statista 2024), it had more than 830 million active users worldwide in 2023. The short-form videos that users can create, watch and share on the platform are extremely attractive for the younger generation. According to Business of Apps (Business of Apps), TikTok's worldwide age demographics reveal that 14.4% of platform users are between 13 and 17 years old, while 34.9% are between 18 and 24 years old.

While some users share funny moments and jokes, business companies use the platform to promote their products. But in recent years, TikTok platform has gained attention for its far less obvious content - educational videos. According to Study.com (Study.com), in a survey of 1,000 US-American users, one out of four utilized the platform for educational purposes. Among these users, 69% reported that TikTok videos helped them complete their homework or homework of their kids. They claim, "with TikTok's plethora of accessible, easy-to-understand video content, the platform is becoming a treasure trove of supplemental educational material" (Study.com).

The education potential of social media, both in general and on some specific platforms, has already attracted significant attention from researchers (van den Beemt et al. 2020; Al-Qaysi et al. 2023; Chugh und Ruhi 2018). A systematic review of 713 studies on social media adoption revealed that most studies collected data from students in business disciplines, with Facebook being the primary application used for educational purposes in the majority of studies (Al-Qaysi et al. 2023). Facebook, especially in higher education context, has been extensively studied (Chugh und Ruhi 2018; Davidovitch und Belichenko 2018). Twitter has also been widely researched, with findings highlighting its potential to enhance student's learning capabilities, improve their motivation and engagement (Evans 2014; Feito und Brown 2018; Malik et al. 2019). These studies suggest that social media can positively contribute to teaching and learning processes. However, the educational potential of TikTok's and the acceptance of this platform for educational purposes remain relatively unexplored.

TikTok has gained a controversial reputation and faced restrictions and bans in the whole range of countries due to privacy, cybersecurity concerns, and malicious content (Mashable 01.12.2023). Despite these issues, some teachers were found to use TikTok in classrooms in order to enhance learning experience, and articles discussing the effectiveness of TikTok for educational purposes have appeared (Escamilla-Fajardo et al. 2021; Gao et al. 2023; Fowler et al. 2022). It was argued that creating and delivering learning content using TikTok could benefit pedagogical methodologies based on nano-learning principles – condensing of micro-content into small units (Khlaif und Salha 2021). A study exploring TikTok's impact in a corporal expression course revealed that TikTok can help to create a motivating learning environment for students, enhance their creativity and curiosity (Escamilla-Fajardo et al. 2021). Another study investigated TikTok's efficacy as a video aid for education to improve learning motivation and oral proficiency among learners (Gao et al. 2023). TikTok has also been recognized as a suitable platform for providing easy-to-digest educational information for students, such as in radiology education (Kauffman et al. 2022), and to address gaps and shortcomings in traditional education, such as providing sexual health information to adolescents in the US as part of sex education (Fowler et al. 2022). Authors assessing TikTok's suitability for radiology education argue that it should not be "summarily dismissed as a silly dancing app" and emphasise its potential to reach a substantial audience , especially those on the early stages of medical education (Kauffman et al. 2022). While TikTok's use in higher education has already received some attention, its potential as an educational platform among 13-17 year old adolescents, who constitute a significant portion of its user base (Business of Apps), remains relatively unexplored.

The objective of our study is to determine whether teenagers use the platform for educational purposes and to assess how they perceive the educational potential of TikTok. We focus on 14–16-year-old teenagers in Gemany. In 2022, TikTok's penetration rate in this country was already 33.6% of Internet users (Statista 2023a). Moreover, the majority of TikTok users in Germany were found among 14-19 year old adolescents, with almost 56% stating that they used the platform (Statista 2023b).

2. Methodology

For this study, we made a survey with 34 teenagers who applied for the adventure education programme "Classroom under Sails" (M=15.59, SD=1.76, 59% female). The participants came from eight out of sixteen regions of Germany. We asked teenagers about their social media use at the end of September 2023 (before the program). Data were collected through the online survey platform SoSci Survey, and teenagers had ten days to respond to our questions at their convenience. We asked teenagers several general closed questions on their TikTok use (e.g., "How often do you use TikTok?" with answer options from "never used" to "several times per hour") and six open questions regarding teenagers' attitudes towards TikTok's use for education (for more details, refer to the results section). The collected data showed no missing values, as all teenagers provided answers to our questions. Responses to open-ended questions varied in lengths from one to eighty words.

3. Results

In our sample, 21% of teenagers (four boys and three girls) reported using TikTok. 11.8% (two boys and two girls) reported using it multiple times a day.

Our questions and teenagers' answers are presented in Table 1. According to teenagers' responses, 9% of all teenagers apply it to learn a new subject that was not enough covered in school. 12% of all teenagers agreed that TikTok has helped them tounderstand better certain content, concepts, or subjects, and one girl has already used TikTok to do her homework.

15% of all teenagers reported that they spoke to a teacher about the educational content on TikTok, and 32% talked to other students about the educational content on the platform. One girl reported that a teacher used or recommended educational content on TikTok.

Table 1: Teenagers answer about their use of TikTok

Topics	Questions	N of positive answers among teenagers	...girls	...boys
TikTok education	Have you ever used TikTok to learn a new subject that was not enough covered in school?	9%	10%	7%
	Have you ever used TikTok to do homework?	3%	5%	0
	Do you think TikTok has helped you to better understand certain content, concepts or subjects?	12%	15%	7%
TikTok	Have you ever spoken to a teacher about the	15%	20%	7%

Topics	Questions	N of positive answers among teenagers	...girls	...boys
exchange	educational content on TikTok?			
	Has a teacher ever used or recommended educational content on TikTok?	3%	5%	0
	Have you ever talked to other students about the educational content on TikTok?	32%	40%	21%

We asked teenagers six open-ended questions regarding their use of TikTok and their perceptions of TikTok as an educational platform. The teenagers' answers are presented below.

3.1 What Educational Content or Learning Videos Have you Seen on TikTok?

The results indicate that teenagers who use TikTok also consume school-relevant content from the platform: learning methods, physical explanations, mathematical tricks, legal topics, astronomy and biology facts, and financial tips. As one girl reported: "I once read a book about astronomy/physics. Later, I discovered that the author also creates TikTok content. I find his videos enlightening". Several teenagers mentioned using TikTok for learning tips, such as drama analysis.

Teenagers also use TikTok for obtaining qualitative news information. One girl wrote: "I found some math explanation videos on TikTok very helpful. Additionally, I enjoy watching TikToks from "Funk" or "Tagesschau"". Funk is a German video-on-demand service operated by the public broadcasters ARD and ZDF and targeting people between the age of 14 and 29 (Funk.net 2024). Funk produces over 70 programs for social media platforms, including TikTok, Snapchat, YouTube, etc., focusing on information and entertainment. "Tagesschau" is a the oldest and most watched news service in Germany, a part of the public-service TV network ARD (Tagesschau.de 2023).

3.2 How do you Find TikTok Helpful for Your Learning?

Here, 47% of teenagers consider TikTok platform to be unsuitable for learning, 29% are unsure as they do not know the platform well enough, 12% find it "partly helpful", and 12% consider it helpful. Among users, more than half find it helpful.

Teenagers who consider TikTok helpful highlight two main reasons. The first is the *speed and ease of access* to information: "Very <important> because one quickly receives the important information". The second is the *brief and easy-to-understand content:* "I find that it is helpful for fundamentals", "Short explanation videos that summarize the content very briefly and comprehensibly", "I find TikTok partially helpful since videos on educational topics provide assistance and are summarized briefly".

Those teenagers who are sceptical about TikTok's potential point out two main shortcomings. The first one is its *distraction potential:* „When you open it, you end up watching just one more video, and in the end, you've learned almost nothing", "There is a significant distraction factor on TikTok", "TikTok also displays many purely entertaining videos". The distraction factor is also the main reason why some teenagers avoid using the platform: "I don't have TikTok, but I believe that TikTok is not the right platform for learning because one easily gets distracted", "I don't have TikTok. Not helpful – it just creates addiction". The reputation of TikTok as an addictive platform stops some teenagers from using it, although one boy mentioned that he, to the contrary, finds TikTok helpful for improving his concentration abilities.

Another point of criticism is the *absence of proper sources*: "I find TikTok to be not very helpful for learning, as it does provide a vast source of information, but often lacks proper sources".

3.3 Do you think TikTok is to be Taken Seriously as a Platform for Knowledge Exchange and Educational Content, or do you Perceive it More as a Purely Entertainment Medium?

Teenagers, both users and non-users, have a clear vision on this topic: here, the majority (47%) think that TikTok is a pure entertainment medium, whereas 44% think that it can be used both for entertainment and education. Interestingly, the proportion is similar between users and non-users. Only two teenagers (non-users) answered that they are uncertain as they do not use TikTok.

Here, teenagers again point out the deficits of the platform. The main obstacle is the platform's *goal to capture users' attention for a long period of time.* As one girl, a regular TikTok user, puts it: "I think that theoretically, it could also be used as an educational platform. However, I believe that the concept of TikTok is not necessarily well-suited for that, as the app is designed for users to spend as much time as possible, and I think it's easy to get distracted". There is a skepsis about the platform goals: "I don't see TikTok as an educational platform! TikTok provides everyone a space to share their knowledge, but ultimately, TikTok is about money and how much time you spend on the app, not about what you learn during that time." There is a clear vision that a boy, who uses TikTok multiple times a week, describes: "I believe TikTok has potential, as short videos are a great way to engage students and deliver content. However, the algorithm would need to prioritize less entertainment-focused videos for this purpose". A non-user girl explains it like this: "I see it more as a pure entertainment medium. However, if changes were made, such as only receiving educational videos on a specific topic when in learning mode, I would find it beneficial."

Another important point, already mentioned in the previous section, is *the transparency of the sources of information*. The *reputation and trustworthiness of information producers* are especially important: "It depends on whether the people whose videos you watch are reputable and trustworthy", „It depends on individual accounts. There are reputable information channels on TikTok, but there are also trolls, conspiracy theorists, and people spreading (populistic) misinformation. I believe the second group prevails because it's favoured by the algorithm", "I consider educational content on TikTok to be less credible because for most individuals, the main focus is on gaining reach and many views. You often get more clicks by addressing an interesting topic, even if it involves spreading false information".

Another problem is the *absence of control over the accuracy of information*: "There is no control over the accuracy of the information, and there's a tendency to simply accept it as "true."'"; "One should double-check all information to ensure its accuracy". One boy summarizes: "Short video platforms are to be taken seriously as they provide access to knowledge for many people who might not seek information through traditional media. However, there are also many misinformation, sometimes malicious or just for fun, that one may not easily distinguish from genuine news".

3.4 How do you Assess the Credibility and Accuracy of Educational Content on Tiktok Compared to Traditional Educational Sources?

Here, 62% of teenagers consider TikTok videos less credible than traditional educational sources, and 15% do not have a specific opinion on this topic. Teenagers report: "I think that a lot of fake news is spread on TikTok <..> I believe this is not the case with traditional educational sources, as they provide references, and the information is typically reviewed before publication". They note, "many things are simply asserted, so one cannot easily believe it. In traditional educational sources, sources are usually provided, and the content is officially reviewed before publication. They are credible". Additionally, „TikTok lacks an efficient control mechanism against fake news, hate, and populism. Publishers, newspapers, and broadcasters have such mechanisms, which usually work efficiently."

At the same time, 24% of teenagers provide a differentiated picture, where the trustworthiness of TikTok videos depends on two main factors. The first one is *the source and author of information*: "I find it very credible with channels like Tagesschau, but with unknown channels, not so much". Another user notes, "Individual users provide sources in their videos, which can be relatively easily checked, making the users more trustworthy". The second factor is *the content type and addressed topic*: "I find educational videos mostly trustworthy; people have no reason to spread misinformation about math equations."

3.5 What improvements or Features Would you Wish for Tiktok to Make it More Effective as an Educational Tool?

Two thirds of teenagers clearly expressed their wishes and explained how they would like the platform to be. Only one-third of teenagers (34%) reported having no clear opinion on this topic, and one user expressed the opinion that TikTok should not become an educational platform.

Teenagers suggested the following improvements for TikTok to make it more effective as an educational tool (several teenagers mentioned more than one topic in their answers):

- Mark credible sources and reliable information (24%): "become more credible", "more credible sources"; "There should be more transparency regarding used sources, for instance, by providing the option to view the sources used in a video", "highlighting particularly helpful and credible videos/channels", "I would fundamentally redesign TikTok so that only qualified individuals can share their knowledge". Teenagers also suggest possible information labelling: "a kind of quality control, conceptually similar to a blue checkmark on Twitter/X"; "authentication for reputable channels",

"...that there's somehow a distinction, marking what is genuinely academic and meant for learning, and what is not".

- Create separated spaces for learning for instance through filters and/or learning settings (21%): "A space for school-related things and a space for leisure"; "To be able to filter specifically for learning content"; "A setting to hide entertainment videos and only display videos with educational content"; "I would wish for the ability to set it to only see educational videos on a specifically chosen topic"; "An additional learning setting that, with a code, blocks all other videos", "One should be able to filter reels on specific topics like education to consume genuinely informative content", "Optional deactivation of the algorithm to avoid getting stuck in one's own filter bubble during research".
- Create more educational content (18%): "more topics and knowledge", "educational videos", "permitting longer videos", "More serious videos, it's always very provocative", "avoiding censorship and discrimination against topics they might disagree with, such as queer issues".
- Make the platform safer (15%): "addressing hate, misinformation, and populism", "make it safer", "more consistent action against misinformation", "<create> a better system to detect fake news", "the company should take stronger measures against misinformation".
- Make the platform less distractive (12%) "less distraction"; "implementing a limit to endless scrolling", "make it less addictive".

3.6 Do you Think TikTok has the Potential as a Supplementary Educational Medium? In What Ways?

The majority of teenagers (59%) answer "no" and "not in its current form" because of *distraction, harmful content* and *the power of algorithms*. As one male user summarises it: "I think TikTok has less potential, as it primarily serves for entertainment for most people and also contains potentially harmful content. The operators would need to make efforts to shift from entertainment to educational videos; otherwise, TikTok has no potential as an educational medium". "I believe that the concept of TikTok is not necessarily well-suited for it, as the app is designed for users to spend as much time as possible, and I think it's easy to get easily distracted." A female non-user: "The idea of short videos with a concise opinion is good, but not when the algorithm only suggests opinions tailored to an individual". Another female non-users also considers TikTok not suitable as an educational medium, but they point out: "I would find a platform similar to TikTok good, but one where only verified educational content is provided"; "Perhaps not TikTok specifically, as it tends to focus more on entertainment. However, digital media, in general, has a chance, as many students find it more engaging and interesting to work with, making them more motivated to learn compared to traditional educational media."

Whereas 12% do not have a special opinion, 29% consider TikTok to have a potential to be a supplementary educational medium: "I believe TikTok has potential, as short videos are a great way to reach students and convey content to them", "as general basics for ideas and initial information, it would be very helpful. However, one should also learn from school or oneself how to handle it"; "I think one could orient oneself towards TikTok in terms of the shortness of the videos. This way, one could make education more interesting for teenagers through very short videos", "Yes, if the information comes from reputable individuals who consistently post the truth".

4. Discussion

In our study, 21% of teenagers reported using TikTok, which aligns with findings from a representative German-wide study indicating that 28% of girls and 22% of boys aged 12 to 19 in Germany stated using the platform in 2023 (Feierabend et al. 2023). One of eight teenagers agreed that TikTok has helped them better understand certain content, concepts, or subjects, with one girl even using TikTok for her homework. One out of three teenagers talked to other students about the educational content on the platform. Teenagers reported consuming school-relevant content from the platform including learning methods, physical explanations, mathematical tricks, legal topics, astronomy and biology facts, and financial tips. It is noteworthy that 9% of all teenagers in our sample, though they reported not using TikTok, mentioned utilizing TikTok videos for learning purposes, such as accessing new methods and physic-related information. One non-user girl also noted that TikTok is used during lessons at her school to initiate discussions. This suggests that some teenagers engage with the platform content without creating profiles; they report being non-users but still watch TikTok videos. This fact could contribute to clarifying the penetration rate discrepancy, as Statista reported 56% of 14 and 19-year-old TikTok users (Statista 2023b).

In our study, 47% of teenagers perceive the TikTok platform unsuitable for learning, while 24% find it either "partly helpful" or "helpful" for learning purposes. Similarly, 47% view TikTok solely as a medium for entertainment, while 44% believe it can serve both entertainment and education purposes. Interestingly, this proportion remains consistent between users and non-users.

Those who consider the platform as beneficial for learning emphasize two main reasons: *the speed and ease of accessing information*, and the *brief and easy-to-understand content*. Short, engaging, and entertaining videos, along with the opportunity to be creative and the sense of community they foster, are the main ingredients driving the platform's strong appeal among younger audiences. TikTok is regarded as "the mirrow of a generation" (Cervi 2021), and "a valuable window into youth experience and cultural production" (Stahl und Literat 2023). The platform's easily understandable and digestible pierces of information have the potential to serve as a powerful learning tool, utilizing its high appeal for educational purposes.

However, teenagers highlight two primary concerns regarding the use of TikTok for learning: its *high potential for distraction* and the *lack of transparency concerning the credibility of sources*. The platform's primary monetary-driven *goal to capture users' attention for as long as possible* poses a major obstacle to effective learning. This distraction potential and the platform's reputation as an addictive medium, driven by powerful algorithms designed to maximize engagement, is a key reason why some teenagers opt to avoid using it.

The second issue concerns the *accuracy of content* and *the lack of source transparency*. It is uncertain whether specific TikTok videos provide reliable information or are misleading. While 62% of teenagers perceive TikTok videos as less credible than traditional educational sources, 24% take a differentiated approach and assess the trustworthiness of TikTok content based on two key factors: *the credibility of the source,* and *the nature of the topic being addressed*. Here, they find mathematical equations less susceptible to misinformation. The credibility of the source is extremely important, as the majority of content on the platform is user-generated, with only a small part produced by private or public entities, such as Funk in Germany, or marketing companies promoting their products. Researchers examining sexual education videos on TikTok note that not all videos provide factual information, they highlight that the platform does not "regulate or oversee the content or provide disclaimers about misinformation or unverified claims" beyond moderating explicit inappropriate content (Fowler et al. 2022). This issue extends beyond sexual education, and is important to all educational content on the platform. There should be a possibility to meet teenagers' informational and educational needs in a safer way. Though specialists try to counteract misinformation, "the ever-growing quantity of content available on TikTok makes responding to all misinformation impractical, and there is no guarantee a user will ever encounter these corrective videos." (Fowler et al. 2022).

The majority of teenagers, both users and non-users, have a clear vision on how they would like TikTok to change to be more suitable for their educational needs. In enhance platform's suitability for learning, several changes could be implemented to make TikTok more effective as an educational tool: marking credible sources and reliable information to ensure transparency and trustworthiness, creating separate learning spaces or introducing filters to facilitate learning environment, increasing the availability of educational content suiting to diverse learning needs, improving platform safety measures and reducing distractions to create a suitable learning environment. In its current state, 29% of teenagers recognize TikTok's potential as a supplementary educational medium, while the majority (59%) view it as unsuitable due to above mentioned limitations. By addressing these concerns and implementing suggested improvements, TikTok could potentially evolve into a more effective educational medium.

5. Conclusions and Limitations

Our study revealed that teenagers who use TikTok also consume school-relevant content from the platform. Those who consider the platform helpful for learning highlight two key reasons: the speed and ease of access to information and the brief and easy-to-understand content. However, the teenagers also point out two main problems regarding the use of TikTok for learning: its high level of distraction and the lack of transparency of sources. Though the majority consider the platform as a purely entertaining medium, 44% of teenagers think that it can be used both for entertainment and education. However, as in its current form only 29% of teenagers consider TikTok having a potential to be a supplementary educational tool. In order to make TikTok more suitable for learning, the following improvements are suggested: mark credible sources and reliable information, create separate space for learning for instance through filters or special settings, increase the availability of reliable educational content, improve platform safety measures and reduce distractions to create a suitable learning environment.

Our study has some limitations. The sample size of 34 teenagers, comprising both users and non-users, is relatively small. A study with more representative sample would be beneficial to provide insights to teenagers' actual use of TikTok for education purposes. Additionally, our assessment relied on self-reported data from teenagers, which may not fully reflect their actual usage patterns.

Our research highlights TikTok's considerable potential as an engaging educational tool for teenagers. However, it faces two primary challenges. The first one lies in balancing educational content with entertaining distractions. The algorithms driving user engagement often lead teenagers to stray from their intended focus, deterring some from using the platform for learning purposes. The second challenge involves ensuring the credibility of content and sources. The solution could be the development of a separate service or space on TikTok offering short, informative videos with entertaining elements, specially tailored for educational purposes. This service could be than utilized in schools without concern that students will drift off-topic, and meet teachers' worries about being perceived as too progressive or too careless. It could also serve as a valuable resource for teachers to explain teenagers complex topics and wake up their interest, both in classroom and at home. Additionally, such a service could address parents' concerns about possible media addiction by providing secure educational space. Another possibility is implementing easy-to-use filters designed to filter educational content for students, although the effectiveness and feasibility of such filtering mechanisms and possible labelling would require profound assessment.

References

Al-Qaysi, Noor; Granić, Andrina; Al-Emran, Mostafa; Ramayah, T.; Garces, Edwin; Daim, Tugrul U. (2023): Social media adoption in education: A systematic review of disciplines, applications, and influential factors. In: *Technology in Society* 73, S. 102249. DOI: 10.1016/j.techsoc.2023.102249.

Anumanthan, Shevany; Hashim, Harwati (2022): Improving the Learning of Regular Verbs through TikTok among Primary School ESL Pupils. In: *CE* 13 (03), S. 896–912. DOI: 10.4236/ce.2022.133059.

Business of Apps: TikTok Revenue and Usage Statistics (Jan 2024 Update). Online verfügbar unter https://www.businessofapps.com/data/tik-tok-statistics/, zuletzt geprüft am 31.01.2024.

Cervi, Laura (2021): Tik Tok and generation Z. In: *Theatre, Dance and Performance Training* 12 (2), S. 198–204. DOI: 10.1080/19443927.2021.1915617.

Chugh, Ritesh; Ruhi, Umar (2018): Social media in higher education: A literature review of Facebook. In: *Educ Inf Technol* 23 (2), S. 605–616. DOI: 10.1007/s10639-017-9621-2.

Comp, Geoffrey; Dyer, Sean; Gottlieb, Michael (2021): Is TikTok The Next Social Media Frontier for Medicine? In: *AEM education and training* 5 (3). DOI: 10.1002/aet2.10532.

Davidovitch, Nitza; Belichenko, Margarita (2018): Using Facebook in Higher Education: Exploring Effects on Social Climate, Achievements, and Satisfaction. In: *IJHE* 7 (1), S. 51. DOI: 10.5430/ijhe.v7n1p51.

Eghtesadi, Marzieh; Florea, Adrian (2020): Facebook, Instagram, Reddit and TikTok: a proposal for health authorities to integrate popular social media platforms in contingency planning amid a global pandemic outbreak. In: *Canadian journal of public health = Revue canadienne de sante publique* 111 (3), S. 389–391. DOI: 10.17269/s41997-020-00343-0.

Escamilla-Fajardo, Paloma; Alguacil, Mario; López-Carril, Samuel (2021): Incorporating TikTok in higher education: Pedagogical perspectives from a corporal expression sport sciences course. In: *Journal of Hospitality, Leisure, Sport & Tourism Education* 28, S. 100302. DOI: 10.1016/j.jhlste.2021.100302.

Evans, Chris (2014): Twitter for teaching: Can social media be used to enhance the process of learning? In: *Brit J Educational Tech* 45 (5), S. 902–915. DOI: 10.1111/bjet.12099.

Feierabend, S.; Rathgeb, T.; Kheredmand, H.; Glöckler, S. (2023): JIM-Studie 2023: Jugend, Information, Medien. Basisuntersuchung zum Medienumgang 12- bis 19-Jähriger. Medienpädagogischer Forschungsverbund Südwest (mpfs). Stuttgart. Online verfügbar unter https://www.mpfs.de/fileadmin/files/Studien/JIM/2022/JIM_2023_web_final_kor.pdf, zuletzt geprüft am 06.02.2024.

Feito, Yuri; Brown, Chris (2018): A practical approach to incorporating Twitter in a college course. In: *Advances in physiology education* 42 (1), S. 152–158. DOI: 10.1152/advan.00166.2017.

Fowler, Leah R.; Schoen, Lauren; Smith, Hadley Stevens; Morain, Stephanie R. (2022): Sex Education on TikTok: A Content Analysis of Themes. In: *Health promotion practice* 23 (5), S. 739–742. DOI: 10.1177/15248399211031536.

Funk.net (2024): Das ist Funk. We are Funk. Online verfügbar unter https://presse.funk.net/das-ist-funk/, zuletzt geprüft am 06.02.2024.

Gao, Sun-Yu; Tsai, Yi-Ying; Huang, Jian-Hao; Ma, Yan-Xia; Wu, Tai-liang (2023): TikTok for developing learning motivation and oral proficiency in MICE learners. In: *Journal of Hospitality, Leisure, Sport & Tourism Education* 32, S. 100415. DOI: 10.1016/j.jhlste.2022.100415.

Kauffman, Lilly; Weisberg, Edmund M.; Fishman, Elliot K. (2022): TikTok for Radiology Education: Is Now the Right Time? In: *Current problems in diagnostic radiology* 51 (6), S. 826–828. DOI: 10.1067/j.cpradiol.2022.06.001.

Kaye, D. Bondy Valdovinos; Zeng, Jing; Wikström, Patrik (2022): TikTok. Creativity and culture in short video. Cambridge, Medford: Polity (Digital media and society series).

Khlaif, Z. N.; Salha, S. (2021): Using TikTok in Education: A Form of Micro-learning or Nano-learning? In: *Interdisciplinary Journal of Virtual Learning in Medical Sciences* (12 (3)), S. 213–218. Online verfügbar unter https://ijvlms.sums.ac.ir/article_47678_c8873a984de4d9c3596440743c0abcdb.pdf.

Malik, Aqdas; Heyman-Schrum, Cassandra; Johri, Aditya (2019): Use of Twitter across educational settings: a review of the literature. In: *Int J Educ Technol High Educ* 16 (1). DOI: 10.1186/s41239-019-0166-x.

Mashable (01.12.2023): Which countries have banned TikTok? A growing list of nations and government bodies are taking action against the app. Online verfügbar unter https://mashable.com/article/tiktok-ban-countries.

Stahl, Catherine Cheng; Literat, Ioana (2023): #GenZ on TikTok: the collective online self-Portrait of the social media generation. In: *Journal of Youth Studies* 26 (7), S. 925–946. DOI: 10.1080/13676261.2022.2053671.

Statista (2023a): Ranking der beliebtesten Social Networks und Messenger nach dem Anteil der Nutzer an den Internetnutzern in Deutschland im Jahr 2022. Februar 2023. Online verfügbar unter https://de.statista.com/statistik/daten/studie/505947/umfrage/reichweite-von-social-networks-in-deutschland/.

Statista (2023b): TikTok users in Germany in 2022, by age group. Febraury 2023. Online verfügbar unter https://www.statista.com/statistics/1337425/tiktok-users-age-group-germany/.

Statista (2024): Number of TikTok users worldwide from 2020 to 2025. Online verfügbar unter https://www.statista.com/statistics/1327116/number-of-global-tiktok-users/, zuletzt geprüft am 31.01.2024.

Study.com: Teaching with TikTok. Study.com. Online verfügbar unter https://study.com/resources/teaching-with-tiktok.html, zuletzt geprüft am 31.01.2024.

Tagesschau.de (2023): About us/ Häufige Fragen zur tagesschau. Online verfügbar unter https://www.tagesschau.de/ueber-uns, zuletzt geprüft am 06.02.2024.

van den Beemt, Antoine; Thurlings, Marieke; Willems, Myrthe (2020): Towards an understanding of social media use in the classroom: a literature review. In: *Technology, Pedagogy and Education* 29 (1), S. 35–55. DOI: 10.1080/1475939X.2019.1695657.

Vaterlaus, J. Mitchell; Winter, Madison (2021): TikTok: an exploratory study of young adults' uses and gratifications. In: *The Social Science Journal*, S. 1–20. DOI: 10.1080/03623319.2021.1969882.

On Presenters and Commenters in YouTube Climate Change Videos

Vered Aharonson[1,2] and Jared Joselowitz[1,3]

[1]School of Electrical and Information Engineering, University of the Witwatersrand, Johannesburg, South Africa

[2]School of Sciences, University of Central Lancashire, Pyla, Cyprus

[3]Department of Electrical and Electronic Engineering, Imperial College, London, UK

Vered.aharonson@wits.ac.za

jared.joselowitz23@imperial.ac.uk

Abstract: Social media videos can promote viewers responsibility to solve social problems such as climate change. Not all aspiring videos, however, are successful in persuading their viewers on the perils involved in climate change and on the need for pro-environmental behaviour. Our study examined attributes that could explain a video's persuasiveness and focused on the video presenter traits. Videos on climate change were sourced from YouTube conjointly with the comments they elicited. The presenters in these videos addressed the negative effects and dangers of climate change and the role of human activity in resolving them. Two attributes were manually coded for each video: the type of presenter in the videos– scientist, politician or celebrity, and their presentation style: blaming, stating the problem, or suggesting a solution. A measure of persuasiveness was computed from the YouTubers comments using sentiment analysis. This computation provided a polarity label – positive, negative, or neutral, for all comments, for each video. Subsets of 50 comments per video were manually coded to validate the computational analysis. The findings indicated that a predominant number of positive-polarity comments was elicited by video presenters who were scientists. Videos that proposed potential solutions to climate change elicited a majority of positive polarity. Politicians and celebrity presenters, as well as blame-oriented videos elicited a larger number of negative-polarity comments. These initial findings imply a potential of sentiment analysis of comments to elucidate which attributes can increase a video's persuasiveness on its viewers. This insight can improve future video production and enhance their influence.

Keywords: Netnography, Persuasiveness, YouTube videos, Climate change, Text analytics

1. Introduction

Social media are often harnessed to promote responsible conduct in support of global social initiatives. As focal point where communities access and interact with information, social media platforms have the potential to nurture behavioural changes on a large scale (Park et al., 2014). By the same token these platforms could be used to study and assess the persuasiveness of the information provided on large populations through social network analysis (SNA). These methods can provide online data and deeper insights into consumers' opinions, motives, and concerns, while facilitating an ethical access to social media community members (Fenton and Procter, 2019). The original use of these methods for marketing purposing was sparsely extended to the promotion of social causes and human betterment (Kanter and Fine, 2010).

Netnography is an SNA method that adapts ethnography to the study of online communities (Kozinets, 2017). In a preliminary study, we employed netnography to evaluate the engagement of social media users with online information on safe behaviour during the COVID-19 pandemic (Aharonson et al., 2022). A set of Youtube video interviews that adressed this topic were evaluated in terms of persuasiveness. Netnography was employed to computationally construct a persuasiveness index from the YouTubers "like" and "dislike" counts. Hypothesising that the persuasiveness is substantially governed by the vocal traits of the presenter (Aharonson et al. 2021), the study focused on acoustic attributes in the speakers' voice, and implied that cepstral attributes can predict the netnographic persuasiveness (Aharonson et al., 2022).

This feasibility study had, however, three limitations. First, although the persuasiveness measure of like-to-dislike ratio was shown to provide quantitative metrics for the interactions that viewers and users have with video content (Broekens and Brinkman, 2009, Sui et al. 2022), it does not consider the textual content of the comment. Moreover, practically, since YouTube how hides the number of dislikes for its videos, this measure cannot be readily applied. The second limitation was the focus on acoustic properties, while organic component of the presenters' speech such as textual attributes can further explain the persuasiveness measure. The identity and role of the presenting person, i.e. politician or scientist, may correspondingly have fundamental impact on the community reaction (Malecki et al., 2021). Lastly, the previous study focused on a South African news network YouTube channel and its YouTubers' reactions.

The present study extends the former one to address the three limitations. The analysis extended the persuasiveness index beyond the community's reactions of "likes" and "dislikes". Natural language understanding methods were employed to extract textual attributes from comments written by the viewers for the persuasiveness index. The study of the presenters' delivery attributes was extended by comparing persuasiveness across three types of presenters, and three types of information delivery styles. Lastly, the videos in the present study were sourced from the global YouTube channel and the netnographic analysis performed on an international community.

Due to an augmented public interest, the present study reverts the analysis to another pertinent global issue – climate change. Social media videos and their communities' reactions on this topic are prolific and long standing. Fundamentally, this topic resembles the COVID-19 one by being universal, and spreading out beyond specific social groups and nations. Both topics entail controversy and elements of fear and blame, as social media users cannot ascertain the scientific information provided by the presenters. Still, in both cases there is a consensus that simple behavioural changes, can potentially do good and make a difference. Video presenters thus need to employ their presentation skills and persuade the viewers of the need for and importance of behaviour change. Systematic SNA can facilitate and improve these presentation skills.

2. Methods

2.1 Dataset Collection

The dataset included YouTube videos, from which presenters' attributes were extracted, and the comments posted under the videos, that served to compute a netnographic community reaction. A list of 200 videos returned when using the keyword "climate change" in YouTube's search engine were sourced. The viewers' comments of each video were scraped using an open-source Python script. The list of 200 videos was sorted by the video number of views using the platform's sorting tool. The database videos were selected from this list based on two criteria: The video had to have at least 200 comments/replies, and at least 90% of the video's comments were in English. A manual selection process was employed to apply an additional criterion – controversial and anti-environmental behavior videos were discarded.

The 150 most popular comments of each video were selected for the dataset. The popularity selection criteria was based on YouTube's "Top comments" sorting function, which considered likes/dislikes, the date the comment was posted, and the number of replies that the particular comment received (Feng and Chen, 2022). Each comment's text data was tagged by the video it was posted under. Data privacy was considered in discarding the identity of the video publisher and personal details of the comment writers from the analysis.

2.2 Videos Attributes Selection

Two presenters' attributes were chosen for the analysis and were manually coded: the role of the presenter and the presentation style. Three categories of presenters were observed in the videos and were manually coded: politicians, high-profile public figure ('celebrities') such as business leaders, artists or social media personalities, and scientists. Similarly, three categories of presentation styles were coded: Videos explicitly blaming an entity, such as political party or country, in the problem, videos suggesting solutions to the problem, and videos stating the effects of climate change.

2.3 Comments Text Analysis

Sentiment analysis was employed on the comments' text using Python's TextBlob package (Loria, 2018). Negative, neutral, or positive sentiment labels were computed for each comment, based on a list of positive and negative words and their semantic orientation. The automated analysis was validated by a human manual coding of 50 randomly chosen comments for each video. A comment was coded as "positive" if its content was in agreement with the negative effects and dangers of climate change and/or expressed the need to change human behaviour. A comment was coded as "negative" if it disagreed with climate change or its effects and/or the need to change human behaviour. A "neutral" label was assigned to comments which did not address the topic of climate change, or did not express neither a positive nor negative stance on the on whether climate change is real and/or on the need to change human behaviour. The congruence between the computerized polarity and the manually coded one was evaluated using Cohen's kappa.

2.4 Video Persuasiveness Labelling

The sentiments polarity extracted from the comments served as proxy for the construction of a persuasiveness label for each video. A video was labeled persuasive if the majority count of its comments were positive, and non-persuasive otherwise. The labels resulted from the manual coding and those computed using sentiment analysis were then compared using Cohen's kappa.

The relations between the video presenters' attributes and their persuasiveness labels were computed using the frequency of each attribute among the two video-label classes – persuasive or non-persuasive.

3. Results

The video selection yielded a dataset of 129 videos.

Cohen's kappa for the agreement between the automated and manual rating of polarity in individual comments was 0.63. The labels of persuasive and non-persuasive videos based on the majority count of positive and negative polarity of their comments, yielded an agreement of 0.78. Sixty-five videos had a majority count of positive-polarity comments and 57 had a majority count of negative-polarity comments. Seven videos had equal quantity of positive and negative polarities, or a majority count of neutral polarity and were omitted from the analysis.

The presenter-attributes frequencies among the persuasive and non-persuasive videos are portrayed in figures 1 and 2, for the presenter role and presenter text style, respectively.

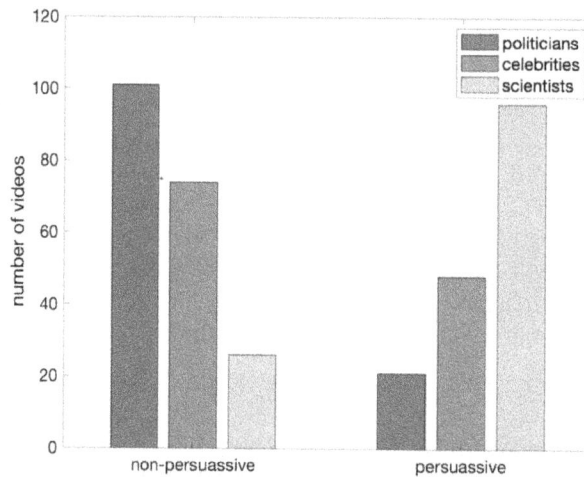

Figure 1: Frequencies of the presenter types in persuasive and non-persuasive videos

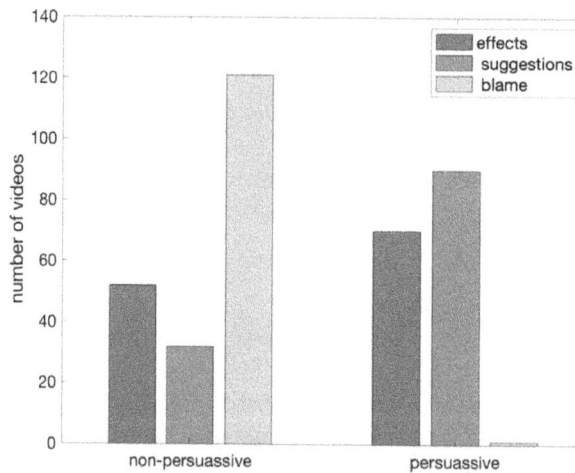

Figure 2: Frequencies of the narrative style types in persuasive and non-persuasive videos

4. Discussion and Conclusions

This study provides a proof of concept for the identification of persuasive and non-persuasive videos on climate change, based on two of their presenters' attributes. Extensive previous research applied social media analysis to extract presenters' attributes in the context of marketing. Our studies follow a growing trend and strive to harness this analysis for promoting responsible behaviour in pertinent global challenges. Whereas most studies involved human participants, and employ either qualitative analysis, or manual coding schemes (Fenton and Procter, 2019), our studies aim to automate this analysis and enable a quantitative view of the entire social media communities' reactions, which could both expedite and improve the analysis. The present study follows our previous ones in elucidating computational measures of persuasiveness based on YouTubers' comments on videos, and the attributes of the videos that contribute to this persuasiveness. The comments polarity, extracted through automated sentiment analysis, yielded a kappa reliability coefficient of 0.63 to the human rating of this polarity. This may result from the fact that the manual coding entailed inference of attitudes from the text, which the preliminary sentiment analysis did not consider. A more comprehensive textual analysis of the individual comments can be applied to test this hypothesis. On the other hand, the persuasiveness label of the *videos*, based on a majority of positive sentiments amongst its comments, yielded a larger agreement of 0.78 between automated and manual coding. This may be explained by the summative nature of this label that overcomes the inner, per-comment, rating disagreement and reflected the overall reaction of the video's viewers' community.

Our preliminary analysis indicate that scientists are more persuasive presenters, and that politicians or other high-profile public figures ("celebrities") are the least persuasive presenters in climate change videos. This implies that viewers may trust scientists more than politicians or celebrities and that scientists are most persuasive presenters in eliciting discussions for taking actions to deal with the climate change problem. This finding is in line with literature showing that scientists are perceived as more trustworthy compared to politicians (Hendriks et al., 2022; Reif et al., 2020, Jin et. al, 2020). The analysis of the video content attribute indicates that videos containing direct blame and quoting the fault in political party, groups or nations, are not persuasive. Videos that contain suggestions and possible solutions to combat climate change were found as more persuasive than videos that only state the effects of climate change rather than providing solutions to help combat the problem.

The full potential of the method proposed in the study, needs to be extended to a plethora of additional persuasive video attributes. This goal, however, necessitates a larger videos dataset. The potential of the methods should be extended to other video platforms such as TikTok to investigate possible platform differences.

Although preliminary, these results offer additional insight into the mechanisms behind online persuasion, within the important context of pro-environmental behaviour. These preliminary findings can channel the future creation of persuasive social-media videos and expand their influence capabilities.

Acknowledgment

The project has received funding from the EU-funded Erasmus+ program "BtheChange" under grant agreement 2022-1-SE01-KA220-HED-000087275.

References

Aharonson, V., Cocker, B., Buisson-Street, K., and Winter, D. (2021) Modelling a Good Delivery of Bad News. In 2021 IEEE 9th International Conference on Healthcare Informatics, pp 224-227.

Aharonson, V. Karpasitis, C. Weinstein, T. (2022) Netnography of Social Media Addresses on COVID-19. European Conference on Social Media, pp 1-6.

Broekens, J. and Brinkman, W.-P. (2009) Affectbutton: Towards a standard for dynamic affective user feedback. 3rd international conference on affective computing and intelligent interaction and workshops, pp 1-8.

Fenton, A. and Procter, C. (2019) Studying social media communities: blending methods with netnography. SAGE Research Methods Cases.

Hendriks, F. Janssen, I. and Jucks, R. (2023) Balance as Credibility? How Presenting One-vs. Two-Sided Messages Affects Ratings of Scientists' and Politicians' Trustworthiness. Health communication Vol. 38 No. 12, pp.2757-2764.

Jin, J. Lam, S. Savas, O. and McCulloh, I. (2020) Approaches for quantifying video prominence, narratives, & discussion: engagement on COVID-19 related YouTube Videos. Proc. IEEE/ACM International Conference on Advances in Social Networks Analysis and Mining pp 811-818.

Kanter, B. & Fine, A. (2010) The networked nonprofit: Connecting with social media to drive change, John Wiley & Sons.

Kozinets, R. (2017) Netnography: Radical participative understanding for a networked communications society. The SAGE handbook of qualitative research in psychology, 374.

Loria, S., 2018. textblob Documentation. Release 0.15, [online] https://buildmedia.readthedocs.org/media/pdf/textblob/latest/textblob.pdf.

Malecki, K.M., Keating, J.A. and Safdar, N. (2021) Crisis communication and public perception of COVID-19 risk in the era of social media. Clinical Infectious Diseases, Vol. 72, pp 697-702.

Park, S. Shim, H.S. Chatterjee, M. Sagae, K. and Morency, L. P. (2014) Computational analysis of persuasiveness in social multimedia: A novel dataset and multimodal prediction approach. Proceedings of the 16th International Conference on Multimodal Interaction, pp 50-57.

Reif A, Kneisel T. Schäfer M. and Taddicken, M. (2020) Why are scientific experts perceived as trustworthy? Emotional assessment within TV and YouTube videos. Media and Communication Vol. 8 No. 1 pp 191-205.

Sui, W. Sui, A. and Rhodes, R.E. (2022) What to watch: Practical considerations and strategies for using YouTube for research. Digital Health Vol. 8, pp 1-13.

Less is More: Stress Detection Through Condensed Social Media Contents

Zeyad Alghamdi[1], Tharindu Kumarage[1], Garima Agrawal[1], Huan Liu[1], and Russell Bernard[2]
[1]School of Computing and Augmented Intelligence, Arizona State University, Tempe, USA
[2]Institute for Social Science Research, Arizona State University, Tempe, USA

zalgham1@asu.edu
kskumara@asu.edu
garima.agrawal@asu.edu
huanliu@asu.edu
asuruss@asu.edu

Abstract: In the digital age, social media has been a go-to platform for stress-related discussions, yielding valuable data to advance the understanding and detection of stress. Swift identification of stress indicators in these online conversations is essential in enabling immediate support and helping to avert subsequent severe mental and physical health issues, especially during global crises such as pandemics and conflicts. Detecting stress in social media posts automatically poses a formidable challenge. While techniques such as supervised Pretrained Language Models (PLMs) and zero-shot Large Language Models (LLMs) based classifiers have demonstrated significant performance, they exhibit limitations, especially on platforms like Reddit. For example, on Reddit, users tend to write lengthy, expressive posts, which causes these methods to often fail to consider the entire context, leading to incomplete or inaccurate assessments of a user's mental health or stress status. To overcome these limitations, we present a new approach to identifying and classifying stress-related discourse on social media. Our approach involves analyzing condensed versions of user posts, such as user-provided summaries or the "Too Long Didn't Read" (TLDR) portion of the original post. We question whether these abridged texts can yield a more accurate classification of stress. In this paper, we make the following contributions. First, we investigate the relationship between the performance of the model's perceived textual context and the length of social media posts. Second, we present a novel approach to use the summarized texts for stress detection. We experiment with different classifiers to evaluate their performance on stress detection accuracy using summarized versus full-length posts. Furthermore, by examining the emotional and linguistic features of the original posts and their summaries, we suggest improvements to current state-of-the-art LLM-based stress classifier prompts, thereby enhancing stress detection capabilities. Finally, when user summaries are absent, we synthetically generate meaningful user post summaries by incorporating the power of LLMs. Our results show that the stress detection performance deteriorates for longer posts, and utilizing the TLDR and summaries improves classification outcomes. We also provide augmented datasets containing human and AI-generated summaries for future research in stress detection on social media.

Keywords: Mental health, Stress detection, Social media, Large language models (LLMs), Linguistic features analysis, Text summarization

1. Introduction

Recent global crises have escalated stress levels, profoundly impacting mental health worldwide. Data from the American Psychological Association (APA, 2023) reveals a significant increase in chronic illnesses and mental health diagnoses since the COVID-19 pandemic, with adults aged 18 to 34 reporting the highest rates. In this digital era, social media platforms have emerged as crucial forums for mental health discourse and support, offering both anonymity and empathy (Sowles, S.J. et al., 2018; Sher, L., 2020). More importantly, these mental health discourses on social media provide a wealth of textual data that can be leveraged for early stress detection. This, in turn, could play a pivotal role in mitigating and addressing severe mental health challenges.

In the field of stress detection on social media, supervised Pretrained Language Models (PLMs) have demonstrated state-of-the-art performance across various platforms, including Twitter and Reddit (Lin, H. et al.,2017; Nijhawan, T. et al., 2022). With the emergence of large language models (LLMs), recent research has presented compelling cases for LLMs serving as superior zero-shot stress classifiers capable of performing effectively across multiple social media platforms(Xu, X., et al., 2023; Lamichhane, B., 2023), alleviating the need for additional fine-tuning, as typically required by PLM-based stress classifiers. However, both fine-tuned PLM and zero-shot LLM-based stress classifiers encounter challenges when confronted with lengthy content. Yang, K., et al. (2023) have noted that models like ChatGPT face difficulties in effectively addressing long contextual posts. Moreover, as shown by Ji, S., et al. (2023), transformer-based models like BERT exhibit inherent limitations in processing long text content, constraining their effective range to a mere 512 tokens. This limitation is significant in the context of social media platforms like Reddit, where posts often exceed this length.

Our research addresses this problem by proposing an innovative approach distinct from direct long-document analysis. We hypothesize that integrating summaries could effectively mitigate the identified limitation for two primary reasons: **1) Conciseness:** Summaries distill the essence of longer posts while preserving crucial information; **2) Availability:** On platforms like Reddit, the prevalent use of "Too-Long-Didn't-Read" (TLDR) sections in lengthy posts presents a readily accessible summary, aiding stress detection. Consequently, our study enhances the established Dreaddit stress dataset (Turcan, E., and Kathleen M. 2019) by incorporating summaries derived from these TLDRs (in our paper, we use 'TLDR' and 'summary' interchangeably). Subsequently, we assess the effectiveness of summaries as an alternative unit of analysis for stress classification in lengthy posts. Furthermore, through a detailed analysis of the psychological, linguistic, and emotional features between these user-generated summaries and the complete posts, we propose modifications to current LLM-based classification prompts to boost stress detection efficacy further.

Additionally, our study investigates the potential of LLMs to produce summaries analogous to human-written TLDRs. The primary aim is to assess whether AI-generated TLDRs could serve as a viable substitute for stress classification in lengthy posts lacking human-authored TLDRs. To this end, we further supplement our dataset with TLDRs generated by ChatGPT. We then benchmark the stress detection performance on AI-generated TLDRs against those written by users. Our comparative analysis reveals that both human and AI-generated summaries significantly improve classification accuracy and F1 scores, particularly in the context of longer posts. In summary, our key contributions are as follows:

- We propose a novel approach for classifying stress using user-provided summary texts as an alternative to analyzing full-length posts.
- We augment the existing LLM-based stress classification prompts by conducting a psychological, linguistic, and emotional feature analysis on user-written posts against their user-written summaries.
- We study the effectiveness of LLM-written summaries for stress classification on longer posts that lack human-authored summaries.
- We release an augmented dataset comprising the original extended post texts, the user-provided summaries, summaries generated by LLMs, and associated features, making it available for other researchers in the field. The code and data are available in our GitHub repository: (*https://github.com/Zeyad-o/TLDR-AISummarizeStress/*)

2. Related Work

2.1 Evolution of Stress Detection Techniques in Social Media

The field of stress detection on social media has evolved substantially over time. Beginning with traditional text analysis methods, such as rule-based systems (Thelwall, M., 2017) and Latent Dirichlet Allocation (LDA) (Khan, A., Ali, R. (2020); Nijhawan, T. et al. (2022)). The scope of stress detection expanded when a new dimension of integrating multimodal data, including images and social network information was proposed by Lin, H., et al. (2014, 2017). Furthermore, Turcan, E., et al. (2021) and Alghamdi Z., et al. (2023), have delved into the role of emotions in stress detection from the poster's perspective. More recent studies have explored emotional disparity in social media comments as a novel approach for stress detection (Alghamdi, Z. et al., (2023)). The advent of LLMs marked a new era, Lamichhane, B. (2023) demonstrated ChatGPT's effectiveness in mental health classification tasks, achieving notable F1 scores. This study highlights ChatGPT's potential for mental health classification roles that are typically reserved for domain-specific models. In parallel, Xu, X., et al. (2023) evaluated multiple LLMs, including GPT-3.5, across various mental health tasks, showing promising results with zero-shot and few-shot prompting despite limitations related to the different LLMs used context window sizes compared to GPT-3.5. Furthermore, Yang, K., et al. (2023) advance this research by focusing on interpretable mental health analysis using LLMs. They address low interpretability of traditional methods by exploring different prompting strategies and the generation of explanations that are close to human performance. Most importantly, they highlight that ChatGPT shows strong in-context learning abilities, but it still falls short of advanced task-specific methods, indicating a need for careful prompt engineering.

2.2 Summarization in Mental Health

The application of summarization in mental health is increasingly being recognized as crucial. It has gained significant recognition for its ability to aid healthcare professionals. Manas, G., et al. (2021) demonstrate the importance of creating semantically relevant summaries from clinical diagnostic interviews. Gao, Y., et al. (2022) investigated how summaries of medical problems can help healthcare stakeholders accurately grasp patient conditions, easing their workload and reducing cognitive biases. Furthering the application of technology in this domain, Li, Hao, et al. (2023) used LLMs to generate concise lists summarizing patients' problems, showcasing the value of LLMs in enhancing the efficiency of patient care. Kim, T., et al. (2023) applied LLMs to summarize psychiatric patients' experiences for clinician dashboards, enhancing patient monitoring. Syed, S., et al. (2023) used multiple LLMs, including GPT3.5 and GPT4, for summarizing extensive social media discussions, focusing on comments. This approach aids in navigating and analyzing complex social media content, demonstrating the practicality of LLMs in mental health and social media contexts. The growing interest in LLMs for text summarization is highlighted by studies from Zhang, Tianyi, et al. (2023), Pu, Xiao, et al. (2023), and Laban, P., et al. (2023). These studies focus on comparing human-generated and LLM-generated summaries, revealing the complexities and potential for further research in this area. While these studies underscore the growing validity of LLM-generated summaries in various contexts, our research focuses on the potential of human-generated summaries, specifically TLDRs, in the realm of stress detection on social media.

3. Methodology

In this section, we first discuss the process used to extract and prepare the data, followed by how the different text sizes were handled. Then, we present our approach for the analysis and classification of the features. For brevity, only the critical aspects of the method are presented here. The overall design and methodology are shown in Figure 1.

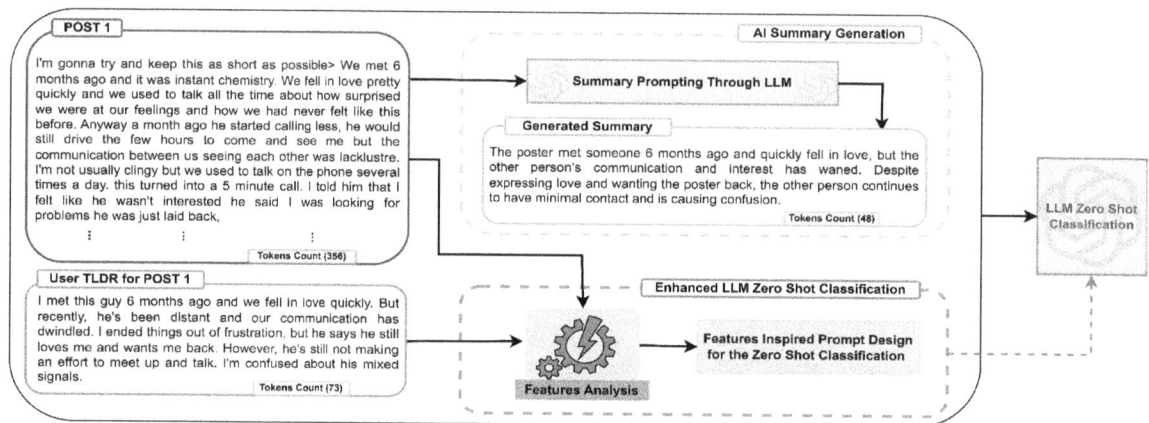

Figure 1: Methodology Pipeline - illustrates the flow of our approach with a sample from our dataset

3.1 Dataset

3.1.1 Dataset extraction

For our analysis, we utilized the Dreaddit dataset, a comprehensive and manually annotated collection of social media posts, specifically from Reddit. This dataset, made publicly available by Turcan, E., and Kathleen M. (2019), is widely recognized for its application in stress detection research. Spanning from January 1, 2017, to November 19, 2018, Dreaddit offers a diverse range of lengthy posts, encompassing various subreddits related to mental health issues, including abuse, anxiety, financial stress, PTSD, and social challenges.

Dreaddit's distinctive quality lies in its focus on everyday stress experiences, as opposed to strictly clinical scenarios, and its inclusion of extensive Reddit posts, which provide a rich insight into the multifaceted nature of stress expression in social media contexts. We utilized the PRAW API (Reddit, 2023) to extract these posts based on their unique IDs. Although the original Dreaddit dataset comprises 2,750 posts with individual classifications, our extraction yielded 1,984 posts, with the reduction mainly due to deletions by users or removals by moderators.

3.1.2 TLDRs extraction

TLDRs are commonly employed by users to encapsulate the essence of their posts. We employed regular expressions to methodically extract TLDRs and user-written summaries, ensuring they were explicit and identified by key phrases such as 'long story short,' 'basically,' 'short story,' among others, or as integral components of the post narratives. Our extraction process prioritized original content, deliberately excluding any edits influenced by subsequent user comments to maintain the authenticity of the posts' sentiment and intended message. This approach was crucial as our objective was to pinpoint early indicators of stress, and incorporating edits that might reflect positive feedback could potentially distort the original context and skew the results. From the initial dataset comprising 1,984 posts, we successfully narrowed it down to a subset of 527 samples that included both the original post text and user-written summaries. It is important to note, however, that not all TLDRs strictly conform to the traditional definition of summaries. Some users tend to list key points or pose questions, aiming to attract readers interested in the core message, who might then choose to engage with the full post or respond based on these highlighted elements.

3.1.3 Augmented dataset

In this work, we developed an augmented dataset that contains the cleaned original social media posts along with both user-generated and AI-generated summaries. This enriched dataset is designed not only for feature extraction and emotional analysis but also to augment the reproducibility of our research. By providing these diverse data elements in a consolidated form, we aim to facilitate future studies in the field of mental health and stress detection.

3.2 Features Extraction

In our study, we used the Linguistic Inquiry and Word Count (LIWC) software (LIWC-22; Boyd, R.L., et al., 2022), a text analysis program. LIWC, known for quantifying psychological and linguistic attributes in text, has been validated for stress detection in previous studies, including Turcan, E. and Kathleen M,.(2019). We employed LIWC's latest version, which extracts up to 118 features from unsegmented posts to maintain contextual integrity. It categorizes words into emotional, cognitive, and structural components, aiding in a comprehensive analysis of psychological constructs in the text. LIWC's ability to assess emotional and cognitive states in social media posts is crucial for detecting early stress indicators in our study.

3.3 Summarization

In this study, we utilized LLMs for summarization with a simple prompt:

"Summarize the following social media post: [POST]".

This approach leverages the model's broad training, enabling it to adapt to various topics efficiently. The use of a straightforward prompt accentuates its capability in zero-shot learning, producing coherent and contextually appropriate summaries. This demonstrates the models' potential to rapidly process diverse mental health topics, and highlight their utility.

3.4 LLM Zero-Shot Classification

The design of our prompts was an integral part of our experiment. Drawing from previous research, the prompts were specifically crafted to align with our task's unique characteristics. This included incorporating expressions of current negative stress as identified in the work of Turcan and McKeown (2019) and Turcan, E., et al. (2021). Based on our dataset text types, we have the following: either post or (post TLDR or summary). Therefore, we use the following zero-shot prompt:

"Is the following [Text Type] indicative of current negative stress or not? Just answer in Yes or No. Don't provide explanations. [POST]".

4. Experimental Setup

Here, we describe the experimental settings used to validate our approach, including the bucketization of the dataset, LLM usage, and stress detection baselines, to support reproducibility.

4.1 Bucketization

To investigate the relationship between stress classification performance and the textual data length, we divided the dataset into three segments into buckets or Quartiles 1, 2, and 3 (Q1, Q2, and Q3) based on the ascending order of token counts in the posts. Each quartile contains approximately one-third of the total dataset. The tokenization of each post was done using the OpenAI tokenizer (Turbo 3.5). Our analysis revealed the following average token counts per quartile:

- Q1 average is 178 tokens (minimum 80, maximum 268).
- Q2 average is 387 tokens (minimum 269, maximum 554).
- Q3 average is 982 tokens (minimum 555, maximum 3,833).

The overall dataset average is 515 tokens. Figure 2 shows the frequency distribution of token count in each quartile.

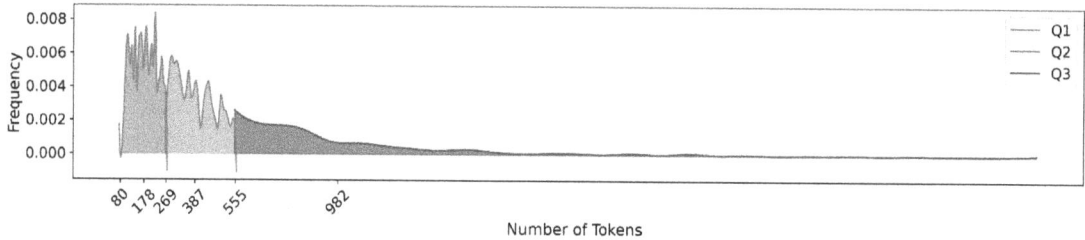

Figure 2: Post-token distribution across the buckets Q1, Q2, and Q3

4.2 LLM Settings

We selected ChatGPT (GPT-3.5) for its balance of capability and cost-effectiveness in the GPT series. With 175 billion parameters, it's refined through reinforcement learning from human feedback. Notably, this model has received appraisals for its performance in studies by Xu, X., et al. (2023) and Lamichhane, B. (2023). As a closed-source model available via OpenAI's API, we integrated the OpenAI library (version 0.28.1) with LangChain for zero-shot LLM prompting. We specifically used *'gpt-3.5-turbo-1106'* to ensure reproducibility. For deterministic classification tasks, we set the temperature to 0, and 0.7 for creative variability in summary generation. We employed LangChain's 'response schema' feature to direct LLM outputs based on input descriptions, using precise instructions for classification and summarization tasks.

4.3 Baseline Stress Classification

As a baseline for our comparative analysis, we used a state-of-the-art PLM-based stress classifier. To be specific, we used the BERT-base model fine-tuned on classifying stress data *('bert-base-cased')*. To ensure the robustness and reliability of our findings, we stratified the dataset by label, implementing an 80/20 split for fine-tuning and testing purposes. The performance metrics were calculated as an average of over 10 distinct runs, enabling a thorough and comprehensive evaluation of the PLM's effectiveness. It is important to note that PLMs have been a cornerstone in stress detection research, with numerous studies leveraging them to understand and classify stress-related content.

5. Experiments and Results

Here, we provide the experiments and analyze the results. We begin with a preliminary analysis of the effect of post-length on stress classification performance, then examine the three research questions in detail, where the role of human and AI-generated summaries in enhancing classification accuracy is discussed, along with a comprehensive performance benchmark. In summary, we address the following key research questions:

- RQ1: Can human-written summaries improve classification?
- RQ2: Are AI-generated summaries effective?
- RQ3: How do summarization approaches compare to baselines?

5.1 Preliminary Analysis - Post Size vs. Stress Classification Performance

We use the Zero-Shot LLM classifier on all the posts in the dataset and focus on evaluating the classification performance, specifically accuracy and F1 score, following the evaluation metrics outlined in related works. We assessed not only the overall performance but also the performance within each defined quartile. As depicted in Figure 3, distinct performance variations across the quartiles were observed. In quartile 1 (Q1), containing shorter posts, the classification performance was notably higher than in quartiles 2 (Q2) and 3 (Q3). Interestingly, Q2 consistently displayed a performance level near the overall average, while Q3, comprising longer posts, showed the lowest performance metrics. The accuracy difference between Q1 and Q3 in zero-shot classification was significant at 22.2%, and a similar trend was noted in the F1 score, with a difference of 15.3%.

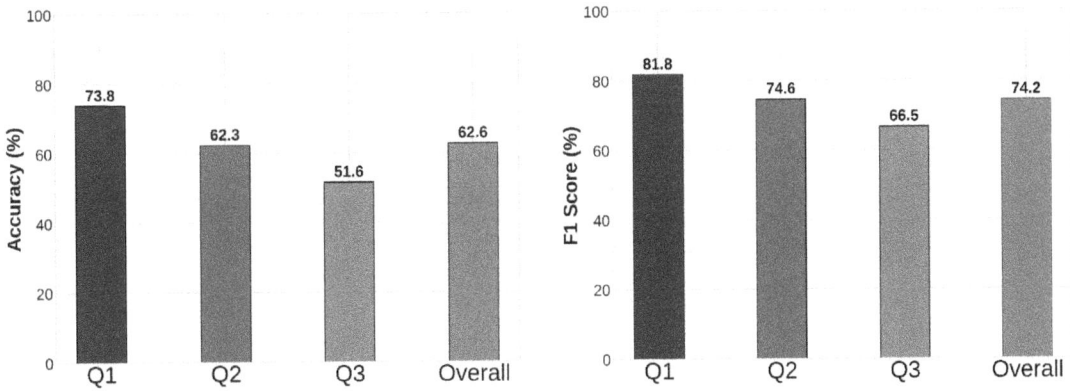

Figure 3: Quartile-Specific and the Overall Performance of Zero-Shot LLM classification

These results indicate that post length impacts classification effectiveness, with performance inversely related to input size. This finding underscores the need for alternative strategies to counteract performance declines associated with longer posts. Consequently, we look into our RQ1: "Can human-written summaries improve classification accuracy?". This question explores whether utilizing human-authored summaries can mitigate the performance drop observed with longer posts. The following section details our approach and findings in addressing RQ1.

5.2 Analysis of Human Written Summaries

Now, we present an analysis of a specific subset of the data comprising social media posts accompanied by user-generated summaries or "TLDRs." This subset consisted of 527 posts, with label distribution at 49% stress and 51% non-stress and an overall average token count of approximately 715 tokens. Notably, this subset predominantly featured longer texts, with 59% falling into Quartile 3 (Q3), 32% in Quartile 2 (Q2), and only 9% in Quartile 1 (Q1). The average token count for the TLDR segments was 44, constituting about 6.16% of the average total length of the original posts.

5.2.1 Stress Classification Performance

As shown in Figure 4, our analysis compared the classification performance using either the full posts or the user-written summaries. Employing the LLM zero-shot classifier, we observed that the summaries outperformed full post classifications, showing a 6.31% increase in accuracy and a 2% increase in F1 score. It suggests that user-generated short summaries could serve as an effective alternative for classifying stress in lengthy social media posts.

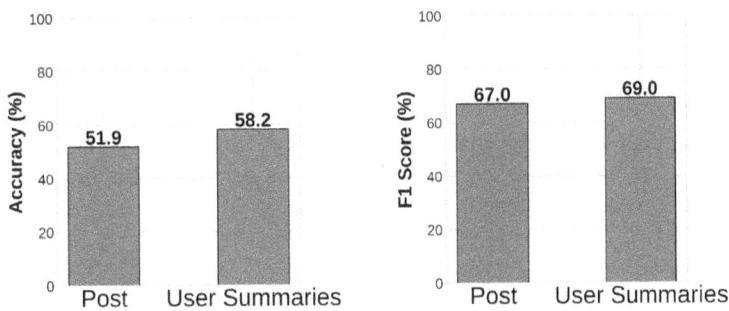

Figure 4: Comparative Performance of Full Posts vs. User-Written Summaries (TLDRs)

5.2.2 Feature Analysis

To further understand these results, it is imperative to understand the dominant characteristics and differences between the original posts and user-generated summaries. To achieve this understanding, we embarked on a comprehensive correlation analysis encompassing 118 features from the Linguistic Inquiry and Word Count (LIWC) tool. We focused on identifying features that exhibited a high correlation to the stress label, that are statistically significant ($P<0.05$) between the two types of texts, summaries, and original posts. Figure 5 shows a Venn diagram illustrating the top 10 features shared and unique to posts and user-written summaries (TLDRs).

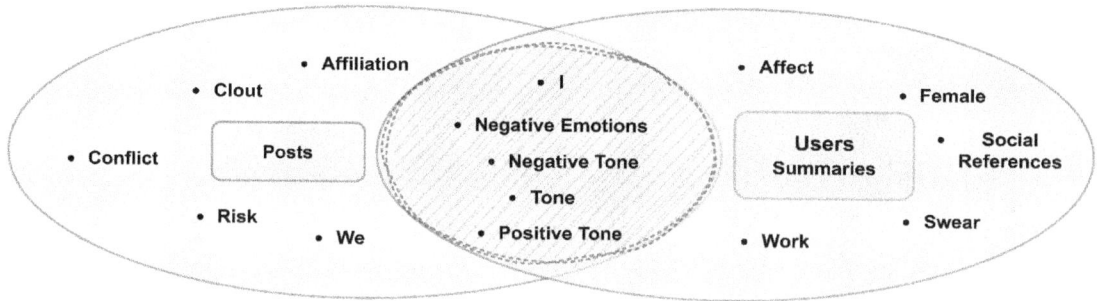

Figure 5: Venn Diagram of the Top 10 Features in Posts vs. User-Written Summaries (TLDRs)

Moreover, analyzing the intersection of features from posts and user-written summaries proves vital. Shared features like 'general Tone', 'Negative Emotions and Tone', 'lack of Positive Tone', and the first person singular pronouns such as ('I') in both posts and summaries are particularly telling. These elements, indicative of negative emotions and a self-centric narrative, are potent stress markers. Furthermore, each text type offers unique insights. Posts often feature elements like 'We', 'Affiliation,' 'Clout,' 'Conflict,' and 'Risk,' which delve into personal dynamics, interpersonal tensions, and perceived threats. On the other hand, the TLDRs, known for their brevity and focus, highlight specific aspects such as 'Female,' 'Work,' and 'Swear,' 'Affect,' and 'Social References'. These features shed light on gender reference, workplace stress, and emotional intensity more directly and succinctly.

5.2.3   Enhanced LLM-Classification

We have leveraged the insights gained from our feature analysis to refine the prompt used in existing LLM-based stress classifiers. Specifically, we have emphasized capturing first-person perspectives and emotional intensity, key elements highlighted by the dominant features shown in Figure 5. Consequently, we have revised the classification prompt, which we denote as the **'enhanced prompt'**:

> *"Given the following social media text (can be either post or post summary or post TLDR), looking from the poster's perspective, only classify if it is indicative of current very severe negative stress as 'Yes' otherwise 'No'. Just answer in 'Yes' or 'No'. Don't provide explanations. Text:[Text Type]"*

Figure 6 shows the enhanced prompt's results, demonstrating an improvement in post-classification accuracy from 51.9% to 57.6% and an increase in performance on human summaries from 58.2% to 60.0%, compared to the generic prompt results in Figure 4.

5.3   Analysis of AI-Generated Summaries

While the above findings are promising, they underscore a practical challenge: not all posts include user-generated summaries. This challenge compels us to explore the feasibility of employing AI-generated summaries as a potential alternative. Here, we try to answer the RQ2: "Can we use AI-generated summaries instead of human-generated summaries?". Figure 6 shows the performance comparison of full posts, human summaries, and AI-generated summaries using enhanced LLM classification.

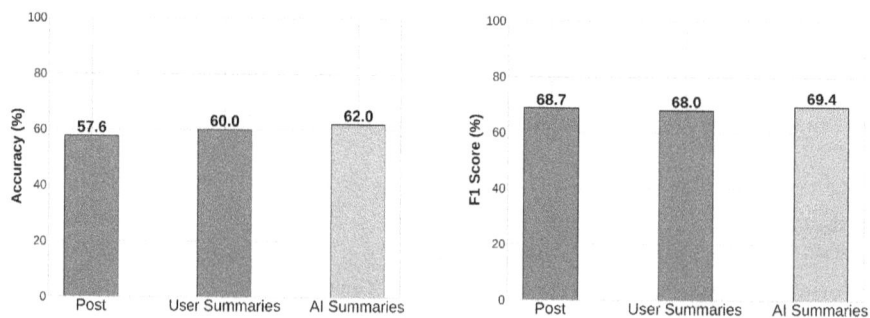

Figure 6: Performance Comparison of Subset Text Types with Zero Shot Enhanced Prompt

These results revealed that while human-written summaries outperformed full posts by 2.4% in classification accuracy, the AI-generated summaries further improved on this by an additional 2%.

Regarding the F1 score, human summaries and posts had similar performance, but AI-generated summaries showed a slightly better F1 score.

To evaluate the resource efficiency of summaries in stress classification, we analyzed token counts within the subset, including human summaries. The average counts were 715 tokens for original posts, 44 for human summaries (6.2% of the total), and 65 for AI-generated summaries (9.1%), as shown in Figure 7.

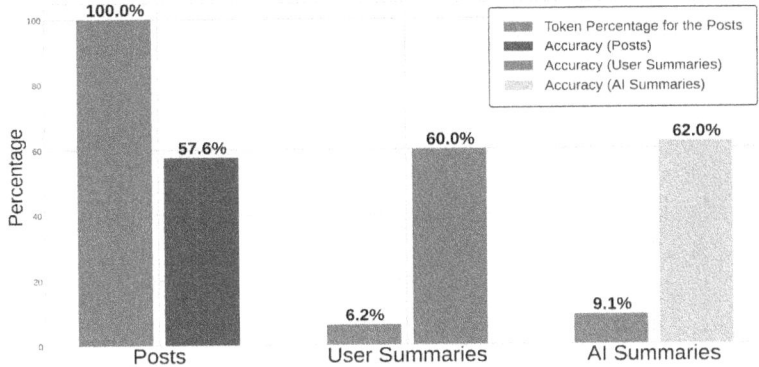

Figure 7: Token Percentage and Performance Comparison for Different Text Types

This analysis yielded two significant insights. First, human-generated summaries, with only 6.2% of the total token count, improved classification accuracy over full posts by 2.4%. More importantly, AI-generated summaries, constituting just 9.1% of the total tokens, outperformed both full posts and human summaries. The marginal increase in token count (2.9%) correlated with a notable 2% accuracy gain compared to human summaries. Thus, AI-generated summaries emerge not only as a valid approach for stress classification but also demonstrate that a slight increase in length can significantly enhance performance.

5.4 Benchmarking Summarization Impact on Classification

To address RQ3: 'How does the summarization approach compare against baseline methods?', we broaden our analysis to encompass the entire dataset. This comparison is critical to understanding the efficacy of our approach across different data buckets or quartiles and the overall performance, as illustrated in Table 1.

We observed that the PLM-based classifier (BERT) was better for the Q2 and Q3 quartiles, though the F1 scores are low. In contrast, the enhanced zero-shot LLM classifier gives the best classification accuracy. The improvement is notable, with a 67.5% accuracy and a 76.4% F1 score.

Table 1: Performance of Posts vs. Generic Summaries in LLMs and PLMs

Classifier / Metric		Q1		Q2		Q3		Overall	
		ACC%	F1%	ACC%	F1%	ACC%	F1%	ACC%	F1%
Post	BERT	73.5	71.3	67.5	63.6	62.0	57.0	66.9	63.6
	Generic Prompt	73.8	81.8	62.3	74.4	51.6	66.5	62.6	74.3
	Enhanced Prompt	78.3	**84.0**	69.2	77.5	54.9	67.9	67.5	76.4
AI Generated Summary	BERT	74.9	73.8	68.2	65.9	61.9	57.7	67.4	64.5
	Generic Prompt	75.3	82.5	65.0	75.6	54.0	67.9	64.8	75.2
	Enhanced Prompt	**78.5**	83.4	**71.5**	**78.1**	**62.4**	**70.3**	**70.8**	**77.4**

Shifting our focus to AI-generated summaries, the application of the zero-shot prompt for the AI-generated summaries we observe the following: i) notable improvement of 2.2% in accuracy and a 0.9% rise in F1 score, and ii) summaries are at least on par with, if not superior to full post classifications. Moreover, the PLM-based baseline on these summaries improved classification in Q1 and Q2, and overall (an increase of 1.7% in accuracy and 1.9% in F1 score) compared to the PLM full post-performance, albeit with a slight dip in Q3 performance. Our analysis concludes that applying the enhanced prompt to AI-generated summaries significantly enhances classification performance. It outperforms the generic zero-shot prompts (8.2% higher accuracy, 3.1% better F1 score) and PLM-based classifications (3.9% more accurate, 13.8% higher F1 score).

6. Limitations and Challenges

Our work, distinct from traditional long document classification, offers an alternative approach where summaries, rather than full-length posts, are utilized for efficient stress analysis. This contribution is particularly crucial considering the complexity and volume of content on social media platforms.

One challenge we encounter is the "black-box" nature of LLMs, which complicates obtaining optimal prompts for classification and summarization tasks. We have attempted to approximate the necessary prompt parameters through feature analysis, but this remains an area that needs further exploration and refinement. We also acknowledge potential limitations in our approach, mainly when dealing with very long texts that may need to be adequately summarized. Our findings showed that the quality of summaries, especially for longer texts (Q3 data), appeared to affect the classification performance negatively when using BERT. This phenomenon suggests that the effectiveness of summarization may vary depending on the text length and warrants additional research.

Another challenge we encounter is the well-known hallucination problem in LLMs (Agrawal, Garima, et al. (2023)). To avoid prompts that can generate hallucinations or unrelated output, we inspected the output generated by the summarization prompts. Multiple graduate students were asked to review around 50-100 randomly selected AI-generated summaries to check the original post's reflection, accuracy, and consistency in the LLMs' summary.

7. Conclusion and Future Work

This research contributes to the growing body of work in mental health analysis on social media, particularly in the context of stress detection. By focusing on the utility of summaries for stress classification, we have demonstrated a practical approach that mitigates some of the challenges posed by lengthy social media content. Our findings indicate that human and AI-generated summaries can serve as viable alternatives to full-length posts for stress detection, with AI-generated summaries showing particular promise due to their scalability and efficiency. This suggests a significant potential for the application of LLMs in mental health monitoring and support systems through social media data. Which complements the usage of summarization of mental health data through medical records and reports.

Our research opens avenues for further investigation into the optimization of LLMs for mental health applications. Future studies could focus on refining summarization techniques to capture the essence of lengthy posts more accurately and expanding the dataset to include a broader range of social media platforms and languages, which could provide a more comprehensive understanding of stress expression in diverse digital environments.

Acknowledgement

This work was supported by the Office of Naval Research under Award No. N00014-21-1-4002. We also appreciate the valuable guidance and support provided by Wildflower Primary Care & Wellness Center. Interpretations, conclusions, and recommendations within this article are solely those of the authors.

References

Agrawal, G., et al. (2023) "Can Knowledge Graphs Reduce Hallucinations in LLMs?: A Survey", arXiv preprint arXiv:2311.07914.
Alghamdi, Z., et al. (2023). "Code RED: Reactive Emotion Difference for Stress Detection on Social Media". No. 10659. EasyChair.
Alghamdi, Z., et al. (2023) "Studying the Influence of Toxicity and Emotion Features for Stress Detection on Social Media", ECSM 2023 10th European Conference on Social Media, Academic Conferences, and Publishing Limited.

American Psychological Association. (2023) "Stress in America." [Online] Available at:
https://www.apa.org/news/press/releases/stress

Boyd, R.L., et al. (2022) "The Development and Psychometric Properties of LIWC-22", Austin, TX: University of Texas at Austin.

Gao, Y., et al. (2022)"Summarizing Patients' Problems from Hospital Progress Notes Using Pre-trained Sequence-to-Sequence Models." Proceedings of COLING. International Conference on Computational Linguistics. Vol. 2022. NIH Public Access.

Ji, S., et al. (2023)"Domain-specific Continued Pretraining of Language Models for Capturing Long Context in Mental Health." arXiv preprint arXiv:2304.10447.

Khan, A. & Ali, R. (2020) "Stress Detection from Twitter Posts Using LDA", International Journal of High Performance Computing and Networking, 16(2-3), pp. 137-147.

Kim, T., et al. (2023) "MindfulDiary: Harnessing Large Language Model to Support Psychiatric Patients' Journaling", arXiv preprint arXiv:2310.05231.

Laban, P., et al. (2023) "SummEdits: Measuring LLM Ability at Factual Reasoning Through The Lens of Summarization", Proceedings of the 2023 Conference on Empirical Methods in Natural Language Processing.

Lamichhane, B. (2023) "Evaluation of chatgpt for nlp-based mental health applications", arXiv preprint arXiv:2303.15727.

Li, H., et al. (2023) "Team: PULSAR at ProbSum 2023: PULSAR: Pre-training with Extracted Healthcare Terms for Summarising Patients" Problems and Data Augmentation with Black-box Large Language Models', The 61st Annual Meeting Of The Association For Computational Linguistics.

Lin, H., et al. (2014) "User-level Psychological Stress Detection from Social Media Using Deep Neural Network", Proceedings of the 22nd ACM International Conference on Multimedia, pp. 507-516.

Lin, H., et al. (2017) "Detecting Stress Based on Social Interactions in Social Networks", IEEE Transactions on Knowledge and Data Engineering, 29(9), pp. 1820-1833.

Manas, G., et al. (2021) "Knowledge-infused Abstractive Summarization of Clinical Diagnostic Interviews: Framework Development Study", JMIR Mental Health, 8(5), e20865.

Nijhawan, T., Attigeri, G., & Ananthakrishna, T. (2022) "Stress Detection Using Natural Language Processing and Machine Learning Over Social Interactions", Journal of Big Data, 9(1), pp. 1-24.

Pu, X., Mingqi, G., & Xiaojun, W. (2023) "Summarization is (almost) Dead", arXiv preprint arXiv:2309.09558.

Reddit. (2023) "PRAW: The Python Reddit API Wrapper", Available from: https://praw.readthedocs.io/.

Syed, S., et al. (2023) "Indicative Summarization of Long Discussions", The Conference on Empirical Methods in Natural Language Processing, pp. 2752–2788, Singapore, Association for Computational Linguistics.

Sher, L. (2020) "The Impact of the COVID-19 Pandemic on Suicide Rates", QJM: An International Journal of Medicine, 113(10), pp. 707-712.

Sowles, S.J., et al. (2018) 'A Content Analysis of an Online Pro-eating Disorder Community on Reddit', Body Image, 24, pp. 137-144.

Thelwall, M. (2017) "TensiStrength: Stress and Relaxation Magnitude Detection for Social Media Texts", Information Processing & Management, 53(1), pp. 106-121.

Turcan, E., Smaranda, M., & Kathleen, K. (2021) "Emotion-infused Models for Explainable Psychological Stress Detection", Proceedings of the 2021 Conference of the North American Chapter of the Association for Computational Linguistics: Human Language Technologies.

Turcan, E., & Kathleen, M. (2019) "Dreaddit: A Reddit Dataset for Stress Analysis in Social Media", Proceedings of the Tenth International Workshop on Health Text Mining and Information Analysis (LOUHI 2019).

World Health Organization. (2023) 'World Mental Health Report', [Online] Available from:
https://www.who.int/teams/mental-health-and-substance-use/world-mental-health-report.

Xu, X., et al. (2023) "Leveraging Large Language Models for Mental Health Prediction via Online Text Data", arXiv preprint arXiv:2307.14385.

Yang, K., et al. (2023) "On the Evaluations of ChatGPT and Emotion-Enhanced Prompting for Mental Health Analysis", arXiv preprint arXiv:2304.03347.

Yang, K., et al. (2023) "Towards Interpretable Mental Health Analysis with Large Language Models", Proceedings of the 2023 Conference on Empirical Methods in Natural Language Processing.

Zhang, T., et al. (2023) "Benchmarking Large Language Models for News Summarization", arXiv preprint arXiv:2301.13848.

Users' Adoption of Social Media Platforms for Government Services: The Role of Perceived Privacy, Perceived Security, Trust, and Social Influence

Lamya Almansoori, Reem Al-Katheeri and Mousa Al-kfairy
College of Technological Innovation, Zayed University, Abu Dhabi, UAE

Mousa.al-kfairy@zu.ac.ae (corresponding author)

Abstract: The rapid integration of social media platforms in government service delivery marks a transformative trend in the digital era. This study investigates the critical factors influencing user adoption of social media for accessing government services, focusing on perceived privacy, perceived security, trust, and social influence. Drawing upon theoretical frameworks of the Unified Theory of Acceptance and Use of Technology (UTAUT), and the Trust-Privacy-Identity (TPI) framework, the research offers a comprehensive understanding of how users perceive and interact with government services on social media platforms. The study emphasises the importance of users' confidence in privacy and security measures, examining how these perceptions shape their willingness to engage with government services online. A key finding of this research is the significant role of Perceived Security and Privacy (PSP) in influencing users' trusting intentions. At the same time, Social Influence (SI) predominantly affects their intention to use these platforms. Additionally, Trusting Intention (TI) is found to be a crucial determinant of users' Intention to Use (IU). Contrary to expectations, the study reveals that Social Influence (SI) does not significantly impact users' trusting intention, and gender does not appear to play a significant role in determining the intention to use or trust intention. The study has important implications for both research and practice. For policymakers and government agencies, understanding that trust and perceived security are central to user adoption. This knowledge is vital for enhancing the effectiveness of government service delivery via social media, ensuring that these platforms are not only accessible but also trusted by the public.

Keywords: S-Government, Social government, Social media, Trusting intention, Behavioural intention

1. Introduction

In the rapidly evolving digital age, integrating social media platforms into government service delivery represents a significant shift, offering new avenues for public engagement and service accessibility. Platforms like Facebook, Twitter, and WhatsApp are increasingly employed by governments worldwide to enhance e-government services, marking a notable trend in digital governance (Khan et al., 2020). This integration, however, brings forth both opportunities and challenges. While social media facilitates greater citizen engagement and transparency, there is a notable gap in empirical research, particularly regarding trust factors and addressing citizens' concerns in this emerging context (Khan et al., 2020).

A critical aspect of this integration is the assurance of data privacy and security. Users' concerns about the handling and protection of their personal information highlight the importance of perceived privacy safeguards (Cho et al., 2019). The apprehension that unauthorised entities might misuse, or access personal data necessitates the establishment of digital trust, achieved through transparent data practices and clear communication about privacy measures (Khan et al., 2021).

The influence of societal norms and peer expectations also significantly shapes user behaviour towards these platforms. The normalization of social media use for government interactions within specific social groups can lead to alignment in user behaviour with community-driven norms (Zubir et al., 2023). This underscores the need to understand the broader social context and its impact on adoption decisions.

Moreover, robust cybersecurity measures are essential in assuring users about their data security. Effective encryption, secure login processes, and vigilant monitoring for threats are crucial in protecting information from unauthorised access and cyber-attacks, fostering a safe environment for user engagement with social media platforms (Khan et al., 2021).

This research aims to comprehensively understand the factors influencing user adoption of social media for government services, focusing on perceived security, privacy, trust, and social influence. This understanding is vital for policymakers, government agencies, and researchers in developing strategies that effectively engage citizens and foster widespread adoption of these digital platforms. Governments' increasing reliance on social media for service delivery underscores the urgency of comprehensively understanding the elements that impact user adoption in this evolving digital landscape.

2. Literature Review

2.1 Related Work

User adoption of government services through social media platforms is a dynamic and multifaceted field, significantly influenced by perceived privacy, security, trust, and social influence. The critical role of these determinants in shaping citizens' willingness to engage with e-government services via social media is evident across various studies. Concerns about the privacy of personal information and the security of online transactions are significant barriers to adoption. Research by Al (2020), Capistrano (2020), and Li (2021) highlights the impact of perceived risk on user decisions, emphasising the need for robust security measures, transparent data handling policies, and effective communication to foster user confidence.

Trust is a cornerstone in the willingness of citizens to use government services through social media. Studies by Al (2020), Madyatmadja et al. (2019), and Méndez-Rivera et al. (2023) consistently point out the critical influence of trust in shaping user attitudes and intentions. This trust encompasses confidence in the government, the social media platforms, and the overall online environment, influenced by information reliability, government process transparency, and personal data security.

User-friendly interfaces and intuitive features are also crucial in building trust for e-government services. Research by Méndez-Rivera et al. (2023) and Mensah (2019) underscores the need for a seamless user experience on social media platforms. Well-designed interfaces that are transparent and easy to navigate can significantly enhance user trust, addressing concerns about complexity and usability. Governments should focus on user-centric design, conduct usability testing, and continuously refine these platforms based on user feedback. The role of social networks in influencing user behaviour is profound. Studies by Capistrano (2020), Khan et al. (2021), and Zubir et al. (2023) demonstrate the significant impact of social influence on the adoption of e-government services through social media. Peer recommendations, family endorsements, and social group norms play a substantial role in accepting these services.

The interconnectedness of trust, security, perceived privacy, and social dynamics in the user adoption process is highlighted in studies by Cho et al. (2019), Kumar et al. (2018), and Sachan et al. (2018). This complex interplay suggests that interventions and strategies to enhance adoption should be comprehensive and multifaceted. Educating users about the benefits, security measures, and privacy controls of e-government services is essential.

However, the existing literature reveals gaps that need addressing. These include the need for broader perspectives, especially concerning marginalised populations (Sachan et al., 2018), exploration of diverse channels beyond traditional websites (Méndez-Rivera et al., 2023), and consideration of gender differences (Li, 2019). Further investigation into the impact of government rules and policies on trust (Madyatmadja et al., 2019) and the influence of emerging technologies on e-government adoption (Madyatmadja et al., 2019) is also necessary.

In conclusion, enhancing user adoption of social media platforms for government services requires a holistic approach. Policymakers and service providers must prioritise factors like perceived privacy, security, trust-building, and leveraging social influence. Future research should explore emerging trends, diverse user segments, and the evolving e-government landscape to develop strategies that resonate with citizens and encourage widespread adoption.

2.2 Conceptual Model and Hypothesises

Figure 1 conceptualises the users' adoption of Social Media platforms for government services. It includes a set of factors such as Social Influence (SI), Perceived Security and Privacy (PSP), Perceived Trust (PT), and Intention to Use (IU). It also assumes that Gender mediates the relationship between Perceived Trust (PT) and Intention to Use (IU). The following paragraphs explain the model in more detail.

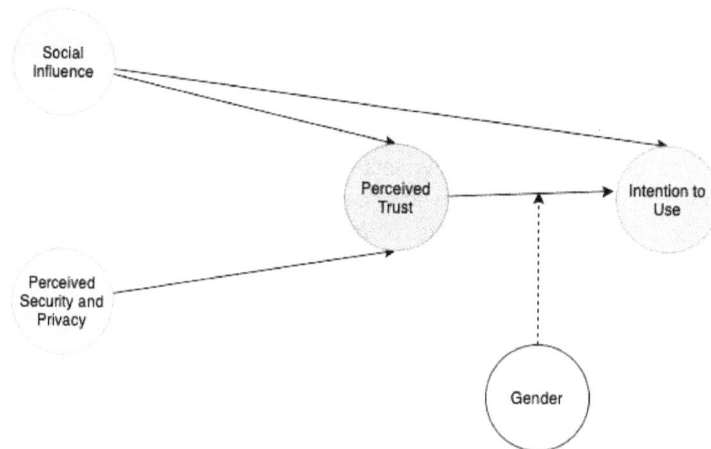

Figure 1: Conceptual Model of Users' Adoption of Social Media Platforms for Government Services

Social influence plays a crucial role in shaping individuals' trusting intentions and intention to use various technologies, products, or services. This phenomenon is particularly evident in information systems, marketing, and organisational behaviour, where those around them often influence the perceptions and behaviours of individuals. In this context, social influence refers to how individuals perceive that essential others believe they should use a new system or technology.

Highlighting the relevance of social influence, Alryalat et al. (2013) conducted a comprehensive study that expanded the Technology Acceptance Model (TAM). They incorporated social influence along with perceived usefulness and perceived ease of use in their model. The study focused on unraveling the factors influencing the intention of Jordanian citizens to adopt e-Government services. The findings revealed a significant outcome, emphasizing that social influence is a substantial factor positively affecting both the perceived usefulness and the intention to use e-government services. This underscores the interconnected nature of social influence in shaping attitudes and behaviors toward technology adoption in various contexts, including e-government services in Jordan.

The Unified Theory of Acceptance and Use of Technology (UTAUT) posits that social influence, performance, and effort expectancy are critical to technology acceptance. This model underscores the significance of social norms and peer influence in shaping an individual's decision-making process regarding technology adoption. Cheung and Lee (2010) highlight how peer pressure and community expectations can significantly sway users' engagement and participation behaviours in digital platforms, emphasising the complex interplay of social dynamics in virtual environments.

In e-commerce and organisational behaviour, the role of social influence is further accentuated. Pavlou and Gefen (2004) emphasise the integral role of social mechanisms like feedback systems and community norms in cultivating user trust. This has been recently confirmed in social commerce in Al-kfairy and Shuhaiber (2022) and Al-kfairy et al. (2023, 2024). In another research, Chang et al. (2017) underscore that trust in social networking services is shaped by the opinions and recommendations of friends, colleagues, and family members. The information and advice shared within social communities have a significant impact on a user's trust in social network services. Thus, we hypothesise the following:

H1a: Social Influence impacts users' intention to use social media for government services.

H1b: Social Influence impacts users' trusting intention (perceived trust) of social media for government services.

The intersection of perceived security and privacy with trusting intentions, particularly in social media usage for government services, is a critical area of study in the digital era. Data security and privacy concerns significantly influence public trust in government-provided services, mainly when these services are accessed through social media platforms. Alkraiji and Ameen (2022) explore these phenomena. They emphasise that the perception of robust security and stringent privacy measures is fundamental in fostering user trust. This trust is particularly pertinent in government services, where the sensitivity of information exchanged heightens privacy concerns. The authors argue that perceived security and privacy act as critical determinants of trust, suggesting that when users believe their data is secure and their privacy is protected, their willingness to engage with government services via social media.

Moreover, Li et al. (2022) investigate the importance of understanding how cultural and generational factors shape privacy concerns. Parallelly, Kanaan et al. (2023) emphasize in their study that security and privacy play pivotal roles in shaping trust when utilizing e-government services. Governments that provide elevated levels of security and safeguard users' privacy are more likely to attract a larger user base for their services. The study highlights that the perception of privacy and security is not uniform across demographics, indicating that government agencies must tailor their social media strategies to effectively address these varying perceptions. These studies collectively underscore the importance of perceived security and privacy in shaping public trust, particularly in the context of utilising social media for accessing government services, and suggest that addressing these perceptions is crucial for successfully implementing and accepting such digital initiatives. Thus, our second hypothesis is:

H2: Perceived Security and Privacy impacts the Trusting Intention of the users in social media platforms for government services.

Trust is a fundamental factor influencing citizens' willingness to engage with government services through social media platforms. Khan et al. (2021) examine this link, highlighting that trust in the government's ability to manage information and protect privacy securely significantly boosts citizens' intentions to use e-government services, including those offered via social media. The study underscores the notion that trust is a precursor to usage intention, suggesting that when citizens trust the government's competence and integrity in handling digital services, they are more likely to utilise these services for various civic engagements. Additionally, Zahid et al.(2022) emphasize that a crucial determinant in the adoption of any technology is trust. When users believe that the government providing services has a legalized website, exhibits credibility, and upholds ethical standards to safeguard their privacy, it enhances trust. Consequently, trust has a substantial impact on users' intentions to utilize e-government services.

Expanding on this theme, Shareef et al. (2019) explore how trust influences the effectiveness of social media as a tool for government-citizen interaction. The study finds that higher levels of trust increase the likelihood of using social media to access government services and enhance the quality of engagement between citizens and government entities. This research indicates that building and maintaining trust is essential for governments to effectively leverage social media platforms. Similarly, researchers like Khan et al. (2018) have indicated trust as a significant factor with a robust impact on shaping citizens' inclination to utilize e-government services through social media platforms. These studies collectively demonstrate the crucial role of trusting intention in shaping the intention to use social media for government services, highlighting the need for governments to foster trust to enhance citizen engagement and participation in digital governance initiatives. Therefore, our last hypothesis is:

H3: Trusting intention impacts users' intention to use social media platforms for government services.

3. Methodology

This study employs a descriptive research design, utilising a survey methodology to gather quantitative data. The primary objective is to understand the role of social influence, perceived security and privacy, and trusting intention in users' adoption of social media platforms for government services.

The target population for this survey is Generation Z, who has experience using social media platforms to communicate with government agencies. A sample size of 103 participants responded to the survey using Google Forms, applying "stratified sampling" to ensure the representativeness of the larger population.

The collected data was analysed using SmartPLS 4. Descriptive statistics was used to summarise the demographic data and the responses to survey items. Inferential statistical analyses, including structural equation modelling, were used to examine the relationships between the different constructs. The level of significance set at $p < 0.05$.

For testing theories on complex relationships between observable and latent variables in conceptual models, structural equation modelling, or SEM, is a flexible statistical technique that is extensively employed in many different fields. Its flexibility in managing complex multivariate interactions, compensating for measurement error, and integrating latent variables to accommodate unobservable notions is what makes it so popular. As a result, it provides a thorough method for empirically evaluating research hypotheses and is a priceless instrument for validating theoretical models and understanding the complex interactions between constructs.

4. Results

Table 1 shows the demographic distribution of the respondents. It shows that the majority of the respondents are female and around the age of 18-22.

Table 1: Demographic Description of the Data

Description	Count	Percentage
Female	72	70%
Male	31	30%
Age (18-22)	83	80.5%
Age (23-26)	18	17.5%
Age (27-30)	2	2%

Moreover, the model reliability and validity test shows that all the cut-off tests were met, indicating that the constructs are consistently accurate and measure what it is intended to measure (Table 2).

Table 2: Constructs Reliability and Validity Tests

Construct	Cronbach's alpha	Composite reliability (rho_a)	Composite reliability (rho_c)	Average variance extracted (AVE)
IU (Intention to Use)	0.921	0.924	0.921	0.701
PSP (Perceived Security and Privacy)	0.831	0.831	0.831	0.711
SI (Social Influence)	0.747	0.759	0.752	0.604
TI (Trusting Intention)	0.891	0.901	0.893	0.628

The path means standard deviations, t-statistics and p-values are presented in Table 3. It shows that the Perceived Security and Privacy (PSP) impacts users' trusting intention, Social Influence (SI) impacts intention to use, and Trusting intention (TI) impacts users' Intention to Use (IU). However, Social Influence (SI) does not impact users' trusting intention, and users' genders do not impact intention to use or trusting intention.

Table 3: Hypothesis Testing

	Sample mean (M)	Standard deviation (STDEV)	T-statistics (|O/STDEV|)	P-values
PSP -> TI	0.729	0.177	4.062	0
SI -> IU	0.357	0.168	2.008	0.045
SI -> TI	0.172	0.189	0.969	0.333
TI -> IU	0.675	0.153	4.499	0
Gender -> IU	0.009	0.052	0.171	0.864
Gender x TI -> IU	-0.088	0.063	1.352	0.177

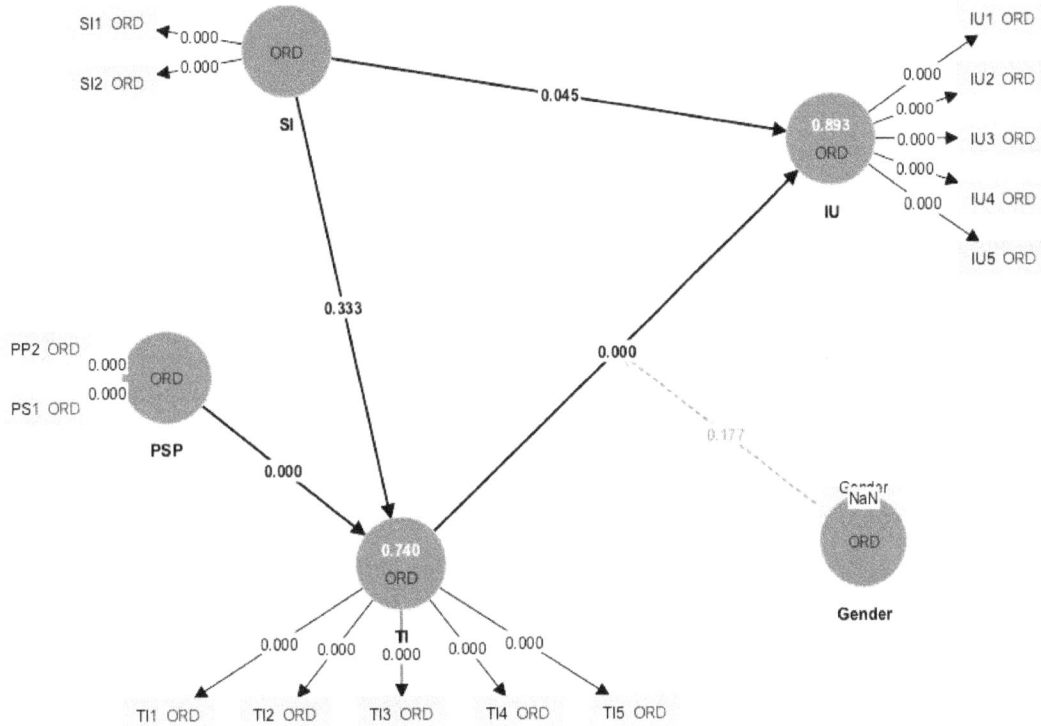

Figure 2:Model Results Representation

5. Discussion of the Results

The relationship between perceived privacy, security, and trusting intention in using social media platforms for government services is a critical area of investigation in today's digital landscape. Research has consistently shown that perceived privacy and security significantly influence users' trusting intentions. Perceived privacy relates to users' beliefs about how their personal information is protected on social media platforms, encompassing concerns of data collection, sharing, and storage. Meanwhile, perceived security entails confidence in the technical and procedural measures aimed to prevent unauthorized access, data breaches, and other cyber threats. These perceptions are fundamental in shaping users' attitudes and intentions towards engaging with government services via social media.

Trust is crucial in adopting technology, particularly in contexts involving sensitive information like government services. When users perceive that a social media platform upholds high levels of privacy and security, their trust in both the platform and the associated government agency increases. This trust is crucial not only for the initial adoption of the service but also for its sustained use. A robust perception of privacy and security reduces the perceived risks associated with using social media for government services, leading to greater user trust and engagement.

The statistically supported relationship between perceived privacy, security, and trusting intention underscores the need for government agencies to prioritise these aspects on their social media platforms. Effective implementation of robust privacy and security measures, coupled with clear communication to the public, is essential for building user trust, a key factor for the successful adoption and effective use of these platforms in delivering government services.

In terms of design, social media interfaces for government services should integrate features that enhance privacy and security, such as secure login processes, encryption, clear privacy policies, and regular security audits. Educating users about the privacy and security measures in place can further enhance their trust. Awareness campaigns or informational content about data protection practices are crucial in this regard.

The relationship between social influence and user behavior in the context of social media for government services is nuanced. While social influence significantly affects the intention to use social media for government services, its impact on trusting intention is more limited. Trust in government services delivered through social media is primarily built on factors such as perceived credibility, security, privacy, and the quality of past interactions with the government. Trusting intention is more deeply rooted in personal experiences and the direct relationship between the citizen and the government, reflecting an individual's own interactions and perceptions of the government's digital competence.On the other hand, the intention to use social media for government services is heavily prompted by social influence. This can be attributed to observational learning and normative pressures often present in social media environments. As Kaplan and Haenlein (2010) describe, social media platforms are inherently social spaces where the actions and opinions of others influence users. Observing others engage with government services via social media can encourage individuals to do the same, as they perceive a normative pressure or benefit in following suit. This phenomenon aligns with the Social Learning Theory, which posits that people learn from one another through observation, imitation, and modelling. Therefore, while trust in the government's digital services might be a personal and direct assessment, the decision to use these services can be heavily influenced by the observed behaviours and endorsements of peers and influential figures within one's social network.

Trust plays a pivotal role in shaping the intention to use social media for government services.In a digital environment where issues like data breaches and misinformation are prevalent, trust acts as a mitigating factor that encourages usage. This is supported by the findings of Welch et al. (2005), who argue that trust in e-government is closely linked to the satisfaction with and subsequent usage of these services. In the context of social media, this implies that when citizens trust the government's ability to deliver services effectively and securely through these platforms, their satisfaction increases, thereby boosting their intention to use them.

Finally, the relationship between trusting intention and intention to use, as well as social influence and intention to use, is generally not mediated by gender. Trusting intention, which reflects confidence in the reliability and integrity of technology, is a fundamental aspect influencing user behaviour, irrespective of gender. Similarly, social influence, the degree to which individuals perceive that essential others believe they should use a new technology, operates independently of gender differences. This is because the mechanisms through which trust and social influence affect technology acceptance are rooted in psychological and social factors that are largely uniform across genders. While there may be variations in the levels of trust or the susceptibility to social influence, these variations are more likely attributed to individual differences, cultural backgrounds, or specific situational factors rather than being inherently tied to gender. Thus, in the context of technology adoption, the core determinants of usage intention – trust and social influence – exert their effects across gender lines, making gender a less significant mediator in this relationship.

6.   Conclusion, Future Research and Research Limitations

This study provides insightful conclusions into user adoption of social media platforms for government services, particularly among Generation Z. The findings underscore the pivotal roles of perceived privacy, security, and trust in shaping users' trusting intentions and subsequent willingness to engage with these platforms. It is evident that when users perceive high levels of privacy and security, their trust in both the platform and the government agency increases, enhancing their intention to use the service. Additionally, the study reveals the significant influence of social norms and peer recommendations on the intention to use these services, although this influence does not extend to trusting intentions. Interestingly, the study also highlights that gender does not significantly mediate the relationship between these factors and the intention to use or trust in social media for government services. These insights are crucial for government agencies and policymakers, emphasising the need for robust privacy and security measures and the importance of leveraging social influence to enhance the adoption of e-government services via social media.

The study, while comprehensive, presents avenues for future research and acknowledges certain limitations. One of the primary limitations is the focus on Generation Z, which may not fully represent the broader population's attitudes and behaviours. Future research could expand the demographic scope to include a more diverse range of age groups, cultural backgrounds, and socio-economic statuses to understand user adoption patterns better. Additionally, the study's reliance on self-reported data could introduce biases, suggesting the need for more objective measures or mixed-method approaches in future research. Exploring the impact of emerging technologies like artificial intelligence and blockchain on users' trust and privacy perceptions could also provide valuable insights. Furthermore, investigating the long-term effects of trust and social influence on the continued use of these platforms would be beneficial. Understanding these dynamics can guide the development of more tailored and effective strategies for engaging citizens through social media in government services.

Acknowledgement

This work was supported by the Zayed University RIF grant activity code R22085.

References

Abdulkareem, A. K., & Ramli, R. M. (2021). Does trust in e-government influence the performance of e-government? An integration of information system success model and public value theory. Transforming Government: People, Process and Policy, [Online] Sep. 09, 2021. Available at: https://doi.org/10.1108/tg-01-2021-0001

Al-kfairy, M. and Shuhaiber, A. (2022,December). The intercorrelations among risk factors and trust dimensions in S-commerce: An empirical investigation from the user experience. In *2022 International Conference on Computer and Applications (ICCA)* (pp. 1-5). IEEE.

Al-kfairy, M., Shuhaiber, A., Al-Khatib, A.W. and Alrabaee, S. (2023). Social Commerce Adoption Model Based on Usability, Perceived Risks, and Institutional-Based Trust. *IEEE Transactions on Engineering Management*.

Al-kfairy, M., Shuhaiber, A., wael Al-khatib, A., Alrabaee, S. and Khaddaj, S. (2024). Understanding Trust Drivers of S-commerce. *Heliyon*.

Al, K. E. (2020). A systematic literature review and a proposed model on antecedents of trust to use social media for e-government services. International Journal of Advanced and Applied Sciences, [Online] Feb. 01, 2020. Available at: https://doi.org/10.21833/ijaas.2020.02.007

Alkraiji, A. and Ameen, N. (2022). The impact of service quality, trust and satisfaction on young citizen loyalty towards government e-services. *Information Technology & People*, 35(4), pp.1239-1270.

Alryalat, M., Dwivedi, Y., Williams, M. and Rana, N. (2013). Examining Role of Usefulness, Ease of Use and Social Influence on Jordanian Citizen's Intention to Adopt E-Government. AIS Electronic Library (AISeL), available at: https://aisel.aisnet.org/ukais2013/4/.

Capistrano, E. P. (2020). Determining e-Government Trust: An Information Systems Success Model Approach to the Philippines' Government Service Insurance System (GSIS), the Social Security System (SSS), and the Bureau of Internal Revenue (BIR). [Online] Jul. 28, 2020. Available at: https://pmr.upd.edu.ph/index.php/pmr/article/view/342

Chang, S.E., Liu, A.Y. and Shen, W. (2017).User trust in social networking services: A comparison of Facebook and LinkedIn, Computers in Human Behavior, available at: https://doi.org/10.1016/j.chb.2016.12.013

Cheung, C.M. and Lee, M.K. (2010). A theoretical model of intentional social action in online social networks. *Decision support systems*, 49(1), pp.24-30.

Cho, S. H., Oh, S. Y., Rou, H. G., & Gim, G. Y. (2019). A Study on The Factors Affecting The Continuous Use of E-Government Services - Focused on Privacy and Security Concerns-. [Online] Jul. 01, 2019. Available at: https://ieeexplore.ieee.org/abstract/document/8935693 (accessed Nov. 09, 2023)

Hu, G., Yan, J., Pan, W., Chohan, S., & Liu, L. (2019). The Influence of Public Engaging Intention on Value Co-Creation of E-Government Services. [Online] 2019. Available at: https://ieeexplore.ieee.org/abstract/document/8793076

Hung, S.-Y., Chen, K. and Su, Y.-K. (2019). The effect of communication and social motives on E-government services through social media groups. Behaviour & Information Technology 39(7), pp. 741–757. Available at: http://dx.doi.org/10.1080/0144929x.2019.1610907

Kanaan, A. (2023). The effect of quality, security and privacy factors on trust and intention to use e-government services, available at: http://m.growingscience.com/beta/ijds/5780-the-effect-of-quality-security-and-privacy-factors-on-trust-and-intention-to-use-e-government-services.html.

Kaplan, A.M. and Haenlein, M. (2010). Users of the world, unite! The challenges and opportunities of Social Media. *Business horizons*, 53(1), pp.59-68.

Khan, S., Ab. Rahim, N.Z. and Maarop, N. (2018). The Influence of Trust in Understanding Citizens' Behavior to Use Social media for E-government Services, available at: https://www.researchgate.net/profile/Sohrab-Khan-2/publication/332554244_The_Influence_of_Trust_in_Understanding_Citizens'_Behavior_to_Use_Social_media_for_E-government_Services/links/5cbd3d134585156cd7a8cd3b/The-Influence-of-Trust-in-Understanding-Citizens-Behavior-to-Use-Social-media-for-E-government-Services.pdf

Khan, S., Umer, R., Umer, S. and Naqvi, S. (2021). Antecedents of trust in using social media for E-government services: An empirical study in Pakistan. *Technology in Society*, 64, p.101400.

Kumar, R., Sachan, A. and Mukherjee, A. (2018). Direct vs indirect e-government adoption: an exploratory study. Available at: https://doi.org/10.1108/dprg-07-2017-0040

Li, W. (2021). The Role of Trust and Risk in Citizens' E-Government Services Adoption: A Perspective of the Extended UTAUT Model. *Sustainability*, [Online] Jul. 09, 2021. Available at: https://doi.org/10.3390/su13147671

Li, Y., & Shang, H. (2020). Service quality, perceived value, and citizens' continuous-use intention regarding e-government: Empirical evidence from China. *Information & Management*, [Online] Apr. 01, 2020. Available at: https://doi.org/10.1016/j.im.2019.103197

Li, Y., & Shang, H. (2023). How does e-government use affect citizens' trust in government? Empirical evidence from China. *Information & Management*, [Online] Nov. 01, 2023. Available at: https://doi.org/10.1016/j.im.2023.103844

Li, Y., Rho, E.H.R. and Kobsa, A. (2022). Cultural differences in the effects of contextual factors and privacy concerns on users' privacy decision on social networking sites. *Behaviour & Information Technology*, 41(3), pp.655-677.

Madyatmadja, E. D., Nindito, H., & Pristinella, D. (2019). Citizen Attitude. [Online] Nov. 05, 2019. Available at: https://doi.org/10.1145/3371647.3371653

Méndez-Rivera, C. A., Patiño-Toro, O. N., Arias, A. V., & Arango-Botero, D. (2023). Factors Influencing the Adoption of E-Government Services: A Study among University Students. *Economies*, [Online] Sep. 04, 2023. Available at: https://doi.org/10.3390/economies11090225

Mensah, I. K. (2019). Factors Influencing the Intention of University Students to Adopt and Use E-Government Services: An Empirical Evidence in China. *SAGE Open*, 9(2), p. 215824401985582. [Online] Apr. 2019. Available at: http://dx.doi.org/10.1177/2158244019855823

Mergel, I. (2013). Social media adoption and resulting tactics in the US federal government. *Government information quarterly*, 30(2), pp.123-130.

Nguyen, T., Nguyen, P., Huynh, H. T. N., Vrontis, D., & Ahmed, Z. (2023). Identification of the determinants of public trust in e-government services and participation in social media based on good governance theory and the technology acceptance model. Journal of Asia Business Studies, [Online] Jul. 18, 2023. Available at: https://doi.org/10.1108/jabs-04-2023-0160

Park, H., & Lee, T. (David). (2018). Adoption of E-Government Applications for Public Health Risk Communication: Government Trust and Social Media Competence as Primary Drivers. *Journal of Health Communication*, 23(8), 712–723. [Online] Aug. 2018. Available at: https://doi.org/10.1080/10810730.2018.1511013

Pavlou, P.A. and Gefen, D. (2004). Building effective online marketplaces with institution-based trust. *Information systems research*, 15(1), pp.37-59.

Sachan, A., Kumar, R., & Kumar, R. (2018). Examining the impact of e-government service process on user satisfaction. Journal of Global Operations and Strategic Sourcing, [Online] Aug. 07, 2018. Available at: https://doi.org/10.1108/jgoss-11-2017-0048

Shareef, M.A., Mukerji, B., Dwivedi, Y.K., Rana, N.P. and Islam, R. (2019). Social media marketing: Comparative effect of advertisement sources. *Journal of Retailing and Consumer Services*, 46, pp.58-69.

Veeramootoo, N., Nunkoo, R., & Dwivedi, Y. K. (2018). What determines the success of an e-government service? Validation of an integrative model of e-filing continuance usage. Government Information Quarterly, [Online] Apr. 01, 2018. Available at: https://doi.org/10.1016/j.giq.2018.03.004

Venkatesh, V., Morris, M.G., Davis, G.B. and Davis, F.D. (2003). User acceptance of information technology: Toward a unified view. *MIS quarterly*, pp.425-478.

Welch, E.W., Hinnant, C.C. and Moon, M.J., 2005. Linking citizen satisfaction with e-government and trust in government. *Journal of public administration research and theory*, 15(3), pp.371-391.

Zahid, H., Ali, S., Abu-Shanab, E. and Javed, H.M.U. (2022), "Determinants of intention to use e-government services: An integrated marketing relation view", Telematics and Informatics, 1 March, available at: https://doi.org/10.1016/j.tele.2022.101778

Zahid, H., Ali, S., Abu-Shanab, E., & Javed, H. M. U. (2022). Determinants of intention to use e-government services: An integrated marketing relation view. Telematics and Informatics, [Online] Mar. 01, 2022. Available at: https://doi.org/10.1016/j.tele.2022.101778

Zubir, M. Z. M., & Latip, M. F. A. (2023). Factors affecting citizens' intention to use e-government services: assessing the mediating effect of perceived usefulness and ease of use. Transforming Government: People, Process and Policy, [Online] Aug. 16, 2023. Available at: https://doi.org/10.1108/tg-04-2023-0040

Online Learning in 280 Characters: Analysing Public Sentiment on Online Learning During COVID-19

Anas Alsuhaibani[1], Mohammed Almotrafi[2], Faisal Alossaimi[1], Ahmad Alhassan[1] and Mohammed Alaklabi[1]

[1]Department of Information Systems, College of Computer Engineering and Sciences, Prince Sattam bin Abdulaziz University, Saudi Arabia

[2]Department of Information Systems, Faculty of Computing and Information Technology, Northern Border University, Saudi Arabia

ah.alsuhaibani@psau.edu.sa
maleinzi@nbu.edu.sa
441050802@std.psau.edu.sa
439051012@std.psau.edu.sa
441050838@std.psau.edu.sa

Abstract: The global COVID-19 pandemic forced a seismic shift towards online learning, replacing conventional in-person education in response to the inherent health risks. This transformation showcased the resilience of educational systems and the transformative potential of technology in breaking geographical barriers and delivering accessible learning opportunities. Despite the pandemic's challenges, it expedited online education developments, heralding a more adaptable, inclusive educational paradigm poised to outlast the pandemic's immediate effects. This study investigates public sentiment and perspectives concerning online learning in Saudi Arabia during the COVID-19 pandemic, using Twitter as a primary data source. By scrutinising tweets and interactions, this study aims to unearth insights into the challenges, advantages, and overall perceptions of online learning amid the pandemic. The analysis of the collected dataset revealed a prevalent negativity at 37.19%, contrasting with 29.37% positive sentiments and 33.43% neutral viewpoints. The primary cause for negative perceptions lies in the difficulties encountered during the shift to online learning, leading to strain on platforms. Nevertheless, positive feedback highlights the efficacy of the online learning system, viewing it as an opportunity for educational development. Neutral tweets often mention platform names, reflecting the nature of the data collected. Key themes in online learning discourse during the pandemic included technological challenges, student engagement, equity, teacher support, and assessment. The study emphasises the potential of Twitter data in identifying obstacles, gauging sentiment, and improving online learning strategies by sharing best practices and tailoring interventions.

Keywords: Sentiment analysis, Online learning, Twitter, COVID-19

1. Introduction

Sentiment analysis has become increasingly important in recent years as the volume of digital data generated by social media, online reviews, and other sources has grown exponentially (Liu, 2012). The ability to analyse this data and extract insights about public sentiment has many applications in areas such as market research, customer feedback analysis (Liu, 2012), brand reputation management, and product development (Dellarocas, Zhang & Awad, 2007). By providing a more nuanced understanding of public opinion, sentiment analysis allows businesses to make data-driven decisions that can improve customer satisfaction, brand perception, and overall business performance. One of the key challenges in sentiment analysis is accurately interpreting short sentences, such as those commonly used on social media platforms like Twitter and Facebook (Pak, & Paroubek, 2010). Global COVID-19 pandemic triggered a significant surge in the adoption of online learning as a response to the disruption of traditional in-person education (UNESCO, 2020). With health concerns rendering physical classrooms unsafe, online learning emerged as a vital alternative, enabling students to continue their education from the safety of their homes (Hodges et al, 2020). This transition highlighted the resilience of educational systems and the transformative power of technology in bridging geographical barriers and providing accessible learning opportunities. Despite the challenges posed by the pandemic, online education advancements were accelerated, leading to a more adaptable and inclusive approach to learning that is expected to endure beyond the pandemic (Darling-Hammond, Hyler, & Gardner, 2020).

This study aims to explore public sentiment and opinions regarding online learning in Saudi Arabia on Twitter during the COVID-19 pandemic. Twitter, as a prominent social media platform, provides a valuable source of real-time data reflecting diverse perspectives on remote education during this unprecedented period. By analysing tweets and interactions, we seek to gain insights into the challenges, benefits, and overall perceptions of online learning during the COVID-19 pandemic. The present study seeks to answer the following questions:

RQ1. How did the sentiment on Twitter towards online learning evolve over the course of the COVID-19 pandemic, and what were the key factors influencing these changes?

RQ2. What were the most frequently discussed topics and issues related to online learning on Twitter during the pandemic?

RQ3. What insights can be gleaned from Twitter data to inform the improvement of online learning strategies and policies for future crises or remote learning scenarios?

2. Literature Review

2.1 Sentiment Analysis

Sentiment analysis, also known as opinion mining, is a process that uses natural language processing, text analysis, and computational linguistics to identify and extract subjective information from text (Young, 2018). It involves analysing the emotional tone or attitude expressed in a piece of text, such as a tweet, review, or news article, and determining whether the sentiment expressed is positive, negative, or neutral (Pang, & Lee, 2012). Sentiment analysis is widely used in various fields, including marketing, customer service, and social media analysis (Liu, 2012), to understand public opinion, identify trends, and make data-driven decisions. One of the most important benefits of sentiment analysis is the ability to analyse people's feedback from various sources, such as social media, reviews, and surveys. By using sentiment analysis, businesses can gain a deeper understanding of customer sentiment and identify areas for improvement. This is particularly helpful for businesses looking to improve their customer service, product offerings, or overall customer experience (Liu, 2012). Sentiment analysis can also be used to monitor brand reputation by tracking the sentiment around the brand (Alsuhaibani, 2018; Pang et al, 2009), identifying any negative sentiment and taking appropriate action to address any issues that may be affecting their reputation. This is especially important in industries where customer trust is crucial, such as healthcare, finance, and technology. By monitoring brand reputation, businesses can stay ahead of the curve and proactively address any issues that may arise. In addition to customer feedback analysis and brand reputation management (Cambria et al, 2014), sentiment analysis can be used to improve marketing and advertising efforts by analysing the sentiment of social media posts. This can help businesses target specific demographics or improve their overall marketing strategy. Sentiment analysis can also be used for competitive analysis by monitoring sentiment around competitors, identifying where they can differentiate themselves and gain a competitive advantage (Dellarocas et al, 2007). Overall, sentiment analysis is an essential tool that can provide valuable insights into public opinion and help businesses make data-driven decisions that can improve customer satisfaction, brand reputation, and overall business performance.

2.2 Online Learning During COVID-19

Online learning pertains to the dissemination of educational materials and teaching via the internet. This mode enables students to enrol in courses and attain qualifications from remote locations, eliminating the necessity for physical attendance at educational institutions. Diverse in its manifestations, online learning encompasses web-centric classes, virtual conferencing, and autonomous learning modules (Singh & Thurman). The global education landscape has been profoundly transformed by the far-reaching impacts of the COVID-19 pandemic, leading to the rapid and widespread adoption of online learning as a critical response (UNESCO. 2020). Facing unprecedented challenges, educational institutions around the world have rapidly shifted from traditional classroom settings to online learning environments (Hodges et al, 2020). This transformation necessitated the creative use of digital technologies, online platforms, and virtual collaboration tools to ensure uninterrupted access to education and maintain educational continuity. The experience of online learning during the COVID-19 pandemic has not only highlighted the resilience of educational systems, but also demonstrated the remarkable adaptability and resourcefulness of both teachers and students (Means et al, 2010). Through effective integration of technology and adoption of online learning, educational institutions have succeeded in providing comprehensive and flexible education, transcending geographical boundaries, and enabling learners to participate in engaging and interactive virtual learning experiences (United Nations, 2020). This transformative approach to education has not only mitigated the disruptions caused by the pandemic but has also accelerated the exploration and implementation of innovative pedagogical practices (Bozkurt et al, 2020), which will continue to shape the future of education beyond the current crisis. The shift to online education amid the pandemic had positive effects, notably increasing enrolment in distance learning courses (Abdelwahed et al, 2023; Zhou, 2024). However, the setup differs between temporary measures and established distance learning programs at universities. Before the pandemic, there were existing online degree programs, but the situation accelerated growth. Data shows a significant rise in registrations, in 2016, there were 21 million registered students on online learning platforms, a number that increased annually by about 7 million over the next two years. However, the pandemic significantly boosted these numbers, with registrations almost tripling in 2020 to 71 million and reaching 92 million in 2021. Course enrolments for online learning also experienced dramatic increases. Pre-pandemic growth was overshadowed by substantial spikes during the pandemic, with enrolment numbers doubling in 2020 and growing by 32% in 2021, culminating in a peak of 189 million enrolments (Zhou, 2024). In the aftermath of the COVID-19 pandemic, online learning has become deeply integrated into Saudi Arabia's educational landscape, offering both students and educators a versatile platform for remote instruction and collaboration. The adoption of online learning tools and platforms continues to expand, facilitating greater flexibility in learning schedules and enhancing access to educational resources across the country (Madani et al, 2023). Many educational institutions in Saudi Arabia have seamlessly integrated virtual classrooms into their curriculum, allowing students to participate in live lectures, discussions, and collaborative projects from the comfort of their homes (Abdelwahed et al, 2023).

2.3 Related Studies

A recent study by Muhammad et al (2021) argued that the COVID-19 pandemic has greatly impacted the online education system, leading to concerns from stakeholders such as parents, teachers, and students. This study investigates the effectiveness of online education by analysing stakeholder sentiment using social media data. The dataset used was obtained from the Twitter API, and various text preprocessing methods were used to clean the tweets. Machine learning algorithms were used to classify positive, negative and neutral reviews. Synthetic Minority Over-sampling Technique (SMOTE), Decision Tree (DT) and Support Vector Machine (SVM) are classification algorithms, Random Forest (RF) is an ensemble learning method, and Valence Aware Dictionary for Sentiment Reasoning (VADER) and lexical resource for sentiment analysis (SentiWordNet) are sentiment analysis tools used in this study. The results show that data normalisation with SMOTE enhances classification accuracy, with DT, SVM, and RF performing well. VADER and SentiWordNet techniques were used to compare performance, with TextBlob showing superior results for data annotation. Furthermore, deep learning models have been found to perform better due to the smaller size of the dataset. When modelling the topic using LSA, concerns emerged regarding uncertainty surrounding the opening date of institutions and the lack of technical skills in rural areas.

Another study by AL-Rubaie et al (2016) focused on the design and implementation of Arabic text classification of the opinions of students at King Abdulaziz University. This study employed algorithms such as SVM and NB (Naive Bayes is a probabilistic machine learning algorithm based on Bayes' theorem). Their analysis showed promising results with students' online comments, revealing that their texts were more traditional and that local Saudi dialects were used more frequently in comments than Modern Standard Arabic (MSA). The best accuracy was achieved by SVM with n-gram feature and class neutral. Future work plans include analysing structured data on the whiteboard and creating a semantic diagram to understand students' behaviours while studying.

A recent study by Zuhri & Aznan (2022) conducted a sentiment analysis about e-learning using Twitter data, focusing on SVM as the most accurate algorithm. SVM achieved a higher accuracy compared to the Linear Regression (LR) algorithm by 3%. However, more research is needed to understand which parameter tuning will lead to better classification results, as the only parameter that was tuned in this project was parameter C (The C parameter tells the SVM optimisation how much a user wants to avoid misclassifying each training example) with different values.

This paper addresses a significant gap in the literature on online learning during the COVID-19 pandemic, namely focusing on Saudi content. While previous studies have explored sentiment analysis and online learning, there remains a lack of comprehensive research that specifically investigates public sentiment and opinions regarding online learning in Saudi Arabia, especially using Twitter data. The distinctive cultural, social, and educational context of Saudi Arabia may significantly influence experiences and perceptions of online learning in this specific setting. Understanding public sentiment and opinions specific to Saudi Arabia is crucial to developing tailored strategies and policies to promote online learning in this country. By examining Twitter data, this paper aims to fill this gap by providing insights into the challenges, benefits, and public perceptions of online learning during the pandemic in Saudi Arabia.

3. Methodology

3.1 Data Collection

The dataset utilised in this study pertains to the domain of online learning in Saudi Arabia during the COVID-19 pandemic. This data was sourced from Kaggle, a prominent online community platform catering to data science and machine learning enthusiasts (Kaggle, 2023). Kaggle served as a valuable resource, providing access to a diverse collection of datasets and supplementary materials essential for the successful execution of this research project. Data acquisition occurred over the time-frame spanning from September 2 to September 17, 2020, encompassing the initial two weeks of the academic year. It is important to note that none of the tweets included in our analysis were duplicated from the same individual within the specified timeframe. Each tweet was treated as a unique data point, contributing to the overall breadth and diversity of the dataset. The dataset was meticulously compiled from four trending hashtags in Saudi Arabia about online learning and COVID-19. These hashtags encompass a total of 1676 records consisting of text Tweets in Arabic, all of which share the same geographic location of Saudi Arabia. These records were structured into 10 distinct data columns, enhancing the richness and depth of the dataset for comprehensive analysis. The first hashtag is #وزارة_التعليم translates to Ministry of Education in English and it is commonly used to discuss news, updates, and initiatives related to the Ministry of Education in Saudi Arabia. The second hashtag is #تعليم_عن_بعد translates to online learning and it is associated with discussions, resources, and experiences related to remote or online education. It became particularly prominent during the COVID-19 pandemic. The third hashtag is #عين which translates to Ain which is the official platform that the Ministry of Education in Saudi Arabia launched during COVID-19 for online education. The fourth hashtag is #تيمز which is related to Microsoft Teams which was highly used by students in their online education and discussion. These hashtags primarily pertain to school pupils rather than university students. Consequently, we expect the data to reflect the opinions of parents of pupils regarding the online learning experience.

3.2 Data Cleaning

Prior to analysing the data, we performed a thorough data cleaning process to ensure the accuracy and reliability of our findings. This involved removing columns that were deemed irrelevant to our research objectives, such as retweet count, hashtags, and the time of a tweet. In addition, we restored words with repeated letters to their original form, such as "خيررر" to "خير". Furthermore, we removed Arabic diacritics, such as "ق", which can appear above or below Arabic letters, to standardise the text and facilitate analysis. For example, "سيّء" was changed back to "سيء". These data cleaning steps were imperative in preparing a high-quality dataset for our research.

3.3 Data Analysis

The data for this study was analysed manually by three researchers who are fluent Arabic speakers. A codebook, containing the three primary emotion dimensions (Table 1) was developed prior to the commencement of coding work. After each coder had completed the analysis of 200 tweets, an interceding reliability check was applied to ensure consistency between the three coders. The test revealed positive results, with an Average Pairwise Percent Agreement of 90.452%, Fleiss' Kappa coefficient of 0.853, and an Observed Agreement of 0.905. Subsequently, the analysis was applied to the whole dataset (1676 tweets).

Table 1: Sentiment Codebook

ID	Code	Definition	Example
0	Neutral	The tweet's content doesn't give a feeling of negativity or positivity.	"لكل تجربة مشاكل ولكن اذا فيه حلول يمكن تجاوز المشاكل" (Every experience has problems, but if there are solutions, the problems can be overcome)
1	Negative	The tweet's content gives a feeling of negativity.	"التعليم الالكتروني غير مجدي وغير نافع" (online learning is useless and ineffective)
2	Positive	The tweet's content gives a feeling of positivity.	"منصة مدرستي يقدم من خلالها جهود عظيمة للامانه يعيش أبناؤنا تجربة تقنيه تعليميه فريدة ومستمتعين فيها جدا" (Madrasati platform is a great platform. Our children live a unique educational technology experience and enjoy it very much)

4. Findings

As illustrated in Figure 1, it is evident that opinions regarding online learning in Saudi Arabia are predominantly negative. The negative sentiment represents 37.19% of the opinions, while the positive sentiment accounts for 29.37%. The remaining 33.43% of opinions were deemed neutral which was interesting. An explanation of this will be presented in the following sections. One of the key reasons behind the negative sentiment is attributed to difficulties faced during the transition to online learning, which resulted in significant strain on the platforms. Consequently, people formed a negative perception at the outset. However, we also discovered positive opinions that praised the effectiveness of the online learning system in Saudi Arabia. Additionally, some individuals initially held neutral opinions but acknowledged the potential for rapid advancements in the field of online learning within the country.

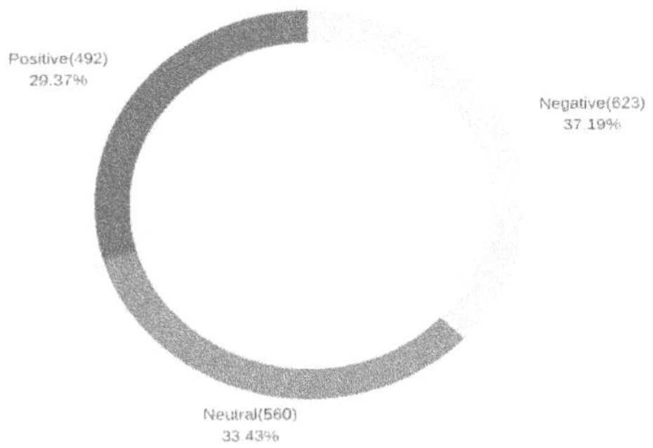

Positive(492)
29.37%

Negative(623)
37.19%

Neutral(560)
33.43%

Figure 1: Tweets distribution over categories

From Figure 2, we can observe that the words "عين", "مدرستي" and "منصه", are repeated in the neutral code. These are the names of the platforms for online learning in Saudi Arabia and this is the reason they appear in this code, as well as in other codes. It is noteworthy that the neutral code appears more frequently than the positive, with the neutral accounting for 33.43% and the positive for 29.37%. This can be attributed to the fact that the existing data included some tweets such as news, advertisements, or responses to tweets. For example, consider the following sentence " لا يوجد فشل تعطل المنصة لا يعني توقف العملية التعليمية يوجد برنامج التيمز و قنوات عين كبدائل للمنصة". The code for this sentence is neutral because it emphasises that even if the educational platform experiences technical issues or malfunctions, the educational process itself should not come to a halt because there are alternative tools like Microsoft Teams "التيمز" and "Ain" channels "عين" available to continue the educational activities. It underscores the importance of adaptability and resourcefulness in ensuring that education continues despite challenges.

Figure 2: Neutral word cloud[1]

---

[1]Word cloud translation: Teachers, Education, Students, Platform, Madrasity platform, Class, Virtual, Ain platform, Ministry, Education, Channels, Mathematics, Primary school, Teams, Online, Sessions and Interactive.

Figure 3 illustrates that this code contains numerous positive Arabic words such as "شكراً" and "بارك", which respectively mean 'thanks' and 'blessing'. The reason for its recurrence is people's praise for the online learning platform and their belief in the success of their education or the education of their children despite the pandemic. They perceive it as an opportunity for the development of education in general in Saudi Arabia. For example, consider the following statement "المنصة شيء جميل ولله الحمد وتساعدنا على الاستمرار بالتعلم رغم الظروف لذلك شكرًا على الجهود". In this example, the student is a positive example who praises the mechanism of online learning, describing it as a wonderful solution for the continuation of education and expressing gratitude for the efforts made for education.

Figure 3: Positive word cloud[2]

In this code, we observe a strong connection between the tweets and their authors. We found that students are usually the main contributors to the tweets in this code. As previously mentioned, the launch of the online learning platform posed significant challenges initially due to server overload and other issues. Students who embarked on online learning found it challenging to adjust to a new system and continued to express a desire to return to in-person study, to which they were accustomed. In this specific example " التعليم عن بعد غير ناجح وخصوصا للابتدائي والمنصه قاصره ولا تفيد والمعلومه لا تصل للطالب بالشكل السليم ولا تستطيع متابعه الطلاب ومتابعه تعلمهم", we classified it as negative because the tweeter appears to lack confidence in the overall success of education, especially for children. They mentioned a lack of a suitable platform and the inability to easily access it to monitor their child's learning.

Figure 4: Negative word cloud[3]

---

[2] Word cloud translation: Successful, Amazing, Honestly, Awesome, Interactive, Efforts, Thanks, Indeed, Nature, Better, Experience, Beautiful, Creativity, Alternatives, Explanation, Activation and Successfully.

[3] Word cloud translation: Failure, No, Very, Platform, We are tired, Education, Nothing, Hopefully, Not enough, Problems, Pressure, Without and Worse.

5. Discussion and Conclusion

This study contributes to understanding how the COVID-19 outbreak in Saudi Arabia has impacted individuals' attitudes toward online learning. Initially, the COVID-19 pandemic elicited mixed reactions on Twitter regarding online learning. Some expressed enthusiasm, while others expressed concerns about technological difficulties and a lack of in-person interaction. The most frequently discussed topics on Twitter regarding online learning during the pandemic included technological difficulties, student engagement, equity and access, teacher support and professional development, and assessment and evaluation. By identifying these obstacles, tracking sentiment and feedback, sharing best practices, including stakeholders, and focusing interventions on specific needs, insights from Twitter data could potentially enhance online learning strategies. The results will highlight opportunities for improvement in distance learning techniques and policies, as well as insights into the evolution of sentiment and significant influencing variables. The study underscores the critical role sentiment analysis plays in influencing instructional strategies and crisis-related decision-making. The findings of this study can aid policymakers and educational institutions in improving current distant learning opportunities and planning for potential future online learning scenarios.

To advance the scholarly conversation, there is a pressing need to scrutinize the effectiveness of targeted interventions aimed at mitigating technological difficulties, enhancing student engagement, promoting equity, bolstering teacher support, and refining assessment practices. This necessitates rigorous empirical inquiry to assess the impact of such interventions on the overall online learning experience. Furthermore, employing complementary qualitative research methodologies alongside quantitative analyses is imperative to gain a comprehensive understanding of the experiential nuances shaping attitudes toward online learning. Future research endeavours could benefit from incorporating qualitative data and engaging a broader spectrum of stakeholders, including educators, examiners, students, and parents, to provide a more nuanced understanding of online learning. Additionally, researchers should consider undertaking cross-cultural studies to discern variations in online learning perceptions across diverse demographic and regional contexts, thereby contributing to a broader understanding of global implications. Strategic policy analyses, coupled with collaborative efforts involving stakeholders, are pivotal for the development of effective strategies that respond to the identified challenges. While the inclusion of emojis could offer an interesting avenue for extending our research in future studies, it is essential to note the scope and limitations of our current analysis. Despite not incorporating emojis in this iteration of our research, we acknowledge the potential value of exploring their role in sentiment analysis and its implications for understanding online discourse more comprehensively. The absence of emojis in this study is due to having them discarded from the dataset when it was initially retrieved from Kaggle.

Acknowledgement

The authors extend their appreciation to the Deputyship for Research & Innovation, Ministry of Education in Saudi Arabia for funding this research work through the project number (IF2/PSAU/2022/02/21727).

References

Abdelwahed, N. A. A., Aldoghan, M. A., Moustafa, M. A., & Soomro, B. A. (2023). Factors affecting online learning, stress and anxiety during the COVID-19 pandemic in Saudi Arabia. International Journal of Human Rights in Healthcare, 16(5), pp. 437-453.

Alhazmi, A. M., (2020). Online Learning in Saudi Arabia During the COVID-19 Pandemic: An Exploratory Study. Journal of Educational Technology Systems. pp. 163-180.

Alotaibi, A. F., Alotaibi, M. S., & Alshahrani, A. S, (2021). The role of online learning during the COVID-19 pandemic: A qualitative study on student perspectives in Saudi Arabia. Education and Information Technologies. pp. 1-18.

Alshumaimeri, Y. A., & Al-Barrak, A., (2020). Distance E-Learning in Saudi Arabia During the COVID-19 Pandemic: An Exploratory Study. Education Sciences. pp. 10-11.

Alsuhaibani, A. (2018). An Investigation of Sentiment and Themes from Twitter for Brexit, 5th European Conference on Social Media ECSM.

Alzahrani, A. I., & Moheeb, A. E, (2020). The Impact of COVID-19 on E-learning: A Case Study of King Abdulaziz University, Saudi Arabia. Journal of Open Innovation: Technology, Market, and Complexity. pp. 146.

Barbosa, L., & Feng, J, (2010). Robust sentiment detection on twitter from biased and noisy data. Proceedings of the 23rd International Conference on Computational Linguistics, pp. 36-44.

Bozkurt, A., Jung, I., Xiao, J., Vladimirschi, V., Schuwer, R., Egorov, G., ... & Paskevicius, M. (2020). A Global Outlook to the Interruptions to Education Due to COVID-19 Pandemic: Navigating in a Time of Uncertainty and Crisis. Asian Journal of Distance Education, n.d.

Cambria, E., & White, B , (2014). "Jumping NLP curves: A review of natural language processing research," IEEE Computational Intelligence Magazine. pp. 48-57.

Darling-Hammond, L., Hyler, M. E., & Gardner, M. (2020). Effective Online Teaching in the Time of COVID-19. Stanford Center for Opportunity Policy in Education., n.d.

Dellarocas, C., Zhang, & Awad, (2007). Exploring the value of online product reviews in forecasting sales: The case of motion pictures," Journal of Interactive Marketing. pp. 23-45.

Hamed AL-Rubaiee, Renxi Qiu, Khalid Alomar and Dayou Li, (2016). Sentiment Analysis of Arabic Tweets in e-Learning.

Hodges, C., Moore, S., Lockee, B., Trust, T., & Bond, A. (2020). The Difference Between Emergency Remote Teaching and Online Learning, n.d.

Kaggle, (2023). online learning Saudi Arabia during covid-19. [Online] Available at: https://www.kaggle.com/datasets/bdo0or/distance-education-saudi-arabi-during-covid19

Liu, B., (2012). Sentiment analysis and opinion mining. Synthesis Lectures on Human Language, pp. 1-167.

Madani, H., Adhikari, A. and Hodgdon, C. (2023), "Understanding faculty acceptance of online teaching during the COVID-19 pandemic: a Saudi Arabian case study", Journal of International Education in Business, Vol. 16 No. 2, pp. 152-166. https://doi.org/10.1108/JIEB-12-2021-0109

Means, B., Toyama, Y., Murphy, R., Bakia, M., & Jones, K. (2010). Evaluation of Evidence-Based Practices in Online Learning: A Meta-Analysis and Review of Online Learning Studies. U.S. Department of Education., n.d.

Muhammad Mujahid 1,†, Ernesto Lee 2,† , Furqan Rustam 1,† , Patrick Bernard Washington , (2021). Sentiment Analysis and Topic Modeling on Tweets about.

Pak, A., & Paroubek, P, (2010). Twitter as a corpus for sentiment analysis and opinion mining. pp. 1320-1326.

Pang, B., & Lee, L, (2009). Opinion mining and sentiment analysis. Foundations and Trends. Information Retrieval, pp. 1-135.

Pang, B., & Lee, L, 2012. Sentiment analysis and opinion mining. Synthesis Lectures on Human Language Technologies. pp. 1-167.

Zhou, L. (2024). ELearning Statistics: The Definitive list in 2024. Luisa Zhou. https://www.luisazhou.com/blog/elearning-statistics/

Instagram Social Media Communication in Pandemic Times: A Deductive Qualitative Analysis of a Portuguese Digital Influencer's Profile

Ana Filipa Costa[1], Teresa Gouveia[2], Nídia Salomé Morais[2] and Rui Raposo[3]
[1]Polytechnic Institute of Viseu, Portugal
[2]Polytechnic Institute of Viseu, CI&DEI - Centre for Studies in Education and Innovation, Portugal
[3]University of Aveiro, Portugal

anafilipacosta24@gmail.com
tgouveia@esev.ipv.pt
salome@esev.ipv.pt
raposo@ua.pt

Abstract: The power of social media as an influential tool is undeniable, and influencer marketing has emerged as a strategic element, introducing innovative methods of communication, promotion, and advertising to support content creators (Brown & Hayes, 2008). In this context, the study aimed to analyze the impact of the COVID-19 pandemic on the communication strategies of Portuguese digital influencer Helena Coelho. The focus was on the content shared on her primary platform, Instagram, widely recognized for influencer marketing. The epidemiological crisis triggered by the pandemic raised the crucial question of how content creators adapted to new ways of communicating with the public. This period of uncertainty imposed significant challenges, forcing creators to reevaluate their communication strategies. To understand these adaptations, the research presented in this paper adopted a deductive qualitative approach, which enabled an in-depth analysis of the content posted by Helena Coelho, a highly followed Portuguese Instagram influencer. A focus group was conducted and included a convenient purposive sample of five female individuals, aged between 22 and 24 years and all active followers of the influencer's Instagram account. The study also resorted to observational research techniques with which 60 Instagram posts, collected between April 1st and April 31st, 2019, and April 1st and April 31st, 2020. This interval was chosen to identify changes in the influencer's communication strategies, covering both pre-pandemic and active pandemic periods. The results revealed that, although the influencer faced challenges due to the lack of common everyday activities during the lockdown, she was able to adjust her communication strategies, engaging the audience through home-produced content such as live streams and challenges, and effectively utilizing hashtags. As a consequence of these adjustments, the influencer experienced a substantial growth in her number of followers and engagement rate on Instagram in 2020 when compared to 2019. The collected and analyzed data indicate that the changes in her communication strategy, due to limitations derived from the pandemic, had a positive impact on her overall results, contributing to her growth and influence in the digital landscape.

Keywords: Social media communication, COVID 19 Pandemic, Instagram, Digital influencer

1. Introduction

The COVID-19 pandemic, one of the most pressing challenges of the 21st century, has had widespread impacts on global health and the economy, accelerating the need for brands to establish a digital presence, especially on social media. In this context, influencers have played a crucial role, standing out for their rise amid pandemic uncertainty (Canton, 2021; Richbourg, 2022).

Social distancing, globally adopted for health reasons, imposed significant adjustments on both businesses and content producers, requiring a reevaluation of their communication strategies. Faced with restrictions, businesses turned to digital marketing as an effective response, enabling consumers to make remote purchases (Fabius et al., 2020). Content producers, including digital influencers, adapted to the circumstances, finding new ways to connect with the audience, often operating from their own homes (Buvár et al., 2022).

Given this scenario, it was considered relevant to analyze possible changes in the communication strategies of Portuguese digital influencer Helena Coelho, based on an analysis of her Instagram content during the pandemic. The research sought to answer the central question: "In what ways did the context of the COVID-19 pandemic influence the communication strategies of the digital influencer Helena Coelho?" To achieve this, the study investigated how the challenges faced by content creators during this period impacted the communicational performance of the digital influencer. Additionally, the study aimed to assess the influence of COVID-19 on Helena Coelho's growth and identify the strategies implemented to maintain relevance in a scenario where social media consumption and information seeking saw a significant increase.

2. Theoretical Framework

The Covid-19 pandemic triggered a crisis that had a significant impact on businesses, compelling them to adapt and develop new forms of communication (Donthu and Gustafsson, 2020). According to Castro et al. (2020), organizations faced the socio-economic impacts resulting from the global crisis caused by the Covid-19 pandemic. Therefore, it became paramount for organizations to adopt new strategies, such as efficient communication, work planning, digital enhancement, telecommuting, and actions aimed at the well-being of their employees, to minimize the harmful effects of the pandemic on the organization.

The pandemic redefined commercial dynamics and daily habits, prompting influencers to adjust. This adjustment became evident during the isolation period, where the increased time dedicated to online content consumption not only boosted follower growth but also strengthened engagement with the audience. This scenario was amplified by the pivotal role of social media, which became an indispensable tool for digital marketing. With technological advances, social media not only enabled consumers to create and share content but also influenced other users, transforming marketing strategies into more effective approaches than traditional ones (Thackeray et al., 2008).

It has become evident that the virtual realm of social networks is advantageous for brands. The act of sharing content has facilitated a deeper understanding of users, their preferences, and needs, thereby enabling a more adaptable market strategy. In this densely populated network of interconnected individuals (Ryan, 2014), the consumption of social media has been significant, experiencing a notable increase during periods of social isolation. Consequently, influencers have had to devise creative strategies employing the tools available on digital platforms. Alves et al. (2020) assert that, during lockdowns, social networks became steadfast allies for many individuals, serving as a means to 'disconnect' from the prevailing circumstances. However, for others, these platforms became a source of anxiety due to the overwhelming influx of information related to the health crisis and the saturation of available activities.

Lincoln (2016) defines digital influencers as individuals who are active online, possessing the ability to shape perspectives and influence the decisions of others through their perceived or real authority, knowledge, position, or relationships. In a parallel perspective, Francalanci and Hussain (2015) characterize influencers as users on social media platforms with a substantial audience (followers). They differentiate the term 'influencers' from the broader concept of 'influence,' which encompasses the social impact derived from the content shared by users across various social media platforms.

Digital influencers, increasingly prominent in Instagram photos, Facebook posts, and YouTube videos, have evolved into celebrities, amassing substantial followings on digital platforms. They now wield the power to influence the choices of their audience, akin to actors, musicians, or politicians. Recognizing this reality, brands are keenly aware of the potential to promote their products through these influencers (Santos, 2018). According to Santos (2020), during the period of social isolation imposed by the pandemic, the interests of digital influencers transformed to align with the cultural moment and adapt to new conditions of content production. Despite the initial impact, influencer marketing has not faded away; professionals have adapted along with the market. Faced with measures to contain the virus, rather than merely adjusting their content and posting routines, digital influencers have taken on the role of disseminating information about precautions and offering tips on dealing with the pandemic. Beyond the realm of digital marketing, this period has yielded positive outcomes for those who focused on education, producing conscious, relevant, and authentic content. Moreover, the audience has displayed increased participation, curiosity, and a propensity for questioning.

With the Covid-19 pandemic, organizations have encountered unprecedented challenges, compelling the need for innovation in their marketing strategies. Wang et al. (2020) define marketing innovation strategies as a company's commitment to developing new marketing tactics or improving existing ones, enabling efficient resource utilization, meeting consumer demand, and creating more value. In this context, the reactive, collective, proactive, or partnership strategies outlined by Wang et al. (2020) have emerged as valuable responses for companies affected by the pandemic. Consequently, organizations have been able to introduce new products and/or services through partnerships with complementary companies. Such collaborations leverage the advantages of both partners, resulting in a 'win-win' outcome. For instance, organizations opting for the partnership strategy developed a unique competitive advantage and were even able to profit from the crisis period. This approach allowed organizations to enter new markets and establish new businesses (Wang et al., 2020). These changes have significantly impacted the digital marketing landscape, leading to exponential growth. Fueled by the necessity to maintain a market presence and adapt to new circumstances, companies have been compelled to invest in online actions. The pandemic, by accelerating the transition to the digital environment, has transformed marketing operations, previously centered on face-to-face approaches. This transformation underscores the growing importance of digital marketing as an essential tool for reaching and engaging consumers in the new normal.

The swift adaptation of organizations, coupled with an astute anticipation of trends in the digital environment and strategic investments in digital marketing, proved decisive for ensuring consumer access to companies during the pandemic. According to Oliveira (2021), digital marketing played a pivotal role in helping companies adjust to circulation restrictions imposed by the pandemic. An exemplary instance of this adaptation was the use of social media as a tool to connect with customers. Through direct communication, the sharing of relevant content, promotions, partnerships with influencers, and targeted ads, companies were able to maintain a strong connection with their clientele during the pandemic.

This transformation in business-customer communication, facilitated by social media platforms, not only sustained commerce during one of the most significant recent economic crises (Oliveira, 2021) but also underscored the influence of these platforms on the online purchasing decision-making process. Borges (2020) emphasized these changes, citing an international study conducted by ISAG - European Business School that unveiled the growing loyalty of Portuguese consumers to online shopping. The study concluded that e-commerce in Portugal is expected to continue its upward trajectory. Additionally, the research highlighted a shift in consumer profiles—individuals who are more sophisticated, tech-savvy, and possess high expectations of brands are emerging. In response, companies must adapt their commercial strategies, the available product offerings, and even the shopping experience to reinforce customer trust and maintain business dynamism (Borges, 2020). With consumers becoming increasingly active on social networks, influencer marketing plays a crucial role, providing brands with a more efficient means of attracting audiences. Social networks have become indispensable in shaping opinions that, in turn, influence customer decisions. Thus, influencer marketing stands as a manifestation of the considerable power wielded by digital influencers with their followers (Antunes, 2020).

3.   Methodology

The methodology employed in this study follows a case study approach, aligning with Sousa's (2009) perspective that deems it appropriate for analyses centered on a single case. The primary advantage of this approach lies in the researcher's capacity to delve into specific events in detail, utilizing various instruments to comprehend the underlying processes. To achieve a comprehensive understanding, we adopted a deductive qualitative approach, which included content analysis of the Instagram account of influencer Helena Coelho and a focus group. Yin (2004) emphasizes that qualitative approaches explore the nuances, contexts, and meanings underlying the data. In this study, we opted for a qualitative approach, utilizing observational research techniques to fulfill the study's objectives. Group interviews were used to gain additional insights and deepen the understanding of the data collected through content analysis.

4.   The Study

The sample selected for content analysis comprised 60 posts, spanning two distinct periods: April 1 to 31, 2019, and April 1 to 31, 2020. This deliberate choice allowed us to delineate two phases in Helena Coelho's profile - before and during the pandemic - to identify potential changes in communication strategies. The sample selection followed an intentional approach, where the digital influencer was chosen deliberately or for convenience, rather than randomly. About ethics on secondary data, all Instagram posts analyzed are in the public domain. Furthermore, all irrelevant personal information for the study was omitted to ensure the influencer's privacy. For content analysis, we employed a grid adapted from previous studies conducted by Segarra-Saavedra and Hidalgo-Marí (2018) and Romo and Aguirre (2020).

Concerning the focus group, a convenience sample of five female participants, aged between 22 and 24 and residing in the city of Viseu, was selected. These individuals use the Instagram platform and are familiar with the content produced by the influencer Helena Coelho. All participants were informed about the purpose of the study and gave their informed consent before participating. Their identities were kept anonymous, and all their responses were treated with confidentiality. In addition, participants were guaranteed the right to withdraw from the study at any time. These ethical principles ensure that the rights and well-being of the participants are protected during the conduct of the study. The focus group took place on October 20, 2022.

5.   Results

The content analysis carried out on the Instagram platform covered various categories, including the number of posts, promotional nature, presence of a human figure, text, other signs, format, interaction, and theme. Upon examining the year 2020, it was observed that the influencer shared 37 posts, indicating an average of more than one post per day. In contrast, in 2019, before the onset of the pandemic, the influencer shared only 23 posts, as depicted in Figure 1.

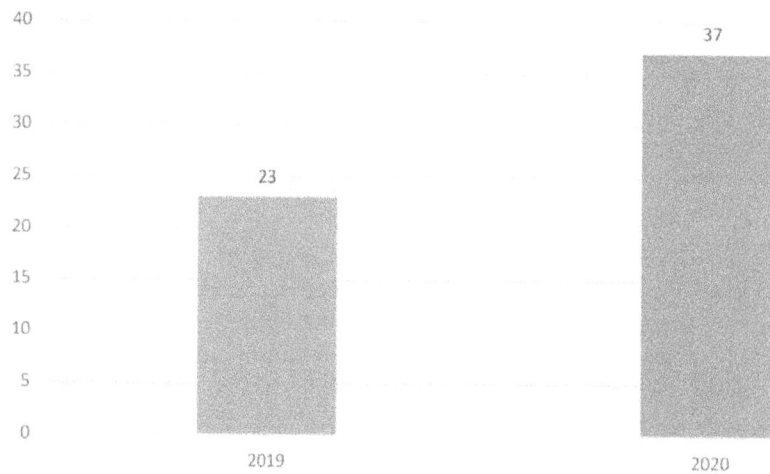

Figure 1*: Number of publications

To evaluate the promotional nature of the content on Instagram, Figure 2 is categorized into three types: explicit mention, implicit mention, and visual presence of the brand. In 2019, out of 23 posts, the influencer shared 13 with an explicit mention, 7 with an implicit mention, and 5 with a visual brand presence. In 2020, among the 37 publications, there were 15 with an explicit mention, 11 with an implicit mention, and 9 with a visual brand presence. This data indicates an increase in promotional posts in 2020 compared to 2019.

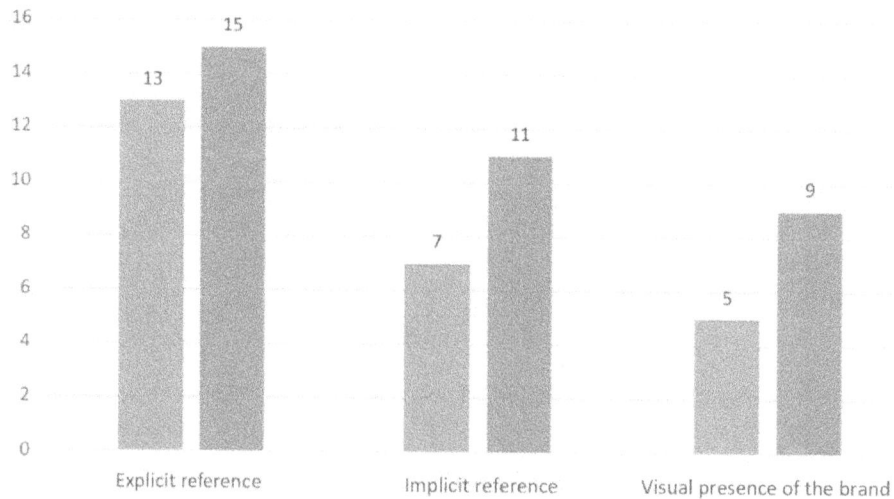

Figure 2*: Promotional character

On the same subject, the focus group aimed to understand participants' reactions to sponsored content. When asked about their responses to sharing advertisements, the participants expressed diverse opinions, with some enjoying it depending on the topic, while others showed indifference.

> Participant 1: *"I personally enjoy watching it. Obviously, it depends on the topic, but for the most part, I enjoy watching it."*

> Participant 2: *"I ignore it. The majority of sponsored products or companies seem forced. But I understand; it's through advertising that they make money. So, I understand, but generally, I ignore it."*

> Participant 3: *"I ignore it. I don't find it genuine. Anyone who truly likes a brand or product doesn't need sponsorship to promote it."*

> Participant 4: *"It doesn't matter to me. Some I like to watch; others don't interest me that much."*
> Participant 5: *"I'm the same; it depends on what's being sponsored. I usually like to see giveaways. Although I never win, I like to take part, especially for trips."*

When asked, 'Can you identify when an influencer's content is produced in partnership with a brand?' the participants provided the following responses:

Participant 1: "Yes, usually the brand appears in the photo or video, and, in addition, when they are sponsorships, they put '#pub'."

Participant 2: "They usually identify the brand."

Participant 3: "Yes, and in most cases, the posts seem forced."

Participant 4: "Of course. Most of the time, yes, because either more influencers are sponsoring the same thing or because it has already appeared in advertising on social media or television."

Participant 5: "When they promote the brand too much, you can tell it's sponsored content."

In response to the question 'Do you trust the influencer's sharing of information/content when it's produced in partnership?', the participants shared the following perspectives:

Participant 1: "There you go, I think she's a professional at what she does. So, when she shares something in the makeup field that I like or want to try, and, importantly, if it's not too expensive, I obviously trust it."

Participant 2: "When she shares clothes from Zara or similar stores, they sell out immediately. I don't know how that's possible. But she seems to be very transparent and always follows her principles. I never thought she'd share anything for more fame because she already has too much."

Participant 3: "I also feel that she's a good professional. When she shares something in her stories and I like the result, I tend to be curious to try it, especially in makeup. It all depends on budgets. She shares a lot from luxury brands, but I know there are others with more affordable prices that are as good or better than the luxury ones."

Participant 4: "She's an influencer with a considerable following and has partnerships with various brands. When she publishes clothing or a makeup product, within a few minutes, they are sold out. Even with the makeup brand she launched, it sold out straight away."

Participant 5: "I trust it. She seems realistic. It's usually not forced, and most of the time, she tries to take things in a more comical tone, which I find kind of funny.

When identifying the presence of human figures in the content (Figure 3), the analysis was categorized into two variables: the presence of the influencer in the publication and others. In 2020, there were 27 publications featuring human figures. In 2019, out of the 23 publications, 18 included the human figure of the content producer.

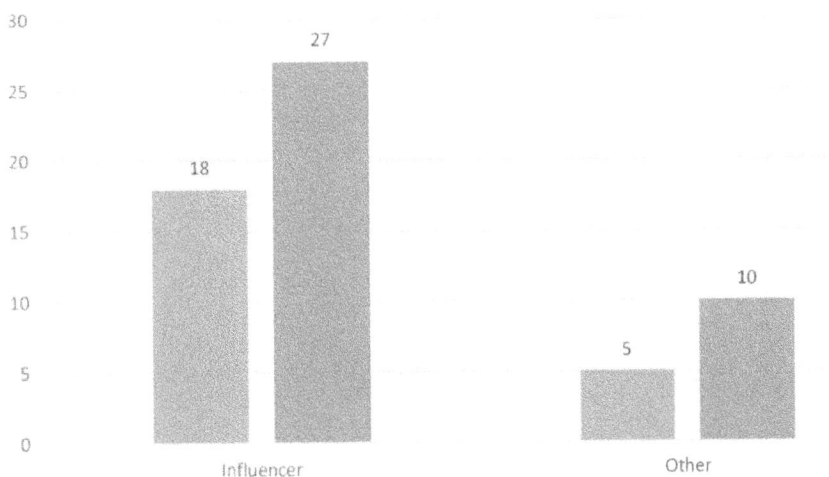

Figure 3: Human representation

In the text category (Figure 4), all publications in both 2019 and 2020 include written content to complement the rest of the content. An important aspect in the text/subtitle category is noted when there is an explicit indication in the description that the publication is in partnership with a brand, or when hashtags such as #pub or #ad are used. As shown in Figure 5, in 2019, 3 publications were identified as paid partnerships, and in 2020, 2 featured promotional content.

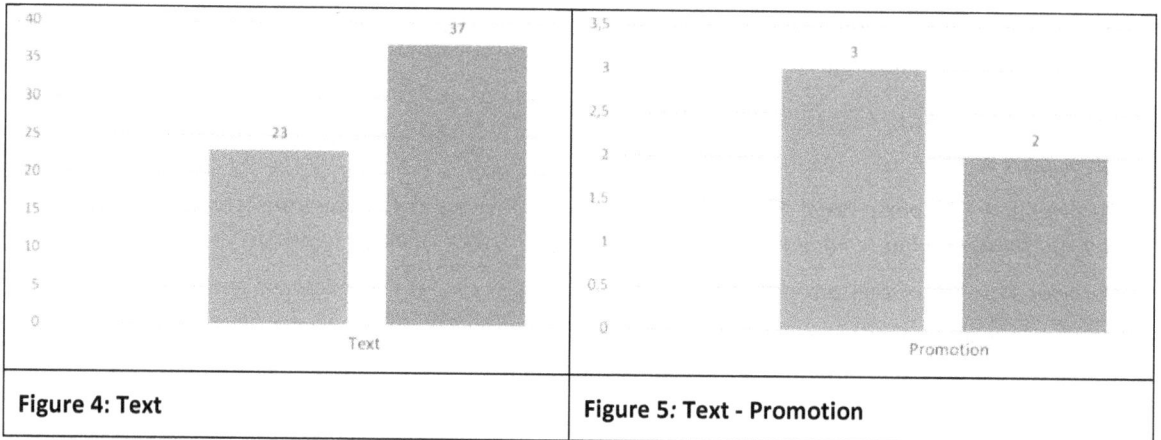

Figure 4: Text	Figure 5: Text - Promotion

In the category of other signs (Figure 6), two components were considered: hashtags and emojis. Hashtags, represented by the symbol (#), are utilized on social media to enhance post visibility by categorizing content on the same topic. In 2019, 17 of influencer Helena Coelho's posts included hashtags, but in 2020, only 8 out of 37 posts featured this sign. In contrast, emojis—small icons representing emotions—were present in both years. In 2019, 20 posts featured emojis, while in 2020, that number increased to 36.

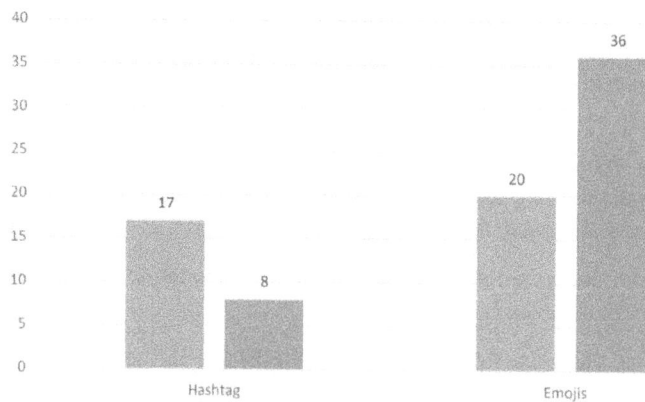

Figure 6: Other signs

Concerning the format of the posts, they were categorized into four types: photography, photo album, video, and reels (short video content, inspired by TikTok). Examining Figure 7, the photo format stands out, with 23 publications in 2020 and 18 in 2019. The second most common format was the photo album, with 5 in 2019 and 6 in 2020. While video is not the influencer's primary format, there were 2 videos in 2019 and only 1 in 2020. The most significant difference occurred in the reels format, introduced in 2019 but explored more extensively in 2020, with 7 publications, whereas none were published in the pre-pandemic year.

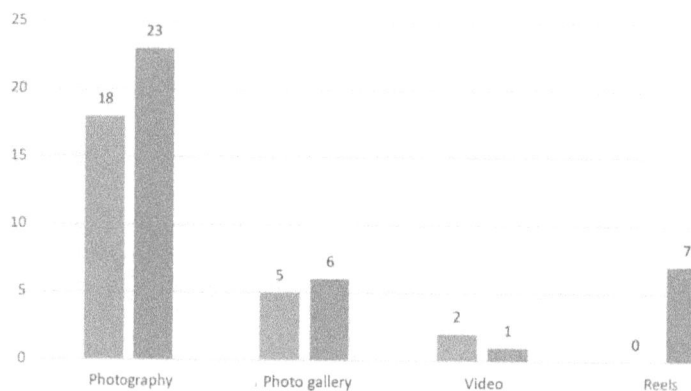

Figure 7: Format

In the focus group, one of the questions centered on the type/format of content most consumed by the participants and the reasons behind their choices. The participants' responses reflect varying individual preferences:

Participant 1: "I prefer reels."

Participant 2: "I also like reels better; it reminds me of TikTok."

Participant 3: "I like to look at the photos."

Participant 4: "I'm also more of a photo fan."

Participant 5: "I prefer watching videos."

In terms of interaction, it's crucial to highlight comments and likes. In 2019, the average number of likes (Figure 8) per post by the influencer was 33,229, increasing to 40,562 in 2020, representing a difference of 7,333 likes. However, in the comments (Figure 9), there is a notable divergence: in 2019, the average was 3,615 comments per post, while in 2020, this number significantly dropped to 420.

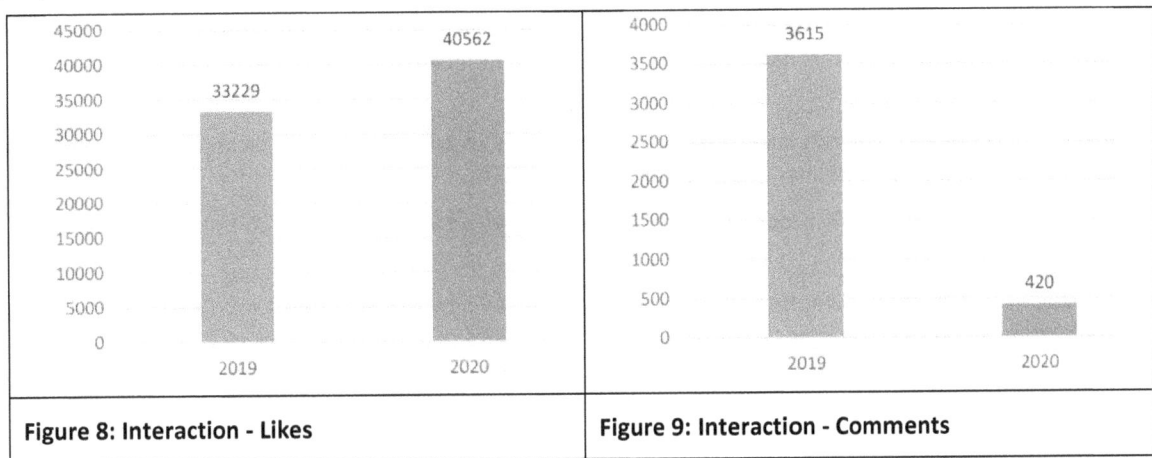

Figure 8: Interaction - Likes   **Figure 9: Interaction - Comments**

Finally, the last category analyzed refers to the themes of the publications (figure 10), where some content covered more than one topic. The topics common to both years were beauty, personal and other. The beauty topic in 2019 had 8 posts, while in 2020 it had 16 posts. In personal posts, of the 23 shared in 2019, it is only mentioned in 4, and in 2020, of the 37 posts, it only appears in 3. The topic of others in 2020 had 14 posts, and in 2019, 12. In 2019, there was 1 post on nutrition, compared to 0 posts in 2020. Covid-19 and health were only covered in 2020, which was to be expected as it was the year we faced the pandemic. Humor was also a topic chosen by the influencer to share in 2020.

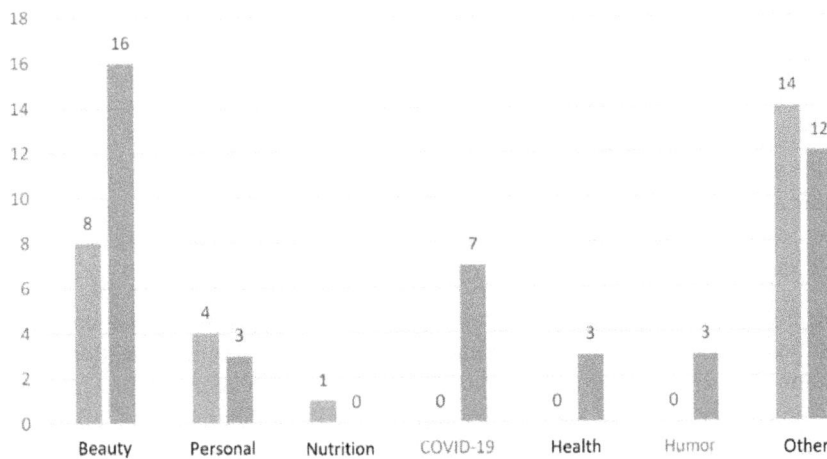

Figure 8: Themes

During the focus group, we explored the participants' preferences for themes in the influencer's publications:

Participant 1: "I'm a fan of everything related to travel. I enjoy seeing where people have been and discovering new places to visit. I'm already thinking about my next trip; I just haven't decided on the destination yet."

Participant 2: "I like to see the more personal side, the day-to-day. I appreciate it when they share recipes. I get a lot of inspiration for dinner or lunch from Instagram."

Participant 3: "I love beauty content, makeup, skincare—everything. I enjoy doing my makeup, always eager to learn new techniques, and I'm constantly on the lookout for new products to try. Instagram is a treasure trove of makeup and fashion content."

Participant 4: "For me, it's more health content. Not only because of my profession, where I need to stay informed about new products, but also because it's the content I find most interesting. I've noticed that with COVID, many brands are increasingly sharing on social media. Have you seen Aspirin's Instagram?"

Participant 5: "I really like to discover the cheapest or most affordable places for planning my next trip. My last trip was to Tenerife in the summer, and I loved it. We stayed in an Airbnb, and it was amazing."

The participants' responses indeed showcase a significant diversity of interests, ranging from travel and personal content to beauty and health. This diversity emphasizes the multifaceted nature of influencer content and the varied preferences of the audience.

When asked, 'Do you feel that influencer Helena Coelho has had to adapt her communication strategies during the pandemic?', the participants shared the following perspectives:

Participant 1: "Of course, it was noticeable that she published more. Since she couldn't share her travels, she started inventing things."

Participant 2: "She began creating exercise videos or challenges with her boyfriend, like the eyeliner challenge in stories with different colors. She gave people clues to guess the next day's color. It seemed like she wanted to maintain her network of followers by creating different ways of generating content while being at home. I honestly found it interesting because, during that period, many people were active on Instagram, and one didn't even know where to turn."

Participant 3: "I didn't notice much of a difference. I think she shared more, of course, needing to maintain engagement, but she could have done different things. Although I thought it was a good initiative to do workouts at home, especially since people couldn't go to the gym."

Participant 4: "Clearly. She was constantly posting things on Instagram, and I think she even posted videos on YouTube, which she hadn't done for a while."

Participant 5: "I know she used to post a lot of stories."

The responses indicate that during the pandemic, Helena Coelho adapted her communication strategies by increasing post frequency and diversifying content with challenges and home exercise videos. Participants' opinions varied on the effectiveness of these changes.

6. Conclusions

This paper presents an investigation aimed at analyzing the impact of the COVID-19 pandemic on the communication strategies of Portuguese digital influencer Helena Coelho. To achieve this goal, methods such as examining Instagram content and conducting a focus group with platform users familiar with the influencer's content were employed.

Based on the results of the content analysis of digital influencer Helena Coelho's Instagram profile, it is evident that the context of the COVID-19 pandemic has impacted the influencer's communication strategies. Changes observed in publication patterns, promotional content, presence of human figures, topics covered, and audience interaction indicate an adaptation to the new reality imposed by the pandemic. The data reveals a significant increase in the number of publications in 2020, possibly reflecting a response to the heightened online activity during periods of confinement and restrictions. In terms of promotional strategies, there was a slight increase in both implicit and explicit mentions of brands. This adjustment suggests a response to the necessity of brand collaborations to sustain the flow of promotional content. Notably, there was an increase in visual brand presence and human figuration in 2020, indicating a potentially more personal and authentic approach in publications - possibly to emotionally connect with the audience during a challenging period. The introduction of the Reels format in 2020 can be interpreted as a response to the trends in short-form content, possibly influenced by the popularity of TikTok during the pandemic. The inclusion of topics related to health, COVID-19, and humor in 2020 reflects a sensitivity to global events and an attempt to stay relevant and connected to the audience's concerns and interests during the pandemic. Although there has been an increase in likes per post, the notable decrease in comments may suggest a shift in audience interactivity, possibly indicating a preference for more visual engagement and overactive participation. Overall, the results of the Instagram profile content analysis suggest that Helena Coelho adapted her communication strategies to the specific needs and dynamics of the pandemic period, demonstrating a conscious effort to maintain relevance and connection with her audience in an ever-changing scenario.

From the focus group results, it is evident that participants noticed a significant increase in the frequency of the influencer's posts during the pandemic. To navigate the limitations imposed by the pandemic, Helena Coelho diversified her content by incorporating home exercise videos/directories and creating challenges. The influencer also gave more prominence to the personal side of her life, as seen in her exercise videos with her boyfriend. Participants perceived that Helena Coelho addressed topics related to the pandemic, such as exercising at home. Given these results, it can be concluded that the influencer has assumed an adaptive approach, responding to the restrictions imposed by the pandemic through a greater online presence, achieved by an increase in the number of posts, diversification of content, and emphasis on more personal aspects of her life.

However, this study has its limitations: the content analysis was carried out during a brief period, and the focus group is small, so their opinions may not be representative of the influencer's followers.

To enhance precision and obtain more in-depth results, future research could include an interview with the influencer herself. This approach aims to capture her perspective on the subject and gain insights into her perception of the continuity of influencer marketing as the preferred choice for brands to communicate with their audiences.

Acknowledgements

This work is funded by National Funds through the FCT - Foundation for Science and Technology, I.P., within the scope of the project Refª UIDB/05507/2020 and DOI identifier https://doi.org/10.54499/UIDB/05507/2020. Furthermore, we would like to thank the Centre for Studies in Education and Innovation (Ci&DEI) and the Polytechnic of Viseu for their support.

References

Alves, A. E. B., Andrade, G. S., Oliveira, J. A., Alves, J. B., & Brandão, N. P. (2020). O uso das redes sociais em época de pandemia - um estudo de caso aplicado em quatro escolas técnicas estaduais de Pernambuco. IV Congresso Internacional de Gestão e Tecnologias. https://doi.org/10.31692/2596-0857.IVCOINTERPDVGT.0079

Antunes, S. (2020). O papel dos influenciadores digitais masculinos no estabelecimento de uma relação entre a marca e o consumidor da geração Millennial. https://repositorio.ucp.pt/handle/10400.14/29528

Borges, A. P. (2020). Comportamento do Consumidor antes, durante e após o período de confinamento: o impacto socioeconómico ao nível internacional. https://www.dinheirovivo.pt/empresas/37-dos-consumidores-admite-aumentar-frequencia-de-compras-online-no-futuro-12894656.htm

Brown, D., & Hayes, N. (2008). Influencer Marketing: who really influences your customers? Amsterdam: Elsevier.

Buvár, Á., Szilágyi, S. F., Balogh, E., & Zsila, Á. (2022). COVID-19 messages in sponsored social media posts: The positive impact of influencer-brand fit and prior parasocial interaction. PLOS ONE, 17(10), e0276143. https://doi.org/10.1371/journal.pone.0276143

Castro, B. L., Oliveira, J., Morais, L., & Gai, M. (2020). COVID-19 e organizações: estratégias de enfrentamento para redução de impactos. Rev. Psicol., Organ. Trab. [online]. 2020, vol.20, n.3, pp. 1059-1063. ISSN 1984-6657. http://dx.doi.org/10.17652/rpot/2020.3.20821.

Canton, H. (2021). United nations conference on trade and development—unctad. In The Europa Directory of International Organizations 2021 (pp. 172-176). Routledge.

Fabius, V., Kohli, S., Timelin, B., & Moulvad Veranen, S. (2020). Meet the next-normal consumer. McKinsey & Company, 1-9.

Francalanci, C., & Hussain, A. (2015). A visual analysis of social influencers and influence in the tourism domain. In Information and Communication Technologies in Tourism 2015: Proceedings of the International Conference in Lugano, Switzerland, February 3-6, 2015 (pp. 19-32). Springer International Publishing.

Donthu, N., & Gustafsson, A. (2020). Effects of COVID-19 on business and research. https://www.sciencedirect.com/science/article/pii/S0148296320303830

Lincoln, J. (2016). Digital Influencer: A Guide to Achieving Influencer Status Online. CreateSpace Independent Publishing Platform. United States: CreateSpace Independent Publishing Platform.

Oliveira, O. P. (2021). A pandemia antecipou tendências do marketing digital. Escola de Gestão e Negócios. Pontifícia Universidade Católica de Goiás. https://repositorio.pucgoias.edu.br/jspui/handle/123456789/2075

Ryan, D. (2014). Understanding Digital Marketing: Marketing Strategies For Engaging The Digital Generation (Vol. 3 Edição). London: Kogan Page.

Richbourg, E. G. (2022). The Coronavirus Pandemic and Participation in the Influencer Economy. https://egrove.olemiss.edu/hon_thesis/2551

Romo, Z. F., & Aguirre, S. I. (2020). Análisis de la gestión de la comunicación de los influencers farmacéuticos españoles en Instagram durante la pandemia del COVID-19. Revista Española de Comunicación en Salud, 9-30.

Santos, J. N. (2018, junho 3). Esta é a máquina que produz os influenciadores. https://eco.sapo.pt/2018/06/03/esta-e-a-maquina-que-produz-os-influenciadores/

Santos, K. J. (2020). Influenciadores Digitais em tempos de pandemia: reputação, performance e responsabilidade. Univerdade do Vale do Rio dos Sinos, GP Comunicação e Cultura Digial, XX Encontro dos Grupos de Pesquisas em Comunicação, 43º Congresso Brasileiro de Ciências da Comunicação, São Leopoldo, RS.

Segarra-Saavedra, J., & Hidalgo-Marí, T. (2018). Influencers, moda femenina e Instagram: el poder de prescripción en la era 2.0. Revista Mediterránea de Comunicación/Mediterranean Journal of Communication, 313-325.

Sousa, A. (2009). Investigação em educação. Lisboa: Livros Horizonte.

Thackeray, R., Neiger, B. L., Hanson, C. L., & McKenzie, J. F. (2008). Enhancing Promotional Strategies Within Social Marketing Programs: Use of Web 2.0 Social Media. Health Promotion Practice, 9(4), pp. 338-343

Wang, Y., Hong, A., Lib, X., & Gao, J. (2020). Marketing innovations during a global crisis: A study of China firms' response to COVID-19. Journal of business research, 116, 214-220.

Yin, R. (2004). Estudos de caso: planejamento e métodos (2ª ed.). São Paulo: Bookman.

From Pixels to Personalities: Identity Formation in Virtual Communities Through Multimodal Communication

Ajita Deshmukh

MIT-ADT University, Pune, India

ajita.deshmukh@mituniversity.edu.in
ajitadeshmukh13@gmail.com

Abstract: Communities of Practice (CoPs) are an important thread in the social fabric of knowledge sharing (Wenger, 2004). Members of CoPs who share a common passion and interact regularly in a bid to improve their discipline and expertise contribute thus to the cohort of knowledge and practice. Recently, due to the transformation of technology this interaction is no longer limited to the physical world but more than often it takes place using communication channels thus breaking the boundaries of time and space. This has led to the rise of the term Virtual Communities of Practice (VCoPs). It is recognised by previous research that it is the informal communication that helps in building and sustenance of a CoP which is more so in the VCoP albeit the hurdles. The members of CoP negotiate their identities on the basis of the communication and move from peripheral membership to the core of the CoP. Similar movement and interactions are also found in VCoP. Multimodal communication forms an integral part of communication. This paper explores the usage of multimodal communication especially emojis, GIFs along with photographs in the formation and negotiation of identities of the members of the VCoP. This study uses discourse analysis to analyse the year-long communication within two VCoPs composed of academicians across India. The findings of the study indicate that use of such multimodal elements of communication contribute towards development of trust needed for knowledge sharing and sustenance of a VCoP and perception of identities within the VCoP.

Keywords: Virtual Communities of Practice , Computer mediated communication, Multimodal communication -Emojis, emoticons and GIF

1. Introduction

Communities of Practice (CoPs) have always been existent but the study of these as part of organisational structure began in the 1980s. CoPs are the social structures that function on the principle of knowledge management thus becoming important elements of "social fabric of knowledge" (Wenger, 2004). Members of these CoPs share a passion for a body of knowledge (domain) and interact frequently (community) in order to make improvements (Practice). It should be noted that it does not mean that the members will necessarily work together in the same space. Knowledge sharing in a CoP leads to situated learning (Lave &Wenger, 1990) which always takes place in context -authentic situations and settings. Organisations, both corporate and academic have found CoPs useful yet challenging to sustain.

Academicians often thrive on the conferences and other academic events in order to look out for furthering of knowledge, find collaborators and develop a sense of community revolving around certain practices. With technological advances, knowledge sharing, opportunities for collaboration have gone beyond the conferences and other academic meetings, breaking boundaries of time and space. Situated learning, an extension of the social learning theory (Vygostsky, 1978) along with Connectivism (Siemens & Downes, 2005) form the basis in case of VCoP since the formation of a VCoP takes place by identifying common "domain" over a network, usually connected in the virtual world. Crampton (2001) emphasises that the requisites for effective communication in order to cultivate mutual knowledge and comprehension become more pressing in case of VCoPs in absence of non-verbal communication.

Communication in the virtual world has seen major transformation from being textual, graphic, pictorial to audio-visual, gestural with stickers, emoticons and emojis to the latest- memes and animated GIFs. These multimodal elements are seen as compensations to non-verbal communication in technology mediated communication and form an integral part of interpersonal communication today.

This paper studies the usage of these elements and its impact on the functioning of the VCoPs using two case studies. These two VCoPs formed of academicians across India (Community), belonging to different subject domains but having a common passion of learner centric education (domain) and using "Learner Centric MOOC model" for the same (Practice). These groups operate over WhatsApp which allows multimodality for communication. This paper analyses the use of emojis, emoticons, gifs, images in the formation of identities, engagement and participation on the movement of members from periphery towards the core.

2.   Related Work

2.1   Virtual Communities of Practice: Communication, Structure and Identities

Through adult life, learning takes place through learning at work (Boud & Middleton, 2003). This learning is also known as situated learning of which communication is a major key. Boud (1999) argues that predominant way of situated learning is through informal communication with peers at work. This informal communication leads the way to share knowledge and improve their discipline and establishes communities of practice. The organisational, social learning theories point out towards communication, especially informal communication as a key element in the functioning and sustenance of all CoPs.

It is through communication that identities are formed, relationships within the CoPs are established, active participation in practices of communities and learning takes place, knowledge is shared and artefacts are created. Social participation in this context involves active participation and building identities within and in relation to these communities. Wenger (1998) has explicitly written about the deep connection between the identities and the practice within the CoPs, highlighting the point that formation of communities of practice involves negotiation of identities as well as the distinction of these identities from self-image. It is through this engagement in the practices and the constant negotiation of identities that the roles get reified within the CoP. There are no 'appointed' people in a CoP or a VCoP and hence they do not come with reification markers. It is through engagement that these reifications and the identities are built up in an ongoing process. A new member usually is at the legitimate periphery stage where their situated learning takes place. Through their engagement and practice, they slowly progress moving in towards the core of the CoP learning the community discipline, aligning their values and behaviours to the norms of the CoP in the process. This movement is not automatic and members may experience hurdles in the movement

Understanding of new members about shared knowledge and the vision of the CoP is constantly negotiated through interpretation of repertoire of language, symbols and genres involved in the communication. In a CoP, members are not merely judged by their knowledge but by their demonstrated ability of reading the local context and acting in ways thereupon that is valued by members of CoP (Contu & Willmott, 2003). Thus, the emphasis is on contextual understanding more than technical knowledge. In recent times, with the development of Web 2.0 technologies, the formation of CoPs is not limited to one organisation or the physical world alone. The term "virtual communities of practice" (VCoPs) has been recognised in the recent literature (Dube et al,2005; Kimble &Hildreth, 2005) where ICT tools are the main channels used for communication and knowledge sharing within the VCoP.

The language of communication used through ICT is characterised by multimodality that includes shorter text to emojis and GIFs which are gesture and emotive expressions. The communication has also become horizontal with the producers also becoming consumers of content and vice-versa. This has set the tone for collaboration and active participation through blogs, comments etc.

2.2   Nonverbal Communication in a VCoP

There has been considerable research on the various aspects of use of emojis, emoticons since their popular use. Research has been done on the analysis of feelings conveyed by the emoji used (Abdellaoui & Zrigui, 2018), frequency of use of emojis by older adults (Briede-Westermeyer & Pérez-Villalobos, 2019) and association of emojis with informal texts (Maíz-Arévalo, 2016). Studies have also been conducted on grammatical tags of emojis (González-Gallardo et al, 2016) as well as for the development of text summaries (Lloret et al,2010). Rodriguez et al (2018) puts forth seven dimensions of usage of emojis and emoticons which are a) aesthetic appeal, b) familiarity, c) visual complexity, d) clarity, e) reflection of positive or negative emotion, f) emotion, and g) the meaning attributed to it.

The distinctive point is the usage of ICT mediated communication (earlier known as Technology Mediated Communication- TMC) that operates differently for each user. This is amplified within the VCoP since every member experiences the VCoP in a different manner, their "realities" being different and hence their interactions within the VCoP would be different as compared to a CoP. This can impact multiple things like trust, sense of belonging as well as extent of comprehension upon which knowledge sharing is based (Kimble, & Wright, 2000; Pan & Leidner, 2003).

CoPs including VCoPs involve informal and formal processes that contribute to knowledge creation and sharing. Multiple activities have been recognised as processes depending upon the structure and the typology of the (V)CoP ranging from mentoring to team work and collaborative activities. In a VCoP, these activities find ground for action, through various tele-communication channels, mostly via the internet in the current era. These could be through open as well as closed social media groups like Facebook, Twitter etc or communication channels like WhatsApp, Telegram etc taking a precedence over email and telephonic conversations. These 'conversations' that happen synchronously as well as asynchronously in a VCoP lack in the non-verbal communication of the physical world. Research shows that this limits the formation as well as perception of identities and affects engagement in a VCoP (Pan & Leidner, 2003, Dube et al, 2005).

Nevertheless, use of multimodal elements of communications in the VCoP attempt to overcome the hurdles of non-verbal communication. These include emojis, emoticons, gifs, images, audio messages, as artefacts that try to imitate the non-verbal communication.

3. The Study

There have been various studies on Communication in CoPs and lately VCoPs but very little research was found to exist on academic VCoP and the role of multimodal communication therein. This study is an empirical, exploratory study of the communication of two VCoPs which comprise academicians across India from various domains and the engagement and movement of members in each of them.

3.1 Research Questions

- Does multimodal communication enhance engagement of members in VCoPs?
- Does the use of emojis, emoticons, gifs and memes contribute to the identity in VCoPs?
- Does multimodal communication enhance ties of members in the VCoP leading to trust and thereby lead to more knowledge sharing within the VCoP?

3.2 Research Methods

The research uses mainly qualitative methods of discourse analysis for the primary data which is the communication on the communication channel used by both the VCoPs under consideration. Notations of observations and discussions with others informally rather than a formal interview were recorded. This helped in further analysis of the identities of VCoPs. The researcher is a member of both the VCoPs and hence this qualitative research involves characteristics of participatory ethnographic research .

The text and the multimodal messages were separately classified for each type and analyzed thematically and for the sentiment analysis. The analysis was done manually and seen in context of the text. The purpose of this exercise was to explore the usage of multimodal communication along with texts for engagement and interpersonal relations

3.3 Research Sample

The sample for this empirical, explorative study comprised two VCoPs formed over WhatsApp. The first VCoP was formed with 24 members chosen on the basis of their involvement in a MOOC Program about Learner Centric MOOC model by the instructor of this MOOC. Out of these 24, 10 members identify themselves as male and 14 female members. The age group of the members varied from 30 years to 50 years of age. The VCoP was formed for the purpose of tasks related to another MOOC program by the same instructor. On the basis of self-initiation from the responses towards tasks, the instructor created another VCoP of 8 members out of these 24 members which showed movement from periphery towards the core. This VCoP1 of 8 members has 3 male and 5 female members. This movement was discovered in a period of 2 months and the establishment of the 2nd VCoP was at an interval of 2 months from that of the first.

4. Data Collection and Analysis

The primary data comprised all the messages -text and multimedia/new media from the WhatsApp Chat over the period of 14 months and 12 months respectively for the VCoP1 and VCoP2 respectively. This data was collected during the year 2021, amidst COVID19 which made WhatsApp groups and other such channels, a necessity.

The exported chat including the multimodal elements and artefacts was subject to: a) for quantitative analysis: WhatsApp chat analyser b) for qualitative analysis: discourse analysis mainly for the non-verbal communication, structure and conversational codes. This data was further coded and subjected to thematic analysis for the identification of patterns and meanings as part of the discourse analysis.

Ethical Considerations

The communication on WhatsApp groups for both the VCoPs are used only for the purpose of this research. The members of the VCoP are aware of this use. Due care has been taken regarding anonymisation to safeguard the privacy of the members of the VCoP. The raw data is secured with a password protected file.

5. Findings and Discussion

Analysis was done on two aspects-the structure and its negotiations of the identities and the usage of multimodal elements. Discourse analysis attempts to provide an insight on how the usage of multimodal elements in the VCoPs affect the interpersonal communication and the negotiation of identities of members within the VCoP.

5.1 Structure and Organisation of the VCoPs of the Study

The structure in both VCoPs was flat and there was openness in communication in both the VCoPs. The members of both the VCoPs belonged to multiple institutions and hence the boundary crossing was high in both the VCoPs. When the boundary crossing is high, it is found that it is difficult to build adequate trust leading to sharing of knowledge (Wenger et al, 2002). The means of ICT have helped in overcoming the gap of time and space and unlike earlier studies that showed physical distance affecting psychological closeness (Wenger et al, 2002), latest research shows that social penetration (Altman & Taylor, 1973) is not particularly dependent upon on physical distance and the higher the self-disclosure in communication, greater are the chances of psychological closeness (Debrot. A, et al ,2017) .

These were closed membership VCoP with members having moderate ICT skills. Both the VCoPs were culturally diverse, since members belonged to regions as well as different professional domains ranging from Medicine to Technology and pure Sciences to Humanities. This brought in rich and diverse perspectives and experiences, it would also mean that the messages would be interpreted with their own cultural filters which are said to be causes for misinterpretations and therefore some hurdles in the communications (Wenger, 2002), especially in a VCoP.

5.2 Analysis of Usage of Multi Modal Elements

On the outset the number of multimodal elements including photographs, emojis and GIFs shared during communication in VCoP1 were lesser than in VCoP2. The general usage of types of messages is shown in fig1. Note: The analyser considers emoji as media.

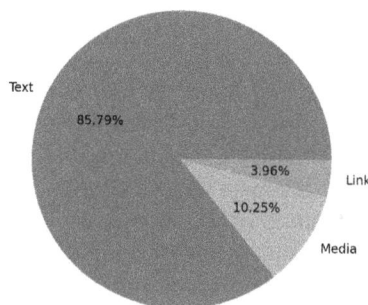

Figure 1: Types of messages in VCoP2

5.2.1   Theme 1: Emoji Accompanying Formal Text

Emojis accompanying text to show formal expressions: applause, congratulations, well done, agreement or best of luck, volunteering

Emojis are used to add and/or compensate for the non-verbal cues in CMC. It was found that the usage of emojis in was more for compensating for absence of non-verbal cues in formal communication. These were used to applaud and appreciate some task done for the group. The emojis used for this purpose were as follows:

VCoP1: 👏 - 42 times, 🙌 - 3   👏 - 22 👍 - 6 times

VCoP2: 👏 - 655 times, 🙌 - 84 times 👏 52 times 👍 - 8 times.

These emojis are found to be repeated in quick succession, mostly in a trio to express emphasis.

The usage of 👍 is found to be the most ambiguous for it is used to wish "best of luck", agreement as well as to express "well done". This necessitates the discourse analysis to set the context for the purpose.

The emojis used in VCoP2 which was formed of self-initiated members which showed movement from periphery towards the core, showed more usage and also more distinction in usage of emojis for the same expression.

The use of emoji for expressing willingness or volunteering for a task was found to be much higher in VCoP1 (🙋 -30) than VCoP2 (🙋 -9). Discourse analysis reveals that the tasks in VCoP2 were taken up or frequently assumed and allotted in accordance with the capabilities of a personnel. Upon discourse analysis, this assumption is found to have reached over the various instances of interaction and completion of tasks that the capabilities and identities within the VCoP2 are established that also assigns roles as per the expertise.

Usage of 👏 was found to be more in VCoP1 for celebration or congratulatory messages than VCoP2 with GIFs taking precedence over 👏 in VCoP2 for the same expression. The cultural context of discourse analysis suggests that this could be due to the fact that this is a neutral, non-personal type of an expression which is considered to be "safe" in a bi-gendered space when there could be mis-interpretations.

"An emoji or emoticon is easy instead of writing words."

"I feel emoji is also my expression. I might be feeling elated and want to use an elaborate emoji rather than just an applause."

" I started interacting more. Seeing emojis meant it is not just a formal work group but also a community, a place to belong freely."

The analysis found that these emojis are used in both VCoPs singularly without any accompanying text. This suggests that members found these emojis to have no other interpretation. Both male and female members in both VCoPs have used these emojis thus eliminating any gender role in its usage in this study.

5.2.2   Theme 2: Emoji Accompanying Informal Text

Emojis accompanying text to show informal expressions- laughter and its types, joy, care and goofed up, frustration, embarrassed.

Research shows that it is the informal non verbal communication that helps to increase collaboration and strengthen ties. The sharing of non-formal expressions and emotions play a key role in building up communication and goes a long way to create the feeling of community.

The number of emojis used for expression of such emotions is lesser in VCoP1 than in VCoP2. This is mainly attributed to the reason that VCoP1 comprises core members where the identities, roles and image of the members is already established. It should be noted that VCoP1 is mainly now dealing with policy level decisions while all daily happenings and conversations around them take place in VCoP2.

Emotion expressed	Emoji used	VCoP1	VCoP2
Joy, amusement	😄 😃 😁	59, 60, 141	143, 60, 346
Laughter, joking, giggling	😂 🤣 😆 😹	60, 32, 10, 16	245, 220, 31, 83
Anger, devilish	😈	1	22
Doubt, questioning	😕 😐	27, 1	89, 19
Relief	😌	101	359
Sorrow, Frustration, annoying	😢 😣 😖 😩 😟	0, 5, 0, 0, 0	5, 28, 3, 46, 30
Love, care and hugs	😍 🤗	24, 7	60, 19

Others- goofed up, embarrassed	😵 👻	8, 0	28,43

As per the discourse analysis, the context of these expressions contribute to the formation of identity as well as image of the member. The affability of the member and the movement of members from periphery towards the core is seen when the other members react to these expressions. The possibility of being able to express these emotions which are largely non formal suggests the existing ties amongst members and opens avenues to strengthen the ties amongst the members and move along together with each other towards the core.

> *"Because of use of the 🦉, I actually completed a pending task. I realised that I had forgotten about it and needed to do it. It conveyed much more than the word 'ASAP'. Also, I didn't see it as threatening. I assume none of us did. In fact, we pulled the leg of the person after the task."*

> *"I felt genuine feelings when person X sent an emoji (😊) on the difficulties I was facing. It was much better than the messages."*

> *"They say, a picture is worth a thousand words. So is an emoji. There is so much difference between the emojis for laughter depending upon the level. We even teased a person for laughing lesser."*

> *"I noticed that it becomes easier for me to collaborate with a person who is expressive even in terms of emoji. I can gauge that a person is busier/not relaxed in absence of use of emojis.."*

There are a couple of members who though are at the periphery have had opportunities of collaborations with the core group due to the ties that were formed over such interaction. It is also noticed that lurking behaviour is common and though acceptable in such online communities, it does not allow the members to undertake movement and negotiate their identities and place in VCoP minimizing their contribution to the VCoP as well as restricting career advancement avenues for themselves.

It is also observed that other than joy, amusement and laughter, other emojis are used by female members of the VCoPs as initiation as well as reaction to an expression. This is attributed again to the cultural identities and background of the members as certain Indian communities are not habitually expressive in emotions.

5.2.3 Theme 3: Photos shared

The main difference in the sharing of these photos is their nature. Around 80% of the photos shared were mainly about announcements, or screenshots related to work. The analysis shows that initiation of sharing of the photos consolidated the identities of members in the VCoP. The interaction later in the group and individually also indicates that members of VCoP2 perceived a structure of the VCoP1 with respect to the people next in command to the instructor within the VCoP2 especially with respect to certain tasks. This is in sync with the theory (Wenger, 2002) where identities are constantly negotiated and perceived even though there is no formal appointment of any person for any role in a VCoP.

Photos included a variety of themes like celebrations at home front, places visited, things of interest or events and even relatable memes.

> *"Seeing the home/artefacts/ food gives a feeling as if you are invited at home. It helped us build the camaraderie."*

> *"It was so new to see a particular delicacy which is not prepared in the region where I stay. I tried cooking it later."*

> *"When we met in reality, it didn't feel as if we were meeting for the first time!"*

The photographs and memes followed a discussion which allowed for some understanding of different cultures of members. Over a period of one year, the interaction enabled the members to understand different aspects of varied culture including celebrations, the lifestyle and food, and even language aspects were noticed being picked up. Both male and female members of the VCoP were found to share photos of non-formal nature in the VCoP, though the percentage of female sharing photos was found to be higher than the male members. The interaction is more of casual nature irrespective of gender. It is also found that the sharing of photos were not always prompted. This hints at the reification of identities as well as rapport enabling removal of silos.

5.2.4   Theme 4: Using GIFs :

GIFs, like emojis, express emotions (Bakhshi et al, 2016), offer different meanings to the viewers and their meanings are often constructed contextually within the community. GIFs are often based on the TV shows and movies and hence have a cultural context to them. These characteristics make GIFs more engaging and hence play a role in interpersonal communication within a VCoP. Usage of GIFs in a VCoP is also dependent upon finding the contextual meaning.

There was an entire story on the events narrated in terms of GIFs. The people involved in that event were part of VCoP1. This depicts not just the creativity but also the study and interpersonal relationship amongst members since the choice of apt GIF depends on the study of each character. This is found to be in line with the research on usage of GIFs which suggest that since GIFs can be interpreted in multiple ways, the usage is restricted to groups either where the contextualisation would be understood and generate an appropriate reaction or where the trust amongst members is high so as to avoid unwanted reactions.

The high number of GIFs used in VCoPs could be indicative of the high level of trust and better interpersonal communication amongst members of VCoPs. Analysis shows that GIFs , like the shared photos but unlike the emojis, are used as communication tactics to initiate and sustain conversation. GIFs were used to show displeasure without the blunt, include some humour and be 'eye-catching' in certain cases. A GIF based story was created on an incident that involved members of VCoP as a humorous take. Analysis reveals GIFs were used in VCoP2 to convey more and a variety of emotions out of reach of the emojis.

> " The GIF story was brilliant. We could laugh and the whole event unfolded in front of our eyes. We didn't feel as if we missed anything."

> "The GIF of embarrassment was useful to show the true feeling and it is easier to convey than the text."

> "GIFs based on films are perfect to show multiple emotions that we experience. We use it often to show our emotion of what happened at work since we all work at different places."

It was found that GIFs allowed the members to have an insight into each other's popular culture. This enabled members of VCoP2 to pick up certain commonly used phrases in their respective cultures thus allowing more intercultural participation which otherwise remains un-imbibed in a formal learning setup.

Figure 2a and 2b: GIFs used to create a story out of an incident in the VCoP

Figure 3a: Expression of consolation

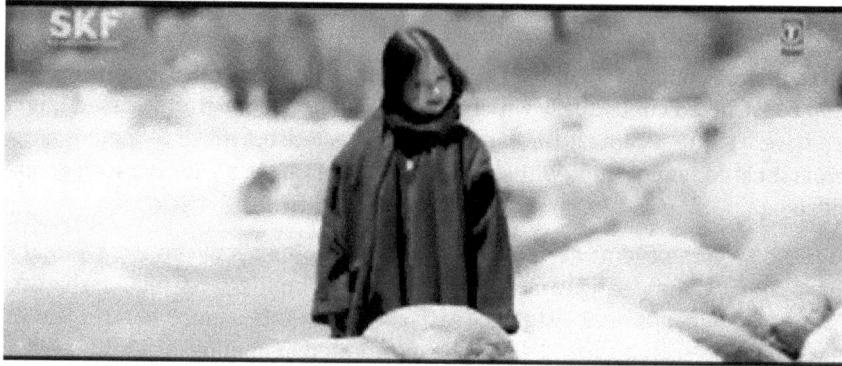

Figure 3b: Expression of persistence

6. Conclusion

The current study investigates the multimodal communication in a VCoP and its effect on the roles and identities of the members and the movement within the VCoP from periphery towards the core of the VCoP. The findings of the study indicate that multimodal communication plays an important function in developing and sustaining interpersonal communication in a VCoP. It suggests that use of emojis and GIFs could enhance the perception of identities and image in the VCoP. The findings also suggest that through the sharing of multimodal elements of communication, allow negotiation of identities to the members of VCoPs. The point highlighted through this study is that such multi modal communication allows for understanding of cultural diversity within multicultural VCoPs and goes a long way in its sustenance. The findings conclude that multimodal communication is an antecedent to trust which is the basis for a VCoP. It is also recommended that VCoPs include and promote multimodal communication in order to strengthen communication and collaboration in the VCoPs.

References

Boud, D. (1999). Situating academic development in professional work: 'using peer learning, Journal for Academic Development, 4(1), 3- 10.

Boud, D. & Middleton, H. (2003). Learning from others at work: communities of practice and informal learning, Journal of Workplace Learning, 15(5), [1] 194-202.

Briede-Westermeyer, J.C.; Pérez-Villalobos, C.E. Aproximación inductiva a la vida cotidiana de adultos mayores de Chile. Interciencia 2019, 44, 332–339.

Burholt, V.;Windle, G.; Gott, M.; Morgan, D.J. Technology-mediated communication in familial relationships: Moderated-mediation models of isolation and loneliness. Gerontologist 2020, 40. [CrossRef] [PubMed]

Churchman, D. (2005). Safeguarding academic communities: Retaining texture and passion in the academy in Carden, P. and Stehlik T. (eds). Beyond communities of practice: Theory as experience, Queensland:Post Pressed.

Ciborra, C. U. & Patriota, G. (1998). Groupware and teamwork in R&D: limits to learning and innovation, R&D Management, 28(1), 1-10.

Contu, A. & Willmott, H. (2003). Re-embedding situatedness: The importance of power relations in learning theory, Organization Science, 14(3), 283-296.

Cramton, C. D. (2001). The mutual knowledge problem and its consequences for dispersed collaboration, Organization Science, 12(3), 346-371.

Creswell, J. W. (1998). Qualitative inquiry and research design: choosing among five traditions, CA Davenport: Sage Publications.

Davenport, T. & Prusak, L. (1997). Working knowledge: How organizations manage what they know. Boston, MA: Harvard Business School Press.

Dubé, L., Bourhis, A. & Jacob, R. (2005). The impact of structuring characteristics on the launching of virtual communities of practice. Journal of Organizational Change Management, 18(2), 145-166.

González-Gallardo, C.E.; Torres, J.M.; Rendón, A.M.; Sierra, G. Perfilado de autor multilingüe en redes sociales a partir de n-gramas de caracteres y de etiquetas gramaticales. Linguamática 2016, 8, 21–29.

Hanisch, Jo. (2006). Virtual communities of practice: A study of communication, community and organisational learning.

Kimble, C. & Hildreth, P. (2005). Dualities, distributed communities of practice and knowledge management, Journal of Knowledge Management, 9(4), 102-113.

Lave, J. & Wenger, E. (1991). Situated learning: Legitimate peripheral participation, Cambridge: Cambridge University Press.

Lesser, E. & Everest, K. (2001). Using communities of practice to manage intellectual capital, Journal of Organizational Change Management, 13(3), 264-274.

Lloret, E.; Palomar, M. Resúmenes de textos: Nuevos retos en laWeb 2.0. Subj. Procesos Cogn. 2010, 14, 113–126.

Pyrko, I., Dörfler, V., & Eden, C. (2017). Thinking together: What makes Communities of Practice work? Human relations; studies towards the integration of the social sciences, 70(4), 389–409. https://doi.org/10.1177/0018726716661040

Rodríguez, F.J.; Ridao, S. La oralidad en educación secundaria. Didáctica. Leng. La Lit. 2012, 24, 341–358.

Rodríguez, D.; Prada, M.; Gaspar, R.; Garrido, M.; Lopes, N. Lisbon Emoji and EmoticonDatabase (LEED): Norms for emoji and emoticons in seven evaluative dimensions. Behav. Res. 2018, 50, 392–405. [CrossRef] [PubMed]

Wenger, E. (2004, January/February). Knowledge management as a doughnut: Shaping your knowledge strategy through communities of practice, Ivey Business Journal, 1-8.

Yarris, L. M., Chan, T. M., Gottlieb, M., & Juve, A. M. (2019). Finding Your People in the Digital Age: Virtual Communities of Practice to Promote Education Scholarship. Journal of graduate medical education, 11(1), 1–5. https://doi.org/10.4300/JGME-D-18-01093.1

Studying the Impact Of D.P.SL Model on Online Identity Management

Pratik Emmanuel[1] and Olufemi Isiaq[2]
[1]Creative Computing Institute, Postgraduate Research, University of the Arts London, UK
[2]Creative Computing Institute, Computer Data Science and AI, University of the Arts London, UK

p.emmanuel1220231@arts.ac.uk
f.isiaq@arts.ac.uk

Abstract: This paper investigates online identities through social media language use, with a focus on classifying online identity within textual conversations. It sheds light on how Demographic (D) groups and Personality (P) impact the use of Social-Media Language (SL) for identity representation online. This study was conducted in 2023 when there were 4.76 billion social media users worldwide, making it essential to study how social media language is used in textual conversations to convey online identity. The study defines social media language as consisting of emoticons/emojis, abbreviations, and mixed language within textual conversations, which have become essential for expressing feelings and emotions during conversations. The D.P.SL based survey conducted for this work aimed to understand how demographic groups and personality are related to social media language. Based on the total number of social media user worldwide, 400 responses (required based on Cochran and Yamane's formulae sample-size calculation) and the survey was distributed across various verified online survey exchange platforms. However, 406 responses were recorded with young people in age groups of 18-24 and 25-34 using social media language more as it has become a part of their social media habits. The study also found that emoticons/emojis and slang abbreviations with letter reduplication were quite common, making conversations lively and funny. Additionally, individuals whose primary language is not English use their native language but type in English for quick communication. Subsequent study is to be conducted using online mock group conversations between participating respondents to further understand correlations, causation, and concurrency on how 'online identity' is managed during online communications via social media language, its context of use, and polarity sentiment.

Keywords: Demographic groups, Personality, Social media language, Online identity management, Mixed languages, Textual conversations

1. Introduction

In recent times, the Internet has now become an indispensable part of our lives, with individuals and businesses relying on it for effective functioning. Social media, which is an offshoot of the Internet, has allowed people to connect with others, be it individuals, organizations, or businesses. Social media users leave behind a trail of their online activity, which can be studied by social media researchers. As of 2023, there were 4.76 billion social media users worldwide, making it crucial to study Social Media Language (SL), which enables people to express their feelings and emotions in textual conversations (Kemp, 2023).

Social media users actively manage their online identity by presenting themselves in a way that influences the opposite person with whom they are conversing. Warburton and Hatzipanagos (2015) define online identity as an individual's social identity that creates a self-impression on others based on the conversation topic. Social media users tend to display their positive self to gain attention from friends and non-friends during textual conversations. Studies show that a person's self-impression varies based on the settings of a particular online platform (McCabe et al., 2005; Gibbs et al., 2006; Heino et al., 2006).

To gain a better understanding of how social media users utilise language to present their online identity, this work is investigating how social media language is used strategically and performatively within textual conversations. This outcome can be used to develop computer-based tools for identifying social media language and understanding online identity. Furthermore, studying a person's online identity formation within text conversation can help researchers understand how the results can be used to improve human-computer interaction, human language translation and text to speech amongst others (Pietro, 2020).

A critical question that arises is whether there is a correlation between demographic groups and personalities with social media language, which can be used to represent identity online. To establish this correlation, we have defined a Null Hypothesis (H0), which states that *demographic groups and personalities do not impact the use of social media language for identity representation online.* An Alternate Hypothesis (H1) states that *demographic groups and personalities do have an impact on the use of social media language for identity representation online.*

2. Method

Before designing the online survey for this work, a literature analysis to investigate related works of other authors was conducted. The academic contribution of this work is D.P.SL (Demographic groups, Personality, Social-Media Language) model to help understand how demographic groups and personalities impact the use of social media language. The survey is cross-sectional meaning it was easy to administer and cost-effective. Also, a JISC Survey tools which is considered safe with regards to data protection was adopted (JISC, 2023).

To begin data collection, the survey was published on survey exchange groups on social media platform Facebook alongside survey exchange websites with multiple social media accounts for verification of their real-world existence and checking their review ratings for further verification (SurveyCircle, 2023; Survey Swap, 2023). Survey exchange is where researchers gain participants for their surveys outside of their friend group, the survey exchange groups on Facebook work by completing surveys of other researchers and sharing a screenshot of the completed survey as proof of completion, and then asking them to complete the needed survey by sharing the survey link with them to which they will respond back with proof of completion. Survey exchange groups on Facebook was the main source of gaining more participants as everyday surveys were exchanged throughout the day and night and the cycle repeated each day for two months. The survey link was also further distributed online by sharing among various groups. Informed consent was also presented to the participants at the beginning of the online survey so they could first read about the research project, then data safety assurance and informed consent before deciding if they wanted to take part in the survey. The contents of the informed consent were derived from the university's informed consent document (Solent, 2023)

2.1 Online Survey Sample Size Calculations (SSC)

Social media users worldwide in 2023 at the time of data collection were 4.76 billion according to a report from 'DataReportal' (Kemp, 2023; Statista, 2023). Industry standard confidence level at 95% was adopted (Hazra, 2017). The margin of error was between 4 – 8% meaning that the range of the population's response may deviate from sample is between 4 – 8%. By adopting these formulas, the Cochran's 1963 formula showed that 384 responses were required for the online survey (Asenahabi and Ikoha, 2023) (Equation 1), whilst Yamane's 1967 formula showed that 399 responses were required (Divakar and Nanjundeswaraswamy, 2021) (Equation 2). Hence, in-total 406 responses were obtained for the online survey during data collection.

2.1.1 Online survey SSC: Cochran's Formula

$$n = \frac{z^2 pq}{e^2}$$

Equation 1: Cochran's Formula.

z = 1.96 for a confidence level of 95%, **(e)** margin of error 5% which is 0.05 and **(p)** population proportion is 0.5 which is 50% (left at default if not known).

z = 1.96, **p** = 0.5, **e** = 0.05

n = 1.96^2 * 0.5 * (1 - 0.5) / 0.05^2

n = 384.16

2.1.2 Online survey SSC: Yamane's Formula

$$n = \frac{N}{K + N(e)^2}$$

Equation 2: Yamane's Formula.

N = Population of study, **K** = Constant (1), **e** = Degree of error expected and **n** = Sample size.

N = 4760000000 (Social media users worldwide).

K = 1

e = 0.05 (5% margin of error (default)).

n = 4760000000 / (1 + 4760000000 * 0.05^2)

n = 399.99

2.2 Online Survey Data Analysis

Statistical tests for hypotheses testing (Section 1.2) were conducted for the survey data analysis. Since, the phase one variables were categorical in-nature, a non-parametric 'Wilcoxon Signed-rank test (WSR)', 'Chi-Square Test of Independence (CSTI)' and 'Correlation Coefficient' test was applied (Table 1).

Table 1: Predictor variables & Target variable

	Variables	Analysis	Tools
Demographic groups. (Predictor)	Language, Age-Groups, Education qualification Vs. Social media Language.	Correlation Coefficient, CSTI & WSR test.	Jupyter Notebook. Python programming language.
Personality. (Predictor)	Personality (OCEAN) Vs. Social media Language.	Correlation Coefficient, CSTI & WSR test.	Jupyter Notebook. Python programming language.
Social media Language. (Target)	All Social media languages (emoticons/emoji, abbreviations and mixed-languages).	Correlation Coefficient, CSTI & WSR test.	Jupyter Notebook. Python programming language.

3. Results

3.1 Correlation Coefficient

The interpretation of the correlation values was carried out as per Table 2 below (Bhandari, 2023).

Table 2: Correlation Coefficient interpretation table

Correlation ranges	Interpretation	Correlation type
-.7 to -1	Very strong	Negative
-.5 to -.7	Strong	Negative
-.3 to -.5	Moderate	Negative
0 to -.3	Weak	Negative
0	None	Zero
0 to .3	Weak	Positive
.3 to .5	Moderate	Positive
.5 to .7	Strong	Positive
.7 to 1	Very strong	Positive

3.1.1 Demographic groups and social media languages

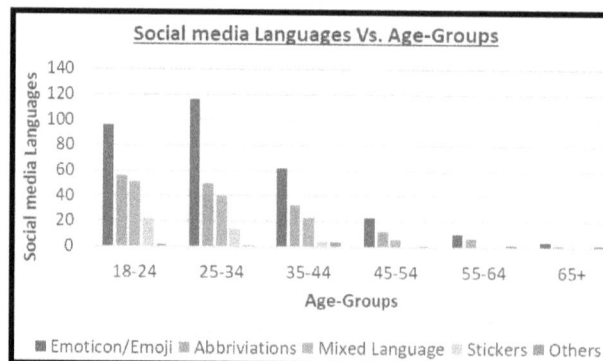

Figure 1: Number of users using social media language as per 'Age-Groups'

The preliminary observation of 'Age-Groups' and 'Social media Language' suggested that as 'Age-Groups' increase so the use of social media language decreases, but the use of 'Emoticons/Emoji', 'Abbreviations' and 'Mixed Language' remains prevalent (Figure 1). Therefore, to understand the significance between variables represented by the P-values, 'Demographic Groups' was broken down, hence Table 3 below shows correlation values and the significance represented by their P-value of each age-groups and 'Social media Language'. The interpretation of the P-value was that if it would be less than $P < 0.05$, then there is a significant relationship (Zach, 2021). The Table 3 below suggests that within 'Demographic Groups', 'Age-Groups' has a significant relation with 'Social media Languages' observed by their P-values. The Table 3 also shows a strong correlation between all six age-groups and 'Social media Languages'.

Table 3: Each of the 'Age Groups' versus the 'Social media Language'

Age Groups	Social media Language				
	Emoticons/Emoji	Abbreviations	Mixed Languages	Stickers	Gifs
18-24 (32.8%)	0.069 (Weak, Positive) P-value: 0.223	0.841 (Very Strong, Positive) P-value: 0.492	0.917 (Very Strong, Positive) P-value: 0.023	0.443 (Moderate, Positive) P-value: 0.021	0.232 (Weak, Positive) P-value: 0.018
25-34 (32.5%)	0.068 (Weak, Positive) P-value: 0.234	0.835 (Very Strong, Positive) P-value: 0.013	0.923 (Very Strong, Positive) P-value: 0.024	0.448 (Moderate, Positive) P-value: 0.074	0.234 (Weak, Positive) P-value: 0.025
35-44 (20.7%)	0.048 (Weak, Positive) P-value: 0.398	0.642 (Strong, Positive) P-value: 0.054	0.768 (Very Strong, Positive) P-value: 0.032	0.632 (Strong, Positive) P-value: 0.237	0.330 (Moderate, Positive) P-value: 0.024
45-54 (7.6%)	0.027 (Weak, Positive) P-value: 0.635	0.324 (Moderate, Positive) P-value: 0.046	0.420 (Moderate, Positive) P-value: 0.076	0.866 (Very Strong, Positive) P-value: 0.019	0.602 (Strong, Positive) P-value: 0.029
55-64 (4.4%)	0.020 (Weak, Positive) P-value: 0.724	0.241 (Weak, Positive) P-value: 0.012	0.313 (Moderate, Positive) P-value: 0.034	0.645 (Strong, Positive) P-value: 0.027	0.816 (Very Strong, Positive) P-value: 0.013
65+ (2%)	0.012 (Weak, Positive) P-value: 0.821	0.158 (Weak, Positive) P-value: 0.041	0.205 (Weak, Positive) P-value: 0.073	0.423 (Moderate, Positive) P-value: 0.058	0.811 (Very Strong, Positive) P-value: 0.026

3.1.2   Personality and social media languages

Table 4: Correlation Coefficient between 'Personality' and 'Social media Language'

Personality	Social media Language				
	Emoticons/Emoji	Abbreviations	Mixed Languages	Stickers	Gifs
Openness	-0.018 (Weak, negative) P-value: 0.723	0.021 (Weak, positive) P-value: 0.671	0.009 (Weak, positive) P-value: 0.848	0.026 (Weak, positive) P-value: 0.593	0.033 (Weak, positive) P-value: 0.503
Conscientiousness	-0.032 (Weak, negative)	0.039 (Weak, positive)	-0.035 (Weak, negative)	0.006 (Weak, positive)	-0.006 (Weak, negative)

Personality	Social media Language				
	Emoticons/Emoji	Abbreviations	Mixed Languages	Stickers	Gifs
	P-value: 0.514	**P-value**: 0.437	**P-value**: 0.491	**P-value**: 0.912	**P-value**: 0.934
Extroversion	-0.037 (Weak, negative) **P-value**: 0.465	-0.032 (Weak, negative) **P-value**: 0.526	0.028 (Weak, positive) **P-value**: 0.572	-0.039 (Weak, negative) **P-value**: 0.424	-0.039 (Weak, negative) **P-value**: 0.431
Agreeableness	-0.008 (Weak, negative) **P-value**: 0.862	0.028 (Weak, positive) **P-value**: 0.577	0.015 (Weak, positive) **P-value**: 0.762	0.029 (Weak, positive) **P-value**: 0.554	0.059 (Weak, positive) **P-value**: 0.238
Neurotic	-0.054 (Weak, negative) **P-value**: 0.28	-0.019 (Weak, negative) **P-value**: 0.71	-0.063 (Weak, negative) **P-value**: 0.20	-0.040 (Weak, negative) **P-value**: 0.42	-0.091 (Weak, negative) **P-value**: 0.07

From Table 4, it can be observed that the correlation coefficient values between 'Personality' and 'Social media Language' suggests that there is a weak relationship between the two variables.

3.2 Wilcoxon Signed-rank (WSR) test for Demographic Groups and Social Media Language

According to the Table 5 below, there is a significant relation between 'Age-Groups' and 'Stickers', and 'Educational Qualification' and all of the 'Social media Languages' as their P-values are less than $P < 0.05$. A significant relation was also observed between 'Language', 'Emoticons/Emoji', 'Mixed Languages' and 'Stickers'. Overall, there is a significant relation between 'Demographic Groups' and 'Social media Language' supported by the WSR test.

Table 5: WSR test between 'Demographic Groups' and 'Social media Language'

Demographic Groups	Social media Language				
	Emoticons/Emoji	Abbreviations	Mixed Languages	Stickers	Gifs
Age-Groups	Statistic: 8789.0 **P-value**: 0.09	Statistic: 4816.0 **P-value**: 0.08	Statistic: 3003.0 **P-value**: 0.06	Statistic: 1824.0 **P-value**: 0.01	Statistic: 486.5 **P-value**: 0.06
Educational Qualification	Statistic: 0.0 **P-value**: 0.01	Statistic: 0.0 **P-value**: 0.04	Statistic: 0.0 **P-value**: 0.02	Statistic: 0.0 **P-value**: 0.04	Statistic: 0.0 **P-value**: 0.01
Language	Statistic: 4958.5 **P-value**: 0.01	Statistic: 10450.0 **P-value**: 0.58	Statistic: 5264.0 **P-value**: 0.04	Statistic: 2002.0 **P-value**: 0.02	Statistic:841.5 **P-value**: 0.07

3.2.1 WSR test on personality vs. social media language

According to Table 6 below, it was observed that there is a significant relation between 'Personality', and 'Social media Language' supported by the WSR test.

Table 6: WSR test between 'Personality' and 'Social media Language'

Personality	Social media Language				
	Emoticons/Emoji	Abbreviations	Mixed Languages	Stickers	Gifs
Openness	Statistic: 0.0 **P-value**: 0.07	Statistic: 0.0 **P-value**: 0.08	Statistic: 0.0 **P-value**: 0.03	Statistic: 0.0 **P-value**: 0.01	Statistic: 0.0 **P-value**: 0.01
Conscientiousness	Statistic: 0.0 **P-value**: 0.02	Statistic: 0.0 **P-value**: 0.06	Statistic: 0.0 **P-value**: 0.02	Statistic: 0.0 **P-value**: 0.01	Statistic 0.0 **P-value**: 0.06

Personality	Social media Language				
	Emoticons/Emoji	Abbreviations	Mixed Languages	Stickers	Gifs
Extroversion	Statistic: 0.0 **P-value: 0.03**	Statistic: 0.0 **P-value: 0.01**	Statistic: 0.0 **P-value: 0.06**	Statistic: 0.0 **P-value: 0.02**	Statistic: 0.0 **P-value: 0.02**
Agreeableness	Statistic: 0.0 **P-value: 0.01**	Statistic: 0.0 **P-value: 0.06**	Statistic: 0.0 **P-value: 0.07**	Statistic: 0.0 **P-value: 0.02**	Statistic: 0.0 **P-value: 0.01**
Neurotic	Statistic: 0.0 **P-value: 0.01**	Statistic: 0.0 **P-value: 0.03**	Statistic: 0.0 **P-value: 0.02**	Statistic: 0.0 **P-value: 0.01**	Statistic: 0.0 **P-value: 0.01**

3.3 Chi-square Test of Independence

3.3.1 Demographic groups vs. social media language

The Chi-square Test of Independence is a non-parametric test to determine if the categorical variables are associated (Jain, 2020). In this phase one the categorical variables are 'Demographic Groups', 'Personality' and 'Social media Language' (Table 1). The Chi-square Test of Independence was performed between 'Demographic groups' and 'Social media Language' to assess the statistical associations between them (Table 7). This test was also performed between 'Personality' and 'Social media Language' (Table 8).

Table 7: The Chi-square Test of Independence between 'Demographic groups' and 'Social media Language'

Demographic Groups	Social media Language				
	Emoticons/Emoji	Abbreviations	Mixed Languages	Stickers	Gifs
Age-Groups	Chi-square value: 5.31 **P-value: 0.37** Degrees of Freedom: 5	Chi-square value: 14.68 **P-value: 0.01** Degrees of Freedom: 5	Chi-square value: 2.04 **P-value: 0.84** Degrees of Freedom: 5	Chi-square value: 4.82 **P-value: 0.04** Degrees of Freedom: 5	Chi-square value: 0.93 **P-value: 0.96** Degrees of Freedom: 5
Educational Qualification	Chi-square value: 4.23 **P-value: 0.37** Degrees of Freedom: 4	Chi-square value: 1.49 **P-value: 0.82** Degrees of Freedom: 4	Chi-square value: 10.69 **P-value: 0.03** Degrees of Freedom: 4	Chi-square value: 0.93 **P-value: 0.92** Degrees of Freedom: 4	Chi-square value: 3.04 **P-value: 0.55** Degrees of Freedom: 4
Language	Chi-square value: 0.21 **P-value: 0.01** Degrees of Freedom: 1	Chi-square value: 0.38 **P-value: 0.53** Degrees of Freedom: 1	Chi-square value: 1.42 **P-value: 0.23** Degrees of Freedom: 1	Chi-square value: 3.18 **P-value: 0.07** Degrees of Freedom: 1	Chi-square value: 1.87 **P-value: 0.17** Degrees of Freedom: 1

In the interpretation of the Chi-square Test of Independence the P-value was observed in which if the P-value would be less than $P < 0.05$, then there is a statistical association between the variables (Brian, 2023). From the Table 7 above, the Chi-square Test of Independence shows that there is an association between 'Age-Groups', 'Abbreviations' $X^2(5, N = 406) = 14.68, p = .01$ and 'Stickers' $X^2(5, N = 406) = 4.82, p = .04$. The test also shows that there is an association between 'Educational Qualification' and 'Mixed Languages', $X^2(4, N = 406) = 10.69, p = .03$. There is also an association observed between 'Language' and 'Emoticons/Emoji', $X^2(1, N = 406) = .21, p = .01$. However, the rest of the results showed that there was no association between 'Demographic groups' and 'Social media Language'.

3.3.2 Personality vs. social media language

Table 8: The Chi-square Test of Independence between 'Personality' and 'Social media Languages'

| Personality | Social media languages | | | | |
	Emoticons/Emoji	Abbreviations	Mixed Languages	Stickers	Gifs
Openness	Chi-square value: 6.55 **P-value**: 0.16 Degrees of Freedom: 4	Chi-square value: 6.47 **P-value**: 0.16 Degrees of Freedom: 4	Chi-square value: 2.88 **P-value**: 0.57 Degrees of Freedom: 4	Chi-square value: 4.89 **P-value**: 0.29 Degrees of Freedom: 4	Chi-square value: 2.75 **P-value**: 0.59 Degrees of Freedom: 4
Conscientiousness	Chi-square value: 3.61 **P-value**: 0.46 Degrees of Freedom: 4	Chi-square value: 1.08 **P-value**: 0.89 Degrees of Freedom: 4	Chi-square value: 3.32 **P-value**: 0.50 Degrees of Freedom: 4	Chi-square value: 1.76 **P-value**: 0.78 Degrees of Freedom: 4	Chi-square value: 4.08 **P-value**: 0.39 Degrees of Freedom: 4
Extroversion	Chi-square value: 5.13 **P-value**: 0.27 Degrees of Freedom: 4	Chi-square value: 2.95 **P-value**: 0.56 Degrees of Freedom: 4	Chi-square value: 1.72 **P-value**: 0.78 Degrees of Freedom: 4	Chi-square value: 3.16 **P-value**: 0.53 Degrees of Freedom: 4	Chi-square value: 10.43 **P-value**: 0.03 Degrees of Freedom: 4
Agreeableness	Chi-square value: 0.64 **P-value**: 0.95 Degrees of Freedom: 4	Chi-square value: 4.14 **P-value**: 0.39 Degrees of Freedom: 4	Chi-square value: 3.24 **P-value**: 0.51 Degrees of Freedom: 4	Chi-square value: 1.56 **P-value**: 0.81 Degrees of Freedom: 4	Chi-square value: 3.92 **P-value**: 0.41 Degrees of Freedom: 4
Neuroticism	Chi-square value: 6.65 **P-value**: 0.15 Degrees of Freedom: 4	Chi-square value: 1.29 **P-value**: 0.86 Degrees of Freedom: 4	Chi-square value: 3.10 **P-value**: 0.54 Degrees of Freedom: 4	Chi-square value: 3.50 **P-value**: 0.47 Degrees of Freedom: 4	Chi-square value: 12.64 **P-value**: 0.01 Degrees of Freedom: 4

From the Table 8 above, the Chi-square Test of Independence shows that there is an association between 'Extroversion' and 'Gifs', $X^2 (4, N = 406) = 10.43$, $p = .03$. The test also shows that there is an association between 'Neuroticism' and 'Gifs', $X^2 (5, N = 406) = 12.64$, $p = .01$. However, the rest of the results show that there is no association between 'Personality' and 'Social media Language'. Overall, the Chi-square Test of Independence revealed that besides few variables, there is no association between 'Demographic Groups' and 'Social media Language', and there is no association between 'Personality' and 'Social media Language'.

4. Discussion

The two hypotheses for this paper relate to understanding the impacts of demographic groups and personality on social media language, it was necessary to prove one of the hypotheses correct by supporting evidence. Hence, the data analysis supports the alternate hypothesis which states that demographic groups and personality does impact the use of social media language, this answers the question. The study also demonstrates a strong positive correlation between demographic groups and personality with social media language.

Therefore, in line with the alternate hypothesis the correlation coefficient values of 'Demography groups' and 'Social media Language' showed that there is a high external validity in terms of the overall population validity, hence the findings can be generalised in real-life settings of the social media user population. However, due to the correlation between the input and output variables such as observed between: 'Age Groups' and 'Social media Language', 'Educational Qualification' and 'Language', it can be deduced that there is also a high internal validity. A high internal validity means a causal relationship between 'Demography groups' and 'Social media Language' further meaning that demography influences the user of social media language. This finding seems to agree with the findings of Veenstra et al (2017) and Abbasova (2019) in which it was found that 60% of their participants preferred English for communication on social media because it was the quickest way to type responses as compared to their own native language. However, a study by Mubarak (2016) showed that people do communicate in their native language but occasionally use English words alongside their native words, or sometimes they type native words in English. Furthermore, the use of abbreviations was also common among the social media users because it enabled them to express their feelings and emotions in text messaging. The similarity between this study and Roni et al (2019) is that both have identified, mixed-languages and abbreviations as common trend among social media users. However, the results also suggests that as age-groups increase so does the use of social media language decreases, but the use of emoticons/emoji, abbreviations and mixed-language remains prevalent, furthermore the data also reveals that the use of mixed-language only remains prevalent up to the age-group 45-54, whereas emoticons/emoji and abbreviations continue to prevail up to the age-group 65+. This finding also agrees with the study of Christa et al (2020) in which 80% of their data collected show that people use abbreviate words like 'But' to 'Bt', 'You' to 'U', 'Text' to 'Txt' etc. for quick and better communication and for quick response.

The analysis of 'Personality' and 'Social media Language' data in this study suggests a high external validity, hence this finding can be generalised to real life settings of social media user population. However, due to some correlation between the input and output variables such as between 'Openness', 'Agreeableness' and 'Social media Language', it can be deduced that there is also a high internal validity. A high internal validity means that there is causal relationship between 'Personality' and 'Social media Language' further meaning that personality does influence social media language. This finding seems to agree with a study from Teresa et al (2009) and Thomas et al (2020), these authors have studied and shown some link between demography, personality and social media, but the focus was only on extraversion when it came to personality. Whilst it could be that extraversion does impact the use of social media as even agreed by Andreassen et al (2012) and Wilson et al (2010), however the results share a new insight between personality and social media language that it is not only extraversion/introversion, but also openness, conscientiousness, agreeableness and neurotic traits which also impacts social media language (Samuel et al, 2003).

5. Conclusion

The study aimed to investigate 'Demographic groups' and 'Personality' impact on social media language which will lead to further research on the development of a computer-sophisticated tool to help identify online identity. The findings of the online survey obtained through statistical analyses and tests provide enough evidence to support the alternate hypothesis which states that 'Demographic groups and Personality impacts the use of social media language which can be used to represent 'identity' online.'. This conclusion was achieved by breaking down demographic groups and personality into independent variables and comparing each of their correlation values to understand their cause-and-effect relation to social media language. These findings will be used further in the research project by focusing on the use of social media language for online identity management in textual conversations. The outcome of the further research will be compared to the phase one data to obtain demographic groups and personality data for the respective participants in the mock conversations, this can also be used to formulate a theory and communication model headed in the path of social media communication using textual conversations and online identity.

References

Abbasova, M. (2019). Language of Social Media: An investigation of the changes that social media has imposed on language use. *9th International Conference on Education, Language and Literature*. Tbilisi, Georgia, pp. 309-313.

Asenahabi, B. and Ikoha, P. (2023). Scientific Research Sample Size Determination. *The International Journal of Science and Technoledge*, vol. 11, pp. 08-12.

Andreassen, S., Torsheim, T., Brunborg, G. and Pallesen, S. (2012). Development of a Facebook Addiction Scale. *Psychological Reports*, vol. 110, pp. 501–517

Brian, B. (2023, March 05). P-Value: What It Is, How to Calculate It, and Why It Matters [Online]. Available from: https://www.investopedia.com/terms/p/p-value.asp#:~:text=Key%20Takeaways,significance%20of%20the%20observed%20difference.

Christa, I. and Mercy, O. (2020). Language use in social media and natural language. *International Journal of Humanities and Social Science*, vol. 10, pp. 1-09.

Divakar, S. and Nanjundeswaraswamy, T. (2021). Determination of Sample Size and Sampling Methods in Applied Research. *Proceedings on Engineering Sciences*, vol. 03, pp. 25-32.

Gibbs, J., Heino, R. and Ellison, N. (2006). Managing impressions online: Self-presentation processes in the online dating environment. *Journal of Computer-Mediated Communication*, vol. 11, pp. 415-441.

Hazra, A. (2017). Using the confidence interval confidently. *Journal of Thoracic Disease*, vol. 9, pp. 4125–4130.

Heino, D., Ellison, B. and Gibbs, J. (2006). Self-presentation in online personals: The role of anticipated future interaction, self-disclosure, and perceived success in Internet dating. *Communication Research*, vol. 33, pp. 152-177.

JISC, (2023, October 10). Online Surveys (formerly BOS) [Online]. Available from: https://www.onlinesurveys.ac.uk/

Jain. R, (2020, May 31). Correlation between Categorical Variables [Online]. Available from: https://medium.com/@ritesh.110587/correlation-between-categorical-variables-63f6bd9bf2f7

Kemp, S. (2023, January 26). Digital 2023: Global Overview Report [Online]. Available from: https://datareportal.com/reports/digital-2023-global-overview-report#:~:text=There%20are%20now%204.76%20billion,growth%20of%20just%203%20percen

Mccabe. D., Yurchisin, J. and Watchravesringkan. (2005). An exploration of identity re-creation in the context of Internet dating. *Social behaviour and Personality*, vol. 33, pp. 735-750.

Mubarak, A. (2016). Learning English as a second language through social media: Saudi Arabian Tertiary context. *International Journal of Linguistics*, vol. 8, pp. 112-119.

Pietro, M. (2020, June 09). Text Analysis & feature engineering with NLP [Online]. Available from: https://medium.com/towards-data-science/text-analysis-feature-engineering-with-nlp-502d6ea9225d

Roni, R. and Perdhani, W. (2019). Generational differences related to linguistic and discourse features of WhatsApp users of texting. *First International Conference on Advances in Education and language,* Malang, Indonesia, pp.1-09.

Samuel, G., Rentfrow, P., Swan, W. (2003). A very brief measure of the Big-Five personality domains. *Methods in Ecology and Evolution*, vol. 27, pp. 504- 528.

Solent, (2023, April 12). Solent Informed Consent [Online]. Available from: https://www.solent.ac.uk/research-innovation-enterprise/documents/informed-consent-form.pdf

Statista, (2023, March 21). Number of internet and social media users worldwide [Online]. Available from: https://www.statista.com/statistics/617136/digital-population-worldwide/

SurveyCircle, (2023, April 14). Find Survey Participants with Survey Circle [Online]. Available from: https://www.surveycircle.com/en/

SurveySwap, (2023, April 14). Find survey respondents now [Online]. Available from: https://surveyswap.io/

Teresa, S., Amber, H., and Homero, Z. (2009). Who interacts on the Web?: The intersection of users' personality and social media use. *Computers in Human Behaviour*, vol. 26, pp. 247-253.

Thomas, B., Hinds, J. and Joinson, A. (2016). How extraversion is related to social media use. *Personality and Individual differences*, vol. 164, pp. 01-11.

Veenstra, A. and Hossain, M. (2017). The uses and gratifications of language in social media among the Indian subcontinental diaspora in the US. *Journal of Intercultural communication research*, vol. 46, pp. 478-496.

Walher, J. (2007). Selective self-presentation in computer-mediated communication: Hyperpersonal dimensions of technology, language, and cognition. *Computers in Human Behavior*, vol. 23, pp. 2538-2557.

Warburton, S. and Hatzipanagos, S. (2015). Digital Identity and Social-Media. 1st ed. Pennsylvania: Information Science Reference.

Wilson, K., Fornasier, S and White, K. (2010). Psychological predictors of young adults' use of social networking sites. *Cyberpsychology, behaviour and social networking*, vol. 13, pp. 173-177.

Social Media use by the Elderly: Friend or foe

Val Hooper

Victoria University of Wellington, New Zealand

Val.hooper@vuw.ac.nz

Abstract: Worldwide, populations are aging, especially in the developed world. In parallel with this increase in the elderly population groups, there has been an increase in the use of social media. However, few studies have explored the use of social media for social engagement by the elderly and the motivations behind such use. The generally accepted age threshold of being elderly is 65 years. Often this coincides with retirement age as well as social pension age. Although this is not always the situation, often the elderly age state is accompanied by changes in economic and social situations. Often transitioning to being elderly presents challenges for those experiencing it, and the question arises as to the extent to which the use of social media can facilitate or hinder that transition. Using a social exchange theoretical lens, as well as that of self-determination theory and privacy calculus, this research was exploratory and qualitative. In-depth personal interviews were conducted with a purposive sample of 20 Eurocentric English-speaking respondents who were over 65 years of age. Some were retired, some were partially employed, some had their own businesses, and some were employed full-time. The gender split was 50:50. The purpose was to explore the use of social media by the elderly and the motivation behind it. In addition, observation of the social media use of the respondents lent further insights into the interpretation of the results. The overwhelming use of social media by the elderly was for social engagement, and the general tenor of posts and responses was one of great positivity. That positive approach was largely driven by self-interest and the implicit understanding that if one posted positive messages or responded positively, there would be a resultant feeling of goodwill and wellbeing in the recipient, and that those well-meant messages would be reciprocated, leading to a feeling of wellbeing in oneself. Although elements of competition, providing purpose to one's life, and honouring privacy concerns of others were additional motivators, the main motivation was for happy social engagement and feelings of personal wellbeing.

Keywords: Elderly, Social media use by the elderly, Self-determination theory, Social exchange theory, Privacy calculus

1. Introduction

Worldwide, populations are aging, especially in the developed world (United Nations, 2023). In parallel with this increase in the elderly population groups, there has been an increase in the use of social media, in general, and amongst those older than 65, in particular (Statista, 2023). In the US, for instance, some 45% of the elderly use social media (Faverio, 2022). However, few studies have explored the use of social media by the elderly and the motivations behind such use.

The generally accepted age of being elderly is 65 years. The age of 65 has often been taken as the mark of 'later life' (Uhlenburg, 2009). Often this coincides with retirement age as well as social pension age (United Nations, 2023). Often the elderly state is accompanied by changes in economic, financial and social situations. Many of the "friends" that one had in the work environment seem to vanish. By then most children have left the home – or even the country; spouses may die; and physical mobility may become reduced. Thus, transitioning to being elderly can present challenges, and the question arises as to how the use of social media can facilitate or hinder that transition.

2. Literature Review

The world's population is ageing. The generally accepted age of being elderly is 65 (United Nations, 2023). Often this coincides with retirement age as well as social pension age. Income is often reduced and unless there is a substantial state support for pensioners and/or the latter have saved judiciously for their retirement, financial burdens can weigh strongly on the individuals (United Nations, 2023). The social environment of the retired person is often severely disrupted, with a reduction from the status accorded the individual. Plus, the readymade social environment of the workplace disappears. Renegotiation of relationships with spouses is often required. Furthermore, becoming elderly often signals reduction in physical ability and mobility. The upshot is that many feel that while retirement signals more time on one's hand to enjoy the things they love doing, the economic and physical constraints frequently limit such opportunities. Added to that, many families are distributed across the world so chances of spending more time with children and grandchildren are limited. Given all that, feelings of loneliness and social isolation can result and together with reduced physical ability, this can lead to depression and a reduction in mental and physical wellbeing. In fact, loneliness has been earmarked as the "hidden killer of older adults" (Coughlan, 2011).

On a more positive note, social media and ICT have enabled many elderly to overcome the challenges of aging and they lead motivated, fulfilling and happy lives (Sohu, 2020; Wilson, 2018)). The feelings of social isolation and loneliness are reduced (Colten et al, 2013); depression is reduced (Jean et al, 2020) and well-being is enhanced (Szabo et al, 2019). Common indicators of a healthier mental state are happiness, increased self-esteem and the loss of loneliness (Ryan and Deci, 2001). Older adults use social media for two main reasons: for socio-emotional use (Coelho and Duarte, 2016) and for informational use (Quinn, 2018).

Initially social media had been used for social reasons. Boyd and Ellison (2007) described social media as web-based services that enabled users to (1) develop a public or semi-public profile within a bounded system, (2) specify a list of other users with whom they are connected, and (3) view and communicate with their list of connections and those made by others within the system. Essentially, individuals manage their self-identity and their relationships on social media. The display of one's friends is what initially differentiated social media from other online media (Boyd and Ellison, 2007). Most people used social media to socialize generally, to keep in contact with existing friends, and to meet new friends (Brandtzaeg and Heim, 2009). However, other opportunities for the use of social media were soon spotted and exploited by all forms of organizations and businesses, social and political causes, governments, and news and entertainment agencies.

There has been considerable research on the use of technology by the elderly and also their informational use. However, there have been a limited number of studies on how the elderly specifically use their social media to enhance their emotional wellbeing, and facilitate the challenges of overcoming the transition of to the elderly state. This research aims to address this gap in knowledge by exploring the use of social media by the elderly.

3. Theoretical Background

This study used a social exchange theoretical lens, as well as that of the privacy calculus theory, and self-determination theory.

The social exchange theory (SET) was introduced by the sociologist, Homans (1958), as a way of explaining the subjective cost-benefit analysis of alternatives in the voluntary exchange for mutual benefit of activities and resources between two individuals. The parties expect to develop and maintain a rewarding relationship. Cropanzano et al (2017) defined the SET as "(i) an initiation by an actor toward the target, (ii) an attitudinal or behavioral response from the target in reciprocity, and (iii) the resulting relationship". The core assumptions are that individuals seek rewards and avoid punishment; and that they seek maximum profit with minimal effort. The SET is a very widely accepted and applied theory in workplace behaviour (Cropanzano and Mitchell, 2005). It also has wide applications in any interpersonal relationships, particularly family and friends.

Aligned with the SET, the privacy calculus theory suggests that an individual's intention to disclose private information is based on a calculation of potentially conflicting factors in light of possible outcomes. It could be construed as a type of risk-benefit analysis (Stone and Stone, 1990). It has been used to examine people's online behaviours, particularly in terms of privacy and security risks.

Yet a further theoretical lens which was useful in this study was self-determination theory. Amongst others, self-determination theory emphasises three basic psychological needs – the need for competence, for relatedness and for autonomy (Ryan and Deci, 2002). Competence refers to the need to feel effective; relatedness refers to the need to feel connected to others and to belong; and autonomy refers to an individual's ability to act according to their own will.

4. Method

The purpose of the study was to explore the use of social media by the elderly and the motivation behind the different uses. This research was exploratory and qualitative, and followed an interpretivist paradigm. In-depth personal interviews were conducted with a purposive sample of 20 Eurocentric English-speaking respondents who were over 65 years of age. They were based in different countries around the world, e.g. the UK, the US, South Africa, New Zealand, Australia. Some were retired, some were partially employed, some had their own businesses, and some were employed full-time. The gender split was 50:50. Ages ranged from 65-88.

In addition, observation of the social media use of the respondents lent further insights into the interpretation of the results. Frequency of postings, extent of friendship circles, number of social media subscribed to; frequency of responses was also noted.

It should be noted that only postings related to individual, private friendships and relationships were covered in this research. Formal communities of practice, and special interest groups, plus business-related groups such as brand communities were excluded.

5. Findings

Very definite categories of social media users emerged from the study. There were the regular posters, many of whom posted something at least once every day and/or at specific times each day such as the beginning of the day. There were the regular respondents who could be counted on to respond to most of the regular posters' posts. Then there were the sporadic posters, who seemed to be selective in what they posted, both in terms of topic and regularity. As with the posters, there were also the sporadic respondents, who did not necessarily respond to each post of a certain poster, or in fact, to the same posters. There were also the passers-on – those who did not actually write anything or create any part of the message but merely passed on something that might appeal to others, such as religious/inspirational messages, recipes, jokes, handy craft hints. Finally, there were the lurkers who observed others' posts avidly but did not care to respond via social media and did so via e-mail instead.

There was no apparent split in number of posts between people living on their own, such as widows, and those living with others, as in an intergenerational family or a care facility. However, those living alone tended to post more regularly, as opposed to spurts of postings.

A brief summary of the findings appears in Table 1 below.

5.1 Target Audience

The general response regarding the target audience of their postings was "anyone who knows/knew me and would be interested in being my friend". This was more broadly expanded upon as catching up and/or communicating.

5.2 Content of Posts

A post consisted predominantly of photo's, videos and other images such as cartoons, media headlines. Invariably these were accompanied by short text comments. Depending on the social media used, so the type of posting content (text or illustration) was prescribed - also the length of the posting.

Although some topic areas received more or less equal attention from males and females in terms of numbers of posts, by and large there was a clear division of topics covered by males and by females.

Both males and females posted a considerable amount of content about their children and grandchildren. However, males tended to post more family group pictures and action shots/videos of their grandchildren performing well at some sport or leisure-time activity. Females tended to post more pictures/videos and information about significant events: birthday celebrations, engagement parties, weddings, births, graduations, prize-givings at schools, special performances/achievements in sport or the performing arts. Females also focused more on posts of their young grandchildren doing "cute" things such as learning to walk/skate, than males.

Table 1: Summary of main findings

Contents of postings		
What is posted		Photos, videos, images, short text
Topics of posts	Male & female	Children & grandchildren; birthday wishes; gardening
	Male	Family groups and action shots; jokes; "male" hobbies and products
	Female	Significant family events, "cute" grandchildren; pets; reunions; "female" hobbies
Posting behaviour – message initiation		
Medium		Facebook
Frequency		Daily
When		First thing in the morning
Why		Achievement; regular regime; would be missed if they broke the pattern of activity; forced productivity; earliness established more opportunities for engagement
Reasons for posting		
Reasons		Keep in touch; share enjoyable information /content; happy experience; inspirational and uplifting; relatively cheap; immediate contact; can see movement and context

Why		Expected of them by their friends; obligation to make others feel loved; convenience
Responses to postings		
What is responded		Brief - single words, short phrases and sentences, emoji's
Topics	Male & female	Always positive
	Male	Achievement oriented
	Female	Appearance oriented
Why		Matter of courtesy; short responses the norm; positive responses expected; positive reciprocity; immediate gratification and positive reinforcement

An interesting aspect of the "family" topic, was the awareness amongst a number of female respondents that they should be cautious about what they posted about their grandchildren, in particular. They were wary of online malpractices, such as stalking and sexploitation, and were conscious of maintaining the privacy of their offspring. Cheryl reported that her daughters and daughter-in-law "freaked" whenever she posted pictures of her grandchildren and she'd been severely reprimanded for doing so. Sandra recounted the many times she'd been lectured to by her children on the need for maintaining the privacy of her young and the consequences of not doing so. This resulted in an inner conflict among many posters because they loved to share the delights of, and pride in, their families but wanted to protect them from harm. On the other hand, some respondents seemed unaware of the potential dangers of posting family pictures and did so with abandon, joy and pride.

Along the lines of family censure, teenage granddaughters, in particular, were reported to be very sensitive about anything that was communicated about them online. Any possible post had to be "cleared" with the relevant grandchild – "it's not even enough for my son or daughter to grant permission" (Felicity) because they get censored as well.

Linked to families, females tended to post many more pictures/videos, in particular, about their pets – and these tended to be smaller, more lapdog type dogs. A number of females, in particular but not exclusively, posted pictures of reunions of school or university friends – and these groups often developed into well-supported online friendship circles. Linked to past contexts, various elderly people had relocated to another country during their lives, and such people often tended to post text or photo's of "the home country", sometimes lamenting the current state of such a country.

Birthday wishes and congratulations of other celebrations featured strongly amongst both males and females. The fact that automatic reminders on some social media helped users to "remember" was an added advantage of social media use. Religious messages or inspirational messages were often posted by females; and although both males and females posted jokes, men tended to do so more than females.

Recent trips also featured strongly, with females tending to focus on this topic much more. Philippa gloried in being referred to as the "Galloping Granny" and even adopted that name for herself. Often these "trip" postings included photo's of social events enjoyed with fellow travellers.

Hobbies, and achievements in this regard, were a very popular topic of postings. Males tended to focus on photography; woodworking; home construction; car/motorbike restoration; fishing. These were usually pursuits where the "product" could be illustrated, rather than actions pursuits such as cycling, walking, etc. Females tended to focus on postings of their arts and crafts - quilting, knitting, crocheting, and general arts and crafts. Photo's of gardens also featured strongly in females' postings.

Interestingly, there were a number of topics that respondents acknowledged they did not post about – business activities/promotion (these were relegated to other business-oriented social media); political propaganda or commentary (although there might be some lampooning of characters like Donald Trump); personal illness and operations (apart from retrospective comments on "full" recovery); and cosmetic surgery they had had done or hair colouring.

5.3 Posting Behaviour (Message Initiation)

By far the preferred social medium was Facebook. This was because it was the "original" social medium, and the social medium that the elderly had become familiar with. It was also seen to serve their purposes and requirements. However, some respondents also used Instagram and WhatsApp and one or two used Tiktok.

Such uses were because grandchildren preferred them, and in the Tiktok instance, use was more as a lurker than a poster.

Many respondents preferred to post on a daily basis and posting on social media was one of the first things they did in the day. They did this for a number of reasons: it was a positive achievement, something they could tick off a list easily; it was relatively quick and easy to accomplish; it gave them a regular regime to follow – a purpose to getting up in the morning; it established a pattern of activity where they would be missed if they skipped a day or two; it forced productivity, especially amongst those inclined to procrastination or slothfulness; and starting early in the day provided more opportunity for responses from others and social engagement in that day.

5.4 Reasons for Posting

The main reason reported for posting was in order to keep in touch, and then to share activities with a wide group of friends and family, as well as introduce friends to one another. The overarching motivation was to share enjoyable content, either news of beloved and important individuals (whom the recipients might well know); happy experiences; or inspirational, encouraging and uplifting messages.

Furthermore, in comparison with the rising postage costs it was a relatively cheap way in which to keep in touch. Plus, the real-time connectivity of certain social media enables immediate contact and communication with friends and family, which can be very gratifying without any delayed gratification. One can also see movement and the respondent's surroundings/context.

Some respondents noted it was "expected" of them by their "friends". It was seen as an obligation to make others feel loved and included. It became almost addictive, something that had to be done. In fact, Sylvia's children and grandchildren complained that, when travelling in Europe, irrespective of how lovely the surroundings were, Sylvia's "main purpose in life" was to find a place with wi-fi so that she could follow her social media activities.

Lastly, birthday reminders/automatic greetings were also convenient ways to ensure that others felt loved and special on their significant days. They were also a convenient alternative to having to go to the shop, buy a card, write a message and post the card. Not only did the convenience benefit mobile respondents but particularly those whose mobility was impaired.

One negative aspect of social media use by the elderly was the overarching concern about privacy/security breaches – particularly of the grandchildren and children. This concern often led to decisions not to post anything to do with their offspring. However, in some cases the privacy concern stretched as far as not posting anything at all to do with personal aspects of one's life.

5.5 Responses and Reasons for Responding

Responses were usually brief, single words, phrases or sentences. There was little actual in-depth engagement/extended communication or opening up of new topics. Postings or responses might often be in the form of pictures, videos, or emojis. Often they were simply an indication of "liking".

Responses were practically always positive. These positive approbations were often just a smiley emoji, a "like" or simply accolades such as "beautiful couple'; "what a lovely family!". Frequently responses to photo's of the original poster referred to physical appearance – "how young you look"; "gosh, what good shape you're in"; "love the new hairstyle". Such personal comments were particularly the case amongst females, while males would comment upon achievements of others such as catching a big fish, building a sundeck, acquisition of a vintage car. Both genders commented on spectacular scenic or wildlife photo's. All respondents felt that a response was expected as a matter of courtesy, and that the typical short response was the expected norm. It made communication very easy. Similarly, positive responses were expected. They were also easy to give – even though sometimes the respondent did not always feel so positive. Once given, however, duty was done and the recipient felt good as did the respondent for sending a positive message. It was thus easy to get someone to feel well-disposed towards you if you "like" them. In fact, spreading positive goodwill was seen to be much easier on social media than the onerous exercise of specially dressing up, travelling to see a friend or family member, spending an obligitary amount of time visiting and then travelling back home again. The frequent, almost immediate response to postings meant immediate gratification and positive reinforcement.

6. Discussion

Although the Findings section reports on what the respondents said, that is the explicit, this section analyses the responses and posting behaviour thematically to gain greater insight into the implicit meanings of the responses.

The overriding tenor of social media use by the elderly was one of positivity. The groups of motivation were all driven by a positive approach and this attitude was also manifested in the norms which guided the postings and responses.

6.1 The Purpose of Social Media use

The purpose of social media use was overwhelmingly to build and nurture friendships (Coelho and Duarte, 2016). This involved catching up and communicating with existing friends/family and making new friends. This is very much in line with the original intentions of social media (Boyd and Ellison, 2007). The assumption was that if you are my "friend" then you would be equally interested in the things and people that are dear to me. Thus, sharing postings of family, grandchildren, beloved pets were assumed to be as precious to the recipient as the poster. Social media were used predominantly as a broadcast medium – disseminating information. Interestingly, when making friends, the original friend remained the fulcrum and was always included in friendship circles that resulted. This indicates a type of loyalty to that original friend.

6.2 Norms

There seemed to be a number of norms that implicitly guided the social media interactions. These norms referred to content of posts, and manner and tone of interaction – the type of behaviour that was expected from posters and what was expected from responders. Posts about business were avoided – so no blatant marketing and no shop talk despite the respondents comprising a number of business people. Posts about politics were avoided, except glancingly or jokingly, such as cartoons about characters like Donald Trump. It seemed that the elderly were aware of the possible differences in political leanings of their friends and did not want to offend them unintentionally. Information about physical operations and illness seemed to be avoided – possibly because of the negative overtone of the potential outcomes. Only happy recoveries were commented upon – again emphasizing the positive. Little was noted about cosmetic surgery or dying their hair. The implication was that the usually rejuvenated appearance was attributable to their natural youthfulness and thus a positive feature to be admired. Responses were usually brief rather than extended engagement.

6.3 Content of Posts

By and large the content of posts focussed on matters close to home and had a decidedly positive orientation. Birthday wishes abounded, together with complimentary comments on how young and lively the birthday person was. Family featured strongly - almost to the extent of boasting and seemingly outdoing their friends with regard to the number, attractiveness, prowess and expertise of their offspring. So, the element of competition and achievement was an underlying motivation (Ryan and Deci, 2001). However, caution and concern about privacy deterred many respondents from posting content about their offspring. The influence of privacy calculus decision making was very evident (Stone and Stone, 1990). Instead, sometimes as a substitute, pets featured commonly in posts. Hobbies and gardens were common content with an element of competition featuring in such posts as well. On the other hand, often common interests in such content led to the formation of common interest groups. Reunions of old school/university friends, as well as people who might have relocated from another country featured frequently, and while there were many laments about the current status of such countries, the overall implication was one of positivity and the good fortune of being in the current country. Trips were often a focus of posts. These created the impression of youthful curiosity; preparedness to explore and learn new things; gregariousness and always being on the go. Here, too, there were elements of competition in terms of places visited (Ryan and Deci, 2001). Linking back to concerns about privacy, the focus seemed very much on caution about postings regarding offspring but yet information was shared about planned trips, especially extended ones, thus compromising any security measures that might have been taken with regard to absences from homes, spending abroad, etc. So, to be positively engaged and admired was more important at that moment than potential security threats – illustrating privacy calculus (Stone and Stone, 1990).

6.4 Motivation for Using Social Media

The main motivations for using social media were the benefits to the self; and the advantages of social media.

The overriding benefit to the self was social engagement (Coelho and Duarte, 2016). Interactions on social media provided company, thereby minimising any feelings of loneliness (Colten et al, 2013). Interactions also provided the opportunity to acknowledge and be acknowledged by others, to praise and be praised (Ryan and Deci, 2001), and to celebrate important dates with others. The positive feelings of involvement, and of being wanted were important. Plus, there was the implicit assurance that messages would be positive and that one would feel good after using social media. There was also the knowledge that responses were usually prompt, if not immediate, so any short-term memory issues would not be challenged. Linked to this implicit recognition of frailty, was the positive attitude of tolerance. Tolerance would be facilitated by the knowledge that the actual engagement could be brief, and offensive postings would be minimal because, deep down, everyone wanted to feel good and they realised that by making others feel good, there would be reciprocity and they would be made to feel good as well. This is an excellent example of the social exchange theory (Homans, 1958; Coprazano et al, 2017).

While experiencing these benefits oneself, there was the rewarding knowledge that one was bestowing all the benefits on others, and such altruistic pleasures were in themselves rewarding.

Yet another beneficial area was that social media engagement brought a purpose to many individuals' lives. It gave them a reason for living; plus it gave them something to do and helped them feel as though they were filling every moment of their lives productively (Deci and Ryan, 2002). It spiced up the competitive elements of some; and gave regularity to the lives of many – something to which they had become accustomed after years of work. Additionally, many saw their own participation as a duty to others, their friends, who needed their dose of positive acclaim or positive inspiration. Such postings were expected and would be missed if not forthcoming.

Regarding the advantages of using social media, the respondents all found mastering social media use relatively easy – which puts pay to the notion that the elderly are technically challenged. One should also remember that many of the younger ones in the sample would have had experience of some fairly advanced IT in business.

The perceived advantages of social media were that they overcame the physical constraints of many elderly people, such as lack of mobility and inability to concentrate for long periods. They enabled one to reach many people all at once, thereby obviating the need for many time-consuming individual communications and even travel (Brandtzaeg and Heim, 2009). Social media were thus seen as a quick and relatively cheap way to give and receive acclaim, approval, acknowledgement - in other words, love. Plus, the ability to see videos and picture/photo's enhanced the appeal of the media, as did features such as birthday reminders.

7. Limitations and Areas for Future Research

This study was exploratory and was conducted amongst a select sector of the elderly population. In future, the elderly of other countries/cultures should be studied. Further exploration is required into the competing uses of social media – other than for social engagement - and how these uses either contribute to the positive effects found in this study or not. In addition, more qualitative research in the form of focus groups should be undertaken as well as quantitative research for further validation of the findings.

8. Conclusion

This research contributes to the theoretical development of social media use motivation by the elderly. It also provides insights into how life of the elderly can be enhanced by social media.

The overwhelming use of social media by the elderly was for social engagement, and the general tenor of posts and responses was one of great positivity. That positive approach was largely driven by self-interest and the implicit understanding that if one posted positive messages or responded positively, there would be a resultant feeling of goodwill and wellbeing, not only in the recipient but also within oneself for making others happy. In addition, the implication was that those well-meant messages would be reciprocated, leading to a feeling of wellbeing in oneself. Topics of posts, behavioural norms, posting and responding behaviour were all driven by the desire for personal happiness. Although elements of competition, providing purpose to one's life, and honouring privacy concerns of others were additional motivators, the main motivation was for happy social engagement and feelings of personal wellbeing.

References

Blau, P.M. (1964) Exchange and Power in Social Life, John Wiley, New York.

Boyd, D. and Ellison, N. (2007) "Social network Sites: Definitions, History and Scholarship", *Journal of Computer-Mediated Communication*, No. 13, pp 210-230.

Brandtzaeg, P.B. and Heim, J. (2009) "Why People Use Social Networking Sites". In Ozok, A.A. & P.Zaphiris (Eds). *Online commission*. Springer-Verlag, Berlin, pp 143-152.

Coelho, J. and Duarte, C. (2016) "A literature survey on older adults' use of social network services and social applications", *Computers in Human Behavior*, No. 58, pp 187–205. https://doi.org/10.1016/j.chb.2015.12.053.

Cotten, S.R., Anderson, W.A. and McCullough, B.M. (2013)" Impact of internet use on loneliness and contact with others among older adults: cross-sectional analysis", *Journal of Medical Internet Research*, Vol 15, No. 2, e39. https://doi.org/10.2196/jmir.2306.

Coughlan, S. (2011, February 1) *Loneliness is "hidden killer" of elderly*. BBC News. https://www.bbc.com/news/education-12324231.

Cropanzano, R., Anthony, E.L., Daniels, S.R. and Hall, A.V. (2017) "Social exchange theory: a critical review with theoretical remedies", *Academy of Management Annals,* No. 11, pp 479–516. doi: 10.5465/annals.2015.0099

Cropanzano, R. and Mitchell, M.S. (2005) "Social exchange theory: an interdisciplinary review", *Journal of Management,* No. 31, 874–900. doi: 10.1177/0149206305279602

Deci, E.L. and Ryan, R.M. (1995) Human autonomy: The basis for true self-esteem. In M. Kernis (Ed.), *Efficacy, agency, and self-esteem* (pp 31–49), Springer.

Faverio, M. (2022) *Share of those 65 and older who are tech users has grown in the past decade*. Pew Research Center. https://www.pewresearch.org/short-reads/2022/01/13/share-of-those-65-and-older-who-are-tech-users-has-grown-in-the-past-decade/

Homans, G.C. (1958) "Social behavior as exchange", American Journal of Sociology, No. 63, pp 597–606. doi: 10.1086/222355

Jeon, G.-S., Choi, K.-W. and Jang, K.-S. (2020) "Social networking site usage and its impact on depressive symptoms among older men and women in South Korea", *International Journal of Environmental Research in Public Health*, Vol 17, No. 8, p 2670. https://doi.org/10.3390/ijerph17082670.

Milne, G.R. and Gordon, M.E. (1993) "Direct mail privacy-efficiency trade-offs within an implied social contract framework", *Journal of Public Policy & Marketing*, Vol 12, No. 2, pp. 206-215.

Murphy, D., Joseph, S., Demetriou, E. and Karimi-Mofrad, P. (2020) "Unconditional positive self-regard, intrinsic aspirations, and authenticity: Pathways to psychological well-being", *Journal of Humanistic Psychology*, Vol 60, No. 2, pp 258–279. https://doi.org/10.1177/0022167816688314

Quinn, K. (2018) "Cognitive effects of social media use: A case of older adults", *Social Media Society*, Vol 4, No. 3, 205630511878720. https://doi.org/10.1177/2056305118787203

Ryan, R.M. and Deci, E.L. (2001) "On happiness and human potentials: A review of research on hedonic and eudaimonic well-being", *Annual Review of Psychology*, Vol 52, No. 1, pp 141–166. https://doi.org/10.1146/annurev.psych.52.1.141

Sohu. (2020, March 18) [*Analysis report of "short video mini programs" for middle-aged and elderly people*]. Sohu. www.sohu.com/a/381003584_114819.

Statista (2023) *Worldwide digital population*. https://www.statista.com/statistics/617136/digital-population-worldwide/#:~:text=Worldwide%20digital%20population%202023&text=As%20of%20October%202023%2C%20there,population%2C%20were%20social%20media%20users.

Statistics Netherlands (2020) *More elderly active on social media* [Webpagina], Statistics Netherlands. https://www.cbs.nl/en-gb/news/2020/04/more-elderly-active-on-social-media.

Stone, E.F. and Stone, D.L. (1990) "Privacy in organizations: theoretical issues, research findings, and protection mechanisms", *Research in Personnel and Human Resources Management*, No. 8, pp 349-411.

Szabo, A., Allen, J., Stephens, C. and Alpass, F. (2019) "Longitudinal analysis of the relationship between purposes of internet use and well-being among older adults", *Gerontology*, Vol 59, No. (1), pp 58–68. https://doi.org/10.1093/geront/gny036.

Uhlenberg, P. ed. (2009) *International Handbook of Population Aging*, Vol. 1, Springer.

United Nations. Department of Economic and Social Affairs (2023) *World social report 2023: Leaving no one behind in an ageing world.*

Wilson, C. (2018) "Is it love or loneliness? Exploring the impact of everyday digital technology use on the wellbeing of older adults", *Ageing and Society*, Vol 38, No. 7, pp 1307–1331. https://doi.org/10.1017/S0144686X16001537

World Health Organization. (2007) Global age-friendly cities: A guide.

Insiders Versus Outsiders: A Comparative Study of Female Politician's Social Media use

Tekla Illés and Zipporah Mwangi

The Department of Communication and Media Science, Corvinus University, Budapest, Hungary

tekla.illes1@gmail.com
zipporahmwangi04@gmail.com

Abstract: In the past, the media had a tendency to neglect women's issues, thereby restricting their visibility concerning development endeavours and political representation. However, this is changing due to technological advancements. Social media offers female politicians access to millions of users, freedom to interact directly with the electorate, bypass gatekeepers and opportunities for self-promotion. This research aims to investigate female politicians' social media use during their legislative terms with a focus on their self-presentation and the policy issues they support. The study involves content analysis of six female politicians from countries with a much lower female representation than their regional counterparts; three from Kenya and three from Hungary who have the highest number of followers on Twitter and Facebook respectively. The data was collected over a three-month period. The visuals were coded using 3 variables based on the *insider* and *outsider* perspective (Gulati 2004) while the text was coded in accordance with the 21 policy agendas defined by the Comparative Agendas Project codebook (Baumgartner 2019). The results indicate that a majority of female politicians in both countries, in the ruling parties presented themselves as *insiders* while those in the opposition presented themselves as *outsiders*. The insiders were majorly characterized by wearing of formal clothing, an important element of statesmanship, that portrays them as ideal candidates. In addition, the insiders' social media use was characterized by original content while outsiders reshared articles and retweets. Both Kenyan and Hungarian female politicians addressed women related policy issues. There were however some differences in social media use and self-presentation between the female politicians of the two countries such as the sharing of personal information and family pictures. The limitation of this study is that it does not fully represent the views and use of social media of all female politicians in Kenya and Hungary.

Keywords: Female politician, Self-presentation, Social media, Insider/outsider, Policy

1. Introduction

The media plays a crucial role in moulding and influencing people's perception, behaviour and attitudes (Kamau, 2010). Traditionally the media has generally ignored women and their issues have been underrepresented with only 21% of the content of the news focusing on women (Oxfam 2006). Female politicians have struggled over the years to gain visibility in the media due to the perpetuation of gender stereotypes of women as victims, sex objects or their inability to address issues of national development (Omtatah 2008). Feminine stereotypes, also known as communal qualities (Mattan and Small 2021) view women as nurturing, compassionate and caring (Prentice and Carranza 2002). However, masculine stereotypes view men as assertive, confident and ambitious, these agentic qualities are associated with good and effective leadership (Mattan and Small 2021). Their appearance: clothing, hair, shoes and purses draw more attention than other weightier issues (Carroll 1994; Falk 2010; Siegel 2009; Watson 2006). With the above in mind, social media therefore is an important tool for female politicians as it offers them access to millions of users, an opportunity to connect and interact directly with the electorate and as a tool for self-presentation (Crawford 2009; Hoffmann et al, 2015; Williams and Gulati 2012). Social media allows politicians to bypass gatekeepers and communicate news that would otherwise not have been aired in traditional news outlets (Bor 2013; Baum and Groelin 2008; Chen 2011; Seidman 2013). While there is research on the gender differences in politicians' online biographies and tone and content of tweets in the United States (Lee 2013; Evans and Clark 2015), political candidates visual presentation on Facebook and Instagram across the United Kingdom, United States of America, Canada, Austria, France, Germany and Norway (Steffan 2020) and gender based stereotypes on twitter and biographies on websites among Canadian and American politicians respectively (Mattan and Small 2021; Lee 2013) there is limited research on female politicians and most especially during their legislative terms (Lee 2013). This research aims to answer the following research questions:

RQ1. How do female politicians use social media?

RQ2. What self-presentation styles do female politicians use on their social media pages?

RQ3. Do female politicians address and promote women related policy issues on their social media pages during their legislative terms?

The study aims at answering the above research questions using case studies of six female politicians in Hungary and Kenya, three from each country who have the largest following on Facebook and Twitter respectively. The number of women in parliament in Hungary and Kenya are at 13% and 23% respectively which is below the regional averages of 31% for Europe and 32% for East Africa (IPU Parline 2023). According to Nemzeti Média és Hírközlési Hatóság (NMHH 2018) 89% of Hungarian internet users are Facebook users, this makes Facebook the most popular social media platform in Hungary (Medve 2023), and it is also used for public debates (Donath 2021). Although the number of Facebook users in Kenya is currently at 10.8 million, political debates mostly take place on Twitter which has 1.35 million users (Kemp 2022; Napoleon Cat 2023). This is further evidenced by a survey that ranked Kenya as the second most active country on Twitter in Africa with over 2 million tweets (Rubadiri 2012).

The paper is structured as follows; the literature review focuses on female politician's social media use, politicians' self-presentation and lastly female politicians in Kenya and Hungary. This is then followed by the method, results and discussion, conclusion and limitations of the study.

2. Literature Review

2.1 Female Politicians' Social Media use

In a survey undertaken by Women in Parliament (2016) to assess social media use by female politicians from 107 countries, results revealed that 61% of all respondents engaged on social media on average less than once a day in each of the following activities: publicizing events and activities, communicating policy positions, sharing new stories, responding to comments, revealing personal information and reviewing comments (WIP 2016). The results also revealed that only one in every four respondents stated they were very knowledgeable on how to effectively use social media (WIP 2016). Knowledge of social media is helpful in recognizing opportunities that could be beneficial such as linking their personal websites to their social media (Zavattaro 2016). This gives the electorate a chance to assess their accomplishments, upcoming activities, their position on certain policies and offer their time and resources to support them (Zavattaro 2016). Results also showed that female politicians were more active during the campaign period, and they reduced or even stopped posting on social media once they obtained a seat in parliament (WIP 2016). Additionally, interactivity has the potential to create stronger bonds with the electorate, growing loyalty and transforming passive supporters into active supporters (McGregor et al, 2016). However, studies have also revealed that politicians tend to use social media as a one-way broadcasting channel (Nulty et al, 2016; Haleva-Amir 2011). Additionally, one of the greatest challenges to consistent posting and interactivity has been the lack of financial resources to update content and engage with the audiences (Molnár 2021).

2.2 Politicians' Self-Presentation

Self-presentation refers to how an individual endeavours to construct a desired persona in their social interactions (Steffan 2020). Goffman (1959) stated that social interaction resembled a theatre stage which had both the front stage and the backstage. The front stage signifies what an individual portrays to the audience while the back stage is what is hidden from the audience (Goffman 1959). The theory of self-presentation has been applied in face-to-face communication (Fenno 1978), websites (Gulati 2004; Lilleker and Koc-Michalska, 2013; Stanyer 2008) and impression management on social media (Jackson and Lilleker 2011). Fenno (1978) investigated how congressmen from the United States presented themselves, they used the *home style* when interacting with the electorate and used the *Washington Style* while on Capitol Hill. In his study on websites, Gulati (2004) found that there were two kinds of presentation styles by politicians: the *Washington Insiders* and *Washington Outsiders*. W*ashington insiders* were portrayed in official settings, dressed in formal attire and had a national theme which included the use of congress seals and symbols of Washington D.C in their images (Gulati 2004). However, *Washington outsiders* were portrayed in local settings, with community sports teams, dressed in casual clothing and often shown meeting with civilians (Gulati 2004). Lastly, Stanyer (2008) found that members of the House of Representatives in the United States shared their private lives more than the members of parliament from Britain.

2.3 Female Politicians in Kenya

During pre-colonial times in Kenya, power was primarily held by men as the African culture was largely patriarchal (Kamau 2010). Although women in Kenya played a role in the fight for independence such as leading peaceful protests, armed resistance (Carrier et al, 2016; Kabira 2012) and leading negotiations that led to independence (Kamau 2010) they were excluded from holding political positions in the first parliament between 1963 and 1969 (Bosire 2017). The introduction of multipartyism and the National women's convention held in

1992 was instrumental in the rise of the number of women in parliament (Bouka et al, 2019). Kenya's 2010 constitution also introduced two provisions in a bid to increase women participation in politics. It created a women's representative seat in each of the 47 counties in Kenya and the two-thirds principle which has only been executed in the County Assemblies but not in the National Assembly. Although these efforts have helped improve the number of women in politics, female politicians continue to face various challenges such as gender-based violence, patriarchal parties, lack of funding for political campaigns, corruption in the nomination process of political parties and socio-cultural presentation of women as subordinate to men (Kabira and Kameri-Mbote 2013; Kamau 2010; Bouka et al, 2019). The elections held in August 2022 showed an improvement in the number of women elected to the National Assembly. There are seven female governors, three female senators and 26 female members of parliament (Tu 2022). However, Kenya is ranked in the 99th position in the world with only 23% of women in parliament which is lower than the regional average of 32% (IPU Parline 2023).

2.4 Female Politicians in Hungary

Women in Hungary received the comprehensive right to vote in 1945 and their numbers continued to grow until 1980 when almost one third of MPs (members of parliament) were female politicians. Hungary could then have been regarded as vanguard among Scandinavian countries that were and still are considered the forefront of gender equality (Koncz 2014). However, in 1985, mainly because of the modernization of the electoral system, the number of female MPs started to decrease due to the introduction of the dual candidate electoral system where the electorate had a greater influence on parliament composition.

In the IPU Parline (2023) ranking, Hungary is the 150th with 13.1% female MPs, while the regional average for Europe is 31%. According to Dahlerup (1988) in order for female politicians to succeed in parliament, their number needs to reach the *critical mass of* 30%, otherwise they are believed to be underrepresented. The current state of the Hungarian parliament can be described by the frequently used term *men's club* or *old boys' network* and an institution where *masculinization* (Craske 2003) takes place. Women and men's strengths lie in different competences, abilities and life experiences; therefore, the ratio of their presence can shape decision-making (Kelemen 2010). This phenomenon has been coined as *"politics of presence"* by Philips (1998: 65) and it declares that without the presence of women, the proper representation of women's interests and related issues cannot be imagined. Another struggle for female MPs is that they must meet a double standard: fulfil the role as a woman and meet the expectations of women as the holder of the given role (Kelemen 2010).

3. Method

This research involves a content analysis of six female politicians' social media platforms, three from Hungary and three from Kenya. Content analysis is considered a scientific tool that can increase our understanding of social phenomena through providing new insight (Krippendorff 2018). In assessing social media use by female politicians, we have restricted this study to address the following through deductive content analysis; consistency in posting and content type (image, text, video, article). To answer our research question on self-presentation we adopted Gulati's (2004) insider versus outsider perspective. Lastly, to assess whether female politicians address and promote women related policy issues during their legislative terms we adopted the CAP codebook (Baumgartner 2019). According to Evans and Clark (2016) environment, education, health and social welfare are considered as women related policy issues.

3.1 Sampling of Female Politicians

We identified three Kenyan and three Hungarian female politicians who had the largest number of followers on Twitter and Facebook respectively during the period starting from September and ending in November of 2022. These female politicians were vying for parliamentary seats in the last election held in April 2022 for Hungary and August 2022 for Kenya. Below is the list of female politicians selected for this study:

- Millicent Omanga (MO)Kenyan politician, 878,800 Twitter followers. She recently lost the elections for the Nairobi County women representative seat to Esther Passaris.
- Esther Passaris (EP) Kenyan politician,741,300 Twitter followers. She is currently the Nairobi County women representative and a member of the *Orange Democratic Movement*.
- Susan Kihika (SK) Kenyan politician, 722,500 Twitter followers. She is the first female governor of Nakuru County and a member of the *United Democratic Alliance* party.
- Dóra Dúró (DD)Hungarian politician, 298,000 Facebook followers. She is an MP affiliated with *Our Homeland Movement*.

- Judit Varga (JV) Hungarian politician,172,000 Facebook followers. She is an MP affiliated with the political party *Fidesz*.
- Tímea Szabó (TSz) Hungarian politician, 167,000 Facebook followers. She is an MP affiliated with *Dialogue for Hungary*.

3.2 Sampling of Posts

Sampling of posts was done manually from September 2022 till November 2022 which resulted in 721 tweets gathered from the Kenyan female politicians and 656 Facebook posts collected from the Hungarian female politicians.

3.3 Coding

The collected posts were coded along eight variables: name of the female politician, date of tweet/post, content type (image, text, video, article), presence or absence of female politician on the image/video, present alone/with crowd/other politicians or family members on the image/video, camera perspective, type of clothing and policy issue. The Kenyan author coded Kenyan female politicians' tweets while the Hungarian author coded Hungarian female politicians' Facebook posts. This was followed by a random selection of 50% of the tweets and posts which were then coded by two external coders so as to test the inter-rater reliability. The percentage agreement for Kenyan tweets was 85% while in the case of the Hungarian sample the percentage agreement was 93%.

3.4 Results and Discussion

RQ1 investigates how female politicians use social media. To answer this question, we analysed the following variables: the number of tweets or posts each politician shared between September and November of 2022 and the type of content they posted. The results for each variable are summarized in Table 1 and explained in detail in the following paragraphs.

Table 1: Variable results

		Kenyan female politicians			Hungarian female politicians		
		MO	EP	SK	DD	JV	TSz
Number of	tweets	52	612	57	-	-	-
	fb posts	-	-	-	240	300	115
Content type	image	46%	63%	88%	47%	73%	50%
	text	50%	21%	10%	29%	14%	20%
	video	4%	16%	2%	11%	13%	25%
	article	-	-	-	12%	-	5%
Present on the content	yes	11%	9%	63%	27%	76%	50%
	alone	66%	11%	6%	58%	39,5%	41%
	with family	-	-	-	10%	0,5%	2%
	with politician(s)	17%	70%	22%	15%	36%	30%
	with general public	17%	19%	72%	17%	24%	27%
Camera perspective	face close up	-	2%	9%	6%	4%	7%
	half bodyshot	34%	53%	55%	56%	80%	62%
	full bodyshot	66%	41%	25%	15%	15%	7%
	long bodyshot)	-	2%	11%	-	-	-

		Kenyan female politicians			Hungarian female politicians		
		MO	EP	SK	DD	JV	TSz
	selfie	-	2%	3%	23%	1%	24%
	formal suits	-	9%	22%	26%	8%	26%
	formal clothing	17%	52%	67%	48%	83%	2%
	casual clothing	50%	13%	5,5%	26%	9%	72%
Clothing	informal clothing	33%	23%	5,5%	-	-	-

Kenyan female politicians tweeted as follows; MO tweeted 0.57 tweets in a day, SK tweeted 0.62 tweets in a day and EP tweeted 6.7 tweets in a day. On the other hand, Hungarian female politicians posted on Facebook as follows: TSz shared 1.2 posts in a day, DD had 2.6 posts in a day, and lastly JV had 3.2 posts in a day. These results indicate that these female politicians have a consistent social media presence as they post between one to six times per day except for two Kenyan female politicians MO and SK whose average daily tweets were below one daily. Previous studies had indicated that female politicians had a tendency to reduce or even stop posting on social media once they got into parliament (WIP 2016) however this is not the case in the findings of this study as the analysed politicians' presence on social media have been consistent even while in parliament. Secondly, the most common content type on Facebook and Twitter were images, followed by text and video, except in the case of MO, whose tweets were predominantly text based. This shows that female politicians are aware of the affordances of these social media platforms and willing to use them to communicate with their constituents. Interestingly, on Facebook female politicians in the opposition also shared articles, while on Twitter EP used retweets to increase visibility with borrowed content. The frequency of posts also relies heavily on the resources available, the more funding one has the higher the chances of hiring a professional team to develop content. This is in line with the empirical results of the study conducted by Molnár (2021), which found that parties with smaller financial resources struggled with updating content on their social media pages and connecting with their audiences through feedback.

RQ2 aimed at assessing how female politicians present themselves on their social media pages. To answer this question, we analysed the following variables: their presence or absence on the content, the camera perspective and their clothing. Four out of the six female politicians were mostly alone in the content that they shared, except for EP and SK, two Kenyan female politicians. A significant difference between the two countries was that Kenyan female politicians did not share images of their family members while Hungarian female politicians did. This is consistent with previous studies that found that congresswomen only shared images of their professional lives and gave low priority to stories about their children or spouses (Benoit et al, 2003; Lee 2013). Additionally, the most common camera perspective for a majority of these female politicians was the half body shot with the exception of MO who was captured in full body shots in a majority of her images. Selfies were more common for the Hungarian female politicians in the opposition than Kenyan female politicians. This may be an indicator of the lack of resources available to hire personnel to curate videos and take photographs which was previously observed with the resharing of articles and retweets. Lastly, clothing was categorized into four main types: formal suits, formal clothing, casual clothing and informal clothing. A majority of these female politicians wore formal suits and formal clothing with the exception of MO and TSz who mostly wore casual clothing. These results indicate that self-presentation based on clothing is related to their insider vis a vis outsider status, except for MO, a Kenyan female politician who is a member of the ruling party, an insider who chose to dress casually. A significant difference in clothing between the two countries is the absence of informal clothing among Hungarian female politicians which is present among Kenyan female politicians although in low percentages.

RQ3 investigated whether female politicians address and promote women related policy issues on their social media platforms. The five most common policy topics addressed by Kenyan female politicians were as follows: Law, crime and family issues, macroeconomics, government operations, health and environment. On the other hand, the five most common policy topics addressed by Hungarian female politicians were as follows: international affairs and foreign aid, education, government operations, health and social welfare. A summary of these results can be found in Figure 1.

Policy	Kenya	Hungary
Macroeconomics	39	17
Civil Rights, Minority Issues, and Civil Liberties	23	17
Health	30	40
Agriculture	17	0
Labor and Employment	5	16
Education	9	76
Environment	29	4
Energy	4	5
Immigration	1	4
Transportation	9	1
Law, Crime, and Family Issues	46	1
Social Welfare	15	31
community Development and Housing Issues	11	4
Banking, Finance, and Domestic Commerce	7	5
Defense	6	20
Space, Science, Technology, and Communications	0	0
Foreign Trade	16	1
International Affairs and Foreign Aid	13	123
Government Operations	34	47
Public Lands and Water Management	13	0
Non-policy related issues- events	141	102
Non-policy related issues-elections	248	115
Non-policy related issues- personal	5	27
Total	**721**	**656**

Figure 1: Policy issues

The results indicate that Hungarian female politicians addressed more women related policy issues (*education, health and social welfare*) as compared to Kenyan female politicians (*health and environment*). However, we suspect that these results are due to the prevailing issues in the countries during the period of this study and not necessarily based on their gender. Since the data collection was in the aftermath of covid-19, some of the health related policy issues were in connection with vaccination laws however, sexual reproductive health issues were also addressed. Secondly, regarding education, Hungary is going through an ongoing education crisis, there is very little financial and human resource in public schools. Thirdly, the social welfare law was modified which has potential dire consequences on the masses. On the other hand, Kenya is going through an environmental crisis due to deforestation hence the emphasis on environmental related policy issues. These results are in line with Hemphill (2020) who found that female politicians are no longer simply addressing women related issues but also address prevailing issues affecting the public.

4. Conclusion

Underrepresentation of female politicians in the media has encouraged female political candidates to turn to social media as a potential platform for sharing their political agenda, connect with the electorate and as a channel for self-promotion. The present research investigated female politicians' social media use, self-presentation and policy issues addressed by Kenyan and Hungarian female politicians. Results show that the analysed female politicians are active on their platforms, they use varied content types and mostly present themselves in line with their insider vis a vis outsider status. Results suggest that female politicians address some policy issues that are considered women related, however, we suspect that this is due to the prevailing issues in their countries and not necessarily gender based. Limitation of this research is that the results cannot be generalized to a majority of female politicians. Future research should expand the study by carrying out longitudinal studies to track changes in female politicians' self-presentation and policy issues addressed during their campaign and legislative terms. The results can also be compared with those of their male counterparts to give a broader perspective on self-presentation and policy issues.

Acknowledgement

The authors would like to express their gratitude to Attila László Nemesi, Lajos Kovács, and Daniel E. Bergan for their valuable insights that greatly contributed to the refinement of this paper. Special thanks to the anonymous reviewer for their constructive feedback, which significantly enhanced the quality of the manuscript.

References

Baum, M. A. and Groeling, T. (2008) "New media and the polarization of American political discourse", *Political Communication*, Vol 25, No. 4, pp 345–365.

Benoit, W. L., McHale, J. P., Hansen, G. J., Pier, P. M. and McGuire, J. P. (2003) *Campaign 2000: A functional analysis of presidential campaign discourse*. Rowman & Littlefield.

Bosire, M. R. (2017) *Political Parties Strategy on Gender Equality in candidates' nomination in Kenya.* Published by CMD Kenya, International IDEA & NIMD.

Bor, S. E. (2013) "Using social network sites to improve communication between political campaigns and citizens in the 2012 election", *American Behavioral Scientist*, Vol 58, No. 9, pp 1195–1213.

Bouka, Y., Berry, M. E. and Kamuru, M. M. (2019) "Women's political inclusion in Kenya's devolved political system", *Journal of Eastern African Studies*, Vol 13, No. 2, pp 313–333.

Carrier, N. and Nyamweru, C. (2016) "Reinventing Africa's national heroes: The case of Mekatilili, a Kenyan popular heroine", *African Affairs*, Vol 115, No. 461, pp 599–620.

Carroll, S. J. (1994) *Women as candidates in American politics*. Indiana University Press.

Chen, G. M. (2011) "Tweet this: A uses and gratifications perspective on how active Twitter use gratifies a need to connect with others", *Computers in Human Behavior*, Vol 27, No. 2, pp 755–762.

Craske, N. (2003) „Visszaférfiasodás" és a neoliberális állam Latin-Amerikában. In: Randall, V. – Waylen, G. (eds.): *Társadalmi nem, politika és állam. Feminista társadalomtudományi tanulmányok*. Jószöveg Műhely Kiadó. Budapest. 142–169.

Crawford, K. (2009) "Following you: Disciplines of listening in social media", *Continuum*, Vol 23, No. 4, pp 525– 535.

Dahlerup, D. (1988) "From a small to a large minority: Women in Scandinavian politics", *Scandinavian Political Studies*, Vol 11, No. 4, pp 275–298.

Donath, A. (2021, September, 10) Facebook's plan to cut back on political content sets up Orbán for re-election .https://www.euractiv.com/section/media/opinion/facebooks-plan-to-cut-back-on-political-content-sets-up-orban-for-re-election/

Evans, H. K. and Clark, J. H. (2016) "You tweet like a girl!" How female candidates campaign on Twitter, *American Politics Research*, Vol 44, No. 2, pp 326–352.

Falk, E. (2010) *Women for president: Media bias in nine campaigns*. University of Illinois Press.

Fenno, R. F. (1978) *Home style: House members in their districts*. Boston, MA: Little, Brown.

Goffman, E. (1959) *The presentation of self in everyday life*. New York, NY: Doubleday.

Haleva-Amir, S. (2011) "Online Israeli politics: The current state of the art", *Israel Affairs*, Vol 17, No. 3, pp 467–485.

Hemphill, L., Russell, A. and Schöpke-Gonzalez, A. M. (2021) "What drives US congressional members' policy attention on Twitter?", *Policy & Internet*, Vol 13, No. 2, pp 233-256.

Hoffmann, C. P., Lutz, C. and Meckel, M. (2015) "Content Creation on the Internet: A Social Cognitive Perspective on the Participation Divide", *Information, Communication & Society*, Vol 18, No. 6, pp 696–716.

Institute of Education and Oxfam (2006) *Working with Media on Gender and Education: A Guide for Training and Planning*. London, OXFAM.

Jackson, N. and Lilleker, D. (2011) "Microblogging, constituency service and impression management: UK MPs and the use of Twitter", *The Journal of Legislative Studies*, Vol 17, No. 1, pp 86–105.

Kabira, W. M (2012) *Time for Harvest: Women and Constitution Making in Kenya*. Nairobi: University of Nairobi Press, 2012.

Kabira, M, W. and Kameri-Mbote P. (2013) Gender issues in electoral politics in Kenya: The unrealized constitutional promise. Published in Ondote C. & Musumba, L. (Eds.) *Balancing the scales of electoral justice-Resolving dispute from 2013 Elections in Kenya and the Emerging Jurisprudence. International Law Development Organisation*, 177–214.

Kamau, N. (2010) *Women and Political Leadership in Kenya: Ten Case Studies*. Nairobi: Heinrich Böll Foundation.

Kelemen, I. B. (2010) "Női képviselők–női képviselet?", *Politikatudományi Szemle*, No. 3, pp 83–103.

Koncz, K. (2014) "Nők a parlamentben, 1990-2014", *Statisztikai Szemle*, Vol 92, No. 6, pp 513–540.

Krippendorff, K. (2018) *Content analysis: An introduction to its methodology*. Sage publications.

Lee, J. (2013) 'You know how tough I am?'Discourse analysis of a US Midwestern congresswoman's self-presentation. *Discourse & Communication*, Vol 7, *No.*3, pp 299–317.

Lilleker, D. G. and Koc-Michalska, K. (2013) "Online political communication strategies: MEPs, e-representation, and self-representation", *Journal of Information Technology & Politics*, Vol 10, No. 2, pp 190–207.

Mattan, A. J. and Small, T. A. (2021) "Worth a Thousand Words: The Study of Visual Gendered Self-Presentation on Twitter", *Canadian Journal of Political Science/Revue Canadienne de Science Politique*, Vol 54, No. 2, pp 477–490.

McGregor, S. C., Lawrence, R. G. and Cardona, A. (2016) "Personalization, gender, and social media: Gubernatorial candidates' social media strategies", *Information, Communication & Society*, Vol *20*, No. 2, pp 264–283.

Medve, F. (2023, February 6) Facebook users in Hungary by age 2023. *Statista*. https://www.statista.com/statistics/1029770/facebook-users-hungary/

Molnar, F. (2021) "A magyar politikai szereplők közösségi média stratégiájának és gyakorlatának összehasonlítása" *Pólusok*, Vol 2, No. 1, pp 31–54

Monthly Ranking of Women in national parliaments. Parline: the IPU's Open Data Platform. (n.d.). Retrieved February 3, 2023, from https://data.ipu.org/women-ranking?month=12&year=2022

Napoleoncat (n.d.). Social media users in Kenya. https://napoleoncat.com/stats/social-media-users-in-kenya/2023/01/

NMHH. (2018) Lakossági internethasználat online piackutatás 2018. https://nmhh.hu/dokumentum/202180/lakossagi_internethasznalat_2018.pdf

Nulty, P., Theocharis, Y., Popa, S. A., Parnet, O. and Benoit, K. (2016) "Social Media and Political Communication in the 2014 Elections to the European Parliament", *Electoral Studies*, No. 44, pp 429–444.

Omtatah, O. O. (2008) T*he Affirmative Action Debate: Developing Winning Strategies, in N. Kamau, Perspectives on Gender Discourse: Enhancing Women's Political Participation*, Nairobi: Heinrich Böll Foundation.

Philips, A. (1998) *The politics of presence*. OUP Oxford.

Rubadiri, V. (2012, January 26) Kenya is Africa's second most active on Twitter. Capital fm. https://www.capitalfm.co.ke/lifestyle/2012/01/26/kenya-is-africas-2nd-most-active-on-twitter/

Gulati, G. J. (2004) "Members of Congress and presentation of self on the World Wide Web", *Harvard International Journal of Press/Politics*, Vol 9, *No.* 1, pp 22–40.

Seidman, G. (2013) "Self-presentation and belonging on Facebook: How personality influences social media use and motivations", *Personality and Individual Differences*, Vol 54, No. 3, pp 402–407.

Siegel, J. M. (2009) "Thank You, Sarah Palin, for Reminding Us: It's Not About the Clothes", *Va. J. Soc. Pol'y & L.*, Vol 17, No. 144.

Stanyer, J. (2008) "Elected representatives, online self-presentation and the personal vote: Party, personality and webstyles in the United States and United Kingdom", *Information, Community & Society*, Vol 11, No. 3, pp 414–432.

Steffan, D. (2020) "Visual self-presentation strategies of political candidates on social media platforms: A comparative study", *International Journal of Communication*, Vol 14, No. 23.

Watson, R. P. (2006) "Madam president: Progress, problems, and prospects for 2008", *Journal of International Women's Studies*, Vol 8, No. 1, pp 1–20.

Williams, C. B. and Gulati, G. J. J. (2012) "Social Networks in Political Campaigns: Facebook and the Congressional Elections of 2006 and 2008", *New Media & Society*, Vol 15, No. 1, pp 52–71.

Zavattaro, S. M. (2016) Some ideas for branding via social media. *Social Media for Government*. Routledge.

Navigating Parenthood Online: Understanding the Complex Dynamics of Sharenting Practices

Beata Jungselius, Maja Fröjelin and Sebastian Johansson

University West, School of Business, Economics, and IT, Trollhättan, Sweden

beata.jungselius@hv.se
maja.frojelin@student.hv.se
sebastian.johansson@student.hv.se

Abstract: In this paper, we focus on the increasingly central visual aspects of documenting and sharing family life as we examine how parents reflect upon "sharenting", i.e. sharing representations of family life in social media. The aim of this paper is to contribute with an empirically supported understanding of activities involved in the social practice of sharenting. We ask: "What activities constitute the practice of sharenting and how do parents perceive, experience, and manage sharenting?" and focus on how parents engage in sharenting and how they experience and manage questions and concerns that occur as they share, and do not share, pictures of their children in social media. We draw upon a thematic analysis of twelve semi-structured in-depth interviews with parents of at least one child in the age of 1-10. Based on our data and in relation to previous research we unpack ambiguous and multifaceted reasonings on sharenting as a complex social media practice. Through rich descriptions and empirical detail, we provide knowledge on key activities involved in sharenting, and present findings following three themes: unforeseeable consequences of sharenting, social media dilemmas of sharenting and strategies for managing sharenting. Lastly, we show how these activities represent expressions of agreed upon idioms of the practice of sharenting and discuss the interplay between contemporary social photography, ICT, and family life. Increased access to, and use of ICT such as smartphones with built-in advanced cameras, leads us to believe that the practice of visually representing family life in a contemporary context comes with a new set of challenges for parents. As the social media landscape is constantly evolving, social media practices, such as sharenting, must be continuously studied to ensure the understanding needed to inform future design, policy, and regulation. This paper present illustrative examples of how this community adopt, make, and negotiate use of social media and the possibilities these ICTs afford.

Keywords: Sharenting, Social media use, Social media practices, Idioms of practice, Social media dilemmas

1. Introduction

The connection between photography and family has always been strong (Cino, 2022), with families curating photos and choosing visual representations of their lives to place in physical photo albums. In the earlier days of amateur photography, photos were usually shared within a small social circle, often through home video showings or slideshows (Chalfen, 1987). While people still engage in similar practices of creating narratives through visual content today, the physical photo albums have mostly been replaced by digital albums. Also, due to the digitalization of photography, photos of family life are usually shared with a greater audience than before. Visual aspects of producing, sharing, and interacting around photographs have become a central part of contemporary social media interaction. Over the recent decade, the number of photos shared daily in social media have tripled and today, a hefty 3.8 billion images are shared on Snapchat, 2.1 billion on Facebook, and 1.3 billion on Instagram daily. Approximately 92,5 % of these are estimated to have been taken and shared using smartphones (Broz, 2023). While the fundamental aspects of the practice of social photography, i.e. how people take, organize, and share photographs (Chalfen, 1987) have been of interest for decades, the digital development of sharing visual content of everyday life has raised new questions and concerns for those seeking to understand contemporary social photography. For this paper, we focus on the parental aspects of social photography, a phenomenon which has previously been described as "sharenting". The term 'sharenting', coined using the words 'share' and 'parenting' (Brosch, 2018), has been defined as the act of "sharing representations of one's parenting or children online" (Blum-Ross & Livingstone, 2017, p. 110). While previous work on sharenting has begun to establish understanding of motives and concerns, less is known about the multitude and variety of activities involved in this social practice and how parents manage and negotiate challenges. In this paper, we focus on how parents engaging in sharenting experience and manage concerns that occur as they share, and do not share pictures of their children in social media. We ask: "What activities constitute the practice of sharenting and how do parents perceive, experience, and manage sharenting?". By unpacking parents' own descriptions of sharenting practices, we describe experienced dos and don'ts of sharenting, unforeseeable consequences of sharenting, dilemmas of sharenting, and strategies for managing sharenting. Finally, we discuss our findings as examples of idioms of this social practice in relation to contemporary social photography.

2.   Related Work

While sharenting is becoming a greater interest for researchers within a variety of fields, more work systematically identifying and describing the activities that constitute the social practice of sharenting is still needed. Previous work has examined and described sharenting from different angles. Most of the existing work have focused on problematic aspects of sharenting, such as implications for privacy (Fox & Hoy, 2019) and children's rights (Brosch, 2018), possible dangers and risks following sharenting (Ferrara et al., 2023, Gatto et al., 2024). In contrast, other scholars have highlighted more desirable outcomes of sharenting, such as information-archiving (Verswijvel et al., 2019) and the possibility to receive social support as a new parent (Archer & Kao, 2018; Barkhuus et al., 2017; Lazard et al., 2019). Most of the previous work has been focusing on sharenting within a Western context, yet some recent work has begun to examine sharenting practices within additional demographics, such as among Middle Eastern (Esfandiari & Yao, 2023) and Turkish (Aydoğdu et al., 2023) parents. Previous work has shown that sharenting is usually motivated by positive interests (Ferrara et al., 2023) and have proven to bring positive outcomes for parents engaging in sharenting. For instance, Lazard et al. (2019) acknowledge that social media has "provided a space for parents to share experiences and receive support around parenting" (Lazard et al., 2019, p. 1). However, the consequences of sharenting have been shown to be complex and difficult do grasp (Ogbanufe et al., 2023), possibly explaining why parents sometimes put their children at risk even when not intending to (Ferrara et al., 2023). A few papers have begun to unpack emotional tensions that parents describe experiencing as they engage in sharenting, such as juggling own self-presentation with protecting of one's children (Holiday et al., 2022) and negotiating and managing privacy (Walrave, 2023). Steinberg (2017) contributes with a solid problematization of the tension that occur for parents as they cherish both the protecting of their children's rights to privacy while also wanting to practice their own right to free speech. Identifying and mapping examples of similar tensions, Cino (2022) show that parents struggle with digital dilemmas and conceptualize these as "Social Media Dilemmas" (SMDs) and include a few dilemmas that parent's associate with governing their families' and children's digital presence (Cino, 2022). Emphasizing this struggle, Cino (2022) writes: "Sharenting is a common habit for parents in the digital age. Despite common discourse describing parents as naïve about it, empirical data supports many of them grapple with digital dilemmas concerning these digital narrations" (Cino, 2022, p. 128).

2.1   The Social Practice of Sharenting

For this paper, we conceptualize sharenting as a social media practice (Jungselius, 2019) when identifying and describing the activities that constitute sharenting. Social media practices refer to the numerous and varied activities that social media users engage in when using social media. These include how people balance, plan and monitor social media interaction before, after and in-between their postings (Jungselius, 2019). In order to be able to engage in social media practices in fulfilling ways, users' need to acquire social media skills (Jungselius, 2019). However, these skills are not static, instead they change as the practices evolve (ibid). Apart from technical skills such as being able to press the right buttons and fill out information for a profile, there are also several social skills that users of social media need to develop to be able to fully engage with social media (ibid). Studying a specific social skill that users of social media develop, knowing how to handle a break-up on Facebook, anthropologist Ilana Gershon introduced the concept of "idioms of practice" (Gershon, 2010). This concept relies on an assumption that communities have shared and often unspoken expectations and refers to "the agreed upon appropriate social uses of technology that people create, learn and negotiate through asking for advice and sharing stories with each other" (ibid, pg. 6) within that community. Also, the idea points to "how people have implicit and explicit intuitions about using different technologies that they have developed with their friends, family members and co-workers" (ibid). Other than learning how to navigate among technical features, there are also a set of social, often implicit, rules that regulate the use of these technologies and which users need to learn to be able to use them in fulfilling ways (Gershon, 2010). As new social media practices emerge, idioms of practice develop through collective discussions, negotiation and social participation among the users who engage in these shared practices (ibid). Extending the existing literature and building upon the theoretical framework conceptualizing social media practices and idioms of practice, we aim to identity and describe idioms of one specific social media practice: sharenting. Taking a qualitative and user-oriented approach, this paper aims to contribute with empirical, detailed knowledge on how parents engage in, and reason on, sharing of pictures of children in social media.

3. Method

In this paper, we ask: "What activities constitute the practice of sharenting and how do parents perceive, experience, and manage sharenting?" and draw upon an interview study where twelve parents were recruited and asked to take part in in-depth, semi-structured interviews on sharenting. The aim was to identify and describe what activities that constitute the social practice of sharenting by contributing with empirically supported and detailed understanding of these activities. Interest in people's own descriptions and a desire for a deeper understanding of people's experiences is often the main motive behind choosing to conduct in-depth interviews (Seidman, 2006). Also, in-depth interviews are often particularly suitable for researchers who want to understand people's underlying motives and strategies in interaction and practice (Dempsey, 2010).

For this study, the participants were recruited through Facebook and Instagram through identical posts posted on three different occasions in March 2023, where parents' meeting the criteria's of having at least one child in the age of 0-10 years old and being a regular user of social media were asked to participate in the study. Prior to the interviews, an interview guide was constructed including questions allowing both general as well as more specific reasonings on sharenting. Beginning the interviews, all informants were given the same, brief, information about the study and informed consent forms was signed. The interviews were audio-recorded and conducted during March-April 2023. Each interview lasted approximately 45-60 minutes. Participants' ages ranged from 26 to 46 years (average age was 36, median age 36,5), nine of them were women and three of them were men.

Informant	Gender	Age	Number of children	Age of children
Informant 1	M	44	1	9
Informant 2	F	37	3	1, 7 and 9
Informant 3	M	26	1	3
Informant 4	F	26	1	3
Informant 5	F	37	2	9 and 11
Informant 6	F	36	2	3 and 5
Informant 7	F	32	2	2 and 4
Informant 8	F	44	2	9 and 12
Informant 9	F	33	2	2 and 4
Informant 10	F	37	2	1,5 and 10
Informant 11	M	34	1	2
Informant 12	F	46	3	7, 12 and 15

Figure 1: The informants

Following the interviews, the audio files were anonymized and transcribed using the built-in voice-to-text feature in Microsoft Office Word to facilitate further analysis. The second and third author completed an iterative thematic analysis (Braun & Clarke, 2006), consulting the first author throughout the process and allowing feedback. It should be mentioned that the data for this paper was initially collected for a bachelor's thesis written by Author 2 and 3 and supervised by Author 1 why parts of the data reported on in this paper have therefore been reported on within that thesis. For this paper however, the data have been analyzed in further detail using the computer-assisted qualitative data analysis software (CAQDAS) NVivo by Author 1 trough a different theoretical lens exploring sharenting as a social practice, which has not been reported on before.

4. Findings: The Dos and Don'ts of Sharenting

From our data, it is clear that the evolvement of digital social photography and increased sharing of representations of family life beyond the immediate family has raised new questions and concerns for parents. We have found numerous examples of ambiguous reasonings as our informants reported both wanting to share photos of their children with their followers on social media, yet also wanting to protect their children's privacy and integrity. When analyzing our data, we noticed that it seemed easier for the informants to describe what they would *not* do, rather than what they actually *do* when they share pictures of their children in social media. Their reasonings on what not to post were explicit, while their reasonings regarding preferred content and ways of sharing photos of children were vaguer. When asked what kind of photos they would never share of their children, we received several rather specific answers. Even when asked the reversed question, i.e. "What kind of pictures would you post of your children?" they referred to what they wouldn't post. We found numerous examples of statements where the informants verbalized their opinions on content that they would never post themselves. These most clearly involved nudity, posting angry or upset children and using one's children for bragging and showing off.

Within the following sections, we will present examples of parents' reasonings on the dos and don'ts of the social practice of sharenting following three themes. Within the first theme, we present findings concerning unforeseeable consequences of sharenting. Secondly, we show examples of social media dilemmas (SMDs) of sharenting found within our data and lastly, we describe strategies used for managing these.

4.1 Unforeseeable Consequences of Sharenting

A central concern raised by multiple informants was the struggle of trying to foresee and manage possible consequences of sharing pictures of their children in social media, even when these are difficult or even impossible to foresee. As shown in previous work, the consequences of sharenting have been difficult do grasp due to its complexity, leading sharenting parents to putting their children at risk, even unintentionally (Ferrara et al., 2023). Although no questions addressing this topic were directly asked during the interviews, each informant mentioned and referred to potential consequences of sharenting. Several mentioned the difficulties of understanding and foreseeing consequences. For example, they said:

"I think there will be consequences, but that it is too early to know what these consequences will be."

(Informant 3)

"My personal opinion on putting out pictures on children under 18 is like, there can be consequences or whatever later on when the child is over 18 and then they might be like: 'why did she put this out, I didn't approve of that.'"

(Informant 11)

"And like that picture that you yourself find cute [...] especially nude pictures I think you need to be careful with, because you don't know where these might end up later."

(Informant 12)

Not being able to foresee the consequences, especially for the child, seem to have an inhibitory impact on their sharenting practices where the informants report on being precautious and safe rather than sorry. All informants acknowledged potential consequences following upon their sharing of photos in social media, and even if they were not certain of what these could turn out to be, they expressed that they need to be guarded against.

4.2 Social Media Dilemmas of Sharenting

While the informants were explicit regarding some content that they would never post themselves, during other reasonings it became clear that the distinction between what was believed to be okay to share and what was not, was not always as clear. As within the work of Cino (2022), our informants described struggling with striving towards conflicting aims. For instance, one informant described a two-folded motive for sharenting:

"You want recognition from others and like, not just the approval in terms of 'look at these cute children' but also approval in terms of being a parent, to share things you want to discuss [...] getting support and cheers and understanding from other parents so that's an additional reason for posting about your children and family life."

(Informant 9)

Another informant elaborated in a similar way when initially describing being very critical towards sharing pictures of children in social media in general, and therefore never doing that herself. However, as she continued talking about sharenting she elaborated in a different direction:

"But in a way you do feel that like, it's a two folded feeling. Because at the same time, I think it's fun to see my friends' children and it's not that I get provoked when I see them or that I am strongly against what they do, it's more like [...] I don't think that it is right to post pictures of one's children but at the same time, I think it is fun to see the children."

(Informant 5)

These informants are acknowledging wanting and getting approval and social support from peers and followers but is also expressing skepticism towards using children to accomplish that. Another interesting example of how a similar kind of SMD was described as one mother talked about her motives for following a certain kind of parent, 'the Pinterest mom'. She described following other mothers on social media and appreciating their postings containing ideas for sleeping routines, meals and recipes, DIY crafts, hobbies and the similar. Later during the interview however, she referred to these mothers again and continued her reasonings, painting a more ambiguous picture. She said:

"I kinda think that you, because you know, you do want to be one of them. You want to do things with your child. Or like, you do want to be one of those Pinterest moms. But then when you get out of this Instagram bubble and like meet reality and it's like [...] how do people have time?"

(Informant 4)

4.3 Managing Sharenting

As with other social media practices, sharenting involves managing social media, before, during, after and in-between postings (Jungselius, 2019). In the previous section, we showed examples of parents experiencing SMDs (Cino, 2022). For this section, we will show how our informants describe meeting, negotiating, and managing these SMDs. From our data, it is suggested that a central part of the sharenting practice takes place before content is shared in social media. We found examples of how parents described having a set of normative 'rules' they follow that they rely upon navigate through their sharenting. Apart from engaging in guiding inner dialogues, other informants described consulting the other parent or other family members guidance:

"...maybe have a dialogue with the family [...] what you think and maybe you discuss some pros and cons, what's best. Or less good so to speak."

(Informant 11)

Another strategy described for managing a will to share pictures of their children with also wanting to protect them was mentioned by multiple informants and included adjusting privacy settings:

"You never know who will watch the pictures, so on Instagram for instance, you can shut it down a bit to be sort of private [...] so that like if you are not friends then they can't see it either."

(Informant 4)

In addition to these examples representing the most commonly described managing activities, we also found examples where the informants described creating additional (private) accounts specifically for sharing pictures of their children, asking others to remove pictures of their own children, reporting other people's postings of sensitive content, anonymizing and hiding or removing identity revealing content (such as hiding faces by adding emojis, blurring faces, only posting pictures of children's hands or backs). These actions all include rather active measures, yet the data also included examples of a slightly different nature. One specifically interesting strategy described was to not press 'Like' on a picture of her children as a way to avoid revealing the identity of her children. She said:

"If I see one on for instance on Instagram or anywhere, then I don't 'Like' it because [...] then I tie them more obviously to me."

(Informant 5)

The informants also referred to involving the children themselves for guidance. However, although they might ask their children, the children do not always have the final say on what will actually be shared:

"If it's a picture of them I would want to talk to them before [...] of course if they say that you should remove that picture, you listen, usually, if it's not a very good picture."

(Informant 1)

This informant explains that if he would consider sharing a picture of his child on social media, he would consult the child first. However, what is interesting within this last example is the ambiguous reasoning here and how the parental ascendancy is highlighted. Even if the child would oppose, there might still be a desire to share the picture.

5. Discussion

For this paper, we conceptualize sharenting as an example of a social media practice that include activities taking place before, after and in-between posting. Following the agreed upon use of idioms of this specific practice, these activities rely on a set of norms which those who engage in the practice have developed through participation, discussion, and negotiation. Increased sharing of family life with a greater audience outside of one's closest family has led to a development of a new set of social media skills for parents. As suggested by Gershon, when people engage in a social digital practice, shared and often unspoken expectations develop (Gershon, 2010). For the practice of sharenting, users have developed expectations of how to act, interact and manage their sharing of photos of their children in social media.

The informants mentioned several ways of managing sharenting, such as consulting others before posting, adjusting the privacy of their profiles or create additional accounts specifically for sharing pictures of their children, asking others to remove pictures of their own children, reporting other people's postings of sensitive content, anonymizing, hiding or removing identity revealing content (such as hiding faces by adding emojis, blurring faces, only posting pictures of children's hands or backs). While these actions all include active measures, we have also presented examples of more 'silent' actions. For instance, one informant described not 'Liking' photos of her children on social media as a way to avoid revealing of the identity of her children. This silent action of acknowledging, yet consciously not 'Liking' a photo due to foreseeing the consequences of doing so (i.e., possibly providing a digital trace that could reveal the identity of the children visible in the pictures) require an understanding of the intertwined and complex relationship between privacy and technology discussed by Ogbanufe et al. (2023) and represents an example of a social media skill (Jungselius, 2019) that develops through engaging in sharenting. Engagement in social media practices have been shown to go beyond the most immediate actions such as pressing the right buttons and include activities that social media users engage in as they balance, plan, and monitor their social media interaction before, after and in-between their postings (ibid). Within our data, we found several examples of how parents engage in sharenting activities before, during and after their most immediate engagement with the social media application used for posting content of their children, leading us to conclude that sharenting is a social media practice that, similar to other social media practices, expands beyond simply taking and sharing pictures and rather involves extensive thought, ambiguous concerns, struggles and negotiating of the practice while creating digital, visual narratives.

Previous work has established that parents engaging in sharenting often struggle with wanting to practice their own right to express themselves while simultaneously aiming to protect their children (Cino, 2022; Steinberg, 2017). Other scholars have shown that sharenting offer comfort and support to parents, providing a sense of belonging to a community, and give children a sense of pride when receiving 'Likes' from family and friends, while also raising concerns in terms of management of privacy risks and consequences difficult to foresee (Ogbanufe et al., 2023). Our data support previous work showing that parents struggle when wanting to express themselves through sharing their everyday life, but also wanting to protect their children's integrity. Ambiguity is central for parents participating in sharenting, and we have found numerous examples of how parents engaging in sharenting negotiate this practice. They admit to appreciating the social support they gain yet also want to protect their children from being overly exposed, especially since the consequences of exposing them are difficult to understand and foresee. They want to show pictures of their children to everyone because they love them and are proud of them, yet they also want to protect them from being subject to dubious purposes. From our data, it is clear that the informants consider it obvious that parents have good intentions, want to protect their children, and respect their own desires and opinions. However, there are also examples of when their children's desires conflict with their own motives and willingness to share pictures of them. As one informant said: *"Of course, if they say that you should remove that picture, you listen...usually, if it's not a very good picture",* highlighting this very dilemma.

6. Conclusion

As people engage in social practices using Information and Communication Technologies (ICTs), they develop an agreed upon appropriate use of them, i.e., idioms of practice (Gershon, 2010). For this paper, we have presented examples of idioms of the practice of sharenting. Some of these expectations of how to behave are explicit (such as not posting pictures involving nudity or the child expressing strong emotions), while others are more implicit (such as not showing off, being cautious, and protecting your children's right to privacy). These activities should be understood as idioms of a practice for a community of users engaging in contemporary social photography. As noted by previous scholars, the link between family and photography has always been strong (Cino, 2022). However, the increased access to and use of ICT such as smartphones with built-in advanced cameras, leads us to believe that the practice of visually representing family life in a contemporary context comes with a new set of challenges and concerns for parents. The findings from this paper suggests that the idioms of the social media practice of sharenting are not static and involve negotiating of current agreed upon ways to use social media, why it is important to continue to follow the evolvement of these practices and study the impacts of living with ICTs have on family-life and parenthood to continue inform future design, policy, and regulation.

7.   Limitations and Future Work

While the notion of limitations in terms of validity, generalizability and transferability is a known concern when conducting qualitative research, the work behind this paper has been conducted with an aim of ensuring quality by emphasizing transparency, engaging in personal and epistemological reflexivity, iterating between empirical detail and "the bigger picture" (Blandford et al., 2016). While some challenges are manageable, others are more difficult to meet. For instance, we cannot ensure that the informants' descriptions capture their actual use, experiences, and opinions. Also, parenthood is sensitive to many and often characterized by strong believes and expectations of how to be a 'good' parent, why there is a risk that the informants adjust their answers accordingly, even if not intending to. Despite limitations, what our findings suggest are valuable in the light of aiming to continue to create in-depth understanding of user needs, practices, perceptions, and experiences to inform design of future ICTs.

References

Archer, C., & Kao, K.-T. (2018). Mother, baby, and Facebook makes three: does social media provide social support for new mothers? *Media International Australia, 168*(1), 122–139. https://doi.org/10.1177/1329878X18783016

Aydoğdu, F., Şanal Güngör, B., Ayhan Öz, T. (2023) Does sharing bring happiness? Understanding the sharenting phenomenon, *Children and Youth Services Review*, Volume 154, 2023, https://doi.org/10.1016/j.childyouth.2023.107122.

Barkhuus, L., Bales, E., & Cowan, L. (2017). Internet Ecologies of New Mothers: Trust, Variety and Strategies for Managing Diverse Information Sources. *Proceedings of the 50th Hawaii International Conference on System Sciences*, 2283–2292.

Blandford, A., Furniss, D., & Makri, S. (2016). *Qualitative HCI Research*. Springer International Publishing. https://doi.org/10.1007/978-3-031-02217-3

Braun, V., & Clarke, V. (2006). Using thematic analysis in psychology. *Qualitative Research in Psychology, 3*(2), 77–101. https://doi.org/10.1191/1478088706qp063oa

Brosch, A. (2018). Sharenting – Why Do Parents Violate Their Children's Privacy? *The New Educational Review, 54*(4), 75–85. https://doi.org/10.15804/tner.2018.54.4.06

Broz, M. (2023, March 10). *Number of Photos (2023): Statistics, Facts, & Predictions*. www.Photutorial.Com. https://photutorial.com/photos-statistics/

Chalfen, R. (1987). *Snapshot versions of life*. Bowling Green State University Popular Press.

Cino, D. (2022). Beyond the Surface: Sharenting as a Source of Family Quandaries: Mapping Parents' Social Media Dilemmas. *Western Journal of Communication, 86*(1), 128–153. https://doi.org/10.1080/10570314.2021.2020891

Dempsey, N. P. (2010). Stimulated recall interviews in ethnography. *Qualitative Sociology*. https://doi.org/10.1007/s11133-010-9157-x

Esfandiari, M. & Yao, J. (2023) Sharenting as a double-edged sword: evidence from Iran, Information, Communication & Society, 26:15, 2942-2960, DOI: 10.1080/1369118X.2022.2129268

Ferrara, P., Cammisa, I., Corsello, G., Giardino, I., Vural, M., Pop, T. L., Pettoello-Mantovani, C., Indrio, F., & Pettoello-Mantovani, M. (2023). Online "Sharenting": The Dangers of Posting Sensitive Information About Children on Social Media. *The Journal of Pediatrics*, 113322. https://doi.org/10.1016/j.jpeds.2023.01.002

Fox, A. K., & Hoy, M. G. (2019). Smart Devices, Smart Decisions? Implications of Parents' Sharenting for Children's Online Privacy: An Investigation of Mothers. *Journal of Public Policy & Marketing, 38*(4), 414–432. https://doi.org/10.1177/0743915619858290

Gatto, A., Corsello, A. & Ferrara, P. (2024) Sharenting: hidden pitfalls of a new increasing trend– suggestions on an appropriate use of social media. *Ital J Pediatr* 50:15. https://doi.org/10.1186/s13052-024-01584-2

Gershon, I. (2010). The breakup 2.0: disconnecting over new media. In *The Australian Journal of Anthropology*. Cornell University Press.

Holiday, S., Norman, M. S., & Densley, R. L. (2022). Sharenting and the extended self: self-representation in parents' Instagram presentations of their children. *Popular Communication, 20*(1), 1–15. https://doi.org/10.1080/15405702.2020.1744610

Jungselius, Beata. (2019). *Using Social Media* [Doctoral dissertation]. University of Gothenburg.

Lazard, L., Capdevila, R., Dann, C., Locke, A., & Roper, S. (2019). Sharenting: Pride, affect and the day-to-day politics of digital mothering. *Social and Personality Psychology Compass, 13*(4). https://doi.org/10.1111/spc3.12443

Ogbanufe, O., Schaupp, L., & Belanger, F. (2023). Sharenting, Parenting, and Identifying: Can Privacy Prevail? *Proceedings of the 56th Hawaii International Conference on System Sciences*, 4453–4462.

Seidman, I. (2006). Interviewing as Qualitative Research. In B. A. Lewis-Beck M S Liao T F (Ed.), *PsycCRITIQUES* (Vol. 37, Issue 7). Teachers College Press. https://doi.org/10.1037/032390

Steinberg, S. B. (2017). Sharenting: Children's Privacy in the Age of Social Media. In *Emory Law Journal* (Vol. 66).

Verswijvel, K., Walrave, M., Hardies, K., & Heirman, W. (2019). Sharenting, is it a good or a bad thing? Understanding how adolescents think and feel about sharenting on social network sites. *Children and Youth Services Review, 104,* 104401. https://doi.org/10.1016/j.childyouth.2019.104401

Walrave, M. (2023). The Translucent Family. In *The Routledge Handbook of Privacy and Social Media* (pp. 165–174). Routledge. https://doi.org/10.4324/9781003244677-19

Unveiling the Influence: Corporate Influencers and Employer Branding in the Skilled Trades Industry

Vanessa Klopf and Carolin Durst

University of Applied Sciences Ansbach, Germany

vanessaklopf@gmx.net
carolin.durst@hs-ansbach.de

Abstract: The skilled trade industry is a significant driving force for the development and prosperity of society and constitutes the backbone of the German economy with its small and medium-sized enterprises. Currently, waiting times for craftsmen stand at approximately three months. This trend is on the rise due to the continued and severe shortage of apprentices and skilled workers. Potential trainees are representatives of Generation Z and best reached through social media channels. Consequently, many companies deliberately utilize corporate influencers in employer branding efforts to win young talents. Corporate influencers have the ability to present specifically job-related content and offer more authentic insights into the daily work environment. However, do they genuinely influence the career preferences of potential trainees? The aim of this study is to investigate if and to what extent corporate influencer influence the perception of the skilled trades industry and career preferences of potential applicants. To investigate the impact of corporate influencers on the perception of the skilled trade industry and the respective career preferences of potential applicants, we conducted a study with 66 students from a secondary school in Germany. (1) First, we measured the perception of the skilled trades industry and career preferences of the participants. (2) Then we exposed them to previously selected content of two corporate influencers from the skilled trades sector. (3) After the exposure, we measured the perception of the skilled trades industry and career preferences of the participants again. For the statistical analysis we used regression analyses and T-tests. The findings of the study show that corporate influencer on social media positively influenced both, the perception of the skilled trades industry and the career preferences of potential applicants. Particularly, insights into daily work routines prove to be effective. Simultaneously, the study reveals that the employer attractiveness of the skilled trades industry in general significantly influences the perception of the industry and enhances applicants' interest in craft professions.

Keywords: Corporate influencers, Employer branding, Career preferences, Recruitment strategies, Skilled trades industry

1. Introduction

The skilled trades sector significantly contributes to society and the economy in its roles as an employer, educator, and economic driver, exerting substantial influence on daily life. Every day, millions of requests, executions, and distributions of artisanal services and products take place. The recipients of this extensive range of offerings include not only private individuals but also the public sector, commerce, and industry. (Zentralverband des Deutschen Handwerks, o.D.).

Although the skilled trades sector is essential for every society as employer, educator, and economic contributor, it has been grappling with significant shortages of skilled workers and an image problem for years (Handwerkskammer Rheinhessen, 2021). The reasons behind the declining number of young individuals opting for an apprenticeship in the skilled trades are multifaceted: demographic shifts, prolonged emphasis in educational policy solely on academic pursuits, as well as the lack of awareness among youths regarding the opportunities within the trades. There is a general lack of appreciation for craftsman professions within society (Eberl, 2022). Zudem herrschen nach wie vor starre Vorurteile über den Sektor. Furthermore, rigid prejudices persist about the sector. Skilled trades are often associated with poor working conditions, high physical exertion, inadequate pay, and insufficient opportunities for advancement and career development, making it an unappealing choice of employment. The integration of innovative technologies in the trades, the earning potential comparable to that of a bachelor's degree holder, and the promising career paths leading to entrepreneurship remain largely unrecognized (Zentralverband des Deutschen Handwerks, 2021).

Despite these challenges, effectively addressing the task of successful talent acquisition has yet to be adequately accomplished. Countering approaches like employer branding and digital recruitment strategies have received little consideration thus far. These factors contribute to a significant bottleneck in the apprenticeship and labor market, bearing far-reaching consequences for the country's economic growth, political climate goals, as well as its energy and mobility transition (Gutensohn & dpa, 2022).

To pursue the desired objectives and alleviate the shortage of skilled workers, it is imperative for the skilled trades to promptly respond and present themselves as attractive employers to attract apprentices. Hence, there needs to be a societal shift in mindset and a greater awareness of the actual circumstances within the skilled trades. Potential apprentices represent Generation Z (born between 1995 and 2010), a demographic best reached through social media channels (Pawlik, 2022; Maas, 2019, p. 59). Companies can employ various strategies on social media to achieve their organizational goals and portray themselves as desirable employers. As an alternative to expensive influencer campaigns, corporate influencers—employees within the company— have proven successful. In contrast to external influencers, they can offer more authentic insights into job-related content and better represent the company as they interact daily with its activities, clients, and products. Major corporations such as Otto, Daimler, or IKEA have already implemented corporate influencer programs (O'Leary, 2023). For instance, the OTTO Group, a leading online retailer, launched a successful internal job ambassador program in 2017, appointing over 100 employees as corporate influencers. After running for over two years, there has been a positive response, with corporate influencers significantly influencing applicants' decisions to pursue employment opportunities at OTTO (Weitzel et al., 2020a, p. 30).

In existing literature, corporate influencers have only been discussed in general or within the context of business-to-business (B2B) scenarios. Specifically, regarding corporate influencers within the skilled trades sector, their influence, and how potential employees perceive them, there is a lack of scientific insights. The same applies to employer branding; while there is existing literature covering the fundamentals and strategies in employer branding, there hasn't been a direct link established to the skilled trades industry. Given this lack of knowledge and the shortage of apprentices in the skilled trades, this study explored how recruiting apprentices from Generation Z in the skilled trades could be successfully executed. In this context, factors influencing how this demographic can be motivated towards trades-based apprenticeships were identified. Furthermore, recommendations for trades-based enterprises were derived from both theoretical insights and practical findings. Consequently, the following research question emerged: *How do corporate influencers influence the perception of the skilled trades sector and the career preferences of potential applicants from Generation Z?*

2. Employer Branding and Corporate Influencer

Employer Branding encompasses all strategies and actions that a company undertakes to position itself as an attractive, credible, and preferred employer, targeting both existing employees and potential applicants (Fournier et al., 2019, p. 22). The objectives of Employer Branding extend beyond recruitment and retention of personnel. Its aim is to construct an employer brand that distinguishes and renders the company an appealing employment option (Meffert, Burmann, & Koers, 2002; Petkovic, 2004 as cited in Wilden et al., 2010, p. 58). A robust employer brand leads to differentiation from competitors and shapes preferences among target audiences (Backhaus & Tikoo, 2004, S. 502; Fournier et al., 2019, p. 24). Additionally, financial advantages such as reduced recruiting expenses and lower turnover and absenteeism rates due to heightened employee loyalty are among the positive effects (Figurska & Matuska, 2013, S. 39; Fournier et al., 2019, p. 25; Sünderhauf, 2022, p. 14). Social media plays a pivotal role in Employer Branding, particularly in engaging young target demographics. Platforms like Facebook, YouTube, and Instagram offer ideal avenues to reach potential applicants and directly engage with them (Kunst, 2023; Lohmeier, 2023; Luoma-aho & Badham, 2023, S. 255). The quality and credibility of the content provided are pivotal in this regard (Meffert et al. 2008, S. 108 as cited in Büttgen & Kissel, 2013, p. 112).

Within the context of Employer Branding and recruiting, employees can serve as brand ambassadors and authentic representatives of the employer brand (Huotari et al., 2015 as cited in Nestler et al., 2021, S. 3). Known as corporate influencers, these individuals are contented employees who share their affiliation with the company on social media platforms, injecting a personal touch (Sünderhauf, 2022, p. 25; Weinländer, 2021, p. 558). In contrast to external social media influencers, corporate influencers are distinguished by their internal position within the company and specific expertise (Enke & Borchers, 2019, p. 267; Schach, 2018, p. 31). Through credible communication about their work routine and employer, corporate influencers contribute to bolstering the employer brand. They expand the company's reach, generate attention, and strengthen employee retention, which positively impacts brand development and overall corporate perception (Sünderhauf, 2022, p. 26; Weinländer, 2021, p. 558).

Selecting and nurturing corporate influencers necessitates clear frameworks, organizational support, and deliberate investments in the knowledge, commitment, and skills of employees (Deutsche Gesellschaft für Personalführung, 2012, p. 111). To effectively engage Generation Z through corporate influencer programs, the content and its messaging must align with their values (Gabrielova & Buchko, 2021, S. 497; Hesse et al., 2019, p. 75). Generation Z values job satisfaction, social responsibility, individuality, and a positive application experience (OC&C, 2019, pp. 16 & 20; Weitzel et al., 2020b, pp. 12 & 19). Extensive use of social media grants companies the opportunity to deploy targeted influencer marketing strategies to reach Generation Z. Authenticity and credibility stand as key values that corporate influencers should convey (Kapitan et al., 2022, S. 342; Kleinjohann & Reinecke, 2020, pp. 18).

3. Research Model and Hypothesis

Employer Branding is a concept closely associated with employer attractiveness. Rohrlack (2019) defines employer attractiveness as the evaluative perception held by employees and external individuals regarding perceived attractive factors (p. 132). Various models have been discussed in the literature, with Ambler and Barrow's (1996) model being frequently cited. Their model applies marketing principles to the merits of employment (Ambler & Barrow, 1996, p. 185) and forms the basis for further developments, such as the model introduced by Berthon et al. (2005) and their scale for determining and operationalizing employer attractiveness (Sivertzen et al., 2013, p. 474).

Nugroho and Liswandi (2018) build upon the model from Berthon et al. (2005) and investigated the impact of employer attractiveness, company reputation, and the use of social media on the intention to apply to a specific company (Nugroho & Liswandi, 2018, p. 553). We used Nugroho and Liswandi's (2018) model as a starting point and adapted it for the skilled trades sector in Germany. In the modified model, the variables are adjusted to examine the influence of employer attractiveness within the skilled trades and corporate influencers on the perception of the skilled trades and the career preferences of potential applicants (see figure 1).

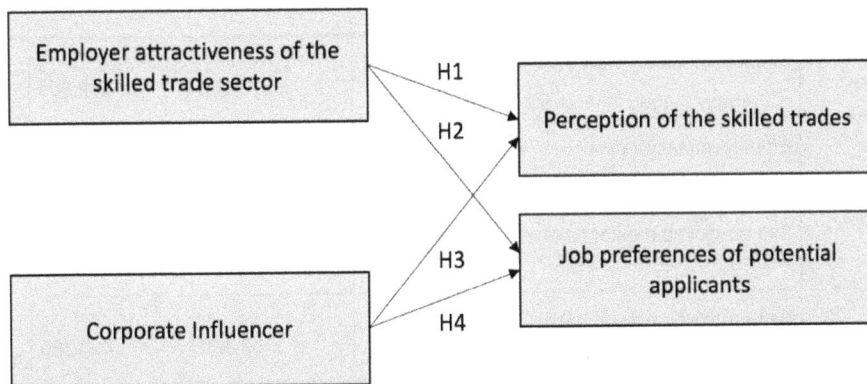

Figure 1: Modified theoretical framework; own illustration based on Nugroho & Liswandi (2018, p. 558)

In the following empirical study, we investigate the following hypotheses:

H1: The employer attractiveness of the skilled trades significantly influences the perception of the skilled trades.

H2: The employer attractiveness of the skilled trades significantly influences the career preferences of applicants.

H3: Corporate influencers significantly influence the perception of the skilled trades.

H4: Corporate influencers significantly influence the career preferences of applicants.

4. Methodology

We conducted a study with 66 students from a secondary school in Germany to investigate the the influence of employer attractiveness within the skilled trades and corporate influencers on the perception of the skilled trade industry and the career preferences of potential applicants. (1) First, we measured the participants' perceptions of the skilled trade industry and their career preferences. (2) We then exposed them to pre-selected content from two corporate influencers in the skilled trades. (3) After the exposure, we measured the participants' perceptions of the skilled trades industry and their career preferences again.

4.1 Selection Process of Corporate Influencers

The identification and selection of corporate influencers in the skilled trade industry were conducted through meticulous internet research, identifying 15 influential personalities from the craft sector on platforms such as Instagram, TikTok, and YouTube. The selection criteria were based on the top three Google search results from reputable sources such as the Handwerksmagazin (Craftsmanship Magazine), the Handwerksblatt

(Craftsmanship Journal), and Online Marketing Rockstars. A detailed table was created, presenting information on the professions, utilized platforms, and the number of subscribers of these influencers. Subsequently, only those influencers were considered as corporate influencers who either tagged or mentioned their employers in their profiles. Following this exclusion process, eight corporate influencers remained, selected for further analysis in the study due to their close association with the company as authentic representatives (see table 1).

Table 1: Overview of the most successful corporate influencers in the skilled trade industry in Germany

Influencer	Profession	Platforms & number of subscribers		
		Instagram	TikTok	YouTube
malermeisterandy	Self-employed master painter & varnisher (Website tagged in Insta-Bio)	104.000	98.500	63.600
dh_ trockenbau	Self-employed drywall installer (Company tagged in Instagram Linktree)	62.300	58.000	126.000
dachdeckerin_chiara	Employed roofer (Company in Insta-Bio tagged)	124.000	123.900	No Account
sandra_hunke	Employed plant mechanic SHK (Company named in Insta-Bio)	146.000	285.100	1740
tschulique	Employed master bricklayer (Company tagged in Insta-Bio tagged)	576.000	902.500	4610
jenni_vom_ dach	Employed master plumber (Company tagged in Insta-Bio tagged)	74.500	93	No Account
cenkinz	Self-employed master hairdresser (Company tagged in Insta-Bio tagged)	235.000	152.000	20.200
brotprofi	Self-employed master baker (Website tagged in Insta-Bio)	99.400	402.300	57.000

The selection of corporate influencers was based on clear criteria to identify two representative individuals from a total group of eight corporate influencers. The established selection objectives encompassed choosing one male and one female corporate influencer actively present on the Instagram and TikTok platforms. This gender-based selection aimed to ensure gender-inclusive and representative portrayal and overcome stereotypical biases within the skilled trade sector. The decision to opt for Instagram and TikTok as platforms for the corporate influencers was rooted in their popularity among the Generation Z target audience and their visual orientation, enabling an engaging and informative presentation of the craft sector. While YouTube was initially considered for identification purposes, it was not further considered due to disparities in usage between male and female corporate influencers.

The final selection of the two pivotal corporate influencers for the survey was conducted based on quantitative and qualitative criteria. The following factors were taken into account:

- Average Engagement Rate of the last ten posts (as of June 15, 2023)
- Average views of the last ten videos (as of June 15, 2023)
- Average posting frequency per month (from January 1 to June 1, 2023)
- Diversity of content within the last 15 posts on Instagram and TikTok (as of June 15, 2023)

Following the evaluation of these criteria, the selected corporate influencers for the survey were Dachdeckerin_Chiara (roofer) and the Brotprofi (baker). Dachdeckerin_Chiara Monteton from Bochum offers an authentic portrayal of construction site realities on her social media channels, showcasing both weaknesses and entertaining aspects. Despite having fewer followers compared to other influencers, her high engagement rate and average views on Instagram demonstrate a strong connection and interest from her target audience. As a roofer, she also acts as a spokesperson for industry-related companies.

The Brotprofi, Ricardo Fischer from Leipzig, is an active master baker and bread sommelier. His videos on Instagram and TikTok aim to enhance appreciation for bread and traditional baking craftsmanship. His high number of TikTok subscribers and active role as an instructor at the Federal Academy of the Bakery Trade reflect his expertise and influence within the industry.

In selecting content for the survey, the focus lies on providing insights into various aspects of the workday. Themes such as daily routines, workspace setup, challenging tasks, and achieved successes are considered. The professional perspective is completed by highlighting craftsmanship skills, expert tips, training opportunities, and current trends. Instagram and TikTok were chosen as ideal platforms, with a deliberate preference for video formats to facilitate a visual understanding. Four videos were chosen per corporate influencer, including two showcasing workday routines, one focusing on professional knowledge, and a specific video for each influencer, with the total length restricted to five minutes to accommodate the survey's timeframe and maintain participants' attention.

4.2 Sampling and Data Collection

Statistical data from 2021 indicates that 42.3 percent of newly signed apprenticeship contracts in the skilled trade sector originate from students in secondary schools, underscoring their significance as the largest group among apprentices (Rimpler, 2021). Therefore, we selected ninth-grade students aged 14 to 16 from secondary schools for our study. Due to their impending decision regarding further educational or career paths, they serve as central recipients for employer advertising and recruitment campaigns. Choosing this target group allows for the early cultivation of awareness regarding the diversity within the craftsmanship sector and the provision of targeted information to support their career orientation. The study took place on June 29th and 30th, 2023, on-site with three ninth-grade classes, accompanied by teachers. Out of a total of 70 students, 66 individuals between the ages of 14 and 17 actively participated in the study and completed the survey (52% female, 47% male, 2% diverse).

The survey design was guided by the Stimulus-Organism-Response (SOR) model (Schaper, 2014, p. 322–323). Within the study, the SOR model was utilized by posing *questions to students before and after* their exposure to corporate influencer videos. This approach aimed to capture changes in their attitudes as a response to the external stimulus, where internal factors (Organism) such as perception, attitudes, and emotions play a role.

The variables were operationalized as follows:

Employer attractiveness of the skilled trade sector (answer on a likert skale)

- How appealing do you find craftsmanship as a potential employer? (very unappealing – very appealing)
- How do you perceive craftsmanship in general? (very negative – very positive)
- How attractive do you find the following two professions (roofer/baker) in general? (very unattractive – very attractive)
- To what extent do the following characteristics apply to jobs in the skilled trades in general? (Does not apply at all – Does fully apply)
- *Skilled trades are generally very attractive.*
- *Skilled trades offer the prospect of a high salary.*
- *Skilled trades have a high social standing.*
- *Skilled trades offer good chances of obtaining an apprenticeship.*
- *Skilled trades offer good training opportunities.*
- *Skilled trades offer good opportunities for career advancement.*
- Please rate the following statements about the skilled trades sector (Do not agree at all – Totally agree)
- *The skilled trades give something back to society.*
- *Working in the skilled trades makes you feel good about yourself.*
- *You have a secure job within the skilled crafts sector.*
- *In the skilled crafts sector, you work with supportive and encouraging colleagues.*
- *The skilled crafts sector values creativity and utilizes the creativity of its employees.*

Perception of the skilled trades (answer on a likert skale)

- How do you perceive the profession of a roofer/baker? (completely disagree – completely agree)

- *I find the profession interesting.*
- *I am interested in training as a roofer/baker.*
- *I can imagine what the daily routine looks like.*

Job preferences of potential applicants (answer on a likert skale)

- I am interested in an apprenticeship in the skilled trade sector. (completely disagree – completely agree)
- I am interested in an internship in the skilled trades sector. (completely disagree – completely agree)
- I would recommend an apprenticeship or internship in craftsmanship to a friend. (completely disagree – completely agree)

Additionally, questions were posed regarding the influencers' social media presence, evaluation of characteristics related to craft professions, and factors influencing career choice. The questionnaire concluded with demographic information, future plans after completing secondary education, and details about prior experiences in craftsmanship.

4.3 Data Analysis and Results

For hypotheses H1 and H2, separate regression analyses were conducted to examine the relationship between the attractiveness of craftsmanship as an employer and the perception of craftsmanship, as well as the job preferences of applicants. The normal distribution of the data was confirmed using the Kolmogorov-Smirnov test.

H1: The employer attractiveness of the skilled trades significantly influences the perception of the skilled trades.

ANOVA

	df	SS	MS	F	Significance F
Regression	1	4,101323733	4,1013237	18,314421	6,38886E-05
Residue	64	14,33213329	0,2239396		
Total	65	18,43345702			

	Coefficients	Standard Error	t Stat	P-value	Lower 95%	Upper 95%	Lower 95,0%	Upper 95,0%
Intercept	1,719419894	0,274431736	6,2653829	3,545E-08	1,171179477	2,2676603	1,1711795	2,2676603
X Variable	0,352410037	0,082347738	4,2795351	6,389E-05	0,187901518	0,5169186	0,1879015	0,5169186

Figure 2: Regression analysis for hypothesis 1

The results for H1 indicate a *significant influence of the attractiveness of craftsmanship as an employer on the perception of craftsmanship*. The significance value (p-value) in the ANOVA table (6.38886E-05) is well below the conventional significance level of 0.05. The multiple correlation coefficient of 0.47169213 suggests a moderate positive correlation (see Fig. 2). An increase in the attractiveness of craftsmanship as an employer leads to a more positive perception of craftsmanship.

H2: The employer attractiveness of the skilled trades significantly influences the career preferences of applicants.

ANOVA

	df	SS	MS	F	Significance F
Regression	1	15,10025539	15,10025539	269,720167	1,234E-24
Residue	64	3,583033322	0,055984896		
Total	65	18,68328871			

	Coefficients	Standard Error	t Stat	P-value	Lower 95%	Upper 95%	Lower 95,0%	Upper 95,0%
Intercept	0,859709947	0,137215868	6,265382852	3,545E-08	0,5855897	1,1338302	0,5855897	1,1338302
X Variable	0,676205018	0,041173869	16,42315946	1,2341E-24	0,5939508	0,7584593	0,5939508	0,7584593

Figure 3: Regression analysis for hypothesis 2

The regression analysis for H2 also demonstrates *significant influence of the attractiveness of craftsmanship as an employer on the job preferences of potential applicants.* The very low p-value in the ANOVA table (1.23413E-24) is well below the significance level of 0.05. The multiple correlation coefficient of 0.89901199 indicates a strong positive correlation, and the coefficient of determination of 0.808 suggests that the attractiveness of craftsmanship as an employer significantly impacts the job preference of applicants (see Fig. 3).

Both hypotheses are confirmed, with H2 showing a notably stronger correlation. This emphasizes the particular significance of the attractiveness of craftsmanship as an employer for the job preferences of applicants.

Hypotheses H3 and H4 are evaluated using dependent sample t-tests, as they involve the same subjects before and after the influence of corporate influencers. The corresponding questions from the questionnaire are reassigned, comparing the questions before and after the influence of corporate influencers.

H3: Corporate influencers significantly influence the perception of the skilled trades.

	Without CI	With CI
Mean	2,879545455	3,236363636
Variance	0,264229021	0,309118881
Observations	66	66
Pearson correlation	0,685221541	
Hypothetical difference of means	0	
df	65	
t Stat	-6,800817496	
P(T<=t) one-tail	1,95E-09	
t Critical one-tail	1,668635976	
P(T<=t) two-tail	3,895E-09	
t Critical two-tail	1,997137908	

Figure 4: T-test for hypothesis 3

We observed a *significant difference in the perception* of the skilled trade sector before and after the influence of corporate influencers. This is evidenced by a clear increase in the mean from 2.87 to 3.23, supported by a t-statistic of 6.80 and a p-value of 1.95E-09 (see Fig. 4). This indicates a significant change, *suggesting that corporate influencers have a notable impact on the perception of craftsmanship.*

H4: Corporate influencers significantly influence the career preferences of applicants.

	Without CI	With CI
Mean	2,444444444	2,570707071
Variance	1,146438746	0,860735561
Observations	66	66
Pearson correlation	0,845493089	
Hypothetical difference of means	0	
df	65	
t Stat	-1,792693201	
P(T<=t) one-tail	0,038837565	
t Critical one-tail	1,668635976	
P(T<=t) two-tail	0,077675129	
t Critical two-tail	1,997137908	

Figure 5: T-test for hypothesis 4

The t-test results for H4 also show a significant difference in the job preferences of applicants before and after the influence of corporate influencers. The mean increased from 2.44 to 2.57, accompanied by a t-statistic of 1.79 and a p-value of 0.03 (see Fig. 4). This change is also significant, indicating that *corporate influencers have a discernible influence on the job preferences of applicants,* albeit with less significance compared to H3.

Our study also provides additional insightful into the factors influencing the career choices of Generation Z. An information day at the respective company, discussions with parents or insights from apprentices on social networks have a strong impact on the individual job decision (see Fig. 6). Thus, these results underscore the importance of authentic insights and personal experiences in the decision-making process regarding a career in the skilled trade sector.

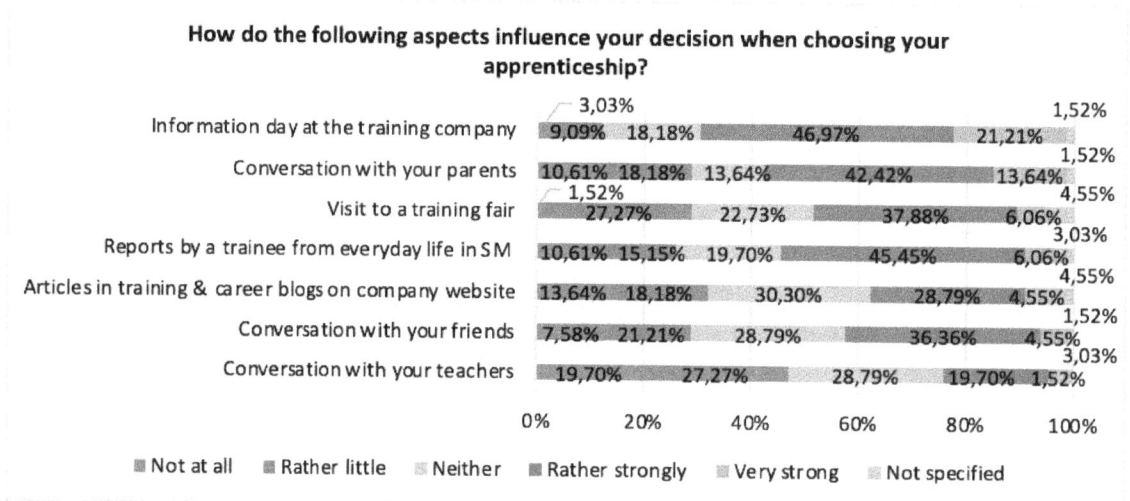

How do the following aspects influence your decision when choosing your apprenticeship?

	Not at all	Rather little	Neither	Rather strongly	Very strong	Not specified
Information day at the training company	9,09%	18,18%	3,03%	46,97%	21,21%	1,52%
Conversation with your parents	10,61%	18,18%	13,64%	42,42%	13,64%	1,52%
Visit to a training fair	1,52%	27,27%	22,73%	37,88%	6,06%	4,55%
Reports by a trainee from everyday life in SM	10,61%	15,15%	19,70%	45,45%	6,06%	3,03%
Articles in training & career blogs on company website	13,64%	18,18%	30,30%	28,79%	4,55%	4,55%
Conversation with your friends	7,58%	21,21%	28,79%	36,36%	4,55%	1,52%
Conversation with your teachers	19,70%	27,27%	28,79%	19,70%	1,52%	3,03%

Figure 6: Factors influencing the career choices of Generation Z

Furthermore, we asked the participants to evaluate the importance of following criteria when considering an apprenticeship in the skilled trades sector. The results show that financial aspects, diverse career and training opportunities, as well as a pleasant work atmosphere, are central for this generation. Regarding corporate influencers, it is evident that students are primarily interested in glimpses into their everyday work life. Additionally, they are inclined to watch mainly artisanal projects and information about training and career opportunities, while product presentations and recommendations are less sought after (see Fig. 7).

What content would you look at from a corporate influencer from the skilled trades sector on social media?

Insights into everyday working life
Presentation of interesting craft projects
Information about training and career opportunities
Information about earning opportunities
Tips and instructions for specialist topics
Testimonials from trainees
DIY Ideas
Dispelling prejudices about the skilled trades sector
Product presentations or recommendations

Figure 7: Preferences regarding corporate influencer content

5. Discussion, Limitations and Implications

The findings of our study show that corporate influencer on social media positively influenced both, the perception of the skilled trades industry and the career preferences of potential applicants. Particularly, insights into daily work routines prove to be effective. Simultaneously, the study reveals that the employer attractiveness of the skilled trades industry in general significantly influences the perception of the industry and enhances applicants' interest in craft professions.

This research presents some limitations that warrant consideration. Firstly, the examination of corporate influencers occurred within an artificially constructed setting, where participants were actively prompted to engage with the influencers and their content. This could potentially distort natural interactions and influence the authenticity of the responses. Secondly, the study was limited to two selected corporate influencers and specific craft professions (roofer and baker), limiting the potential diversity and generalizability of the results across the broad spectrum of craftsmanship. Furthermore, the diversity in presentation styles of the influencers posed challenges in result comparison, as varying content strategies, styles, and tones could affect individual perceptions and reactions of the participants. Thirdly, the participants were exclusively recruited from a specific school (secondary school), potentially limiting the generalizability of the results to other schools or educational institutions. Lastly, the influence of social background and parental educational expectations on the affinity toward craftsmanship remains unaccounted for. These limitations emphasize the necessity for a cautious interpretation of research findings and highlight areas that could be further investigated in future studies.

Despite the limitations, this study presents significant insights and derives the following key recommendations for craftsmanship enterprises:

- **Employer branding and positioning:** A clear employer positioning is essential for positive employer branding. Developing a distinct Employer Value Proposition supports this by highlighting the uniqueness of the company and the benefits offered to employees. Particularly relevant are attractive earning opportunities, diverse career and training options, and a positive work atmosphere.
- **Presence on social media:** The results underscore the significance of a strong presence on social media, especially on platforms like Instagram, to effectively reach the adolescent target audience. Emphasizing specific craft career prospects and providing authentic insights into the everyday work life are pivotal elements.
- **Corporate influencers for employer branding:** The study emphasizes the importance of corporate influencer marketing as an effective tool to enhance employer attractiveness and attract young potential applicants to craftsmanship. Their role as ambassadors for craft businesses can positively impact apprentice recruitment. Specifically, apprentices can serve as influential corporate influencers by providing authentic insights into their training and daily work routines.
- **Actively engage parents:** The role of parents in the career orientation process is significant. Craft businesses should develop targeted measures to actively involve parents in the recruiting process. Information sessions and parent evenings can help address concerns and convey the benefits of a craft apprenticeship.
- **Support from governing bodies:** Due to the limited experience of many craft businesses in relevant areas (employer branding, social media, corporate influencer marketing), support from governing institutions such as trade chambers is crucial. Training programs and workshops can impart the necessary knowledge and practical skills to implement successful strategies and enhance the presence as an attractive employer.

Overall, these recommendations indicate that targeted implementation can strengthen not only individual enterprises but also sustainably enhance the image of the skilled trade sector as a whole.

For future research in the domain of corporate influencers and their influence, extensions to different age groups, integration of diverse student groups, and a long-term analysis could offer relevant research perspectives. Additionally, focusing on specific target groups, such as women and foreign professionals in craftsmanship, and considering the role of female corporate influencers as promotional instruments in investigations, could be considered.

References

Ambler, Tim und Barrow, Simon (1996): „The employer brand" *Journal of Brand Management*. (*4*) (1996), 185–206. doi:10.1057/bm.1996.42

Backhaus, Kristin und Tikoo, Surinder (2004): „Conceptualizing and researching employer branding" Career Development International. (9)Nr. 5 (2004), 501–517. Emerald Group Publishing Limited doi:10.1108/13620430410550754

Büttgen, Marion und Kissel, Patrick (2013): Der Einsatz von Social Media als Instrument des Employer Branding. In R. Stock-Homburg (Hrsg.), *Handbuch Strategisches Personalmanagement*. (S. 107–124). Wiesbaden: Springer Fachmedien Wiesbaden. doi:10.1007/978-3-658-00431-6_7

Deutsche Gesellschaft für Personalführung (Hrsg.) (2012): *Employer Branding: die Arbeitgebermarke gestalten und im Personalmarketing umsetzen*. Reihe: DGFP-PraxisEdition (2. Aufl.). Bielefeld: Bertelsmann.

Eberl, Jens (02.03.2022): „Wie das Handwerk um Personal kämpft" *tagesschau.de*. Verfügbar unter: https://www.tagesschau.de/wirtschaft/konjunktur/handwerk-arbeitsmarkt-101.html [08.02.2023].

Enke, Nadja und Borchers, Nils S. (2019): „Social Media Influencers in Strategic Communication: A Conceptual Framework for Strategic Social Media Influencer Communication" *International Journal of Strategic Communication*. (*13*)Nr. 4 (2019), 261–277. doi:10.1080/1553118X.2019.1620234

Figurska, Irena und Matuska, Ewa (2013): „Employer branding as a human resources management strategy" Human Resources Management. Nr. 7 (2013), 35–51.

Fournier, Jana, Dürig, Uta-Micaela, Peters, Kai und Weers, Jan-Philipp (2019): Marke und Branding. In G. Hesse & R. Mattmüller (Hrsg.), *Perspektivwechsel im Employer Branding*. (S. 19–54). Wiesbaden: Springer Fachmedien Wiesbaden. doi:10.1007/978-3-658-26208-2_2

Gabrielova, Karina und Buchko, Aaron A. (2021): „Here comes Generation Z: Millennials as managers" Business Horizons. (64)Nr. 4 (2021), 489–499. doi:10.1016/j.bushor.2021.02.013

Gutensohn, David und dpa (03.07.2022): „Fachkräftemangel: Sechsstellige Zahl an Handwerkern fehlt" *Die Zeit*. Verfügbar unter: https://www.zeit.de/arbeit/2022-07/fachkraeftemangel-handwerk-baubranche-ausbildungen [08.02.2023].

Handwerkskammer Rheinhessen (03.05.2021): Studie zu Fachkräftemangel im Handwerk. *Handwerkskammer Rheinhessen*. Verfügbar unter: https://www.hwk.de/studie-zu-fachkraeftemangel-im-handwerk/ [23.09.2023].

Hesse, Gero, Mayer, Katja, Rose, Nico und Fellinger, Christoph (2019): Herausforderungen für das Employer Branding und deren Kompetenzen. In G. Hesse & R. Mattmüller (Hrsg.), *Perspektivwechsel im Employer Branding*. (S. 55–104). Wiesbaden: Springer Fachmedien Wiesbaden. doi:10.1007/978-3-658-26208-2_3

Kapitan, Sommer, Van Esch, Patrick, Soma, Vrinda und Kietzmann, Jan (2022): „Influencer Marketing and Authenticity in Content Creation" *Australasian Marketing Journal*. (30)Nr. 4 (2022), 342–351. doi:10.1177/18393349211011171

Kleinjohann, Michael und Reinecke, Victoria (2020): *Marketingkommunikation mit der Generation Z: Erfolgsfaktoren für das Marketing mit Digital Natives*. Reihe: essentials. Wiesbaden: Springer Fachmedien Wiesbaden. doi:10.1007/978-3-658-30822-3

Kunst, Alexander (2023): „Soziale Netzwerke in Deutschland 2022" *Statista*. Verfügbar unter: https://de.statista.com/prognosen/999733/deutschland-beliebteste-soziale-netzwerke [13.05.2023].

Luoma-aho, Vilma und Badham, Mark (2023): Handbook on Digital Corporate Communication. Edward Elgar Publishing.

Lohmeier, L. (2023): „Social-Media-Plattformen - Anteil der Nutzer nach Altersgruppen in Deutschland 2022" *Statista*. Verfügbar unter: https://de.statista.com/statistik/daten/studie/543605/umfrage/verteilung-der-nutzer-von-social-media-plattformen-nach-altersgruppen-in-deutschland/ [13.09.2023].

Maas, Rüdiger (2019): *Generation Z für Personaler, Führungskräfte und jeden der die Jungen verstehen muss: Ergebnisse der Generation-Thinking-Studie*. München: Hanser.

Nestler, Lisa, Hoffmann, Clara und Poeppelbuss, Jens (2021): „Understanding and defining the corporate influencer in business-to-business sales – first insights from an interview study" European Conference on Information Systems. (2021). Research-in-Progress Papers. 26.

Nugroho, A. und Liswandi, L. (2018): „The Influence of Employer Attractiveness, Corporate Reputation and the Use of Social Media towards Intention to Apply for a Job" *International Journal of Management, Accounting and Economics*. (5)Nr. 7 (2018), 553–565.

O'Leary, Emily (20.01.2023): „Corporate Influencer: Best Practices und Beispiele" *HubSpot*. Verfügbar unter: https://blog.hubspot.de/marketing/corporate-influencer [08.02.2023].

OC&C (2019): „Eine Generation ohne Grenzen: Generation Z wird erwachsen." Verfügbar unter: https://www.occstrategy.com/media/1904/eine-generation-ohne-grenzen_.pdf [10.06.2023].

Pawlik, V. (07.12.2022): „Generationen - Häufigkeit der Nutzung von Social Media (z.B. Facebook, Twitter, Instagram, WhatsApp) 2020" *Statista*. Verfügbar unter: https://de.statista.com/statistik/daten/studie/1137640/umfrage/umfrage-zur-haeufigkeit-der-nutzung-von-social-media-nach-generationen/ [08.02.2023].

Rimpler, René (2021): „Wirtschaftlicher Stellenwert des Handwerks 2021" Verfügbar unter: https://www.zdh.de/daten-und-fakten/kennzahlen-des-handwerks/wirtschaftlicher-stellenwert-des-handwerks-2021/ [08.02.2023].

Rohrlack, Kirsten (2019): Wie erhöhen Sie Ihre Chancen, geeignete Mitarbeiter zu gewinnen? *Lösungsorientierte Mitarbeitergewinnung*. (S. 131–170). Wiesbaden: Springer Fachmedien Wiesbaden. doi:10.1007/978-3-658-24084-4_4

Schach, Annika (2018): Botschafter, Blogger, Influencer: Eine definitorische Einordnung aus der Perspektive der Public Relations. In A. Schach & T. Lommatzsch (Hrsg.), *Influencer Relations*. (S. 27–47). Wiesbaden: Springer Fachmedien Wiesbaden. doi:10.1007/978-3-658-21188-2_3

Schaper, Niclas (2014): Theoretische Modelle des Arbeitshandelns. In: Springer-Lehrbuch *Arbeits- und Organisationspsychologie*. (S. 321–345). Berlin, Heidelberg: Springer Berlin Heidelberg. doi:10.1007/978-3-642-41130-4_20

Sivertzen, Anne-Mette, Nilsen, Etty Ragnhild und Olafsen, Anja H. (2013): „Employer branding: employer attractiveness and the use of social media" (D.L.V. de C. Dr Stuart Roper Dr Francisco Guzman, Hrsg.)*Journal of Product & Brand Management*. (22)Nr. 7 (2013), 473–483. . Emerald Group Publishing Limited doi:10.1108/JPBM-09-2013-0393

Sünderhauf, Vincent (2022): *Employer Branding für KMUs: Wie Sie als Arbeitgeber zu einer attraktiven Marke werden*. Reihe: essentials. Wiesbaden: Springer Fachmedien Wiesbaden. doi:10.1007/978-3-658-38853-9

Weinländer, Markus (2021): Corporate Influencing in B2B – Die eigenen Mitarbeiter als Markenbotschafter in sozialen Medien einsetzen. In U. Seebacher (Hrsg.), *Praxishandbuch B2B-Marketing*. (S. 557–576). Wiesbaden: Springer Fachmedien Wiesbaden. doi:10.1007/978-3-658-31651-8_21

Weitzel, Dr Tim, Maier, Dr Christian, Weinert, Dr Christoph, Pflügner, Katharina, Oehlhorn, Caroline, Wirth, Jakob et al. (2020a): „Recruiting Trends 2020: Employer Branding" (2020). Verfügbar unter: https://www.uni-bamberg.de/fileadmin/uni/fakultaeten/wiai_lehrstuehle/isdl/Recruiting_Trends_2020/Studien_2020_03_Employer_Branding_Web.pdf

Weitzel, Dr Tim, Maier, Dr Christian, Weinert, Dr Christoph, Pflügner, Katharina, Oehlhorn, Caroline, Wirth, Jakob et al. (2020b): „Generation Z - die Arbeitnehmer von morgen" (2020). Verfügbar unter: https://www.uni-bamberg.de/fileadmin/uni/fakultaeten/wiai_lehrstuehle/isdl/Recruiting_Trends_2020/Studien_2020_05_Generation_Z_Web.pdf

Wilden, Ralf, Gudergan, Siegfried und Lings, Ian (2010): „Employer branding: strategic implications for staff recruitment" *Journal of Marketing Management*. (*26*)Nr. 1–2 (2010), 56–73. . Routledge doi:10.1080/02672570903577091

Zentralverband des Deutschen Handwerks (13.01.2021): „„Die Wahrnehmung des Handwerks hat sich massiv gesteigert."" Verfügbar unter: https://www.zdh.de/presse/veroeffentlichungen/interviews-und-statements/die-wahrnehmung-des-handwerks-hat-sich-massiv-gesteigert/ [08.02.2023].

Zentralverband des Deutschen Handwerks (o.D.): „Das Handwerk in Deutschland" Verfügbar unter: https://www.zdh.de/daten-und-fakten/das-handwerk/ [08.02.2023].

The Impact of Artificial Intelligence on Social Media

Peter Krajčovič

The Faculty of Mass Media Communication, University of Ss. Cyril and Methodius in Trnava, Slovakia

peter.krajcovic@ucm.sk

Abstract: Artificial intelligence is having a dramatic impact on a variety of industries, including marketing and marketing communications. Its use enables the optimization of marketing activities and increases efficiency not only within large corporations, but also in small and micro businesses. On social media, AI plays a significant role in content creation, post scheduling, campaign analysis and other aspects. Implementing AI tools into social media management can be a key element for improving the performance and effectiveness of marketing communications. This paper examines the impact of AI on social media from the perspective of using AI in an SME environment. It analyses the current state of the art, the authors' perspectives and the results of empirical studies. It concludes with recommendations for the use of specific AI-based tools that businesses can use in social media management.

Keywords: Artificial intelligence, Marketing communication, SMEs, Social media

1. Introduction

The use of artificial intelligence and tools such as chat GPT has dramatically increased in popularity in many areas within marketing and marketing communications. According to Columbus (2020), the importance of AI in marketing is confirmed by the estimate that by 2023, 30% of customer service organisations will deliver proactive customer service using AI-enabled process orchestration and continuous intelligence.

The artificial intelligence (AI) market is expected to grow significantly over the next decade, according to a number of sources. According to Thormundsson (2023), the AI market is expected to grow from $241.8 billion in 2023 to nearly $740 billion in 2030, a compound annual growth rate of 17.3%.

According to Next Move Strategy Consulting (2023), its value of around $208 billion in 2023 is expected to grow ninefold by 2030, reaching around $1.85 trillion. In fact, the AI market covers a wide range of industries, including healthcare, education, finance, media and marketing. The rate of adoption and use of the technology is increasing worldwide. Chatbots, image-generating AI and mobile applications are among the major trends that will enhance AI in the coming years.

Artificial intelligence-based tools are a way to answer questions and solve problems in a variety of areas related to marketing communications and sales strategy. As the experience of AI users and companies grows, so do the demands and expectations of marketers to increase the effectiveness of marketing communications. Despite some doubts, concerns and a number of unanswered questions, it is clear that AI will have a fundamental impact on marketing, not only in large corporate environments, but also in small and micro businesses. In fact, it brings entirely new possibilities to the marketing of these businesses. It can personalise content, improve communication outcomes, provide feedback and innovate the use of social media itself.

Using a range of AI-based tools, marketers can create tailored content, measure results faster and more accurately, and provide feedback, and all in much less time than before. Information and data on the use of AI by small and micro businesses is still relatively scarce. However, it is clear from the above that AI is having a significant impact on how users interact with social media and how content is presented to them. AI increases personalisation and efficiency on social media, but also raises issues of privacy and transparency. Examples from the field show that AI is now being used by many brands to improve communication, personalise content, enhance customer service and manage reputation on social media.

This paper analyses the impact of artificial intelligence on social media. It examines the extent to which AI has influenced the use of social media for marketing communications and the trends it is bringing. The author presents the results of several empirical studies on the state of AI use within companies and their marketing communications on social media. At the same time, he provides an overview of the current state of the art in academic research.

2. Methodology

Offering an overview of the most important aspects shaping the use of artificial intelligence on social media, the following part of this study focuses on a relatively wide range of issues. To explore the current state of this problematic and the current state of using AI by enterprises, we refer to the existing body of knowledge and academic research, as well as a number of documents and reports to discuss the using of AI for marketing and marketing communications. The reflection below employs the basic methods of meta-analysis, logical reasoning, and synthesis for presenting the individual findings, specific practical examples used to better explain the using of AI, as well as inductive and deductive reasoning and wider generalization.

3. Artificial Intelligence and Social Media

Social media is one of the main industries where marketers can use artificial intelligence to improve both performance and efficiency. According to Sadiku et al. (2021), artificial intelligence is a fundamental part of how today's social networks work. AI technologies offer the ability to increase productivity, identify new trends, reach a wider audience, find out what works for your niche, track performance and optimise campaigns in real time.

According to Kaput (2022), AI is a fundamental part of how today's social networks work. This is why AI-based tools are so widely used in marketing. Facebook uses a variety of AI tools to enhance each user's experience. Instagram uses artificial intelligence to identify and suggest visuals and images. Snapchat uses AI technology in the form of computer vision to monitor facial features and then apply filters to the face in real time. LinkedIn uses the power of AI to recommend connections, suggest job openings, provide specific posts in the feed and suggest people to follow. According to Sadiku et al (2021), the use of artificial intelligence in social media is growing at an unprecedented rate and is constantly transforming social media.

Many authors (e.g. Agnihotri, 2020; Chintalapati and Shivendra, 2022; Huang and Roland, 2021) point to the growing importance of artificial intelligence in marketing and social media. According to Sarmiento (2020), AI is used to continuously collect and analyse data on social media activity. According to Chui et al. (2018), AI will continue to influence social media networks as the technology develops and evolves. The combination of AI and social media is proving to be highly beneficial for businesses.

Anandvardhan (2021) emphasises that AI is playing a dominant role in defining how social media works today. Argan et al. (2022) point out that AI algorithms can predict consumer expectations and desires at scale, and can apply consumer behaviour theories and variables to improve advertiser-user interactions. According to Quadros (2020), the benefits that AI can bring to social media include (1) increased audience engagement, (2) greater efficiency, (3) smarter advertising, (4) refined content targeting, (5) reduced marketing costs with better return on investment, (6) AI-powered chatbots, (7) increased security, (8) cost reduction, (9) increased revenue, and (10) a competitive tool.

According to Resqi (2022), there has been an increase in the number of publications dealing with marketing communication in the period 2015 to 2022. The author emphasises that marketing communication studies over the last two years refer to marketing through social media.

In the literature we can find several examples of the influence of AI on social media. Pariser (2011) talks about personalised content. This includes recommending posts and advertisements that are relevant to each individual user. Examples are personalised views on platforms such as Facebook or YouTube. An example is Netflix's algorithm that suggests movies and shows based on the user's viewing history. Go et al. (2009) talk about sentiment analysis. AI analyses the sentiment of comments and posts on social media to measure public opinion. Gao et al. (2019) talk about bots and chatbots. Artificial intelligence can be used to create bots and chatbots that can interact with users on social media. Davidson et al. (2017) talk about content filtering. AI is used to filter content on social media to remove inappropriate or dangerous posts. Castillo et al. (2011) talk about trend prediction. AI analyses social media data to predict trends and viral events. Goodfellow et al (2016) talk about ad management. AI helps you better target your social media ads and maximise their effectiveness.

4. Use of Artificial Intelligence and Social Media by Enterprises

According to Sadiku et al (2021), social media has moved away from its traditional role as a platform for people to interact and connect. Today, smart companies are using social media for e-commerce, customer service, marketing, public relations and more. AI applications on social media platforms include text analysis, image analysis, spam detection, social insights, advertising, and data collection.

According to Kietzmann et al. (2018), AI's reasoning capabilities mean that it can uncover personality, tendencies, values, and needs from social media users' comments and posts. Sarmiento (2020) emphasises that companies are making better use of social media through AI. With the help of AI, data about your social media activity is continuously collected and analysed. Social media is currently being used to infer social behaviour and derive trends in combination with big data analytics tools.

According to Rodgers (2021), current developments and figures also point to the importance of AI in marketing and the high likelihood that this synergy will continue to grow in the future. More than 75% of consumers already use an AI-powered service or device. By 2021, AI marketing is expected to grow by 53%. By 2023, we expect global digital advertising to reach $517.51 billion, with AI accounting for 80% of this sum.

Many companies are already using AI to personalise their websites, emails, social media posts, videos and other materials to better respond to customer demands (Khokhar, 2019). According to Budiyanto et al. (2022), social media is widely used not only for the purpose of conducting transactions, but also to provide users with the ability to showcase the goods or services they offer. Social media is also more focused on the process of brand presentation (branding) by marketers to potential consumers and more focused on the process of brand recognition, known as branding.

With the rise of AI over the past few decades, more and more companies are turning to machine learning programmes to streamline their operations and open up more opportunities for improvement within their businesses. According to a report by Tractica (2020), AI is recognised as the most influential technology for business, with an expected growth from $10.1 billion in 2018 to $126 billion by 2025.

Artificial intelligence is being used by many brands today to improve communications, personalise content, provide better customer service and manage social media reputation. Netflix uses AI to personalise content for its users. Algorithms track what movies and shows users have watched and recommend additional content based on that. This approach increases customer engagement and loyalty (How Netflix Uses AI to Predict Your Next Binge-Worthy Show, n.d.). Facebook uses AI to filter content and identify inappropriate posts and spam. This improves user experience and security on the platform (How Facebook Uses Artificial Intelligence, n.d.). Amazon uses AI to improve customer service through chatbots. These chatbots can answer customers' questions and help them select products (How Amazon Uses AI for Customer Service, n.d.). Coca-Cola uses chatbots on platforms such as Facebook Messenger to communicate with customers. They help answer questions, manage complaints and provide information about new products (Coca-Cola Turns to Facebook Messenger for Chatbot Customer Service, n.d.). Starbucks uses artificial intelligence to analyse customer feedback on social media. This provides important insights into what customers think about their products and services (How Starbucks Uses Artificial Intelligence for Customer Engagement, n.d.). Airbnb uses AI to rate hosts and guests. This helps to ensure credibility and safety on the platform (How Airbnb Uses AI and Big Data, n.d.). Sephora has created a social media chatbot to enhance the shopping experience. Users can consult with the chatbot and receive product recommendations (How Sephora's Chatbot is Making Personalisation Easier for Customers, n.d.). Nestlé uses AI to monitor discussions about its products on social media. This allows them to respond immediately to customer questions or complaints (How Nestlé Uses AI for Social Media Monitoring, n.d.).

The use of artificial intelligence in small and micro businesses is an equally important aspect of modern business. According to Kaput (2021), artificial intelligence supports greater customer engagement on social media, while AI applications can help managers increase revenue and reduce costs in their businesses.

According to the European Commission (2020), 78% of companies say they know what the term artificial intelligence means, while only 7% do not know and 15% are unsure. Looking at Europe as a whole, companies tend to fall into one of two camps: 'adopters' (42%), who are currently using at least one AI technology, and 'non-adopters' (40%), who are not currently using AI and do not intend to use any of the AI technologies (at least in the next two years).

According to the report – New Report Shows Marketers Lack the Education, Training to Effectively Adopt Artificial Intelligence (n.d.), the majority of marketers know the importance of AI to their business, but 70% of respondents believe a lack of training and education is a barrier to adopting AI in marketing.

According to Gartner survey – Gartner Survey Shows 37 Percent of Organisations have Implemented AI in Some Form (n.d.), 37% of organisations are using AI for content curation and management. According to Gartner, 37% of organisations have implemented AI in some form.

Gartner (2019) also shows interesting results: 37 % of organizations have implemented AI in some form. The survey revealed that the number of organisations implementing artificial intelligence (AI) has increased by 270 % in the last four years, and tripled in the last year. It also found that organisations across all industries are using AI in a variety of applications, but are struggling with an acute talent shortage.

In 2020, 7% of EU enterprises with at least 10 employees were using AI applications. While 2% of enterprises used machine learning to analyse big data internally, 1% analysed big data internally using natural language processing, natural language generation or speech recognition. A chat service, where a chatbot or virtual agent generates natural language responses to customers, was used in 2% of enterprises. The same proportion of enterprises, 2%, used service robots, which are characterised by a certain degree of autonomy, e.g. to carry out cleaning, dangerous or repetitive tasks, such as removing toxic substances, sorting items in the warehouse, assisting customers in shopping or at payment points, etc. (Eurostat, 2021).

According to the Enehano report (2023), 5.2% of Slovak companies used AI applications in 2021, which puts Slovakia ahead of its neighbours. However, there is still a large group of companies in Slovakia that are not yet using artificial intelligence. Slovakia is still behind the EU average of 7.9%.

The previous survey conducted by Krajčovič (2023) on a sample of 78 Slovak micro-enterprises shows that more than 60% of companies have come across the term artificial intelligence. Almost 30% of the companies have come across the term but do not know exactly what it means and how it is used. Artificial intelligence has been used by 37%, but outside of business activities. No company is using AI for marketing or marketing communications. However, in more than 30% of cases, entrepreneurs said they did not know what benefits artificial intelligence could bring them. Lack of experience and knowledge are among the most common and biggest barriers to adopting artificial intelligence tools.

A study by Bunte, et al. (2021) found that lack of expertise, start-up costs and time investment, infrastructure, resources, experience, and company size are major challenges in implementing AI in SMEs.

5. Suggestions and Recommendations for SMEs in Using AI Tools for Social Media

Based on the results of previous studies and academic papers, the use of artificial intelligence in business is very important, not only for large, but also for small and medium enterprises. Very often, especially in the case of small businesses, and even more often in the case of micro-businesses, we can encounter several barriers and problems when using AI tools. This is also the case when using artificial intelligence to manage social media.

According to Sarmiento (2020), social media is one of the main areas where marketers can boost both performance and efficiency by using AI. The study conducted by Popovic et al. (2018) shows that AI can help micro and small businesses create personalised advertising based on customer data.

Bhalerao et al. (2022) suggest that if SMEs do not adopt available technologies, they may lose their competitive position. The authors also explore issues related to the challenges and benefits of AI adoption in SMEs.

To facilitate the use of AI in social media management and support its integration, especially in micro and small business environments, we provide some recommendations in the form of specific AI-based tools that can be used by these businesses in practice:

- Circleboom Publish

Streamlines social media management across platforms and accounts. It provides a versatile post generator and can be integrated with OpenAI (Chat GPT). Using this tool simplifies content creation by providing AI-generated images and text that can be published to managed social media.

In addition, this tool is designed to efficiently schedule, design and publish posts, allowing users to seamlessly manage multiple social media accounts at once. It also allows users to create and design images, text and captions, and enhance posts with trending and relevant hashtags.

- Content Studio

Makes it easy to create Instagram captions, generate tweet ideas, inspirational quotes or content for entire posts. It also offers a variety of AI-generated images for individual social media posts, as well as a number of ready-made templates that can be used to create original posts.

Using AI, the tool can suggest relevant and popular hashtags for posts, make posts more visually appealing by analysing the tone of the text and adding appropriate emoticons, or create eye-catching images for your social posts by simply entering text descriptions.

- Cortex

Helps you publish optimised content. It also recommends when and how often to publish posts based on historical metrics. It also generates detailed competitive analysis and provides a dashboard with an interface that highlights posts and a publishing schedule. It also identifies the colours that appeal most to audiences when submitting one or more photos, helping you to make the best decision.

- Flick

Allows you to create social media content faster and at scale. It speeds up the process of brainstorming, writing and scheduling posts for marketing managers. It can also help generate original and engaging ideas based on a variety of topics. Other features include: scheduling, hashtag creation and campaign analysis.

- Heyday

This conversational AI social media tool interacts with users in real time. It allows you to have the highest quality interactions while improving the user experience.

- Lately

Allows you to extract context from a larger collection of content, which can then be used to create social posts that promote that content. Other features include social media project planning and management, and metrics analysis.

- Linkfluence

Allows you to monitor and analyse all managed social media channels. It also provides valuable insights that make it easier to understand social media audiences. It also measures the evolution of brand identity on social media before setting smart targets, and predicts and analyses customer trends.

- QuillBot

Allows you to summarise and paraphrase existing content into entirely new versions, which means it can help you create new content. Compatible with multiple web browsers and text editors. It preserves the original context when rewriting. At the same time, it can help to improve vocabulary, which also enriches individual posts.

- Socialbakers

This AI-driven social media management platform provides advanced audience insights, expanding the possibilities of using social networks for marketing and marketing communications. This tool also offers: advanced audience statistics, intelligent scheduling and optimal posting times or multi-channel social media account management.

- Wordstream

This tool allows you to improve the performance of your ads online, including social media. It helps evaluate PPC ads on social networks and provides data-driven recommendations. It is useful for businesses of all sizes, including those involved in online sales and marketing.

6. Conclusion

Artificial intelligence has penetrated, or is gradually penetrating, all industries, with a dramatic impact on their development and direction. In the field of marketing and marketing communications, it offers opportunities to streamline individual marketing activities - from planning to the implementation of strategic solutions. AI makes it easier, faster and more efficient to implement individual activities, increasing their applicability even in the environment of small and micro enterprises, which generally lack resources in terms of both human and financial resources, as well as experience in implementing marketing solutions.

The impact of AI on social media is also significant. AI is helping social media marketers create engaging content, schedule posts effectively, segment content, analyse campaigns and more. According to the 2020 Social Media Industry Benchmark Report (2020), success in social media is about much more than getting the most comments or likes: it's about increasing engagement and growing or maintaining the percentage of your audience that is engaged as you grow your audience. This is why it is essential to incorporate AI tools into social media management and use them to their full potential when communicating with your customers. Social media marketing is one of the key areas where marketers can improve both performance and efficiency through the use of artificial intelligence. AI extracts more value and engagement from every online conversation that takes place on social media channels.

The use of artificial intelligence in the environment of small and micro enterprises can therefore be a key element in the process of increasing their competitiveness and achieving their goals, without radically increasing expenditure on the services of advertising or communication agencies. With the help of AI tools, they will be able to carry out many of the activities for which they were previously unable. At the same time, the use of AI can help such businesses overcome other barriers associated with the use of social media or AI - indeed, several studies show the limited ability to use them in the environment of small and micro enterprises.

In this paper, in addition to these aspects, we have also highlighted the importance and relevance of using AI in marketing communications. We have presented the current scientific knowledge and the authors' views on this issue, as well as the results of empirical studies on the use of AI in business environments.

A particularly specific situation in this direction can be found in the environment of micro-enterprises in Slovakia. According to the survey conducted by Krajčovič (2023) at the end of last year, none of the business entities used artificial intelligence for marketing and marketing communication. Although, according to the results of the Eurostat (2021) survey, companies in Slovakia use AI systems the most of all V4 countries, these are mainly medium and large companies with a technological or technical focus.

The use of artificial intelligence in the process of social media management and social media marketing communication can ultimately also help to use these communication channels more efficiently. The benefit for small and micro businesses can therefore be an overall improvement in marketing communication activities. The importance and need for the use of artificial intelligence in this area is also demonstrated by the fact that AI for the social media market is predicted to grow to more than $2.1 billion by 2023 (Anandvardhan, 2021).

Acknowledgement

The article is a result of the scientific project APVV-22-0469 entitled "Roadmap of a digital platform providing AI (Artificial Intelligence) automation of decision-making processes in the field of communication strategy".

References

2020 Social Media Industry Benchmark Report. (2020). Retrieved March 4, 2022, from https://www.rivaliq.com/blog/social-media-industry-benchmark-report/#title-financial-services

Agnihotri, R. (2020). Social media, customer engagement, and sales organizations: A research agenda. Industrial Marketing Management, 90, 291–299. https://doi.org/10.1016/j.indmarman.2020.07.017

Anandvardhan. (2021). Role of Artificial Intelligence in Social Media Marketing. International Journal of Business Analytics & Intelligence, 9(1 & 2), 34–40.

Argan, M., Dinc, H., Kaya, S., & Argan, M. T. (2022). Artificial Intelligence (AI) in Advertising: Understanding and Schematizing the Behaviors of Social Media Users. ADCAIJ: Advances in Distributed Computing and Artificial Intelligence Journal Regular Issue, 11(3), 331-348

Bhalerao, K., Kumar, A., Kumar, A., & Pujari, P. (2022). A study of barriers and benefits of artificial intelligence adoption in small and medium enterprise. Academy of Marketing Studies Journal, 26, 1-6.

Budiyanto, A., Pamungkas, I. B., & Praditya, A. (2022). Pengaruh Media Sosial Terhadap Minat Beli dan Keputusan Pembelian Konsumen; Analisis Bibliometrik. Jurnal Ekonomi dan Manajemen, 8(2), 133–142.

Bunte, et al. (2021). A study of barriers and benefits of artificial intelligence adoption in small and medium enterprise. Academy of Marketing Studies Journal, 26(1), 1-6.

Castillo, C., Mendoza, M., & Poblete, B. (2013). Predicting information credibility in time-sensitive social media. Internet Research, 23(5), 587-617. DOI:10.1108/IntR-05-2012-0095

Chintalapati, S., & Pandey, S. K. (2022). Artificial intelligence in marketing: A systematic literature review. International Journal of Market Research, 64(1), 38–68. https://doi.org/10.1177/14707853211018428

Chui, M., et al. (2018, November 28). Applying artificial intelligence for social good. Retrieved from https://www.mckinsey.com/featured-insights/artificial-intelligence/applying-artificial-intelligence-for-social-good

Coca-Cola Turns to Facebook Messenger for Chatbot Customer Service. (n.d.). Chatbots Magazine. https://chatbotsmagazine.com/coca-cola-turns-to-facebook-messenger-for-chatbot-customer-service-30b365d073c0

Columbus, L. (2020). Six Areas Where AI Is Improving Customer Experiences. Forbes. Retrieved March 27, 2022, from https://www.forbes.com/sites/louiscolumbus/2020/04/29/six-areas-where-ai-is-improving-customer-experiences/?sh=3b939103f5bc

Davidson, T., Warmsley, D., Macy, M., & Weber, I. (2017). Automated hate speech detection and the problem of offensive language. In Proceedings of the 11th International AAAI Conference on Web and Social Media (ICWSM '17), Vol. 17 (pp. 512–515).

Enehano. (2023, April 20). Slovensko vo využívaní umelej inteligencie predbehlo susedov. Technológie však nemôžu fungovať bez ľudí. https://www.enehano.sk/blog/napisali-o-nas-slovensko-vo-vyuzivani-umelej-inteligencie-predbehlo-susedov-technologie-vsak-nemozu-fungovat-bez-ludi

European Commission. (2020). European Enterprise Survey on the Use of Technologies Based on Artificial Intelligence. https://www.ipsos.com/sites/default/files/ct/publication/documents/2020-09/european-enterprise-survey-and-ai-executive-summary.pdf

Eurostat. (2021, April 13). Artificial intelligence in EU enterprises. Retrieved from https://ec.europa.eu/eurostat/web/products-eurostat-news/-/ddn-20210413-1?redirect=%2Feurostat%2Fhome%3F

Gao, J., Bi, W., Liu, X., Li, J., & Shi, S. (2019). Generating multiple diverse responses for short-text conversation. In Proceedings of the AAAI Conference on Artificial Intelligence (pp. 6383-6390).

Gartner Survey Shows 37 Percent of Organizations have Implemented AI in Some Form. (n.d.). Retrieved April 25, 2021, from https://www.gartner.com/en/ newsroom/press-releases/2019-01-21-gartner-sur¬vey-shows-37-percent-of-organizations-have

Gartner. (2019, January 21). Gartner Survey of More Than 3,000 CIOs Reveals That Enterprises Are Entering the Third Era of IT. Retrieved from https://www.gartner.com/en/newsroom/press-releases/2019-01-21-gartner-survey-shows-37-percent-of-organizations-have

Go, A., Huang, L., Bhayani, R., & Huang, L. (2009). Twitter sentiment classification using distant supervision. CS224N Project Report, Stanford.

Goodfellow, I., Bengio, Y., Courville, A., & Bengio, Y. (2016). Deep Learning. MIT Press Cambridge.

How Airbnb Uses AI and Big Data. (n.d.). Becoming Human. https://becominghuman.ai/how-airbnb-uses-ai-and-big-data-40e959f57e77

How Amazon Uses AI for Customer Service. (n.d.). Digiday. https://digiday.com/marketing/amazon-turning-ai-chatbots-customer-service/

How Facebook Uses Artificial Intelligence. (n.d.). Algorithmia Blog. https://algorithmia.com/blog/how-facebook-uses-artificial-intelligence

How Nestlé Uses AI for Social Media Monitoring. (n.d.). IDG Connect. https://www.idgconnect.com/interviews/1506117/nestl%C3%A9-ai-monitoring-its-social-media-mentions

How Netflix Uses AI to Predict Your Next Binge-Worthy Show. (n.d.). OpenAI Blog. https://blog.openai.com/how-netflix-uses-ai-to-predict-your-next-binge-worthy-show/

How Sephora's Chatbot is Making Personalization Easier for Customers. (n.d.). PYMNTS.com. https://www.pymnts.com/news/retail/2019/sephora-personalization-chatbot-ai-messaging-beauty/

How Starbucks Uses Artificial Intelligence for Customer Engagement. (n.d.). Relevance. https://www.relevance.com/how-starbucks-uses-artificial-intelligence-ai-machine-learning-for-customer-engagement/

Huang, M.-H., & Rust, R. T. (2021). Engaged to a robot? The role of AI in service. Journal of Service Research, 24(1), 30–41. https://doi.org/10.1177/1094670520902266

Kaput, M. (2021). 9 AI Tools to Streamline Your Social Media Strategy. Retrieved March 27, 2022, from https://blog.hubspot.com/marketing/ai-social-media-tools

Kaput, M. (2022). What Is Artificial Intelligence for Social Media? Marketing AI Institute. Retrieved March 27, 2022, from https://www.marketingaiinstitute.com/blog/what-is-artificial-intelligence-for-social-media

Khokhar, P. (2019). Evolution of artificial intelligence in marketing, comparison with traditional marketing. Our Heritage, 67(5), 375–389.

Kietzmann, J., Paschen, J., & Treen, E. (2018). Artificial intelligence in advertising: How marketers can leverage artificial intelligence along the consumer journey. Journal of Advertising Research, 58(3), 263-267.

Krajčovič, P. (2024). The use of artificial intelligence in the marketing communications of micro-enterprises. In T. Klieštik (Ed.), Globalization and its socio-economic consequences: 23rd international scientific conference (pp. xx-xx). Žilina: Žilinská univerzita v Žiline. (in press)

New Report Shows Marketers Lack the Education, Training to Effectively Adopt Artificial Intelligence. (n.d.). Retrieved April 23, 2021, from https:// www.marketingaiinstitute.com/blog/2021-state-o f-marketing-ai-report-launch

Next Move Strategy Consulting. (2023). Artificial intelligence: Global opportunity analysis and industry forecast 2022-2023. Retrieved from https://www.nextmsc.com/report/artificial-intelligence-market

Pariser, E. (2011). The Filter Bubble: What the Internet is Hiding from You. Penguin.

Popovic, A., Hackney, R., & Tassabehji, R. (2018). The Impact of Artificial Intelligence in Marketing. Journal of Business Research, 98(2), 261-276.

Quadros, M. (2020, September). Artificial intelligence in social media marketing. Retrieved from https://www.socialbakers.com/blog/ai-in-social-media

Resqi, M. (2022). Marketing Communications: A Bibliometric Study In The Use Of Technology And Social Media For Marketing [Komunikasi Pemasaran: Studi Bibliometrik Dalam Penggunaan Teknologi Dan Media Sosial Untuk Pemasaran]. Volume 3, (October), 4194–4203.

Rodgers, S. (2021). Themed issue introduction: Promises and perils of artificial intelligence and advertising. Journal of Advertising, 50(1), 1–10.

Sadiku, M. N. O., Ashaolu, T. J., Ajayi-Majebi, A., & Musa, S. M. (2021). Artificial Intelligence in Social Media. International Journal of Scientific Advances, 2(1), 2708-7972.

Sarmiento, H. (2020, May). How artificial intelligence can benefit the social media user. Clyste. https://medium.com/clyste/how-artificial-intelligence-can-benefit-the-social-media-user-aeaefd24e0a7

Thormundsson, B. (2023, October 26). Artificial Intelligence (AI) market size/revenue comparisons 2018-2030. Retrieved from https://www.statista.com/statistics/941835/artificial-intelligence-market-size-revenue-comparisons/

Peter Krajčovič

Tractica Research Report. (2020). Artificial Intelligence for Telecommunications Applications. https://omdia.tech.informa.com/topic-pages/artificial-intelligence

Social Media Narratives: Addressing Extremism in Middle Age (SMIDGE)

Jason Lee, Sara Wilford, Raouf Hamzaoui and Nitika Bhalla
De Montfort University, Leicester, UK

jason.lee@dmu.ac.uk
sara@dmu.ac.uk
rhamzaoui@dmu.ac.uk
nitika.bhalla@dmu.ac.uk

Abstract: This paper examines the ongoing work of a three-year Horizon Europe project titled 'Social Media Narratives: Addressing Extremism in Middle Age' (SMIDGE). The project will cover aspects of the following areas: ethical dimensions, review of the literature (including conspiracy theories, misinformation and extremism online), co-designing of quantitative surveys, stakeholder engagement through qualitative focus groups, national nuances, changing technological issues, platform use and regulations. We take this analysis as a case study template that we believe will be useful to researchers in this field and potentially policy makers, especially from a multidisciplinary and transnational perspective. The project is split into four phases; Phase 1 - Understanding the landscape, profiling content and users, Phase 2 - Understanding the 'attractiveness' of the narrative, Phase 3 - Creating counter narratives and Phase 4 - Guidelines and policy briefs: spreading the word. We will unpack the challenges and opportunities of this approach for social media analysis and its real-world impact on democracy. Once the initial phase is completed in year one, we will start to construct counter-narratives to combat extremism in this context. This will take the form of creating counter videos and a documentary, as well as producing a series of podcasts and webinars. Furthermore, the outputs of the empirical research will inform and feed into the development of educational and training materials, guidelines and recommendations, as well as policy briefs that can be useful to policy makers, researchers, security professionals, journalists and beyond. The outputs from the SMIDGE project will provide evidence-based content, tools and resources that will directly help to counter extremist narratives from multiple perspectives. This will enable a greater understanding of the specificities and characteristics of those in the middle-age category, specifically those aged 45-65 years, and their vulnerability to extremism online.

Key words: Social media, Middle-age, Extremism, Counter narratives, Misinformation

1. Introduction

Extremist narratives have found an ever-expanding outlet online, with many willing participants who both produce and spread misinformation and conspiracy theories. Effective countermeasures need to be multi-level, multidisciplinary, and multi-sector. This growing phenomenon is having a direct impact on perceptions of democratic institutions (Christodoulou and Iordanou, 2021), trust in science and democracy, and can lead to calls for direct action (Jan 6th, 2021, incursion in USA) to overthrow or disrupt democratically elected governments. In Europe, misinformation about Covid-19 has created demands for ever stricter controls on the movement of people and protests against restrictions and vaccines. Such protests have also attracted members of a wide range of extremist and conspiracy theory groups. Extreme, often authoritarian and populist political discourse is becoming ever more mainstream (Lee, 2018). Politicians, often middle-aged, vie to gain media attention and social media support by acknowledging and often amplifying the misleading messages inherent in the content whereby 'the underlying force of extremism seems best understood as the 'quest for personal significance'' (Cichocka et al., 2023). Often seen as 'strong leaders' and 'anti-woke', such politicians use extreme and fear-inducing messaging to portray themselves as saviours of the masses from 'those who would wish to do you harm'. In understanding those who fall victim to fake news and misinformation and extremism, it has been recognised that it is no longer just a 'youth problem' (Pauwels, 2021), and those who may be at risk of being drawn into extremist content are also likely to be older adults. These people may take different routes to extremism than younger people, hence the focus of our work.

The middle-aged are invisible, and this is reflected both in the lack of research, but also in the focus on youth that is evident across society. For example, young people have long been the target and focus of much of mainstream media and commerce (Aas, 2006; Brandtzæg, 2012; Buckingham, 2007; Hoadley et al., 2010; Skarpa and Garoufallou, 2021), a trend that has only accelerated since the advent of the internet. The evidence of this is everywhere, from the exclusive use of young people to promote and market consumer goods, to the exclusion of older people in advertising (Eisend, 2022). It is rare to see older people advertising anything that is not directly targeted to them (like elder care services, retirement homes, hearing aids, etc.). Despite the financial weight of middle-aged people, products are not generally marketed to them (Leonard, 2014; Prabhaker, 2000; Slootweg and Rowson, 2018), suggesting that 'in the visual market, it is as if getting older means being moved to the margins of visibility' (Fernandez-Ardevol and Grenier, 2022). This short-sighted approach means that a whole swathe of people is excluded or sidelined.

The problems with sidelining or ignoring certain demographic groups are manifold. When people feel excluded, they may consider that they are no longer important or relevant in society, which, in turn, makes the fringes appear more welcoming. The use of social media and other forms of online community building provides opportunities for people to feel useful, to feel wanted and valued, and to get involved, as 'older adults often prioritise interpersonal goals over accuracy, they primarily use technology to connect with others, rather than to gain new information' (Sims et al., 2017). While these groups are often benign and offer support and encouragement in very positive ways, they sometimes work to feed the feeling of exclusion, offer targets to blame, such as asylum seekers and climate protestors, and distract from the real causes of their distress, which may lead them to 'circulate fake news with specific social goals in mind' (Brashier and Schacter, 2020 p. 217). These goals can be for political or business power, and such misinformation may not only reinforce preconceived prejudices and biases but may prove useful in providing justification for ideological policy making.

Those in middle-age are not the 'digital natives' of later generations and are still relying on TV and traditional routes of information such as newspapers. They distrust mainstream sources of information (Reich, 2021) and at the same time are engaging with online media. This means that while they are potential targets and victims of online misinformation and conspiracy theories, they lack the tools and skills to identify the differences between truth and misinformation (Jiang, 2016). This group of adults at risk of extremism are often self-taught, use their own lived experiences to make judgements about the validity of sources, and may have been involved in extremist activities in their youth (Lee, 2018). They also may perceive themselves as relatively tech and life-savvy, with no need to be educated further. For example, a 2021 study of older men in Malta and their engagement with the University of The Third Age stated that 'there exists no evidence that older men find it 'uncool' to be associated with lifelong learning, *as is the case in middle-age…*', (Formosa, 2022, emphasis added). The study provides insight into older, retired men's engagement with learning, but provides no further discussion about the middle-aged men who consider learning to be 'uncool'.

Attempts by authorities to do so may further fuel distrust and disengagement or be seen as evidence of attempts at manipulation. Those who are susceptible to cults and conspiracy theories, such as QAnon, Anti-Vax, New World Order and so on, are generally more distrustful and cynical (Hughes and Machan, 2021) and may experience 'high individual narcissism but low self-esteem' (Cichocka et al., 2016), alongside low educational achievement (van Prooijen, 2017), although we posit that within the 45-65 age group there is also a subset of well-educated people with decision or policy-making power. This means that people in this age group do not always adhere to the current understanding about those who are perceived to be vulnerable to extremism. These factors make this demographic particularly hard to reach, under-researched, and their specific characteristics, drivers and rationale rarely explored.

Education and awareness raising initiatives are usually targeted at young people and so are often not relatable to those in middle-age (Pauwels, 2021 p. 10). Further, training and education resources are not generally made available to older people, even if they were inclined to engage with them. The Ofcom media literacy initiatives library identifies 123 initiatives for media literacy education, tools and other resources of which only three are specifically aimed at older people, and 29 at the general public (Ofcom, 2023). The lack of dedicated learning resources for a huge section of society is undoubtedly contributing to the relatively poor digital literacy among middle-aged and older adults (van Deursen and van Dijk, 2014). While it is understandable that many of the key resources are dedicated to educating the young, as they need to navigate the future, it is potentially hugely damaging for a significant proportion of highly influential members of society to be left largely unaware of and vulnerable to misinformation, which can have a significant impact if it is then used as justification for key decision-making.

An example of this is the 15-minute city concept devised by Professor Carlos Moreno and which won the OBEL award in 2021 (OBEL, 2021). The idea behind the 15-minute city is that cities should be re-designed, so that access to daily needs (housing, work, food, health, education, culture, and leisure) is within the distance of a 15-minute walk or bike ride. This greatly reduces car traffic and CO2 emissions and increases the health and well-being of residents (Moreno et al., 2021). However, the idea was seized upon as a threat to modern life and a restriction on freedom (Morris and Ullmann, 2023; Zuidijk and Rudgard, 2023). Even though the idea was misrepresented, the resulting furore led to UK government policy being made on the basis of a conspiracy theory (Walker, 2024).

This research goes beyond the current state of the art by focusing on a specific group of under-researched individuals. These individuals play significant roles in proliferating misinformation and conspiracy theories. They are also becoming increasingly extreme in their online rhetoric and are beginning to directly question democratic values, preferring an authoritarian and often violent solution to achieve their goals. This research explores this multifaceted target group through an intersectional lens, i.e., delving into the interactions between this age group, plus other categories of identity, in particular the gender differences, and power positioning in social hierarchies, which go beyond the essentialist perception of this group from the outside.

SMIDGE will develop robust and research-informed content and learning resources that can be integrated into training for journalists, police and security agencies; provide counter narratives to foster reflexivity in middle-aged people who are currently excluded from educational initiatives and may not engage with the traditional approaches (Pauwels, 2021); and develop webinars and provide guidelines and recommendations for policymakers and other professionals. A Responsible Research and Innovation (RRI) approach will include co-creation involvement of all relevant stakeholders (police and training authorities, journalists, civil society organisations, policy makers, general public). This will ensure a human-centred and ethical development of counter narratives to extremist online content.

Online social media sites provide a space where extremist views are shared and discussed and may result in negative behaviour in the physical world. For example, in 2019, an extremist in Christchurch, New Zealand, entered two mosques and shot and killed fifty-one people. Prior to the attack, he had announced his intentions on the imageboard 8Chan, which has now closed down. On 8Chan, users were anonymous, and the image-board fostered an environment where extreme violence, hate, racism, homophobia and misogyny were rampant. Since the board was shut down in 2019 (and reborn for a brief moment under the name 8kun), the extremism that grew out of 4Chan and 8Chan/8kun has become increasingly woven into more mainstream social media platforms, making these ideas accessible to a much larger audience. Today, media users who have never been on 4Chan or other message boards can still engage with extremist content, but they often do so as part of their everyday media practices on mainstream social media platforms such as Facebook, YouTube, TikTok and X (formerly Twitter). The embedding of extremist material into mainstream platforms means that countering such material and viewpoints may in some ways be easier due to the relatively accessible nature of the mainstream sites. However, the sheer size, scope and reach of these platforms may also make it difficult to capture (Moor, 1997).

SMIDGE aims to achieve a truly in-depth understanding of the major factors contributing to the present rise of extremist narratives and their influence on mainstream worldviews, discourses and policies across Europe. We will particularly focus on those between the ages of 45 and 65, who are an under-researched group, but who are also susceptible to being drawn into extremist content, and may either be disenfranchised on the one hand, or in positions of power on the other. The work will go beyond discipline-specific excellence, to draw on perspectives and expertise across and between disciplines, including anthropology, psychology, sociology, law, ethics, data science, computing, education, media studies, and security studies. SMIDGE aims to produce and disseminate alternative narratives in the form of counter-videos, memes and other micro-content and to promote reflexivity in the target stakeholders. However, to ensure that the content created is informed by an understanding of the characteristics and nature of extremism, SMIDGE will engage in a new and innovative approach to the production of counter-narratives to extremist material, drawing on previous work but not remaining within it. For the first time, using empirical work, SMIDGE will produce counter-content, educational tools and policy recommendations, which will promote first-and second-order reflexivity in both those vulnerable to extremist material and those tasked to address the issues.

A further tightening of focus to middle-aged people and involving them in a co-creative approach to creating the counter-content is a new, RRI-based methodological approach to counter-extremism. The creation of the content will be politically neutral, and the co-creation activities will provide guidance to avoid bias, which is one of the charges made against mainstream media (Reich, 2021). By also targeting key professional stakeholder groups (journalists, policing and security professionals, policymakers, educators, researchers), SMIDGE will also provide new insights, tools and reflexive approaches to understanding and addressing online extremism in those of middle-age.

SMIDGE will provide a new approach to tackling misinformation and extremism in media, by using the tools, format and approach used by those creating the extremist content to inform our own creations (part of our work therefore includes understanding the complex characteristics that make such videos attractive). This approach means that there will be a greater likelihood that such messaging would be viewed positively by the target group.

We are carrying out the following activities and a brief explanation is given here: i) exposure to alternative messaging, promotes reflection and greater awareness and exposure to targeted counter-narratives, and this will encourage those in middle-age who are vulnerable to extreme messaging, to re-consider critically the type of media they view; ii) produce educational resources and training including a MOOC (massive open online course), webinars, and tools for security professionals, journalists and educators to also elicit reflexivity in their approaches and understanding, and therefore become better able to counter online extremism risk in those aged 45-65; iii) develop guidelines and recommendations and policy briefs for decision-makers, to provide evidence-based solutions as part of a toolkit to address online extremism.

These resources will be disseminated through engagement with a wide range of stakeholder networks, including RAN (Radicalisation Awareness Network), European Foundation for Democracy and ISD (Institute for Strategic Dialogue), Age Platform Europe, UK Police, AGICOM, European Press Association, Foundation Porticus, Danish Centre for Prevention of Extremism, the Italian Rete Nazionale per il Contrasto ai Discorsi e ai Fenomeni d'Odio, the Council of Europe supported No Hate Speech Campaign, and the tools developed will aid decision-makers to make effective policy to address the grooming process that leads people to online extremism.

A social network and sentiment analysis will be undertaken to inform the creation and distribution of the media. SMIDGE advances the state of the art by providing counter-narrative media and guidelines to provide tools for governments to push back on misinformation and extremism online, while at the same time eliciting first- and second-order reflexivity to gain greater insight and awareness. To achieve its key goal, addressing the impact of these narratives on mainstream worldviews and limiting their impacts, the SMIDGE project will take an RRI approach to the work and will draw on the various sources of the RRI discourse i.e European Commission, 2012; (Stilgoe et al., 2013; Von Schomberg, 2011). It is acknowledged that there are ongoing debates around RRI (Owen et al., 2012), but we posit that this approach provides an open and pluralist perspective that aims to align science, research and innovation with a view to strengthening societal influence and thereby fostering scientific excellence. The concept of RRI as meta-responsibility (Stahl et al., 2017) provides the theoretical anchor point for our approach. The SMIDGE approach aims to elicit both first-order and second-order reflexivity.

First-order reflexivity enables the gathering, interpretation, critique and understanding of an issue or topic. First-order reflexivity is, in part, the reason why some people may be drawn into misinformation online. Misinformation or extremist material may be so convincing that the initial reaction is that; 1. the material is to be taken seriously; 2. an interpretation is made that the claims being made are true (this may be due, in part, to having prior beliefs and experiences confirmed, such as the belief that the Government cannot be trusted to tell the truth), which then convinces the viewer that; 3. the videos or content are providing the truth, leading to ; 4. a belief that the videos reflect reality. This way of thinking may then lead to a desire to act in some way, to either raise others' awareness (sharing, commenting, etc.) or even to direct action, such as protesting and possibly acts of violence.

When second-order reflexivity is employed, each interaction and reflection is re-considered through an acknowledgement of the context in which it sits and is a key part of the RRI process (Gianni et al., 2019). Further, integrating a gender and intersectional perspective into this frame enables the gathering, interpretation, critique and understanding of the explored topics, by taking into consideration how the interaction between identity characteristics shape individual experiences, representations and epistemologies, as well as how structures and discourses impact on these individuals in a 'qualitatively different way' (Crenshaw, 1991). Through understanding the interactions of responses and characteristics, cultural influences and personal experience, SMIDGE will provide stakeholders with the tools to elicit a greater understanding of the drivers and triggers for being vulnerable to misinformation with a focus on those in middle-age. 1. With regard to the content being viewed, second-order reflexivity provides a momentary pause to be taken before deep diving into extremist/conspiracy theory material. 2. Within training and educational tools such as a MOOC for journalists, it raises awareness of the specific drivers, factors and contexts that lead people down the path towards extremism, and second order reflexivity through lateral reading, aids journalists to more effectively contextualise, understand and report on the issues of misinformation and online extremism. 3. Understanding one's own cultural drivers, as well as understanding personal motivations can go a long way towards enabling critical and reflexive thinking.

2. Case Study

The SMIDGE project is divided into four phases.

Phase 1 - Understanding the landscape, profiling content and users

Phase 1 includes a comprehensive horizon scanning and theoretical analysis of the scope, extent and nature of online extremist material. SMIDGE takes a multi-disciplinary approach, and so the examination takes a broad view to enable greater understanding of the context in which extremism online has permeated society, threatening democratic institutions and trust. The first of two literature reviews covers social, political, philosophical, psychological, technical and legal developments from 2016 (Cambridge Analytica scandal, the rise of Trump, and Brexit vote). They include specific analysis of the literature regarding technology use and acceptance by those in middle-age (45-65 years) and their involvement in social media and the online extremist narrative. In addition, we analyse the popular conspiracy and fake news content published online during this period. We review and analyse the technologies used by individuals engaging with this content. This work provides the starting points and sets the parameters for the quantitative analysis work, which includes a social network analysis and a textual analysis of the reach and engagement with extremist material on YouTube, Twitter and Telegram. Phase 1 also includes a qualitative study through data scraping of content and textual analysis of social media extremist material. Finally, Phase 1 will collate and classify characteristics of existing videos and content to create a searchable database and an open data portal. This will help to identify key factors associated with online extremist material.

Phase 2 - Understanding the 'attractiveness' of the narrative

Phase 2 of the project involves key empirical data collection, and will include an online survey, focus groups and interviews with the 45-65 age group. We will develop, pilot-test and conduct an online survey to understand attitudes, beliefs, and the ability to critically evaluate extremist media. The survey development will be informed by the literature review in Phase 1. Five hundred participants will be drawn from the community, aiming to reach a diverse sample of middle-aged individuals. This will consider variables such as nationality, education, employment, occupation, as well as their intersections, which the literature review has identified as influential to individuals' beliefs. Participants will be recruited according to demographic requirements. None of the participants will be selected based on their known extreme political or personal views. On the contrary, SMIDGE aims to provide targeted counter narratives that will facilitate greater reflection on this content, thereby discouraging people from starting this journey.

Participants will be drawn from organisations such as Age Network and other groups or networks that offer services or advice for older working people, regardless of their political or societal viewpoint. In addition to the survey and drawing on early findings, two focus groups in each of the six focus countries will be carried out. These focus groups will represent the diverse countries of origin of the partners (Denmark, UK, Greece/Cyprus, Kosovo, Italy, Belgium) and reflect the potential for diverse opinions across different areas of Europe. The two groups are 'citizens/users' and 'journalists/bloggers/content creators'. We will examine the features participants find attractive and convincing in social media, as well as what helps shape attitudes and propensity to engage with extremist material. At the focus groups, we will invite the participants to help us to identify those key characteristics that make such content attractive. This work will provide key indicators for understanding what attracts people to online extremism. As noted, much work has been done in this area, particularly focusing on young people (Petersen and Peters, 2020). However, this study will be the first of its kind to address this particularly under-researched demographic.

Phase 3 - Creating the counter narratives

Phase 3 of the project involves the creation of counter narratives and content specifically designed for the 45-65 age group. The understanding of the landscape will be informed by the initial literature review. It will be kept current and relevant through the second horizon scanning exercise and the creation and continuation of the database. The work undertaken will provide demographic specific insights and psychological understanding, including those uncovered during the co-creation exercise, to provide targeted and specific approaches to the creation of counter videos and micro-content. The second set of focus groups in the final year, will involve participants engaging with the created media, to provide their insights and observations through the process of watching while talking, thereby further engaging participants in the co-creation approach and eliciting second-order reflexivity. This time, their insights will directly inform revisions to content. In the case of videos, this may include editing or clarification in the form of subtitled additions or notes. One task will focus on using this content to create training materials and resources for journalists, security trainers and others who are directly trying to address the problems of misinformation and online extremism. These materials will be delivered as a set of resources for educational and other organisations, and a MOOC to enable broader engagement with online counter-extremism materials and training.

Phase 4 - Guidelines and policy briefs: spreading the word

Drawing on the previous three phases, guidelines and recommendations for policy and decision-makers will be produced. First, the requirements for guidelines (Wilford, 2019) will be identified. This will be informed by the RRI requirements for guidelines tool developed by DMU in the GREAT project GA n°321480, which has also been used in the development of guidelines for Universal Design for Learning (UDL), thereby further disseminating EU funded work. This approach will enable the guidelines, recommendations and policy briefs being developed to be tailored and targeted towards the stakeholders, and will be formatted and developed with the key recipients.

3. Conclusion

Middle-aged people are frequently influential decision makers, yet have often remained invisible in research, and can be vulnerable to online extremist narratives which SMIDGE is aiming to address. With the advancing spread of conspiracy theories, some of which now inform policy decisions, are influenced by disinformation and extremist narratives online. The SMIDGE project will analyse and address extremist discourse and narratives across Europe through social network analysis, textual, and content analysis. The key insights from the empirical research, such as online surveys and focus groups, probe the psychological, national, demographic and intersectional aspects in Europe and the UK. A broad range of stakeholder engagement activities feed into our co-production of counter-narratives, a documentary, plus guidelines and training resources. Finally, SMIDGE will promote reflexivity and design tools for researchers, policy makers, journalists and security professionals.

Acknowledgements

Grant Agreement Number 101095290. Funded by the European Union. Views and opinions expressed are however those of the author(s) only and do not necessarily reflect those of the European Union or European Research Executive Agency (REA). Neither the European Union nor the granting authority can be held responsible for them

The UK participant in Horizon Europe Project SMIDGE is supported by UKRI grant number 10056282 (De Montfort University).

Fact sheet https://cordis.europa.eu/project/id/101095290

Project website: https://www.smidgeproject.eu

References

Aas, K., 2006. 'The body does not lie': Identity, risk and trust in technoculture. *Crime, Media, Culture: An International Journal*, 2(2), 143–158. https://doi.org/10.1177/1741659006065401

Brandtzæg, P.B., 2012. Social Networking Sites: Their Users and Social Implications — A Longitudinal Study. *Journal of Computer-Mediated Communication*, 17, 467–488. https://doi.org/10.1111/j.1083-6101.2012.01580.x

Brashier, N.M., Schacter, D.L., 2020. Aging in an Era of Fake News. *Current Directions in Psychological Science*, 29, 316–323. https://doi.org/10.1177/0963721420915872

Buckingham, D., 2007. *Youth, Identity, and Digital Media*. The MIT Press, Cambridge, MA.

Christodoulou, E., Iordanou, K., 2021. Democracy Under Attack: Challenges of Addressing Ethical Issues of AI and Big Data for More Democratic Digital Media and Societies. *Frontiers in Political Science,* 3.

Cichocka, A., Marchlewska, M., de Zavala, A. G, 2016. Does Self-Love or Self-Hate Predict Conspiracy Beliefs? Narcissism, Self-Esteem, and the Endorsement of Conspiracy Theories. *Social Psychological and Personality Science,* 7, 157–166. https://doi.org/10.1177/1948550615616170

Crenshaw, K., 1991. Mapping the Margins: Intersectionality, Identity Politics, and Violence against Women of Color. *Stanford Law Review,* 43, 1241–1299. https://doi.org/10.2307/1229039

Eisend, M., 2022. Older People in Advertising. *Journal of Advertising*, 51, 308–322. https://doi.org/10.1080/00913367.2022.2027300

Fernandez-Ardevol, M., Grenier, L., 2022. Exploring data ageism: What good data can('t) tell us about the digital practices of older people? *New Media & Society*, 0(0). https://doi.org/10.1177/14614448221127261

Gianni, R., Pearson, J., Reber, B. (eds), 2019. *Responsible Research and Innovation: From Concepts to Practices*, Routledge, London.

Formosa, M., 2022. From invisibility to inclusion: Opening the doors for older men at the University of the Third Age in Malta. *Gerontology & Geriatrics Education*, 43, 443–455. https://doi.org/10.1080/02701960.2021pa.1913413

Hoadley, C.M., Xu, H., Lee, J.J., Rosson, M.B., 2010. Privacy as information access and illusory control: The case of the Facebook News Feed privacy outcry. *Electronic Commerce Research and Applications*, 9, 50–60. https://doi.org/10.1016/j.elerap.2009.05.001

Hughes, S., Machan, L., 2021. It's a conspiracy: Covid-19 conspiracies link to psychopathy, Machiavellianism and collective narcissism. *Personality and Individual Differences,* 171, 110559. https://doi.org/10.1016/j.paid.2020.110559

Jiang, M., Tsai, H.Y.S., Cotten, S.R., Rifon, N.J., LaRose, R. and Alhabash, S., 2016. Generational differences in online safety perceptions, knowledge, and practices. *Educational Gerontology*, 42(9), 621-634.

Lee, J., 2018. *Nazism and Neo-Nazism in Film and Media*. Amsterdam University Press, Amsterdam.

Leonard, J., 2014. Gen X and Social Media: Stuck in the Middle. *Business Community*. https://www.business2community.com/social-media-articles/gen-x-social-media-stuck-middle-0939476 (accessed 22.1.24).

Moor, J. 1997. Towards a theory of privacy in the information age. *Computers and Society*, 27-32.

Moreno, C., Allam, Z., Chabaud, D., Gall, C., Pratlong, F., 2021. Introducing the "15-Minute City": Sustainability, Resilience and Place Identity in Future Post-Pandemic Cities. *Smart Cities*, 4, 93–111. https://doi.org/10.3390/smartcities4010006.

Morris, S., Ullmann, J., 2023. What is a 15-minute city? How the urban-planning idea is tangled in conspiracy Evening Standard [WWW Document]. URL https://www.standard.co.uk/news/uk/15-minute-city-urban-planning idea-conspiracy-theory-misinformation-b1062266.html (accessed 1.25.24).

OBEL, 2021. 2021 Winner: The 15-minute city. OBEL AWARD. URL https://obelaward.org/2021-winner-the-15 minute-city/ (accessed 1.25.24).

Ofcom, 2023. Media literacy initiatives library. Ofcom. https://www.ofcom.org.uk/research-and-data/media-literacy-research/approach/evaluate/toolkit/initiatives-library (accessed 10.03.24).

Owen, R., Macnaghten, P., Stilgoe, J., 2012. Responsible research and innovation: From science in society to science for society, with society. *Science and Public Policy*, 39, 751-760. https://doi.org/10.1093/scipol/scs093

Pauwels, A., 2021. Contemporary manifestations of violent right-wing extremism in the EU: An overview of P/CVE practices. Luxembourg: Publications Office of the European Union.

Petersen, K.S., Peters, R. L. A, 2020. Desk research: Mapping knowledge on prevention of extremism online amongst children and young people. (Original title: Desk research: Kortlægning af viden om forebyggelse af ekstremisme online blandt børn og unge). Nationalt Center for Forebyggelse af Ekstremisme.

Prabhaker, P.R., 2000. Who owns the online consumer? *Journal of Consumer Marketing*, 17, 158–171. https://doi.org/10.1108/07363760010317213.

Reich, R., 2021. What's really wrong with the mainstream media. *The Guardian*, 9 December *What's really wrong with the mainstream media | Robert Reich | The Guardian* (accessed 26.02.2024).

Sims, T., Reed, A.E., Carr, D.C., 2017. Information and Communication Technology Use Is Related to Higher Well-Being Among the Oldest-Old. *The Journals of Gerontology: Series B*, 72, 761–770. https://doi.org/10.1093/geronb/gbw130.

Skarpa, P.El., Garoufallou, E., 2021. Information seeking behavior and COVID-19 pandemic: A snapshot of young, middle aged and senior individuals in Greece. *International Journal of Medical Informatics*, 150, 104465. https://doi.org/10.1016/j.ijmedinf.2021.104465.

Slootweg, E., Rowson, B., 2018. My generation: A review of marketing strategies on different age groups. *Research in Hospitality Management*, 8, 85–92.

Stahl, B., Obach, M., Yaghmaei, E., Ikonen, V., Chatfield, K., Brem, A., 2017. The Responsible Research and Innovation (RRI) maturity model: Linking theory and practice. *Sustainability*, 9, 1036. https://doi.org/10.3390/su9061036.

Stilgoe, J., Owen, R., Macnaghten, P., 2013. Developing a framework for responsible innovation. *Research Policy*, 42, 1568–1580. https://doi.org/10.1016/j.respol.2013.05.008.

van Deursen, A.J., van Dijk, J.A., 2014. The digital divide shifts to differences in usage. *New Media & Society*, 16, 507–526. https://doi.org/10.1177/1461444813487959.

van Prooijen, J.-W., 2017. Why Education Predicts Decreased Belief in Conspiracy Theories. *Applied Cognitive Psychology*, 31, 50–58. https://doi.org/10.1002/acp.3301.

Von Schomberg, R. (ed.), 2011. Towards responsible research and innovation in the information and communication technologies and security technologies fields. Available at SSRN: https://ssrn.com/abstract=2436399.

Walker, P., 2024. Ministers prioritised driving in England partly due to conspiracy theories. The Guardian https://www.theguardian.com/uk-news/2024/jan/10/shift-from-15-minute-cities-in-england-partly-due-to-conspiracy-theories (accessed 11.03.24).

Wilford, S., 2018. First Line Steps in Requirements Identification for Guidelines Development in Responsible Research and Innovation (RRI). *Systemic Practice and Action Research*, 31, 539–556. https://doi.org/10.1007/s11213-018-9445-z.

Wilford, S.H. 2019. Responsible Research and Innovation: Using the Requirements Tool for Stakeholder Engagement in Developing a Universal Design for Learning Guidelines for Practice. *Sustainability*, 11, 2963.

Zuidijk, D., Rudgard, O., 2023. What Are 15-Minute Cities and Why Is Britain's Conservative Party Suddenly Talking About Them? *Bloomberg Law News*, 3 October.

Social Media as a Communication Strategy for Regional and Local Tourism: A Portuguese Case Study

Marlene Loureiro

University of Trás-os-Montes and Alto Douro, Portugal

mloureiro@utad.pt

Abstract: Investing in social media should be seen as a strategic asset in communicating and publicising tourism. In fact, more and more social media, especially social networks, are a winning bet for communicating and publicising tourist destinations. Based on these premises, this research aims to answer the following research question: "What is the importance of social media, especially social networks, as a local tourism communication strategy?". To answer this question, we analysed the communication of two local institutions: on the one hand, a local authority, a public institution; and, on the other hand, a local accommodation, a private institution, seeking to analyse how local authority policies use social media to communicate and publicise local tourism. To complement this, the opinion of the tourist public on the impact of social media on their choices was analysed. In this way, we sought to answer the following objectives: 1) to understand the importance of social media for communicating and publicising tourism; 2) to describe the main digital platforms used for communicating and publicising tourism; 3) to ascertain the importance of social media as a strategy for communicating and publicising tourism in Portugal. The data obtained showed that social networks are increasingly being used by institutions as a strategy for communicating and publicising tourism. On the other hand, they are also a source of advice and decisions when it comes to choosing a tourist destination. On this last point, the opinions shared on social networks and the role of influencers as determining factors in the final decision and choice are particularly important.

Keywords: Social media, Social networks, Communication, Strategy, Tourism

1. Introduction

Tourism is currently an activity that is completely "rooted in society" and in the world. As a human activity, tourism is one of the areas that has attracted the most interest and different perspectives (Almeida, 2003). Tourism is studied by various sciences and each has its own point of view on the concept. Generally speaking, tourism can be defined as all the lawful activities carried out by visitors as a result of travelling, the attractions and means that give rise to them, the facilities created to satisfy their needs and the phenomena and relationships that result from one or the other (Cunha, 2010). According to the same author, Cunha (2010), tourism has become one of the most dynamic activities in the world, not only economically but also culturally and socially.

In Portugal, the tourism sector is one of the fastest growing in recent years, having contributed significantly to the development of the territory, the growth of the economy and the valorisation of culture and traditions. According to the official website of Turismo de Portugal (2022), the tourism sector is a fundamental economic activity for generating wealth and employment in Portugal, given that in 2019 it accounted for 15.3% of GDP (Seguro, 2021a). However, in 2020 this figure fell to 8.0% (Seguro, 2021b), as a result of the arrival of the COVID-19 virus, which forced the temporary closure of various tourist services such as accommodation, catering, air transport, among others. Fortunately, in 2021, some of these restrictions were eased, which allowed some tourist activities to be more active. For this reason, in 2021 the tourism sector accounted for 10.1 per cent of national GDP, a significant increase on the previous year, but still far from the figure reached in 2019.

Bearing in mind the importance of tourism in Portugal and, therefore, the need to strategically plan communication to promote and publicise tourism, social media has increasingly emerged, especially after the Covid-19 pandemic, as a key strategy in promoting tourist destinations. This exploratory study therefore aims to demonstrate how social media has been used to promote local tourism in Portugal. In fact, regional and local tourism is booming in Portugal, and so we started with a case study in the city of Fafe, in the north of Portugal, as a way of exemplifying and portraying how social media has been used as a tool for publicising and promoting regional and local tourism.

2. Theoretical Framework - the Potential of Social Media in Tourism Promotion

Strategic communication planning for the promotion of tourist destinations aims to make them stand out from their competitors by promoting unique experiences, telling the stories of the people and the places, thus presenting their culture. In this way, it aims to captivate future visitors through difference, uniqueness, "personality" and hospitality. Therefore, the ultimate goal of tourism communication strategy will always be to influence or persuade the behaviour of potential tourists so that they visit and contribute revenue to the economic growth of the destination (Mendes and Teixeira, 2019).

In this sense, according to Blichfeldt (2017), tourist destinations are understood as places where tourists travel, at the centre of this concept lie commercial interests received in the form of revenue that tourism can generate for the destination through its ability to attract tourists who will spend money on the various products, services and experiences during their stay. Thus, according to Teruel and Viñals (2012), the strategic communication plan can serve local communities as a comprehensive tool for managing, planning and promoting tourist destinations, achieving the level of development desired by the community.

That said, the company/institution or tourist brand has the task of building loyalty or captivating tourists, influencing the decision-making process and making a lasting impression on the experiences they have had, with the aim of getting them to recommend and return. In view of this, resorting to more emotional strategies is likely to be more effective, since tourists seem to have some resistance to making choices based solely on rational elements. Therefore, according to Mendes and Teixeira (2019), the tourism communication of a destination should adopt rational argumentative elements, but also emotional arguments that stimulate sensations.

Strategic communication in the tourism context is primarily a question of identifying the many existing stakeholders and including all the relevant voices in the plan that is being communicated about a particular place, a particular destination or a particular subject (Blichfeldt, 2017).

On the other hand, the internet, which has given rise to a new space for communication, sociability, organisation and transactions, but also a new market for information and knowledge (Levy, 1999), has become a focus for the tourism sector, playing an increasingly important role in the strategic promotion of destinations. In this sense, tools such as a website and social networks are essential for developing an effective plan to publicise local recreational assets. The purpose of these tools is to provide visitors/users with a range of information that might make them want to visit the physical place they are seeing virtually. Following this line of thought, López et al. (2016) state that new communication technologies are a cross-cutting element in the evolution of tourism and have therefore become indispensable tools for the promotion and dissemination of tourist destinations.

The consumer is currently considered the protagonist of social media, since blogs, opinion forums, social networks (such as Facebook, Twitter, Instagram, etc.) enable direct and instantaneous communication, without geographical or time barriers, without intermediaries and without filters (Wichels, 2014). In this context, consumers/users become creators of multimedia content, giving a new dimension to public opinion, which encourages interactivity, sharing, hypertextuality, without hierarchical structures, without traditional gatekeepers (Wichels, 2014). Therefore, the consumer of tourism products or services should be seen as an agent integrated into a network of relationships, with the ability to transmit opinions and complaints.

What's more, with the help of the Internet, consumers/tourists have become "experts" on certain subjects or products through a simple Google search (for example). Following the same reasoning, Xiang and Gretzel (2010) state that due to the huge amount of information available, searching has become an increasingly dominant mode in travellers' use of the Internet. However, according to the same authors, with the huge amount of information available, the Internet becomes an important platform for the exchange of information between the consumer and industry suppliers (e.g. hotels and tourist attractions), intermediaries (e.g. travel agents), "controllers" (e.g. governments and administrative bodies), as well as many non-profit organisations, such as destination marketing organisations.

According to Wichels (2014), the internet has led to the "democratisation" of tourist information on networks such as Facebook and Instagram, since, for example, large hotel chains are now living in the same "space" as small hostels, something that would otherwise not be possible due to their limited marketing and communication budgets. Although this social media terrain is somewhat unstable, many authors and communication agencies recognise the advantages of good positioning on social media. In fact, it is the "utopia" of communication turned into reality, i.e. companies have at their disposal a network of consumers who adhere to advertising campaigns, promote and share products, making them go viral.

TripAdvisor, Booking and Airbnb are the best examples of user-generated content management platforms specialising in the tourism sector, with great worldwide prestige. These platforms have a high number of participants and contributors, so many tourists consult the comments and evaluations made by other users before making a final decision about their trips (Amaral *et al.*, 2015). These platforms therefore guarantee the credibility of the reviews they provide and are currently essential tools in travel planning. However, of the three platforms mentioned, TripAdvisor is the most comprehensive, as it gathers the opinions of millions of people on various tourism products and services, such as accommodation, catering and airlines. In this context, the concept of "word of mouth" applies, which, according to Hennig-Thurau *et al.* (2004), consists of any positive or negative statement made by potential, actual, or former customers about a product or company, which is made available to a multitude of people and institutions via the Internet. On the other hand, from the point of view of tourism product and service companies, Wichels (2014) points out that TripAdvisor offers the possibility of interacting directly with consumers and also identifying problems/weaknesses in their products and services, allowing them to take measures to correct, improve and also make adjustments to communication and marketing campaigns.

As far as municipal organisations are concerned, ICTs can offer a range of potential, since they build a kind of grand information structure capable of covering all the themes, spaces and actors of the city; from its history and heritage to the most trivial information on accommodation and catering (Moragas, 2015). In view of this, in the local context, Jiménez and San Eugenio (2009) state that there is an emitter who, consciously or unconsciously, creates a certain image of a place. It acts as an antenna that emits concepts, attributes, values, impressions, smells and visual impacts that configure the image of a space.

Town halls and local/regional tourism promotion organisations use their websites to attract potential visitors by promoting a cultural and recreational offer. In other words, websites are tools that help the managers of a destination to attract tourists to their localities, whether through the provision of information, the establishment of dialogue between interested parties or the systematisation of the tourist service offer, including access to links to hotels and tour operating companies (Alencar *et al.,* 2011).

In fact, in the last decade, the tourism industry has grown dramatically and now occupies a very important place in the economic and social panorama of many countries. This has happened due to a number of factors. Among them, according to Piñeiro-Naval and Serra (2018), there are two that seem to be particularly important: the increase in supply and diversification of tourist services (with cultural and natural tourism as the main "rivals" of mass tourism), as well as the use of ICT and the Internet in the strategic promotion of destinations, a fact that allows tourists, who use them, to plan their trips and select their leisure experiences autonomously, based on their own interests and motivations.

In fact, Web 2.0 applications, in particular social networks, are powerful platforms for connecting with, attracting and retaining customers, as well as transforming communication strategies in the tourism sector. In fact, social networks, more than a technology, are a reality that has grown and gained a multidisciplinary action that is difficult to assimilate in all its sectors of intervention. Social media has a notorious and progressive influence on numerous development sectors, especially the economic sector, which includes tourism. Therefore, active and efficient communication and information management are, in fact, the main factors for its operation and success. To complement this, Gonçalves *et al.* (2021) state that today, access to the Internet and the ever-increasing use of social media applications has led to a change in the strategy used to promote tourist destinations, with most of the information about them now being user-generated content.

Therefore, the number of users of social networks is gaining more and more ground, consequently, tourism consumption through virtual means has increased. According to Mendes and Teixeira (2019), the applications that most influence e-tourism are social networks, Facebook, Instagram and Twitter, as well as TripAdvisor, Expedia, Rumbo and Booking.

According to Zeng and Gerritsen (2014), the most significant actions most exploited by social media users are: making informed decisions about travelling, searching for trips, interacting with other tourists and service providers and sharing personal experiences.

Following the same line of thought, Gonçalves *et al.* (2021) state that social media have become for tourists: a) reliable sources of travel information; b) influencers in decision-making; and c) interfaces for interaction with service providers.

Over time, consumers have become more demanding when it comes to information about the service or product they want. They therefore turn to social networks because they offer tourists greater comfort and flexibility. In this sense, the promotion of a destination through social media has become a marketing opportunity for the place to be visited since Web 2.0, through digital platforms, provides mechanisms for direct participation, thus transforming visitors into the main agents of choice for their destination. Therefore, according to Toffler (2006), the tourist has gone from being a consumer to playing the dual role of consumer and producer, the "prosumer".

According to Sousa (2014), the sharing of experiences on social networks among tourists guarantees the credibility of tourist destinations, but it can also jeopardise the lack of success of others. In other words, promotion/advertising via social media has strengths as well as weaknesses. That said, it is essential to develop an effective and objective strategy in which the brand is strong, persuasively highlighting the offers. However, according to Bolotaeva and Cata (2011) Issues such as aggressive advertising, lack of e-commerce abilities, invasion of user privacy, and certain legal pitfalls, among others, can be major disruptions to social network advertising.

In short, the connection between tourism and social media makes up a perfect system for working together, since tourism combined with social media generates manifestly positive progress (Mendes and Teixeira, 2019). What's more, tourism without the Internet or digital networks/platforms was somewhat limited, its reach was more restricted and it didn't have the strength to encourage tourists to travel to previously unknown destinations. So, these platforms/networks are an efficient contributor to global tourism, as they facilitate the promotion of products and services, and consequently influence the composition of an image that is more desirable to future/new tourists who are looking for destinations that are talked about and distinctive.

3. Methodology

This exploratory study takes the following research question as its starting point: "What is the importance of social media, especially social networks, as a local tourism communication strategy?". To answer this question, we analysed the communication of two local institutions from Fafe: on the one hand, a local authority, a public institution; and, on the other hand, a local accommodation, a private institution, seeking to analyse how local authority policies use social media to communicate and publicise local tourism. To complement this, the opinion of the tourist public on the impact of social media on their choices was analysed. In this way, we sought to answer the following objectives: 1) to understand the importance of social media for communicating and publicising tourism; 2) to describe the main digital platforms used for communicating and publicising tourism; 3) to ascertain the importance of social media as a strategy for communicating and publicising tourism in Portugal.

To achieve these objectives, we carried out a case study analysis of the tourism communication of the Municipality of Fafe, in comparison with the two neighbouring municipalities - Vieira do Minho and Póvoa de Lanhoso, in the north of Portugal. Firstly, we carried out a content analysis of its social media: website and social networks. Secondly, we analysed social media presence of a local accommodation in that municipality. And finally, questionnaire surveys were administered to residents, with a convenience sample of 116 individuals, in order to ascertain the effectiveness of the tourism communication strategies adopted. We chose for convenience the municipality of Fafe as a case study, comparing it with neighbouring municipalities, as it exemplifies the panorama of regional and local tourism in Portugal.

4. Results

4.1 Analysing Social Media: Website and Social Networks

The comparative analysis of the websites of the municipalities of Fafe, Póvoa de Lanhoso and Vieira do Minho evaluates factors related to accessibility, ease of use of the websites, type and quality of information, appearance, reliability and interactivity. To do this, the "Website Quality Framework" developed by Mota and Losada (2018) was used. Table 1 below shows a comparative analysis of the three municipalities mentioned above.

Table 1: Analysing the quality of websites (Self elaboration)

Items		Fafe	Póvoa de Lanhoso	Vieira do Minho
		Nr.	Nr.	Nr.
Accessibility	Nr. of idioms	0	0	1
	Adapted to different devicess[1]	1	1	1
	Adapted for people with special needs[1]	0	1	1
Facility of use	Navegability[2]	1/2	2/3	2/3
	Internal search (search engine)[1]	0	1	1

Items		Fafe	Póvoa de Lanhoso		Vieira do Minho
		Nr.	Nr.		Nr.
	Direct link tourism[1]	1		1	1
Type and quality of information	Links to other companies[1]	1		1	1
	Tourism enquiry [1]	1		1	1
	Online virtual graphic materials [1]	1		1	1
	Downloadable virtual graphic materials [1]	1		1	1
	Videos/audios available online [1]	0		0	1
	Useful advice (visit/accommodation/how to get there)[1]	1		1	1
	Tourism maps [1]	0		0	1
	Events diary [1]	0		1	1
Appearance	Aesthetics [2]	1/2		3	3
	Logo/brand image[1]	1		1	1
	Logo *Slogan*[1]	0		0	0
Fiability/ trust	Programming errors [1]	1		1	1
	Maintenance/Update[1]	0		0	0
Interactivity	Nr. of social networks	2		4	4
	Nr. of active social networks	2		4	4

[1]0: No; 1: Yes

[2]1: Hostile/Bad; 2: Fair; 3: Very Intuitive/Good; 4: Very Good

With regard to analysing the social networks Facebook and Instagram of the Municipality of Fafe, the first three months of the year 2022 (January, February and March) and three summer months (June, July and August) of the same year, in order to understand the uses of social networks in communicating with the public. Table 2 shows the accounting and division of publications by category, as well as the number of followers on the social networks (Facebook and Instagram) of the Municipality of Fafe.

Table 2: Analysis of the Social Networks of the Municipality of Fafe (Self-elaboration)

Categories	Fafe			
	Facebook		*Instagram*	
	From January to March	From June to August	From January to March	From June to August
Nr. of followers (19/12/2022)		31 mil		5647
Total of posts	178	396	63	49
Tourism	8	3	18	-
Culture/Events	59	188	28	27
Initiatives	3	42	1	9
News	27	49	9	3
Public utilities	9	10	-	3
Awareness	5	18	1	1
Commemorative	9	-	2	-
Newsletters/Announcements	15	19	2	1
Others	43	67	2	5

The Municipality of Fafe currently has around 31,000 followers on the social network Facebook and 5,647 followers on the social network Instagram. In terms of activity, the municipality analysed is more active on Facebook than on Instagram, considering the number of posts made.

As far as categories are concerned, there are three that stand out in terms of the number of posts on both of the analysed municipality's social networks: culture/events, other and news.

With regard to the "Tourism" category, another table 3 was created for this one, in order to understand the types of posts made by the Municipality of Fafe regarding the tourism sector. However, before that, it is important to mention the total number of publications in this category. So, from January to March there were 8 posts on Facebook and 18 on Instagram and from June to August there were 3 posts on Facebook and none on Instagram.

Table 3: Analysis of posts in the "Tourism" category (Self elaboration)

Tourism Posts				
Sub-categories	Fafe			
	Facebook		Instagram	
	From January to March	From June to August	From January to March	From June to August
Videos	1			
Promotional images	2		16	
Suggestions		2		
Support / Initiatives		1	1	
Attendance at trade fairs	5		1	

4.2 Case Study of a Local Accommodation

With regard to the presence of Casa da Avó local accommodation on social media, this local accommodation's social media commitment began in 2018 on the Facebook platform, seeking to promote this tourist destination. At the time of the research, this local accommodation has a website and the social networks Facebook and Instagram. The period of analysis was between 1 July 2021 and 1 April 2022. The main data that stand out are:

- The website was mostly accessed by mobile phones, with around 90 clicks, which corresponds to 66.7% of accesses from this device. It is therefore vital to pay attention to the layout of the website elements for this type of device. The number of accesses from computers represents around 33.3%, with 45 clicks.
- The number of accesses to the website at the end of the analysis was around 160, the majority of which came from Instagram, leading with 41.3% (66 clicks) of accesses.
- Social networks were the main stage for promoting the local accommodation website.
- The website is like a shop window that showcases what's on offer, giving visibility to products and services, thus avoiding geographical boundaries.
- Increased investment in local accommodation's social platforms, including: creating a routine of posts, interacting with followers, identifying the location, sharing news on the website and answering messages on social media accounts.
- The increase in posts on social networks has brought with it an increase in interactions and visits to social networks. The creation of content and the regularity of posts may be responsible for these results.

4.3 Survey Main Results

The questionnaire was answered by 116 people from the municipality of Fafe, with the aim of finding out how well they know their municipality is publicising tourism on social media. Of our sample, only 22 people don't follow any of the municipality's social networks, the most followed being Facebook. 53 individuals believe that the municipality's social networks are being well managed, as opposed to 43 individuals who do not believe that they are being well managed. Nevertheless, the overwhelming majority agree that Fafe's social networks are a good way of promoting the municipality for tourism (65.5 per cent of respondents (76 individuals) agree and

20.7 per cent (24 individuals) agree completely). Likewise, the vast majority of respondents agree that the municipality should invest more in social media as a way of promoting the municipality for tourism (62.6% (73 individuals) agree and 19.8% (23 individuals) completely agree).

The same results do not apply to the website, since the majority of respondents (66 individuals) do not visit the municipality's website regularly, only 43 individuals visit it frequently, and 7 individuals have never visited the municipality's website. Similarly, the majority of respondents agree that the Fafe municipality's website is a good way of promoting the municipality in terms of tourism (53.4% (62 respondents) agree and 9.5% (11 respondents) completely agree). As a result, 85.3 per cent (99 individuals) of those surveyed believe that social networks are a more effective way of promoting the municipality for tourism. However, only 14.7 per cent of respondents (17 individuals) consider the website to be a more effective medium.

5. Discussion of Results

As organisations, municipalities play a leading role in the social, economic, environmental and cultural planning of their municipalities, and consequently make an influential contribution to local and regional development, not just by providing public services. In fact, the main missions of communication in municipalities are to inform citizens, work on the positive image of the municipality, boost the municipality in the economic and social spheres, promote tourism, encourage culture and sport, and commit to residents that the name of their municipality is taken across borders thanks to its distinctiveness and the primacy of complementary strategic actions (Pinto, 2016).

Consequently, local councils and local/regional tourism promotion organisations use their websites and social networks to attract potential visitors by promoting their cultural and recreational offerings. Or rather, they use these tools to provide visitors/users with a range of information that might encourage them to want to visit the place. In particular, websites build a kind of information structure capable of covering all kinds of issues, places and actors/agents in the city, such as its history and heritage, but also more common information such as accommodation and catering (Moragas, 2015). The website of the Municipality of Fafe proves this, as it provides the contact details (email, telephone and postal address) of local businesses such as restaurants, hotels, tour operators, among others, as well as other useful information such as opening hours, the average price (in the case of restaurants) and their geographical coordinates.

In this sense, according to Fernández-Poyatos *et al.* (2012), with the development of new technologies, organisations' websites have become "business cards" which, as well as communicating, are important access tools for users. That said, the aesthetics of a website's homepage is a factor to be taken into account, as it is the user's first contact with the site. In this respect, the website of the Municipality of Fafe is somewhat neglected and could have presented its information and content in a more attractive way. However, it is interesting to note that it has a contemporary logo, not limited to using the traditional coat of arms, but it does not have a slogan next to its logo. The existence of these elements (slogan and logo) is indispensable when creating any brand, in this case a territorial brand.

Therefore, the information made available online is a decisive factor in choosing a tourist destination, so websites must be easy to access, intuitive, allow simple navigation and be adapted to users' criteria and needs. The website of the Municipality of Fafe fulfils some of these requirements since, in general, its navigability can be classified as regular. However, as far as accessibility is concerned, it doesn't provide a personalised translation of the content into other languages and, consequently, it doesn't take into account the possibility of a visit from an international audience, limiting the use of the website to a national audience or Portuguese readers. On the other hand, the website moulds itself to different devices such as smartphones and tablets, but does not adapt its content according to the standards developed by the W3C. In fact, in the context of public administration, municipal websites have become, in part, the official tourist representatives of the locations, as recognised by the majority of respondents, even though many of them do not regularly visit the Fafe Municipality website.

On the other hand, when it comes to social media, the Municipality of Fafe uses the social network Facebook more than Instagram, which can be seen in the total number of posts made (Facebook - 574 posts; Instagram - 112 posts) in the periods analysed above (January to March 2022 and June to August 2022). This trend is also reflected in the number of followers, as the Municipality of Fafe has 31,000 followers on Facebook and 5,647 followers on Instagram.

With regard to tourism, social networks play a central role as they are a great resource for promoting the destination and, consequently, are a powerful marketing tool for the place, as the respondents and the local accommodation case study showed. In this vein, Mendes and Teixeira (2019) point out that "the link between social media and tourism is an impeccable system for working together, as tourism propagates clearly positive progress when it is linked to social media".

Events, according to Marujo (2012), act as promotional tools for the image of the place or region as a tourist destination to be consumed, "in other words, when well planned and well publicised, they create a positive image, thus promoting the destination". In addition, special events provide the opportunity for a leisure, social or cultural experience that can be enjoyed together by the resident community and tourists (Marujo, 2014). It should also be noted that the promotion of events/culture is one of the categories that received the most attention on the Fafe Municipality's social networks.

Tourist destinations use communication in order to stand out from their competitors, promoting unique experiences, telling the stories of the people and places, and thus making their culture known. In fact, it is relevant to compare the municipal communication in the tourism sector carried out by the Municipality of Fafe with other municipalities in the region with similar characteristics, in this case with the municipalities of Póvoa de Lanhoso and Vieira do Minho. Inevitably, there were both similarities and differences. That said, all the municipalities analysed use social networks and institutional websites as a means of communication and tourism promotion. However, unlike the municipality of Fafe, the municipalities of Póvoa de Lanhoso and Vieira do Minho have exclusive digital platforms for tourism promotion.

6.   Conclusions

Tourism is one of the sectors that needs this communication capacity to generate revenue, emphasising the dissemination of information using communication tools. In local tourism, the use of social media can often guarantee a company's notoriety and survival. In fact, as our research shows, both public institutions, municipalities and private institutions are increasingly relying on social media as a strategy for publicising and promoting tourism. On the other hand, as our sample recognised, citizens, fully integrated into social media and the digital universe, increasingly use and value what is published on social media, not only by tourism promoters, but also by other tourists, their peers.

The data obtained showed that social networks are increasingly being used by institutions as a strategy for communicating and publicising tourism. On the other hand, they are also a source of advice and decisions when it comes to choosing a tourist destination. On this last point, the opinions shared on social networks and the role of influencers as determining factors in the final decision and choice are particularly important.

References

Alencar, S.; Cruz Aguiar, E.; Kovacs, M. H.; Andrade, F. G. (2011) *Imagen de los destinos turísticos en los portales gubernamentales. Análisis de tres localidades brasileñas.* Internet. https://www.redalyc.org/pdf/1807/180722700007.pdf 2776 (retrieved on 27th of April 2022).

Almeida, P.J.S. (2003) *A Contribuição da Animação Turística para o Aumento das Taxas de Ocupação de Uma Região.* Internet. https://ria.ua.pt/handle/10773/1493?locale=pt_PT (retrieved on 3rd of October 2022).

Amaral, F.; Tiago, T.; Tiago, F.; and Kavoura, A.(2015) *Comentários no TripAdvisor: Do que falam os turistas?.* Internet. https://www.dosalgarves.com/index.php/dosalgarves/article/view/80 (retrieved on 05th of October 2022).

Blichfeldt, B. S. (2017) *Strategic Communication in Tourism.* Internet. https://www.sdu.dk/en/om_sdu/institutter_centre/c_tik/publikationer (retrieved on 4th 3rd of October 2022).

Bolotaeva, V., and Cata, T. (2011) *Marketing Opportunities with Social Networks.* Internet. https://ibimapublishing.com/articles/JISNVC/2011/409860/ (retrieved on 16th of May 2022).

Cunha, L. (2010) *A Definição e o Âmbito do Turismo: um aprofundamento necessário.* Internet. https://recil.grupolusofona.pt/handle/10437/665 (retrieved on 20th of August 2021).

Fernández-Poyatos, M.D; Aguirregoitia-Martínez, A.; and Boix-Martínez, B. (2012) *The way of Saint James and the Xacobeo 2010 in the tourism websites of the Spanish autonomous communities.* Internet. http://rua.ua.es/dspace/handle/10045/19635#vpreview (retrieved on 13th of October 2022).

Gonçalves, P.; Raposo, R.; and Roque, V. (2021) *Estratégias de comunicação baseadas no Facebook: o caso do Posto de Turismo da Praia da Barra.* Internet. https://proa.ua.pt/index.php/rtd/article/view/8507/18061 (retrieved on 22nd of June 2022).

Hennig-Thurau, T.; Gwinner, K. P.; Walsh, G.; and Gremler, D. D. (2004) *Electronic word-of-mouth via consumer-opinion platforms: What motivates consumers to articulate themselves on the Internet?.* In: *Journal of Interactive Marketing* 18(1): 38–52.

Jiménez Morales, M., and San Eugenio, J. (2009). *Identidad territorial y promoción turística : la organización de eventos como estrategia de creación, consolidación y difusión de la imagen de marca del territorio.* Internet. https://ojs.ehu.eus/index.php/zer/article/view/2776 (retrieved on 27th of April 2022).

Lévy, P. (1999) *Cibercultura.* Tradução: Carlos Irineu da Costa. Edição brasileira. São Paulo: Editora 34.

López, M. T.; Altamirano, V.; and Valarezo, K. (2016) *Comunicación turística colaborativa 2.0: promoción, difusión e interactividad en las webs gubernamentales de Iberoamérica*. Internet. http://nuevaepoca.revistalatinacs.org/index.php/revista/article/view/811/1236 (retrieved on 27th of April 2022).

Martínez, A. A. (2005) *Relaciones públicas y gabinetes de comunicación*. Internet. https://ddd.uab.cat/pub/analisi/02112175n32/02112175n32p117.pdf (retrieved on 13th of January 2022).

Marujo, N. (2014) *Turismo e eventos especiais: a festa da flor na Ilha da Madeira*. Internet. https://www.tmstudies.net/index.php/ectms/article/view/699 (retrieved on 14th of March 2023).

Marujo, N. (2012) *Turismo, Turistas E Eventos: O Caso Da Ilha Da Madeira*. Internet. https://dspace.uevora.pt/rdpc/handle/10174/14150 (retrieved on 14th of March 2023).

Mendes, G.; e Teixeira, S. J (2019) *Turismo, património e cultura na era das redes sociais: Um estudo de caso. #Viajamos para partilhar*. Internet. https://proa.ua.pt/index.php/rtd/article/view/20480 (retrieved on 5th of May 2022).

Moragas, M. (2015) *Cruce de caminos. Tecnologías de la comunicación y convivencia en la ciudad global*. Internet. https://telos.fundaciontelefonica.com/archivo/numero100/tecnologias-de-la-comunicacion-y-convivencia-en-la-ciudad-global/?output=pdf (retrieved on 27th of April 2022).

Mota, G., e Losada, N. (2018) Promoção turística nos websites municipais: O caso da região do Douro (NUT III). Internet. https://www.review-rper.com/index.php/rper/article/view/485 (retrieved on 21st od September 2022).

Piñeiro-Naval, V.; e Serra, J.P. (2018) *O potencial turístico da web local. Uma análise à comunicação digital das autarquias portuguesas*. Internet. https://www.researchgate.net/publication/328171959_O_potencial_turistico_da_web_local_Uma_analise_a_comunicacao_digital_das_autarquias_portuguesas (retrieved on 25th of February 2022).

Pinto, P. M. M. (2016) Comunicação autárquica nos municípios da Terra Quente Transmontana. Dissertação de Mestrado. Vila Real: UTAD.

Seguro, P. (2021[a]) *Conta Satélite do Turismo | 2019*. Internet. https://travelbi.turismodeportugal.pt/turismo-em-portugal/conta-satelite-do-turismo-2019/ (retrieved on 3rd of October 2022).

Seguro, P. (2021[b]) *Conta Satélite do Turismo | 2020*. Internet. https://travelbi.turismodeportugal.pt/turismo-em-portugal/conta-satelite-do-turismo-2020/ (retrieved on 3rd of October 2022).

Sousa, C. (2014) *A Influência da Internet na escolha de um Destino Turístico*. Internet. https://silo.tips/download/a-influencia-da-internet-na-escolha-de-um-destino-turistico (retrieved on 16th of May 2022).

Teruel, L., and Viñals, M. J. (2012) "Internet applications for strategic communication, tourism and local communities in relation to heritage". In: M.T. Albert, M. Richon, M. J. Viñals, e A. Witcomb (Eds.), *Community development through World Heritage*. UNESCO, World Heritage Papers 31: 54-60.

Turismo de Portugal. (s.d.[a]) *Organização da área do Turismo em Portugal e principais parceiros institucionais*. Internet. http://www.turismodeportugal.pt/pt/Turismo_Portugal/Organizacao_Parceiros/Paginas/default.aspx (retrieved on 13th of June 2022).

Turismo de Portugal (s.d.[b]) *Missão e visão*. Internet. http://www.turismodeportugal.pt/pt/quem_somos/Organizacao/Missao_Visao/Paginas/default.aspx (retrieved on 13th of June 2022).

Turismo de Portugal (2022) *Visão geral*. Internet. http://www.turismodeportugal.pt/pt/Turismo_Portugal/visao_geral/Paginas/default.aspx (retrieved on 3rd of October 2022).

Wang, Y. (2008) *Web-based Destination Marketing for Management and Implementation*. In: *International Journal of Tourism Research* 10: 55–70.

Wichels, S. (2014) *Comunicação Turística:desafios e tendências na contemporaneidade. Estudo de Caso: Tenerife*. Internet. https://eg.uc.pt/handle/10316/26209 (retrieved on 4th of October 2022).

World Travel Awards (s.d.) *World Travel Awards Winners*. Internet. https://www.worldtravelawards.com/winners/2020 (retrieved on 4th of September 2022).

Xiang, Z., and Gretzel, U. (2010) *Role of social media in online travel information search*. In: *Tourism Management* 31(2): 179–188.

Zeng, B.; and Gerritsen, R. (2014) *What do we know about social media in tourism? A review*. Internet. https://www.researchgate.net/publication/260033314_What_do_We_Know_About_Social_Media_in_Tourism_A_Review (retrieved on 16th of May 2022).

Design of a Disinformation Awareness Digital Game

Clara Maathuis[1], Frederick Janssens[2] and Ebrahim Rahimi[1]
[1]Open University of the Netherlands, Heerlen, The Netherlands
[2]Independent Researcher, Belgium

clara.maathuis@ou.nl
frederick.janssens.BSc@gmail.com
ebrahim.rahimi@ou.nl

Abstract: Social media is the digital canvas where users' thoughts, ideas, and voices converge, and are being brought to the world. It is the environment where individuals and groups are connected and empowered in ways that were previously unimaginable. Nonetheless, the users are exposed and engage without knowledge or willingly to various social media manipulation mechanisms like disinformation and misinformation which have the potential to influence their believes, behaviour, and attitudes. Although social media represents a valuable arena for connectivity and expressivity to the younger generation, it also poses risks like access to sensitive information and exposure to altered or false narrative and misleading content which can shape young minds in ways that are detrimental to critical thinking and overall well-being. To combat these, it is crucial for families and teachers as well as the educational system to promote security awareness, digital literacy, and critical thinking to high school students. Since research and practitioner initiatives and programs are in an incipient phase to tackle such threats, this research aims to design a digital game for security awareness regarding broken authentication and social bots to high school students. To achieve this objective, a transdisciplinary approach is considered by merging methods from cyber security awareness, social media manipulation, software engineering, game-based learning, and computer science education domains using the Design Science Research methodology. This research strives to contribute to building responsible efforts that bring and/or strengthen awareness and resilience to social media security threats of adolescents to assure a safe digital domain.

Keywords: Disinformation, Misinformation, Cyber security awareness, Social media, Game-Based learning

1. Introduction

"We can only see a short distance ahead, but we can see plenty there that needs to be done." (Alan Turing)

The proliferation of cyber security incidents became a global pressing societal concern, especially within the social media realm. Primer cyber threats in this realm are targeting data and human behaviour and believes through information access and information manipulation operations (ENISA, 2023a). An increasing trend in this direction that escalates the complexity of the security landscape is represented by the persuasion of targeting authentication mechanisms that serve as the first line of defence against unauthorized access through broken authentication exploits and the deployment of social bots that represent automated software agents designed to mimic human interactions for producing/amplifying dis/misinformation among users (UNICEF, 2021; Fard & Maathuis, 2021; Kaur & Ramkumar, 2022; Pastor-Galindo, Marmol & Pérez, 2022). As these threats continue to evolve in sophistication and scale, there is an urgent need for building and adopting intelligent, adaptive, and robust cyber security programs and solutions that counter and further prevent them. Nevertheless, effectively countering and preventing such multifaceted challenges implies firstly awareness and education of users (Zwilling, 2022) concerning their action and impact (Caramancion et al., 2022) through public awareness campaigns, professional training courses, and tailored educational programs (ITU, 2018). Given their reliance on digital platforms for activities like education, communication, and entertainment as well as their implicit vulnerability, cyber security awareness is vital for adolescents since they are in a forming stage of development, and they lack the necessary experience, emotional and cognitive maturity to deal with social media threats (Lazer et al., 2018; Smith & Ali, 2019) like unauthorized access to sensitive information, and content manipulation. While dedicated efforts for building and implementing cyber security awareness solutions that facilitate digital safety and media literacy (IRIS Plus, 2022) are proposed by various academic, governmental, and private stakeholders, they are limited in relation to dedicated tailored solutions to adolescents/high school students. This represents the knowledge gap that this research tackles adopting a multidisciplinary approach by means of designing a digital game for raising cyber security awareness of high school students focusing on disinformation social bots and broken authentication threats.

To achieve the aim of this research, the Design Science Research methodology is used to build the design architecture of a cyber security awareness digital game (Hevner et al., 2004; Peffers et al., 2007; Ibrahim & Jaafar, 2009). Accordingly, this research aims to bring a contribution to ongoing academic and professional efforts for building cyber security awareness tailored to children, and in particular high school students, to increase their resilience, responsibility, and media literacy skills in relation to evolving cyber threats that the social media domain embeds using gaming technologies as this approach previously showed valuable results and is considered enjoyable by high school students.

The outline of this article is structured as follows. Section 2 sets the background of this research and discusses relevant related studies. Section 3 discusses the methodological approach considered in this research. Section 4 presents the design of the game architecture that this research proposes. At the end, Section 4 provides concluding remarks and future research perspectives.

2. Background and Related Research

In its future vision on cyber threats, ENISA (2023b) stresses that both state and non-state actors are increasing their technological capabilities and that by 2023, they continue to expand their disinformation efforts using bots and deepfakes as part of influence operations and campaigns. Accordingly, ENISA (2021) calls for collaboration, cooperation, and coordination of governmental, professional, and scientific cyber security efforts on building tailored awareness strategies, programs, and solutions. In the Netherlands, cyber security awareness campaigns are carried out at national level through efforts that the Ministry of Security and Justice direct in respect to producing and enhancing awareness of civilians and municipalities by cooperating with police and private sector players like Google, Facebook, Microsoft, and telecommunication companies, while the Ministry of Economic is raising security awareness among companies and entrepreneurs. This reflects the importance of media literacy that social media users need to have to critically evaluate and use information before transforming it into knowledge. Hence, users, and in particular children and young people need to be aware of aspects like the source of information, the ways how the information received represents the world, and further what kind of implications these could have (Glas et al., 2023). Quayyum, Cruzes & Jaccheri (2021) conduct a systematic literature review on the importance of cyber security awareness among children in relation to existing risks and provide a series of awareness mechanisms that could be developed to allow them to avoid and/or mitigate them. The authors identify the following core risks: online privacy, online harassment, stranger danger, social engineering, content related, sexual solicitation, technology-based threats, economic, Internet addiction, and password practice and management. In the systematic literature review conducted by Zhang-Kennedy & Chiasson (2021) on cyber security awareness and education tools, the authors stress the need to develop gaming and media solutions for building and supporting awareness and education of people in a structured manner following clear design and evaluation principles. The study proposes the following research agenda: focus on impactful and current educational topics, consider interdisciplinarity, integrate a rigorous evaluation methodology without jeopardizing users' security and privacy (i.e., ecological validity), consider users' motivation and engagement, establish a consistent reporting template, and embed various cultural perspectives.

Shamsi (2019) investigates the effectiveness of cyber security awareness programs for students aged 8 to 10 years old based on interviews conducted with teachers and students. The results position the online safety, authentication, privacy, online strangers, and cyber bullying among the core issues that children deal with online. At the same time, while the results of the two parts are similar, the children emphasize cyber bullying more based on their own experiences. Nevertheless, as Bada, Sasse & Nurse (2019) stresses, cyber security awareness campaigns can fail due to (i) personal factors such as tiredness, perceived control, and self-regulation, and (ii) cultural and environmental factors like perception of risk, social disruption, and positive/negative perception of the outcomes.

Hart et al., (2020) propose Riskio, a tabletop serious game for increasing cyber security awareness of people without technical background working as employees in various organizations and students. In this game, the users play scenarios that cover a broad range of cyber attacks for whom they need to define proper countermeasures based on existing standards and learn in a fun and enjoyable environment that promotes players' active learning (i.e., constructivism learning theory). Yasin et al., (2018) develop a serious game for security requirements education of university students and young professionals focusing on understanding security concepts, analysing them in real life situations, and motivating players for further learning and remaining updated on future developments of security issues. This is done by presenting the cyber-attack mechanism which starts from identifying the target, searching, and finding a vulnerability to be exploited, and preparing the attack surface using a scenario-based learning approach. Literat, Chang & Hsu (2020) design for primary school students two serious games named Fakeopoly and Lying Geese based on the Monopoly and Buffalo games, respectively. While the first game focuses on production and sharing fake news, the second game focuses on the story of the fake news including the writer and reader roles and deciding the trustfulness of the news story. Along these lines, Giannakas, Kambourakis & Gritzalis, (2015) develop a cyber security education and awareness game for K-6 (Kindergarten to sixth grade – elementary school) students aiming at providing understanding of general security concepts and attacks. Given the young age of the target audience, the study considers attention, relevance, confidence, and satisfaction are core design elements. With a broader target audience, Jin et al. (2018) build a cyber security training named GenCyber for K-12 (Kindergarten from 5-6 years old to twelfth grade – up to 17-18 years old) students for raising cyber security awareness and providing understanding to what safe online behaviour means and implies aiming at increasing diversity in the US cyber security workforce by focusing on social engineering, online behaviour security, and defence strategy.

Micallef et al. (2021) developed Fakey, an online fake news awareness game directed to a general online audience. The game is online available since November 2019, adopts a human-centred computing approach by including users' needs, goals, and expectations since the design phase. In the assessment process, the study included semi-structured interviews to evaluate the interaction and the achievement of learning objectives. A human-centred approach is also taken by Mikka-Muntuumo & Peters (2021) who propose an online game for engaging both high school students and their teachers, parents, and caregivers for producing and sustaining online safety awareness focusing on core threats like identity theft and cyber bullying. Considering a different implementation perspective, Paraschivoiu et al. (2021) propose an escape room AR game for fake news education of high school students and young adults that contains quizzes with multiple-choice questions, matching games, and minigames, a chatbot for narrative storytelling, and an exploration mode. The game focuses on the following four pillars for assuring a balance between challenge and skill: (i) learning that captures knowledge, skills, and attitude elements, (ii) storytelling which provides engagement with the narrative, (iii) gameplay which refers to the activities taken in the game (mechanics), (ii) dynamics, and (iii) and emotional responses (affection). Using web technologies, Olano et al. (2014) built a web-based game named Security Empire for high school students for building cyber security awareness skills in a setting of building a green energy company. The skills imply issues regarding unsafe links, encryption auction bids, authentication and software downloads, integrity checks of system software, antivirus protection up-to-date, and selection of strong passwords. Addressing university students, Wu et al. (2021) propose an information awareness security online game that focuses on general security awareness aspects like social media use, information handling, and password management. The study assesses the attitude and intention to comply with the game security principles and measures if gender differences can be seen in this process. Based on the results obtained, the authors did not see an increase in interest of students towards further engaging and approaching information security topics and did not see a difference in gender among engaging with the content among the participants.

In relation to social media trolls, Lees et al. (2023) built an online game named Spot the Troll Quiz addressed to a general audience tailored to generating and sustaining awareness to social media trolls. As a response to the infodemic phenomenon born and further developed in the Covid-19 pandemic, Cernicova-Buca & Ciurel (2022) proposed a paper-based game for university students for disinformation awareness during crisis such as the Covid-19 pandemic aiming at increasing fake news awareness skills and promoting media literacy. As a professional effort, Common Sense (2018) developed the Digital Passport which is a web-based educational game for digital awareness to primary school students in relation to issues like password protection and online sharing using a series of mini games. Focused on disinformation awareness, Urban, Hewitt & Moore (2018) developed a web-based game named Fake it to make it that helps identifying and simulating common fake news techniques, analysing potential disinformation, understanding how fake news are created and spread, and provide players ways to distinguish fake news from real news. A similar tool called Bad News is proposed by Barabas (2023) where the users can engage in building and spreading disinformation for reflecting on the implications of their actions, and further gaining insights in these mechanisms.

The studies above discussed are summarized in Table 1 for capturing their goals, direct target audience as well as educational, gaming, implementation, and evaluation methods. Based on this extensive literature review, one can see that limited attention is provided to building cyber security awareness gaming solutions to K-6 and K-12 students or primary and secondary school students in relation to social media threats like social bots and broken authentication. This represents the knowledge gap that this article aims to tackle through a gaming approach given its effectivity in previous awareness settings and appreciation by high school students.

Table 1: Core elements and methods of the related studies

Article no	Aim	Target audience	Educational method	Gaming method	Implementation method	Evaluation method	Reference
1	Cyber security awareness on attack and defence mechanisms	Non-technical employees of organizations (primary) and university students (secondary)	Constructivism learning theory (e.g., motivation, experimentation, responsibility, feedback)	Game design (e.g., planning, collaboration, game turns, tokens, scoring)	Multiplayer card game	Three experiments with 14, 15, and 12 players, respectively	(Hart et al., 2020)
2	Security requirements education	University students and professionals	Scenario based learning (planning, communication, problem solving) using the Bloom taxonomy	Game design (e.g., planning, rules, characters, scoring)	Multiplayer card game in English and Chinese languages	One experiment with 16 players	(Yasin et al., 2018)
3	Fake news awareness	Primary school students between 10-14 years old	Learning by participatory game design (reflection, discussion, and participation)	Participatory game design	Multiplayer board game	Two experiments both with three players on two different games	(Chang & Hsu, 2020)
4	Cyber security training	K-12 students	Scenario based learning	Participatory game design	Single-player game developed in Unity 3D	One experiment with 181 high school students	(Jin et al., 2018)
5	Fake news awareness	General audience	Scenario based learning	Game design	Single player game developed in Python, Javascript, and Django	Ongoing as it is online available since November 26, 2019	(Micallef et al., 2021))
6	Fake news	High school and young adults	Scenario based learning	Game design (learning, storytelling, gameplay, and user experience)	Single-player escape-room AR game developed in Unity 3D	An experiment with 49 high school and young adults	(Paraschivoiu et al., 2021)
7	Online safety awareness	High school students	Scenario based learning	Game design	Single-player online game	Two experiments: first where 29 high school students and teachers ranging between 7 to 35 years old, second with 18 teachers, parents, and caregivers.	(Mikka-Muntuumo & Peters, 2021)
8	Information security awareness	University students	Experimental learning	Gamification for learning (e.g. points, levels, and leaderboards)	Single-player online game	One experiment with 110 university students ranging between 18 to 21 years old	(Wu et al., 2021)

9	Cyber security education and awareness	K-6 students	Game-based learning and Instruction Design Model	Game design (e.g., challenge, points, mini games)	Single-player mobile game built using the Android Development Kit and libGDX game engine	One experiment with 43 elementary school students aged between 9 to 11 years old	(Giannakas, Kambourakis & Gritzalis, 2015)
10	Cyber security education	High school students	Game-based learning	Game design	Multi-player online game	One experiment with high school students	(Olano et al., 2014)
11	Troll detection awareness	General audience	Experimental learning	Game design	Single-player online game	Multiple experiments with 2847 players of various age	(Lees et al., 2023)
12	Disinformation awareness	University students	Game-based learning	Game design	Single-player paper and online game	One experiment with 50 university students	(Cernicova-Buca & Ciurel)
13	Digital security awareness	Primary school students	Game-based learning	Game design	Single-player online game	Ongoing web-based functional game	(Common Sense, 2018)
14	Disinformation, troll detection awareness	General audience	Game-based learning	Game design	Single-player online game	Ongoing web-based functional game	(Urban, Hewitt & Moore, 2018)
15	Disinformation, troll detection awareness	General audience	Game-based learning	Game design	Single-player online game	Ongoing web-based functional game	(Barabas, 2023)

3. Research Methodology

The fast-paced advancements of cyber attackers and their corresponding threats overscore the awareness and readiness of existing scientific and professional efforts on building cyber security awareness, education, and training of the younger generation of students, as already discussed in the previous section of this article. This represents the knowledge gap that this research aims to address by designing a cyber security awareness digital game for high school students/adolescents focusing on social bots and broken authentication threats. To this end, the following research questions are formulated:

- RQ1: Which cyber security awareness games that focus on disinformation social bots and broken authentication exist for high school students?
- RQ2: How to design a disinformation social bots and broken authentication cyber security awareness game for high school students?

Given the scope of creating innovative artefacts that address real-world problems through an iterative design, the Design Science Research methodology is applied in this research considering the perspective illustrated in Figure 1, as follows (Hevner et al., 2004; Peffers et al., 2007; Ibrahim & Jaafar, 2009):

- Problem identification and motivation: extensive literature review was carried out in the fields of cyber security, software engineering, gaming, and computer science education domains to identify relevant studies, methods, design requirements, and metrics. Accordingly, scientific literature and practitioner and governmental publications were considered based on combinations of keywords like disinformation, social bot, broken authentication, security awareness, and game. In this process, the IEEE Digital Library, ACM Digital Library, Scopus, Wiley, and Google Scholar scientific databases were queried, and only English documents were included.
- Game design: based on the results obtained in the previous research phase, the core concepts, methods, and techniques are established to build the architecture of the game which is proposed in this article.
- Evaluation: in this research, the evaluation will be carried out when the game is developed with high school students in a setting established by the Dutch-Belgium research partners respecting the ethical assessment that was conducted and approved by the ethical committee of the university.
- Dissemination: the initial results of this research are presented focusing on the architecture of the game as described in this article.

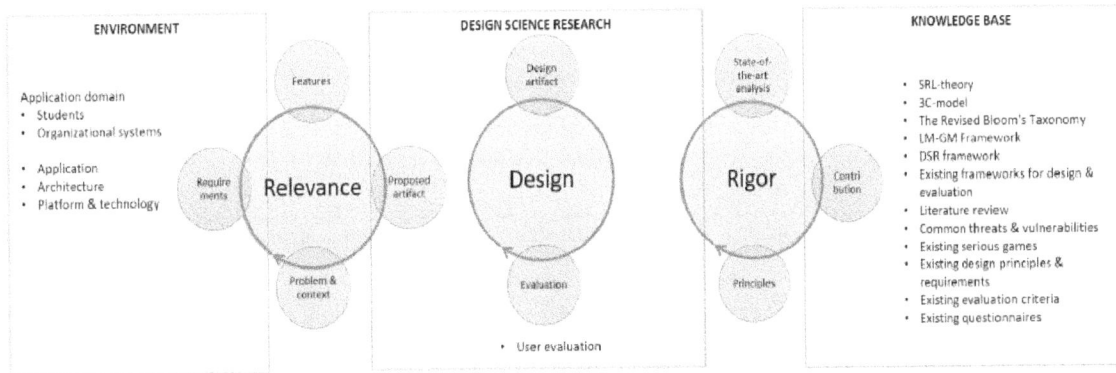

Figure 1: Research methodology application based on Hevner et al. (2004)

4. Digital Game Design

The design of a cyber security awareness game is a thoughtful process as it plays a pivotal role in developing it as it directly influences users' engagement and knowledge retention. This implies clearly establishing its target audience, learning goals, scenarios and content development, implementation choices, user interface, and the overall aesthetic aspects. Accordingly, the design requirements are established based on a set of corresponding technical and educational requirements and principles. Based on the extensive literature review conducted in this research and addressed in the previous section of this article, the following design requirements and principles are captured in Table 2, are tailored to the target audience of this research, and are considered for the game proposed. Next to these, taking into consideration the technical core of the game proposed, the ISO/IEC 25010: 2011 Systems and software engineering standard (ISO, 2011) is considered for assuring a proper quality and evaluation mechanism of the game. Furthermore, the instances considered in Table 1 are further elaborated in respect to the design of the game proposed in this research:

Educational and gaming methods: scenario-based learning and gamification design using the 3C-model are considered in this research (challenge, choices, and consequences of these choices) (Kuhlmann, 2019). This approach aims to challenge students to reflect on their choices for triggering their understanding about the learning materials, and further encouraging self-reflection and raising awareness in various settings.

Implementation and evaluation methods: the game will be implemented in Java and use MySQL as a relational database management system. Moreover, a series of scenarios are built inside the game considering effectiveness, game enjoyment, and usability as core evaluation criteria (Zhang-Kennedy & Chiasson, 2021).

Learning goals: the primary goal is to propose a game that increases the cyber security awareness of adolescents in relation to social bots and broken authentication cyber threats. Accordingly, the following core learning objectives are defined:

- Differentiate between credible and misleading information spread through disinformation campaigns.
- Explain and assess common patterns, functionalities, and tactics employed by social bots.
- Understand and apply corresponding mechanisms for controlling and/or avoiding engagement and the action of social bots.
- Understand and assess common vulnerabilities of authentication mechanisms in social media.
- Explain and assess the implications of broken authentication threats in social media.
- Understand and apply relevant mechanisms for assuring safe authentication in social media.

Table 2: Overview of requirements/principles

Design Requirement/Principle Categories	Design Requirement/Principle Description	Article No
1	Consider realistic scenarios that enhance learning and facilitate critical thinking	(Yasin et al., 2018; Maathuis et al., 2023)
2	Use the Bloom taxonomy	(Yasin et al., 2018)
3	Provide real-time feedback	(Wolfenden, 2019)
4	Consistency (the information presented is consistent), integrity (learning-by-doing), explicit or inferred aspects, and stand-alone assessments. Consistency in tracking and reporting progress.	(Zhang-Kennedy & Chiasson, 2021; Khader, Karam & Fares, 2021)
5	Guide and provide explanations to the user.	(De Troyer & Janssens, 2014)
6	Distinguish between mandatory and optional components of the game.	(De Troyer & Janssens, 2014)
7	Provide alternatives, visualize them, change them, and relate them to the impact of their choices.	(De Troyer & Janssens, 2014)
8	Easy to use graphical interface and provide feedback to users.	(De Troyer & Janssens, 2014)
9	Assess the effectiveness of the game by measuring the (i) usability and satisfaction, (ii) learning/knowledge acquisition, and (iii) impact on future online behaviour. Assess the effectiveness of the game by measuring (i) its adaptability to current situations, (ii) usability reducing the cognitive load and time spent, (iii) usability through easy to learn, efficient to use, and re-playability/re-usability, and (iv) learning considering an active and collaborative learning approach and measure the performance.	(Quayyum, Cruzes & Jaccheri, 2021) (Shamsi. 2019)

Game narratives and rules: the game uses and will be assessed in respect to its quality and effectiveness in relation to three use case scenarios: register, login, and game play. The narratives of the use cases capture real-world situations allowing the developers to foster understanding and the players to experience the consequences of their choices and actions in a simulated user-friendly controlled environment. The architecture of the game narratives is captured in Figure 2 below. Specifically, the game use cases contain the following elements:

- *Preconditions:* the student is already logged in.
- *Postconditions:* the student played one or more challenges.
- *Scenario logic:* the student selects the level of a topic -> the student starts a challenge -> the system presents the current challenge with its choices -> the student submits a choice -> the system verifies the choice -> the system presents consequences and feedback -> the system updates achievements and progress -> the system shows additional learning material -> if desired, the student selects additional learning material -> repeat until the current level of a topic is finished.
- *Additional rules:* in all the following cases the system records all states at events: (i) at any moment, the student can abort the game, (ii) in case of system failure, (iii) at any moment, the student can make a note, (iv) at any moment, the student can select informational help, and (v) the student can skip the additional learning material provided.

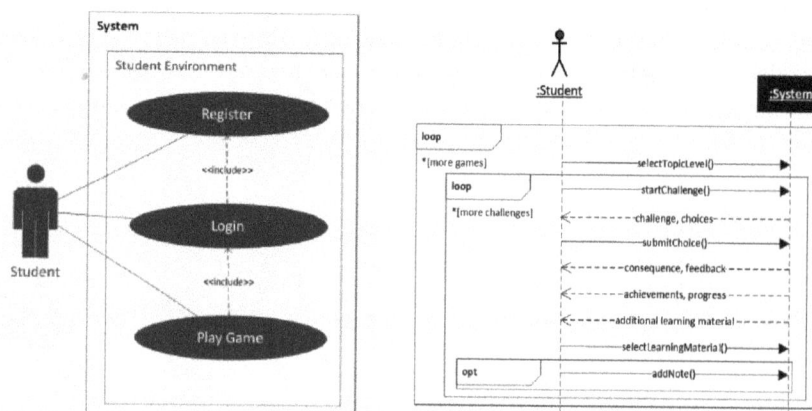

Figure 2: Use case diagram

Game architecture: this serves as the foundational framework that describes the overall user experience, feedback mechanism, educational effectiveness, and information flow between its core components. The architecture of the game proposed is illustrated in Figure 3 and has a modular structure allowing modular updates and extensions that enable the game to remain current with emerging cyber threats developments. Hence, the game architecture encompasses the following three layers:

- *Presentation layer:* represents the interface through which players interact with the game, containing graphics, user interface, and interactive elements. The implementation of this layer is done in JavaFX and FXML. JavaFX is a Java framework for developing cross-platform client applications with immersive media and graphical content, and FXML (Effects Extended Markup Language) is an XML-based language for defining the structure of the JavaFX interfaces.
- *Domain layer:* represents the backbone of the game as it contains the core logic and rules that govern the game while managing players' progression and feedback, in other words, it assures the alignment between the game mechanics and learning objectives of the game. The implementation of this layer is done in Java programming language.
- *Data layer:* represents the place where the game data is stored, retrieved from, and operated on for actions like creating players' profile, tracking players' performance, and scenario outcomes. Herein, MySQL is the relational databased management system used for managing and querying the data.

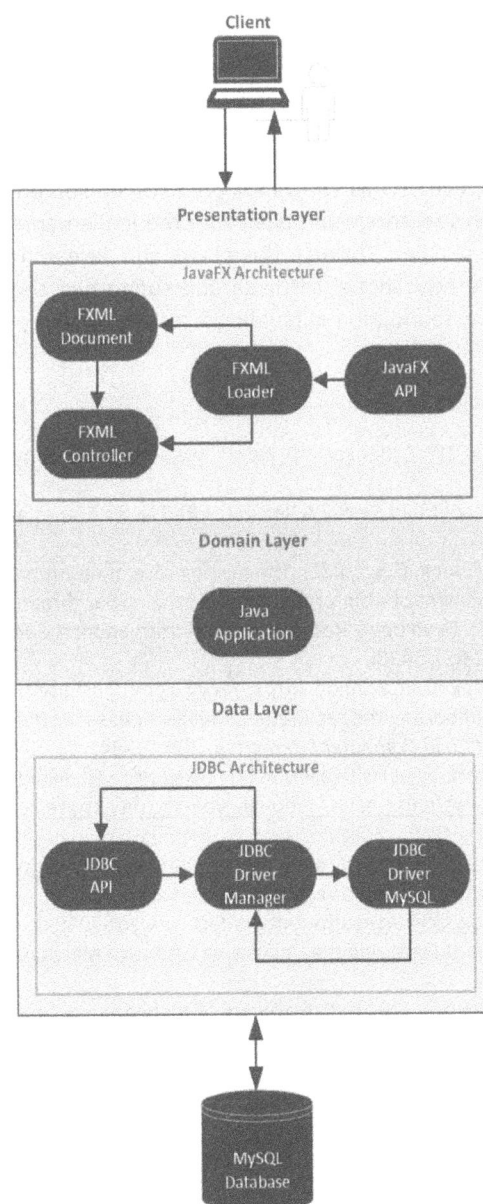

Figure 3: Game Design Architecture

5. Conclusions

While the advent of new technologies ushered unprecedent opportunities for connectivity and innovation across various societal domains, concomitant with these advancements are the uprising and escalating risks that reveal the importance and urgency of cyber security awareness. Although cyber security strategies and programs exist at regional, national, and local/organizational levels, they primarily focus on core assets like the infrastructure and corresponding systems and tools used, and only secondarily, on people (Tatum, 2023). Given the dynamism, complexity, and uncertainty that surround cyberspace (i.e., the digital domain), preventing, detecting, and responding in an effective manner to advanced, intelligent, and sophisticated threats is difficult as the threat landscape is continuously evolving and its effects cross the digital borders into the physical/human realm. Hence, cultivating cyber security awareness supports behaviour change and media literacy by building knowledge, skills, and resilience against cyber threats. Nevertheless, given the fact that children are digital natives being naturally drawn to social media platforms and content, they are also the most vulnerable and exposed ones to various cyber threats like authentication and disinformation as they lack cognitive maturity and discernment skills to navigate the digital sphere in a safe and responsible way (Maathuis & Chockalingam, 2022).

Based on the extensive literature review conducted in this research, efforts for building and enhancing cyber security awareness to primary and secondary schools through tools tailored to their cognitive abilities and age are in an incipient phase considering academic, governmental, or professional approaches and settings. It is then the aim of this research to tackle this knowledge gap and societal need by designing a cyber security awareness digital game for building and enhancing cyber security awareness among high school students in relation to cyber threats like social bots and broken authentication, which represent top cyber threats in the social media realm at global level. To achieve this aim, the architecture design of a cyber security awareness digital game is proposed in this research as the fundament for implementing the game using the Design Science Research methodology. This research continues with the implementation and evaluation of the game with high school students in real settings. Through this effort, this research strives to contribute to bringing cyber security awareness into the educational curricula and supporting the development of digital literacy programs tailored to children as the foundation of building a secure, privacy preserving, and responsible digital citizenship from an early age.

References

Bada, M., Sasse, A. M., & Nurse, J. R. (2019). Cyber security awareness campaigns: Why do they fail to change behaviour? *arXiv preprint arXiv:1901.02672*.

Barabas, R. (2023). What's the News About Bad News? A Review of Bad News Games as a Tool to Teach Media Literacy. *Libri, 73*(4), 283-292.

Caramancion, K. M., Li, Y., Dubois, E., & Jung, E. S. (2022). The missing case of disinformation from the cybersecurity risk continuum: A comparative assessment of disinformation with other cyber threats. *Data, 7*(4), 49.

Cernicova-Buca, M., & Ciurel, D. (2022). Developing Resilience to Disinformation: A Game-Based Method for Future Communicators. *Sustainability, 14*(9), 5438.

Common Sense (2018). Digital Passport Educator Guide. https://www.commonsense.org/

De Troyer, O., & Janssens, E. (2014). Supporting the requirement analysis phase for the development of serious games for children. *International Journal of Child-Computer Interaction, 2*(2), 76-84.

ENISA (2021). National cyber security strategies: with a vision on raising citizens' awareness. https://www.enisa.europa.eu/news/enisa-news/national-cybersecurity-strategies-with-a-vision-on-raising-citizens2019-awareness

ENISA (2023a). ENISA Threat Landscape 2023. https://www.enisa.europa.eu/publications/enisa-threat-landscape-2023

ENISA (2023b). Identifying emerging cyber security threats and challenges for 2030. https://www.enisa.europa.eu/news/cybersecurity-threats-fast-forward-2030

Fard, A. E., & Maathuis, C. (2021). Toward Capturing the Underlying Offensive Mechanisms of Social Manipulation: A Data Model Approach.

Giannakas, F., Kambourakis, G., & Gritzalis, S. (2015). CyberAware: A mobile game-based app for cybersecurity education and awareness. In *2015 International conference on interactive mobile communication technologies and learning (IMCL)* (pp. 54-58). IEEE.

Glas, R., van Vught, J., Fluitsma, T., De La Hera, T., & Gómez-García, S. (2023). Literacy at play: an analysis of media literacy games used to foster media literacy competencies. *Frontiers in Communication, 8*, 1155840.

Hart, S., Margheri, A., Paci, F., & Sassone, V. (2020). Riskio: A serious game for cyber security awareness and education. *Computers & Security, 95*, 101827.

Hevner, A. R., March, S. T., Park, J., & Ram, S. (2008). Design science in information systems research. *Management Information Systems Quarterly, 28*(1), 6.

Ibrahim, R., & Jaafar, A. (2009, August). Educational games (EG) design framework: Combination of game design, pedagogy and content modeling. In *2009 international conference on electrical engineering and informatics* (Vol. 1, pp. 293-298). IEEE.

IRIS Plus (2022). User empowerment against disinformation online. European Audiovisual Observatory.

ISO (2011). ISO/IEC 25010:2011 – System and software engineering standard. https://www.iso.org/standard/35733.html

ITU (2018). ITU Regional Workshop for Europe and CIS on Cybersecurity and Child Online Protection.

Jin, G., Tu, M., Kim, T. H., Heffron, J., & White, J. (2018). Game based cybersecurity training for high school students. In *Proceedings of the 49th ACM Technical Symposium on Computer Science Education* (pp. 68-73).

Kaur, J., & Ramkumar, K. R. (2022). The recent trends in cyber security: A review. *Journal of King Saud University-Computer and Information Sciences, 34*(8), 5766-5781.

Khader, M., Karam, M., & Fares, H. (2021). Cybersecurity awareness framework for academia. *Information, 12*(10), 417.

Kulhmann (2009). Build branched e-learning scenarios in three simple steps. https://blogs.articulate.com/rapid-elearning/build-branched-e-learning-scenarios-in-three-simple-steps/

Lees, J., Banas, J. A., Linvill, D., Meirick, P. C., & Warren, P. (2023). The Spot the Troll Quiz game increases accuracy in discerning between real and inauthentic social media accounts. *PNAS nexus, 2*(4), pgad094.

Lazer, D. M., Baum, M. A., Benkler, Y., Berinsky, A. J., Greenhill, K. M., Menczer, F., ... & Zittrain, J. L. (2018). The science of fake news. *Science, 359*(6380), 1094-1096.

Literat, I., Chang, Y. K., & Hsu, S. Y. (2020). Gamifying fake news: Engaging youth in the participatory design of news literacy games. *Convergence, 26*(3), 503-516.

Maathuis, C., & Chockalingam, S. (2022). Responsible digital security behaviour: Definition and assessment model. In *European Conference on Cyber Warfare and Security* (Vol. 21, No. 1).

Maathuis, C., Kerkhof, I., Godschalk, R., & Passier, H. (2023). Design Lessons from Building Deep Learning Disinformation Generation and Detection Solutions. In *European Conference on Cyber Warfare and Security* (Vol. 22, No. 1, pp. 285-293).

Micallef, N., Avram, M., Menczer, F., & Patil, S. (2021). Fakey: A game intervention to improve news literacy on social media. *Proceedings of the ACM on Human-Computer Interaction, 5*(CSCW1), 1-27.

Mikka-Muntuumo, J., & Peters, A. N. (2021). Designing an Interactive Game for Preventing Online Abuse in Namibia. In *2021 3rd International Multidisciplinary Information Technology and Engineering Conference (IMITEC)* (pp. 1-6). IEEE.

Olano, M., Sherman, A., Oliva, L., Cox, R., Firestone, D., Kubik, O., ... & Thomas, D. (2014). {SecurityEmpire}: Development and evaluation of a digital game to promote cybersecurity education. In *2014 USENIX Summit on Gaming, Games, and Gamification in Security Education (3GSE 14)*.

Paraschivoiu, I., Buchner, J., Praxmarer, R., & Layer-Wagner, T. (2021). Escape the Fake: Development and evaluation of an augmented reality escape room game for fighting fake news. In *Extended Abstracts of the 2021 Annual Symposium on Computer-Human Interaction in Play* (pp. 320-325).

Pastor-Galindo, J., Marmol, F. G., & Pérez, G. M. (2022). Profiling users and bots in Twitter through social media analysis. *Information Sciences, 613*, 161-183.

Peffers, K., Tuunanen, T., Rothenberger, M. A., & Chatterjee, S. (2007). A design science research methodology for information systems research. *Journal of management information systems, 24*(3), 45-77.

Quayyum, F., Cruzes, D. S., & Jaccheri, L. (2021). Cybersecurity awareness for children: A systematic literature review. *International Journal of Child-Computer Interaction, 30*, 100343.

Al Shamsi, A. A. (2019). Effectiveness of cyber security awareness program for young children: A case study in UAE. *Int. J. Inf. Technol. Lang. Stud, 3*(2), 8-29.

Smith, D. T., & Ali, A. I. (2019). YOU'VE BEEN HACKED: A TECHNIQUE FOR RAISING CYBER SECURITY AWARENESS. *Issues in Information Systems, 20*(1).

Tatum, D. (2023). *Gamification of security awareness training programs: a literature* (Doctoral dissertation, Georgia State University).

UNICEF (2021). Digital misinformation/disinformation and children. https://www.unicef.org/globalinsight/stories/digital-misinformation-disinformation-and-children

Urban, A., Hewitt, C., & Moore, J. (2018). Fake It to Make It: Game-based Learning and Persuasive Design in a Disinformation Simulator. In *Conference: Association for Educational Communications and Technology*.

Wolfenden, B. (2019). Gamification as a winning cyber security strategy. *Computer Fraud & Security, 2019*(5), 9-12.

Wu, T., Tien, K. Y., Hsu, W. C., & Wen, F. H. (2021). Assessing the effects of gamification on enhancing information security awareness knowledge. *Applied Sciences, 11*(19), 9266.

Yasin, A., Liu, L., Li, T., Wang, J., & Zowghi, D. (2018). Design and preliminary evaluation of a cyber security Requirements Education Game (SREG). *Information and Software Technology, 95*, 179-200.

Zhang-Kennedy, L., & Chiasson, S. (2021). A systematic review of multimedia tools for cybersecurity awareness and education. *ACM Computing Surveys (CSUR), 54*(1), 1-39.

Zwilling, M., Klien, G., Lesjak, D., Wiechetek, Ł., Cetin, F., & Basim, H. N. (2022). Cyber security awareness, knowledge, and behavior: A comparative study. *Journal of Computer Information Systems, 62*(1), 82-97.

The Possible Role of Digital Platforms in Information Operations

Niina Meriläinen

Faculty of Management and Business, Tampere University, Finland

Faculty of Social Sciences (SOC) Tampere University, Finland

Niina.merilainen@tuni.fi

Abstract: We have less knowledge of digital platforms in relation to credible information, news, and information operations among young people. While young people use digital platforms, do they consider themselves targets of information operations, false information, and news? The results tell us that young people use various digital platforms as sources of credible information and news. Young participants said they could never fall prey to fake news and information operations while trusting content creators, such as influencers on digital platforms, without verifying their agendas, backgrounds, funding, or motives. No one wondered if, at any point, any influencers might work for a hostile actor, entity, or state. Misinformation and disinformation, or fake news and information operations, did not concern young people. Confirmation biases were never admitted, since young participants trusted their instincts to find truthful information and news. The power of AI, machine learning, algorithms, advertising, bots, and influencers was discussed to a lesser degree. At worst, this has implications for democratic states.

Keywords: Information operations, Social media, Internet, Value framing, Influencers

1. Introduction

Young people use digital platforms such as various social media apps, discussion forums, and Internet sites as sources for fun, information, and news, as well as to participate globally and locally (Bergström & Belfrage, 2018; Pietilä, 2022; Oser et al., 2013; Meriläinen, 2021; 2022). User-centric research and design of the digital platforms enable a better experience and usability (Pietilä, 2022; Pietilä et al., 2019Ma). Together with artificial intelligence (AI) and various other digital means, the possibilities to connect and make an impact are vast. Young people can connect, participate in varying degrees, and find, create, and consume entertainment, information, and news. Young people claim ownership of digital platforms and their content (Meriläinen, 2022). Digital platforms also have various negative impacts on youth and the world (Nilan et al., 2015; Parris et al., 2022; Markey et al., 2022; Amichai-Hamburger & Ben-Artzi, 2003). Yet we have less knowledge of digital platforms in relation to credible information, news, and information operations among young people. While young people use digital platforms, do they consider themselves easily misled by false information and news, or targets of information operations? Shallcross (2017) and Meriläinen (2023) highlighted the need for research on digital platforms and information operations. Related to the topic, this study asks, in their own minds, are young people prone to information operations online? Does confirmation bias play a role in the consumption of content that is deemed credible? What possibilities does this create possibilities for information operations and divisions in societies by local and international hostile actors?

The research questions for this study are:

RQ1: Who produces credible information and news for young people?

RQ2:Is the content on digital platforms considered a source for information operations?

Next, the related works are presented briefly. This is followed by the introduction of empirical data gathering. Following this, the results, discussion, and conclusions are presented.

2. Related Works

2.1 Value Framing and Credible Information

Framing is based on values and beliefs that guide every actor's behaviour, thinking, and communication, thus creating various understandings and archetypes (Meriläinen et al., 2023) such as youth and online content creators. This has great importance in creating salience and credibility in connection with confirmation biases, thus seeking credible and trusting information, news, and actors that align with a person's pre-existing values and beliefs. The theoretical choice of combining the fields of communication and political sciences with ICT (information and communication technology) has been made to create a new outlook on digital platforms in relation to confirmation biases, information operations among youth. Personal value framing connects our values and beliefs to the truthful information we sense and how we decode it in our thinking (Brewer and Gross, 2005; Shen and Edwards, 2005; Schemer et al, 2012; Slothuus, 2010). As Banks et al (2021) state that we live in a polarized world with media feeds. Thus, confirmation biases guide us toward the information and news as well as content creators we trust based on our values and beliefs. Aligned with confirmation bias, value framing affects how people, such as youth, view reality (Brewer and Gross, 2005) and the credibility of digital platforms and content creators as sources of truth and information. Framing is a powerful tool aimed at other actors, such as people, governments, and organizations, and how they view issues, events, and other actors. Please see more: (Lewin, 1947; Bachrach and Baratz, 1962; Cohen, 1963; Entman, 1993; Kilburn, 2009; Lippmann, 1922; McCombs, 1997; Stone and McCombs, 1981). With their chosen forms of communication, fashion, and behaviour, actors influence others by placing emphasis on chosen language, values, and beliefs, which means that the salience of an actor's language, values, and beliefs are transferred as salient to other actors, who then adopt them as reality in their own thinking. This process is called the transfer of salience in the communication context (McCombs and Reynolds, 2002), where personally salient information and news are shared and believed. These can be used to direct young people to use digital platforms and to consume information from these platforms as truths from chosen content creators, such as influencers worldwide.

2.2 Credible Information and Information Operations

Information operations utilize information as a tool to achieve various endgames. As information is generally regarded as a soft power, it may be most effectively implemented in times other than force-on-force military conflict, where, depending on its intent and objectives, information can be used to inform, persuade, threaten, or confuse audiences (Iasiello, 2017). Although different interpretations exist between academic disciplines, some argue that there is no strict definition of what information is. Information is used to create various realities and influence states, nations, and individuals online and offline (Chochowski, 2022) and is a tool in information operations. In relation to Madden (2000), information does present facts that actors accept as truths if the content aligns with their personal value framing. In addition, believed credible actors and confirmation biases are useful tools in information operations. In some cases, people are forced to accept information and news as truth, for example, by suppression or state- and actor-led power. Moreover, information, who shares it, and how it is perceived and accepted are linked to actors' credibility and the platforms where communication occurs. For example, social media platforms may be credible platforms for various young people (Meriläinen, 2021; 2022), but not for adults. Digital platforms are fertile soil for fake news and information operations (Van Der Linden et al., 2020). Information operations have been discussed in relation to fake news, elections, and social movements (Darraj et al., 2017; Davey et al., 2018; Briant, 2022). These operations are always participatory in nature when people partake in shaping and spreading them and the information they use. Furthermore, information operations are often discussed in the context of military and national defence (Turan, 2018; Thomas, 1998; Cox, 2006) also in social media environments. Yet, as Crawford (1999) says, information operations and warfare are too important to be left to the military. Access to digital networks creates a downward adjustment of established power differentials at all levels of society (Crawford, 1999). Content creators may be an alluring part of these operations.

In information operations, various types of information, including disinformation and misinformation, are disseminated through various forms of communication and platforms, both online and offline. Disinformation is false information that is deliberately intended to mislead and make untrue facts, while misinformation is false or inaccurate information where facts are wrong (APA, 2023). These can be combined and called fake news. Weedon et al (2017) define them as actions taken by organized actors, such as governments or non-state actors, to distort domestic or foreign political sentiment to achieve a strategic and/or geopolitical outcome. Information operations can use a combination of methods, for example, disinformation, false news, or networks of fake accounts aimed at manipulating public opinion (Weedon et al, 2017). Starbird et al (2019) argue that online information operations are participatory in nature, where messages spread through—and with the help of—online crowds and other information providers. Much like strategic communication, which uses framing, Starbird et al (2019) assert that strategic information operations are efforts by individuals and groups, including state and non-state actors, to manipulate public opinion and change, while others associate them with elections (Darraj et al, 2017; Davey et al, 2018). These operations are a global phenomenon with political, social, psychological, educational, and cybersecurity dimensions (Starbird et al, 2019). Referring to Hyman and Sheatsley's (1947) study on why information campaigns can sometimes fail, modern information campaigns and information operations do not vary much from theories on information campaigns since they are dependent on prior attitudes and beliefs. While young people are active online, how, if at all, do they regard information operations and do they fall for them?

3. Empirical Research Setting

This research relies on empirical data produced by young people. The empirical data comes from explorative empirical research conducted with vocational schools in n=8 municipalities in Western, Central, and Eastern Finland during February 2021–February 2024. During this explorative empirical research phase, n=366 young vocational school students between the ages of 16 and 29 were invited to be anonymous and volunteer research participants. Young participants produced the empirical data for this research either in written or spoken form in n=53 research workshops. The results of this study are drawn from empirical data via qualitative content analysis to formulate an understanding of how young vocational secondary school students regard information, news, actors, various digital platforms, and their perceptions of credibility and information operations. Research permits were granted by either vocational schools or cities and by the anonymous research participants.

Authors such as Pietilä et al. (2021) and Lazar et al. (2010) discuss the different ways to apply interviews and open discussion with young people in the realms of HCI (human-computer interaction) and multidisciplinary research. This research is qualitative and explorative in nature. Please see the in-depth look at the data gathering on Meriläinen (2022; 2021). Explorative research can be defined as a study with the intention of generating evidence that is needed to decide whether to proceed to the next phase of the research (Hallingberg et al., 2018). The explorative research method was chosen to develop multidisciplinary research protocols to conduct research with the youth, based on limited power relations between the adult researcher from the university and the young participants. To respect the young people's anonymity, their names, fields of study, and the names of the participating municipalities are not stated here. In this age of digital platforms, bullying, harassment, and violence, there is a possibility that the young participants could be identified using open-source information.

4. Results and Discussion

The results of the theoretical and empirical multidisciplinary research show that young research participants value the idea of the Nordic democratic state while using various digital platforms to shape their understanding of facts and fiction. Everyone out of all the n=366 volunteer research participants, from liberals to conservative Christians, used various digital platforms as a source for credible information and news as well as to participate politically. The most credible, trustworthy, and used platforms were Instagram, Discord, Reddit, TikTok, YouTube, and various other message boards and Internet pages, as well as gaming. Often these were used together; while gaming on one screen, social media platforms, such as TikTok and Discord, were open on another screen where credible content was consumed and shared. Several Finnish and international influencers, ranging from liberals to conservatives, were sources of credible information and news. Influencers were regarded as being a new generation of politicians who are on the side of the youth, while officials, traditional media, and journalists were not. The possible deception by influencers, or them being used as useful idiots in information operations, was not detected. Rather, it was seen as impossible.

Young research participants relied on a certain archetype of themselves as "us" aligned with trusted influencers, while adults, officials, journalists, and mainstream traditional media presented the archetype of "them," the ones fundamentally against the youth. Misinformation, disinformation, or information operations did not concern young people. They did not perceive themselves as targets for these. They said they could distinguish truth from fiction. Faith in one's ability to utilize critical media literacy was strong. They explain that they are native Internet and social media users, while claiming that people over 40 years old are not. Thus, people over 40 years old can be targets of information operations, while youth cannot.

Confirmation bias was never discussed. Yet, the truths were always aligned with existing personal values and beliefs. Confirmation biases were always denied when I specifically asked about them. However, based on the empirical data, confirmation biases guided the usage of digital platforms and the information and content creators the research participants trusted. Yet, the power of AI, algorithms, advertising machine learning, and bots was discussed, but only to some degree. AI and algorithms were seen as a means of personal and political control and coercion by those in power, so-called the global elite or the World Economic Forum, which kept people under control. A few young participants said that they have no other choice but to consume forced, false, and outdated information because AI and algorithms keep "people under control by force."

Young participants said they could never fall prey to fake news and information operations while trusting influencers on digital platforms without verifying their agendas, backgrounds, funding, or motives. No one wondered if, at any point, any influencers might work for hostile actors, entities, or states. This issue must be further researched in the coming months. Credibility and trust were related to: 1) the person's own values and beliefs; 2) the content creators' credibility; 3) the usability of the platforms; and 4) the credibility of the digital platforms. User-centric design (Pietilä, 2022) and framing of actors' communication hold an enormous advantage in reaching young people. This opens the door for future research in HCI and information operations.

The deception on digital platforms goes beyond consuming or being targets of false information. It forces you to become something you are not by using AI technology and filters to alter your looks and behaviour to better fit the current fashionable (western) standards of beauty, behaviour, and truth. There is indeed a need for discussions of normative values and beliefs in the era of fake news, information operations, the power of influencers, Trumpism, and institutionalized disregard for human rights. At least in the Global North, policymakers seem to pay lip service to the global threat of information operations on digital platforms, or it extends to simply condemning TikTok or Meta. Simultaneously, companies continue to facilitate grave abuses of human rights, create platforms for information operations, and make a handsome profit. Meanwhile, young participants laughed at entertaining content and filters on digital platforms while consuming content tailored to them on the FYP (For You Page) via algorithms.

Based on the empirical data, influencers on various digital platforms have a strong influence on young people. These actors may work independently, as a collective, or for someone else. They may simply build a personal brand in an individualistic world. Or they may also receive funding and directives from unknown actors or states. Young people look for help, truths, information, and role models on digital platforms and participate politically locally and globally online. They trust entertaining information tailored to match their values and beliefs without acknowledging any confirmation biases. They do not trust content creators that do not match their social or political belief systems. Information produced by the so-called wrong side is inherently disregarded as fake news. Here are the vast possibilities for actors wanting to conduct small- or large-scale information operations: With the help of user-centric design and focus research coupled with algorithms, AI, and bots, at best, various actors can create credible and entertaining content that corresponds with the biases, values, and beliefs of young people from various backgrounds. This has enormous potential for influencing societies via information operations, which are not regarded as warfare that can threaten democratic development of states.

The transfer of information and news (McCombs and Reynolds, 2002; Roberts et al., 2002) from various online platforms was evident. Young participants said they accepted the information and news from digital platforms as truth if they believed it to be true, if their friends liked it, and if the content creator was entertaining, credible, and seemed to be speaking the truth. The same applies to fake news (Allcott and Gentzkow, 2017); it is accepted if it *feels* right personally. Indeed, the empirical results correlate with the theoretical framework that people believe information to be true based on their personal value framing. Information must also come from trusted sources (Brewer and Gross, 2005; Shen and Edwards, 2005; Schemer et al., 2012; Slothuus, 2010; Meriläinen and Vos, 2013). Entertainment is a strong attribute for creating credible information and news online. Similar results were found in the earlier research (Meriläinen, 2021), which coincides with Granholm (2016) and Pietilä (2022), who argued that young people use digital platforms to be active and as part of their everyday lives. Young participants connect their online and offline lives and activities. Social media and the Internet were discussed often as one entity. Only after being asked, the young participants specified which digital platforms they used.

The power of influencers, for example, on YouTube, Instagram, and TikTok, is enormous for young people. They are seen as idols, entertaining, and credible in the world, where grownups are trying to dimmish and downplay the viability and smartness of young participants. Influencers communicate in ways that are understandable and relatable to young people. This may mean communication, for example, behaviour, looks, the tone of voice, Internet slang, or visual styles ranging from entertaining to serious and everything in between. Moreover, several attributes affect the credibility of online influencers, such as credibility and attractiveness (Balaban and Mustăţea, 2019). These enable extensive and versatile information operations if the content is created to appeal to young people from various backgrounds and political ideologies. Young people feel like they are being attacked, not by information operations but by adults over 40 years old. This is where the power of influencers on digital platforms lies. They can connect with young people in ways that parents, teachers, journalists, and officials cannot. The roles of fashion, behaviour, and credibility as well as user-centric design should not be overlooked when researching digital platforms, information operations, and the future of democratic development of societies globally.

According to Mejova et al. (2020), in the online world, different narratives, news, and actors from fields ranging from politics to business are competing for clicks. Previously, young people argued that anything goes online as long as you get clicks. (Meriläinen, 2022; 2023). Information operations are complicated and complex projects that aim to impose one's perception of reality on the other side of conflict (Chochowski, 2022). Indeed, information operations do not choose political or social sides but have, for example, utilised social media to promote various causes, from #blacklivesmatter to #bluelivesmatter (Briant, 2022). Starbird et al. (2019) argued that online information operations are participatory in nature, where messages spread through—and with the help of—online crowds and other information providers. In addition, Briant (2022) stated that during the US 2016 elections, Russia conducted various information operations by creating clandestine accounts, while others may have infiltrated social and political movements, such as the #BlackLivesMatter and #BlueLivesMatter movements. Thus, information operations do not need to create new divisions but rather utilise existing divisions and discourses in their operative tactics, which can have lasting effects on democratic societies. Based on these results, the divisions are between youth and adults, which creates a vast possibility for information operations. Young people believe and spread the content they consume online. They may thus spread content, which is part of information operations, as part of larger hybrid operations. As young people were involved in various political movements, from liberals to conservative Christians, they were willing to act on behalf of their ideology. The arena for information and actions was firstly digital. When pressed about the truthfulness of their values, beliefs, and ideologies, most of the participants noted that everything is online, thus their political actions and audiences are there. Once you have your own truth and audience set online, you can start the movement offline. Thus, in this way, the online and offline worlds come together.

However, while relying heavily on digital platforms and content creators, some young participants were nonetheless critical of various digital platforms. Pages like Reddit or Wikipedia were not to be trusted since anyone could add and edit the content. Also, social media platforms such as Instagram and TikTok were considered dangerous because nothing is real or to be trusted because of fake news, deep fakes, opinions framed as truthful information, and other negative effects such as bullying and hate speech. Here we have a dichotomy. As earlier research (Meriläinen, 2022) argued, young people noted that both traditional print and social media can be used as propaganda either by the state or by the editorial and "owning classes." This critique did not explicitly expand to content creators such as influencers on digital platforms. Online influencers were seen as free of outside money, or "the owning class" or World Economic Forum. While information operations are sociotechnical phenomena that rely on a variety of actors and structures to successfully disseminate problematic kinds of information (Arif and Wilson, 2019), the reality of misinformation and disinformation was not fundamental for the young participants. The role of algorithms was discussed by a handful of research participants. For these young people, algorithms were stronger than their own will to not consume the content online. Most commonly, the algorithms on Google and YouTube raised questions among young participants. Critical media literacy must be further studied in the future. Although in the large minority, some young participants noticed they were being directly influenced on particular social media, such as Instagram or TikTok, by known influencers and unknown actors such as AI or bots. A few young participants despised these unknown actors and their motives. Those belonging to this minority stated that algorithms, AI, or bots were unknown to them, yet they made them consume information and various goods, such as podcasts and content, online. This content then provided forcefully trusted information for young participants. Yet, they did not have the means to further elaborate on how they are influenced or to so-called fight these powerful actors.

To conclude, based on the empirical data, content creators such as influencers from various political sides, coupled with the right kind of fashion, behaviour, communication, user-centric research, AI, algorithms, bots, ads, and entertainment, as well as endless funding, have a strong influence on young people. These actors may work independently or for someone else. They may receive funding and directives from unknown actors or states in attempts to shake democratic states as part of hybrid operations. Young people look for truth and information role models on digital platforms. They trust information tailored to match their values and beliefs without admitting any confirmation biases towards influencers, information, or news online. Here are the vast possibilities for actors wanting to conduct small- or large-scale information operations: This has enormous potential for influencing societies and can, at worst, threaten democratic states and values for decades.

Funding: This research has been funded by Kone Foundation Finland.

Acknowledgements

I wish to thank the reviewers and young research participants.

References

Allcott, H. and Gentzkow, M. (2017) "Social media and fake news in the 2016 election", Journal of economic perspectives, Vol 31, No. 2, pp 211-236.

Albarracin, D. and Wyer Jr, R. S. (2000) "The cognitive impact of past behavior: influences on beliefs, attitudes, and future behavioral decisions", Journal of personality and social psychology, Vol 79, No. 1.

American Psychological Association, APA (2023) Misinformation and disinformation. [Online]. https://www.apa.org/topics/journalism-facts/misinformation-disinformation

Amichai-Hamburger, Y. and Ben-Artzi, E. (2003) "Loneliness and Internet use", Computers in human behavior, Vol 19, No. 1, pp 71-80.

Bachrach, P. and Baratz, M.S. (1962) "Two faces of power", The American Political Science Review, Vol 56, No. 4, pp 947-952.

Balaban, D. and Mustăţea, M. (2019) "Users' perspective on the credibility of social media influencers in Romania and Germany", Romanian Journal of Communication and Public Relations, Vol, 21, No. 1, pp 31-46.

Bergström, A and Belfrage, M. J. (2018) "News in social media", Digital Journalism, Vol 6, No. 5, pp 583-598.

Brewer, P. R. and Gross, K. (2005) "Values, framing, and citizens' thoughts about policy issues: Effects on content and quantity", Political Psychology, Vol 26, No. 6, pp 929-948.

Chochowski, K. (2022) "Legal aspects of information operations in Poland", Journal of Scientific Papers ''Social Development and Security'', Vol 12, No. 2, pp 1-11.

Cohen, B.C. (1963) *The Press and Foreign Policy*, Princeton University Press, Princeton.

Cox, J. L. (2006) "Information Operations in Operations Enduring Freedom and Iraqi Freedom: What Went Wrong?", School of Advanced Military Studies, United States Army Command and General Staff College.

Crawford, B. C. H. (1999) "Information warfare: Its application in military and civilian contexts", The Information Society, Vol 15, No. 4, pp 257-263.

Darraj, E., Sample, C. and Cowley, J. (2017) "Information operations: The use of information weapons in the 2016 US presidential election" In Proceedings of the 16th European Conference on Cyber Warfare and Security, pp 92-101.

Davey, J., Saltman, E. M. and Birdwell, J. (2018) "The mainstreaming of far-right extremism online and how to counter it: A case study on UK, US and French elections." In *Trumping the mainstream*. Routledge, pp 23-53.

Entman, R.M. (1993) "Framing: toward clarification of a fractured paradigm", Journal of Communication, Vol 43, No. 4, pp 51-58.

Granholm, C. (2016) "Blended Lives: ICT talk among vulnerable young people in Finland", Young, Vol 24, No. 2, pp 85-101.

Gray, L. (2018) "Exploring how and why young people use social networking sites", Educational Psychology in Practice, Vol 34, No. 2, pp 175-194.

Hallingberg, B., Turley, R., Segrott, J., Wight, D., Craig, P., Moore, L., Murphy, S., Robling, M., Simpson, S.A. and Moore, G. (2018) "Exploratory studies to decide whether and how to proceed with full-scale evaluations of public health interventions: a systematic review of guidance", Pilot and Feasibility Studies, Vol 4, No. 1, p 1-12.

Hyman, H. H. and Sheatsley, P. B. (1947) Some reasons why information campaigns fail. Public opinion quarterly, Vol 11, No 3, pp 412-423.

Iasiello, E. J. (2017) "Russia's improved information operations: from Georgia to Crimea," The US Army War College Quarterly: Parameters, Vol 47, No. 2, pp 7.

Jung, K. 1968, Symbolit. Piilotajunnan kieli. Translated by Rutanen M. Helsinki: Otava. (In Finnish)

Kamler, E.M. (2013) "Negotiating narratives of human trafficking: NGOs, communication and the power of culture", Journal of Intercultural Communication Research, Vol 42, No. 1, pp 73-90.

Kilburn, H.W. (2009) "Personal values and public opinion", Social Science Quarterly, Vol 90, No. 4, pp 868-885.

Lapadat, L., Balram, A., Cheek, J., Canas, E., Paquette, A. and Michalak, E.E. (2020) "Engaging youth in the bipolar youth action project: community-based participatory research", Journal of Participatory Medicine, Vol 12, No. 3, pp 1-24.

Lazar, J., H. J. Feng, and H. Hochheiser. (2010) Research Methods in Human-Computer Interaction. Chichester: Wiley.

Lewin, K. (1947) "Frontiers in group dynamics II. Channels of group life; social planning and action research", Human Relations, Vol 1, No. 2, pp 143-153.

Lippmann, W. (1922) *Public Opinion*, Macmillan, New York, NY.

Madden, A. D. (2000) "A definition of information", In Aslib Proceedings, Vol 52, No. 9, pp 343-349.

Markey, C. H. and Daniels, E. A. (2022) "An examination of preadolescent girls' social media use and body image: Type of engagement may matter most", Body Image, Vol 42, pp 145-149.

McCombs, M. (1997) #Building consensus: The news media's agenda-setting roles", Political communication, Vol 14, No. 4, pp 433-443.

McCombs, M., Reynolds, A. (2002) "How the news shapes our civic agenda" In Media effects: Routledge. pp 17-32.

Mejova, Y., Kalimeri, K., and Morales, G. D. F. (2023), Authority without Care: Moral Values behind the Mask Mandate Response. arXiv preprint arXiv:2303.12014.

Meriläinen, N. and Vos, M. (2013) "Framing issues in the public debate: the case of human rights", Corporate Communications: An International Journal, Vol 18, No. 1, pp 119-134.

Meriläinen, N. (2021) "My participation is often dismissed: how vocational school students participate in society," in Teaching Civic Engagement Globally, eds. E. C. Matto, A. R. M. McCartney, and E. A. Bennion (Washington, DC: American Political Science Association, New Hampshire), pp 359–373.

Meriläinen, N. (2022) "The Problems of the drifting young people – first look of framing of vocational school students in Finnish media", On Horizon Vol 30, pp 57–81.

Meriläinen, N., Hiljanen, M., & Rautiainen, M. (2023) Archetypes of youth as vectors in power relations From praises to information operations. Frontiers in Political Science, 5, 1228838.

Meriläinen, N. (2023) "Information operations do not worry me" – The Role of Credible Information on Digital Platforms. Journal of Information Warfare, 22(4), 93–112.

Middaugh, E., Bowyer, B. and Kahne, J. (2017) "U suk! Participatory media and youth experiences with political discourse", Youth & Society, Vol 49, No. 7, pp 902-922.

Nilan, P., Burgess, H., Hobbs, M., Threadgold, S., & Alexander, W. (2015) "Youth, social media, and cyberbullying among Australian youth: "Sick friends"", Social Media+Society, Vol 1, No. 2, pp 1-12.

Oser, J., M. Hooghe and S. Marien. (2013) "Is Online Participation Distinct from Offline Participation? A Latent Class Analysis of Participation Types and Their Stratification", Political Research Quarterly, Vol 66, pp 91–101.

Parris, L., Lannin, D. G., Hynes, K. and Yazedjian, A. (2022) "Exploring social media rumination: associations with bullying, cyberbullying, and distress", Journal of interpersonal violence, Vol 37, No. 5-6.

Pietilä, I. (2022), Studies of Digital Solutions Supporting Societal Participation of Youths. Doctoral Dissertation.

Pietilä, I., Varsaluoma, J., & Väänänen, K. (2019) Understanding the digital and non-digital participation by the gaming youth. In *Human-Computer Interaction–INTERACT 2019: 17th IFIP TC 13* International Conference, Paphos, Cyprus, September 2–6, 2019, Proceedings, Part II 17. Springer International Publishing. pp 453-471.

Pietilä, I., Meriläinen, N., Varsaluoma, J. and Väänänen, K. (2021) "Understanding youths' needs for digital societal participation: towards an inclusive Virtual Council", Behaviour & Information Technology, Vol 40, No. 5, pp 483-496.

Roberts, M., Wanta, W. and Dzwo, T. H. (2002) "Agenda setting and issue salience online", Communication research, Vol 29, No. 4, pp 452-465.

Schemer, C., Wirth, W. and Matthes, J. (2012) "Value resonance and value framing effects on voting intentions in direct-democratic campaigns", American Behavioral Scientist, Vol 56, No. 3, pp 334-352.

Schoenfeld, A. H. (1983) "Beyond the purely cognitive: Belief systems, social cognitions, and metacognitions as driving forces in intellectual performance", Cognitive science, Vol 7, No. 4, pp 329-363.

Shallcross, N. J. (2017) "Social media and information operations in the 21st century", Journal of Information Warfare, Vol 16, No. 1, pp 1-12.

Shen, F. and Edwards, H. H. (2005) "Economic individualism, humanitarianism, and welfare reform: A value-based account of framing effects", Journal of Communication, Vol 55, No. 4, pp 795-809.

Slothuus, R. (2010) "When can political parties lead public opinion? Evidence from a natural experiment", Political Communication, Vol 27, No. 2, pp 158-177.

Starbird, K., Arif, A and Wilson, T. (2019) "Disinformation as collaborative work: Surfacing the participatory nature of strategic information operations", Proceedings of the ACM on Human-Computer Interaction, 3(CSCW), pp 1-26.

Stone, G.C. and McCombs, M.E. (1981) "Tracing the time lag in agenda-setting", Journalism Quarterly, Vol 58, No.1, pp 51-55.

Thomas, T. L. (1998) "Dialectical versus empirical thinking: Ten key elements of the Russian understanding of information operations", The Journal of Slavic Military Studies, Vol 11, No. 1, pp 40-62.

Turan, S. (2018) "The Internet and social media as Information Operations and Public Relations Tools for the Turkish Armed Forces. Doctoral dissertation, Monterey, CA; Naval Postgraduate School.

van Der Linden, S., Roozenbeek, J., & Compton, J. (2020) "Inoculating against fake news about COVID-19. Frontiers in psychology", Vol. 11, pp 1-7.

Walters, S. (1994) "Algorithms and archetypes: evolutionary psychology and Carl Jung's theory of the collective unconscious", Journal of social and evolutionary systems, Vol 17, No. 3, pp 287-306.Weber, R., & Crocker, J. (1983) "Cognitive processes in the revision of stereotypic beliefs", Journal of personality and social psychology, Vol 45, No. 5, 961.

Weedon, J., Nuland, W., & Stamos, A. (2017) Information operations and Facebook. [Online] https://fbnewsroomus. files. wordpress. com/2017/04/facebook-and-information-operations-v1. pdf

Exploratory Study: Social Media Impact on Mental Health Perception in Colombian Gen Z

Luisa Fernanda Manrique Molina and Camilo Andrés Ramírez Roja

Business Administration Department, Pontificia Universidad Javeriana, Bogotá, Colombia

manrique.luisa@javeriana.edu.co
ramirezcamilo@javeriana.edu.co

Abstract: This exploratory study aimed to discern and comprehend the social media usage patterns and their perceived impact on mental health among Generation Z students at a Colombian university. Employing a mixed methods approach, data were collected from 361 Colombian Gen Z individuals. A focus group guide and a self-reported questionnaire, informed by focus group results, were utilized to evaluate diverse constructs. Qualitative data underwent iterative categorization (IC), while quantitative data underwent statistical analysis using SPSS software. Participants predominantly utilized social media for communication and entertainment, with indications of a link between social media use and anxiety. However, participants did not perceive social media as significantly influential in their decision-making processes or relationships. Notably, female participants reported higher anxiety levels. This study of Colombian Gen Z freshmen unveiled social media's notable influence on body image, mental health, and social rewards. It underscores the necessity for tailored interventions to foster positive online experiences, address gender-specific challenges, and reassess brand engagement strategies within this demographic. Additionally, it highlights the need for further research within the Colombian university context. Though the employed instrument exhibited acceptable validity and reliability levels, future research could benefit from enhancements. This paper represents the initial endeavor to analyze social media consumption among Generation Z in Colombia through a mixed methods approach. Examining social media consumption patterns and their impact on mental health contributes to academic discourse on this relationship, informing the design of appropriate pedagogic strategies while considering reported gender differences. This study contributes valuable insights into the intricate interplay between social media use and mental health among Colombian Gen Z students. Addressing these dynamics is pivotal in formulating targeted interventions and strategies to support the mental well-being of this demographic within university settings. Future investigations should focus on refining measurement tools and delving deeper into nuanced aspects of social media's influence on mental health within educational environments.

Keywords: Generation Z, Social media apps consumption, Mental health perceptions, Colombia, Social networks, Anxiety

1. Introduction

Several studies report global mobile phone usage at 68% and active social media engagement at 59% of the total population (DataReportal, 2023; Broadbent et al, 2017). Colombians spend an average of 9 hours daily online, ranking fourth globally (Pasquali, 2020). Specifically, Colombia ranks second for social media exposure, averaging 3 hours 46 minutes daily (Roa, 2019, 2021), which is significantly higher than the global average of 1 hour 15 minutes (Melo, 2023). This high exposure underscores the necessity for a deeper understanding of social media consumption among Colombian youth, and how it could be vital for businesses, policymakers, and educational institutions.

Generation Z, succeeding Generation Y, refers to the population born spanning the mid-1990s to mid-2000s (Dwivedula et al, 2019, p. 11). They exhibit unique traits, including realism, skepticism toward institutions, and a strict work-life separation (Bontekoning, 2019; Gentina, 2019). This group are of particular interest to researchers as they can be considered the first global cohort due to their digital immersion, regional studies, like those in Europe, contribute to a nuanced understanding of media influence (Vyugina, 2019; Scholz and Rennig, 2019). Despite general trends have been found, differences across cultures demand further exploration (Allahverdi, 2022; Davison et al, 2023).

Amid concerns globally about rising social media addictions, comprehending Generation Z's consumption patterns becomes crucial (Salo et al, 2018). Exploring their interactions with social media—how it influences their behavior, entertainment, and mental well-being—is essential (Davison et al, 2023). However, cultural variations necessitate diverse population studies (Salo et al, 2018). Researchers advocate for mixed methods to mitigate social desirability bias, underscoring the need for a balanced approach (Fisher, 1993; Salo et al, 2018).

This study aims to probe into Generation Z's social media usage patterns and its impact on mental health at a Colombian university, employing an exploratory mixed methods approach.

2. Literature review

2.1 Connecting Social Influence and Gratification Theories to Life Satisfaction in the Age of Social Media

Life satisfaction is regarded as a fundamental aspect of well-being (Vate-U-Lan, 2020). People inherently seek social interaction, with social ties often serving as an indicator of both life satisfaction and well-being (Valenzuela et al, 2009; McLaughlin et al, 2010). The advent of social networks has greatly facilitated human interaction, resulting in an increased global user base (Raza et al, 2020). It is plausible that individuals who actively engage on social networking platforms experience greater feelings of connectedness and heightened levels of satisfaction and well-being. Therefore, it is conceivable that college students with lower life satisfaction may increase their interaction on social networks, thereby experiencing enhanced well-being and increased social confidence (Valkenburg et al, 2006; Ellison et al, 2007; Valenzuela et al, 2009).

The social influence theory (Kelman, 1958) posits that an individual's behaviour is significantly influenced by the collective behaviour of society, indicating a profound societal impact on an individual's actions. The gratification theory (Blumler and Katz, 1974; Blumler, 1979) outlines how people utilize different media to fulfil various needs, including the pursuit of entertainment and relaxation, maintenance of personal relationships, self-discovery, and identity formation, and staying informed about current events. Understanding these needs and the degree of satisfaction provided by various media channels, including social networks, is vital (Currás-Pérez et al, 2013).

2.2 Generation Z, Their Social Media Consumption and Vulnerability to Negative Health Effects

Generation Z is arguably the most internet-dependent generation and the primary users of social networks. Since their inception, social networks have been developed to connect people worldwide, regardless of their location. This rapid development has significantly influenced and changed the communication habits of Generation Z, shaping their interactions through the internet. In terms of social media consumption, several studies have found that among the youngest European group, WhatsApp, YouTube, TikTok, Snapchat, and Instagram are the most popular platforms (Bontekoning, 2019; Gentina, 2019). On the other hand, American Generation Z relies on Instagram and Twitter as their main platforms for staying informed and keeping up with others (Seemiller and Grace, 2016, 2019). Interestingly, Generation Z students only use Facebook in a marginal way. It appears that the presence of their parents and family members on this social network is a significant factor influencing this behaviour. Several studies have indicated that Facebook is predominantly used by parents (Generation X and Baby Boomers) and is no longer considered relevant for Generation Z (Scholz and Rennig, 2019, p. 280; Seemiller and Grace, 2019).

In the Colombian context, recent studies report that 67% of Gen Z engage with brands to influence product innovation, and 71% only buy from brands they trust completely. Of the 33% who prefer to be anonymous online, 63% said they actively manage data sharing and privacy settings according to their preferences; this includes 63% of Gen Z. Furthermore, many Colombian consumers place great value on the appearance of personal success and achievement. Twenty-seven percent of respondents express this sentiment, a figure consistent with the global average. Additionally, 24% of Colombian Gen Z consumers prefer to use a brand or company's social media account or website to find information about a brand or product. Furthermore, 39% of Colombian Gen Z feel that more of their everyday activities will shift to in-person interactions in the future (Euromonitor International, 2023).

However, previous research has demonstrated that compulsive social media use still has a significant impact on physical and mental health, including sleep, affect, self-esteem, well-being, and overall functioning, particularly among adolescents (Cheng and Li, 2014; Li et al, 2023; Turel et al, 2016). Furthermore, the adverse effects of increased reliance on social media can have long-lasting consequences at the individual level. As social media has become a primary source of information, particularly during the pandemic, users across different age groups, and especially Generation Z, have become more vulnerable to issues such as misinformation, loneliness, anxiety, envy, narcissism, and depression (Andreassen et al, 2017; Singh et al, 2020).

There is a gap in the literature concerning the controversies surrounding the nature and outcomes of the primary uses of social media (Davison et al, 2023). Some studies suggest that following other people on social networks can serve to maintain interpersonal connections, but it can also transform into digital voyeurism (Mäntymäki and Riemer, 2014, 2016). Furthermore, research on the relationship between social anxiety and social media use remains inconclusive, as highlighted by Erliksonn et al (2020). They advocate for the utilization of self-report measures specifically adapted to the context of social media, which could enhance research efforts.

3. Methodology

The methodology for this exploratory study followed a mixed methods approach, starting with a qualitative phase to inform the design of the questionnaire. The aim was to identify usage patterns and gain insight into social media consumption among Generation Z and their perceptions regarding mental health implications at a Colombian University. The combination of qualitative and quantitative insights helped construct a more holistic understanding of the complexities that surround Generation Z's perceptions of mental health in the Colombian context.

3.1 Qualitative Methods

3.1.1 Data collection

For the qualitative phase, a focus group was conducted with seven freshmen students aged between 19 and 20 years old. A purposive sampling method was used as participants needed to meet specific criteria related to social media usage. The focus group utilized projective techniques, including sentence completion and third-person questions. A total of 31 questions were asked, with a focus on understanding the participants' perceptions of social network use, potential mental health implications, and the impact of social networks on social interactions. A $10 financial incentive was raffled among all participants. Initially, three focus groups were planned, one with freshmen and the other with senior students. However, due to insufficient participation, only one focus group was held.

3.1.2 Analysis of the focus group

For the focus group analysis, the entire session was first transcribed. Then, during the review of the transcript, recurring and important themes that emerged from the participants were identified (Smithson, 2000). The iterative categorization (IC) technique is applicable for both inductive and deductive coding and can accommodate various analytical methods employed in research, such as thematic analysis, content analysis, and narrative analysis (Neale, 2016). This iterative process allows findings to emerge from the participants' discourse (Neale, 2016; Srivastava and Hopwood, 2009), which are then coded.

3.2 Quantitative Methods

3.2.1 Measures

For the quantitative phase, a questionnaire with 39 questions was administered through the Qualtrics platform. The purpose of this questionnaire was to gather insights into individuals' ideas and perceptions regarding the subjective levels of anxiety and isolation caused by excessive use of social networks, in relation to mental health and social interactions. The questionnaire included items on demographic data, the selection of potential mental impairments associated with social networks, and scales ranging from 3 to 10 categories to measure these constructs (Davison et al, 2023). As there was no validated questionnaire available in Spanish for the constructs to be assessed, part of the proposal by Critikián and Núñez (2021) was used as a criterion. Additionally, some items and scales were adapted from other studies (Anderson and Wood, 2023; Davison et al, 2023).

Our sample consisted of 361 participants recruited also through purposive sampling to meet the criteria of social media use. Out of 393 questionnaires, 9 participants were excluded as they reported not being social network users, 7 participants claimed to be social network users but did not answer any questions about their usage, and 16 participants did not complete the questionnaire, resulting in a total of 361 responses analysed. Table 1 provides a summary of the participants' demographics. Statistical analyses were conducted using SPSS version 26 software.

Table 1: Participant demographic characteristics (n=361)

Characteristic	n°	% of n
Age		
Less than 18	48	13.30%
18 -20	132	36.57%
20 -23	74	20.50%
More than 23	107	29.64%

Characteristic	n°	% of n
Gender		
Female	196	54.29%
Male	161	44.60%
No binary/other	2	0.55%
Prefer don't say	2	0.55%

4. Results

4.1 Qualitative Results

Based on the focus group analysis, several key findings have emerged:

1. The use of social media by participants, primarily to present their idealized image and alleviate boredom.
2. The influences of social networks on young people. Interestingly, they tend to deny high influence on Gen Z and perceive themselves as mature individuals.
3. Possible effects on mental health, which can be attributed to inadequate emotional management and immaturity.

4.1.1 Main Findings

All participants agreed that social interactions predominantly occur through social networks. However, they acknowledged that these interactions could involve information manipulation and the presentation of an idealized image. Nestor (Male, 20, #3) stated:

Thanks to social networks, people have been able to socialise more and expand their social circle. However, personal relationships are much stronger face-to-face, as they allow for emotional ties to be established.

The participants recognized that social networks could perpetuate the idea of a "perfect life" by allowing individuals to modify their lives and physical appearance. Silvana (Female, 20, #4) expressed:

People seek to show a life, which in most cases is not the real one, with the sole purpose of having social acceptance or demonstrating different aspects of life to an audience that may not be completely known.

While the participants acknowledged that social networks and digital media could potentially influence everyday decisions, they did not consider them as determinants or causes for their actions. They did not believe that social networks have a significant influence on their lives. Silvana (Female, 20, #4) elaborated:

The fact that social networks do not possess influence in the personal lives of their users is acquired over time; this is because when you start using social networks at a young age, the influence is much greater, either in terms of the number of likes or the appearance of people on them. However, as time goes on, people start to acquire their own style and get into the mindset that they should be accepted for who they are and how they are.

Participants expressed the belief that younger individuals, such as children or adolescents, are more susceptible to influence due to their limited personal development and maturity. Consequently, social networks do not exert a significant influence on their daily lives.

When interviewees were questioned about how social networks could affect users' mental health, most effects were attributed to inadequate emotional management and insufficient maturity to cope with the various aspects associated with social network use. Carlos (Male, 19, #5) stated that:

People who are still in the process of maturing and use social networks may not have fully established what they seek in life. When they see influencers presenting perfect bodies or lives, these individuals can experience mental health issues. Modifying social media content to project a perfect life, without sufficient maturity or emotional management, can negatively affect users' mental health and self-image.

Regarding the duration of social network usage, respondents reported spending approximately 4 to 6 hours a day, which can extend up to 10 hours, particularly when they feel bored. Carlos (Male, 19, #5) commented:

Most of the time, social networks are used as a means of distraction during moments of boredom.

Social networks can contribute to self-comparison among young people. All participants agreed that many young individuals compare themselves and desire the physical appearance of others due to societal beauty standards and the desire for social acceptance. Carlos (Male, 19, #5) emphasized this issue, explaining:

When observing different individuals, including their physical appearance and body shape, many people develop a desire to possess the same physical attributes. Society instils numerous stereotypes regarding beauty and social acceptance.

The study further explored the mental health effects of social networks by engaging participants in a sentence completion task. The results indicated that the participants associated the effects with stereotypes and insecurities, while another linked them to depression. Additionally, respondents identified anxiety problems as the primary cause, and connected them to self-esteem issues. Thus, according to participants' perspectives, anxiety problems and self-esteem issues emerged as the predominant factors impacting mental health.

Finally, participants shared their overall perspectives on social networks, acknowledging both the advantages and disadvantages that arise from their use, which depend on how individuals engage with them, their maturity, and their age. Interviewees recognized the awareness people have regarding the implications of using social networks and the changes that have occurred in social interactions in today's society. The frequent use of electronic devices has had an impact on social relationships. Silvana (Female, 20, #4) expressed:

Within contemporary society, social paradigms cannot be completely eliminated, as they are an inherent and enduring factor in our social fabric.

4.2 Quantitative Results

4.2.1 Reliability and factor analysis

To assess the reliability and validity of the data set and instrument, Cronbach's alpha measure of internal consistency (Cronbach, 1951) was utilized to determine the construct's alpha value. For exploratory studies, a value of 0.6 is deemed acceptable (Garson, 2013; Hair, 2019; Hoque et al, 2018; Nunnally, 1975). With a Cronbach's alpha coefficient of 0.635, surpassing the threshold of 0.6, the required reliability for the model is achieved. An exploratory factor analysis (EFA) test was conducted to validate the questionnaire. The Kaiser-Mayer-Olkin (KMO) index was 0.64, exceeding the recommended value of 0.6 (Kaiser, 1970), and Bartlett's Test of Sphericity (Bartlett, 1954) reached statistical significance ($\chi2$ =3,519.69, p<.001), indicating that our data were suitable for factor analysis. The results of the initial analysis revealed six factors with Eigenvalues over 1, explaining 10.50%, 10.05%, 9.22%, 7.71%, 5.46%, and 5.1% of the variance, respectively. The reliability of the derived factors from the validity analysis is presented in Table 2.

Table 2: Descriptive statistics and construct reliability

Components/constructs	M	Sd	Cronbach's α
Frequency of use	2.166	0.299	0.28
Level of anxiety/insecurity	2.571	1.904	0.74
Use of social networks	3.047	0.849	0.35
Social isolation and beliefs	4.120	0.781	0.60
Favorite social networks	3.902	1.220	0.75
Level of satisfaction	4.029	0.911	0.82

Note: acceptable Cronbach's alpha coefficient >.6

4.2.2 Correlation analysis

To examine the relationship between the time of use and beliefs regarding social network usage, specifically in relation to anxiety and social isolation, a Pearson correlation analysis was conducted. In terms of the number of followers, young individuals demonstrated a positive correlation between a higher number of followers and the duration of their presence on the social network (r = 0.138, p = 0.009), as well as their daily usage of social networks (r = 0.247, p < 0.001). Conversely, a lower sense of isolation when interacting face-to-face with others was associated with a larger number of followers (r = -0.119, p = 0.025).

Regarding the daily use of social networks, there was an inverse association with the perception of isolation resulting from social network usage (r = -0.204, p < 0.001), as well as the belief in increased problems related to depression, anxiety, and self-esteem (r = -0.127, p = 0.016). Moreover, young individuals associated feelings of isolation on social networks with an increased belief in depression, anxiety, and self-esteem problems (r = 0.223, p < 0.001), as well as the belief in isolation during face-to-face interactions with others (r = 0.225, p < 0.001). Additionally, both beliefs in increased problems and isolation demonstrated a strong positive correlation (r = 0.499, p < 0.001).

Subsequently, the same perceptions of young individuals were assessed in relation to self-reported anxiety levels. In the context of social networks, particularly Instagram, young individuals reported higher levels of anxiety and insecurity with increased daily use (r = 0.170, p = 0.001). Similar findings were observed for TikTok (r = 0.157, p = 0.003), along with a stronger belief in anxiety correlating with a higher number of followers (r = 0.127, p = 0.016). Furthermore, Twitter (r = 0.105, p = 0.048), Pinterest (r = 0.201, p < 0.001), and WhatsApp (r = 0.115, p = 0.030) also showed a positive association between increased daily use and higher perceived anxiety and insecurity among young individuals. Conversely, YouTube demonstrated a negative correlation between belief in anxiety and insecurity and the amount of time spent on the platform (r = -0.135, p = 0.010). Notably, young individuals did not establish any significant relationship between these perceptions and anxiety or insecurity while using Snapchat.

4.2.3 Sex and gender differences

To examine potential sex and gender differences, a t-test was conducted to compare the perceptions of social beliefs and social isolation between males and females. Participants who did not indicate their gender or identified as non-binary were excluded from the analysis due to the small number of participants, as indicated in Table I. Gender exhibited statistically significant differences in perceptions of social isolation caused by social networks, with women (M = 4.40, SD = 0.783) scoring higher than men (M = 4.21, SD = 0.912), t(df = 353) = 2.154, p = 0.032, d = 0.230. However, no sex differences were observed in beliefs regarding increased problems associated with social networking or in feelings of isolation during face-to-face interactions.

The perceived level of anxiety for each social network was then assessed. Females reported a higher level of anxiety perception (M = 3.65, SD = 3.225) compared to males (M = 2.88, SD = 3.226) for TikTok, t(df = 355) = 2.154, p = 0.025, d = 0.239, and Pinterest (female, M = 1.41, SD = 2.459; male, M = 0.65, SD = 1.424), t(df = 355) = 3.651, p < 0.001, d = 0.370. Conversely, for Twitter, males reported a higher level (M = 2.62, SD = 3.132) of anxiety compared to females (M = 1.70, SD = 2.844), t(df = 355) = -2.862, p = 0.004, d = -0.308.

5. Discussion

Participants highlighted the adaptability of social networks in moulding lives and appearances to match convenience, aligning with research by Valencia et al (2021) and Burnell et al (2022). These studies assert societal beauty standards drive the use of filters to modify appearances. Internet and social media impact young minds, fostering impulsivity and hampering inhibitory functions (Patil et al, 2021), potentially fuelling desires to conform to evolving beauty norms (Burnell et al, 2022).

However, Critikián and Núñez (2021) and Martínez-Martínez et al (2022) underscore a contradiction in perceptions. Social networks induce rapid gratification, triggering a sense of satisfaction akin to reinforcing events (Xu et al, 2022). Positive social rewards may drive increased social media usage among youth (Anderson and Wood, 2023), influenced by factors such as gender and parental involvement (Keresteš and Štulhofer, 2020). Investigating this contradiction is imperative.

Participants raised mental health concerns stem from the interplay of anxiety and low self-esteem, where low self-esteem fuels anxiety (He, 2022; Vahedi and Saiphoo, 2018). Extensive social media use is linked to diminished health-related quality of life (Davison et al, 2023).

Moreover, participants reported using social networks during boredom, an area underexplored concerning its impact on well-being (Huang, 2017). Usage time correlates more strongly with loneliness than self-esteem, indicating a need for further studies on its relation to life satisfaction, an indicator of psychological well-being.

Raza (2020) notes social identity's role in bolstering self-esteem among college students, driving their social network usage. Gender disparities in network use are linked to social relationships, body image, cyberbullying, and lower physical activity among females during adolescence (Keresteš and Štulhofer, 2020).

Surprisingly, contrary to expectations (Ismail et al, 2021), participants did not express brand engagement or purchase intentions through social media. Instead, they associated influence with negativity and immaturity.

This research reveals the intricate interplay between social media usage patterns and social rewards, particularly among Colombian Gen Z college students. The insights gained can inform the development of tailored interventions and strategies to foster mindful and balanced social media usage within the university setting. Educators' involvement in designing intellectually stimulating activities could prevent boredom in the learning process.

Identifying gender-specific challenges related to social media usage among Colombian Gen Z university students, such as preoccupation with body image and experiences of cyberbullying, underscores the need for gender-specific support mechanisms and inclusive online environments in Colombian universities.

In conclusion, participants' insights illuminate the flexible nature of social networks in shaping lives and appearances, revealing contradictions in their perceived impact on satisfaction and mental well-being. Addressing these inconsistencies requires further scholarly attention.

References

Allahverdi, F.Z. (2022) "Relationship between perceived social media addiction and social media applications frequency usage among university students", *Psychology in the Schools*, Vol 59, No. 6, pp 1075–1087, https://doi.org/10.1002/pits.22662.

Anderson, I.A. and Wood, W. (2023) "Social motivations' limited influence on habitual behavior: Tests from social media engagement", *Motivation Science*, Vol 9, No. 2, pp 107–119, https://doi.org/10.1037/mot0000292

Andreassen, C.S., Pallesen, S. and Griffiths, M.D. (2017) "The relationship between addictive use of social media, narcissism, and self-esteem: Findings from a large national survey", *Addictive Behaviors*, Vol 64, pp 287–293, https://doi.org/10.1016/j.addbeh.2016.03.006.

Bartlett, M.S. (1954) "A Note on the Multiplying Factors for Various Chi-Square Approximations", *Journal of the Royal Statistical Society: Series B (Methodological)*, Vol 16, No. 2, pp 296-298. https://doi.org/10.1111/j.2517-6161.1954.tb00174.x.

Blasco-Fontecilla, H. (2021) "El impacto de las redes sociales en las personas y en la sociedad: redes sociales, redil social, ¿o telaraña?", *Tarbiya: Revista de investigación e innovación educativa*, Vol 49, pp 97-110, https://doi.org/10.15366/tarbiya2021.49.007.

Blumler, J.G. (1979) "The role of theory in uses and gratifications studies", *Communication Research*, Vol 6, No. 1, pp 9-36.

Blumler, J.G. and Katz, E. (1974) "The uses of mass communications: current perspectives on gratifications research", Sage Annual Reviews of Communication Research, Vol. III, ERIC Number: ED119208.

Bontekoning, A. (2019) "Generation Z in the Netherlands: Updating Aging Organisations", in Scholz, C. and Rennig, A. (Eds.), *Generations Z in Europe: Inputs, insights and implications, The Changing Context of Managing People*, Emerald Publishing, Bingley UK, pp. 127–148, https://doi.org/10.1108/978-1-78973-491-120191015.

Broadbent, E., Gougoulis, J., Lui, N., Pota, V. and Simons, J. (2017) "Generation Z: Global Citizenship Survey", [online] Varkey Foundation, https://www.varkeyfoundation.org/media/4487/global-young-people-report-single-pages-new.pdf.

Burnell, K., Kurup, A. R., and Underwood, M. K. (2022) "Snapchat lenses and body image concerns", New Media & Society, Vol 24, No. 9, pp 2088-2106, https://doi.org/10.1177/1461444821993038.

Cheng, C. and Li, A.Y. (2014) "Internet addiction prevalence and quality of (real) life: a meta-analysis of 31 nations across seven world regions", *Cyberpsychology, Behavior, and Social Networking*, Vol 17, No. 12, pp 755–760, https://doi.org/10.1089/cyber.2014.0317.

Chevalier Naranjo, S. (2022) "¿Cuántos latinoamericanos usan las redes sociales para informarse?", [online], Statista https://es.statista.com/grafico/27010/uso-de-las-redes-sociales-para-consultar-las-noticias-en-america-latina.

Critikián, D. M., and Núñez, M. M. (2021) "Redes sociales y la adicción al like de la generación z", *Revista de Comunicación y Salud*, Vol 11, pp. 55-76, https://doi.org/10.35669/rcys.2021.11.e281.

Cronbach, L.J. (1951) "Coefficient alpha and the internal structure of tests", *Psychometrika*, Vol 16, No. 3, pp 297–334, https://doi.org/10.1007/BF02310555.

Currás-Pérez, R., Ruiz-Mafé, C., & Sanz-Blas, S. (2013) "Social network loyalty: evaluating the role of attitude, perceived risk and satisfaction", *Online Information Review*, Vol 37, No. 1, pp 61-82, https://doi.org/10.1108/14684521311311630.

DataReportal (2023), "Digital 2023: Global Overview Report", [online] DataReportal – Global Digital Insights https://datareportal.com/reports/digital-2023-global-overview-report.

Davison, J., Bunting, B. and Stewart-Knox, B. (2023) "The mediating effect of food choice upon associations between adolescent health-related quality of life and physical activity, social media use and abstinence from alcohol", *Health and Quality of Life Outcomes*, Vol 21, No. 1, p 46, https://doi.org/10.1186/s12955-023-02129-7.

Dwivedula, R., Singh, P., and Azaran, M. (2019) "Gen Z: where are we now, and future pathways", *Journal of HRM Human Resource Management*, Vol 20, No. 2, pp 28-40.

Ellison, N. B., Steinfield, C., and Lampe, C. (2007) "The benefits of Facebook "friends:" Social capital and college students' use of online social network sites", *Journal of computer-mediated communication*, Vol 12, No. 4, pp 1143-1168, https://doi.org/10.1111/j.1083-6101.2007.00367.x.

Erliksson, O.J., Lindner, P. and Mörtberg, E. (2020) "Measuring associations between social anxiety and use of different types of social media using the Swedish Social Anxiety Scale for Social Media Users: A psychometric evaluation and cross-sectional study", *Scandinavian journal of psychology*, Vol 61, No. 6, pp 819–826, https://doi.org/10.1111/sjop.12673.

Euromonitor International (2023) "Consumer Lifestyles in Colombia", [online] Passport, Euromonitor International https://www.portal.euromonitor.com/Analysis/Tab.

Fisher, R.J. (1993), "Social Desirability Bias and the Validity of Indirect Questioning", *Journal of Consumer Research*, Vol 20, No. 2, p 303, https://doi.org/10.1086/209351.

Garson, G.D. (2013), *Validity and reliability*, Statistical Associates Publishers, Asheboro USA.

Gentina, E. (2019) "Generation Z in France: Reverse Socialisation and Social Engagement", in Scholz, C. and Rennig, A. (Eds.), *Generations Z in Europe: Inputs, insights and implications, The Changing Context of Managing People*, Emerald Publishing, Bingley UK, pp 109–126, https://doi.org/10.1108/978-1-78973-491-120191014.

Hair, J. F, Black, C. W, Babin, B. J, and Anderson, R, E. (2009) *Multivariate data analysis*, Pearson Prentice Hall, USA.

He, X. (2022), "Relationship between Self-Esteem, Interpersonal Trust, and Social Anxiety of College Students", *Occupational Therapy International*, Vol 2022, p. 8088754, https://doi.org/10.1155/2022/8088754.

Hoque, A. S. M. M., Siddiqui, B. A., Awang, Z. B., and Baharu, S. M. A. T. (2018) "Exploratory factor analysis of Entrepreneurial orientation in the context of Bangladeshi small and medium Enterprises (SMEs)", *European Journal of Management and Marketing Studies*, Vol 3, No. 2, pp 81-94, https://doi.org/10.5281/zenodo.1292331.

Huang, C. (2017) "Time Spent on Social Network Sites and Psychological Well-Being: A Meta-Analysis", *Cyberpsychology, Behavior, and Social Networking*, Vol 20, No. 6, pp 346–354, https://doi.org/10.1089/cyber.2016.0758.

Ismail, A.R., Nguyen, B., Chen, J., Melewar, T.C. and Mohamad, B. (2021) "Brand engagement in self-concept (BESC), value consciousness and brand loyalty: a study of generation Z consumers in Malaysia", *Young Consumers*, Vol. 22, No. 1, pp 112–130.

Jenkins, R. H., Shen, C., Dumontheil, I., Thomas, M. S., Elliott, P., Röösli, M., and Toledano, M. B. (2020) "Social networking site use in young adolescents: Association with health-related quality of life and behavioural difficulties", *Computers in human behavior*, Vol 109, p 106320, https://doi.org/10.1016/j.chb.2020.106320.

Kaiser, H.F. (1970), "A second generation little jiffy", y. *Psychometrik*, Vol 35, pp 401-415, https://doi.org/10.1007/BF02291817.

Kereteš, G., and Štulhofer, A. (2020), "Adolescents' online social network use and life satisfaction: A latent growth curve modeling approach", *Computers in Human Behavior*, Vol 104, p 106187, https://doi.org/10.1016/j.chb.2019.106187.

Lagla, G. A. F., Chisag, J. C. C., Moreano, J. A. C., Pico, O. A. G., and Pulloquinga, R. H. M. (2017) "La influencia de las redes sociales en los estudiantes universitarios", *Boletín Redipe*, Vol 6, No. 4, pp 56-65.

Li, L., Xu, D. D., Chai, J. X., Wang, D., Li, L., Zhang, L., Lu, L., Ng, C. H., Ungvari, S. L. M., and Xiang, Y. T. (2018) "Prevalence of Internet addiction disorder in Chinese university students: A comprehensive meta-analysis of observational studies", *Journal of behavioral addictions*, Vol 7, No. 3, pp 610-623, https://doi.org/10.1556/2006.7.2018.53.

Mäntymäki, M. and Riemer, K. (2014) "Digital natives in social virtual worlds: A multi-method study of gratifications and social influences in Habbo Hotel", *International Journal of Information Management*, Vol 34, No. 2, pp 210–220, https://doi.org/10.1016/j.ijinfomgt.2013.12.010.

Mäntymäki, M. and Riemer, K. (2016) "Enterprise social networking: A knowledge management perspective", *International Journal of Information Management*, Vol 36, No. 6, pp 1042–1052, https://doi.org/10.1016/j.ijinfomgt.2016.06.009.

Martínez-Martínez, F. D., González-García, H., and González-Cabrera, J. (2022) "Student's social networks profiles, psychological needs, self-concept and intention to be physically active", *Behavioral Psychology*, Vol 30, No. 3, pp 757-772, https://doi.org/10.51668/bp.8322310n.

McLaughlin, D., Vagenas, D., Pachana, N. A., Begum, N., and Dobson, A. (2010) "Gender differences in social network size and satisfaction in adults in their 70s", *Journal of Health Psychology*, Vol 15, No. 5, pp 671-679, https://doi.org/10.1177/1359105310368177.

Melo, M.F. (2023) "Más de tres horas diarias dedicadas a las apps" [online], Statista, https://es.statista.com/grafico/29846/tiempo-medio-diario-que-usuarios-dedican-a-distintas-aplicaciones.

Neale, J. (2016) "Iterative categorization (IC): a systematic technique for analysing qualitative data", *Addiction*, Vol 111, No. 6, pp 1096-1106, https://doi.org/10.1111/add.13314.

Nunnally, J.C. (1975) "Psychometric Theory. 25 Years Ago and Now", *Educational Researcher*, Vol 4, No. 10, pp 7-21.

Patil, A. U., Madathil, D., and Huang, C. M. (2021), "Age-related and individual variations in altered prefrontal and cerebellar connectivity associated with the tendency of developing internet addiction", *Human Brain Mapping*, Vol 42, No. 14, pp 4525-4537, https://doi.org/10.1002/hbm.25562.

Pasquali, M. (2020) "¿Cuántas horas al día pasamos conectados a internet?", [online], Statista, https://es.statista.com/grafico/22701/tiempo-medio-de-uso-diario-de-internet.

Raza, S. A., Qazi, W., Umer, B., and Khan, K. A. (2020) "Influence of social networking sites on life satisfaction among university students: a mediating role of social benefit and social overload", *Health Education*, Vol 120, No. 2, pp 141-164, https://doi.org/10.1108/HE-07-2019-0034.

Roa, M.M. (2019) *"La adicción a las redes sociales en el mundo"*, [online], Statista, https://es.statista.com/grafico/18988/tiempo-medio-diario-de-conexion-a-una-red-social.

Roa, M.M. (2021) *"Más de 70 países han bloqueado o restringido el acceso a redes sociales desde 2015"*, [online], Statista, https://es.statista.com/grafico/24035/paises-segun-sus-practicas-de-bloqueo-a-plataformas-de-redes-sociales.

Salo, J., Mäntymäki, M. and Islam, A.N. (2018) "The dark side of social media – and Fifty Shades of Grey introduction to the special issue: the dark side of social media", *Internet Research*, Vol 28, No. 5, pp 1166–1168, https://doi.org/10.1108/IntR-10-2018-442.

Scholz, C. and Rennig, A. (2019) *Generations Z in Europe: Inputs, insights and implications, The Changing Context of Managing People*, Emerald Publishing, Bingley UK.

Seemiller, C. and Grace, M. (2016) *Generation Z goes to college*, Jossey-Bass Inc.U.S, New York USA.

Seemiller, C. and Grace, M. (2019) *Generation Z: A century in the making*, Routledge Taylor and Francis Group, Milton, New York USA

Singh, S., Dixit, A. and Joshi, G. (2020) "Is compulsive social media use amid COVID-19 pandemic addictive behavior or coping mechanism?", *Asian journal of psychiatry*, Vol 54, p 102290, https://doi.org/10.1016/j.ajp.2020.102290.

Smithson, J. (2000) "Using and analysing focus groups: Limitations and possibilities", *International Journal of Social Research Methodology*, Vol 3, No. 2, pp 103–119, https://doi.org/10.1080/136455700405172.

Srivastava, P. and Hopwood, N. (2009) "A Practical Iterative Framework for Qualitative Data Analysis", *International Journal of Qualitative Methods*, Vol 8, No. 1, pp 76–84, https://doi.org/10.1177/160940690900800107.

Turel, O., Romashkin, A. and Morrison, K.M. (2016) "Health Outcomes of Information System Use Lifestyles among Adolescents: Videogame Addiction, Sleep Curtailment and Cardio-Metabolic Deficiencies", *PLOS ONE*, Vol 11, No. 5, p. e0154764, https://doi.org/10.1371/journal.pone.0154764.

Vahedi, Z., and Saiphoo, A. (2018) "The association between smartphone use, stress, and anxiety: A meta-analytic review", *Stress and Health*, Vol 34, No. 3, pp 347-358, https://doi.org/10.1002/smi.2805.

Valencia Ortiz, R., Cabero Almenara, J., Garay Ruiz, U., and Fernández Robles, B. (2021) "Problemática de estudio e investigación de la adicción a las redes sociales online en jóvenes y adolescentes", *Revista Tecnología, Ciencia y Educación*, Vol 18, pp. 99-125.

Valenzuela, S., Park, N., and Kee, K. F. (2009) "Is there social capital in a social network site?: Facebook use and college students' life satisfaction, trust, and participation", *Journal of computer-mediated communication*, Vol 14, No. 4, pp 875-901, https://doi.org/10.1111/j.1083-6101.2009.01474.x.

Valkenburg, P. M., Peter, J., and Schouten, A. P. (2006) "Friend networking sites and their relationship to adolescents' well-being and social self-esteem", *CyberPsychology & Behavior*, Vol 9, No. 5, pp 584-590, https://doi.org/10.1089/cpb.2006.9.584.

Vate-U-Lan, P. (2020) "Psychological impact of e-learning on social network sites: Online students' attitudes and their satisfaction with life", *Journal of Computing in Higher Education*, Vol 32, No. 1, pp 27-40, https://doi.org/10.1007/s12528-019-09222-1.

Vyugina, D. (2019) "How McLuhan Would Have Talked to Us: The Extension of Generation in the Global Village", in Scholz, C. and Rennig, A. (Eds.), *Generations Z in Europe: Inputs, insights and implications, The Changing Context of Managing People*, Emerald Publishing, Bingley UK, pp. 39–40, https://doi.org/10.1108/978-1-78973-491-120191003.

Xu, H., Phan, T. Q, and Tan, B. C. (2022) "Why are people addicted to SNS? Understanding the role of SNS characteristics in the formation of SNS addiction", *Journal of the Association for Information Systems*, Vol 23, No. 3, pp 806-837, https://doi.org/10.17705/1jais.00735.

An Analysis of Online Bulletin Board Discussions Using Posting Transitions

Minoru Nakayama[1], Satoru Kikuchi[2] and Hiroh Yamamoto[2]
[1]Tokyo Institute of Technology, Tokyo, Japan
[2]Shinshu University, Matsumoto, Japan

nakayama@ict.e.titech.ac.jp

Abstract: Online discussion transitions were analysed as a means of furthering the development of critical thinking disposition of students and their attitude toward disaster mitigation. The discussion was organised as an additional learning activity during a fully online course. The participant's posted messages were analysed using a network analysis technique in order to promote discussion and learning performance. The posting chain was represented as an adjacency matrix and posting relationships were analysed. The results suggest that discussant's activity shows a hierarchical structure, with some participants posting in response to lecturer's instructions. Posting participants were classified into several clusters, and these characteristics were analysed. Though single-posting participants were not active discussants, their characteristics, including their learning performance, could be readily recognised correctly during the analysis.

Keywords: Online discussion, Network analysis, Critical thinking, Student's characteristics, Learning activity

1. Introduction

The ability to think critically may help people make assessments during emergencies such as natural disasters or social unrest. In order to develop this ability, theoretical procedures have been discussed (Rychen and Salganik, 2003; Kikuchi 2018). A practical activity to train critical thinking disposition (CTD) is suitable for certain types of discussions, including online forums (Ekahitanond, 2013; Trehan et al., 2017) has been recognised. Since the effectiveness of online discussions has been demonstrated (Kusumi and Tanaka, 2008; Leh et al., 2012), the authors have been conducting surveys of participant's CTD abilities and individual characteristics (Nakayama et al. 2021, 2022a, 2022b, 2023). However, evaluation of discussion activity is not easy because the discussion depends on the mutual relationships between discussants or on the topic presented. Though some lexical content analyses were introduced to extract the quantitative contents of discussions, assessment of individual performance was not easy (Nakayama et al. 2016; Teranishi et al. 2017).

Student's discussion activities have been analysed using qualitative and quantitative approaches, in particular some issues of the discussion style are discussed discussion style are examined through the change of the lesson format from face-to-face to online (Smith, 2019; Julien and Dockwah, 2020). In order to promote the discussion activity, collaboration by students and procedures that support discussion groups are required. These points have been examined through practical analyses and case study assessments (Gasparic and Pecar, 2016). In addition to the conventional analysis of the progress of discussions, more dynamic assessments using mathematical analysis of the transitions of speakers or postings (Li et al. 2022), or lexical analysis of discussion contents (Zara et al. 2018) would be preferred. Also, more anatomical approaches are required to extract the structure of discussions (Han and Xu, 2022). These analyses may reveal the developing progress necessary to acquire CTD abilities.

As discussion activity may depend on the development of robust communication, some relationships involving speaking-out or posting and reviewing the opinions of others may provide information about participant's individual contributions. Therefore, any analyses of activity where participants present their own opinions in discussions shows the ongoing stage of development of the desired disposition rather than simply analysing overall posting frequency or posted sentences.

In this paper, participant's discussion activities on a bulletin board, such as posting transitions, were analysed in order to understand their learning activity. The following topics will be addressed:

- Online discussion activity during participant's message exchange process was analysed using a network analysis technique in order to examine discussion activity that would further the ability to develop critical thinking disposition.
- By extracting discussion characteristics from a bulletin board, individual posting behaviour was classified and **the** ability to participate in discussions was evaluated using measured individual characteristics.

In order to analyse relationships between posting behaviour and individual characteristics, survey data from two years of classes at a Japanese university was introduced.

2. Method

The development of critical thinking disposition was observed during a regularly scheduled on-demand style fully online course at a university in Japan (Nakayama et al., 2021, Nakayama et al. 2023).

2.1 Learning Settings

The course was entitled the Psychology of Natural Disaster Mitigation and Prevention, and consisted of 15 sessions. Learning performance of participants was evaluated using several activities, such as weekly confirmation tests and report assignments. The course has been provided in fully online style since 2020. The lecturer recorded videos of his lectures in advance, and the video clips for each session were delivered using an LMS. The main methods of learning assessment during the course were online tests and report essay writing. The participant's essay reports were evaluated by the course lecturer using a rubric which was presented to participants in advance. The number of registered students was above 400. The valid number of essay report submissions was 440 in 2022, and 364 in 2023. In order to encourage better understanding of the subject matter, all participants were invited to participate in online discussions. Online discussion boards were available throughout the course, and participants could obtain additional marks which contributed to their final mark. This opportunity represented a significant incentive for students.

2.2 Survey Metrics

In order to extract the characteristics of participants in the class, the following inventories were surveyed during the course. In addition to individual characteristics such as personality and literacy, these are the targeted scales for critical thinking and disaster prevention abilities. In this project most metrics were measured continuously (Nakayama et al. 2021, 2022b), and some new metrics were introduced for the purpose of the current research. Though every metric has an independent measurement scale, rating comparisons between scales are not intended as a purpose of the research. These ratings will be compared using metrics of online posting activities in the following sections of the paper.

2.2.1 Personality (Big5)

Scores of participant's personalities were measured using a shortened version of the Big5 inventories, which consists of 10 question items (Kawamoto et al. 2015). The factors which were extracted were Extroversion (P1), Conscientiousness (P2), Neuroticism (P3), Openness (P4), and Agreeableness (P5). The factor scores of the Big5 use 7-point scales (1-7).

2.2.2 Literacy of science and technology (LST)

Kawamoto et al (2013) developed an inventory of science and technology literacy which is based on a survey of scientific literacy. It consists of 10 questions, from which four factors were extracted from the answers: Life-centered (LST-1), Sciencephile (people who are interested in science and technology) (LST-2), Logic-oriented (LST-3), and Authoritarian (LST-4). The LSTs were scored using a 4-point scale (1-4). Four clusters of LSTs were also defined in order to compare behavioural attitudes toward Social Science issues using the four dimensional factor scores (Kawamoto et al. 2013).

2.2.3 Critical thinking disposition (CTD)

Hirayama and Kusumi (2004) developed a Japanese inventory of behaviour exhibited during development of critical thinking. Four factors from the inventory were extracted: Awareness of logical thinking (CTD-1), Inquiry-mindedness (Inquisitiveness) (CTD-2), Objectiveness (Objectivity) (CTD-3), and Evidence-based judgment (CTD-4). These CTDs were scored using a 5-point scale (1-5). These metrics were surveyed twice, during the first and second halves of the course. The differential scores between the two surveys are also used in the following analysis, and the sum of the four factor scores is referred to as the CTD meta metric.

2.2.4 Disaster-prevention consciousness (DPC)

These inventories were developed to measure attitude toward disaster-prevention consciousness, and consisted of 20 question items using a 6-point Likert scale (1-6) (Ozeki et al. 2017). The total score is defined as the summation of scores for the 5 aspects (imagination for disaster situations, a sense of crisis about disasters, the degree to which other participants were spoken to, interest in disaster, anxiety, with the minimum score being 20 and the maximum score being 120. This metric was also surveyed twice during the course, and the two scores were compared.

2.2.5 Weekly test scores (WTS)

The lecturer recorded videos of his lectures in advance, and the video clips for each session were delivered using the university LMS (a Moodle learning management system). All communications such as assignment submissions, online tests, essay report reviews and follow-up surveys were conducted using the LMS. Learning performance was evaluated using online evaluations such as short written tests which asked about course session topics (WTS).

2.2.6 Essay Report and Comments

An essay report task was assigned in order to evaluate student's in class performance, and was to be marked as part of their overall final grade assessment.

2.3 Discussion Activity Measure

Transitions of messages posted on the bulletin board were recorded. The record can be extended to a path of messages responding to a previous posting. The relationship between participants who posted is summarised as an adjacency matrix, as shown in Figure 1. In this matrix, columns and rows show individuals and the frequency of their messages which are responses is noted as a component. If the initial posting seems to be a self-tweet, then the posting is recorded as a diagonal component.

The features of online discussions recorded over two years are summarised in Table 1. Both the number of participants and the level of activity posting threads in 2023 is less than in 2022, as the activity may depend on participant's level of interest in the course content and motivation, even though all course environmental factors are the same.

```
1 5 1 2 1 3 3 1 0 1 1 0
0 5 1 2 1 3 2 2 0 1 1 0
0 1 0 2 1 1 0 0 1 0 0 0
0 1 2 4 0 0 0 1 0 0 0 0
0 1 1 0 1 1 0 0 0 0 0 1
0 0 0 0 0 4 0 1 0 1 0 0
0 2 0 0 0 2 1 0 0 0 0 0
0 2 0 1 0 0 1 0 0 0 0 0
0 0 0 0 0 0 0 0 1 0 0 0
0 0 0 0 0 0 0 0 0 1 0 0
0 0 0 0 0 0 0 0 0 0 1 0
0 0 0 1 0 0 0 0 0 1 0 0
0 0 0 0 0 0 0 0 0 0 1 0
```

Figure 1: An example of Adjacency matrix (a part of transaction in 2023 survey)

Table 1: Basic features of online discussion activities in two years

Year	2023	2022
Active members	364	440
N of participants for discussion (% in total)	34 (9.3%)	127 (28.9%)
one posting participant (% of participants)	20 (58.8%)	64 (50.4%)
threads	20	62
mean post frequency	2.85	2.37
max posting	20	12

3. Results

3.1 Summarising Discussion Network

Network analysis was introduced in order to illustrate posting activity. Here, all transactions in 2023 are summarised as a directional graph in Figure 2(a). All nodes are labelled with the numbers of each participant. The number "1" shows a lecturer who has joined as a facilitator. A self-loop shows initial postings by participants. Most initial presenters seem to post frequently as participants. Participants with single postings are located in the peripheral region, as shown by a single arrow line. These participants simply followed the postings of others. The network illustration can be also converted into a circle layout. As Figure 2(b) shows, more than half of the participants are represented as followers of the initial postings. As Table 1 shows, more than half of the participants were participants with single postings. In all discussions during the course, the number of discussion participants is limited. Figures 3(a) and 3(b) show focused networks for frequent submitters (i.e., a frequency more than 1). Even these participants are divided into several groups by their posting frequency.

3.2 Participant Clustering

As shown in the previous section, the behaviour of participants varies between individuals. In order to extract features of posting behaviour, a clustering technique is applied to the summarised adjacency matrix using a measure of betweenness centrality for nodes on the graph (Ognyanova, 2016). The dendrogram in Figure 4(a) summarises sub-groups which are similar. The horizontal axis represents the number of participants. The number "1" indicates postings by the lecturer. The summarised clusters are marked using colours on the graph illustration in Figure 4(b). The frequent posting communication cluster which includes the lecturer's posts in the centre of the graph can be extracted and marked, and the remaining parts are presented as additional small clusters.

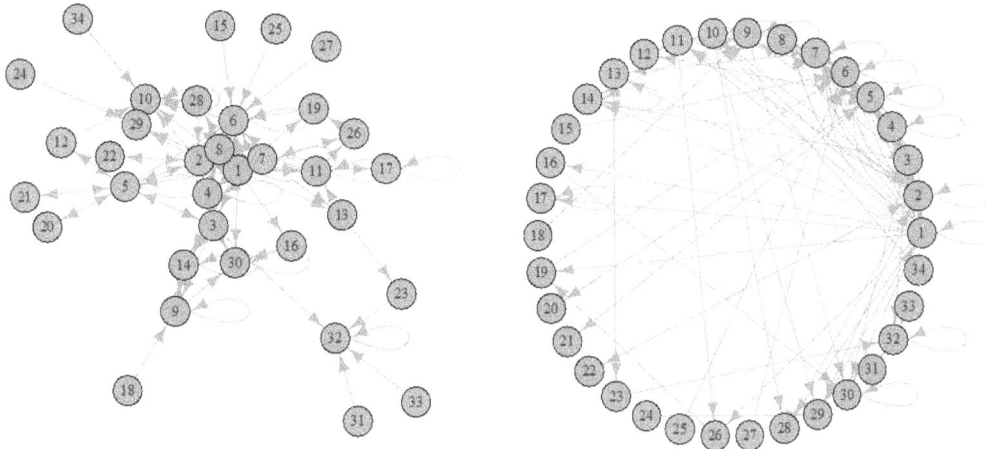

Figure 2: Network illustrations for all transaction in 2023 survey as a graph (a) and a circle layout (b)

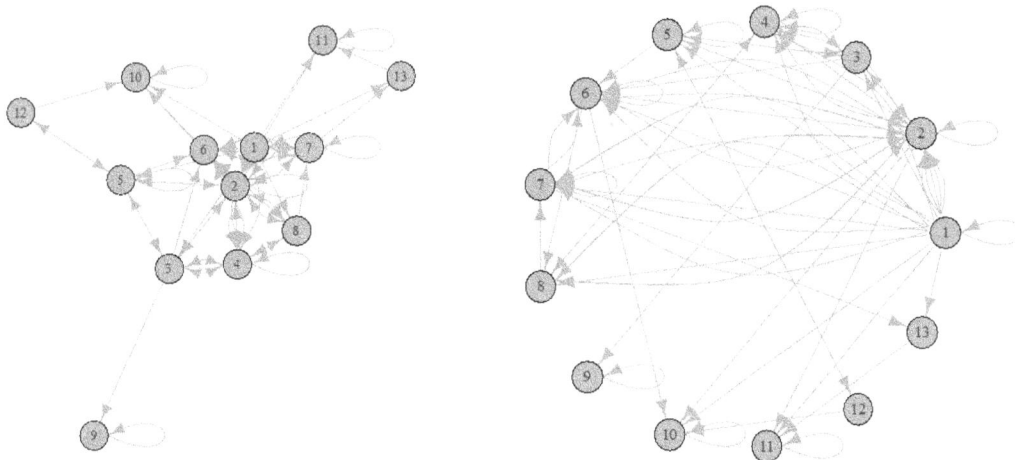

Figure 3: Illustration with selected participants (postings>1) in 2023 survey as a graph (a) and a circle layout (b)

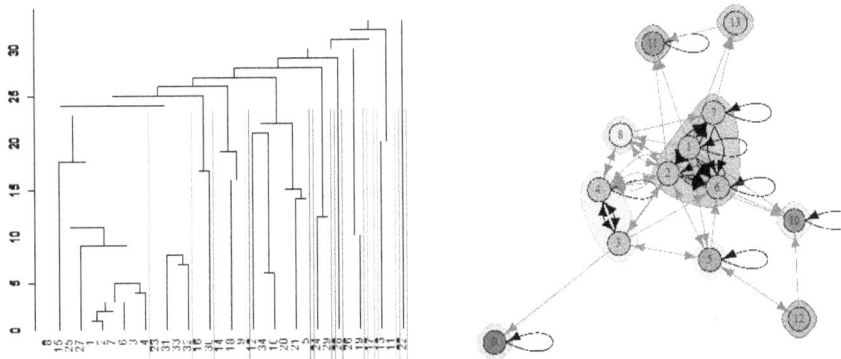

Figure 4: Illustrations of cluster analysis for 2023 survey, with dendrogram results in (a) and (b) showing cluster markings on Figure 3(a)

These analyses are applied to transactions of postings in the 2022 survey. The results are shown in Figures 5(a) and 5(b). In both results, the first major cluster includes the lecturer, as some participants responded to the lecturer's instructions. The sub-groups containing the most frequent communications were extracted as a cluster during the analysis.

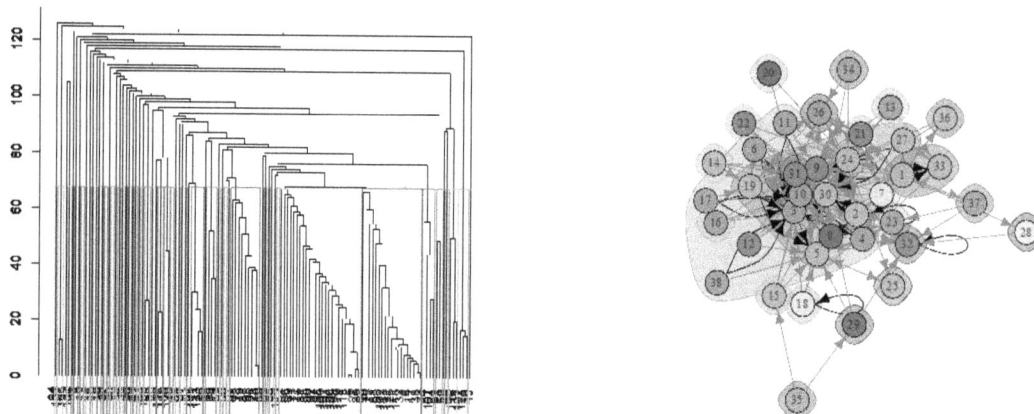

Figure 5: Illustrations of cluster analysis for 2022 survey, with dendrogram results in (a) and (b) showing cluster markings of selected posting participants.

3.3 Participant's Characteristics and Learning Performance

In order to extract features of classified clusters of postings by participants, surveyed metrics from individual responses are compared. In regards to the results of cluster analysis for the two surveys in 2023 and 2022, mean scores of metrics are compared between major clusters. Small clusters are merged as "Other" clusters. The results are summarised in Table 2 for the 2023 survey and in Table 3 for the 2022 survey. To confirm the differences between clusters, one-way ANOVA of each metric is conducted, however there are no significant differences because the number of participants is small. In comparing mean scores of metrics, the highest values are marked using bold face. The highest values appear mostly for clusters without clust:1, which includes the lecturer.

Table 2: Statistics of 2023 survey

Student's characteristics	Clust:1(10)	Clust:2(6)	Clust:3(3)	Clust:4(2)	Others (13)
PS1: Extroversion	3.4	5.0	**5.8**	3.3	4.5
PS2: Conscientiousness	3.0	3.0	2.8	**5.5**	2.8
PS3: Neuroticism	4.6	4.3	4.0	4.5	**5.1**
PS4: Openness	4.0	4.7	**4.8**	2.5	3.8
PS5: Agreeableness	3.3	2.8	**3.5**	3.0	3.2
KG1: Life-centered	3.7	3.4	**4.3**	4.0	3.9
KG2: Sciencephile	3.5	4.0	**4.3**	3.0	3.6
KG3: Logic-oriented	3.3	3.7	4.0	3.0	**4.1**
KG4: Authoritarian	3.2	2.9	3.2	3.0	**3.5**
CTD1: Critical Thinking Disposition-1st survey	14.1	13.9	**15.2**	**15.2**	13.8
CTD2: Critical Thinking Disposition-2nd survey	13.9	13.9	14.1	**16.1**	14.3
DPC1: Disaster-prevention Consciousness-1st survey	76.4	84.5	**94.0**	84.5	86.0
DPC2: Disaster-prevention Consciousness-2nd survey	76.6	81.0	73.5	75.5	**83.2**
WTS: Weekly Test Score	920.0	733.3	793.3	**940.0**	743.3
Report essay score	80.6	**84.1**	75.0	77.5	77.3
Mean posting frequency	8.4	2.5	2.0	2.0	1.0

Table 3: Statistics of 2022 survey

Student's characteristics	Clust:1(18)	Clust:2(25)	Clust:6(9)	Others (74)
PS1: Extroversion	4.2	**4.4**	3.4	4.0
PS2: Conscientiousness	3.8	3.5	**4.0**	3.4
PS3: Neuroticism	4.5	4.7	**5.0**	4.7
PS4: Openness	3.8	**4.0**	3.3	3.9
PS5: Agreeableness	**3.1**	2.6	3.0	3.0
KG1: Life-centered	3.7	**3.8**	3.5	3.7
KG2: Sciencephile	3.5	3.4	**3.6**	3.5
KG3: Logic-oriented	3.1	**3.4**	3.0	**3.4**
KG4: Authoritarian	3.3	3.0	**3.5**	3.3
CTD1: Critical Thinking Disposition-1st survey	**14.7**	14.4	13.5	14.2
CTD2: Critical Thinking Disposition-2nd survey	13.8	**14.3**	13.9	13.7
DPC1: Disaster-prevention Consciousness-1st survey	83.3	85.3	**85.6**	82.2
DPC2: Disaster-prevention Consciousness-2nd survey	84.9	85.0	85.3	81.5
WTS: Weekly Test Score	758.9	855.2	**875.6**	835.1
Report essay score	**80.3**	78.8	80.0	79.6
Mean posting frequency	3.1	2.0	1.9	2.4

It is interesting that the characteristics and performance of participants who responded to the lecturer's postings do not show higher numerical values. The highest scores for weekly tests (WTS) appear on a cluster which shows the highest score for conscientiousness (PS2). Also, the posting frequency of these clusters is not the highest of all of the clusters. This suggests that simple enhancement of participant's frequent postings of their own opinions may not contribute to a participant's understanding of critical thinking ability and learning performance.

4. Discussion

Discussion activity is believed to aid in development of critical thinking disposition and objectiveness, which are based on behaviour during disaster mitigation. To enhance discussion activity in response to the large number of participants, an extended community was organised using a bulletin board as a virtual space. Also, the lecturer used this to lead and to encourage discussion by participants.

In regards to the previous studies, frequent participation and posting activity in response to the lecturer's invitation were preferred during online discussions. Our previous study has also confirmed that participants with multiple postings show better performance during learning (Nakayama et al. 2023).

This paper examines the detailed relationship between posting behaviour and individual characteristics or learning performance, even though the number of participants was limited. In regards to our hypothesis, participants with frequent postings who sympathise with the lecture's postings were expected to show a better level of performance than with the previous results. Participant's performance within a cluster which includes the lecturer do not always show the highest averages for metrics. Participants in clusters without the most frequent number of postings also achieved better performance during the surveys in both years **these** were conducted.

Though there were no significant differences in survey metrics, the results reveal an interesting piece of evidence. Participants who did not post frequently also joined the discussions, and might have observed the activity of discussants who posted frequently while posting only a few times themselves. This phenomenon seems similar to the situation known as "legitimate peripheral participation" (Lave & Wenger, 1991). Since discussion participants may gain some actual knowledge without even postings any messages of their own, their participation activity should be evaluated affirmatively.

These procedures will be a subject of our further study.

5. Summary

Posting transitions between participants in online discussions were evaluated in order to extract the developmental progress of individuals regarding critical thinking disposition during a fully online course, using a network analysis technique to understand the progress of the exchange of opinions.

Participant's posted message transitions were summarised as an adjacency matrix, and the posting relationships were analysed. The results suggest that discussants joined as a hierarchical structure, and that some participants posted in response to the lecturer's instructions. Participants who posted were classified into several clusters, and the participant's characteristics and learning performances were analysed. The result suggests that participants whose postings frequently synchronised with the lecture's postings did not always show the highest levels of performance in the metrics surveyed. Since some of the remaining clusters of participants showed better performance, more multi-level support for participants is required.

As these results do not coincide with the hypotheses, a more detailed analysis will be required.

Acknowledgement

This research was partially supported by the Japan Society for the Promotion of Science (JSPS), Grant-in-Aid for Scientific Research (KAKEN, 21K18494: 2021-2024).

References

Ekahitanond, V. (2013) Promoting University Students Critical Thinking Skills Through Peer Feedback Activity In An Online Discussion Forum, Alberta Journal Of Educational Research, 59(2), Pp. 247-265.

Gasparic, R.P., Pecar, M. (2016) Analysis Of An Asynchronous Online Discussion As A Supportive Model For Peer Collaboration And Reflection In Teacher Education, J. Information Technology Education: Research, 15, 377-401.

Han, M., Xu, J. (2022) In-Depth Analysis Of College Students' Online Discussion Interaction Based On Behavior Sequence, Proc. Icdel 2022, 184-189.

Hirayama, R. And Kusumi, T. (2004) Effect Of Critical Thinking Disposition On Interpretation Of Controversial Issues: Evaluating Evidences And Drawing Conclusions, Japanese Journal Of Educational Psychology, 52, Pp. 186-198.

Julien, G., Dookwah, R. (2020) Students' Transition From Face To Face Learning To Online Learning At Higher Education: A Case Study In Trinidat And Tobago, Educational Research And Reviews, 15(8), Pp487-494.

Kawamoto, S., Nakayama, M. And Saijo, M. (2013) Using A Scientific Literacy Cluster To Determine Participant Attitudes In Scientific Events In Japan, And Potential Applications To Improving Science Communication, Jcom, 12(1), Pp. 1-12.

Kawamoto, T., Oshio, A., Abe, S., Tsubota, U., Hirashima, T., Ito, H., And Tani, I. (2015) Age And Gender Differences Of Big Five Personality Traits In A Cross-Sectional Japanese Sample, The Japanese Journal Of Developmental Psychology, 26(2), Pp. 107-122.

Kikuchi, S. (2018) How To Recognize Cognitive Biases In Risk Perception In Case Of Disasters -Applying Cognitive Psychology To Reduce Damages In Disasters, Journal Of The Japan Landslide Society, Vol. 55, No. 6, Pp. 286-292.

Kusumi, T. And Tanaka, Y. (2008) A Development Of Critical Thinking Ability During A Class Of English For Specific Purpose, Jaep Annual Meeting, Pf2-35.

Lave, J., Wenger, E. (1991) Situated Learning: Legitimate Peripheral Participation, Cambridge University Press, Cambridge, Uk.

Leh, Asc., Kremling, J., Nakayama, M. (2012) Effects Of The Use Of The Blog And Discussion Board On Online Teaching And Learning, Society For Information Technology & Teacher Education International Conference, 574-579.

Li, S., Poysa-Tarhonen, J., Hakkinen, P. (2022) Patterns Of Action Transitions In Online Collaborative Problem Solving: A Network Analysis Approach, Intern. J. Comput.-Support. Learn, 17:191-223.

Nakayama, M., Leh, Asc., Santiago, R. (2016) Effectiveness Of Online Discussion As A Learning Activity In A Postgraduate Course, Proc. Of Ecsm2016, Pp. 249-257,

Nakayama, M., Kikuchi, S., And Yamamoto, H. (2023) Characteristics Promoted In Order To Develop Student's Critical Thinking Disposition In Online Discussions During A Fully Online Course, Proc. Of Ecel 2023, Pp. 212-218.

Nakayama, M., Uto, M., Kikuchi, S., And Yamamoto, H. (2022a) Evaluation Of Essays And Comments For Developing Thinking Ability During A University Course, In Proc. Psychology Learning Technology In November, 2022, Pp.1-16.

Nakayama, M., Kikuchi, S., And Yamamoto, H. (2022b) Development Of Critical Thinking Disposition Using An Online Discussion Board During A Fully Online Course, Proc. Of Ecel 2022, Pp. 295-301.

Nakayama, M., Kikuchi, S., And Yamamoto, H. (2021) The Development Of Critical Thinking Disposition During Two Online Styles Of Learning, Proc. Of Ecel 2021, Pp. 314-320.

Ognyanova, K. (2016) Network Analysis And Visualisation With R And Igraph, http://Kateto.Net/Netscix2016

Ozeki, M., Shimazaki, K. And Yi, T. (2017) Exploring Elements Of Disaster Prevention Consciousness: Based On Interviews With Anti-Disaster Professionals, Journal Of Disaster Research, Vol.12, No.3, Pp. 631-638.

Rychen, D.S. And Salganik, L.H. (2003) Key Competencies For A Successful Life And A Well-Functioning Society, Hogrefe & Huber Publishers, Boston, Usa.

Smith, T.W. (2019) Making The Most Of Online Discussion: A Retrospective Analysis, International J. Of Teaching And Learning In Higher Education, 31(1), Pp.21-31.

Teranishi, A., Nakayama, M., Wyeld, T., Mohamad, E.A. (2017) Effectiveness Of Social Media Communication In Game Development Study Using Team-Based Learning, Ecsm 2017, Proc. Of Ecsm 2017, Pp. 289-296.

Trehan, S., Sanzgiri, J., Li, C., Wang, R., And Joshi, R.M. (2017) Critical Discussions On The Massive Open Online Course (Mooc) In India And China, International Journal Of Education And Development Using Information And Communication Technology (Ijedict), 13(2), Pp. 141-165.

Zarra, T., Chiheb, R., Faizi, R., Afia, A.E. (2018) Student Interactions In Online Discussion Forums: Visual Analysis With Lda Topic Models, Proc. Iopal' 18, Pp. 1-5.

Thinking Through Targeting: Social Media an Effective Tool for Influencing People and Society

Daniel Ionel Andrei Nistor

National defence University "Carol I", Bucharest, Romania

dan.nistor.rp@gmail.com

Abstract: Every day, a wide range of stakeholders target us on social media platforms in an attempt to influence our decisions and behaviour. These stakeholders might be politicians hoping to win over support from the public and secure votes, organizations trying to convey the benefits of their decisions and actions to us as citizens, or commercials trying to sell us something. We absorb new media content, and it can be difficult to distinguish between fake and real news in this redundant environment with widespread data invasion. Beginning with the INSCOP opinion survey from 2023, which investigates Romania's exposure to propaganda and disinformation, our goals are to analyse how audiences were affected by the disinformation narratives in Ukrainian war context, and look at the current social media trends related to this topic using the analytical techniques made available by new media instruments. We want to highlight how social media is the main channel used in Romania for disseminating false information, and we also want to draw attention to the connections that can be made between those who spread false information and the traits of the individuals they are trying to reach. The present paper is part of a larger PhD research program that focuses on consolidating a society's security culture through better institutional strategic communication; therefore, all the findings will be used to this end.

Keywords: Targeting audience, Social media, Disinformation, Narrative, Influence

1. Introduction

We witness social media weaponization. Over 61% of the global population uses social media, which means over 4.95 billion people spend an average of 2 hours 24 minutes per day on it. The Milgram experiment with six degrees of separation can be used to examine how many social media users connect instantly (Hâncean, 2018). Over 12 months (starting in October 2022), approximately 215 million new users have joined social media, resulting in annualized growth of 4.5%, at an average rate of 6.8 new users every single second. By 2023 global social media advertising spending is expected to reach $207 billion, with the US spending $72.33 billion, China $71.38 billion, and the UK $9.7 billion (Bagadiya, 2023). Even though we all know social media is important for communication, most of us don't see it as a tool for influence, manipulation, and targeting in order to change our behaviour or societal standards, and we don't even consider the possibility that we might be victims.

Think of social media in terms of its capacity to influence, as employed by a malicious actor to target a certain audience. Meta claims "5.3 billion global Internet users, with 3.71 billion using at least one Meta app per month." This means 70% of Internet users use Facebook, Instagram, Messenger, or WhatsApp, and many use multiple platforms. With over "1 billion Stories uploaded every day throughout Facebook and a potential advertising reach of 2.08 billion people" (Newbery, 2023), the influence is not only in the number of users but also in the massive amount of data and information. Most subjects are unprepared for what Bittman called the "evil doctor approach of disinformation" (Kalensky, 2022).

Imagine how quickly a brief targeting message can reach a large audience. Privacy delays source identification if the malign actor sends the message in large private groups and redistributes it in large public groups and pages, making it difficult to find the message's origin and spreading map to resend it to the initial audience. If you are not in the bubble, you will not find out about the message.

Manipulated, false, and misleading information can threaten public safety, community cohesion, trust in institutions and the media, public acceptance of science's role in policy development and implementation, economic prosperity, global influence, and government, constitution, and democratic processes (GCS, 2021). BREXIT, vaccination campaigns, and the US election and Cambridge Analytica scandal (Bârgăuanu, 2018) also seem to be examples. Algorithms and AI help companies exploit digital user behaviour to increase sales. A new level of consumerism in which users buy things they don't need and set the stage for algorithms to change their consumption patterns so that they require something that doesn't even exist on the market yet (Ioana, 2023).

2. The System in the System - how to fit the Audience Inside

Regardless of whether our objective is to safeguard the audience from being influenced and manipulated or if we assume the role of a malicious actor with the intent to project influence to affect behavior and decisions, it is imperative to master the art of the targeting process. This encompasses the techniques, tactics, and strategies employed, along with a profound understanding of cultural nuances and specificities. Of paramount importance is a comprehensive knowledge of the information environment's dynamics and the ability to seamlessly integrate within the audience's context. We delve into the strategies employed by malicious actors in relation to current trends on social media platforms – encompassing everything from the deployment of chatbots and influencer marketing to the nuances of fact-checking.

2.1 Information Environment

Modern information environments are more complex due to the convergence of physical, cognitive (human-centric), and informational (data-centric) dimensions (FM 3-13, 2016), especially social media. Physical and virtual realities collide in this digital ecosystem, fostering disinformation. Social media influences global opinions. Disinformation campaigns change platform content and narratives. These efforts aim to sway public opinion and weaken society. Thus, understanding and navigating the many layers of the information environment requires a sophisticated strategy that considers physical presence, cognitive effect, and social media quality and purpose.

2.2 Characteristics of Audience and Target Analysis

When considering the influence of the target analysis audience (TAA), the notion may prompt us to consider psychological operations, which are defined as „*planned psychological activities that use various methods of communications and other means on a specific (approved) audience in order to influence perceptions, attitudes and behaviour,* thereby *affecting the achievement of political and military objective"* (AJP-3.10.1, 2007). TAA is a planned process that changes audience perceptions and attitudes to achieve a goal, so audience is a mean.

Consider applying this strategy to a specific audience on one or more social media platforms. A textbook psychological operation has three main steps: set objectives and define target audiences (TA); create, approve, and deliver influence messages to TA; and evaluate effectiveness (FM3-05.302, 2005). The key is to calibrate the message on affecting behaviour because people focus more on values, particular individuals, items, phenomena, and circumstances that can generally meet their wants (UK GCS, 2022) and socio-cultural factors and prior experience influence decisions and actions.

We must analyse demographic profiles of individuals by age, gender, educational background, and geographical regions more susceptible to disinformation campaigns when analysing the targeting audience. Psychographics and behavioural patterns of targeted individuals are important because psychological traits, beliefs, values, and motives make some people more susceptible to disinformation. Understanding audiences, context, instruments, and adversary objectives is crucial to targeting audiences, which is done defensively to prevent malign influence and protect domestic audiences. Defensive or offensive actions target the opponent to diminish, reduce, or annihilate his ability to act (Nistor, 2023). We must study online behaviour, including social media use, conspiracy theories, and confirmation bias, which often differs from real life.

Moving from individuals to communities, certain communities and social groups are especially vulnerable to disinformation because of societal differences such as political polarization, ethnic and religious conflicts, and socioeconomic inequality. Groups act different from individuals and are characterized by „impulsivity, mobility and irascibilities of the masses", (Le Bon, 2022), and this is especially true on social media, where certain groups are turned into communities based on similar interests, emotions, habits, and jobs.

2.3 Malicious Actors and Influence Strategies

We should consider state-sponsored actors, state actors, ideologically driven groups, and for-profit entities when considering malicious actors who use social media to spread false information and influence public opinion (Prier, 2017). To counter them, we must also investigate their motivations, affiliations, and goals. This will help us identify harmful actors' content generation methods, such as misleading narratives, conspiracy theories, and emotional messages. Provocateurs in online discussion forums, blogs, and social media can spread disinformation, as can governments, corporations, unethical news outlets, and others (Global Security Initiative, 2023). In 2018, Oxford University and Grafika (US) presented to the US Senate Intelligence Committee "that Russia's Internet Research Agency had launched an extended attack on the United States by using computational propaganda to misinform and polarize US voters" (Smith, 2019) using Facebook, Twitter, and YouTube data.

The cyber domain extension changed how we see audiences and target audience processes because it has five layers—cognitive, service, semantic, and syntactic—that can manifest differently on devices, networks, and people, affecting target audience identities from rational to emotional, virtual or physical (Sartonen et all, 2016). Even when discussing information warfare or the exploitation of social media, the media is essential for audience targeting because it offers a means of both influencing people through hostile propaganda or malicious information and counterinfluenceing them by informing, educating, and debunking. In order to "persuade and induce the sympathy of potential allies, and simultaneously spread confusion, uncertainty, and distrust in the enemy's population," social media serves as both the environment and the means of doing so (Pelletier, 2022).

Other methods include manipulating social media algorithms to spread false narratives, impersonation and identity deception, using fake accounts to make the message seem credible, well-known, and trusted, and creating fictitious personas. Malicious actors use cognitive biases, emotional triggers, and fear, wrath, and empathy to manipulate and persuade audiences. The malicious influence could be a cross-border campaign, campaign in which actors seek to influence audiences in different countries. Those campaigns are often is difficult to be linked with the end user beneficiary, because cybersecurity and hybrid warfare consists in multiple action, overlayed and covered, and there is the need to maintain the balance of international relations.

2.4 Trends in Social Media – From Chatbots and Deepfake to Microtargeting, Social Activism, Influencers Marketing and Fact Checking

Deepfakes and synthetic media are a major social media trend and concern. Deepfake, AI-generated realistic audio, video, and text content, can be used for political disinformation, fraud, and identity theft. AI can recognize speech, convert text to audio, and analyse feelings, "a processing of the inflections of our voices to the point where it knows when we are angry or joyful, angry or indifferent" (Măruță, 2023). AI generates text and images quickly, fuelling disinformation campaigns. Technology threatens reporting credibility by blurring fact and fiction. Adobe promised to remove the fake AI war photos from the Mideast and Ukraine after the Washington Post revealed them (Stein, 2024). Using chatbots to answer user questions instantly and increase customer interactions became common practice. The changing landscape of social media influence requires understanding how AI-driven interaction affects user behaviour and decision-making. Microtargeting and personalized content delivery are common on social media because highly performant algorithms and user data analysis enable tailored messages based on preferences, behaviours, and demographics. Influencer marketing targeted high-profile celebrities on social media, promising exclusivity, private jet travel, partying on a private island, and meeting the reality of crowded beaches, tropical rain, and casserole sandwiches. Billy McFarland, an influencer and marketer, launched a bold Instagram campaign that resulted in a scammer being sentenced to six years in prison and $26 million in damages (Frier, 2020).

Social media remains crucial to activism and social movements. The Black Lives Matter movement and climate activism demonstrate social media's ability to mobilize large-scale social change campaigns. Measurement or limitation of harmful messages is difficult, especially for hate speech. Levy (2021) states that "Hate speech is still an issue on banning and implementing because of lack of context" because we must consider not only the ideology and intention of the message, but also the semantics, cultural, and social context of the environment. It's easy to see how difficult it is to assess because it's not just about the words, but also the pictures, videos, or combination of them (Levi, 2021). Social media platforms like Twitter (X), Instagram, and TikTok allow activists to organize protests and raise awareness. This type of influence campaigns also raises privacy concerns and questions about echo chambers and filter bubbles (Arguedas et all 2022) fuelled in part by confirmation bias, which favour info that reinforces existing beliefs (GCF Global, 2024).

Misinformation and disinformation persist on social media. Fighting disinformation has increased as malicious actors spread false narratives. Fact-checking groups, social media platforms, and independent fact-checkers debunk false statements. The UK Governmental Service Communication launched the RESIST 2 Counter Disinformation Toolkit (GCS, 2021) to teach subjects how to detect, warn, counter, and protect against disinformation. The approach has worked in Romania, where UK professionals trained MFA and MOD staff. The relationship between disinformation and fact-checking is crucial to understanding the social media ecosystem.

2.5 Combating Disinformation: The Changing Roles of Social Media, Government, and Non-Governmental Organizations

State institutions, non-governmental organizations, and network security are working to protect audience by educating them and developing detection and enforcement tools, awareness and education programs, or for combating disinformation. On the six months of 2022, Facebook took action on 2.8 billion fake accounts. A record of 2.2 billion fake profiles were removed by platform in the first quarter of 2019 (Dixon, 2023).

Rather than changing the underlying beliefs, social media platforms have implemented several measures to make people less likely to share misinformation under the principle of balance between free speech and protection of citizens' rights. Articles marked as "disputed" are displayed less prominently on Facebook, allowing fewer people to view and share them. These articles are also labelled as "disputed" or "misleading", making them less socially acceptable to share (GCS Behavioural Science, 2022).

„Social media companies remain unable to prevent commercial manipulators from undermining platform integrity. Buying manipulation remains cheap. The price today is roughly one third of the price in 2018 (Fredheim et all, 2023). Overall, no platform has improved since 2021 and their ability to prevent manipulation has decreased.

Several sources can be researched to verify the veracity of information or news, including verification platforms (Munteanu, 2022) such as BBC Reality Check and AFP Fact Check - content in English- or Veridica, AFP Verified, and ANTI-FAKE - content in Romanian- (Eurocomunicare, 2022), a signal being that the news remains only online, not being broadcast in the mainstream media.

Regarding Shaping Europe's digital future, the EU consider that "large-scale disinformation campaigns are a major challenge for Europe and require a coordinated response from EU countries, EU institutions, online platforms, news media and EU citizens". Disinformation is addressed by several Commission initiatives: The Communication on 'tackling online disinformation: a European approach' provides tools to combat disinformation and protect EU values; the Action plan on disinformation: strengthens EU capability and cooperation in the fight against disinformation; and the European Democracy Action Plan: establishes online platform obligations and accountability (European Union, 2022).

State institutions, non-governmental organizations, and network security professionals are educating users and developing tools to identify and prevent disinformation, but the problem is significant and complicated. Social media platforms cannot prevent manipulation and commercial exploitation of their systems, even after detecting and reducing controversial content. Facebook's increased content removal shows a growing awareness and responsiveness to disinformation, but these platforms' manipulation-prevention efficiency has not improved.

Additionally, verification platforms and fact-checking services help consumers verify information. The ease with which these platforms can be manipulated and the need for ongoing technology and user education to combat disinformation are the ongoing challenges.

3. Research Statement (Question), Instruments and Methods

In our study, we will undertake a comprehensive analysis and correlation of datasets derived from a variety of sources, including: (1) a national opinion poll conducted by INSCOP, (2) three studies by Global Focus, and (3) data extracted from Crowdtangle, an analytical tool utilized for monitoring and analyzing social media channels.

1. The opinion poll, administered by INSCOP Research—a reputable public opinion research institute in Romania with over two decades of experience known for its methodological rigour—employed the interview research method via telephone questionnaires. The sample comprised 1,100 individuals, stratified to representatively cover significant socio-demographic categories (including sex, age, occupation) of the non-institutionalized Romanian population aged 18 and over. The poll achieved a maximum permissible error margin of ±3.0% and a confidence level of 95%. Commissioned by the New Strategy Center, this survey aimed to gather Romanians 'perspectives on various issues, such as the war in Ukraine, the Israel-Hamas conflict, and the country's membership in NATO and the EU.

2. Additionally, our research incorporates and correlates findings from three Global Focus studies, which are: (A) "Monitoring report on the evolution of the main pro-Kremlin voices on Facebook. Early warning" (2022), (B) "Propaganda Without Borders – A study of pro-Kremlin propaganda among far-right and radical voices in Hungary, Poland, Romania, and Serbia" (2022), and (C) "Resilience of the disinformation ecosystem: how pro-Russian voices adjust when banned by Facebook. Case study: Diana Sosoaca" (2023). These studies provide a statistical analysis of social media data, track the evolution of trends and tendencies, and deconstruct the process of disinformation narrative formation, from their amplified peak to the origin.

3. The detailed methodology of employing Crowdtangle, an analytical tool, is elaborated in Chapter 4 ("Case Analysis"). Rationale for Selection: The chosen analytical elements reflect the significant impact and relevance of the subject matter. Through the prism of Romanian public perception on pivotal issues, these studies not only furnish sociologically measured data but also offer insights into

methods of analysis, identification of trends, and recommendations for both understanding the target audience's process and devising strategies for the prevention and combat of misinformation trends.

The INSCOP national opinion poll, conducted in December 2023, measures Romanians' main concerns, the country's European and Euro-Atlantic orientation, how the perpetrators of the Ukraine war are perceived, and disinformation exposure. We plan to analyse how these figures are reflected in social media. We also want to track central narratives that have shaped Romanians' views and propaganda and disinformation since the Ukraine crisis began. We analyse pool data and correlate it with primary storylines in the Ukrainian war.

Working data from March and November 2023 Romanian INSCOP country survey

In November 2023, 49.8 % of Romanians saw Russia as the main aggressor in the Ukraine war, down 21.4 % from 71.2 % in May 2022. While US and Ukraine blame grew, those blaming increased from 10.4% in May 2022 to 14.6% in November 2023. While 64.7 % think Russia should withdraw and return occupied territories to Ukraine, 24.5 % think Ukraine must concede Russia significantly in order to resolve the conflict. Russia's chances of winning the war dropped 15.8% (from 50.3% in May 2022 to 34.5% in November 2023), while Ukraine's chances rose 6.5 %.

Romania perceives Russia as the biggest threat, with 56.4%, followed by Hungary (8.6%), the US (8.2%), China (6.6%), and Ukraine (4.0%). In response to the next question about Romania's relationship with the EU/USA, 57.9% believe Romania is a colony of both, while 35.4% disagree. Fifth in national concerns is the Ukraine conflict (9% in November 2023, down from 12% in May 2022), preceded by price increases (23.6%), corruption (21.5%), personal and family health (18.1%), and education (14.3%).

In terms of information sources about the Ukraine war, television is still the most popular (53.3%), followed by social media (16.5%), newspapers and websites (17.2%), and those who are uninterested in the subject (17.2%). (11.7 %). In terms of the accuracy of information circulating in Romania about the Ukraine war, 29.8% believe it is mostly true, 42.1% believe it is mostly false, and 20.8% do not follow the events. Regarding news source credibility, television is regarded as very reliable by 29.5% and untrustworthy by 67.8%; trust in websites and news websites increased from 15.2% in May 2022 to 21.9% in November 2023. Trust in news received on Facebook and other social networks increased from 7.8% to 11.6%, while 32.6% went from having very little trust (a drop from 84.8% to 55.8%) to being uninterested in responding or not following the subject.

4. Romanian Case

Despite the fact that 80% of Romanians believe the country should follow the West in terms of democracy and freedom, more than 60% of the most recent INSCOP respondents believe that "Romania became a UE and US colony." This data raises the question *"Could disinformation campaigns and ultranationalist narratives spreading on social media be influencing Romanians' attitudes in that direction?"*

We spoke with a research NGO that has access to social media monitoring technology to put this story to the test. We used Google trends to monitor how the the interest in the Ukrainian conflict changed since the beginning of the war for a more accurate corroboration. The NGO Global Focus Center's senior analyst Rufin Zamfir prepared and extracted data from the program and coded the narrative *"Romania is a colony of the West/EU" disinformation narrative"*, using Bolean operators, and we have created a string containing the coded context (European Union and other terms used by channels/pages/personalities spreading disinformation) and the coded subject (the alleged colony status): (occident OR Occidentului OR occidentul OR UE OR "Uniunea Europeana" OR "uniunii europene" OR Bruxelles OR Bruxellesul OR "Bruxelles-ul" OR "von der leyen" OR Ursula OR Borel OR borell OR Germania OR Franta OR Berlin OR berlinul OR Paris OR Parisului) AND (colonie OR colonia OR sclavi OR supusi OR sclavilor OR "de mana a doua" OR umiliti OR umilite OR vasala OR vasal OR vasali)" (Zamfir, 2024). After that, we ran it through Facebook, using CrowdTangle Program (Global Focus).

We also looked at Global Focus's "Monitoring report on the evolution of key pro-Kremlin voices on Facebook. Early warning "(Global Focus, 2022), a study that concentrates on current trends in pro-Kremlin narratives on Facebook in Romania, emphasizing the critical roles of specific far-right and pro-Russian actors and media outlets.

5. Findings, Results and Interpretation

The interest over Ukraine in Romania, as expressed in Google searches from the beginning of the war until today it naturally declined, not just as the general population lost interest in the war but as the general public started to refine their searches (eg. and not referring generic on term „Ukraine", by searching the places of the battles, or names of the military or political leaders).

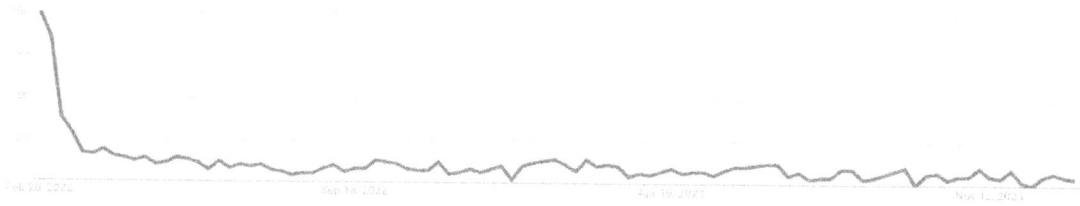

Figure 1: Interest in Ukraine War, from February 24th, 2022- January 13th, 2024, Source: from Google Trends, 2024

Figure 2: Interest in Ukraine War, detailed from January 8th, 2022- January 13th, 2024, Source: Google Trends, 2024

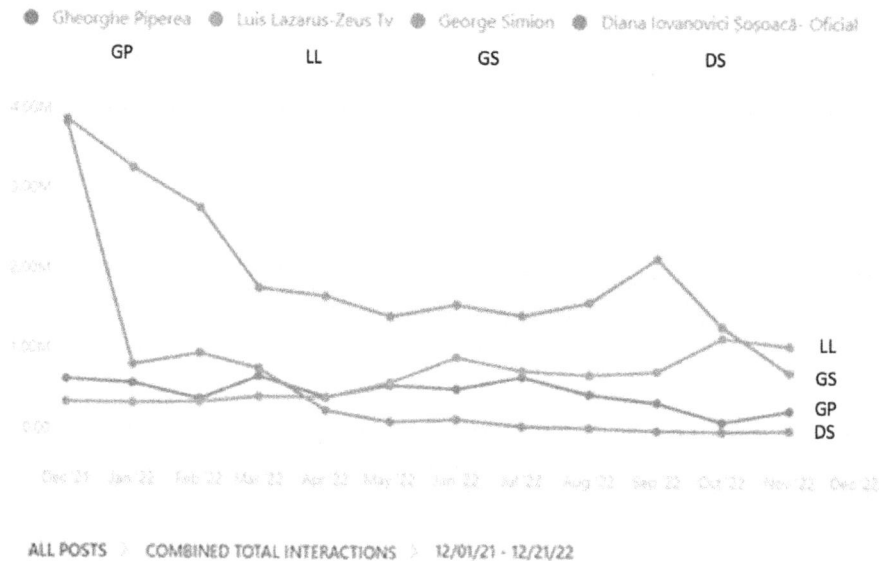

Figure 3: Evolution in 2022 of the main far right actors on Facebook. Extract from Crowdtangle. Source: Global Focus – „Monitoring report on the evolution of the main pro-Kremlin voices on Facebook"

Figure 3 highlights Zeus TV's rise as a prominent far-right and pro-Kremlin voice, surpassing Diana Șoșoacă and George Simion, between now and 2022. They criticize Ukraine rather than Russia in their pro-Russian positions. Although George Simion (GS) and Diana Șoșoacă (DS) were once considered prominent radicals, organizations like Zeus TV (LL) is gaining popularity. This requires a new approach to poisonous rhetoric and deception.

INTERACTIONS   POSTS
136,114   1,594

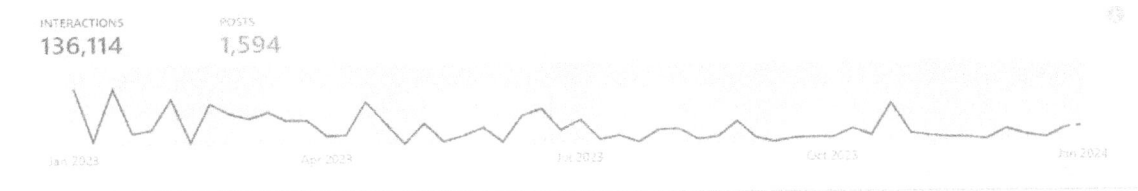

Figure 4: Facebook data on disinformation coded narrative "Romania is a colony of the West/EU" retrieved from Crowdtangle, 2024. Source: Global Focus

INTERACTIONS   POSTS   EXTENDED 3-MONTH TIME PERIOD
27,039   422

Figure 5: Facebook data on disinformation coded narrative "Romania is a colony of the West/EU" retrieved from Crowdtangle, 2024. Source: Global Focus

It appears the topic is soaring. Figure 5 demonstrated that in December 2023, at least one-third of all disinformation posts on Facebook occurred during a given year. Everything is linked and exploited to demonstrate Romania's status as an EU colony. "The leaders of the European Commission are nuts. George Simion, the president of the AUR political party, states that "they brought inflation, poverty, and a fake pandemic while Romania needs hospitals, roads, and half the country is impoverished" (Digi24, 2023). German protests were cited by pro-Russian Romanian senator Șoșoacă (SOS political party) as evidence of EU nefarious intentions (Șoșoacă, 2023). According to a 2022 study, Simion and Șoșoacă are regarded as the most dangerous far-right voices because they are pro-Kremlin, anti-Ukraine, and (Global Focus, 2022).

By cross-referencing national poll results with data gleaned from Google Trends and Crowdtangle we can see that popular opinion of the Ukraine war's main aggressor has changed significantly. Russia was blamed 21.4% less between May 2022 and November 2023, while the US and Ukraine were blamed more. The effectiveness of disinformation tactics, shifting geopolitical narratives, or war fatigue may have led to a more nuanced or muddled view of the fight. It also symbolizes public opinion's change in response to world events and media portrayals.

Romanians still considers Russia as the biggest threat, which supports the majority view that Russia should leave Ukraine. Most Romanians believe the EU and US dictate too much. This emotion, along with the Ukraine war being ranked lower than internal matters, shows how national identity, sovereignty, and media narratives interact. Television and, increasingly, social media are crucial to creating these impressions due to the public's mistrust of information.

Television remains the most popular source of Ukraine war information (53.3%), but 67.8% believe it is inaccurate. Social media (16.5%) and new media (17.2%) gain trust and credibility from 7.8% to 11.6% and 15.2% to 21.9%, respectively (new media). The findings emphasize television as the main source of Ukraine war information, despite the fact that most people distrust it. This contradiction may be due to a lack of reliable sources or overreliance on conventional media. The rise in trust in websites and social media for news is a progressive move toward digital sources, but they still struggle with credibility. This trend shows the changing media landscape and the difficulty of obtaining credible information. The public's mixed faith in different media reflects its struggles to fight disinformation and identify trustworthy news sources in a changing information landscape.

6. Conclusions

We must understand the complexity of the information environment and social media's role as a component of its physical, cognitive, and informational. It emphasizes the difficulty of fighting disinformation and deception and the use of psychological operations to influence audience behaviour. Malign actors shaping narratives and new technologies like deepfakes and microtargeting complicate matters. Despite these challenges, audience research and fact-checking reduce the impact of false narratives, showing the dynamic nature of disinformation and misinformation combat in the digital age.

To highlight the data's discrepancy, we used the misleading narrative "Romania has become a colony of the EU and the US." Despite the fact that 57.9% of Romanians answered YES to the question "Do you believe Romania has become a colony of the EU and the US?" an overwhelming majority of Romanians (56.6%) believe Russia is a real threat and that the pro-European and Euro-Atlantic path is the right direction, with 76.7% believing Romania should remain in the EU and NATO (79.8%). Malicious social media actions may explain this paradox. Meanwhile, the number of social media users has increased while the lack of interest in the issue has decreased.

Identification and mitigation of disinformation is difficult in the fast-changing world of social media, where users are constantly bombarded with information and disinformation is fought on an education gap. Closed accounts and strict regulations may seem like good solutions, but they are not enough. Education is the best option. It gives people the skills to navigate information overload. This process is like a skier masterfully navigating a mountain course between flags while maintaining speed and balance. Social media users don't have time to review every post. Therefore, they must learn to instinctively avoid harmful and malicious content. By teaching users the right skills, they can exercise their free will, balancing regulation and user satisfaction. This emphasises the need for a digitally literate society that can critically evaluate information and make informed decisions.

7. Suggestions and Recommendations

To combat disinformation, legal frameworks, education, transparency, and key player collaboration are needed. Governments and social media companies collaborate to create and enforce anti-disinformation rules that respect free speech. Educational programs that emphasize media literacy in curriculum and public awareness campaigns are crucial. This helps people analyse content and understand social media's complexity. Social media platforms must also follow ethical, transparent practices like content moderation, fact-checking, and content algorithm transparency. Civil society advocates for accountability and raises awareness of disinformation risks.

Governments, law enforcement, cybersecurity experts, social media companies, and civil society must work together to fight disinformation. This multidimensional strategy should improve authority cooperation to identify and respond to disinformation, cybersecurity to protect sensitive data, and digital literacy to build community resilience. These initiatives together protect individual rights and promote an educated, responsible society against disinformation in the digital age.

8. Way Ahead

The present paper is part of a larger PhD research program that focuses on consolidating a society's security culture through better institutional strategic communication. All the findings will be used to emphasize the strong links between communication, security culture and audience; how this can be targeted to be influenced and educated in order to increase resilience.

References

AJP-3.10.1(A) (2007), Allied Joint Doctrine for Psychological Operations (NATO)

Arguedas, A.R., Robertson, C.T., Fletcher, R., Nielsen, R.K. (2022) Echo chambers, filter bubbles, and polarisation: a literature review, Reuters Institute, retrieved from https://reutersinstitute.politics.ox.ac.uk/sites/default/files/2022-01/Echo_Chambers_Filter_Bubbles_and_Polarisation_A_Literature_Review.pdf, DOI: 10.60625/risj-etxj-7k60, accessed on November 12, 2023

Bârgăoanu, A. (2018), Fakenews. Noua Cursă a înarmării, Evrika Publishing, Bucuresti

Bagadiya, J. (2023), 200+ Social Media Statistics and Facts Of 2023, retrieved from https://www.socialpilot.co/blog/social-media-statistics, accessed on 23 December 2023

Digi24 (2023), The political discourse, https://www.digi24.ro/stiri/actualitate/politica/discurs-halucinant-al-lui-simion-comisia-europeana-este-condusa-de-minti-bolnave-ne-au-adus-inflatie-saracie-o-pandemie-inventata-2436877, accesed on September 3rd, 2023

Dixon, S. J.(2023), Facebook: fake account removal, https://www.statista.com/statistics/1013474/facebook-fake-account-removal-quarter/, accesed January 3rd, 2024

European Union (2022), Tackling online disinformation, https://digital-strategy.ec.europa.eu/en/policies/online-disinformation, accesed on December 27th, 2023

Eurocomunicare (2022), Psihologia dezinformării: Cum este relativizat războiul din Ucraina: 5 tehnici înșelătoare, retrieved from https://www.antifake.ro/psihologia-dezinformarii-cum-este-relativizat-razboiul-din-ucraina-5-tehnici-inselatoare/, accesed on September 22nd, 2023

FM 3-05.302 (2005), Tactical Psychological Operations Tactics, Techniques, And Procedures (US)

FM 3-13 (2016) Information operations, (US), https://www.globalsecurity.org/military/library/policy/army/fm/3-13/fm3-13_2016.pdf

Fredheim, R., Bay, S., Dek, A., Stotze M., Haiduchyk, T., (2023), Social Media Manipulation 2022/2023: Assessing the Ability of Social Media Companies to Combat Platform Manipulation, https://stratcomcoe.org/publications/social-media-manipulation-20222023-assessing-the-ability-of-social-media-companies-to-combat-platform-manipulation/272, accesed on September 17th, 2023

Frier, S. (2020), #NOFILTER, Povestea Instagramului, Corint Books, București

GCF Global (2024), What is an echo chamber?, retrieved from https://edu.gcfglobal.org/en/digital-media-literacy/what-is-an-echo-chamber/1/, accesed on January 3rd, 2024

Global Focus (2022), Monitoring report on the evolution of the main pro-Kremlin voices on Facebook. Early warning, https://www.global-focus.eu/2023/01/monitoring-report-on-the-evolution-of-the-main-pro-kremlin-voices-on-facebook-early-warning/, January 9th, 2023

Global Focus (2022), Propaganda Without Borders – A study of pro-Kremlin propaganda among far-right and radical voices in Hungary, Poland, Romania and Serbia, https://www.global-focus.eu/2022/10/propaganda-without-borders-a-study-of-pro-kremlin-propaganda-among-far-right-and-radical-voices-in-hungary-poland-romania-and-serbia/, October 14th, 2022

Global Focus (2023), Resilience of the disinformation ecosystem: how pro-Russian voices adjust when banned by Facebook. Case study: Diana Sosoaca, https://www.global-focus.eu/2023/03/resilience-of-the-disinformation-ecosystem-how-pro-russian-voices-adjust-when-banned-by-facebook-case-study-diana-sosoaca/, June 22nd, 2023

Global Security Initiative (2023), Narrative, Disinformation and Strategic Influence, retrieved from https://globalsecurity.asu.edu/expertise/narrative-disinformation-and-strategic-influence/

Google Trends, (2024), https://trends.google.com/trends/explore?geo=RO&q=war%20in%20Ukraine&hl=en, accessed on January 13th, 2024.

Hâncean, M.G. (2018), Rețelele de socializare în era Facebook. O analiză sociologică, Polirom, Bucuresti

INSCOP (2023), Opiniile românilor despre războiul din Ucraina, conflictul Israel – Hamas, apartenența la NATO și UE, retrieved from https://www.inscop.ro/decembrie-2023-sondaj-de-opinie-inscop-research-la-comanda-new-strategy-center-opiniile-romanilor-despre-razboiul-din-ucraina-conflictul-israel-hamas-apartenenta-la-nato-si-ue/?fbclid=IwAR0xsxu9YcHiRUKVBPOWIRz0Keg-xJ4dmkMF5soLLttRPGGgxgkub_0J1zE

Ioana, C (2023), Surveillance capitalism sau când algoritmii ne spun ce și când să cumpărăm. Cât de liber mai e liberul arbitru pe internet?, https://panorama.ro/surveillance-capitalism-date-cookies-algoritmi/?utm_source=b365&utm_campaign=crosspromo&utm_medium=website, accessed on November 29th, 2023

Kalenský, J. (2022), Disinformation and the 'Evil Doctors', retrieved from https://cepa.org/article/disinformation-and-the-evil-doctors/, accesed on January 7th, 2024

Levy, S. (2021), Facebook, povestea din spatele unui brand de success, RAO, București

Măruță, M. (2023), Identitatea virtuală, cum și de ce ne transformă rețelele de socializare, Humanitas, București

Nistor, D. (2023), Target Audiences' Characteristics and Prospective in Countering Information Warfare. European Conference on Cyber Warfare and Security. 22. 623-630. 10.34190/eccws.22.1.1169.

Newberry, C. (2023), Marketers Need to Know in 2023 retrieved from https://blog.hootsuite.com/facebook-statistics/, accessed January 17, 2023

Pelletier, J., 2022. Intelligence, information warfare, cyber warfare, electronic warfare – what they are and how Russia is using them in Ukraine. *The Conversation: Science + Technology; Boston*

Prier, J. (2017), Commanding the Trend: social media as Information Warfare, Strategic Studies Quarterly, Vol. 11, No. 4 (WINTER 2017), Air University Press, retrieved from https://www.jstor.org/stable/10.2307/26271634

Sartonen, M., Huhtinen, A.-M., & Lehto, M. (2016). Rhizomatic Target Audiences of the Cyber Domain. Journal of Information Warfare, 15(4), 1-13, retrieved from https://www.jinfowar.com/subscribers/journal/volume-15-issue-4/rhizomatic-target- audiences-cyber-domain, accesed on September 9th, 2023

Smith, B. and Brown C.A. (2019), Tool and weapons, the promise and peril of digital age, Hodder&Stoughton Publisher, London

Sosoaca D. (2023), https://www.facebook.com/DianaSosoacaOficial/videos/1119305106112316/, accesed on November 3rd, 2023

Stein, J. (2024), AI Disinformation – We Need New Defenses, retrieved from https://cepa.org/article/ai-disinformation-we-need-new-defenses/, accessed on January 9th, 2024

Strategic Thinking (2022), Proiectul Agenda România 2050 - Viitorul României pornind de la opiniile românilor, Capitolul 6: Securitatea națională a viitorului, retrieved from www.strategicthinking.ro, June 22nd, 2023

UK GCS (2021), Government Communication Sistem, RESIST 2 Counter Disinformation Toolkit, https://gcs.civilservice.gov.uk/wp-content/uploads/2021/11/RESIST-2-counter-disinformation-toolkit.pdf

UK GCS Behavioural Science (2022), *The Wall of Beliefs*, A toolkit for understanding false beliefs and developing effective counter-disinformation strategies, UK Team Cabinet Office, retrieved from https://gcs.civilservice.gov.uk/wp-content/uploads/2022/09/Wall_of_Beliefs_-publication.pdf, November 23rd, 2023

Exploring Social Media Metrics: A Comprehensive Literature Review on Assessing Post-Digitalisation Outcomes in Companies from a People-Centric Perspective

Fortune Nwaiwu, Linda Newnes and Susan Lattanzio

Mechanical Engineering, Faculty of Engineering and Centre for People-Led Digitalisation, Bath, UK

Fn351@bath.ac.uk

L.B.Newnes@bath.ac.uk

sl2091@bath.ac.uk

Abstract: Assessment of post-digitalisation outcomes in companies remains a pressing concern for stakeholders in industry, and metrics from social media engagements could offer valuable insights that may be beneficial from a people-centric perspective. Yet, there remains a significant lack of comprehensive exploration of these metrics. This review evaluates the state of the art of academic literature on the subject of social media engagement as evaluative indicators of the outcome of digitalisation in companies. Drawing from a people-centric perspective, a qualitative methodological approach examined peer-reviewed articles selected for the literature review. Results underscore the nuanced interplay between social media engagement metrics and post-digitalisation outcomes and offers valuable theoretical and practical insights beneficial to stakeholders both in industry and the academia. The study concludes by advocating for a deeper, more industry-specific exploration of engagement metrics in assessing post-digitalisation outcomes in companies.

Keywords: Digitalisation, Metrics, Employee, Workforce, Customers, Social media, Literature review

1. Introduction

Social media platforms have transformed how companies interact with their customers, particularly in terms of how companies collect data on their customers, as well as giving them better opportunities to shape their brand identity. Within specific industry sectors, the use of social media metrics in assessing the impact of the implementation of digitalisation on business organisations has emerged as an area of research interests within the academia (Ornstein, 2012; Cao et al., 2016; Carter and Eger, 2021). While existing research has provided insights into discrete aspects of social media and digitalisation within business organisations, there remains a conspicuous gap in comprehensively exploring the spectrum of social media metrics that can be employed as evaluative tools for assessing post-digitalisation in companies operating across different industry sectors.

This paper aims to bridge this gap by critically assessing the role of social media engagement among the workforce of a company as indicators of the impacts of digitalisation across organisational domains in the company. The study adopts a people-centric focus considering that evidence from previous research efforts acknowledges and emphasises the active roles of employees, customers, and stakeholders in the digitalisation journey of a company, and highlights their impact and interactions within the digital sphere (Goswami et al., 2013; Cardon and Marshall, 2015). The objective of this research is to critically examine existing evidence to gauge the extent to which social media engagement within the workforce of a company can provide useful evidentiary metrics that can be in evaluating the effects of digitalisation across organisational domains in a company.

Taking into consideration the diverse range of metrics, the assessment revolves around the measurement of digital process adoption, efficiency enhancement, and overall competitiveness. Furthermore, the study delves into the role of employees as digitalisation ambassadors, scrutinising how their active engagement through social media channels contributes significantly to the outcomes of digitalisation initiatives. Additionally, the paper investigates the profound effects of customer and stakeholder feedback shared on social media platforms, assessing their impact on shaping, and refining a company's digitalisation strategies. By recognising social media as a dynamic repository of invaluable consumer sentiments and insights, this study endeavours to uncover how these inputs influence and optimise digitalisation efforts within the manufacturing landscape.

This study considers the following research questions relevant to achieving the objectives of the study: How effectively have social media engagement metrics been applied in assessing post-digitalisation outcomes across core organisational domains in business organisations? And what impact does the workforce's engagement on social media platforms have on the outcomes of company digitalisation initiatives? Both research questions will enable the study to achieve its objectives by assessing the effectiveness of social media metrics in evaluating post-digitalisation outcomes across diverse organisational domains, and critically investigating the role of a company's workforce either as barriers or enablers of the company's digitalisation initiatives.

This study adopts a qualitative methodological approach that combines desk research with critical literature review in assessing state of the art evidence from peer-reviewed academic sources. The research offers valuable insights into the use of social media platforms for multi-stakeholder engagements and its pivotal role in shaping digitalisation outcomes in business organisations. Results from the study contributes both theoretically and practically to the ongoing academic discourse by providing a nuanced understanding of how metrics from social media platforms serve as instrumental evaluative tools in assessing the outcomes of digitalisation in companies.

2. Literature Review and Theoretical Foundation for the Study

A range of studies have explored the use of social media metrics in assessing post-digitalization outcomes in companies from a people-centric perspective. Hallock, Roggeveen and Crittenden (2019) and Boujena *et al.* (2021) both emphasise the importance of customer engagement as a key metric. Hallock, Roggeveen and Crittenden (2019) further highlights the need for firms to define and assess engagement, while Boujena *et al.* (2021) discusses the gaps in understanding customer engagement and its impact on social media performance. Yoon *et al.* (2018) further supports the significance of digital engagement metrics, they found a positive correlation between the volume and tone of Facebook comments and company revenue. Nistor (2011) provides a theoretical framework for understanding people's behaviour on social media, drawing on the Theory of Reasoned Action and the Technology Acceptance Model.

The fusion of social media platforms with modern business landscapes has resulted in a paradigm shift in customer-company interactions, reshaping how brands curate their identities and gather customer insights (Cao *et al.*, 2015, 2016; Hanna, Kee and Robertson, 2017). While Ornstein (2012) and Cao et al. (2016) acknowledge the transformative effect of social media on customer-company interactions and brand identity, Ornstein (2012) situates the discourse firmly within the lens of workforce social media engagement within the workplace as distinct entities with agency beyond the dictates of organisational policy. However, the research of Cao et al. (2016) presents more relevant findings in terms of workforce social media engagement within the workplace. Results from their research shows that social media usage by the workforce of a company can promote the formation of employees' social capital indicated by network ties, as well as promote a sense of shared vision and trust, which, in turn, can lead to knowledge transfer and better collaboration among the workforce of the company. Also, Cardon and Marshall (2015) presents an interesting dimension to the subject. They argue that while traditional communication channels are used more frequently and considered more effective for team communication, company employees who fall into the demographic classification of Gen X and Gen Y are more favourably disposed to using social networking tools as their primary medium for team communication.

Men, O'Neil and Ewing (2020) conducted research on the effects of internal social media usage on employee engagement, and results from their studies shows that employees' use of internal social media contributes to an enhanced level of perceived transparency of the organisation and organisational identification, which in turn, leads to employee engagement. However, a recurrent theme that continues to emerge from previous research is that of the pivotal roles of employees, customers, and other relevant stakeholders in a company's digitalisation journey (Cardon and Marshall, 2015; Breunig, 2016; Hallock, Roggeveen and Crittenden, 2019). This highlights a bias and preference by companies towards understanding customers better via social media engagements, hence the use of customer-centric social media metrics as crucial evaluative tools that reflects the customers' perspectives of the company's value offerings over that of their employees' perceptions of the impact of digitalisation on various organisational domains, efficiency gains, and competitiveness of the company within its industry sector. For industry stakeholders, they consider feedback from their customers on social media platforms as influential inputs that should shape their digital strategies (Muñoz-Expósito, Oviedo-García and Castellanos-Verdugo, 2017; Men, O'Neil and Ewing, 2020).

Effective utilisation of social media metrics in post-digitalisation assessment remains a key area for exploration, and understanding the role of a company's workforce (either as barriers or enablers) of digitalisation, makes the need for further investigation necessary (Ornstein, 2012; Cardon and Marshall, 2015; Cao *et al.*, 2016). To get a better understanding of how these metrics translate into tangible business impacts, Muñoz-Expósito, Oviedo-García and Castellanos-Verdugo (2017) makes the connection between customer and stakeholder feedback shared on social media platforms and its influence on shaping post-digitalisation outcomes in a company. They argue that the benefits of a high level of customer engagement will lead to superior organisational performance outcomes such as sales growth, cost reductions, brand referrals, enhanced consumer contributions for collaborative product development processes, enhanced co-creative experiences, and higher levels of profitability for the company.

Cao *et al.* (2016) applies the media synchronicity theory (MST) in arguing that synchronicity exists among people when they work together at the same time with a shared focus. According to them, at the core of MST lies five objective capabilities in the conceptualisation of a medium that influences the level of synchronicity: transmission velocity: the speed to which a medium can transmit a message; parallelism: the extent to which a medium enables information from multiple senders to be transmitted simultaneously; symbol sets: the number of ways in which the information can be conveyed; rehearsability: the extent to which a medium enables the sender to rehearse or adjust the message before sending; and reprocessability: the extent to which a message can be re-examined or processed again by the receiver. While Quish (2010) adopts a novel approach which he describes as "Utility Media- digital workforce platforms" in explaining the use of social media within the workplace to create richer relationships by driving engagement among the workforces. This approach consists of three factors - Recruitment Relationship Marketing whereby companies social media platforms such as Facebook and LinkedIn to 'fish in the ocean' for talent when needs arise; Enterprise Learning whereby companies leverage social media platforms provide opportunity for socially engaging experiences like online gaming or gamification (Bonsón and Ratkai, 2013; Yoon *et al.*, 2018; Haziri, Nwaiwu and Chovancová, 2019) for formal training, while mobile applications should be explored for quick fix question and answers (Q&A); and finally, Employee Engagement via social media platforms in ways to ensure that social or hierarchical barriers within companies are broken down.

These studies collectively underscore the value of customer engagement and digital metrics in evaluating post-digitalisation outcomes. However, the existing body of research surrounding social media metrics and post-digitalisation in companies, though extensive, remains segmented and lacks a comprehensive exploration of the diverse metrics crucial for assessing the outcomes of digitalisation in business organisations. Despite these findings, a prevalent bias is apparent favouring customer-centric social media metrics over employee perspectives in evaluating digitalisation impacts. This emphasises the need for a more comprehensive and balanced exploration of social media metrics, encompassing both customer and employee dimensions, to effectively evaluate post-digitalisation outcomes and its impact across organisational domains.

3. Methodology

The research adopts a qualitative methodological approach in reviewing relevant literature to evaluate state of the art evidence from peer-reviewed academic sources. It begins with desk research to identify peer-reviewed literature on the subject of social media metrics and post-digitalisation outcomes in business organisations. The desk research used both the Scopus and Web of Science academic database which are reputable sources of peer-reviewed journal articles. The initial search employed the following keywords to yield the desired results – digitalisation, metrics, employee, workforce, customers, social media. The results were uploaded unto Rayyan, an intelligent research collaboration online platform useful for conducting literature reviews and systematic reviews. This enabled a quick turnaround time especially in terms of eliminating duplicate articles. The Rayyan platform was also used to process and compare articles in terms of title, keywords, and abstracts, the combined dataset contained articles from multiple sources. This is followed by a critical literature of the peer-reviewed journal articles identified from the desk research (Jesson and Lacey, 2006; Stigmar, 2016). The selection criteria for articles were established to ensure the inclusion of academic papers pertinent to the research questions, excluding practitioner articles due to their differing analytical constructs and form compared to academic journal papers. This step aims to establish a foundational understanding of the subject matter by incorporating diverse perspectives and theoretical lenses. All selected articles which subjected to purposive sampling and selection criteria to ensure that they have social media engagement metrics and post-digitalisation outcomes within business organisations as their primary research focus.

The review specifically focused on identifying gaps, inconsistencies, and emerging trends related to using social media engagement metrics of a company's workforce as a means of assessing post-digitalisation outcomes in the company. This purposive selection process ensured that the selected studies covered variables associated with social media metrics in the context of digitalisation in business organisations. A total of 15 articles were selected from the pool of 90 articles identified. The articles that were selected for examination, were published over the period between 2013 to 2023, this ensured a comprehensive understanding of the subject matter based on recent state of the art research outputs. The method of data collection involved impartial cross-referencing of major journals in the field, followed by a meticulous analysis of cross-references. This approach aimed to minimise subjectivity in the selection criteria and capture the totality of the literature to comprehend the internal dynamics of discourse within the academic realm.

The detail of selected articles was deconstructed and organised into key categories using a comparative table, this made it possible for a comprehensive analysis. The categories included paper details (Author – Journal – Year of publication), type of relationship, perspective (customer, employee, or both), nature or type of company's business activities, country from which the sample was drawn, methodology and sample information, and findings related to social media metrics and post-digitalisation outcomes. In addition, a deliberate effort was made to simplify the data and enhance comparability among studies by categorising findings into the following three distinct categories: antecedents of post-digitalisation outcomes, dimensions of social media metrics, and consequences of social media engagement on post-digitalisation outcomes. This tabulated form aimed to provide future researchers with a framework for constructing theoretical models and comparing findings across different variables and methodologies. It is pertinent to state that some level of subjectivity was inevitable in this process. However, rigorous cross-checking against the original articles was conducted to ensure consistency, objectivity, and the legitimacy of observations derived from the comparative tables. This meticulous approach was fundamental in attempting to create valid and comparable data for a comprehensive analysis of the role of social media engagement metrics in post-digitalisation outcomes within business organisations. The triangulation of methodological approaches provides a comprehensive, multi-faceted analysis of the interplay between social media metrics and post-digitalisation outcomes in business organisations (Carter *et al.*, 2014; Abdalla *et al.*, 2018).

4.   Results and Discussions

Results from the critical literature review and comparative analysis of peer-reviewed literature on social media engagement metrics and post-digitalisation outcomes in business organisations yielded comprehensive insights into the intricate interplay between these variables. This section presents and discusses a synthesis of findings derived from the reviewed studies, and outlines the significant themes, patterns, and implications that emerged from the analysis. The structure and organisation of the results is intended to elucidate the multifaceted impacts of social media engagements of a company's workforce as well as that of their customers on assessing post-digitalisation outcomes in the company, this underscores its relevance across various organisational domains. The critical analysis and examination of diverse studies focusing on the subject under investigation revealed nuanced perspectives regarding the effectiveness of the workforce of a company's social media metrics in assessing how digitalisation affects various aspects of the company and contributes to a deeper understanding of how social media engagement among the employees of the company influences and shapes digitalisation initiatives across core organisational domains.

The discussion herein delineates key insights gleaned from the critical literature review, delving into the implications of social media metrics on the efficiency gains, competitiveness, and overall organisational dynamics post-digitalisation. By examining the interconnectedness between social media metrics and post-digitalisation outcomes, this discussion aims to offer valuable implications for businesses seeking to leverage these insights in shaping effective digital strategies and fostering enhanced organisational performance. Table 1 provides a summary of key findings in the literatures included in the review.

Table 1: Summary of key findings in the literatures included in the review (source: authors)

Title of Article	Year	Journal	Reference	Notes
A set of metrics to assess stakeholder engagement and social legitimacy on a corporate Facebook page	2013	Online Inf. Rev.	(Bonsón and Ratkai, 2013)	The study sought to propose and validate metrics for evaluating stakeholder engagement on corporate Facebook pages, demonstrating their validity and adaptability across other social media platforms.
How to measure engagement in Twitter: advancing a metric	2017	Internet Res.	(Muñoz-Expósito, Oviedo-García and Castellanos-Verdugo, 2017)	The study proposes a novel metric for gauging engagement on Twitter, with the aim of aiding companies in refining their engagement strategies through a new analytical approach for the social media platform (Twitter, now X).

Title of Article	Year	Journal	Reference	Notes
Social Media Use in Research: Engaging Communities in Cohort Studies to Support Recruitment and Retention	2015	JMIR Research Protocols	(Farina-Henry, Waterston and Blaisdell, 2015)	The study evaluates Social Media usage within the context of the National Children's Study. It demonstrates the feasibility of metrics for content and engagement analysis on Facebook and offers insights for optimising future posts and engaging online communities.
Attracting Comments: Digital Engagement Metrics on Facebook and Financial Performance	2018	Journal of Advertising	(Yoon *et al.*, 2018)	The study investigates how social media engagement affects a company's business performance, how user comments on company Facebook posts influence company revenue of S&P 500 companies over a five-year time span (from 2010 to 2015). Results show a positive correlation between engagement volume and sentiment with company revenue, guiding potential future research directions.
Visibility and vulnerability in online marketing practices	2021	Journal of Cultural Economy	(Carter and Eger, 2021)	The study explores how users' perceptions of engagement metrics influence content creation on social media, results from the study shows that tactics enhancing metrics also prompt users to disclose personal and vulnerable information in online interactions.
Exposure to Social Engagement Metrics Increases Vulnerability to Misinformation	2020	ArXiv	(Avram *et al.*, 2020)	The study reveals that exposure of other users to a user's social media engagement metrics elevates susceptibility to misinformation, and it emphasises the need for platforms to reconsider displaying these metrics to mitigate the spread of false information.
Off the Court: Examining Social Media Activity and Engagement in Women's Professional Sport	2021	International Journal of Sport Communication	(Piché and Naraine, 2021)	The study evaluates the social media engagement of the Women's National Basketball Association, results from the study reveals a heightened interaction during the season compared to off-season periods, suggesting a need for sustained engagement strategies.
Social Networks' Engagement During the COVID-19 Pandemic in Spain: Health Media vs. Healthcare Professionals	2020	International Journal of Environmental Research and Public Health	(Pérez-Escoda *et al.*, 2020)	The research explores the relationship established between the population in general and digital media in particular through the measurement of engagement. Results from the study shows that the pandemic accelerated the transformation of communication in general and created new challenges for stakeholders in the communication industry, as well as higher education institutions.
Multi-Emotion Detection in Social Media Post using Lexicon-Driven Approach	2020	Conference Proceedings: International Conference on Digital Transformation and Applications, 2020	(Yow *et al.*, 2020)	This research examines how various content types on popular social media platforms influence customer engagement metrics, results from the study reveals that media and content type significantly impact audience interactions, potentially affecting real-world purchasing behaviour.
Social Media Analytics: Instagram Utilization for Delivering Health Education Messages to Young Adult in Indonesia	2021		(Mukti and Putri, 2021)	The study analyses the Centre for Indonesia's Strategic Development Initiatives' (CISDI) social media marketing impact on health messages. Results from the research reveals engagement rates metrics averaging 14.43% on trending issues like sex education, engaging 10,266 individuals in their classes. The study concludes that social media utilisation benefits CISDI in engaging audience and moves them to participate in their cause.

Title of Article	Year	Journal	Reference	Notes
The use of social networking platforms for sexual health promotion: identifying key strategies for successful user engagement	2015	BMC Public Health	(Veale *et al.*, 2015)	The study examines successful strategies for sexual health promotion on Facebook and Twitter. Findings show that active, interactive profiles have higher levels of user engagements by adopting regular multimedia and celebrity/influencer involvement.
Effectiveness of social media marketing on enhancing performance: Evidence from a casual-dining restaurant setting	2019	Tourism Economics	(Li, Kim and Choi, 2019)	The study investigates the impact or influence of social media engagement on customers in casual-dining restaurants, the results reveal variations among metrics across platforms and promotional activities and indicates their positive influence on restaurant performance. The study offers valuable insights for marketing decisions.
What KPIs Are Key? Evaluating Performance Metrics for Social Media Influencers	2019	Social Media + Society	(Gräve, 2019)	The study examines challenges associated with influencer marketing, and the results reveals that professionals rely on reach and interactions as primary metrics. Comment sentiment also significantly correlates with content evaluation, and this challenges the adequacy of traditional quantitative metrics.
Firm-level perspectives on social media engagement: an exploratory study	2019	Qualitative Market Research: An International Journal	(Hallock, Roggeveen and Crittenden, 2019)	The study investigates the perception of companies of customer engagement on social media platforms. The results highlight measurable metrics like growth, interactions, and subscribers. It also outlines propositions for defining engagement, social media breadth, and its strategic usage, thereby suggesting the need for clearer engagement definitions and platform choices for fostering customer interaction.
Synergies between Social Media Features and User Engagement to Enhance Online Brand Visibility - A Conceptual Model	2013	Information Systems & Economics eJournal	(Goswami *et al.*, 2013)	The research investigates the relationship between social media features, user engagement, and online brand visibility, and proposes a conceptual model that uses a social media-user engagement matrix, as well as proposing metrics to measure online brand visibility, aiming to contribute to understanding their synergies and effective measurement.

Findings from the critical analysis of the selected literature reveals a variety of interesting perspectives in relations to how previous research efforts into the subject of social media metrics as a frame of reference for assessing the impact of digitalisation in companies. Results from the study conducted by Yoon *et al.* (2018) established a positive correlation between engagement metrics and the revenue of companies, their research was focused on companies from S&P 500 list, their research provides valuable insights but within a constrained scope because of the absence of in-depth exploration of various engagement metrics' impact across diverse organisational domains.

5. Conclusion

The study shows that while significant efforts have been made in conducting research into the subject of social media engagements, the scope and focus on applying metrics from the use of social media by the workforce of a company as an evaluative lens into assessing post-digitalisation outcomes is still an area of research that has not been adequately explored. A typical example is reflected in the research efforts of Bonsón and Ratkai (2013) who adopts an approach which in itself does not focus on assessing post-digitalisation outcomes in companies, but proposes metrics that they believe can be valuable for stakeholders in industry to use in evaluating stakeholder engagements on social media platforms, with particular focus on corporate Facebook pages, and demonstrating their validity and adaptability across social media platforms. The approach adopted by Bonsón and Ratkai (2013) can be argued to be pre-digitalisation because it is constrained by the fact that it seeks to analyse all-encompassing stakeholders' engagements on corporate social media platform with a view to helping the company get a better understanding of the perceptions of their stakeholders which in this case is more inclined towards the perception of the company's customers.

Yow *et al.* (2020) highlighted the impact of content types on audience engagement but failed to delve into broader influences on brand performance. While the research by Mukti and Putri, 2021) (2021) explored social media's impact on health messages. Results from their research offers valuable insights into engagement rates and audience participation. In addition, Li, Kim, and Choi (2019) investigated social media's influence on restaurant performance but did not thoroughly explore specific metrics' effects across diverse platforms, the limitation of their research can also be seen from the focus on financial performance of companies. Gräve (2019) examined influencer marketing metrics but could further explore alternative metrics for comprehensive evaluations. Hallock, Roggeveen, and Crittenden (2019) conducted research which focused on analysing company's perspectives on social media engagement; however, the lack of offer deeper insights into industry-specific metrics and strategies presents a challenge which significantly limits the value derivable from their research findings. Goswami (2013) proposed a model without empirical validation, requiring further exploration and verification of practical applicability. In summary, while these studies offer valuable insights, there remains a need for comprehensive analyses to understand the broader implications of engagement metrics in the assessment of post-digitalisation from a people-centric perspective in business organisations. This would enable companies to benefit from a less subjective dataset that is often neglected. Based on the review of extant literature on the subject of social media metrics used in assessing post-digitalisation outcomes in Companies from a people-centric perspective, it can be inferred that there are two broad categories of people centric metrics: those that are focused on the employees and another group focused on the customers. It can also be inferred that companies tend to pay more priority to the customer facing metrics when compared to the employee facing metrics. This has significant implications in practice for companies who embark on digitalisation initiatives as they only tend to see one side of the picture of their digitalisation initiatives while largely ignoring the other aspect which is equally consequential as the workforce of a company is a vital resource relevant to its overall wellbeing.

Acknowledgements

The work reported in this paper was undertaken as part of the Made Smarter Innovation: Centre for People-Led Digitalisation, at the University of Bath, University of Nottingham, and Loughborough University. The project is funded by the Engineering and Physical Sciences Research Council (EPSRC) Grant EP/V062042/1.

References

Abdalla, M.M. *et al.* (2018) 'Quality in Qualitative Organizational Research: Types of Triangulation as a Methodological Alternative', *Administracao-Ensino e Pesquisa*, 19(1), pp. 66–98. doi:10.13058/raep.2018.v19n1.578.

Avram, M. *et al.* (2020) 'Exposure to social engagement metrics increases vulnerability to misinformation', *arXiv preprint arXiv:2005.04682* [Preprint].

Bonsón, E. and Ratkai, M. (2013) 'A set of metrics to assess stakeholder engagement and social legitimacy on a corporate Facebook page', *Online Information Review*, 37(5), pp. 787–803. doi:10.1108/OIR-03-2012-0054.

Boujena, O. *et al.* (2021) 'Customer engagement and performance in social media: a managerial perspective', *Electronic Markets*, 31(4), pp. 965–987. doi:10.1007/s12525-020-00450-3.

Breunig, K.J. (2016) 'Limitless learning: assessing social media use for global workplace learning', *The Learning Organization*, 23(4), pp. 249–270. doi:https://doi.org/10.1108/TLO-07-2014-0041.

Cao, X. *et al.* (2015) 'The role of social media in supporting knowledge integration: A social capital analysis', *Information Systems Frontiers*, 17(2), pp. 351–362. doi:10.1007/s10796-013-9473-2.

Cao, X. *et al.* (2016) 'Exploring the influence of social media on employee work performance', *Internet Research*, 26(2), pp. 529–545. doi:https://doi.org/10.1108/IntR-11-2014-0299.

Cardon, P.W. and Marshall, B. (2015) 'The Hype and Reality of Social Media Use for Work Collaboration and Team Communication', *International Journal of Business Communication*, 52(3), pp. 273–293. doi:https://doi.org/10.1177/2329488414525446.

Carter, D. and Eger, E.K. (2021) 'Visibility and vulnerability in online marketing practices', *Journal of Cultural Economy*, 14(4), pp. 373–387. doi:10.1080/17530350.2021.1879212.

Carter, N. *et al.* (2014) 'The use of triangulation in qualitative research.', *Oncology nursing forum*, 41(5), pp. 545–547. doi:10.1188/14.ONF.545-547.

Farina-Henry, E., Waterston, L.B. and Blaisdell, L.L. (2015) 'Social Media Use in Research: Engaging Communities in Cohort Studies to Support Recruitment and Retention.', *JMIR research protocols*, 4(3), p. e90. doi:10.2196/resprot.4260.

Goswami, A. *et al.* (2013) 'Synergies between social media features and user engagement to enhance online brand visibility - A conceptual model', *International Journal of Engineering and Technology*, 5, pp. 2705–2718.

Gräve, J.-F. (2019) 'What KPIs Are Key? Evaluating Performance Metrics for Social Media Influencers', *Social Media + Society*, 5(3), p. 2056305119865475. doi:10.1177/2056305119865475.

Hallock, W., Roggeveen, A.L. and Crittenden, V. (2019) 'Firm-level perspectives on social media engagement: an exploratory study', *Qualitative Market Research: An International Journal*, 22(2), pp. 217–226. doi:10.1108/QMR-01-2017-0025.

Hanna, B., Kee, K.F. and Robertson, B.W. (2017) 'Positive Impacts of Social Media at Work: Job Satisfaction, Job Calling, and Facebook Use among Co-Workers', *SHS Web of Conferences*. Les Ulis: EDP Sciences PP - Les Ulis. doi:https://doi.org/10.1051/shsconf/20173300012.

Haziri, F., Nwaiwu, F. and Chovancová, M. (2019) 'Assessing the Dissimilarities of Game Mechanics on Albanian Working-Class Consumers', in. doi:10.7441/dokbat.2019.032.

Jesson, J.K. and Lacey, F.M. (2006) 'How to do (or not to do) a critical literature review', *Pharmacy education*, 6(2), pp. 139–148.

Li, J. (Justin), Kim, W.G. and Choi, H.M. (2019) 'Effectiveness of social media marketing on enhancing performance: Evidence from a casual-dining restaurant setting', *Tourism Economics*, 27(1), pp. 3–22. doi:10.1177/1354816619867807.

Men, L.R., O'Neil, J. and Ewing, M. (2020) 'Examining the effects of internal social media usage on employee engagement', *Public Relations Review*, 46(2), p. 101880. doi:https://doi.org/10.1016/j.pubrev.2020.101880.

Mukti, O. and Putri, N. (2021) 'Social Media Analytics: Instagram Utilization for Delivering Health Education Messages to Young Adult in Indonesia', *Jurnal PROMKES*, 9, p. 36. doi:10.20473/jpk.V9.I1.2021.36-43.

Muñoz-Expósito, M., Oviedo-García, M.Á. and Castellanos-Verdugo, M. (2017) 'How to measure engagement in Twitter: advancing a metric', *Internet Research*, 27(5), pp. 1122–1148. doi:10.1108/IntR-06-2016-0170.

Nistor, C. (2011) 'A Conceptual Model for the Use of Social Media in Companies', *SSRN Electronic Journal* [Preprint]. doi:10.2139/ssrn.1898670.

Ornstein, D. (2012) 'Social Media Usage in the Workplace Around the World - Developing Lami and Practices', *Business Law International*, 13(2), pp. 120,195-207. Available at: http://libproxy.bath.ac.uk/login?url=https://www.proquest.com/scholarly-journals/social-media-usage-workplace-around-world/docview/1173720136/se-2?accountid=17230.

Pérez-Escoda, A. *et al.* (2020) 'Social Networks' Engagement During the COVID-19 Pandemic in Spain: Health Media vs. Healthcare Professionals.', *International journal of environmental research and public health*, 17(14). doi:10.3390/ijerph17145261.

Piché, M.C. and Naraine, M.L. (2021) 'Off the Court: Examining Social Media Activity and Engagement in Women's Professional Sport', *International Journal of Sport Communication* [Preprint]. Available at: https://api.semanticscholar.org/CorpusID:245927896.

Quish, R. (2010) 'Social Media: Creating Richer Relationships in the Workplace', *People and Strategy*, 33(3), pp. 7–8. Available at: http://libproxy.bath.ac.uk/login?url=https://www.proquest.com/trade-journals/social-media-creating-richer-relationships/docview/763403002/se-2?accountid=17230.

Stigmar, M. (2016) 'Peer-to-peer teaching in higher education: A critical literature review', *Mentoring & Tutoring: partnership in learning*, 24(2), pp. 124–136.

Veale, H.J. *et al.* (2015) 'The use of social networking platforms for sexual health promotion: identifying key strategies for successful user engagement', *BMC Public Health*, 15(1), p. 85. doi:10.1186/s12889-015-1396-z.

Yoon, G. *et al.* (2018) 'Attracting Comments: Digital Engagement Metrics on Facebook and Financial Performance', *Journal of Advertising*, 47(1), pp. 24–37. doi:10.1080/00913367.2017.1405753.

Yow, L. *et al.* (2020) *Multi-Emotion Detection in Social Media Post using Lexicon-Driven Approach*. doi:10.56453/icdxa.2020.1008.

Exploring the Potential and Challenges of WhatsApp Focus Groups in Qualitative Consumer Research: A Case Study of Sustainable Eating

Virpi Oksman, Tom Tamlander, Marjoriikka Ylisiurua and Anu Seisto
VTT Technology Centre of Finland, Espoo, Finland

virpi.oksman@vtt.fi
tom.tamlander@vtt.fi
marjoriikka.ylisiurua@vtt.fi
anu.seisto@vtt.fi

Abstract: The emergence of digital technologies has opened new methods for engaging consumers, conducting focus groups, and gathering research material online. One such method is the use of smartphone-based mobile messaging platform WhatsApp, which allows real-time discussions and diary-type studies. Nevertheless, the potential of WhatsApp focus groups as a research method necessitates further exploration. This paper analyses the advantages and limitations of employing WhatsApp-based focus groups in qualitative consumer studies related to sustainable eating. Specifically, we will examine the effectiveness, interaction, and quality of research materials obtained through this method in previous studies. To carry out our study, we organized a focus group in Finland utilizing the WhatsApp-based platform with a pre-selected panel of 24 participants. The study explored barriers to sustainable food choices among so-called imperfect consumer segments. Based on our observations, mobile focus groups offer a fruitful method for studying consumer insights due to the direct and non-hierarchical communication channels they provide between participants and researchers. However, it is crucial to acknowledge that materials acquired through mobile groups may be less extensive than those obtained through traditional focus groups. Participants often rely on emojis and emoticons to convey meaning, which may pose challenges in terms of text-based coding, categorization, and software utilization. Furthermore, the fragmented nature of messages presented another challenge in analysing the collected material. Additionally, when employing WhatsApp focus groups as a method, careful preparation of the question route is necessary to ensure the production of high-quality research materials.

Keywords: Mobile focus groups, WhatsApp, Consumer studies, Sustainable consumption, Healthy eating

1. Introduction

In recent years, qualitative consumer research has significantly shifted towards using mobile and online platforms to gather data and insights. This shift has been driven by the proliferation of smartphones and the increasing popularity of messaging applications, such as WhatsApp, which have become integral parts of people's daily lives. As a result, researchers have begun to explore the potential of using WhatsApp-based focus groups in consumer studies.

Focus groups, in general, can be helpful when researchers want to understand people's thoughts and insights on specific topics. The interaction between participants can elicit data and ideas that might not be discovered with traditional structured interviews. Different methods of participation in product and service development have been developed for decades in several fields of science and evidence of the successful use of social media tools in user-centric design has been available for several years (Friedrich, 2013; Mensonen *et al.*, 2014). From the perspective of potential participants, social media tools are everyday life tools used for communicating with friends and family, organising events, sharing opinions, and collecting individuals to act together. Hence, using them as research platforms does not require additional skills and no additional downloads from the participants. In addition, online focus groups, particularly through mobile applications, can be a time-saving and economical approach to collecting qualitative data, especially when the research design relies on collecting multiple types of materials (Rivaz, Shokrollahi, and Ebadi, 2019). Mobile focus groups can thus make research participation convenient, at least for those familiar with mobile apps such as the widely utilised WhatsApp (Chen and Neo, 2019).

In addition to real-time discussions, diary-type studies have become more accessible due to the widespread use of smartphones (Kimhy, Myin-Germeys, and Palmie, 2012; Lukoff *et al.*, 2018). Smartphones can be used to automatically collect mobile sensing data to infer, predict, and summarise people's daily activities and behavioural patterns (Liao *et al.*, 2014). They can be used for gathering data on specific tasks. Additionally, mobile focus groups can facilitate the collection of rich and varied data. Researchers can elicit more detailed materials by integrating multimedia elements such as images, videos, and interactive exercises. This multimedia approach can enhance the overall engagement and quality of data gathered, leading to more robust findings.

Moreover, digital tools, such as large language models (LLM), can be used to analyse the data collected efficiently, e.g., creating persona descriptions based on the data collected.

However, further investigation is required to fully explore the potential of WhatsApp focus groups as a research method. In addition, every research context to gather qualitative data is different, and some basic principles can guide researchers in using these tools effectively. This paper explores the potential of the online focus group method in qualitative consumer studies based on literature and an empirical study. The starting points are the findings about the effectiveness, interaction, and quality of research materials acquired through mobile focus groups found in the previous research. Furthermore, through our own case study experience, we analyse how suitable mobile focus groups are for gathering data in a consumer case study.

The paper is organized as follows. The next section discusses previous research, focusing on the benefits and limitations of mobile focus groups as a research tool. Section three provides an outline of our target group and a description of the mobile focus group platform. Section four presents the findings, and the following sections the discussion and conclusions.

2. Previous Research on the Advantages and Limitations of Mobile Focus Groups

In the 21st century, the widespread adoption of online social interaction has spurred the development and diversification of online research tools. This expansion is particularly evident in the context of behavioral lifestyle changes in food consumption and sustainability. Researchers now have a wide range of methods to choose from, each offering unique advantages. One approach involves capitalising on the pervasive nature of online platforms, allowing researchers to observe and intervene in online life. Several studies (Oksman *et al.*, 2016; Närvänen *et al.*, 2018; Potter *et al.*, 2023) exemplify the utilisation of this method. Alternatively, researchers can opt for specifically designed online research platforms (Komonen and Seisto, 2022; Van der Merwe *et al.*, 2019; Graça *et al.*, 2019; Vainio *et al.*, 2016). Moreover, researchers can also combine multiple online platforms to prompt sustainable behavior using one tool, while collecting experiences through another tool (Kymäläinen, Seisto, and Malila, 2021)

Virtual focus groups have emerged since the early 2000s, offering several benefits over face-to-face focus groups (Stewart and Williams, 2005; Keen, Lomeli-Rodriguez, and Joffe, 2022). They share the qualities of conventional focus groups in that they afford a purposeful social interaction in generating research material (Stewart and Williams, 2005; Kymäläinen, Seisto, and Malila, 2021). However, virtual focus groups offer greater flexibility in terms of scheduling, as participants can engage in discussions at their convenience, reducing scheduling conflicts (Almujlli *et al.*, 2022; Morgan and Lobe, 2015). Furthermore, online platforms serve as valuable research management tools by facilitating participant recruitment (Lazzarini *et al.*, 2016).

A more recent introduction to the researcher palette, mobile focus groups, utilize smartphones to conduct research remotely. This method has gained popularity due to its convenience and cost-effectiveness (Rupert *et al.*, 2017). One of the primary benefits of mobile focus groups is their ability to overcome geographical limitations. They engage participants in their everyday settings, which helps especially inform the study of daily household food-related practices (Lukoff *et al.*, 2018). Further, they help to reduce the expenses and effort of research management associated with travel, venue rental, and refreshments (Keen, Lomeli-Rodriguez, and Joffe, 2022). Moreover, using specifically designed online platforms eliminates the need for transcription services, as conversations are automatically recorded and transcribed (Morgan and Lobe, 2015). This reduces the time and effort needed for data preparation and analysis.

In addition, mobile focus groups have the advantage of being a familiar way of communication to many potential participants (Colom, 2022). A defining functionality of WhatsApp is the creation and use of messaging groups, which helps create a sense of community and connection (Church and De Oliveira, 2013). A further advantage of mobile focus groups compared to real-life focus groups is the potential for increased anonymity and a reduced social desirability bias as the participants communicate behind their nicknames (Chen and Neo, 2019). Mobile focus groups are a direct and non-hierarchical communication channel between participants and researchers (Chen and Neo, 2019), and may help foster contemplation of sensitive topics that may cause a barrier to sustainable consumption (Topping, Douglas, and Winkler, 2021). Participants may thus feel more comfortable expressing their opinions and difficulties in an anonymous group setting, leading to more honest and reliable data.

Despite these benefits, some limitations should be considered. One primary concern is potential technical difficulties and the resulting exclusion of less technologically savvy participants. This potential for a digital divide is a limitation when certain populations may not have access to or feel comfortable using mobile devices and online platforms. This can result in a biased sample that may not represent all the demographics of the target population. Researchers should be mindful of this limitation and consider other methods to ensure inclusivity in their research (Poliandri *et al.*, 2022). Even technically fluent participants may encounter issues with their mobile devices or face challenges navigating the online platform. These issues can disrupt the flow of the discussion and affect the quality of data collected (Poliandri *et al.*, 2022). In addition, some participants may feel a lack of trust regarding digital platforms and have concerns about the security of the services, especially regarding personal or sensitive topics (Kaihlanen *et al.*, 2022). Moreover, text-based online interaction often relies on emojis and emoticons to replace words and convey meaning, making interpretation more difficult (Walther and D'Addario, 2001). Furthermore, the lack of non-verbal cues in mobile focus groups may limit the depth of understanding. In face-to-face interactions, researchers can closely examine individuals' physical gestures, facial cues, and vocal intonations. Conversely, mobile focus groups exclusively rely on written exchanges, potentially resulting in a diminished grasp of subtleties and contextual intricacies (Chen and Neo, 2019).

Furthermore, it should be noted that mobile focus groups are not exempt from ethical considerations. Similar to conventional face-to-face focus groups, ethical concerns such as confidentiality and privacy matters may arise (Sim and Waterfield, 2019). Furthermore, previous studies employing WhatsApp and Messenger as research tools have demonstrated a dearth of attention toward research ethics and data protection, particularly regarding end-to-end encryption (Manji *et al.*, 2021). It is worth highlighting the potential solutions to these issues through the implementation of data safety measures and adherence to ethical protocols, including participant anonymity and informed consent.

In conclusion, in previous research, mobile focus groups present a multitude of advantages as a research methodology, encompassing the circumvention of geographical constraints, enhancement of participant convenience and comfort, and cost reduction. Subsequent sections will explicate further our approach, target demographic, and findings about mobile focus groups.

3. The Target Group and Method

To test the suitability of mobile online focus groups in consumer studies, we organised a focus group study using WhatsApp and Messenger-based platforms with a pre-selected consumer panel in April 2023 in Finland. The focus group was conducted to research and support behaviour change toward sustainable food consumption.

3.1 The Target Group

The focus of this study encompassed a specific subset of individuals referred to as "imperfect" consumers. In the initial stages of our investigation, we successfully identified a group exhibiting restricted tendencies in selecting environmentally friendly or health-conscious food choices yet displaying an increasing inclination towards embracing sustainable and nutritious dietary practices. This group presents a significant knowledge-behavior disparity, rendering them an opportune cohort to examine insights and experiences about the transition toward sustainable and healthy eating patterns.

The preceding study was based on a segmentation analysis of sustainable food behaviors among 1,000 Finnish consumers. The study used the COM-B modeling approach (Michie, Stralen, and West, 2011) to assess factors influencing sustainable food behaviors and identified four consumer groups. The study found that consumers engaging in sustainable consumption, in general, were more likely also to choose sustainable food protein options and were willing to pay a premium for sustainable products. From the larger segmentation study, 28 participants were selected for a focus group study based on their criteria as "imperfect consumers" from the age group of 18- to 65-year-olds, diverse educational and professional backgrounds, and locations. Later, we excluded four participants who were less active during the first week and did not respond to the assignments and polls.

3.2 The Platform and the Study Design

In the platform (Fig. 1), participants were able to write comments anonymously under nicknames, see each other's comments, and respond to them. Before joining the discussions, the participants received an information letter regarding the purpose of the research and handling of the data according to GDPR (EU General Data Protection Regulation) and were asked for consent.

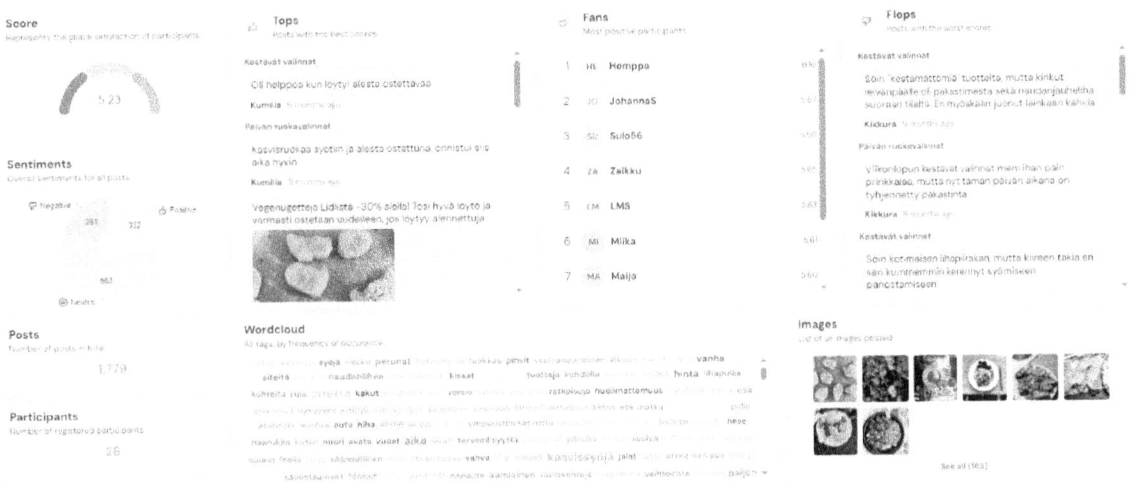

Figure 1: WhatsApp and Messenger-based platforms used for mobile focus group discussion

Initially, a diary study utilizing the WhatsApp platform was conducted to gather data. A total of 24 participants were assigned tasks and instructed to document their daily routines by exchanging images and engaging in activities that promote sustainable eating for two weeks. Subsequently, from this initial group, 20 participants participated in a two-hour real-time online focus group session. The session was moderated by two researchers who ensured the smooth progression of the conversation. Before the commencement of the session, questions were formulated regarding sustainable food behavior, food wastage, and grocery shopping. Furthermore, the facilitators were afforded the chance to delve into intriguing subjects that surfaced during the discussion, thereby posing impromptu questions. The collected research materials underwent a comprehensive analysis guided by thematic examination and descriptive coding techniques, facilitated by the utilization of NVivo software.

4. Findings

4.1 WhatsApp Diary Study

The participants were instructed to respond to topics regarding their food behavior and provide photos of their daily food choices through the online platform for two weeks. Comments and pictures were collected chronologically. The diary allowed to write about participants' priorities to make food consumption more sustainable.

Participants received daily timed reflective questions via WhatsApp. The tasks concerned for instance daily food choices and reflections on how the participants succeeded in following a sustainable diet:" *Tell us what you had for breakfast or lunch today. Take a photo. (7 a.m.) Tell us how you managed to make sustainable choices today. What was successful and what was an obstacle? (9 p.m.)*"

The diary encompassed several food-related tasks, enabling respondents to report barriers, facilitators, and feelings connected to task completion. We received in all 184 photos from the participants through the platform. Food photos were included in various tasks, such as daily self-assessments (Fig 2), and cooking tasks.

Figure 2: Photos of breakfast/lunch as a part of a sustainable eating WhatsApp diary study

The daily journal format encouraged participants to consider more detailed topics related to sustainable food consumption such as food shopping, and food waste management. At the end of the day, the participants responded to reflective inquiries through WhatsApp and described how they felt about the tasks and if there were some barriers. For instance, in the task of preparing vegetarian food, some participants raised budget concerns:

"The challenge for families is to find affordable dishes that are still tasty."

Additionally, some participants found vegetarian recipes to be complicated:

"When I searched for vegetarian recipes, many of them were unfamiliar and unappetising."

To address the lack of non-verbal cues in WhatsApp's functionality, sentiment analysis was carried out on each task about household cooking activities using NVivo's autocode function. This analysis captured cues related to emotions associated with the performance of cooking tasks.

In the context of a diary study, WhatsApp was found to offer several notable advantages, despite certain limitations. These benefits included the ability to the opportunity to ask detailed questions about the participants' photos and reflections and engage in real-time discussions, which represented an innovative approach to the collection of consumer insights. In addition, in the diary study, the polls were used to categorise respondents based on their personal goals for sustainable food consumption and the challenges of choosing sustainable foods in grocery stores. Notably, the study revealed that participants were able to develop new vegetarian recipes and successfully incorporate them into their cooking routines. Furthermore, through the polls, we were able to identify potential enablers and barriers to engaging in sustainable food behaviors among the target group, utilising the COM-B behavioral theory (Michie, Stralen, and West, 2011) as a framework to investigate daily reflections on food choices. The polls segmented respondents into groups to understand their motivations and capabilities for choosing sustainable food. The coding of themes provided insights into the challenges faced and the level of success in cooking activities by different types of 'imperfect consumers'. This supported further the creation of personas with Chat GPT.

4.2 WhatsApp Chat Session

During the hour two-hour real-time chat session, we received 400 responses from the participants. This communication was non-hierarchical, evenly distributed among the participants, and open, letting everyone share their views and respond to each other's messages.

Moderator: Do you have a favorite waste recipe?

R1: There is very little waste in a two-person household, it is easy to buy and cook food appropriately.

R2: For buttermilk cake, buttermilks, creams, yogurts, fillings...

R3: You can put milk whose date is getting old in the pancakes.

R4: A couple of days ago I made a sauce where I mixed salsa, sweet chili, and ketchup leftovers. You can also try any fillings for the tortillas. It's easy to hide leftovers in oven foods, e.g., with pasta.

R5: We don't have any wastege, the chickens/dog and the cat eat what people leave.

R6: Mash and porridge leftovers for rolls.

R7: Pizza and omelette with salty toppings.

R8: I have used the ResQ application and thus reduced waste.

R9: Pizza or some kind of stew as wastege food. And casseroles. Roots and many vegetables that are near the end date can be well immersed in them.

R10: The pizza is really good.

R11: My favorite pastime is making leftover mashed potatoes into fritters.

R12: Pizza is always a good wastage food.

It is worth noting that through WhatsApp chat we were able to effectively engage also non-tech-savvy groups with clear instructions and providing sufficient response time. To ensure a smooth flow of conversation, we had to consider the pace of slower participants. The semi-structured nature of the platform allowed for the exploration of intriguing topics, and WhatsApp's flexibility enabled repeated assessments that captured changes in attitudes and preferences before and after study., the platform's ability to accommodate wider participation increased convenience for respondents with diverse daily schedules.

One notable limitation identified in the study pertains to the lack of detail in the messages exchanged during the moderated chat session. This limitation posed challenges in terms of effectively managing and analysing the data. The fragmented nature of the conversations on WhatsApp, combined with the presence of multiple messages addressing a single topic, made it difficult to organize and analyse the responses efficiently. To address this challenge, meticulous data preparation was implemented. This involved consolidating significant responses obtained from scattered messages. To facilitate this, a simple crosstab table was created in Excel during the data preparation phase. This table served as a reference, linking the scattered messages to the respective respondents and relevant questions (See Table 1).

Table 1 Example of data preparation procedure in Excel

Username	Comments	1. What would ease sus choice and food blogs?	2. What type of informatio n would benefit instore?	3. Can you read product labels, for example?	4. Do you have a favourite recipe?	5. Have you tried any plant-based products?	6. Would it be easier to choose sustainabl e food in	7. Are locally produced food products available	8.How much do your family, friends or relatives
Respondent 1	You would need m	1							
Respondent 1	Yes, I'm apparently	1							
Respondent 1	Children usually su	1							
Respondent 1	The guidance in the store was			1					
Respondent 1	That's good								
Respondent 1	You can put milk whose date is getting old in the pan				1				
Respondent 1	I've looked at them, but haven't bought them					1			
Respondent 1	We didn't like the tofu either					1			
Respondent 1	Neither do I						1		
Respondent 1	In the Valma store, you can get dairy products, etc., cheaply							1	
Respondent 1	I get eggs from a local hen							1	
Respondent 1	In the summer, we grill with my sister's family at the same time and there have been no problems								1
Respondent 1	I also take leftovers to work the next day								
Respondent 1	Fish is terribly expensive in the store							1	
Respondent 1	We can also have the fish in the lake because no one wants to gut and put them in							1	
Respondent 1	Cats do thank you for fresh fish							1	
Respondent 1	Fiksu Ruoka is often blocked and cannot get the order through							1	
Respondent 1	I go to blueberry in the summer and they are good for children and friends								1
Respondent 1	Well, the wife stays in the raspberry in the backyard								1
Respondent 1	Strawberries are laborious to keep, so they have been left out								1

This facilitated seamless retrieval and examination of the reconstructed comments within the NVivo software tool, without encountering any data gaps. Nevertheless, it is important to acknowledge that the incorporation of time stamps could have potentially mitigated certain obstacles encountered. Unfortunately, the time stamps were not exportable from the discussion platform along with the comments, thereby hindering their inclusion in the analysis.

4.3 Further Analysis with Large Language Models

Incorporating large language models (LLM), like Chat GPT, can be utilised for enhancing the complexity of research findings alongside human reasoning of discovered rationales. The LLM has been found to improve the objectivity of human reasoning in topic coding and content analysis when studying qualitative data (Bano *et al.*, 2024). In the focus group study, LLM was used alongside NVivo to validate the manually coded topics by respondents' answers with basic prompting to contextualise the questions in the analysis (Tai *et al.*, 2023). This provided an additional layer of quality assurance to guarantee precise coding procedures that are typically conducted by comparing the discovered topics between researchers. If gaps or incomplete components were identified, the LLM's capabilities were utilised to generate new topics, thus refining the analytical framework to a higher degree. Incorporating LLM aided in refining the creation of detailed personas, which are fictional representations of segments of actual people within a population (Pruitt and Grudin, 2003) (Fig.3).

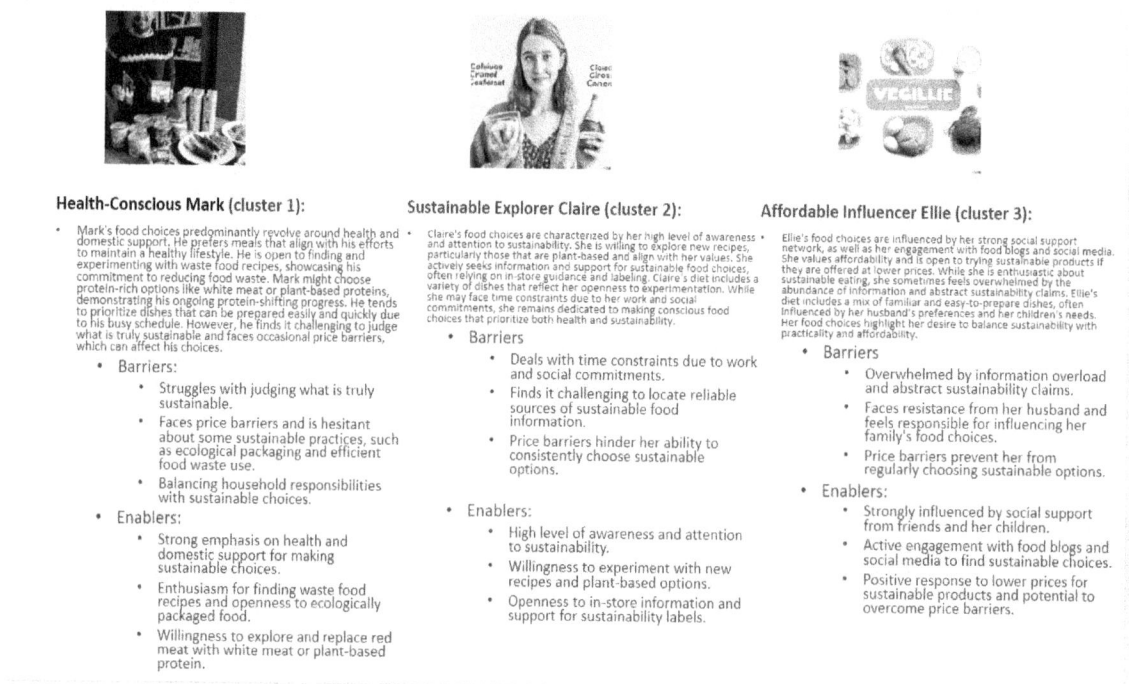

Health-Conscious Mark (cluster 1):

- Mark's food choices predominantly revolve around health and domestic support. He prefers meals that align with his efforts to maintain a healthy lifestyle. He is open to finding and experimenting with waste food recipes, showcasing his commitment to reducing food waste. Mark might choose protein-rich options like white meat or plant-based proteins, demonstrating his ongoing protein-shifting progress. He tends to prioritize dishes that can be prepared easily and quickly due to his busy schedule. However, he finds it challenging to judge what is truly sustainable and faces occasional price barriers, which can affect his choices.
  - Barriers:
    - Struggles with judging what is truly sustainable.
    - Faces price barriers and is hesitant about some sustainable practices, such as ecological packaging and efficient food waste use.
    - Balancing household responsibilities with sustainable choices.
  - Enablers:
    - Strong emphasis on health and domestic support for making sustainable choices.
    - Enthusiasm for finding waste food recipes and openness to ecologically packaged food.
    - Willingness to explore and replace red meat with white meat or plant-based protein.

Sustainable Explorer Claire (cluster 2):

- Claire's food choices are characterized by her high level of awareness and attention to sustainability. She is willing to explore new recipes, particularly those that are plant-based and align with her values. She actively seeks information and support for sustainable food choices, often relying on in-store guidance and labeling. Claire's diet includes a variety of dishes that reflect her openness to experimentation. While she may face time constraints due to her work and social commitments, she remains dedicated to making conscious food choices that prioritize both health and sustainability.
  - Barriers:
    - Deals with time constraints due to work and social commitments.
    - Finds it challenging to locate reliable sources of sustainable food information.
    - Price barriers hinder her ability to consistently choose sustainable options.
  - Enablers:
    - High level of awareness and attention to sustainability.
    - Willingness to experiment with new recipes and plant-based options.
    - Openness to in-store information and support for sustainability labels.

Affordable Influencer Ellie (cluster 3):

- Ellie's food choices are influenced by her strong social support network, as well as her engagement with food blogs and social media. She values affordability and is open to trying sustainable products if they are offered at lower prices. While she is enthusiastic about sustainable eating, she sometimes feels overwhelmed by the abundance of information and abstract sustainability claims. Ellie's diet includes a mix of familiar and easy-to-prepare dishes, often influenced by her husband's preferences and her children's needs. Her food choices highlight her desire to balance sustainability with practicality and affordability.
  - Barriers:
    - Overwhelmed by information overload and abstract sustainability claims.
    - Faces resistance from her husband and feels responsible for influencing her family's food choices.
    - Price barriers prevent her from regularly choosing sustainable options.
  - Enablers:
    - Strongly influenced by social support from friends and her children.
    - Active engagement with food blogs and social media to find sustainable choices.
    - Positive response to lower prices for sustainable products and potential to overcome price barriers.

Figure 3: Example of persona descriptions of three types of imperfect consumers using AI tools (Chat GPT 3.5) to provide insight into the barriers and enablers of sustainable food behavior

5. Discussion

In our study, the WhatsApp platform helped to collect a comprehensive dataset and materials to form nuanced consumer insights. The integration of WhatsApp as a communication tool allowed for real-time discussions and diary-style reflections, which has been applied to previous research on the topic (Chen and Neo, 2019). WhatsApp provided a more straightforward and ubiquitous sharing of insights and instant inclusion of photos of daily food choices and cooking activities, compared to specifically designed, asynchronous discussion platforms (Kymäläinen, Seisto, and Malila, 2021). Despite its limitations, WhatsApp proved to be a valuable tool for gathering consumer insights on barriers preventing sustainable food choices. WhatsApp focus groups allowed immediate and continuous interaction between the study participants and the researchers, enabling an intimate exploration of consumer attitudes and behaviors. This direct and non-hierarchical communication fostered a sense of comfort and openness among participants, leading to authenticity and candidness.

However, it is essential to note that materials acquired through WhatsApp focus groups may be less verbose and extensive than traditional face-to-face or video focus groups. Further, while emoticons are a common feature in contemporary digital interactions and conversations (Walther and D'Addario, 2001), they may pose challenges to the analysis of the material, particularly when it comes to text-based coding, categorisation, and software-based analysis. Researchers must be cautious in interpreting and analysing the briefest messages and the non-verbal cues, as they may not always accurately reflect the intended meaning of the participants, especially out of context. In addition, the fragmented nature of messages can pose challenges and extra effort to manage research data in further analyses.

Another limitation of WhatsApp focus groups, which is also found in previous studies, is the potential for the digital divide, particularly with older or less technologically savvy individuals. This can lead to difficulties in participation and potential bias in the sample (Colom, 2022). Even though WhatsApp-based focus groups may be inaccessible to some groups, we found that also non-tech-savvy groups can successfully participate if they are given enough time to respond and clear instructions. However, it should be noted that our research is limited to Finland, where the digital divide between the population is not significant and thus the results could be different in other countries.

Moreover, WhatsApp focus groups necessitate careful question route preparation when employing them as a research method to produce high-quality research materials. Clear and concise questions are easy to understand and respond to in the short-message medium. The absence of visual cues and non-verbal communication in mobile focus groups may require additional clarification and guidance from the researchers to ensure that participants fully understand the questions and can provide meaningful responses.

5. Conclusion

In conclusion, mobile focus groups offer a promising approach to qualitative consumer research. They provide convenience, flexibility, and the potential for more authentic and unbiased responses. By leveraging the benefits of mobile and digital technologies, researchers can gather rich and varied data that can lead to deeper insights into consumer attitudes and motivations. While there are limitations to consider, mobile focus groups have the potential to enhance the field of qualitative consumer research and contribute to a better understanding of consumer behavior. However, researchers must be mindful of the limitations of using mobile technology, such as the reliance on emojis and emoticons, potential technical issues, and the need for careful question route preparation and supporting those participants, who are not as technically savvy and may need more time to participate in the conversation. By understanding these limitations, researchers can harness the benefits of mobile and WhatsApp-based focus groups to generate valuable insights into future research on sustainable consumption.

References

Almujlli, G. *et al.* (2022) 'Conducting Virtual Focus Groups During the COVID-19 Epidemic Utilizing Videoconferencing Technology : A Feasibility Study', 14(3). Available at: https://doi.org/10.7759/cureus.23540.

Bano, M. *et al.* (2024) 'Large language models for qualitative research in software engineering : exploring opportunities and challenges', *Automated Software Engineering*, pp. 1–12. Available at: https://doi.org/10.1007/s10515-023-00407-8.

Chen, J. and Neo, P. (2019) 'Texting the waters: An assessment of focus groups conducted via the WhatsApp smartphone messaging application', *Methodological Innovations*, 12(3). Available at: https://doi.org/10.1177/2059799119884276.

Church, K. and De Oliveira, R. (2013) 'What's up with WhatsApp? Comparing mobile instant messaging behaviors with traditional SMS', *MobileHCI 2013 - Proceedings of the 15th International Conference on Human-Computer Interaction with Mobile Devices and Services*, pp. 352–361. Available at: https://doi.org/10.1145/2493190.2493225.

Colom, A. (2022) 'Using WhatsApp for focus group discussions: ecological validity, inclusion, and deliberation', *Qualitative Research*, 22(3), pp. 452–467. Available at: https://doi.org/10.1177/1468794120986074.

Friedrich, P. (2013) *Web-based co-design Social media tools to enhance user-centred design and innovation processes*. Aalto university. Available at: https://doi.org/https://aaltodoc.aalto.fi/server/api/core/bitstreams/c844e519-8439-497b-9038-b0109554b6c7/content.

Graça, J. *et al.* (2019) 'Consumption orientations may support (or hinder)transitions to more plant-based diets', *Appetite*, 140(February), pp. 19–26. Available at: https://doi.org/10.1016/j.appet.2019.04.027.

Kaihlanen, A.M. *et al.* (2022) 'Towards digital health equity - a qualitative study of the challenges experienced by vulnerable groups in using digital health services in the COVID-19 era', *BMC Health Services Research*, 4, pp. 1–12. Available at: https://doi.org/10.1186/s12913-022-07584-4.

Keen, S., Lomeli-Rodriguez, M. and Joffe, H. (2022) 'From Challenge to Opportunity: Virtual Qualitative Research During COVID-19 and Beyond', *International Journal of Qualitative Methods*, 21, pp. 1–11. Available at: https://doi.org/10.1177/16094069221105075.

Kimhy, D., Myin-Germeys, I. and Palmie (2012) 'Mobile assessment guide for research in schizophrenia and severe mental disorders', *Schizophr Bull* [Preprint]. Available at: https://doi.org/10.1093/schbul/sbr186.

Komonen, P. and Seisto, A. (2022) 'Consumers anticipating futures beyond the pandemic: A qualitative study', *Futures*, 142(August), p. 103019. Available at: https://doi.org/10.1016/j.futures.2022.103019.

Kymäläinen, T., Seisto, A. and Malila, R. (2021) 'Generation z food waste, diet and consumption habits: A finnish social design study with future consumers', *Sustainability (Switzerland)*, 13(4), pp. 1–14. Available at: https://doi.org/10.3390/su13042124.

Lazzarini, G.A. *et al.* (2016) 'Does environmental friendliness equal healthiness? Swiss consumers' perception of protein products', *Appetite*, 105, pp. 663–673. Available at: https://doi.org/10.1016/j.appet.2016.06.038.

Liao, J. *et al.* (2014) 'Smart Diary : A Smartphone-based Framework for Sensing , Inferring and Logging Users ' Daily Life', (c), pp. 1–13. Available at: https://doi.org/10.1109/JSEN.2014.2331970.

Lukoff, K. *et al.* (2018) 'TableChat: Mobile food journaling to facilitate family support for healthy eating', *Proceedings of the ACM on Human-Computer Interaction*, 2(CSCW). Available at: https://doi.org/10.1145/3274383.

Manji, K. *et al.* (2021) 'Using WhatsApp messenger for health systems research : a scoping review of available literature', (April), pp. 774–789. Available at: https://doi.org/10.1093/heapol/czab024.

Mensonen, A. *et al.* (2014) 'Novel services for the publishing sector through co-creation with users', *Journal of Print and Media Technology Research*, 3(4), pp. 279–290. Available at: https://www.jpmtr.org/JPMTR-0414-ggA.pdf.

Van der Merwe, S.E. *et al.* (2019) 'Making sense of complexity: Using sensemaker as a research tool', *Systems*, 7(2), pp. 3–7. Available at: https://doi.org/10.3390/systems7020025.

Michie, S., Stralen, M.M. Van and West, R. (2011) 'The behaviour change wheel : A new method for characterising and designing behaviour change interventions The behaviour change wheel : A new method for characterising and designing behaviour change interventions', 42(April).

Morgan, D.L. and Lobe, B. (2015) 'Chapter 9 Online Focus Groups David Morgan and Bojana Lobe', (March).

Närvänen, E. *et al.* (2018) 'Creativity, aesthetics and ethics of food waste in social media campaigns', *Journal of Cleaner Production*, 195, pp. 102–110. Available at: https://doi.org/10.1016/j.jclepro.2018.05.202.

Oksman, V. *et al.* (2016) 'Vitality as a life style trend in blogs: a netnographic approach', in Christine Bernadas and D. Minchella (eds) *Proceedings of ECSM2016*. Caen: Academic Conferences and Publishing International Limited Reading, UK 44-118-972-4148, pp. 258–266. Available at: https://doi.org/https://books.google.fi/books?id=1DaeDAAAQBAJ&pg=PA259.

Poliandri, D. *et al.* (2022) 'Dematerialized participation challenges : Methods and practices for online focus groups'.

Potter, C. *et al.* (2023) 'Effects of environmental impact and nutrition labelling on food purchasing: An experimental online supermarket study', *Appetite*, 180(April 2022), p. 106312. Available at: https://doi.org/10.1016/j.appet.2022.106312.

Pruitt, J. and Grudin, J. (2003) 'Personas: practice and theory', in *DUX '03*, pp. 1–15. Available at: https://doi.org/https://dl.acm.org/doi/10.1145/997078.997089.

Rivaz, M., Shokrollahi, P. and Ebadi, A. (2019) 'Online focus group discussions: An attractive approach to data collection for qualitative health research', *Nursing Practice Today*, 6(1), pp. 1–3. Available at: https://doi.org/10.18502/npt.v6i1.386.

Rupert, D.J. *et al.* (2017) 'Virtual versus in-person focus groups: Comparison of costs, recruitment, and participant logistics', *Journal of Medical Internet Research*, 19(3). Available at: https://doi.org/10.2196/jmir.6980.

Sim, J. and Waterfield, J. (2019) 'Focus group methodology : some ethical challenges', *Quality & Quantity*, 53(6), pp. 3003–3022. Available at: https://doi.org/10.1007/s11135-019-00914-5.

Stewart, K. and Williams, M. (2005) 'Researching online populations: The use of online focus groups for social research', *Qualitative Research*, 5(4), pp. 395–416. Available at: https://doi.org/10.1177/1468794105056916.

Stremmel, G. *et al.* (2022) 'Vegan labeling for what is already vegan: Product perceptions and consumption intentions', *Appetite*, 175(February), p. 106048. Available at: https://doi.org/10.1016/j.appet.2022.106048.

Tai, R.H. *et al.* (2023) 'Use of Large Language Models to Aid Analysis of Textual Data', *bioRxiv preprint* [Preprint]. Available at: https://doi.org/https://doi.org/10.1101/2023.07.17.549361.

Topping, M., Douglas, J. and Winkler, D. (2021) 'General Considerations for Conducting Online Qualitative Research and Practice Implications for Interviewing People with Acquired Brain Injury', 20, pp. 1–15. Available at: https://doi.org/10.1177/16094069211019615.

Vainio, A. *et al.* (2016) 'From beef to beans: Eating motives and the replacement of animal proteins with plant proteins among Finnish consumers', *Appetite*, 106, pp. 92–100. Available at: https://doi.org/10.1016/j.appet.2016.03.002.

Walther, J.B. and D'Addario, K.P. (2001) 'The impacts of emoticons on message interpretation in computer-mediated communication', *Social Science Computer Review*, 19(3), pp. 324–347. Available at: https://doi.org/10.1177/089443930101900307.

Exploring Content Moderation Research: Insights from a Bibliometric Analysis

Ozlem Ozan and Ali Rıza Sadıkzade
Yasar University, İzmir, Türkiye

ozlem.ozan@yasar.edu.tr
ali.riza.sadikzade@gmail.com

Abstract: Rapid technological advances have intensified user-content interactions, leading to real-world consequences and the implementation of complex regulation mechanisms such as AI filtering and industrial and user moderation. This study aims to introduce the contemporary topics surrounding the subject by comprehensively examining the content moderation research by conducting a bibliometric analysis of 202 publications between 2016 and 2023 from the Web of Science and Scopus databases. This study aims to identify the influential authors, universities, countries, journals, funding agencies, network maps of keywords, and co-authorship. The findings of this study demonstrate that the Queensland University of Technology is the most influential in the field. The United States of America, England, and Australia are the most productive countries. The National Science Foundation and the European Research Council are the most supporting funding institutions. New Media & Society, Social Media + Society, and Big Data & Society are the most influential journals. Ysabel Gerrard is the most productive author. Seven clusters occur in author collaboration networks. The network map of the keywords suggests that researchers mainly focus on social media; Facebook, Instagram, YouTube, and Twitter are the most investigated platforms. There is a shift from transparency to hate speech and misinformation among the research themes. The academic research has exhibited a consistent upward trajectory since 2016. Given the demonstrable momentum of interest in this field, it is reasonable to anticipate a further increase in research with a diverse array of academic disciplines.

Keywords: Content moderation, Bibliometric analysis, Bibliometric data, Social media

1. Introduction: Internet, Social Media, and Content Moderation

The internet's pervasive integration into daily life has blurred the lines between online and offline experiences, prompting extensive discussions on its multifaceted implications. As the internet's salience grows, discussions span a wide range, from the positive effects of social media, such as enhanced connectivity and access to diverse opinions, to concerns like increased polarization and manipulative misinformation (Wike et al. 2022).

Beyond organic issues, political actors leverage the internet to advance their agendas, employing tactics like disinformation campaigns witnessed in the 2016 US Presidential Election (Ferrara et al. 2020). The online landscape also poses challenges at personal and interpersonal levels, including data privacy, copyright, internet scams, and cyberbullying.

Given these issues, safeguarding online individuals and communities has become imperative. Legislative efforts, such as the US Communications Decency Act's Section 230, passed in 1996, aimed to limit online platform liabilities, although tech companies actively reviewed content to protect their user base (Angwin and Grassegger, 2017; Caplan 2018). Recent discussions point to an increased institutional authority, as seen in legislative examples like the European Union's Digital Services Act and Germany's NetzDG law.

The content moderation market has grown substantially, reflecting the heightened need for online safeguarding. Content moderation involves diverse methods, from algorithmic processes to user cooperation and active moderation teams (MSNBC 2021; Veglis 2014).

While typically executed by platforms, content moderation also involves online service providers enforcing ethical guidelines on clients and engaging in the moderation process (Byman 2022). Moderation methods vary based on platform size and financial structure, with larger platforms employing extensive moderation teams (Caplan 2018; Liu et al. 2022). Challenges persist, including concerns about the adequacy of human moderators in understanding content nuances and potential biases in moderation processes (Debre and Akram 2021).

Despite the rich insights from cited studies, comprehensive articles scarcely summarize the content moderation discourse. Therefore, the primary objective of this study is to conduct a bibliometric analysis of the literature, summarizing contemporary discussions through bibliographic analysis of academic articles. This research aims to contribute valuable insights for future researchers examining the evolving landscape of content moderation.

2. Methodology

This section covers research methodology adapted from the Preferred Reporting Items for Systematic Reviews and Meta-Analyses (PRISMA) framework (BMJ 2021), which mainly includes the key elements as rationale and aim of the research, search strategy (database selection, search terms, inclusion, and exclusion criteria), study selection (screening process, data extraction), data analysis, results, discussion, and conclusion.

2.1 Rationale and aim of the Research

This research conducts bibliometric analysis to assess the literature structure on content moderation. Bibliometric analysis, as defined by Broadus (1987), involves the quantitative study of published or bibliographic units. Zupic and Čater (2015) characterize bibliometrics as a quantitative method for describing, evaluating, and monitoring research.

In the contemporary context, the enhancements in computer programs, such as VOSviewer, GEPHI, Bibexcel, and CiteSpace II, along with the establishment of reputable databases like Web of Science and Scopus, have rendered bibliometric analysis more fruitful (Cobo et al. 2011; Zupic and Čater 2015). Therefore, bibliometric analysis effectively addresses the trends and issues in the literature on content moderation, which is essential for fostering a positive, safe, and constructive online environment.

In this context, the research aims to answer the following questions:

- RQ1: What is the growth pattern of publications in content moderation? Which years have seen significant increases or decreases in publication outputs?
- RQ2: Which authors had the highest publication productivity and citations in content moderation?
- RQ3: What is the co-authorship network structure among authors in content moderation? Can we identify central authors, communities, or specific collaboration patterns?
- RQ4: Which journals hosted the most research on content moderation?
- RQ5: Which institutions and countries have contributed the most to the literature on content moderation?
- RQ6: Which articles on content moderation have received the highest number of citations?
- RQ7: What are the most frequently used keywords in articles on content moderation, and how have these keywords evolved? What does the co-occurrence network of keywords reveal about thematic clusters and relationships?
- RQ8: How have research topics related to content moderation evolved?

2.2 Search Strategy

2.2.1 Database selection

We systematically searched for relevant articles in the Web of Science (WOS) and Scopus databases, comprehensively covering academic literature across various disciplines.

2.2.2 Search terms

Choosing an effective search strategy was crucial for identifying relevant research on content moderation, given the diverse terminology and lack of standardized keywords within the field. We initially experimented with combining controlled vocabulary terms and keywords, but this approach included irrelevant studies. We adopted an iterative approach to optimize results, ultimately selecting a strategy focused on "content moderation" within the Author Keywords field of both WOS and Scopus. This strategy allowed us to capture a broader range of research while minimizing false positives, as studies explicitly mentioning content moderation in their author keywords are more likely to be relevant to our analysis.

2.2.3 Inclusion and exclusion criteria

We included the studies if they meet the following criteria: (1) Published in peer-reviewed journals, (2) Address content moderation as a primary focus or a significant component, (3) Available in English, and (4) Accessible as Full-text. Studies that did not meet these criteria were excluded.

2.3 Study Selection

2.3.1 Screening process

The authors of the study conducted the screening of titles and abstracts independently to identify potentially eligible studies.

2.3.2   Data extraction

The standardized metadata provided by WOS and Scopus databases for bibliometric analysis is used to collect relevant information from each included study. Extracted data included Authors, Article Title, Journal Name, Author Keywords, Abstract, Author Address, Funding Text, Cited References, Cited Reference Count, Total Times Cited Count, Publisher, Publisher Address, International Standard Serial Number (ISSN), Year Published, Digital Object Identifier (DOI), Web of Science Categories, Research Areas, and other relevant details. Further data for RQ3 (such as h-index, country, and subject areas of journals) has been collected from the Scimago Database.

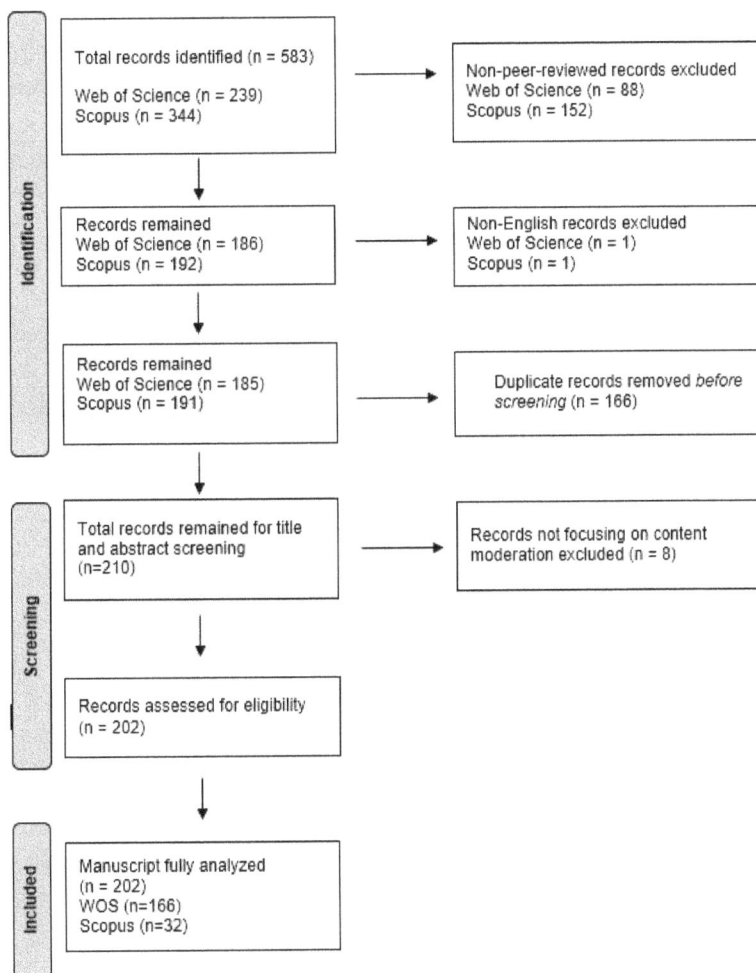

Figure 1: PRISMA framework of the study

2.4   Data Analysis

We uploaded extracted data as RIS files to Zotero Reference Management Software to detect duplicate records of WOS and Scopus databases. After the identification of duplicates, we combined WOS and Scopus files manually with MS Excel and analyzed them with VOSviewer Bibliometric Analysis Software.

The bibliometric analysis uses publication metrics (e.g., average vs. total and single- vs. multi-authored publications), Citation metrics (e.g., average vs. total citations), and publication-citation metrics (e.g., h-index) for science mapping of the studied field. Science mapping includes the following methods to examine social networks based on contributors and knowledge clusters based on cited/citing publications and keywords (Lim and Kumar 2024): (1) Co-authorship analysis, (2) Co-citation analysis, (3) Bibliographic coupling analysis, (4) Co-occurrence of keywords analysis, (5) Citation analysis and (6) PageRank analysis. Furthermore, performative statistics relating to institutions (e.g., Universities and funding programs) can also be analyzed within bibliometrics (Benckendorff and Zehrer 2013; Michael Hall 2011).

In this context, we used the following analyses to overview and inspect the networks and connections among themes related to content moderation as well as classify the literature, highlighting conceptual structures that could produce insights through mapping:

- Descriptive statistics based on metrics in RQ1, RQ2, RQ3, RQ4, R5, R6, R7, R8
- Co-authorship analysis (authors and countries) in R3
- Bibliographic coupling analysis in R6
- Co-occurrence of keywords analysis in R7, R8

3. Results

3.1 RQ 1: Growth Pattern of Publications by Year

According to the results presented in Figure 2, there has been a steady increase in publications between 2016-2022. The number of publications peaked in 2023 with a noticeable momentum. The number of publications in 2023 is approximately equal to the total number in the last three years. This increase also aligns with the discussion presented in the introduction about increasing attention to safeguarding the internet.

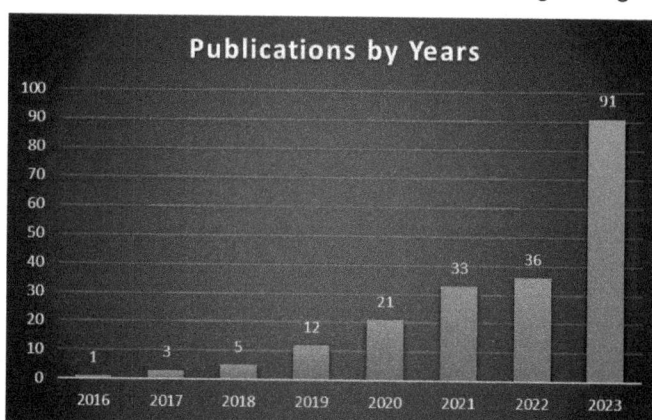

Figure 2: Growth pattern of publications by years

3.2 RQ 2: Authors who had the highest publication productivity

The author with the highest publication productivity is Y. Gerrard, with five publications, followed by S.M. West and N. Suzor, with four publications. The University of Sheffield, the University of Southern California, and the Queensland University of Technology (QUT) are noticeable institutions with which the top three productive authors are affiliated. Additionally, Y. Gerrard, S.M. West, and R. Gorwa exhibit more significant influence and broader citation impact. In the authors' disciplines, it is noticeable that social sciences have the overwhelming majority, including sociology, communication and journalism, political sciences, and law.

Table 1: 10 Authors with the most publication

Name	Number of Publication*	Affiliation	Department	Total Citations	Avg Citations
Y. Gerrard	5	University of Sheffield	Sociological Studies	176	35.2
S. M. West	4	University of Southern California	Annenberg School for Communication and Journalism	246	61.5
N. Suzor	4	QUT	Faculty of Law	104	26
R. Gorwa	3	University of Oxford	Department of Politics and International Relations	243	81
T. Gillespie	3	Cornell; Microsoft	Department of Communication	142	47.3
A. Matamoros-fernandez	3	QUT	School of Communication	54	18
G. M. Masullo	3	University of Texas at Austin	School of Journalism and Media	39	13

Name	Number of Publication[*]	Affiliation	Department	Total Citations	Avg Citations
Bright, J.	3	University of Oxford	Oxford Internet Institute	39	13
M. J. Riedl	3	University of Texas at Austin	School of Journalism and Media	35	11.6
J. E. Gray	3	QUT	Creative Industries Faculty	19	6.3

* Authors' affiliations and departments are taken from the publications; their current affiliations may differ from this list.

3.3 RQ 3: Networks among Authors

The co-authorship analysis reveals collaboration among 27 authors distributed across seven clusters, Figure 3. Clusters 1, 2, 3, 4, and 7 include seven authors listed in the top ten productive ones. S. M. West and N. Suzor are in Cluster 1. J. E. Gray is in Cluster 2; Y. Gerrard and A. Matamoros-Fernandez are in Cluster 3. R. Gorwa is in Cluster 4. Finally, T. Gillespie is in Cluster 7. According to the co-authorship analysis among countries, the USA, England, Australia, Germany, and Brazil are the most collaborative in content moderation, as shown in Figure 4.

Figure 3: Co-authorship network among authors

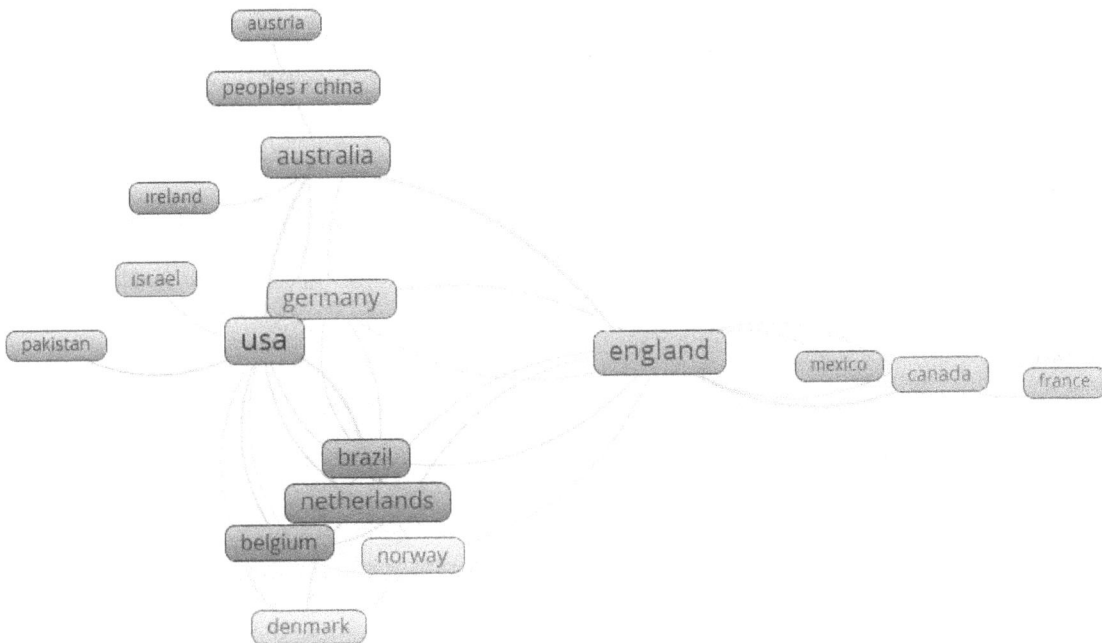

Figure 4: Co-authorship network among countries

3.4 RQ 4: Top Journals in Content Moderation Research

Ninety-nine journals have contributed to the subject in the given timeframe. According to the results in Table 2, New Media & Society has the highest citation number and H-Index. Furthermore, 10.91% (n=22) of the publications of the local dataset were published in this journal. On the other hand, Big Data & Society has the highest average citation rate per paper and published 4.46 % (n=9) of the publications in this field of study.

Table 2: Top Journals

Top 10 Journals	Number of Publications	Total Citations	Avg. Citation	H-Index
New Media & Society	22	479	21.7	136
Social Media + Society	16	215	13.4	54
Big Data & Society	9	269	29.8	57
International Journal of Communication	9	58	6.4	52
Policy and Internet	9	122	13.5	38
Information Communication & Society	7	34	4.8	101
Internet Policy Review	7	146	20.8	24
Journal of Digital Media & Policy	7	85	12.1	9
Media Culture & Society	5	28	5.6	78
Computer Law & Security Review	4	32	8	49
Total	**95**	**1468**	**15.45**	

As for the countries of the journals, 35.35% (n=35) of the journals are published in the United Kingdom, followed by 27.27% (n=27) in the United States and 11.11% (n=11) in the Netherlands.

3.5 RQ 6: Publications Which Have Received the Highest Number of Citations

Most of the most cited papers are written by the authors who have contributed the most. Similarly, they are in the journals that have contributed most to the field by the number of publications. Additionally, the keywords provided in Table 3 illuminate the scope of these articles. Notably, the most cited articles predominantly belong to the domain of social sciences. Keywords such as internet policy, platform transparency, online protest, transparency, artificial intelligence, platforms, and demonetization are prevalent in these highly cited works.

Table 3: Top 10 publications based on the number of citations

Author(s)	Total Citations	Journal	Title	Keyword(s)
Gorwa et al. 2020	185	Big Data & Society	Algorithmic content moderation: Technical and political challenges in the automation of platform governance	algorithms, artificial intelligence, content moderation, copyright, platform governance, toxic speech
West 2018	139	New Media & Society	Censored, suspended, shadowbanned: User interpretations of content moderation on social media platforms	accountability, content moderation, free expression, social media, survey, transparency, user studies
Gerrard 2018	99	New Media & Society	Beyond the hashtag: Circumventing content moderation on social media	algorithms, Anorexia, content moderation, eating disorders, hashtags, Instagram, Pinterest, pro-ana, social media, Tumblr
Caplan and Gillespie 2020	75	Social Media + Society	Tiered Governance and Demonetization: The Shifting Terms of Labor and Compensation in the Platform Economy	apocalypse, advertising, content moderation, demonetization, digital intermediaries, platforms, YouTube
Flew et al. 2019	63	Journal of Digital Media and Policy	Internet regulation as media policy: Rethinking the question of digital communication platform governance	media policy, digital platforms, platform capitalism, content moderation, classification, media regulation, intermediaries, platform governance

Jhaver et al. 2019	59	ACM Transactions on Computer-Human Interaction	Human-Machine Collaboration for Content Regulation: The Case of Reddit Automoderator	content moderation, automated moderation, automod, platform governance, mixed-initiative, future of work
Katzenbac 2019	58	Internet Policy Review	Algorithmic governance	transparency, automation, politicization, regulation, social ordering, governance, predictive policing, content moderation, algorithmic governance
Zeng et al. 2017	47	Policy & Internet	How Social Media Construct "Truth" Around Crisis Events: Weibo's Rumor Management Strategies After the 2015 Tianjin Blasts	Internet censorship, online rumor, content moderation, emergency communication, online protest, collective action
Gillespie et al. 2020	46	Internet Policy Review	Expanding the debate about content moderation: scholarly research agendas for the coming policy debates	content moderation, platforms, internet policy, social media, regulation
Suzor et al. 2019	46	International Journal of Communication	What Do We Mean When We Talk About Transparency? Toward Meaningful Transparency in Commercial Content Moderation	content moderation, platforms, transparency, due process

The bibliographic coupling analysis, with the minimum number of citations of a document parameter set at 15, reveals collaboration among 33 documents distributed across four clusters, Figure 5. Our analysis indicated that the field is not monolithic but encompasses distinct research areas. Cluster 1, the red one, focuses on Online Dynamics, covering communication, social dynamics, governance, and emotional impact. It bridges the gap between technical moderation mechanisms and the socio-cultural aspects of online interactions. Cluster 2, the green one, highlights the interplay between governance, technology, and societal implications of content moderation, focusing on regulatory frameworks, technological innovations, and ethical considerations. Cluster 3, the blue one, addresses Algorithmic Governance and Expression. It explores the relationship between algorithmic governance, freedom of expression, and socio-cultural dimensions, focusing on ethical, legal, and technological aspects of content moderation, particularly algorithmic decision-making. Cluster 4, the yellow one, explores the impact of social media on mental health awareness, advocacy, and specific health issue discussions.

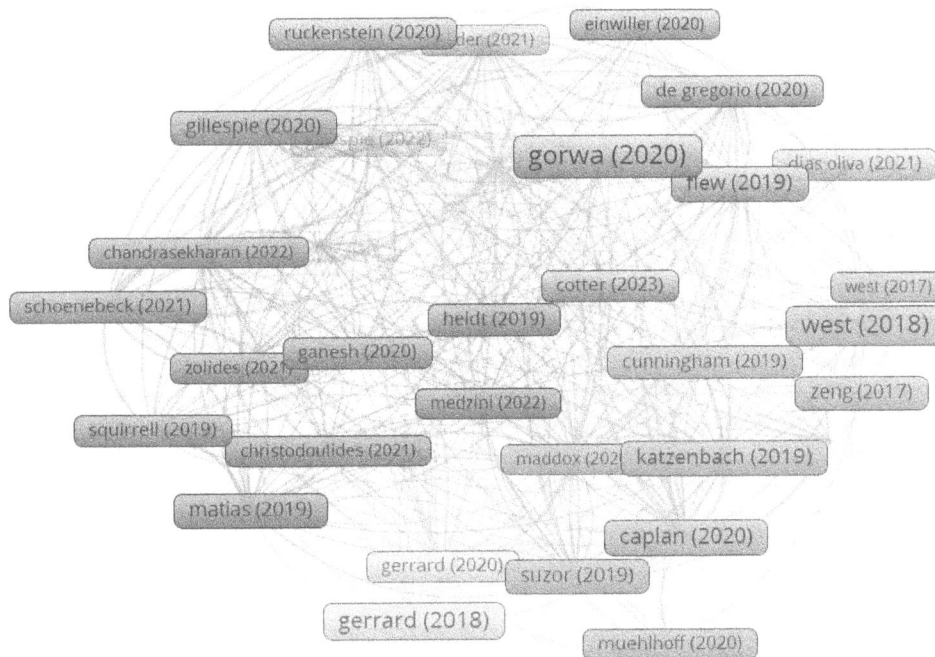

Figure 5: Bibliographic coupling analysis of publications

While each cluster has a unique thematic emphasis, common themes like governance and regulation appear prominently in Clusters 2 and 3, reflecting the ongoing discourse on legal and ethical aspects. Terms related to online behavior, such as communication and social dynamics, indicate a shared interest in understanding user interactions across all clusters. On the other hand, the clusters differ in their theme specificity. Cluster 1 covers a comprehensive range of topics, providing a holistic overview of content moderation research. In contrast, Clusters 2 and 3 delve into more specialized areas, with Cluster 2 focusing on governance and technology and Cluster 3 exploring algorithmic governance and freedom of expression.

The diversity within these clusters highlights the interdisciplinary nature of content moderation research. Researchers approach content moderation from various angles, from technical aspects to legal and ethical considerations, social dynamics, and mental health advocacy. This diversity underscores the need for collaborative efforts integrating insights from different clusters to develop comprehensive and effective content moderation strategies.

3.6 RQ 5: Institutions and Countries That Have Contributed the Most to the Literature on Content Moderation

According to the results shown in Table 4, the University of Oxford is the leading university in content moderation studies. QUT follows it. The University of Amsterdam is in third place. However, it has a low impact, with the most minor citations per publication.

According to the results shared in Table 5, seven of the ten institutions that funded research are governmental institutions. Despite being the most prominent research funder regarding the number of projects it supports, the European Union ranks among the least influential organizations with a comparatively low average citation rate. Canada's Social Sciences and Humanities Research Council is the most influential organization, with 30.2 average citation rates. The Australian Research Council has the third-highest average citation (22.1). Microsoft stands out as the most successful non-governmental funding agency, boasting the highest citations per publication, 39.3. In comparison, Microsoft and Google appear more notable than Meta and Twitter, which funded only two.

Table 4: Top 10 Universities

Top 10 Universities	# of Publications	Total Citations	Avg. Citations
University of Oxford	12	294	24.5
Queensland University of Technology	12	264	22
University of Amsterdam	10	54	5.4
University of Michigan	8	120	15
Cornell University	5	111	22.2
University of Sheffield	5	179	35.8
University of Pennsylvania	4	21	5.75
University of Southern California	6	193	32.1
University of Texas Austin	4	51	12.7
University of Sydney	4	72	18.5
Total	70	1363	

Table 5: Top 10 Funding organizations of the research

Funding Organizations	# of Publications	Total Citations	Avg. Citations
European Union	10	61	6.1
Social Sciences and Humanities Research Council of Canada	7	212	30.2
National Science Foundation	7	131	18.7
Australian Research Council	6	133	22.1
Israel Science Foundation	3	33	11
Microsoft	3	119	39.3

Funding Organizations	# of Publications	Total Citations	Avg. Citations
Research Council of Norway	3	13	3.3
William and Flora Hewlett Foundation	2	24	12
Google Inc	3	14	4.6
Dutch Research Council	2	8	4
Total	38	687	18.1

*Funding programs under "European Union" include: European Research Council, European Union Tailor, European Union, European Commission Joint Research Centre, and European Union Nextgenerationeu Prtr

**Funding programs under "Google Inc" include Google Inc and Google - Project Be Positive Under The 2019 Google Org Impact Challenge on Safety Call

3.7 RQ 7: Keyword Analysis

A keyword represents the main topics explored in the document, aiding in indexing and categorization for readers. The dataset has 628 keywords, with the top 3 being social media, platform governance, and Facebook. 1.5 egocentric network analysis of the "Content Moderation" keyword, with a minimum occurrence parameter set at 5, revealed six clusters representing topic relationships, Figure 6. These clusters depict relationships among topics, with the thickness of connecting lines indicating the strength of keyword pairs, and the nodes' size signifies the keyword's frequency. Each cluster shows the interconnectedness and thematic cohesion among keywords within the broad context of content moderation.

Cluster 1: Legal and Regulatory Aspects: The keywords of this cluster are artificial intelligence, copyright, digital platforms, the Digital Services Act, free speech, freedom of expression, hate speech, online platforms, and platform regulation. This cluster focuses on the legal and regulatory aspects of content moderation. It covers topics like the legal implications of artificial intelligence, copyright issues, and the role of regulations in governing digital platforms. Terms like hate speech and freedom of expression suggest a focus on balancing regulatory measures with preserving free speech online.

Cluster 2: Technological and Platform-Specific Focus: The keywords of this cluster are algorithms, Instagram, machine learning, misinformation, platform governance, and YouTube. Cluster 2 centers on technological aspects of content moderation and emphasizes algorithms, machine learning, and the problems posed by misinformation. Platform-specific terms such as Instagram and YouTube suggest a focus on understanding and addressing content moderation challenges unique to these platforms.

Cluster 3: Algorithmic Governance and Transparency: The keywords of this cluster are algorithmic governance, de-platforming, platforms, regulation, social media platforms, and transparency. This cluster emphasizes the intersection of algorithmic governance, transparency, and regulatory measures in content moderation. Terms like de-platforming suggest a focus on the decisions made by platforms regarding removing certain content or users. Social media platforms indicate a broader consideration of these issues within the social media landscape.

Cluster 4: Platform-Specific Analysis: The keywords of this cluster are Facebook, self-regulation, and Twitter. Cluster 4 focuses on specific social media platforms—Facebook and Twitter. It suggests a detailed examination of content moderation issues within these platforms, including considerations of self-regulation and policies implemented by these companies to manage content.

Cluster 5: *Human Rights and Social Media*: The keywords of this cluster are human rights and social media. This cluster emphasizes the intersection of content moderation with human rights considerations. It suggests exploring the impact of content moderation practices on users' rights within the context of social media.

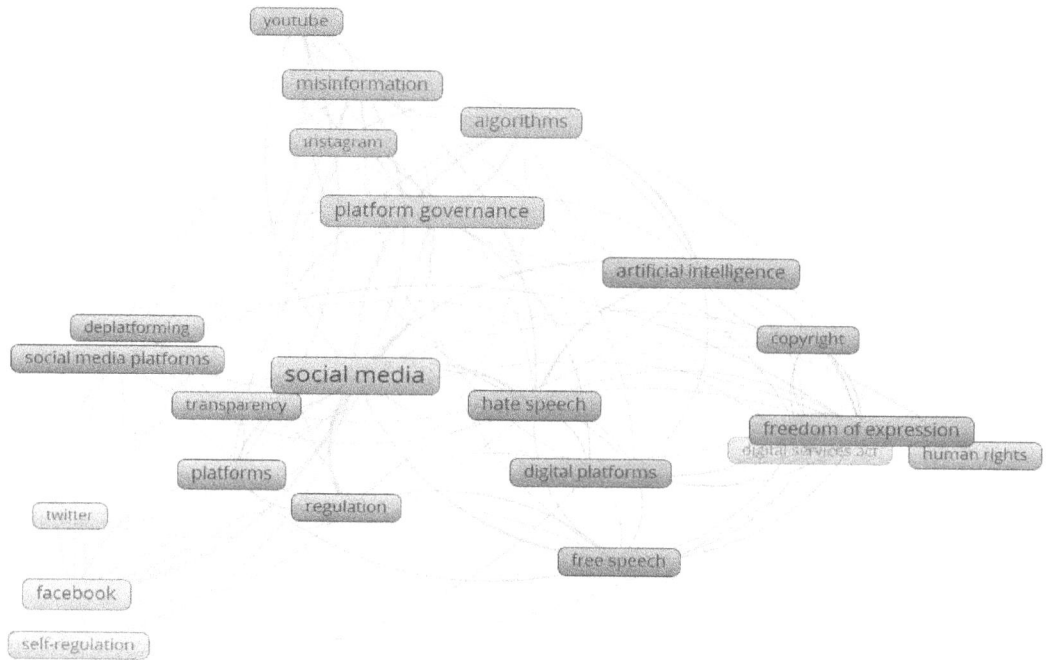

Figure 6: Thematic clusters and relationships among keywords

The network analysis reveals the multidimensional nature of the field, including legal, technological, platform-specific, governance, and human rights aspects.

3.8 RQ8: Analysis of Research Trends

1.5 egocentric network analysis was conducted on the keyword Content Moderation with a minimum occurrence parameter set at five. Overlay visualization was utilized to monitor the evolution of research trends over the past three years, Figure 7. In early 2020, the focus was on transparency. By late 2020, the emphasis had shifted to algorithms. In early 2021, the main areas of interest were free speech and platforms, while later in the year, the focus expanded to platform governance, social media, YouTube, human rights, artificial intelligence, copyright, and regulation. The trend continued to evolve in early 2022, with research centering on self-regulation, the Digital Services Act, Instagram, Twitter, Facebook, and freedom of expression. In late 2022, the focus shifted to hate speech and digital platforms. Early 2023 saw an emphasis on misinformation, and by late 2023, the main areas of interest were social media platforms and deplatforming.

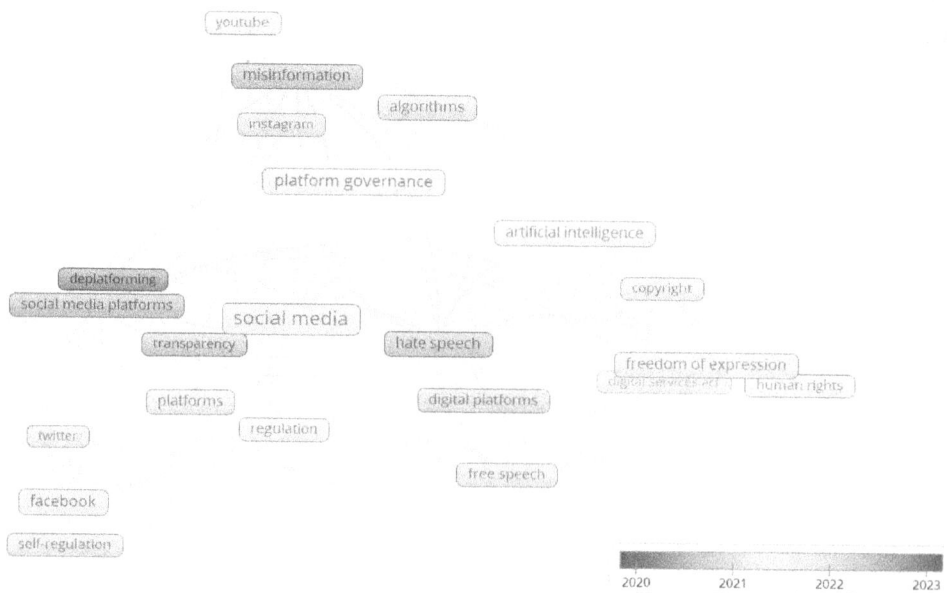

Figure 7: Research trends between 2020 and 2023

The trends culminated in late 2022 when research interest prominently shifted towards deplatforming, misinformation, hate speech, and social media platforms in 2023. This trajectory highlights content moderation research's dynamic and adaptive nature, reflecting an evolving response to emerging challenges and contemporary issues within the digital landscape.

4. Discussion and Conclusion

Internet integration necessitates formal and informal measures to maintain a secure and positive online and offline environment. Thus, content moderation has become a vital topic today. Our analysis reveals a rise in publications on content moderation, particularly in 2023, corresponding with its increased significance due to the surge in hate speech and misinformation during the global COVID-19 pandemic and election periods. Keyword trends point to the complex relationship between the internet, social media platforms, and democratic ideals. The emphasis on transparency in early 2020 suggests a shared effort to increase openness and accountability online, but the subsequent shift towards algorithms raises questions about the impact of automated content moderation systems.

Social media platforms, seen as tools for democratization, play a crucial role in global discourse. The keyword trends reflect a progression from a focus on free speech and platforms to a broader exploration of platform governance, social media dynamics, and algorithmic impacts on various aspects such as human rights, artificial intelligence, and regulation. However, the trends also highlight concerns about algorithmic recommendation systems' potential threats, such as fostering environments conducive to hate speech and misinformation spread.

Research predominantly focuses on major platforms like Facebook, YouTube, Twitter, and Instagram. This focus might inadvertently reinforce capital-driven models and neglect alternative platforms or narratives.

Prominent authors and institutions from Australia, England, and the USA dominate content moderation research, suggesting expertise and collaboration concentration in these regions. In contrast, countries unprepared for AI may face challenges in dealing with the ethical and legal considerations related to evolving content moderation practices.

In conclusion, while the internet and social media platforms offer potential for a more democratic world, content moderation research trends indicate potential threats to democracy. Algorithm-driven polarization of online spaces can lead to environments that limit exposure to diverse perspectives. Addressing this requires a nuanced approach that balances algorithmic content curation benefits with democratic values preservation. Initiatives prioritizing transparency, user agency, and algorithmic accountability are vital, as is ongoing interdisciplinary research and collaboration among scholars, policymakers, and platform developers. Prioritizing transparency, user agency, and algorithmic accountability can help navigate the complex landscape of content moderation and mitigate the unintended consequences of algorithmic systems, harnessing the internet and social media platforms' potential to contribute positively to democratic discourse and global idea exchange.

References

Angwin, J. and Grassegger, H. (2017) "Facebook's Secret Censorship Rules Protect White Men From Hate Speech But Not Black Children", *ProPublica,* [online], 28 June. https://www.propublica.org/article/facebook-hate-speech-censorship-internal-documents-algorithms

Benckendorff, P. and Zehrer, A. (2013) "A Network Analysis of Tourism Research". *Annals of Tourism Research, Vol* 43, October 2013, pp 121-149.

Broadus, R. N. (1987). "Toward a definition of 'bibliometrics'", *Scientometrics*, Vol 12, pp 373–379. https://doi.org/10.1007/BF02016680

Byman, D. (2022) "Content Moderation Tools to Stop Extremism", *Lawfare,* [online], https://www.lawfaremedia.org/article/content-moderation-tools-stop-extremism

Caplan, R. (2018) "Content or Context Moderation? Artisanal, Community-Reliant, and Industrial Approaches", Data & Society, [online], https://datasociety.net/library/content-or-context-moderation/

Cobo, M.J., López-Herrera, A.G., Herrera-Viedma, E. and Herrera, F. (2011) "Science mapping software tools: Review, analysis, and cooperative study among tools". *Journal of the American Society for Information Science and Technology,* Vol 62, no. 7, pp 1382–1402. https://doi.org/10.1002/asi.21525

Debre, I. and Akram F. (2021) "Facebook's language gaps weaken screening of hate, terrorism". *The Associated Press*, [online], 26 October, https://apnews.com/article/the-facebook-papers-language-moderation-problems-392cb2d065f81980713f37384d07e61f

Ferrara, E., Chang, H., Chen, E., Muric, G. and Patel, J. (2020) "Characterizing social media manipulation in the 2020 US presidential election", *First Monday,* [online], https://doi.org/10.5210/fm.v25i11.11431

Lim, W. M. and Kumar, S. (2024) "Guidelines for interpreting the results of bibliometric analysis: A sensemaking approach", *Global Business and Organizational Excellence*, Vol 43, No. 2, pp. 17–26. https://doi.org/10.1002/joe.22229

Liu, Y., Yildirim, P. and Zhang, Z. (2022) "Implications of Revenue Models and Technology for Content Moderation Strategies", *Marketing Science, Vol* 41, No. 4, pp. 403–419. https://doi.org/10.1287/mksc.2022.1361

Michael Hall, C. (2011) "Publish and perish? Bibliometric analysis, journal ranking and the assessment of research quality in tourism", *Tourism Management*, Vol 32, No. 1, pp. 16–27. https://doi.org/10.1016/j.tourman.2010.07.001

MSNBC (2021) "Why Content Moderation Costs Social Media Companies Billions". *MSNBC*, [online], 27 February, https://www.youtube.com/watch?v=OBZoVpmbwPk (Accessed: 9 February 2024)

BMJ, 2021;372:n71 https://doi.org/10.1136/bmj.n71

Veglis, A. (2014) *Moderation Techniques for Social Media Content in* Meiselwitz, G. eds. *Social Computing and Social Media*. Cham: Springer International Publishing, pp. 137–148.

Wike, R., Silver, L., Fetterolf, J., Huang, C., Austin, S., Clancy, L. and Gubbala, S. (2022) "Social Media Seen as Mostly Good for Democracy Across Many Nations, But US is a Major Outlier", *Pew Research Center*, [online], 22 January, https://www.pewresearch.org/global/2022/12/06/social-media-seen-as-mostly-good-for-democracy-across-many-nations-but-u-s-is-a-major-outlier/

Zupic, I. and Čater, T. (2015) "Bibliometric Methods in Management and Organization", Organizational Research Methods, Vol 18, No. 3, pp. 429–472. https://doi.org/10.1177/1094428114562629

Summarizing User Comments on Social Media Using Transformers

Afrodite Papagiannopoulou and Chrissanthi Angeli

School of Engineering, University of West Attica, Athens, Greece

apapagiannop@uniwa.gr
angeli@uniwa.gr
c_angeli@otenet.gr

Abstract: Social media and smart technology have invaded our daily lives. They are increasingly used to express feelings and opinions, to publish news, to support public debates on various issues and events. User comments under each post are a key factor in making economic, political and business decisions. Managing their sheer volume is an almost impossible task. Therefore, summarization seems crucial. Recent years have shown that abstractive summarization has achieved great results in the field of document summarization by producing more human-like summaries. Unlike formal documents, social media conversations face four challenges: 1) tend to be informal, consisting of slang expressions and special characters, 2) show deviations from the original theme and dependencies on previous opinions, 3) since they are short, they lack lexical richness and, 4) contain redundant and repetitive information, resulting in confusion among readers. We address these challenges by developing a system that generates abstractive summaries from pools of user comments under a specific social media post, using Transformers. Unlike previous works that do not rely on user comment pools and draw data from Reddit, Twitter or "Sina Weibo" platforms only, we use a Facebook dataset. We first reshape the raw dataset in a meaningful way for summary generation and we apply some basic pre-processing. Then, we define a task that deals with grouping comments according to the post title. A summary is generated for each group (pool) of comments. Our model is evaluated using ROUGE scores between the generated summary and each comment on the thread.

Keywords: Social media, Social comments, Abstractive summarization, Neural networks, Transformers

1. Introduction

Social media through smart technology is widespread and has become an integral part of our daily lives as it is used to communicate, express feelings, advertise, post news, political, economic and social exchanges. Social media's role in public life is very important as posts and comments shape public opinion on a variety of important issues. It has been observed that people's opinions expressed through social networks are more direct and representative than those expressed in face-to-face communication. The data exchanged in social media is a cornerstone of research because we can extract patterns of social behaviour that can be used for social, business and government decisions. Creating summaries on social media comments seems crucial for the retrieval of useful knowledge in a reasonable time period.

Summarization means converting the content of a long text into a smaller one, preserving the meaning of the original text. There are different ways to write a summary. It can be done either manually or using algorithms and artificial intelligence techniques. The latter is called "Automatic text summarization" and is an area that has attracted the interest of researchers especially in recent years (Gupta, S. and Gupta, S.K., 2019). There are two main categories of summarization techniques: a) extractive and b) abstractive (Nenkova, A. and McKeown, K., 2012) Extractive summarization finds the most important words or sentences from the original text by considering statistical and linguistic features. Then rearranges them in the correct order and produces the summary text. Abstractive summarization, on the other hand, is based on the meaning of the document and is created by either formulating new sentences or rewording existing ones with new words (Varma, V., Kurisinkel, L.J. and Radhakrishnan, P. 2017). Target text is produced by analyzing the semantic information of the original text. With deep analysis and reasoning, new sentences are created from the original text (Rachabathuni, P.K., 2017).

Initially, most summarization work was done with extractive summarization because of its simplicity. In recent years, however, this field has stagnated as it was observed that extractive summaries lacked fluency, coherence and the meaning of the original text. Producing high quality summaries that were grammatically correct, consistent, concise and informative were deemed necessary. For this reason, researchers turned their attention on abstractive summarization which, despite its complexity, still satisfies the above limitations, creating human-like summaries (Suleiman, D., and Awajan, A., 2020).

Artificial intelligence and Deep Learning techniques have been successfully applied to summarization with excellent results. By introducing the transformer model in (Vaswani et al, 2017), the traditional sequence-to-sequence model has drastically improved in terms of both accuracy and training time. Sequential processing is being replaced by parallel processing, the simple embeddings from the positional embeddings and self-attention to multi-head attention. The attention mechanism is not a term that appeared with the emergence of transformers. But when combined together their power took off. Thus, we selected the Transformer model as our basic model for training and fine-tuning. In the field of social media summarization, there is limited research which builds abstractive text summarization systems based on transformers. Unlike these works that mainly generate summaries from Reddit, Twitter or "Sina Weibo" platforms, our approach aims to go beyond and to create a post-level summary of pools of comments and sub-comments. Our goal is to include all comments and not the most liked or those characterized by linguistic richness. Additionally, since each social media platform is unique with its own particularity on posting and commenting (Ghanem, F.A., Padma, M.C. and Alkhatib, R., 2023), we aim to expand our research to platforms other than Reddit and Twitter. The dataset we are looking at in this paper is Facebook news posts accompanied by user comments under each post.

This paper illustrates the design of our system, based on T5 pre-trained model. The rest of the paper is organized as follows: Section 2 presents a review of the research done so far on social media summarization using transformers. Section 3 illustrates our model description. Section 4 shows the experimental methodology, Section 5 discusses the results achieved so far and finally section 6 contains concluding remarks and our future work.

2. Related Work

As the internet began to conquer our daily lives in the area of news, information and opinion exchange, scientists focused on creating summaries of web posts, microblogs, and social networks. They first used probabilistic and optimization methods to generate a summary. Indicative works have been done on Twitter posts; the first is introduced by (Sharifi, B., Hutton, M-A. and Kalita, J., 2010), (Sharifi, B., Inouye, D., and Kalita, J.K., 2014) where the model automatically generates a summary by applying a Phrase Reinforcement (PR) algorithm adding the TF-IDF technique to it. The second (Chong, F., Chua, T., Asur, S., 2021) is based on two models the Decomposition Topic Model (DTM) and the Gaussian Topic Model (GDTM) exploit the temporal correlation between tweets under predicted conditions to produce a concise and information-rich summary of events.

With the development of Artificial Intelligence, NLP also started gaining attention from researchers. The main reason for turning to these techniques has been a) their abilities to support the large volume of data circulating on the internet, and b) the powerful computing power available today. Various deep learning models including Convolutional Neural Networks (CNN), Recurrent Neural Networks (RNN) and Long-Term Memory (LSTM) RNNs have been used in the field of natural language generation. Indicative examples are research works such as of (Gao et al, 2019) which introduces a sequence-to-sequence model based on CNN and Bi-RNN creating abstractive summaries of social media. Work by (Liang, Z., Du, J. and Li, C., 2020) has created abstractive summaries of social media based on Attentional Encoder-Decoder RNNs. An additional hidden layer is used before the encoder where the model decides which information is useful and which should be removed. Another work introduced by (Wang, Q. and Ren, J., 2021) proposes a model of summary-aware attention mechanism that produces abstractive summaries. This mechanism has managed to overcome the particularity of social media content. In (Bhandarkar, P., Thomas, K. T., 2023) abstractive summaries are produced using an RNN which combines sequence-to-sequence and the attention approach. The model also uses LSTM as an encoder and decoder to build summaries. With the attention layer in this architecture the decoder is allowed to have more direct access to the input sequence.

The use of transformers and attention mechanism (Vaswani et al, 2017) has been a pivotal point in deep learning applications. The idea has been adopted by many researchers and has been extended to all NLP tasks (Gupta, A., Chugh, D. and Katarya, R., 2022). The social media summarization field is still in its infancy. We recognize, so far, the following aspects that refer to abstractive summaries on social media using transformer models: A framework using a pre-trained BERT-based model as encoder and a non-pre-trained transformer model as a decoder, had been introduced by (Li, Q. and Zhang, Q., 2020). This project produces abstractive Event Summarization on Twitter. An event topic prediction component helps the decoder to focus on more specific aspects of posts. In order to produce more coherent summaries and exceed the limit of 512 tokens taking into account only the most liked comments. In the work of (Tampe, I., Mendoza, M. and Milios, E., 2021) a multi-document text summarization scenario that includes meaningful comment detection, extending previous single-document approaches is proposed. The proposed model uses pre-trained BERT as encoder and a transformer as a decoder. This architecture is extended with an attention encoding level that is fed with user preferences. Attention encoding focuses on comments with the highest social impact. Comments are rated as important based on user preferences. Finally (Blekanov, I. S., Tarasov N. and Bodrunova, S. S., 2022) introduces a Transformer-based abstractive summarization model which creates summaries in three languages from posts and comment pools. The datasets used have been downloaded from Reddit and Twitter. In this work T5 and LonFormer are fine-tuned and compared with BART. In addition, they apply enlarged Transformer-based models on Twitter data in three languages (English, German, and French) to discover the performance of these models on data with non-English text. In (Rawat et al, 2021) an abstractive summarization model was presented which used a transformer model to generate individual sentence summaries of review texts. Then a combination of Universal Sentence Encoder, statistical methods and graph reduction algorithm was used to select the most relevant sentences to best represent the whole text in the summary.

3. Methodology

Our system's design, based on Transformers, aims to generate abstractive summaries from pools of user comments under a specific social media post. Unlike prior works that generate summary for each comment we create a post-level summary of pools of comments and sub-comments. First, we focus on creating coherent and meaningful summaries of pools of user comments, since they present greater specificity, in terms of a) the nature of the language, b) their conceptual grouping and c) their dynamic upgrading. Second, unlike the other research works that consider only two social media platforms, Reddit and Twitter, our goal is to explore how different data sets and training models can be developed. For summarizing pools of user comments under social media posts, we used transformer model architecture as explained in (Vaswani et al, 2017). Transformers give state-of the-art results on various NLP tasks, such as sentiment analysis, language translation and text summarization. The main components of our system are:

3.1 Transformer Encoder-Decoder Architecture

Encoder-decoder architectures are widely used for developing neural networks. It can handle inputs and outputs both of which consist of variable-length sequences admirably. Therefore, these architectures, although they are applied in many fields, are best suited for problems related to natural language understanding and text generation, such as translation and summarization. In other words, they perform immensely in sequence-to-sequence modelling. The encoder takes as input a sequence of variable length and transforms it into a numerical representation that captures the important information from the input. This numerical representation constitutes the hidden state and is of fixed length. Subsequently, the decoder maps the fixed-shape coded state into a variable-length sequence to generate the output (Figure 1).

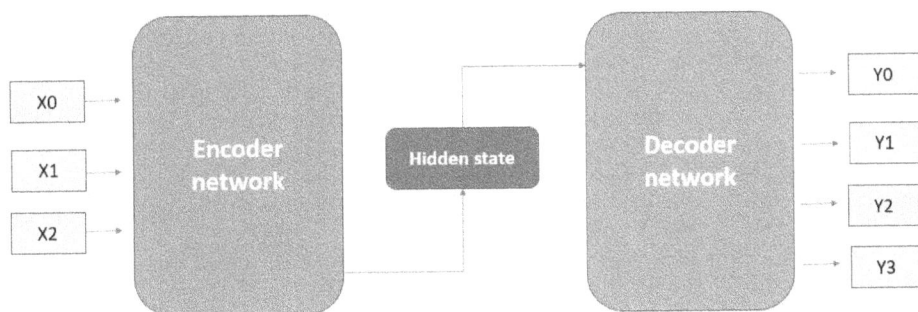

Figure 1: Encoder-Decoder architecture (Vitalflux.com/encoder-decoder-architecture-neural-network)

3.2 Model Explanation

Starting our approach, we compared three pre-trained transformer models (T5, BART and PEGASUS) for their performance in generating summaries of our dataset (Rawat A., and Singh Samant, S., 2022). What these pre-trained models have in common is that they generate abstract summaries and use the encoder-decoder transformer architecture that performs best in text generation tasks. The results showed very good behaviour from all three models with the T5 giving the best. Without excluding the performance study of the other models, we started with T5 by feeding and training it with data from Facebook, specifically with news posts and their respective comments.

As we have already mentioned earlier, user posts and comments on social media are of particular interest when it comes to creating summaries. First of all, they are short, lack verbal and linguistic richness and tend to be informal, consisting of slang expressions and special characters. Secondly, they present deviations from the original theme and dependencies on previous views. Finally, they contain redundant and repetitive information, resulting in confusion to readers. For this reason, their pre-processing is deemed necessary in order to improve the performance of the model. Based on the topic of the post we create lists of comments ignoring parts that do not add meaning to the sentence such as short words, links, abbreviations and emoji. The proposed approach consists of the following steps:

- Data collection using Facebook.
- Preprocessing using regex libraries.
- Post-level classification of user comments using Python.
- Feed the transformer-based encoder with the lists of texts using Pytorch library.
- Feed this encoding to the Transformer decoder using Pytorch library.
- Produce the summary text
- Validate the predicted summary using ROUGE metrics.

For the creation of our system we decided to use the pre-trained models rather than building a model from scratch because pre-trained models: a) can give much better results, with careful pre-processing of the data, b) provide a learning base on which they can tune many different data sets and c) can create new models with a small change in the training session and fine-tuning, leading us to faster results (Blekanov, I. S., Tarasov N. and Bodrunova, S. S., 2022). Particularly our system creation is based on the T5 pre-trained model. T5 - stands for "Text-to-Text Transfer Transformer" (Raffel et al, 2021) and is an encoder-decoder model. It converts all problems into text-to-text format and can be trained or fine-tuned either for supervised or unsupervised data.

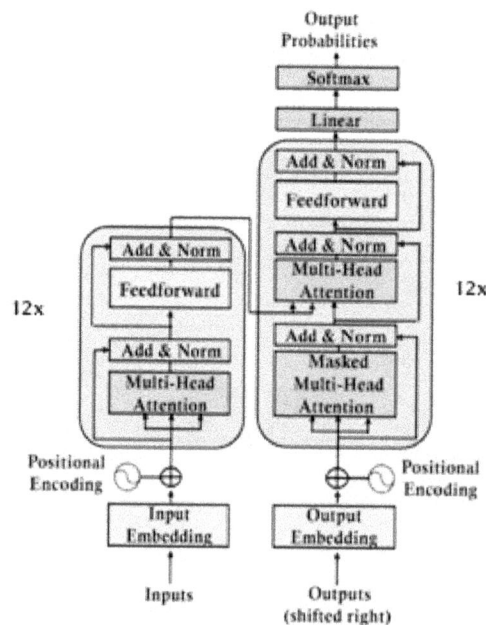

Figure 2: Transformer architecture

It is characterized as a task-agnostic model since it is suitable for any NL task, such as Translation, Language Inference, Information extraction and Summarization. Its training procedure is based on teacher forcing. It has an input sequence and a target sequence.

For the purpose of our work, it is trained and fine-tuned for text summarization from social media. The input sequence of our system is fed to the encoder which in turn the target sequence is fed to the decoder. More specifically: The input sequence is tokenized and processed to convert every word into a unique numeric id using *body_input_ids* with *body_attention_masks.* Then in the embedding layer the transformer uses learned embeddings to transform the input tokens into vectors of 512.

Encoder part: The encoder is comprised of two major components: a multi-head attention mechanism which is followed by normalization and a feed-forward neural network. The Multi-head Attention is based on a scale dot-product attention which creates a vector of every input word. Once it is applied 8 times it generates several vectors for the same word. This helps the model to capture different representations of the words' relations in the sentence. The different attention-based matrices generated by the multiple heads are summed and passed through a linear layer to reduce the size to a single matrix.

Decoder part: The decoder side has a lot of shared components with the encoder side. It takes in two inputs: the output of the encoder (*summary_input_ids*) and the output text shifted to the right (*generated_ids*). Then it applies multi-head attention twice with one of them being "masked" (*summary_attention_masks*). The dictionary at the final layer of the decoder should have the same size as the target dictionary, our case 128. Finally, the softmax function is applied indicating the probability of each word to be present in the output.

4. Experimental Methodology

4.1 Dataset

Finding the right datasets to generate social media summaries is a really complex task. Several social media platforms place restrictions on data download. For those that are open, the data must be reformatted to meet the needs of the project. From our research we have seen that different social media platforms meet different performances. Therefore, we have used a Facebook dataset for the development of our system. The data pertains to posts of Facebook's news, each of which is accompanied by user comments and sub-comments. The raw data consists of the following 7 columns with a total of 1,781,576 rows. Essentially, our interest is limited to 3 columns: 'message', 'post_title', 'post_number' where 'post_title' and 'post_number' identify a specific post while the 'message' column represents the comments of users under the post. After the dataset was downloaded, the first step was to apply a basic pre-processing to it before entering it into the model. As we mentioned above, raw social network data contain special characters, emoticons, and referral links. Pre-processing involves cleaning the data from unnecessary and useless elements that would have led us to undesirable results. Using the python NLTK and regex libraries, we removed punctuation, special characters, emoji strings and links, as well as NULL values. The second step of pre-processing concerns the grouping of data according to the topic of discussion. Our goal is to generate a summary from a set of user comments related to a specific post-topic. Based on the post title, the data dictionary is reformatted to isolate user comments for each post into separate lists of different sizes. The new data set is the input of our model.

Experimental Setup

The Transformer model was trained on PyCharm with NVDIA GeForce 4070 GPU with 12 BG RAM. For simplicity, we used the 1/3 of our dataset (1,781,576 rows), since it is converted into lists of group-comments. We considered all sentences of each list with a summary length of 128. The dataset is split into Train, Validation and Test with 80%, 20% and 10% ratio size respectively. We trained our model based on the traditional T5-base 12-layer pre-trained model with 12 attention heads and depth of feed forward network as 3072. The dropout rate set to 0.1 and the AdamW optimizer we used is set to 1e-3. The model was trained for 12 epochs with batch size set to 64. We calculate the Train, Validation and Validation PPL loss to assess the performance of the model. Finally, we have used the Rouge score metrics to evaluate the model.

5. Results

Trying to make the right decision on which pre-trained model is more suitable for our dataset, we have started comparing three pre-trained models: BART (Lewis et al, 2019), PEGASUS (Zhang et al, 2020) and T5 (Raffel et al, 2021). Since there is a variety of pre-trained models that have achieved great results on many NLP tasks, HuggingFace hub (Wolf et al, 2020), settling on these 3 because they meet the constraints below: a) they are transformer-based, b) they have encoder-decoder architecture and c) they produce abstractive summaries. Applying these models to our data set before clustering, we obtained that T5 had the best performance. Thus, we have started our study by applying this model to our own dataset. Our main goal is to produce summaries that are accurate and coherent. In addition, T5 is a modern model that has already been successfully used in summary studies, but in the field of social media it is less explored. This is an initial estimate for our own model design, but by enriching our study with additional assumptions to optimize the results, the pre-trained models will be re-evaluated for their performance.

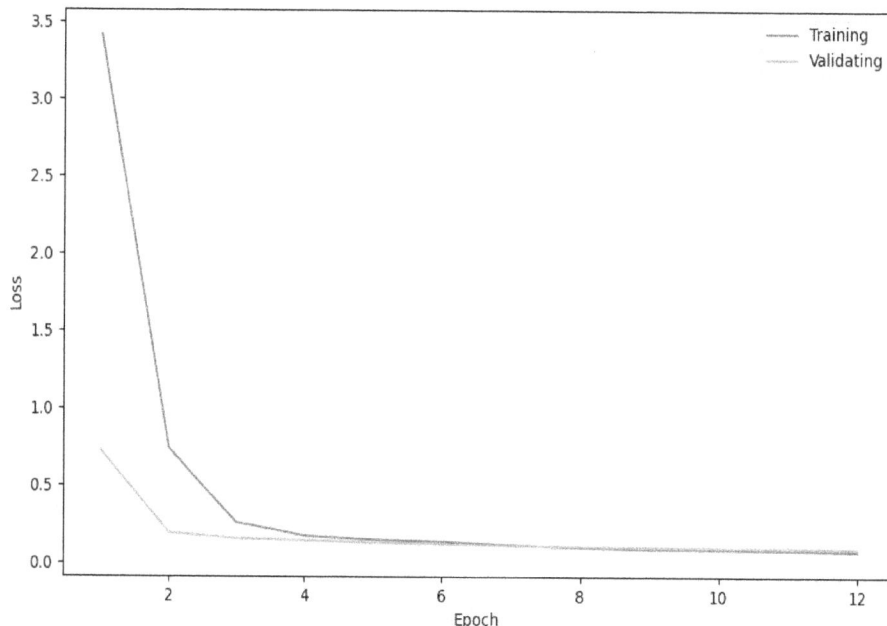

Figure 3: Train and Validation Loss

In order to assess the performance of our model, we have calculated loss. Loss quantifies the error produced by the model and it is one of the most important factors in deep learning and neural networks. After splitting the dataset into Train, Validation and Test subsets we have measured the Training and Validation loss for all the samples. As it is obvious in Figure 3 both metrics are decreasing gradually. Furthermore, the gap between validation and train loss shrinks after each epoch. This is because as the network learns the data, it also shrinks the regularization loss (model weights), leading to a minor difference between validation and train loss. Consequently, with most of our data samples it gains a good fit.

In order to evaluate the text summary produced by our system we used Rouge. The Recall-Oriented Understudy for Gisting Evaluation, ROUGE (Lin, C.-Y., 2004) is a metric for evaluating an automatically produced summary against reference summaries. It is a widely used set metrics and software package for evaluating automatic summarization. At this stage of our work Rouge compares the system-generated summary against each comment in the thread. The results are shown in Table 1. To get a better quantitative value, we compute precision, recall and F1 score. As is obvious from the results, recall is quite high which means that the reference summary has been captured by the system-generated summary. Precision gives a proportion of 0.514-0.520 of words suggested by the predicted summary that actually appears in the reference summary. On the other hand, recall gives a proportion of 0.849-0.854 of words in the reference summary captured by the predicted summary. Both of them lead to a harmonic mean f1-score of 0.640-0.645. Knowing that Rouge scores must range from 0-1 with 1 being the best value and therefore the most ideal summary, we conclude that these results look quite good for our text summarization system. It is important to notice a high Rouge score means that the system captures the most important information to put in the summary. This, on the other hand, doesn't lead us to a high-quality summary because it may contain biased text. Therefore, the evaluation of the quality of the produced text is a very complex process where the dimensions and limitations of each system must be taken into account.

Table 1: Rouge Score Results

	rouge1	rouge2	rougeL
P	0.520	0.514	0.519
R	0.854	0.849	0.854
F	0.646	0.640	0.645

6. Conclusion and Further Work

As can be seen from the measurements so far, we come to two main conclusions. First, the learning rate of the model has a good fit according to our dataset. Both the training and validation sets start with high values due to lack of learning but as they are trained the errors decrease and we have a smoothing of the curves, until in the end where they even out. Thus, the model is properly trained and can give correct results. Also, as seen from Rouge scores, the summaries generated from user comments on each post are quite satisfactory. As with all research works, however, there are areas for improvement. Earlier in this paper we pointed out that, at this stage, our model is evaluated using ROUGE scores between the generated summary and each comment in the thread. Therefore, further research would be done to compare the system-generated summary with the human-generated summary. ROUGE only works on overlays. If we only want to stick to calculated scores then a score of 1 would indicate the perfect summary. But this would only happen if both summaries had the same n-grams. Furthermore, rouge performs better on models that produce extractive summarization. Since our model focuses on paraphrasing thus producing abstractive summarization, our research will be extended to more modern tools and techniques that can achieve better results. For the purposes of this project, we have used data from facebook that correspond user comments under specific posts. A certain amount of data is manageable by the model, enabling the system to learn, train and give certain results. However, a robust mechanism can be developed to allow the desired flexibility in the model to further learn and perform on large-scale data. Most of the research work in the field of social networks has been done using data from the platforms Reddit and Twitter. Wanting to go beyond the limits and check the data of other platforms, we used Facebook data streams. However, knowing that each platform is unique and presents particularities both in the way it posts information and in the way users react, more research could be done to expand the behaviour and effectiveness of summary models for every platform.

Acknowledgements

The publication fees were totally covered by the University of West Attica.

References

Bhandarkar, P., Thomas, K. T. (2023) "Text Summarization Using Combination of Sequence-To-Sequence Model with Attention Approach", *Springer Science and Business Media Deutschland* GmbH: 283–293, 2023, doi:10.1007/978-981-19-3035-5_22.

Blekanov, I. S., Tarasov N. and Bodrunova, S. S. (2022)"Transformer-Based Abstractive Summarization for Reddit and Twitter: Single Posts vs. Comment Pools in Three Languages". *Future Internet 2022*, 14(3), 69. https://doi.org/10.3390/fi14030069

Chong, F., Chua, T., Asur, S. (2021) "Automatic Summarization of Events from Social Media". *Proceedings of the International AAAI Conference on Web and Social Media*, 7(1), 81-90. https://doi.org/10.1609/icwsm.v7i1.14394.

Gao, S., Chen, X., Li, P., Ren, Z., Bing, L., Zhao, D. and Yan, R. (2019) "Abstractive Text Summarization by Incorporating Reader Comments". *In The Thirty-Third AAAI Conference on Artificial Intelligence (AAAI-19)*, 33(01):6399-6406

Ghanem, F.A., Padma, M.C. and Alkhatib, R. (2023) "Automatic Short Text Summarization Techniques in Social Media Platforms". *Future Internet 2023*, 15(9), 311. https://doi.org/10.3390/fi15090311

Gupta, S. and Gupta, S.K. (2019) "Abstractive summarization: An overview of the state of the art". *Expert Systems with Applications 121*, 49–65.

Gupta, A., Chugh, D. and Katarya, R. (2022) "Automated News Summarization Using Transformers", *In Sustainable Advanced Computing*, 2022, Volume 840. ISBN: 978-981-16-9011-2.

Han, X., Zhang, Z., Ding, N., Gu, Y., Liu, X., Huo, Y., Qiu, J., Yao, Y., Zhang, A., Zhang L., et al., (2021) "Pre-trained models: Past, present and future," *AI Open*, vol. 2, pp. 225–250.

Lewis, M., Liu, Y., Goyal, N., Ghazvininejad, M., Mohamed, A., Levy, O., Stoyanov, V. and Zettlemoyer, L. (2019) "BART: Denoising Sequence-to-Sequence Pre-training for Natural Language Generation, Translation, and Comprehension". In *Proceedings of the 58th Annual Meeting of the Association for Computational Linguistics*, pages 7871–7880, online. Association for Computational Linguistics. https://aclanthology.org/2020.acl-main.703

Li, Q. and Zhang, Q. (2020) "Abstractive Event Summarization on Twitter". *In The Web Conference 2020 - Companion of the World Wide Web Conference*, WWW 2020, Association for Computing Machinery: 22–23, doi:10.1145/3366424.3382678.

Liang, Z., Du, J. and Li, C. (2020) "Abstractive social media text summarization using selective reinforced Seq2Seq attention model," *Neurocomputing*, **410**, 432–440, doi:10.1016/j.neucom.2020.04.137.

Lin, C.-Y. (2004) "ROUGE: A Package for Automatic Evaluation of Summaries". *In Text Summarization Branches Out,* pages 74–81, Barcelona, Spain. Association for Computational Linguistics.

Nenkova, A. and McKeown, K. (2012) "A survey of text summarization techniques", *In: Aggarwal, C., Zhai, C. (Eds) Mining Text Data*. Springer, Boston, MA. https://doi.org/10.1007/978-1-4614-3223-4_3

Rachabathuni, P. K. (2017) "A survey on abstractive summarization techniques". *In Inventive computing and informatics (ICICI), international conference on* (pp. 762765). doi: 10.1109/ICICI.2017.8365239.

Raffel, C., Shazeer, N., Roberts, A., Lee, K., Narag, S., Matena, M., Zhou, Y., Li, W. and Liu P. J. (2021) "Exploring the Limits of Transfer Learning with a Unified Text-to-Text Transformer". *In The Journal of Machine Learning Research,* Volume 21, Issue 1, 2019. ISSN: 1532-4435.

Rawat A., and Singh Samant, S. (2022) "Comparative Analysis of Transformer based Models for Question Answering". *2nd International Conference on Innovative Sustainable Computational Technologies (CISCT),* Dehradun, India, 2022, pp. 1-6, doi: 10.1109/CISCT55310.2022.10046525.

Rawat, R., Rawat, P., Elahi V. and Elahi, A. (2021) "Abstractive Summarization on Dynamically Changing Text," *2021 5th International Conference on Computing Methodologies and Communication (ICCMC),* Erode, India, 2021, pp. 1158-1163, doi: 10.1109/ICCMC51019.2021.9418438.

Sharifi, B., Hutton, M-A. and Kalita, J. (2010) "Summarizing Microblogs Automatically". In *Human Language Technologies: The 2010 Annual Conference of the North American Chapter of the Association for Computational Linguistics,* pages 685–688, Los Angeles, California. Association for Computational Linguistics.

Sharifi, B., Inouye, D., and Kalita, J.K. (2014) "Summarization of Twitter Microblogs". *The Computer Journal,* Volume 57, Issue 3, March 2014, Pages 378–402, https://doi.org/10.1093/comjnl/bxt109

Suleiman, D., and Awajan, A. (2020) "Deep Learning Based Abstractive Text Summarization: Approaches, Datasets, Evaluation Measures, and Challenges," *Mathematical Problems in Engineering,* doi:10.1155/2020/9365340.

Tampe, I., Mendoza, M. and Milios, E. (2021) "Neural Abstractive Unsupervised Summarization of Online News Discussions". *In: Arai, K. (Eds) Intelligent Systems and Applications. IntelliSys 2021. Lecture Notes in Networks and Systems,* vol 295. Springer, Cham.

Varma, V., Kurisinkel, L.J. and Radhakrishnan, P. (2017) "Social Media Summarization", *In A practical Guide to Sentiment Analysis,* Chapter 7 pp.135-153.

Vaswani, A., Shazeer, N., Parmar, N., Uszkoreit, J., Jones, L., Gomez, A.N., Kaiser, L. and Polosukhin, I. (2017) "Attention Is All You Need". *In 31st Conference on Neural Information Processing Systems (NIPS 2017),* Long Beach, CA, USA., June 2017.

Wang, Q. and Ren, J. (2021) "Summary-aware attention for social media short text abstractive summarization," Neurocomputing, **425**, 290–299, doi:10.1016/j.neucom.2020.04.136.

Wolf, T., Debut, L., Sanh, V., Chaumond, J., Delangue, C., Moi, A., Cistac, P., Rault, T., Louf, R., Funtowicz, M., Davison, M., Shleifer, S., von Platen, P., Ma, C., Jernite, Y., Plu, J., Xu, C., Le Scao, T., Gugger, S., et al.. (2020) "Transformers: State-of-the-Art Natural Language Processing". *In Proceedings of the 2020 Conference on Empirical Methods in Natural Language Processing: System Demonstrations,* pages 38–45, online. Association for Computational Linguistics.

Zhang, J., Zhao, Y., Saleh, M. and Liu, P.J. (2020) "PEGASUS: Pre-training with Extracted Gap-sentences for Abstractive Summarization". *In ICML'20: Proceedings of the 37th International Conference on Machine Learning,* July 2020, Article No.: 1051, Pages 11328–11339.

Uses, Perceptions and Impacts of Instagram: A Study with Young Higher Education Students

Telma Pereira[1], Nídia Salomé Morais[2], Rui Raposo[3] and Teresa Gouveia[2]
[1]Polytechnic Institute of Viseu, Portugal
[2]Polytechnic Institute of Viseu, CI&DEI - Centre for Studies in Education and Innovation, Portugal
[3]University of Aveiro, Portugal

temarisa18@gmail.com
salome@esev.ipv.pt
raposo@ua.pt
tgouveia@esev.ipv.pt

Abstract: Given the evidence that young people have a very active presence on social networks, especially Instagram (Kemp, 2022), it is important to study this phenomenon and understand what drives young people to use this social network to share content, especially photos and audiovisual content. The study presented was guided by the following research questions: What is Instagram used for by university students? How does Instagram impact and influence youth perceptions regarding everyday life? From a methodological perspective, the case study resorted to a mixed methodology. Data was collected through a questionnaire and a focus group from undergraduate students from a public higher education institution in Portugal. The study collected data from 89 respondents, mostly female and aged between 19 and 22. The results revealed that Instagram is one of their favourite social networks and is where they spend the most time daily, mainly to keep in touch with friends and family and find new content. Participants affirmed that they don't use social media to feel accepted, validated or integrated. This shows that they use social media to reinforce what they already know and feel through the feedback they receive from shared content. Even though most state that they don't engage in getting likes, comments or reactions on their shared content, the participants in the study admit that this is a consequence and are happy with the feedback they receive. The study, although limited to a sample of students from a single higher education institution, enabled the researchers to understand better some engagement habits that currently take up little under one-fourth of the users' daily time while awake. The sheer fact that users spend so much time on this social media platform daily, sometimes with little or no positive impact on other activities, has already been outlined as an issue worth tackling in future studies.

Keywords: Instagram, Uses, Impacts, Youth, Higher education

1. Introduction

According to the 2022 Digital Global Overview Report, it is young people between the ages of 16 and 24 who spend the most time on social networks, with females spending an average of 3 hours and 13 minutes a day and males 2 hours and 43 minutes (We are social, 2022). The report also shows that Instagram is the fourth most used social network globally and is a favourite among young people. Instagram allows users to share different types of content, especially photographic content, which leads users to focus mainly on sharing photos. This social network achieved great success after its launch in October 2010, partly due to the possibility of creating and editing content directly on the application.

The aforementioned data points to a specific age group and shows that young people have the most active presence on social networks, especially Instagram, a social network that is increasingly present in the day-to-day life of this younger generation. Moreover, it is outlined that younger users are excessively concerned with posting photos and the feedback they receive for those same photos. In this context, it is important to study this phenomenon further and understand what drives young people to use Instagram to share content, especially photographs. It is also important to understand how they behave on Instagram and the impacts associated with its use, especially regarding approval and validation by other users.

Given the evidence mentioned above, this project was guided by the following research questions: "What is Instagram used for by young higher education students? How does Instagram impact and influence their perceptions regarding everyday life?". This article summarises the work conducted and some of the results obtained.

2. Theoretical Framework

Nowadays, young people have behaviours that distinguish them from other generations regarding digital practices. They use digital media in a multitasking way since technologies are at the epicentre of their lives (Amaral et al., 2017). In a research carried out by the same authors that aimed to understand the practices and consumption of Portuguese people, it was possible to conclude that, of the 1,814 young people surveyed, almost

90 per cent used the internet daily, which shows a strong presence of online activities in their everyday lives. Social networks are also heavily used by young people who spend a large part of their time in these spaces (Portugal & Souza, 2020), mainly due to the ease with which they can access them on their mobile phones (Ferreira, 2018). According to Vilela (2019), the internet and social media have countless advantages and are a new world full of possibilities and opportunities. Social networks play an important role in the lives of young people since, by creating private or public accounts, they can interact with each other (Cardoso, 2022) in an open or more dissimulated manner. Many interaction processes that young people have, from a social, cultural, or educational nature, are derived from activities linked to social networks such as Instagram (Amaral et al., 2017).

Instagram, in a nutshell, is a social network that promotes user interaction mainly through relatively simple tasks through content such as photos and videos (Silva, 2018) and that enables its users to communicate by resorting to actions such as liking and sharing content, comment and post copyrighting, and intricate editing. Simply uploading or taking a photo and publishing it is considered the ground zero competency for a newbie on Instagram. It quickly gives way to trimmed-to-detail publications with effects, trendy soundtracks, and deep and eye-catching quotes or life lessons to be shared with the world. On social networks like Instagram, young people can express themselves and share their interests, opinions and needs with others (Portugal & Souza, 2020), developing and consuming content from other users and sharing ideas and information (Cardoso, 2022). Worldwide, the app is the second favourite social network for users aged between 16 and 64 and is the favourite of both female and male users (We are Social, 2022). In Portugal, according to 'The Portuguese and Social Networks 2022' study, Instagram is one of the digital spaces most used by young people aged between 15 and 24, who use the application daily for several hours (Marketeer, 2022).

It can be said that globally and in Portugal, Instagram is the most successful social media among the younger generations and has even been voted a favourite. According to Alegria (2019), this phenomenon is due to the already-mentioned functionalities combined into the app and leaves no need to use any other application. A study by Huang and Su in 2018 among 307 university students revealed that the respondents used Instagram mainly to see posts by other users, especially entertainment posts and the possibility of socially interacting. It was also possible to conclude that gender and professional background influenced their reasons for using it. For example, in terms of professional background, design students use social networks to be inspired and see other work, while engineering students use them mostly to follow their friends' updates. According to the same authors, Instagram users post various photos to get comments and likes, as it triggers their need to seek social validation.

Vilela (2019) believes that the use of Instagram directly influences young people's lifestyles, learning, thinking, and interacting with other people. Its misuse and excessive use can have negative impacts and consequences on their lives, especially if there is a related dependency, i.e. a constant need to be connected to Instagram. According to Köse and Doğan (2019), Instagram dependency is characterised by behavioural addiction, and, according to their research with 325 students from three universities in Istanbul, they found that young women spent the most time on the social network using it for entertainment and leisure purposes.

By using Instagram daily, young people can trigger insecurities about their perception of their bodies. According to Vieira (2019), there are currently standards that categorise people, so it is crucial and almost mandatory that they look good and have a good body image. A study carried out in Brazil involving 212 female adolescents concluded that the use of social networks, especially Instagram, is associated with dissatisfaction with the body image of adolescents (Lira et al., 2017), which indicates the negative impact that this application has on the lives of young people, especially female adolescents.

The use of social media also leads young people to compare themselves with other users through the information they see in photographs, videos posted, descriptions, likes and comments, and these comparisons can affect their well-being. Hwang (2019) also mentions that social networks generally make it possible to obtain information about other people, especially friends and acquaintances, making them platforms for social comparison. According to the same author, young people compare themselves to others negatively and positively. When they compare themselves negatively with other users, it's in the sense that they want to become more like them. In other words, they consider themselves inferior to them because they're not like them, which can lead to feelings of envy. By positively comparing themselves, they feel that the people they are comparing themselves to are inferior and, therefore, have a feeling of superiority. They tend to feel good in these situations, and their self-esteem improves. According to Jan et al. (2017), these comparisons can be called downward and upward, respectively. A study carried out by the authors among 245 university students who use

Instagram concluded that there is an association between the use of the social network and social comparison, i.e. as soon as they enter the app, younger users automatically start comparing themselves with other users, showing a particular negative impact associated with their use. It also showed that the amount of time per day they spend on Instagram and the frequency with which they open the app influence all types of social comparison.

As to comparisons made on social networks, it's important to mention that, as well as being made with friends and acquaintances, they can often be made with so-called digital influencers or celebrities. Nowadays, we can see digital influencers' existence and strong presence on various social networks. These users have made the platform their primary form of work and share their daily lives, from the clothes they wear to where they go. Digital influencers usually have a high profile and exert a great deal of influence over their followers, so they always try to highlight the most positive side of their personality and their lives in their posts, ending up showing a life and a way of behaving that is not entirely real and true, making young people unable to realise what is real and what is not (Vieira, 2019).

By using the app every day and several times throughout the day and by comparing their lives with what they see shared in their feeds, young people can start to experience symptoms linked to low self-esteem, depression and dissatisfaction with life since social comparison has an impact on their self-perception and the way they evaluate themselves. A positive self-image can be linked to high self-esteem, while if a young person has a negative self-image, they can develop low self-esteem, so the act of comparison triggers a set of reactions that need to be considered.

Research has shown that social networks are often places where young people try to boost their self-esteem, and many of them use them and spend part of their time in these spaces precisely because they have low self-esteem. Hawi and Samaha (2016) and Köse and Doğan (2019) observed in their research that there is a negative correlation between levels of self-esteem and addiction to social networks, i.e. users with low self-esteem use social networks more than users with high self-esteem. In this sense, a study carried out in Indonesia with 259 participants showed that individuals who find it difficult to build social relationships in the "real world" due to low self-esteem try to connect with people on other social networks, especially Instagram (Rahardjo & Mulyaani, 2020). Based on the results of these studies, it is possible to identify that in many cases, it is low self-esteem and other external factors, such as inhibition and social anxiety, that often lead people to use these media. Andreassen et al. (2016) shared the same opinion as they stated, based on the results of their 2016 study, that people use social media to gain more self-esteem by posting photos and consequently trying to get likes and comments or to escape from low self-esteem, as on social media they can communicate online through a screen rather than face-to-face.

3. Methodology

In methodological terms, we chose to carry out a case study, which, as the name suggests, describes a particular reality. The case study provides an in-depth approach to the subject under study since specific and detailed information is collected. This type of study, therefore, made it possible to apply data collection techniques such as questionnaires and focus groups.

Using a mixed approach in this project, quantitative data was collected through a questionnaire survey, while qualitative data was collected through a focus group. Both approaches were best suited for gathering data and information associated with our study's objectives.

As Santos and Henriques (2021) point out, using a questionnaire makes it easy to reach students quickly. It is, however, more impersonal, according to Coutinho (2014), and, therefore, it must be prepared with care regarding its questions, size, layout and overall appearance.

A focus group was also held to complement and clarify the data obtained through the questionnaire. According to Sá et al. (2021), a focus group is a data collection technique consisting of a group discussion on a particular topic chosen by the researcher. This technique aims to obtain information that could not be gathered, for example, by interviewing just one person, and it allows results to be achieved more easily than individual interviews. However, all the techniques can complement each other (Sá et al., 2021).

4. The Study

The sample of participants in the study included undergraduates from the ESEV School of Education (Portugal), from different degrees. The sample for this investigation is considered a convenience sample since the individuals were selected conveniently, i.e. it would be easier to reach the youth as they attended the same school as the researcher. In addition, the individuals were also selected intentionally, since in this type of sampling, individuals are chosen because they represent the population to which the study is directed, allowing the researcher to select who will be included in the sample.

The questionnaire was available online for one month (April 2023) and shared with 1st, 2nd and 3rd-year students from ESEV's undergraduate programmes. During this period, 89 completed questionnaires were collected, with 80.9% (71) female and 16.9% (15) male participants, as seen in Table 1. The questionnaire was answered by students aged between 18 and 25 or over. Of the 89 participants, students aged 19 and 20 were the most represented, making up 23.6% of the total sample. These were followed by students who were 21 (19.1%) and those who were 25 or over (12.4%) (Table 1). As for the focus group, 6 students were selected to participate. Once the availability of the participants and the researcher was agreed on, the place, time and day were selected, and the focus group took place on the 11th of May, 2023.

Table 1: Participant's age and gender

Gender	f	%
Female	72	80.9
Male	15	16.8
I'd rather not say	2	2.2
Age	f	%
18	5	5.6
19	21	23.6
20	21	23.6
21	17	19.1
22	10	11.2
23	3	3.4
24	1	1.1
25	11	12.4

Regarding the distributions of participants according to the degree attended, Table 2 shows that students from the Basic Education and Social Education degrees were the most participative, with a total of 34 students (38.2%) from the Basic Education course and 21 students (23.6%) from the Social Education course. This was followed by 14 students from Advertising and Public Relations (15.7%), 12 from Sports and Physical Activity students (13.5%) and 6 from Social Communication (6.7%).

Table 2: Participants by course and year

Course	f	%
Cultural Performance Arts	1	1.1
Plastic Arts and Multimedia	1	1.1
Social Communication	6	6.7
Sport and Physical Activity	12	13.5
Basic Education	34	38.2
Social Education	21	23.6
Advertising and Public Relations	14	15.7

Since the questionnaire was aimed at students in the 1st, 2nd and 3rd years of the degrees taught at the ESEV, it was possible to get responses from all years, with 39.3% (35) of the students attending the 2nd year, 31.5% (28) saying they were enrolled in the 3rd year, and the remaining 29.2% attending the 1st year (Table 3).

Table 3: Participants by course and year

Year	f	%
1st	26	29.2
2nd	35	39.3
3rd	28	31.4

5. Results

Concerning the students' use of social networks, the questionnaire data showed that the social networks where students spend the most hours (between 3 and 4 hours or more a day) are Instagram (34), WhatsApp (32) and TikTok (22). The social networks where students spend the fewest hours (less than 1 hour a day) are Messenger (67), Facebook (64), Pinterest (58), Snapchat (56) and BeReal (51). The social networks where most students say they don't have an account are Telegram (48), as seen in Figure 1.

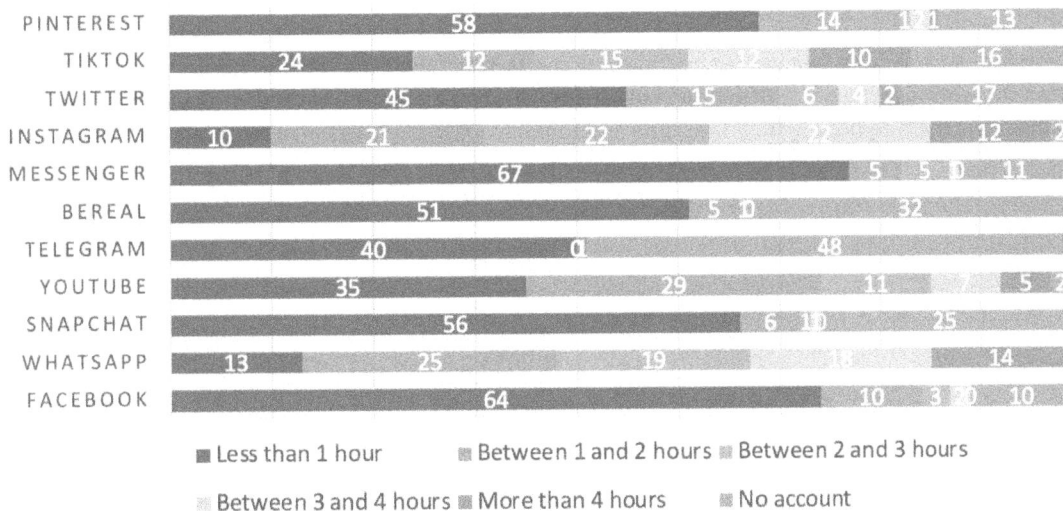

Figure 1: Time spent by students per day on different social networks

Through the same question asked in the focus group, which was intended to find out which social network was most used by the students, the data obtained corroborates what was obtained through the questionnaire. Instagram once again stands out in the participants' responses:

Student 1- *"Instagram. I spent 5 minutes on it today, but my daily average is 1.5 hours."*

Student 2- *"Instagram. I spent 1 hour but only on Instagram because I don't use any other social networks."*

Student 3- *"Instagram. I was on TikTok for 1.5 hours and 9 minutes."*

Student 4- *"Instagram. I was on for 12 minutes."*

Student 5- *"Instagram."*

Student 6- *"Instagram. I was on for 17 minutes."*

Regarding the frequency with which students use social media, based on the objectives and reasons for using it, Figure 2 shows that many students 'always' and 'often' use social media to occupy their time (47) because it's fun (45), it helps them relax (45) and are used when they feel happy (41). Of the participants, 40 said they sometimes use social media when frustrated, 39 students when happy, and 36 students sometimes to escape boredom and loneliness.

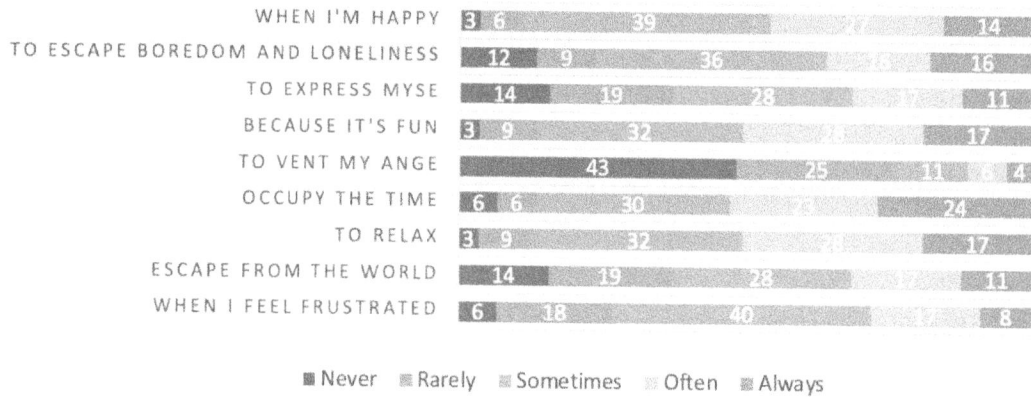

Figure 2: Frequency and reasons to use social networks

Figure 3, referring to the purposes for which students use Instagram, shows that the possibility of keeping in touch with friends and family stands out, followed by the fact that Instagram allows them to find new content, with most students also agreeing. The other reasons mentioned by more than half of the students were that Instagram allows them to occupy their free time and to follow public figures and influencers.

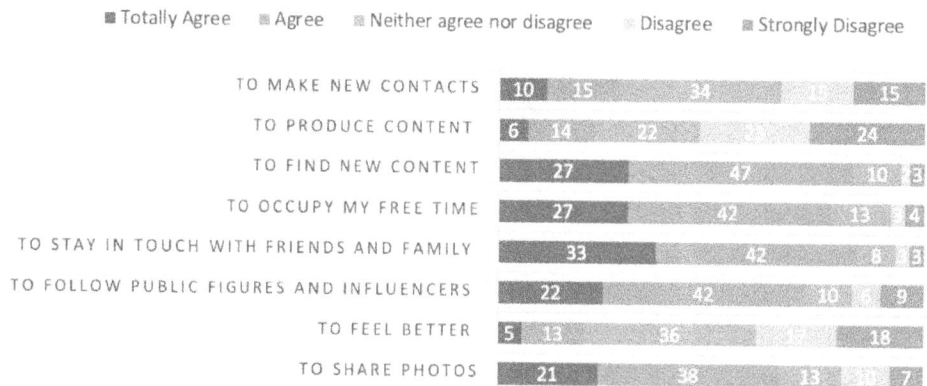

Figure 3: Purposes for which students use Instagram

We also tried to understand what emotions students felt after using Instagram. Figure 4 shows that the student's perceptions about their positive emotions after using this social network are joy (39), satisfaction (34) and excitement (30) since the students classified these as positive emotions that they felt "always" and "often" after using Instagram.

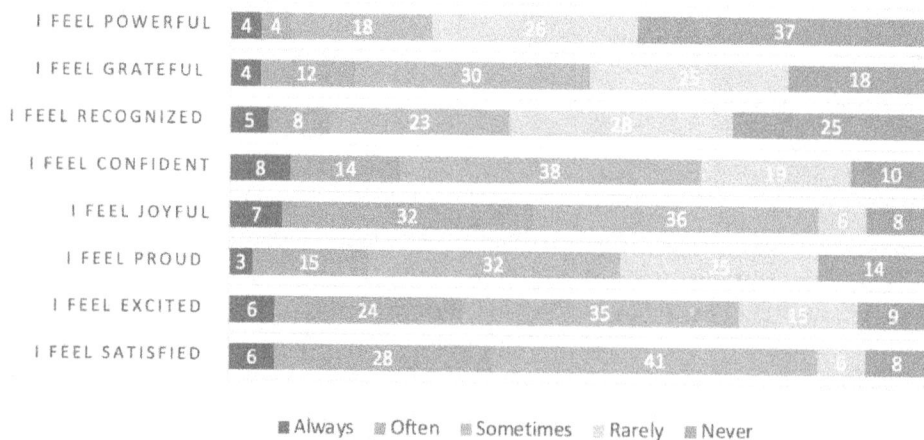

Figure 4: Student's perceptions about their positive emotions

By analysing the results shown in Figure 5, it can be seen that 46 participants do not think that Instagram has a negative impact on their self-esteem (20 disagree, and 26 totally disagree with the statement). Regarding the statement "Instagram has a positive impact on my self-esteem", no student totally agreed with it, and only 20 students agreed. It's important to mention that the majority neither agreed nor disagreed with the statement. Concerning the statement "Instagram has no impact on my self-esteem", 32 students answered affirmatively using the "agree" and "totally agree" options, while 35 "disagree" and "totally disagree".

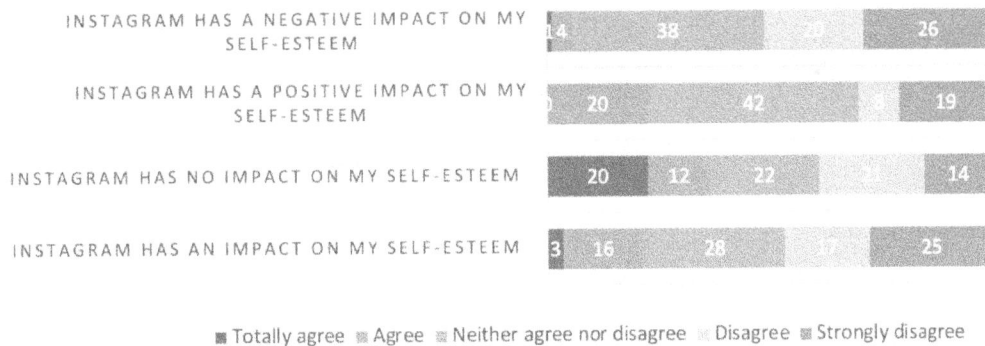

INSTAGRAM HAS A NEGATIVE IMPACT ON MY SELF-ESTEEM	4	38	20		26
INSTAGRAM HAS A POSITIVE IMPACT ON MY SELF-ESTEEM		20	42	8	19
INSTAGRAM HAS NO IMPACT ON MY SELF-ESTEEM	20	12	22		14
INSTAGRAM HAS AN IMPACT ON MY SELF-ESTEEM	3	16	28	17	25

■ Totally agree ■ Agree ■ Neither agree nor disagree ■ Disagree ■ Strongly disagree

Figure 5: Impacts associated with the use of Instagram

During the focus group, we tried to understand what drives students to share photos on Instagram. The questions asked were: "What makes you publish photographs? Under what circumstances and why do you do it? Both in stories and in the feed," to which the students responded:

Student 2- *"To congratulate someone on their birthday. In memory of someone who is no longer here."*

Student 5- *"When I'm travelling."*

Student 1- *"I do a lot of dance work, and I can publicise my work and reach more people. To make contacts (...) So that people in the industry can also share and exchange ideas, contacts and information about castings. It's not working, but I'm sharing what I do through Instagram."*

Student 5- *"I don't think it's a social network just for entertainment, but for people who use it professionally."*

Student 3- *"It's not a question of validation, but for example, I post a photo because I feel good, but I prefer to post make-up videos, so I end up sharing the photos to diversify the feed and reach more people so that they can go to the page and watch the videos. Even though the accounts have much more reach, the photos get more attention in the feed."*

During the focus group, the content shared made it clear that students post photos in their feeds and stories in different circumstances, namely when they want to congratulate friends on their birthdays while travelling. They also do so when they want to share their passions, both for entertainment and professionally. However, when they share photos, they do so because they feel good about themselves.

The questionnaire also sought how students feel after posting a photo on Instagram (Figure 6).

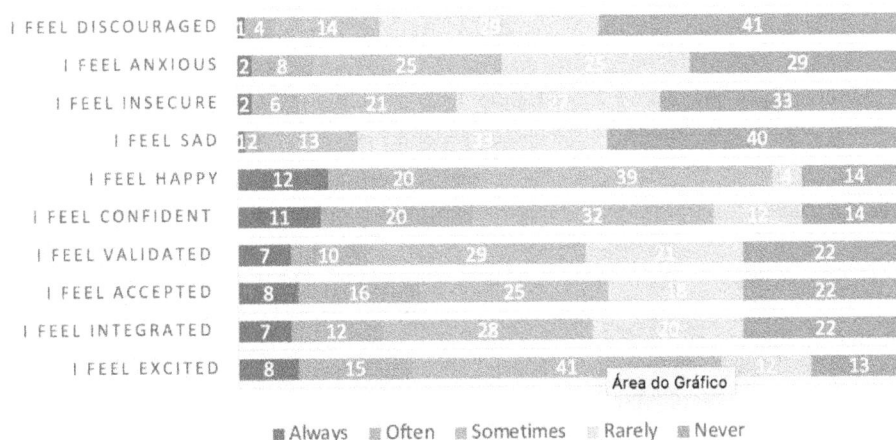

I FEEL DISCOURAGED	1 4	14			41
I FEEL ANXIOUS	2 8	25			29
I FEEL INSECURE	2 6	21		33	
I FEEL SAD	1 2	13		40	
I FEEL HAPPY	12	20	39		14
I FEEL CONFIDENT	11	20	32		14
I FEEL VALIDATED	7	10	29		22
I FEEL ACCEPTED	8	16	25		22
I FEEL INTEGRATED	7	12	28		22
I FEEL EXCITED	8	15	41		13

Área do Gráfico

■ Always ■ Often ■ Sometimes ■ Rarely ■ Never

Figure 6: Student's perceptions about how they feel after posting a photo on Instagram

Figure 6 shows that considering a set of emotions, the students' positive emotions were happiness, confidence and acceptance. As can be seen above, after posting a photo, students feel "always" or "often" happy (32), confident (31) and accepted (24). In addition, 39 participants also said they felt pleased "sometimes". As to the more negative emotions, the ones least mentioned by the participants by choosing "never" and "rarely" options were sadness (73) and discouragement (70).

The focus group also endeavoured to obtain answers regarding how students feel after posting photos by asking the question, "If you could describe in one word how you feel after posting a photo, both in stories and in the feed, what would it be? And why?" the following answers were obtained:

> *Student 6- "Anxiety."*
>
> *Student 5- "Anxiety."*
>
> *Student 3- "Nervousness."*
>
> *Student 1- "Not anxiety. I feel enthusiasm."*
>
> *Student 4- "Joy. I shared it because I feel beautiful."*

Through the answers given by the students during the focus group, emotions such as "anxiety", "nervousness", "enthusiasm" and "joy" emerged. The students who said they felt "enthusiasm" and "joy" justified their choices because they like what they usually publish and don't feel insecure about their shared content. On the other hand, the students who said they felt anxious and nervous specified that they felt this way when thinking about the feedback they would receive on their shares.

6. Conclusions

The research presented in this paper aimed to identify the uses, perceptions, and impacts of Instagram use by a sample of young university students from Portugal. The developed case study, conducted with a literature review and the application of two data collection instruments, a questionnaire survey and a focus group, allowed us to collect quantitative and qualitative data that shed some light on the matter. The questionnaire results show that Instagram is one of the students' favourite social networks and the one they spend the most time on daily. The time spent on Instagram is 3 to 4 hours or more, according to most of our respondents. Results are concurrent with those obtained by recent research (Marketeer, 2022; We are Social, 2022; Obercom, 2023) that point to frequent use of this social network by young people of similar ages to the participants in the research presented. The growth of users in the 18 to 24 age group was highly pronounced in Instagram's remarkable growth. The reports reveal that in 2023, Instagram was used by 72.0% of these young people, making it the most popular social network in this age group, surpassing YouTube in 2022 (Obercom, 2023). The Digital 2023 Global Overview Report also confirms the popularity of this social network among young people of these ages by showing that a total of 517.7 million users aged 18 to 24 (32.0% of Instagram's total ad audience) use Instagram and "the "typical" internet user spends almost 2½ hours each day using social media platforms, comparing to more than one-third of our total online time" (Kemp, 2023, s.p.). Another research also pointed out that young people between the ages of 16 and 24 spend the most time on social networks, with females spending an average of 3 hours and 13 minutes a day and males 2 hours and 43 minutes (We are Social, 2022).

Given that users are both content consumers and producers in the context of social media, the study also identified that the social network where students post most often is Instagram, while Facebook is falling behind and is less used by students and more frequently used by older people. Despite recent data indicating that Facebook remains the most significant active social media platform in many countries around the world (Kemp, 2024), it seems that younger people are less likely to be using Facebook and Twitter (renamed X) than they were a decade ago (Anderson, Faverio & Gottfried, 2023).

A closer look into what students use Instagram for shows that it is mainly used to keep in touch with friends and family and to find new content. The conclusions obtained in our study are in line with those reported by the Digital 2023 Global Overview Report, which suggests that among the top seven reasons for using social media, the first is to keep in touch with friends and family, followed by spending free time, reading new stories and looking for content (kemp, 2023).

The data also shows that students don't use social networks to feel accepted, validated or integrated. They don't use Instagram, for instance, in search of any social approval or validation. However, although students say they are not looking for likes, comments or reactions to their shares, the participants in the study admit that this is a consequence. Although they don't share for this purpose, they are happy with the feedback they receive, which acts as a "confirmation" of what they already know and feel about what they post, especially regarding the photos they share. From an emotional point of view on how they think and view social networks, it was possible to conclude that students feel positive emotions more readily than negative emotions after using Instagram. The most selected were joy, satisfaction, and enthusiasm. They also associated Instagram with sharing, leisure, fun, inconstancy, validation and sharing. Based on these results, there is strong evidence that, in general, Instagram can positively impact the well-being of the students who took part in the study. The study concluded that much of what was answered regarding emotions and the use of social networks mostly gravitated around Instagram, probably because it was the most used network by our sample of students. Although these conclusions seem encouraging, suggesting that Instagram can provide a sense of connection and support, it is essential, as Beyari (2023, p. 8) says, "to be aware of its potential negative impacts on mental health. In light of these findings, it may be beneficial for individuals to set limits on their social media use and prioritise activities that promote mental well-being, such as physical exercise and social interaction with friends and family."

Lastly, the information collected through the questionnaire and the focus group also allows us to conclude that students post photos above all when they feel good about what they share. They do so mainly on Instagram because it is their friends' social network. After sharing photos, students tend to feel positive emotions such as happiness, confidence and acceptance. However, some who mentioned feeling anxious and nervous attributed it to the pressure felt regarding the feedback they may receive. These results corroborate those obtained by Beyari (2023) in the sense that "(…) social media can have both positive and negative effects on mental health, depending on how it is used and the specific features that are engaged with. It is therefore important for young people to be aware of the potential risks and to use social media in a balanced and responsible manner" (p. 9).

In general, the contributions of this research are mainly to have allowed the identification of trends in the use of Instagram by young university students, as well as to understand the impacts of the use of this social network on the emotional level, communication and sharing of content. Since its conclusion, the study presented has provided additional research questions and challenges that, in collaboration with young higher education students, are already contributing to a better understanding of the phenomenon easily recognised as an intrinsic part of the higher education landscape. Current and future research is looking at these issues, and our future work will undoubtedly follow along these lines and be developed within this context.

The study, although limited to a sample of students from a single higher education institution, enabled the researchers to understand better some engagement habits that currently take up little under one-fourth of the users' daily time while awake. The sheer fact that users spend so much time on this social media platform daily, sometimes with little or no positive impact on other activities, has already been outlined as an issue worth tackling in future studies.

Acknowledgements

This work is funded by National Funds through the FCT - Foundation for Science and Technology, I.P., within the scope of the project Refª UIDB/05507/2020 and DOI identifier https://doi.org/10.54499/UIDB/05507/2020. Furthermore, we would like to thank the Centre for Studies in Education and Innovation (Ci&DEI) and the Polytechnic of Viseu for their support.

References

Alegria, A. (2019). Relação entre a utilização de redes sociais e a literacia em saúde mental positiva de jovens: um estudo exploratório sobre o Instagram. Repositório Institucional da Universidade Católica Portuguesa. http://hdl.handle.net/10400.14/29943

Amaral, I., Reis, B., Lopes, P., & Quintas, C. (2017). Práticas e consumos dos jovens portugueses em ambientes digitais. Estudos Em Comunicação, 24, 107–131. https://doi.org/10.20287/ec.n24.a06

Anderson, M., Faverio, M. & Gottfried, J. (2023). Teens, Social Media and Technology 2023. https://www.pewresearch.org/internet/2023/12/11/teens-social-media-and-technology-2023/

Andreassen, C., Pallesen, S., & Griffiths, M. (2016). The relationship between addictive use of social media, narcissism, and self-esteem: Findings from a large national survey. Addictive Behaviors, 64, 287–293. https://doi.org/10.1016/j.addbeh.2016.03.006

Beyari, H. (2023). The Relationship between Social Media and the Increase in Mental Health Problems. Int. J. Environ. Res. Public Health 2023, 20, 2383. https://doi.org/10.3390/ijerph20032383

Cardoso, D. (2022). Influência do tempo de acesso e quantidade de redes sociais utilizadas na insatisfação com a imagem corporal, no comportamento alimentar e na autoestima dos adolescentes. Lume- Repositório Digital. https://doi.org/http://hdl.handle.net/10183/241570

Coutinho, C. (2014). Metodologia de Investigação em Ciências Sociais e Humanas – Teoria e Prática (2ed.). Almedina.

Ferreira, R. (2018). Redes Sociais Digitais: usos e estratégias dos jovens portugueses. In L. M. França et al. (Eds.), Consumo Cultural e Redes Sociais (pp. 173–200). Criação Editora.

Hawi, N., & Samaha, M. (2016). The Relations Among Social Media Addiction, Self-Esteem, and Life Satisfaction in University Students. Social Science Computer Review, 35(5), 576–586. https://doi.org/10.1177/0894439316660340

Huang, Y., & Su, S. (2018). Motives for Instagram use and topics of interest among young adults. Future Internet, 10(8). https://doi.org/10.3390/fi10080077

Hwang, H. (2019). Why social comparison on Instagram matters: Its impact on depression. KSII Transactions on Internet and Information Systems, 13(3), 1626–1638. https://doi.org/10.3837/tiis.2019.03.029

Jan, M., Soomro, S., & Ahmad, N. (2017). Impact of Social Media on Self-Esteem. European Scientific Journal, ESJ, 13(23), 329–341. https://doi.org/10.19044/esj.2017.v13n23p329

Kemp. S. (2022). Digital 2022: Portugal. Datereportal. https://datareportal.com/reports/digital-2022-global-overview-report

Kemp. S. (2023). Digital 2023: Global Overview Report. https://datareportal.com/reports/digital-2023-global-overview-report

Kemp. S. (2024). No, Social Media Is Still Not Dying In 2024. https://datareportal.com/reports/digital-2024-deep-dive-social-media-is-still-growing

Köse, Ö., & Doğan, A. (2019). The Relationship between Social Media Addiction and Self-Esteem among Turkish University Students. Addicta: The Turkish Journal on Addictions, 6(1), 175–190. https://doi.org/10.15805/addicta.2019.6.1.0036

Lira, A., Ganen, A., Lodi, A., & Alvarenga, M. (2017). Uso de redes sociais, influência da mídia e insatisfação com a imagem corporal de adolescentes brasileiras. Jornal Brasileiro de Psiquiatria, 66(3), 164–171. https://doi.org/10.1590/0047-2085000000166

Marketeer. (2022). Instagram é a rede social mais utilizada pelos jovens em Portugal. https://marketeer.sapo.pt/instagram-e-a-rede-social-mais-utilizada-pelos-jovens-em-portugal/

Obercom. (2023). Retrato digital de Portugal - Caracterização e tendências de utilização das redes sociais – 2015 a 2023. https://obercom.pt/wp-content/uploads/2023/09/Retrato_redes_sociais_2023_FINAL6Set.pdf

Portugal, A., & Souza, J. (2020). Uso das redes sociais na internet pelos adolescentes: uma revisão de literatura. Revista Ensino de Ciências e Humanidades, 4(2), 262–291. https://periodicos.ufam.edu.br/index.php/rech/article/view/7966/5673

Rahardjo, W., & Mulyani, I. (2020). Instagram addiction in teenagers: The role of type D personality, self-esteem, and fear of missing out. Psikohumaniora: Journal Penelitian Psikologi, 5(1), 29-44. https://doi.org/10.21580/pjpp.v5i1.4916

Sá, P., Costa, P., & Moreira, A. (2021). Reflexões em torno de Metodologias de Investigação- recolha de dados (1ed.). UA Editora. http://hdl.handle.net/10773/30772

Santos, R., & Henriques, S. (2021). Inquérito por questionário: contributos de conceção e utilização em contextos educativos. (1.ª ed.). Universidade Aberta. https://doi.org/10.34627/3s9s-k971

Silva, M. (2018). Espelho meu, espelho meu: o culto ao corpo e a promoção de ideais de beleza no Instagram e os efeitos sobre a autoimagem corporal das mulheres. Universidade de Brasília. https://bdm.unb.br/handle/10483/22037

Vieira, A. (2019). Instagram: Possíveis influências na construção dos padrões hegemônicos de Beleza entre mulheres jovens. Centro Universitário de Brasília. https://repositorio.uniceub.br/jspui/handle/prefix/13440

Vilela, B. (2019). Jovens e redes sociais- Efeitos no desenvolvimento pessoal e social. Biblioteca Digital do Instituto Politécnico de Bragança. http://hdl.handle.net/10198/20576

We are Social. (2022). Digital 2022: Another Year of Bumper Growth. https://wearesocial.com/uk/blog/2022/01/digital-2022-another-year-of-bumper-growth-2/

Fostering Global Wellness: Harnessing Social Media to Enhance Cross-Cultural Trust to propel Medical Tourism Ensuring Economic Growth

A S Poornima[1] and Srikant Subramanian[2]

[1]Sri Ramachandra Faculty of Management Sciences, SRIHER, Chennai, India
[2]Blue Star Limited

poornima@sriramachandra.edu.in
poornimaas@yahoo.com
srikantnpi@yahoo.com

Abstract: The "Heal in India" initiative, initiated by the Government of India and fortified by a dedicated web portal, is the fulcrum of India's strategy to boost medical tourism. Apart from its impact on healthcare, this initiative is a compelling economic growth catalyst. By positioning India as a preferred destination for international healthcare seekers, the initiative stimulates foreign exchange inflows, creates employment opportunities, and contributes to the growth of ancillary sectors such as hospitality and tourism. Medical travel, a burgeoning universal trend, involves people seeking healthcare services across transnational borders. India ranked 10th on the Medical Tourism Index 2020-21, securing twelfth position globally and fifth in Asia-Pacific for wellness tourism. Accredited healthcare facilities contribute to this accolade, including 1400 National Accreditation Board for Hospitals & Healthcare Providers (NABH) accredited hospitals and 40 Joint Commission International (JCI). The "Heal in India" initiative, complemented by a dedicated web portal, emphasizes the Indian government's commitment to medical tourism. Developing trust among likely medical tourists is quintessential as it creates confidence in the quality, safety, ethical standards and transparency of healthcare, overwhelmingly influencing the choice of medical tourism destination. Social media can nurture trust among potential medical tourists, in some way contributing to economic growth in medical tourism destinations by augmenting reputation and visibility, thereby enticing a steady influx of patients through positive word-of-mouth marketing. Trustworthiness authenticated through informative content that is transparent influences decision-making, leading to increased patient inflow and revenue generation. Adapting content to align with cultural subtleties builds trust and increases the appeal of a destination, expanding its clientele with an economic impact extending to ancillary industries. Thus, within social media, vital for healthcare marketing, this study advocates leveraging online platforms such as Facebook (Meta), Twitter, and Instagram to foster trust among potential medical tourists. Steered by Hofstede's Cultural Dimensions Theory, which explores communication styles, power distance, uncertainty avoidance, and individualism/collectivism, this research establishes a nuanced conceptual framework for tailoring social media content strategies based on Individualism/collectivism dimension. In individualistic cultures, content highlighting personal testimonials and individual success stories may resonate, building trust in the provider's expertise. Conversely, collectivist societies may favour content emphasizing community and shared experiences, establishing trust through collective endorsement. The dimension of indulgence/restraint directs content tone, with culturally attuned approaches aligning with societal values. By integrating these cultural insights into social media content strategies, healthcare marketers can effectively build trust, ensuring resonance with diverse audiences in the medical tourism landscape. This study proposes a robust conceptual framework aligning social media content strategies with cultural nuances, cultivating trust among varied global audiences. The synthesis of Hofstede's theory and tailored social media approaches emerges as a potent means to reinforce India's position as a preferred destination for medical tourism and advance the broader discourse on cross-cultural healthcare communication.

Keywords: Heal in India, Medical tourism, Economic growth, Healthcare marketing, Social media, Trust-building, Cultural dimensions, Cross-cultural communication, Healthcare destinations

1. Introduction

In an era marked by escalating healthcare costs, prolonged waiting periods, and regulatory complexities in developed nations (Medhekar, 2018), India emerges as a beacon, drawing global attention as a premier destination for medical tourism. This burgeoning trend is not just a testament to India's advanced allopathic therapies seamlessly interwoven with time-honoured traditions (Medhekar, 2020) but a transformative force with immense economic potential, job creation prospects, and a model of cross-ministerial collaboration (Shandilya et al., 2021; Subbaraman et al., 2021).

Central to India's meteoric rise in medical tourism is the visionary "Heal in India" initiative, a concerted government effort fortified by an exclusive website. Beyond the immediate healthcare implications, this initiative stands as a catalyst, promising economic prosperity through job creation, increased foreign exchange inflows, and the flourishing of ancillary sectors such as hospitality and tourism.

However, the efficacy of the Heal in India strategy pivots on robust information dissemination concerning the nation's medical infrastructure. John et al. (2018) illuminate medical tourism providers' crucial role in engaging with online users and shaping travel decisions. While these providers excel in maintaining customer intimacy, the untapped potential exists to stimulate deeper customer involvement and glean invaluable insights.

This study significantly contributes to global society by highlighting the extensive societal benefits available to medical tourists engaging with India. In aligning with the United Nations' Sustainable Development Goals (SDGs), particularly those related to good health and well-being (SDG 3), this research underscores its commitment to ensuring wellness for global citizens while contributing to the broader agenda of creating a more interconnected and a healthy world. (SDG 17).

1.1 Statement of Purpose

As global tourists increasingly turn to social media for health-related information, particularly in the context of Indian hospitals, the pressing need for comprehensive knowledge dissemination in the global medical tourism business becomes evident. This paper goes beyond the confines of conventional medical discourse. It aims to intricately explore the cross-cultural trust dynamics in social media marketing, which is so essential for the medical tourists choosing medical tourism destination. Through an in-depth analysis of existing literature and discussions, the study seeks to build a conceptual framework of building trust in cross cultural context through Social media.

1.2 Objectives of the Study

This study aims to achieve the following objectives:

- Analyze the factors influencing trust formation and perception on social media platforms, considering cultural nuances and variations.
- Develop a comprehensive cross-cultural trust model within the realm of social media, drawing upon Hofstede's cultural trust theory.
- Provide insights and recommendations for enhancing cross-cultural trust-building strategies in social media environments, catering to diverse user backgrounds and preferences.

2. Literature Review

Since the advent of Social media, many authors have studied the impact of social media on the consumption of various services. Medical tourism is not exempt. This section provides an overview of diverse studies from 2010 to date, examining the multifaceted dynamics of medical tourism, social media's impact on healthcare, and factors influencing consumer behaviour. This timeframe was chosen to encapsulate the rapid evolution and widespread adoption of social media across diverse business sectors. Additionally, it encompasses a period marked by significant growth in academic research focused on understanding the impact and implications of social media in various domains. The studies encompass themes such as patient trust, satisfaction, technological innovation, the role of social media in healthcare branding, and the impact of COVID-19 on vaccine tourism, collectively contributing to a comprehensive understanding of the evolving landscape in medical tourism and social media marketing of healthcare.

2.1 Use of Social Media to Build Trust In Medical Tourism

In exploring various dimensions of medical tourism, several studies have consistently identified trust as a pivotal factor influencing the decisions and behaviours of medical tourists. Mechinda et al. (2010) emphasized the critical role of trust in shaping the attitudinal loyalty of medical tourists, particularly highlighting its significance for hospital tourists. This sentiment was echoed by Crooks et al. (2015), who delved into the impact of medical tourism on the trust relationship between physicians and patients, emphasizing that trust becomes vulnerable when patient decisions contradict the best interests of physicians. Furthermore, Moslehifar et al. (2016) evaluated the trust features of top medical tourism websites, underscoring the importance of trust in the online health information sought by medical tourists.

Interestingly, the transformative role of social media in fostering trust has emerged as a consistent theme across multiple studies. Anita et al. (2013) emphasized social media's low-cost nature and diverse forms, presenting it as a valuable tool in health promotion and education. Claster et al. (2015) highlighted the critical role of up-to-date information provided by social media platforms, offering real-time insights into medical tourists' perceptions and concerns. Vidyanata (2022) substantiated this by demonstrating that social media marketing activities generate Brand Trust, mediating between social media activities and purchase decisions in the healthcare industry.

Furthermore, Kaewkitipong et al. (2021) identified trust in the foreign healthcare system as a significant factor in the context of vaccine tourism. Balouchi and Aziz (2023) provided empirical evidence that various factors, including self-efficacy, contribute to the belief in using social media for medical travel planning, reinforcing the role of trust in online information sources.

The synthesis of these studies suggests that trust is a crucial factor for medical tourists, influencing their decisions and behaviours. The multifaceted nature of trust encompasses aspects such as trust in healthcare providers, online health information, and the foreign healthcare system. Importantly, social media emerges as a facilitator of trust, providing real-time information, fostering brand trust, and contributing to the overall trustworthiness of medical tourism services. As the medical tourism industry continues to evolve, cultivating and enhancing trust, mainly through social media channels, can be a strategic imperative for healthcare providers and destination marketers seeking to attract and retain medical tourists.

2.2 Trust

Trust, a fundamental concept in various disciplines, represents a willingness to rely on an exchange partner in whom one has confidence (Morgan and Hunt, 1994). In medical tourism, trust manifests itself in different contexts, from consumers trusting information provided by healthcare organizations (Järvenpää et al., 2006) to relying on e-commerce platforms for online transactions (Gefen and Straub, 2004). Cultural dimensions, particularly Individualism and collectivism, significantly influence the meaning and perception of trust. Research by Hofstede (1980) suggests that consumers from individualistic countries exhibit a higher level of trust in information provided by healthcare organizations than those from collectivistic countries. This cultural context is crucial in understanding the diverse impacts of trust on individuals across different nationalities.

Cross-cultural studies by Zaheer and Zaheer (2005) and Yin et al. (2019) underscore the importance of cultural dimensions in shaping trust imbalances and influencing consumer behaviour in various contexts. Jenkner et al. (2022) emphasized that cultural dimensions play a crucial role in shaping trust, particularly in situations requiring the disclosure of sensitive health information. The findings highlight the intricate nature of trust across different nationalities, affecting social interaction, business relationships, and consumer behaviour.

In the broader context of e-commerce, trust is multifaceted, encompassing dimensions like credibility, integrity, reliability, and confidence (Pavlou et al., 2007). Trust in online environments is influenced by technical competence, concerns over opportunistic behaviours, and website quality (Davidavičienė et al., 2020). Cultural dimensions play a pivotal role in shaping trust in e-commerce, emphasizing the need to consider these dimensions when examining trust and social interaction (Jenkner et al., 2022).

In social media marketing, trust is complex and influenced by information exchange and community interactions (Puspaningrum, 2020). Trust in social media platforms like Facebook (Meta) is built upon consumer experiences within interactive communities, involving credibility, care, empathy, and consumers' previous interactions with the brand (Vingirayi, 2021). Trust in social media plays a mediating role between social media marketing and purchase intentions (Ibrahim et al., 2023). Moreover, interpersonal trust between users within online communities contributes to brand trust and loyalty (Anastasiei & Chiosa, 2018).

Understanding the cultural dimensions of Individualism and collectivism is crucial in delineating the nuances of trust. In certain cultures, Individualism places importance on information-based trust, where the reliability and performance of the brand play a pivotal role. Conversely, collectivist cultures may emphasize community-based trust, where interpersonal relationships within the community significantly influence trust in social media marketing and brand loyalty. The review indicates that the Individualism/Collectivism construct underscores the importance of considering cultural dimensions in understanding trust. For countries high in Individualism, information-based trust becomes crucial, emphasizing reliability and performance. Community-based trust, rooted in interpersonal relationships, holds significance in collectivist countries. The complex interplay of these trust dimensions shapes consumer behaviour in medical tourism, e-commerce, and social media marketing, providing essential insights for fostering trust and enhancing experiences in these diverse contexts. Hence, Hofstede's cultural dimensions theory emerges as this research paper's apt and comprehensive theoretical framework. The theory's emphasis on individualism-collectivism provides a nuanced understanding of how cultural norms and values impact trust, with individualistic societies favouring information-based trust and collectivist societies leaning towards community-based trust. In the critical decisions of medical tourism, the virtual transactions of e-commerce, and the interactive nature of social media marketing, Hofstede's framework

3

offers a robust lens to decipher the cultural intricacies influencing trust. By employing this theory, the research not only gains depth in exploring the multifaceted nature of trust but also provides valuable insights for stakeholders in these industries, emphasizing the significance of cultural dimensions in fostering trust and enhancing experiences across different cultural contexts.**Theoretical Framework**

3.1 Hofstede's Cultural Dimension Theory

Hofstede's Cultural Dimensions Theory, with its six dimensions impacting cross-cultural management studies, challenged the assumption of universally applicable management practices. Despite criticisms, the theory has endured, shaping the examination of global management theory over decades.

Individuals in highly individualistic cultures prioritize pleasure-seeking, while those in collectivistic cultures value conformity (Roth, 1995). Cultural differences influence the impact of others on consumer decisions, with collectivist cultures, like Hispanic consumers in the United States, being more susceptible to social influence (Nicholls et al., 1997).

Examining the cultural scale by Hofstede (1980), the USA ranks first in Individualism, indicating a highly individualistic society, while India ranks around 40, depicting a collectivistic society. Consequently, elements influencing brand trust through social media may significantly vary between the two societies. Men and Tsai (2012) investigated how companies use social network sites in culturally distinct countries, emphasizing the nuanced impact of cultural dimensions on social media usage for brand trust. This reinforces the relevance of Hofstede's theory in understanding cross-cultural dynamics in contemporary business practices.

3.2 Use of Hofstede's Cultural Dimensions Theory in Context of Social Media.

Hofstede's Cultural Dimensions Theory sheds light on the interplay between cultural dimensions and trust in social media marketing. These dimensions, encompassing Power Distance, Individualism vs. Collectivism, Masculinity vs. Femininity, Uncertainty Avoidance, Long-Term vs. Short-Term Normative Orientation, and Indulgence vs. Restraint, shape behaviors within societies. Marketers, armed with insights from these dimensions, can tailor social media strategies to resonate globally. The theory, linked with social media, influences information-based and community-based trust dynamics.

Studies like Mcknight et al. (2002) and Guftométros and Guerreiro (2021) explore trust measures in e-commerce and online environments, revealing how cultural dimensions impact trust perceptions. Yin et al. (2019) and Abbas and Mesch (2015) emphasize the significance of cultural dimensions in social interaction, trust, and purchase intention in social commerce.

In social media marketing, Individualism vs Collectivism aligns with Information-Based Trust, relying on facts and transparency, while Community Interactions-Based Trust corresponds to collectivist values built through shared experiences and communal interactions (Guftométros & Guerreiro, 2021). These dimensions, rooted in cultural values, provide frameworks for understanding trust in social media marketing, especially in the context of medical tourism.

This research aims to enhance understanding of how individualistic and collectivist tendencies influence trust in social media interactions in medical tourism, laying the groundwork for informed hypothesis formulation.

3.3 Hypothesis Development and Model Formulation

Hofstede (1980) emphasized that Individualistic cultures emphasize autonomy, personal achievement, and independence. Individuals from these cultures may be more inclined to engage in content that provides detailed information transparency and addresses their needs and preferences in social media. On the other hand, collectivist cultures prioritize group harmony, shared experiences, and communal well-being. This collectivist orientation may lead individuals from such cultures to seek content that emphasizes community interactions, endorsements, and collective benefits. The cultural dimension's theory suggests that the cultural dimension of individualism-collectivism will influence the engagement patterns with social media content on various SNS sites. Hence, we frame our first Hypothesis as

> *H1: Potential medical tourists from individualistic cultures would engage more with the information and remunerative posts of social networking platforms than the potential medical tourists of Collectivist cultures.*

In the social media marketing landscape, trust unfolds as a dynamic interplay between information exchange and community interactions (Puspaningrum, 2020). Platforms like Facebook (Meta) intricately construct trust through consumer experiences within interactive communities involving credibility, care, empathy, and past brand interactions (Vingirayi, 2021). Studies by (Sousa & Alves, 2019), (Mele et al., 2021), and Myungkeun et al. (2017) underscore the transformative impact of social media on consumer behaviour, particularly in the context of medical tourism. Crooks et al. (2015) provide a comprehensive understanding of the challenges faced by family physicians while navigating the intricate landscape of medical tourism. Their work offers valuable insights into the delicate balance required to support effective decision-making. Ghanem et al. (2020) make a strong case for the imperative nature of diversifying the forms of trust within the tourism sector, as they play a crucial role in mediating the adoption of information systems (IS).

Drawing from these insights, it can be inferred that Social media marketing communications seem poised to evoke information-based trust more prominently in potential medical tourists from individualistic cultures than their counterparts from collectivist cultures. This alignment resonates with the observed positive association between trust in foreign healthcare systems and the intention of travellers to recommend medical tourism, as evidenced by Kaewkitipong et al. (2021). Furthermore, Guftométros and Guerreiro's (2021) study on the impact of cultural differences on social media behaviour, viewed through the lens of cultural dimensions theory (Hofstede, 1980), suggests that medical tourists seeking content from individualistic cultures may lean towards trusting information-rich content, addressing their individual needs. Hence, we frame our second and third Hypothesis as

> *H2: Information-rich social media content induces higher trust levels in potential medical tourists from individualistic cultures than collectivist cultures.*

> *H3: Social media content fostering extensive community interaction induces higher trust levels in potential medical tourists from collectivist cultures than those from individualistic cultures.*

Robinson (1996) said that collectivist societies value consensus, which makes them loyal to the dominant brand. Research into the symbolic meaning of brands indicates that brand names are an essential symbol of group identity in collectivistic societies (Johannson—et. al (1994). Previous literature has found that the degree to which other people influence consumer trust is a factor that may affect brand attitudes across national cultures. Particularly Nicholls. et al. (1997) show that a collectivist subculture (Hispanic consumers in the United States) tends to be more susceptible to social influence than an individualistic subculture (their Anglo counterparts). For example, collectivist consumers considered friends' influence essential in choosing a favoured brand. In their work, Ibrahim et al. (2023) provided evidence that trust in social media mediates between social media marketing and purchase intentions. Anastasiei & Chiosa (2018) proved that interpersonal trust between users within online communities contributes to brand trust and loyalty. Again, from Hofstede's Cultural dimensions theory,

We frame our fourth and fifth hypotheses as

> *H4: Information-based trust would mediate the relationship between social media marketing communications and medical tourism destination trust in potential medical tourists from individualistic cultures rather than those from collectivist cultures.*

> *H5: Community Interaction trust would mediate the relationship between Social media marketing communications and Medical tourism Destination Trust in potential medical tourists from Collectivist cultures than the potential medical tourists of individualistic cultures*

3.4 The Conceptual Model

From the Proposed Hypothesis, we derive our proposed model as follows.

5

The Conceptual model

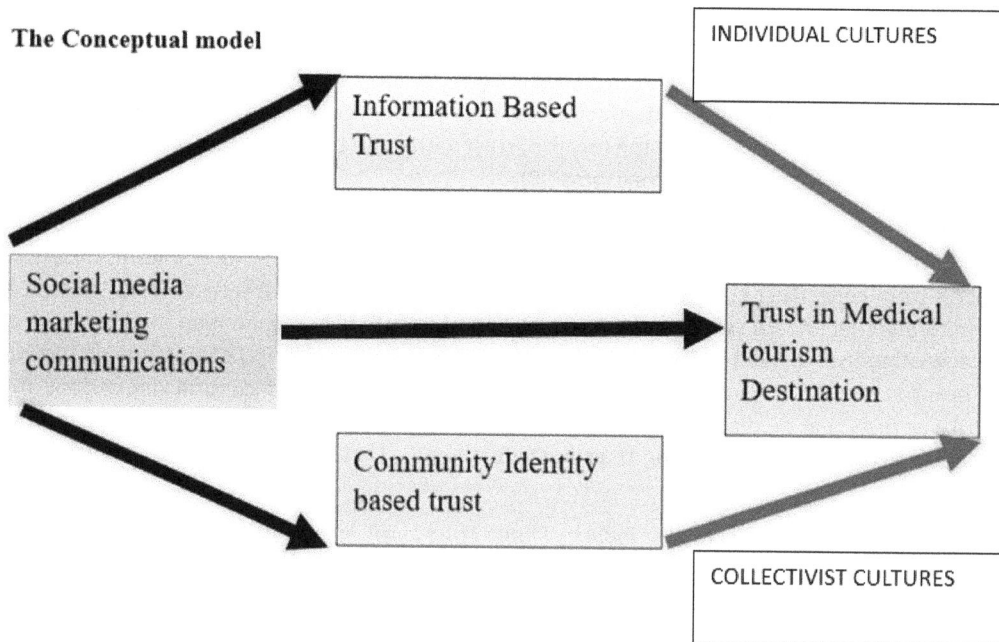

4. Findings of the Study

Based on the objectives of the study, We find

- Cultural nuances and variations significantly influence trust formation on social media.Factors such as communication styles, social norms, and individualistic vs. collectivistic values impact how trust is perceived and established.
- The study develops a comprehensive cross-cultural trust model for social media in context of medical tourism, integrating Hofstede's cultural trust theory. This model identifies key dimensions of trust influenced by cultural factors, as information based trust and Community based trust and offers a framework for understanding trust dynamics in diverse cultural contexts.
- The Insights from the study provide valuable recommendations for enhancing cross-cultural trust-building strategies on social media platforms.Strategies suggested include tailoring communication approaches, fostering cultural sensitivity, and leveraging cultural values to build trust among diverse user backgrounds and preferences.

5. Contribution of the Study

The study significantly advances theory in three key areas:

- **Cultural Dimensions Integration:** By applying Hofstede's Cultural Dimensions Theory, it explores cross-cultural trust in medical tourism's social media marketing, revealing how Individualism and Collectivism influence trust perceptions.
- **Nuanced Trust Understanding:** It distinguishes between Information-Based Trust and Community Interaction-Based Trust, offering insights into the intricate nature of online trust, especially in medical tourism.
- **Cross-Cultural Social Media Insights:** Through analyzing responses across different cultural backgrounds, it provides valuable insights for crafting effective strategies that resonate with diverse global audiences in medical tourism.

6. Limitations and Scope for Further Research

Addressing these limitations and pursuing these avenues for further research can enhance the depth and breadth of knowledge in the intersection of cultural dimensions, trust, and social media marketing in medical tourism.

- **Cultural Generalization:** While focusing on Individualism and collectivism, the study may oversimplify cultural diversity. Future research should explore additional dimensions like power distance or uncertainty avoidance for a more comprehensive analysis.
- **Contextual Constraints:** Findings may be specific to medical tourism and social media marketing. Generalizing to other industries or platforms should be approached cautiously. Examining trust dynamics across various sectors could reveal sector-specific nuances.
- **Cross-Cultural Dynamics:** The study mainly explores trust between individualistic and collectivist cultures. Further investigation into subcultures within these categories could provide deeper insights.
- **Lack of Empirical Support:** The model lacks empirical validation. Future studies should employ scales and conduct empirical research for validation.

7. Conclusion

In conclusion, this study advances the understanding of cross-cultural dynamics in trust formation within social media marketing for medical tourism. Integrating Hofstede's Cultural Dimensions Theory unveils nuanced insights into the influences of Individualism and collectivism on Information-Based Trust and Community Interaction-Based Trust. Despite certain limitations, the findings offer valuable implications for marketers navigating diverse cultural contexts, emphasizing the importance of tailored strategies in building trust. This research lays a foundation for further exploration, urging future studies to expand cultural dimensions, delve into industry-specific dynamics, and employ qualitative approaches to comprehend trust in this evolving landscape comprehensively.

References

Abbas, R., & Mesch, G. S. (2015). Cultural values and Facebook use among Palestinian youth in Israel. Computers in Human Behavior, 48, 644-653.

Anastasiei, B. and Chiosa, A. R. (2018). Antecedents of word-of-mouth communication and purchase intention on facebook. Journal of Marketing and Consumer Behaviour in Emerging Markets, 2/2018(8), 33-45. https://doi.org/10.7172/2449-6634.jmcbem.2018.2.3

Crooks, V. A., Li, N., Snyder, J., Dharamsi, S., Benjaminy, S., Jacob, K. J., ... & Illes, J. (2015). "you don't want to lose that trust that you've built with this patient...": (dis)trust, medical tourism, and the canadian family physician-patient relationship. BMC Family Practice, 16(1). https://doi.org/10.1186/s12875-015-0245-6

Davidavičienė, V., Markus, O., & Davidavičius, S. (2020). Identification of the opportunities to improve customer's experience in e-commerce. Journal of logistics, informatics and service science, 42-57.

Delgado-Ballester, Elena, José L., Munuera-Alemán & Maria J., Yagüe-Guillén (2003). Development and Validation of a Brand Trust Scale, International Journal of Market Research, 45, 35–53

Djatmiko, T. and Novianto, A. (2016). The impact of brand image, brand trust towards brand loyalty of indosat telecommunication operator customer in bandung. Proceedings of the 1st UPI International Conference on Sociology Education (UPI ICSE 2015). https://doi.org/10.2991/icse-15.2016.43

Ghanem, M., Elshaer, I. A., & Shaker, A. (2020). The successful adoption of is in the tourism public sector: the mediating effect of employees' trust. Sustainability, 12(9), 3877. https://doi.org/10.3390/su12093877

Hahn, I. S., Scherer, F. L., Basso, K., & Santos, M. B. d. (2016). Consumer trust in and emotional response to advertisements on social media and their influence on brand evaluation. Brazilian Business Review, 13(4), 49-71. https://doi.org/10.15728/bbr.2016.13.4.3

Ibrahim, B., Aljarah, A., Hazzam, J., & Elrehail, H. (2023). Investigating the impact of social media marketing on intention to follow advice: the mediating role of active participation and benevolence trust. FIIB Business Review, 231971452211479. https://doi.org/10.1177/23197145221147991

Izogo, E. E., Mpinganjira, M., Karjaluoto, H., & Liu, H. (2021). Examining the impact of ewom-triggered customer-to-customer interactions on travelers' repurchase and social media engagement. Journal of Travel Research, 61(8), 1872-1894. https://doi.org/10.1177/00472875211050420

Jackson, T. (2020). The legacy of geert hofstede. International Journal of Cross Cultural Management, 20(1), 3-6. https://doi.org/10.1177/1470595820915088

Järvenpää, S., Tractinsky, N., & Saarinen, L. (2006). Consumer trust in an internet store: a cross-cultural validation. Journal of Computer-Mediated Communication, 5(2), 0-0. https://doi.org/10.1111/j.1083-6101.1999.tb00337.x

Jenkner, C., Ravi, N., Gabel, M., & Vogt, J. (2022). Trust in data-requesting organizations—a quantitative analysis on cultural antecedents and individual-level perceptions. The Electronic Journal of Information Systems in Developing Countries, 88(4). https://doi.org/10.1002/isd2.12208

Johansson, J.K., Ronkainen, I.A. and Czinkota, M.R., 1994. Negative country-of-origin effects: The case of the new Russia. Journal of International Business Studies, 25(1), pp.157-176.

John, M., Smith, J., Williams, L., & Brown, A. (2018). The crucial role of medical tourism providers in shaping travel decisions. International Journal of Tourism Management, 22(4), 167-184.

7

Kaewkitipong, L., Chen, C., & Ractham, P. (2021). Examining factors influencing covid-19 vaccine tourism for international tourists. Sustainability, 13(22), 12867. https://doi.org/10.3390/su132212867

Kao, D. (2009). The impact of transaction trust on consumers' intentions to adopt m-commerce: a cross-cultural investigation. Cyberpsychology & Behavior, 12(2), 225-229. https://doi.org/10.1089/cpb.2008.0212

Khu, S. and Sukesi, S. (2020). Analysis of the effect of brand experience on brand loyalty through brand satisfaction and brand trust in wakoel rempah restaurant surabaya. Ekspektra : Jurnal Bisnis Dan Manajemen, 4(1), 65-83. https://doi.org/10.25139/ekt.v4i1.2656

Kwon, J., Jung, S., Choi, H., & Kim, J. (2020). Antecedent factors that affect restaurant brand trust and brand loyalty: focusing on us and korean consumers. Journal of Product &Amp; Brand Management, 30(7), 990-1015. https://doi.org/10.1108/jpbm-02-2020-2763

Lee, D. and Dawes, P. (2005). guanxi, trust, and long-term orientation in chinese business markets. Journal of International Marketing, 13(2), 28-56. https://doi.org/10.1509/jimk.13.2.28.64860

Li, S., Xu, W., & Yin, J. (2023). Cross-cultural differences in retracted publications of male and female from a global perspective. Scientometrics, 128(7), 3805-3826. https://doi.org/10.1007/s11192-023-04717-2

Martinčević, I., Črnjević, S., & Klopotan, I. (2022). Novelties and benefits of fintech in the financial industry. International Journal of E-Services and Mobile Applications, 14(1), 1-25. https://doi.org/10.4018/ijesma.2022010107

Matzler, K., Grabner-Kräuter, S., & Bidmon, S. (2008). Risk aversion and brand loyalty: the mediating role of brand trust and brand affect. Journal of Product & Brand Management, 17(3), 154-162. https://doi.org/10.1108/10610420810875070

Medhekar, A. (2018). Escalating healthcare costs, prolonged waiting periods, and regulatory complexities in developed nations. Journal of Global Healthcare Trends, 12(3), 45-56.

Medhekar, A. (2020). India's advanced allopathic therapies seamlessly interwoven with time-honoured traditions. International Journal of Integrative Medicine, 18(2), 112-128.

Mele, E., Kerkhof, P. v. d., & Cantoni, L. (2021). Analyzing cultural tourism promotion on instagram: a cross-cultural perspective. Journal of Travel &Amp; Tourism Marketing, 38(3), 326-340. https://doi.org/10.1080/10548408.2021.1906382

Men, L.R. and Tsai, W.H.S., 2012. How companies cultivate relationships with publics on social network sites: Evidence from China and the United States. Public Relations Review, 38(5), pp.723-730.

Money, R.B., Gilly, M.C. and Graham, J.L., 1998. Explorations of national culture and word-of-mouth referral behavior in the purchase of industrial services in the United States and Japan. Journal of marketing, 62(4), pp.76-87.

Myron Guftométros & João Guerreiro, 2021. "The effects of cultural differences on social media behaviour," International Journal of Internet Marketing and Advertising, Inderscience Enterprises Ltd, vol. 15(4), pages 412-428.

Myungkeun, S., Noone, B. M., & Mattila, A. S. (2017). A tale of two cultures: consumer reactance and willingness to book fenced rates. Journal of Travel Research, 57(6), 707-726. https://doi.org/10.1177/0047287517713722

Nicholls, J.A.F., Roslow, S. and Dublish, S., 1997. Hispanic and non-Hispanic mall shoppers: Segmentation by situational variables and purchase behaviors. Journal of Segmentation in Marketing, 1(1), pp.57-73.

Özdemir, E. and Sonmezay, M. (2020). The effect of the e-commerce companies benevolence, integrity and competence characteristics on consumers perceived trust, purchase intention and attitudinal loyalty. Business and Economics Research Journal, 11(3), 807-821. https://doi.org/10.20409/berj.2020.283

Puspaningrum, A. (2020). Social media marketing and brand loyalty: the role of brand trust. Journal of Asian Finance Economics and Business, 7(12), 951-958. https://doi.org/10.13106/jafeb.2020.vol7.no12.951

Robinson, S.L., 1996. Trust and breach of the psychological contract. Administrative science quarterly, pp.574-599.

Roth, A.E. and Erev, I., 1995. Learning in extensive-form games: Experimental data and simple dynamic models in the intermediate term. Games and economic behavior, 8(1), pp.164-212.

Roth, M.S., 1995. The effects of culture and socioeconomics on the performance of global brand image strategies. Journal of Marketing Research, 32(2), pp.163-175.

Salam, A. F., Iyer, L., Palvia, P., & Singh, R. (2005). Trust in e-commerce. Communications of the ACM, 48(2), 72-77. https://doi.org/10.1145/1042091.1042093

Sitta, D., Faulkner, M., & Stern, P. (2018). What can the brand manager expect from facebook?. Australasian Marketing Journal, 26(1), 17-22. https://doi.org/10.1016/j.ausmj.2018.01.001

Shandilya, R., Gupta, A., Patel, K., & Singh, N. (2021). Transformative force with immense economic potential, job creation prospects, and a model of cross-ministerial collaboration. Journal of Health Economics and Policy, 34(4), 223-240.

Sousa, B. and Alves, G. M. M. (2019). The role of relationship marketing in behavioural intentions of medical tourism services and guest experiences. Journal of Hospitality and Tourism Insights, 2(3), 224-240. https://doi.org/10.1108/jhti-05-2018-0032

Srikant, P.A. and Sathyanarayan, K., 2016, July. Effect of Social Media in Building Trust: An Empirical Study on Face Book Platform. In 3rd European Conference on Social M di R h Media Research EM Normandie, Caen, France (p. 483).

Subbaraman, S., Kumar, A., Sharma, P., & Reddy, M. (2021). The visionary "Heal in India" initiative: A concerted government effort fortified by an exclusive website. Medical Tourism Review, 28(1), 78-92.

Triandis, H.C. and Gelfand, M.J., 1998. Converging measurement of horizontal and vertical Individualism and collectivism. Journal of personality and social psychology, 74(1), p.118.

Vingirayi, I. (2021). The effect of brand image on customer choices in the zimbabwean food industry. Journal of Business Management and Economics, 09(02), 09-20. https://doi.org/10.15520/jbme.v9i02.3243

Wu, X. and Shen, J. (2018). A study on airbnb's trust mechanism and the effects of cultural values—based on a survey of chinese consumers. Sustainability, 10(9), 3041. https://doi.org/10.3390/su10093041

Yang, J. and Lee, H., 2002. Identifying key factors for successful joint venture in China. Industrial Management & Data Systems.

Yin, X., Wang, H., Xia, Q., & Gu, Q. (2019). How social interaction affects purchase intention in social commerce: a cultural perspective. Sustainability, 11(8), 2423. https://doi.org/10.3390/su11082423

Zaheer, S. and Zaheer, A. (2005). Trust across borders. Journal of International Business Studies, 37(1), 21-29. https://doi.org/10.1057/palgrave.jibs.8400180

9

Municipalities and Their Use of Social Media as Communication Tools: An Overview of Some Current Practices in the Aveiro Region In Portugal

Rui Raposo[1], Nídia Salomé [2], Teresa Gouveia[2], and Ana Silva[1]
[1]University of de Aveiro, DigiMedia - Digital Media and Interaction Research Centre, Portugal
[2]Polytechnic Institute of Viseu, CI&DEI - Centre for Studies in Education and Innovation, Portugal

raposo@ua.pt
salome@esev.ipv.pt
tgouveia@esev.ipv.pt
borges.anacarolina@ua.pt

Abstract: Social media has gradually evolved into a phenomenon that transcends its purely technical nature and has become an almost ubiquitous part of the communication activities of our modern society, playing an essential role in numerous sectors, such as public administration, where its potential as a communication tool has helped local authorities to develop agile and easily accessible communication channels with their communities. Traditional communication strategies using leaflets, local television, newspaper and radio advertising, and even the authorities' institutional website are being replaced by more engaging communication strategies based on social media. The research presented in this paper took up the challenge of mapping and analysing during a short period the online presence of the 11 municipalities of the Intermunicipal Community of the Region of Aveiro (CIRA) in Portugal in terms of their use of social media as tools for communicating with their constituents and others living in the region. The information collected focused on the municipalities' activities on Facebook, Instagram, Twitter, and YouTube. Particular attention was paid to consistency and coherence of communication, engagement, and shared content. An empirical study was conducted based on quantitative information collected over 30 days through a web-based web analytics tool, with further review of some of the data collected by the researchers directly from each municipality's social media profile. The results show that municipalities are engaged in developing communication strategies and activities on social media, providing audiovisual content is becoming more critical, and followers are more engaged with audiovisual content and issues less related to political and administrative matters. The information gathered shows that followers are more engaged with content about cultural and sports-related news and that there is still room for improving the use of YouTube for sharing information about each municipality. The results also suggest municipalities can improve their current practices by developing their communication team's new communication design skills. These conclusions have already been shared with decision-makers to help them improve current practices and design future communication strategies based on concepts linked to new media and transmedia experiences.

Keywords: Social media, Communication, Engagement, Local government, Transmedia

1. Introduction

Social media has gradually grown into a phenomenon that strands beyond its sheer technological essence and has become an almost omnipresent piece of our modern society's communication activities. This hard-to-ignore reality, on the verge of a ubiquitous existence, has made it difficult to keep up with transdisciplinary dynamics due to their complexity, reach and depth. Social Media has gained a relevant role in numerous sectors, such as public administration, in which its potential as a communication tool has aided local government bodies in developing agile and easily accessible communication channels with their communities.

Local government has gradually begun to understand social media's relevance to engaging with communities and their constituents. The study conducted aimed to answer the following research questions: "What are the current practices adopted by the municipalities members of the Intermunicipal Community of the Region of Aveiro as to their presence on social media and their use as communication tools?" This paper presents examples of current practices and provides insight that may contribute to improvements and strategy design that may be used to take advantage of the potential presented by social media in local government communication activities. Some of its content may eventually be used as a reference point for similar assessments as to what is being done in other communities, thus contributing to the construction of some critical thought about the subject and providing tools for more active citizenship. The research presented in this paper took on the challenge of mapping and analysing the online presence of the 11 municipalities of the Intermunicipal Community of the Region of Aveiro (CIRA) in Portugal as to their use of social media as tools for communicating with their constituents and other people living in the region. The information collected focused on the municipalities' activity on Facebook, Instagram, Twitter and YouTube. Special attention was given to communication consistency, coherence, engagement, and shared content issues. The information was collected over 30 days using Fan Page Karma, a web-based web analytics tool, and direct observation and information collection from each municipality's social media profile with a comparison table with over 30 quantitive and qualitative indicators.

2. Theoretical Framework

The number of social media users has increased since a little after 2005. Despite the rise, fall, takeover, and diminishing of many social media networks and platforms, it has kept a steady pace and welcomed new generations of users. These new generations of social media users and a broad scope of other users who have used social media regularly for quite some time are currently the fabric of the local communities where the local government bodies work. For several reasons, traditional communication strategies that use leaflets, local TV stations, newspaper and radio ads and even the government bodies' institutional websites are being replaced by closer and more engaging communication strategies based on social media.

According to a study by Kietzmann, Hermkens, McCarthy, and Silvestre (2012), social media can effectively communicate with municipalities. The study found that municipalities can use social media to increase transparency, facilitate public participation, and improve customer service. A study by Arshad and Khurram (2020) found that the information provided on social media within this context played an important role in perceived transparency, trust in agency, perceived responsiveness, and online political participation. This relation is also found in other studies conducted in other parts of the world (Graham & Avery, 2013; Elison & Hardey, 2014; Lin & Kant, 2021; Padeiro et al., 2021; Torres et al., 2023).

Overall, research suggests that social media can be a valuable communication tool for municipalities, allowing them to increase transparency, improve customer service, and foster trust and engagement with citizens. However, there are cases in which engagement and freedom to express concerns and opinions are concepts still under development if, as in some cases, the social media platforms are managed by the government itself (Medaglia & Zhu, 2017; Zhang & Guo, 2021) Recent studies have, however, attempted to demonstrate some shifts in previous approaches (Zhang et al, 2023) that are still to be proven as widespread and a permanent change in the right direction towards a more democratic, free thought and open opinion relation between governmental bodies and the citizens. As in the case of individual users who opt to use social media as an extension of their real offline persona, municipalities must carefully manage their social media presence to avoid potential negative effects, such as spreading misinformation or creating conflicts. In the case of municipalities, this concern is closely linked to avoiding problems with their constituents. Municipalities must develop strategies for monitoring and moderating their social media accounts to ensure effective and appropriate platform use and manage conflicts that may surface with their users or even among them. Overall, the research reviewed suggests that social media can be a valuable communication tool for municipalities, but it must be managed carefully to avoid potential adverse effects. The content provided by municipalities on social media is highly relevant and influences not only the engagement rates achieved but also the construction and consolidation of relationships built on the foundations of trust and transparency. It is undeniable that audiovisual content is king and leads any given study to focus on the type of content consumed on the leading social media platforms (Kemp, 2022). User-generated content (UGC) has gained popularity throughout the years, and there has been an increase in studies involving local government bodies that are tapping into the valuable contribution that this type of content may provide for city planning and engaging with both resident and non-resident users (Ramadhani & Indradjati, 2023; Gryszel et al., 2023). To a certain extent, this trend may provide a sense of authenticity to the content and contribute to a sense of belonging between users and the municipality. Many municipalities have considered the main trends in using social media as a communication tool when designing their online presence.

The following are but a few of some trends that have been outlined in recent years and that are still up-to-date:

- Audiovisual content is king on social media, and users tend to prefer watching content instead of reading;
- Social media platforms are organic and change over time, which implies that communication strategies must be reviewed systematically and adjusted accordingly (Hruska & Maresova, 2020; Li et al., 2021);
- User-generated content and community building are critical issues for social media success (Santos, 2022);

- Artificial intelligence and machine learning are being used more frequently in social media management and content creation (Henman, 2020; Kerr et al., 2020; Anantrasirichai & Bull, 2022);
- Users are provided with information tailored to their profile (Winter et al., 2021; Zarouali et al., 2022);
- Content and conflict moderation is an enormous challenge that has to be tackled by municipalities if they want to build a relationship with their constituents based on trust and transparency (Gorwa et al., 2020; Rossini, 2022);
- Being on all trending social media platforms is highly time-consuming. It must be adequately assessed as to its implications and both positive and negative impacts on the municipality's image.

This theoretical framework enabled the study conducted and presented in the following sections to design the methodology which guided the work conducted.

3. Methodology

The research presented in this paper took on the challenge of an empirical study aimed at mapping and analysing the online presence of the 11 municipalities of the Intermunicipal Community of the Region of Aveiro (CIRA, 2023) in Portugal as to their use of social media as tools for communicating with their constituents and other people living in the region. As for the methodology adopted, the empirical study carried out consisted of a comparative analysis using a set of 31 indicators listed in Table 1, partly considering the work carried out by one of the authors of this article (Vieira & Raposo, 2020; Raposo, 2022), for the analysis and deconstruction exercise of the 11 municipalities analysed. These indicators were distributed into four main categories (Presence, Fans and Followers, Content published, and Engagement). The indicators were chosen and their clustering into the four main categories enabled the researchers to establish a clear image of: i) what characterized each municipality as to its presence on social media platforms; ii) What was the size of their following and its growth dynamic; iii) What each municipality posted on each social media platform (number, frequency, type of content, coherence, language); iv) and the type of engagement and its rate on each platform. A portion of the comparison grid is illustrated in Figure 1.

Table 1: List of all the indicators used for the comparative analysis and their categorization

Presence	Fans and Followers
Social platforms with active profiles	Number of fans for each profile – Total number
Profile name coherence	Fan growth
Profile links shared on the official website	Number of followers
Page performance index	The follower growth,
Content published	**Engagement**
Posts published per day,	Post likes
Post structure coherence	Post comments
Language used in posts	Post shares
Posts with photos	Post mentions
Posts with videos	Post impressions
Reels	Feedback to comments posted by followers or fans
Posts with links to other media	Videos most interacted with
Reposts from other sources	Photos most interacted with
	Links most interacted with
	Reels most interacted with
	Reposts most interacted with
	The total of engagement actions with each profile,
	the engagement rate of each profile,
	The engagement rate of each post
	the reach rate of each post

Metrics Overview			Oct 1, 2022 - Oct 31, 2022				
Profile	Network	Page Performance Index	Fans	Follower Growth (in %)	Post Interaction	Posts per day	Link
Município de Aveiro	FACEBOOK	13,0%	52676	0,17%	0,13%	1,4	https://www.facebook.com/municipiodeaveiro
Câmara Municipal de Ovar	FACEBOOK	29,0%	24291	0,49%	0,21%	1,4	https://www.facebook.com/cm.ovar
Município de Águeda	FACEBOOK	26,0%	24277	0,38%	0,32%	1,1	https://www.facebook.com/cmagueda
Município da Murtosa	FACEBOOK	39,0%	24189	0,51%	0,59%	0,9	https://www.facebook.com/municipiodamurtosa
Município de Ílhavo	FACEBOOK	31,0%	21430	0,26%	0,26%	2,5	https://www.facebook.com/camaramunicipalilhavo
Município de Vagos	FACEBOOK	12,0%	21345	0,09%	0,1%	2,8	https://www.facebook.com/municipiovagos
Município de Anadia	FACEBOOK	38,0%	20314	0,46%	0,13%	4,4	https://www.facebook.com/municipioanadia
Município de Estarreja	FACEBOOK	22,0%	20048	0,24%	0,19%	1,9	https://www.facebook.com/estarrejamunicipio
Município de Albergaria-a-Velh	FACEBOOK	40,0%	18151	0,41%	0,21%	3,5	https://www.facebook.com/municipiodealbergariaavelha
Município de Oliveira do Bairrc	FACEBOOK	63,0%	15377	0,84%	0,27%	4,0	https://www.facebook.com/oliveiradobairro.municipio
Município da Murtosa	INSTAGRAM	20,0%	4373	0,48%	1,72%	0,5	https://www.instagram.com/municipiodamurtosa
Município de Vagos	INSTAGRAM	10,0%	4246	0,19%	0,69%	1,0	https://www.instagram.com/municipiovagos
Município de Estarreja	INSTAGRAM	30,0%	3616	0,78%	1,02%	1,2	https://www.instagram.com/estarrejamunicipio
Município de Sever do Vouga	FACEBOOK	83,0%	3514	1,97%	1,58%	2,0	https://www.facebook.com/municipioseverdovouga

Figure 1: A small portion of the comparison grid used in the study

Figure 2 illustrates the process followed when carrying out the study. The information collected focused on the municipalities' activity on Facebook, Instagram, Twitter and YouTube. Special attention was given to communication consistency, coherence, engagement, and shared content issues. The information was collected over 30 days, during October 2022, using Fan Page Karma, a web-based Web analytics tool, and direct observation and information collection from each municipality's social media profile with a comparison table with 31 indicators combining both quantitive and qualitative data.

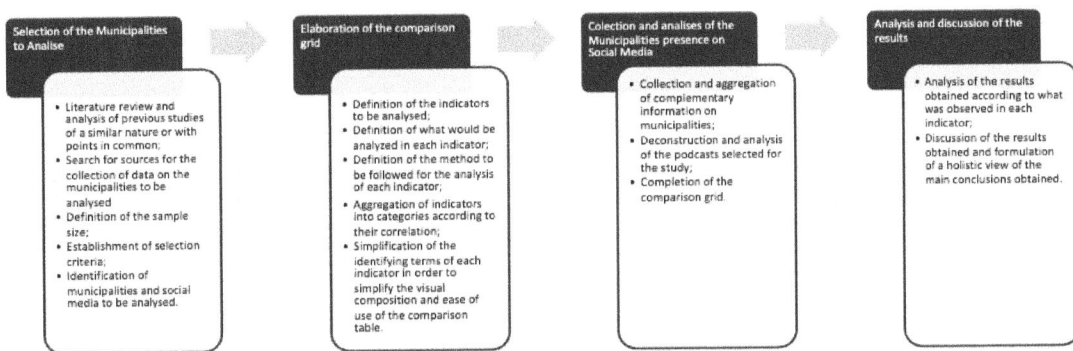

Figure 2: Stages of the study and tasks carried out

As mentioned, the 11 municipalities chosen are part of Portugal's Intermunicipal Community of the Aveiro Region. All municipalities were considered eligible for the study, and all complied with the basic criteria of having some online presence on social media platforms. In some cases, there was the need to search for some of the social media profiles that were not listed on each of the municipality's official websites. The sample of municipalities included in the study and the link to their official website are presented in Table 2.

Table 2: The sample of municipalities included in the study

Municipality	Website link
Município de Aveiro	https://www.cm-aveiro.pt/
Município de Ovar	https://www.cm-ovar.pt/pt/Default.aspx/
Município de Águeda	https://www.cm-agueda.pt/
Município da Murtosa	https://www.cm-murtosa.pt/
Município de Ílhavo	https://www.cm-ilhavo.pt/
Município de Vagos	https://www.cm-vagos.pt/
Município de Anadia	https://www.cm-anadia.pt/
Município de Estarreja	https://www.cm-estarreja.pt/
Município de Albergaria-a-Velha	https://www.cm-albergaria.pt/
Município de Oliveira do Bairro	https://www.cm-olb.pt/
Município de Sever do Vouga	https://www.cm-sever.pt/

4. The Study

As illustrated in Figure 1, the study comprised four moments, each with its purpose and period within the overall work conducted. Although the analysis stage of the study occurred during the whole month of October, the sample selection and the development of the comparison grid were developed over a month before the analysis stage. This enabled the research team to collect all the information regarding the municipalities' online presence and confirm if the profiles collected were, in fact, official profiles and not false profiles posing as official ones. There was also some attention dedicated to what may be considered discarded or forsaken profiles, which may be understood as profiles created at some point by a member of the municipality team but then left online unattended instead of being shut down. We opted to keep these forsaken profiles on our comparison list when there were no alternative profiles on the same social media platform. We chose to do so because, despite being left without any tending to, it was up and online. During October, the profiles collected and included in the comparison grid were monitored every week, and additional activities, such as reading the content of newly published posts and viewing videos recently uploaded, were completed to form a better understanding of the type of content published. It was interesting to find out that, at the time, most of the municipalities had inconsistent information on their official websites. With this, we mean that even though they have a presence on multiple social media platforms, most of them are not mentioned on the official website. This, of course, led to the need to spend some time on each social media platform to try and identify if each municipality had an up-and-running profile on Facebook, Instagram or any of the other more commonly used social media platforms. Much to the researchers' surprise the municipalities were falling short of properly sharing with their website visitors what other official communication channels could be found online. Table 2 illustrates an example of this inconsistency regarding each municipality's presence on Instagram during October 2022. Some of these inconsistencies have been reviewed since then while others are still in place.

Table 3: Example of inconsistencies regarding each municipality's presence on Instagram and the link provided on their official website during October 2022

Municipality	Official Instagram account	Link provided on website
Município de Aveiro	https://www.instagram.com/municipiodeaveiro/	No link
Município de Ovar	https://www.instagram.com/municipioovar	https://www.instagram.com/municipioovar/
Município de Águeda	https://www.instagram.com/agueda.tv	No link
Município da Murtosa	https://www.instagram.com/municipiodamurtosa	No link
Município de Ílhavo	https://www.instagram.com/municipio_de_ilhavo	https://www.instagram.com/municipio_de_ilhavo/
Município de Vagos	https://www.instagram.com/municipiovagos	https://www.instagram.com/municipiovagos/
Município de Anadia	https://www.instagram.com/municipioanadia	No link
Município de Estarreja	https://www.instagram.com/estarrejamunicipio	https://www.instagram.com/estarrejamunicipio/
Município de Albergaria-a-Velha	https://www.instagram.com/municipiodealbergariaavelha	https://www.instagram.com/cineteatroalba/
Município de Oliveira do Bairro	https://www.instagram.com/oliveiradobairro.municipio	https://www.instagram.com/oliveiradobairro_municipio/
Município de Sever do Vouga	https://www.instagram.com/municipioseverdovouga	No link

There are other examples of this type of inconsistency regarding Facebook and YouTube that may be easily solved and contribute to improving each municipality's visibility on each of these social media platforms. The empirical nature of the study conducted did not provide data or information regarding the reasons behind these issues still open to improvement. An additional issue identified and which may also be subject to further analysis is the fact that some of the profiles created by each municipality are given different names and branding. Probably the most evident case is the municipality of Águeda summarized in Table 3 that, for some reason, uses an Águeda TV brand on some of its official social media profiles such as Instagram and YouTube while in others use the more institutional cmagueda brand. We mustn't ignore the possibility that the profile name may have already been taken when this municipality chose to create an account, but there is a relevant difference between cmagueda and aguedatv worth reviewing for the sake of brand consistency and coherence.

Table 4: Example of brand inconsistency regarding the Municipality of Águeda's presence on various social media platforms during October 2022

Município de Águeda	
Social media platform	Link to Social Media profile
Facebook	https://www.facebook.com/cmagueda
Instagram	https://www.instagram.com/agueda.tv
YouTube	https://www.youtube.com/channel/UC5MCZycylopJ6YWI79pZMGQ
Twitter	https://www.twitter.com/cmaagueda

Despite these inconsistencies and some difficulty in finding each municipality's official online presence, the study ended up collecting a diverse list of social media profiles that are, as a whole, presented in Table 4. It was interesting to see that at the time, all the municipalities had both a Facebook page and an Instagram profile, but not all had a YouTube channel, and less than half had a Twitter profile. While the relevance of having a Twitter profile now rebranded as X is debatable yet understandable due to its time-consuming nature, especially in small social media communication teams, the fact that not all municipalities have a YouTube channel is worth outlining. The time and effort put into creating good audiovisual content and properly managing a YouTube channel is probably as demanding, if not more, than other social media platforms. However, besides its relevant role in sharing information about the municipality's present and future activities, it may also play an important role in preserving and promoting the municipality's past. For this reason alone, it is worth looking at it from a different angle when discussing its importance as a communication tool.

Table 5: Summary of the number of Municipalities with an official presence on Facebook, Instagram, Youtube and Twitter during October 2022 the corresponding percentage with the sample

Municipalities (11)	Number of Municipalities with an official presence	Percentage of Municipalities with an official presence
Official Facebook pages	11	100%
Official Instagram profiles	11	100%
Official Youtube Channels	9	82%
Official Twitter profiles	5	45%

The results attained after thoroughly filling in the comparison grid are presented and discussed in the next section of this paper.

5. Results

The results attained with the work developed in this study may be analysed according to the data collected during October 2022, the picture it painted, and the reflections derived from what was learned with that same data. If we merely look at the data and try to establish a set of main conclusions contained within an established period, we may look at the results as instances of our sample's presence and activity on a set of social media platforms. Table 5 clearly shows that Facebook is the social media platform on which the sample of municipalities was most active, with a total of 688 posts, averaging a total of 25 per day, closely followed by Instagram, with 410 posts and an average of about 13 posts per day. YouTube and Twitter, on the other hand, had little or no content creation activities during the month included in the study. This clearly shows the municipalities' preference regarding their social media presence. However, it corroborates the idea that, at least in the case of YouTube, the time and effort involved in producing audiovisual content may lead municipalities to focus on other platforms, such as Facebook and Instagram. The content analysis did, on the other hand, show that some of the content published on Facebook could easily find its way onto YouTube, thus increasing the content published on the municipality's channel and, at the same time, contributing to its archiving, preservation and future retrieval for reuse.

Rui Raposo et al.

Table 6: Summary of the average and total number of posts published by the sample during October 2022 on Facebook, Instagram, YouTube and Twitter

Social Media Platform	Average number of posts per day	Total number of posts during October 2022
Facebook	25	688
Instagram	13	410
Youtube	0,4	12
Twitter	0,2	5

Although the total number of posts on Facebook and Instagram shows some activity, it is worth outlining that not all municipalities produce the same publication patterns. Table 6 clarifies the most and least active municipalities on, in this case, Facebook.

Table 7: Summary of the average and total number of posts published on Facebook by each municipality during October 2022

Municipality	Average number of posts per day	Total number of posts during October 2022
Município de Anadia	4,5	126
Município de Oliveira do Bairro	3,9	108
Município de Vagos	3,8	106
Município de Albergaria-a-Velha	2,9	82
Município de Ílhavo	2,6	72
Município de Estarreja	2,3	65
Município de Aveiro	1	27
Município da Murtosa	1,2	34
Município de Águeda	1,1	31
Município de Sever do Vouga	1,0	28
Município de Ovar	0,3	9

One may think that posting many times will result in high engagement rates when, in reality, that is not the case. For instance, when considering Instagram, having a larger number of followers will not grant you a great engagement rate even if you publish less content to engage with. Table 7 proves this point by showing that, for example, The Murtosa Municipality, despite its 4373 followers on Instagram and 16 posts during the month considered in the study, was only able to reach a 0,9% engagement rate. A result similar to Aveiro, which had less than half of Murtosa's followers and only 6 more posts. Regarding engagement, Anadia and Ílhavo stand out with an engagement rate of around 5% and a similar number of followers. Anadia, however, posted more than twice as much as Ílhavo, which means that the latter got more engagement with less posting effort. This also provides evidence that by selecting the right content, there is no need to overflow your social media profile with much content. Less may mean more, and this is a great example.

Table 8: Summary of the engagement rate, number of followers (most to least) and total of posts published by each municipality during October 2022

Municipality	Engagement rate	Followers	Total of posts during October 2022
Município da Murtosa	0.9%	4373	16
Município de Vagos	0.6%	4246	31
Município de Estarreja	1.1%	3616	37
Município de Oliveira do Bairro	2.2%	2801	79
Município de Aveiro	1.0%	1913	22
Município de Águeda	0.5%	1361	11
Município de Anadia	5.4%	1306	130
Município de Sever do Vouga	0.0%	1183	0

Municipality	Engagement rate	Followers	Total of posts during October 2022
Município de Ílhavo	4,9%	1113	61
Município de Albergaria-a-Velha	2,4%	118	24

As for the type of content, most published pictures are the most posted (Figure 3) and the most interacted with, probably due to the need for some users to click on the picture to see it in full-screen mode.

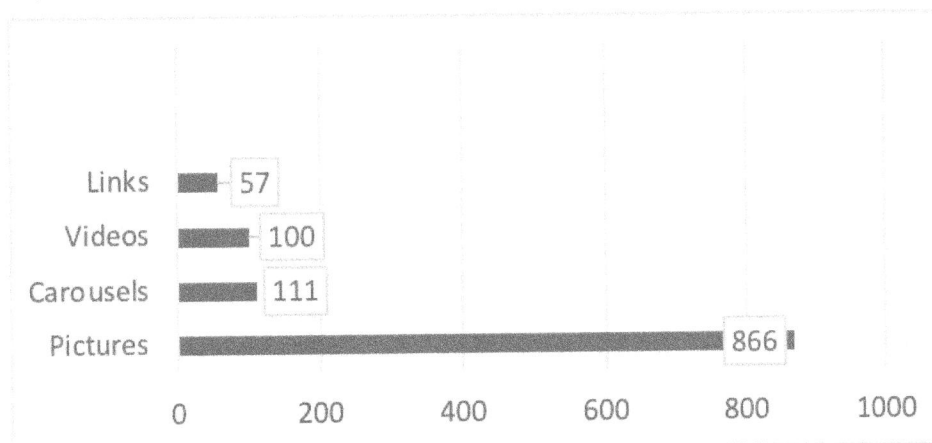

Figure 3: Type of content most published by each municipality during October 2022

It was interesting to see that the content that most interacted with, apart from pictures or videos, always included a personal story that may have touched base with the users' memories or gastronomical preferences (Figure 4). This engagement is a great pointer regarding the content these municipalities should share on their social media profiles and other more formal information. Keeping engaged with the constituents is a great way to establish communication and, in due time, create relations based on trust.

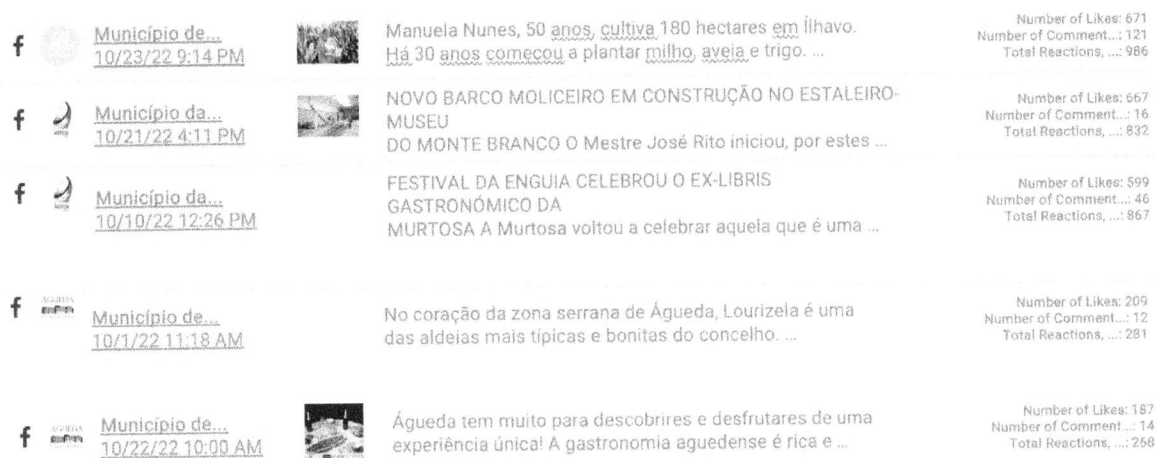

Figure 4: Examples of some of the posts most interacted with content during October 2022

These results and others to be published soon enabled the research team to draw the conclusions presented in the following section.

6. Conclusions

According to the results obtained from the study conducted, we may state that the municipalities from CIRA are concerned with developing communication strategies and activities on social media, that there is a growing concern with providing audiovisual content, and that followers engage more with posts which include pictures and audiovisual content and with topics less linked to political and purely administrative issues. Information collected shows that followers are more engaged with content about personal stories and cultural and gastronomic news something already identified in a study by Perea (Perea, Bonsón & Bednárová, 2021). There is, however, room for improvement as to the correction of inconsistencies linked to municipality branding on social media, rethinking the municipality's presence online by focusing on fewer platforms rather than trying to be everywhere but with little or no content or clear goals, understanding that their official website is a fundamental starting point for finding them on social media and the first alternative to making the user waste time searching for them online. It is also evident that most of the municipalities considered should improve their editorial guidelines for their presence on social media by further normalizing content such as post structure, the use of #tags and the tone of the language used (Stone & Can,2020). The analysis conducted allowed the research team to identify that certain types of content, like videos about positive actions in local communities and associations, attracted a lot of attention and engaged a wider number of followers and fans. This should be something that municipalities may tap into as anchor content capable of attracting attention and a way of promoting a greater connection with their constituents (Faber, 2022). As a side-effect, other content may earn greater visibility. Working on this concept of Return on Engagement may also help promote connections with the municipality's constituents, which may help promote citizen participation in other forms beyond the typical online comments and opinions about everything but doing nothing in the real world. Attracting and involving the constituents in offline activities, attracting at the same time their attention toward municipal management and improving government-to-citizen relationships through call-to-action initiatives posted and promoted on their social media is also worth promoting (Sarantis et al., 2022). Mayors and their clear perception of the relevance of this effort are essential for tackling this challenge for they are the main decision-makers in these local governance bodies (Giacomini & Simonetto, 2020). The study also enabled the team to perceive that YouTube is underused and even its current use falls short of what it may be used for. As aforementioned, municipalities may resort to YouTube as a means to preserve, promote and discuss the territory's tangible and intangible heritage. A holistic analysis of the results also suggests municipalities may improve their current practices by developing their communication team's competencies in communication design for new media. This may, however, be a challenge due to possible limited resources as in the cases identifiable other studies previously conducted (Silva et al., 2019; Stone et al., 2024) Much of the work presented in this paper may contribute to the improvement of some of the practices identified in the study and the design of future communication strategies based on concepts closely knit with new media and transmedia experiences as practices useful for bridging the municipalities goals and ideas with their constituents and local communities. The study conducted has room for more in-depth research by adding the qualitative analysis of both the content posted by the municipalities and the comments provided by their followers and fans, structured interviews with the people responsible for managing the municipalities' presence on social media, a comparative analysis of social media activity over a longer period and a comparative analysis between municipalities according to the indicators adopted for this study. These possibilities may be considered as both limitations of the work done and opportunities for future studies.

References

Anantrasirichai, N. and Bull, D., 2022. Artificial intelligence in the creative industries: a review. *Artificial Intelligence Review*, pp.1-68.

Arshad, S. and Khurram, S., 2020. Can the government's presence on social media stimulate citizens' online political participation? Investigating the influence of transparency, trust, and responsiveness. *Government Information Quarterly*, 37(3), p.101486.

Ellison, N. and Hardey, M., 2014. Social media and local government: Citizenship, consumption and democracy. *Local Government Studies*, 40(1), pp.21-40.

Faber, B., 2022. A Tale of Three Technologies: A Survival Analysis of Municipal Adoption of Websites, Twitter, and YouTube. *Digital Government: Research and Practice*, 3(3), pp.1-20.

Fan Page Karma website, n.d. *Fan Page Karma website*. [Online] Available at: https://www.fanpagekarma.com/ (Accessed: 8 December 2023).

Giacomini, D. and Simonetto, A., 2020. How mayors perceive the influence of social media on the policy cycle. *Public Organization Review*, 20, pp.735-752.

Gorwa, R., Binns, R. and Katzenbach, C., 2020. Algorithmic content moderation: Technical and political challenges in the automation of platform governance. *Big Data & Society*, 7(1), p.2053951719897945.

Graham, M. and Avery, E., 2013. Government public relations and social media: An analysis of the perceptions and trends of social media use at the local government level. *Public Relations Journal*, 7(4), pp.1-21.

Gryszel, P., Pełka, M. and Zawadzki, P., 2023. The Use of Social Media in City Marketing Communication with Residents and Tourists–User Segmentation. *Polish Journal of Sport and Tourism*, 30(1), pp.27-32.

Henman, P., 2020. Improving public services using artificial intelligence: possibilities, pitfalls, governance. *Asia Pacific Journal of Public Administration*, 42(4), pp.209-221.

Hruska, J. and Maresova, P., 2020. Use of social media platforms among adults in the United States—behavior on social media. *Societies*, 10(1), p.27.

Intermunicipal Community of the Aveiro Region (CIRA) website, n.d. [Online] Available at: https://www.regiaodeaveiro.pt/ (Accessed: 8 December 2023).

Kemp, S., 2022. *Digital 2022: Portugal*. [Online] Available at: https://datareportal.com/reports/digital-2022-global-overview-report (Accessed: 8 December 2023).

Kerr, A., Barry, M. and Kelleher, J.D., 2020. Expectations of artificial intelligence and the performativity of ethics: Implications for communication governance. *Big Data & Society*, 7(1), p.2053951720915939.

Kietzmann, J., Silvestre, B., McCarthy, I. and Pitt, L., 2012. The social media phenomenon: towards a research. *Journal of Public Affairs*, 12(2), pp.109-119.

Li, F., Larimo, J. and Leonidou, L.C., 2021. Social media marketing strategy: definition, conceptualization, taxonomy, validation, and future agenda. *Journal of the Academy of Marketing Science*, 49, pp.51-70.

Lin, Y. and Kant, S., 2021. Using social media for citizen participation: Contexts, empowerment, and inclusion. *Sustainability*, 13(12), p.6635.

Medaglia, R. and Zhu, D., 2017. Public deliberation on government-managed social media: A study on Weibo users in China. *Government Information Quarterly*, 34(3), pp.533-544.

Padeiro, M., Bueno-Larraz, B. and Freitas, Â., 2021. Local governments' use of social media during the COVID-19 pandemic: The case of Portugal. *Government information quarterly*, 38(4), p.101620.

Perea, D., Bonsón, E. and Bednárová, M., 2021. Citizen reactions to municipalities' Instagram communication. *Government Information Quarterly*, 38(3), p.101579.

Ramadhani, I.S. and Indradjati, P.N., 2023. Toward contemporary city branding in the digital era: conceptualizing the acceptability of city branding on social media. *Open House International*.

Raposo, R., 2022. Os podcasts enquanto experiência multimédia e transmedia: Uma análise comparativa de podcasts portugueses e brasileiros. *VISUAL REVIEW. International Visual Culture Review/Revista Internacional de Cultura Visual*, 10(3), pp.1-21.

Rossini, P., 2022. Beyond incivility: Understanding patterns of uncivil and intolerant discourse in online political talk. *Communication Research*, 49(3), pp.399-425.

Santos, M.L.B.d., 2022. The "so-called" UGC: an updated definition of user-generated content in the age of social media. *Online Information Review*, Vol. 46 No. 1, pp.95-113. [Online] Available at: https://doi.org/10.1108/OIR-06-2020-0258Sa

Sarantis, D., Soares, D., Susar, D. and Aquaro, V., 2022, October. Local e-Government Development: Results of an international survey. In *Proceedings of the 15th International Conference on Theory and Practice of Electronic Governance* ,pp. 391-396.

Silva, P., Tavares, A.F., Silva, T. and Lameiras, M., 2019. The good, the bad and the ugly: Three faces of social media usage by local governments. *Government Information Quarterly*, 36(3), pp.469-479.

Stone, J.A. and Can, S.H., 2020. Linguistic analysis of municipal twitter feeds: Factors influencing frequency and engagement. *Government Information Quarterly*, 37(4), p.101468.

Stone, J.A., Flanders, K.J., Robles, P. and Can, S.H. (2024), Strategic measurement and evaluation of municipal social media: insight from front-line personnel in the United States, *Transforming Government: People, Process and Policy*, Vol. 18, no. 1, pp. 103-117. Available at: https://doi.org/10.1108/TG-07-2023-0090

Torres, P., Augusto, M. and Rodrigues, T., 2023. The mechanisms that make social media effective in building citizens' trust on local government. *Digital Policy, Regulation and Governance*, 25(2), pp.138-152.

Vieira, J. and Raposo, R., 2020. Audiovisual content production for MOOCs: a comparative analysis of current practices. In: *ICERI2020 Proceedings* (pp.2730-2737). IATED.

Winter, S., Maslowska, E. and Vos, A.L., 2021. The effects of trait-based personalization in social media advertising. *Computers in Human Behavior*, 114, p.106525.

Zarouali, B., Dobber, T., De Pauw, G. and de Vreese, C., 2022. Using a personality-profiling algorithm to investigate political microtargeting: assessing the persuasion effects of personality-tailored ads on social media. *Communication Research*, 49(8), pp.1066-1091.

Zhang, C., Zhang, D. and Shao, H.L., 2023. The softening of Chinese digital propaganda: Evidence from the People's Daily Weibo account during the pandemic. *Frontiers in psychology*, 14, p.1049671.

Zhang, Y. and Guo, L., 2021. 'A battlefield for public opinion struggle': how does news consumption from different sources on social media influence government satisfaction in China? *Information, Communication & Society*, 24(4), pp.594-610.

User-Generated Content in Tourism: Could it Impact Brand Equity and Intention to Visit?

Sara Santos[1], Sónia Ferreira[2] and Maria Vasconcelos[3]
[1]Research Centre in Digital Services (CISeD) – Instituto Politécnico de Viseu, Portugal
[2]Center for Studies in Education and Innovation, ESEV - Instituto Politécnico de Viseu, Portugal
[3]ESEV - Instituto Politécnico de Viseu, Portugal

ssantos@esev.ipv.pt
sonia.ferreira@esev.ipv.pt
pv23756@esev.ipv.pt

Abstract. The Internet has changed communication and created significant challenges for the tourism and hospitality sectors. Due to the abundance of tourist destinations available, competition is fierce. Therefore, destinations must devise strategies to set themselves apart and strengthen customer brand equity by providing informative and engaging content on digital platforms, specifically social media, with millions of users. Web 2.0 allows users to generate and distribute information through user-generated content and e-word-of-mouth as trustworthy sources for tourist information that can significantly influence travellers' decision-making process. Therefore, businesses must share pertinent information and incentivize online customer feedback on social media platforms where ideas and opinions are highly valued. These can influence a potential tourist's decision to visit, which makes them critical to destination promotion. Effective communication is essential in shaping consumer opinion and fostering strong customer relationships. This study analyses whether user-generated content impacts brand equity and visitation intentions. It utilized a quantitative approach, using a survey to collect data from tourists and potential tourists of Portugal's Central Region. The sample size consisted of 515 participants. The collected data was then analyzed statistically with the assistance of Smart PLS 3.3.2 software. Based on the results, it was found that user-generated content has an impact on destination awareness, perceived quality, and intention to visit.

Keywords: User-Generated content, Brand equity, Intention to visit, Tourism

1. Introduction

Incorporating technology into our everyday lives has led to businesses seamlessly transitioning online, enhancing customer interactions. This shift towards novel communication avenues enabled by technological developments has facilitated new social connections. Marketers and customers can effortlessly connect on digital platforms, and companies must comprehend their client's needs to maintain a strategic online presence that caters to personalized content suggestions or guidance. The Internet has significantly impacted tourism, with digital marketing influencing customer decisions. Travellers use online and offline resources to plan trips, making it easier than ever to select and book hotels or vacation packages through online platforms and social media.

Nowadays, users exhibit a critical and opinionated attitude towards brands, products, services, and experiences. The trust in fellow travellers' reviews is high, emphasizing the importance for businesses to share pertinent information while encouraging user-generated content. Individuals can now create their digital footprint by writing reviews of restaurants, lodgings, or airlines and sharing text, images, and videos about their experiences. Such information is deemed more credible than that supplied by the corporation due to its authenticity and impartiality. This enables potential travellers to make informed decisions through insights gained from others' feedback and recommendations. Positive customer opinion creates consumer-based brand equity (CBBE), adding value to goods/services (Cervova & Vavrova, 2021). The destination's communication, from both entities and tourists, influences the consumer's perception and intention to visit (Fu et al., 2016). Therefore, tourism organizations should disseminate compelling material that is pertinent and stimulate user sharing. Due to the participative nature of consumers on social networks and the significance of opinion-sharing in tourism, it was vital to investigate if user-generated content impacts brand equity and visitation intentions.

2. Literature Review

2.1 User-Generated Content

User-generated content (UGC) is defined as user-generated material distributed to a large audience through social media or other channels (Tirunillai & Tellis, 2012). Because it presents an unbiased perspective and has no immediate financial interest to the provider, user-generated content is frequently seen as more reliable than corporate-produced content (Cheong & Morrison, 2008). This type of content is only considered accurate, truthful, and genuine when not controlled by a corporation (Sawaftah et al., 2021). Both consumers and businesses can benefit from using user-generated material. It offers precise consumer data and can be utilized to determine what people desire (Timoshenko & Hauser, 2019). Companies frequently encounter UGC regarding their products and services online as more people use the digital world, and many support its spread (Yang et al., 2019). This indicates that businesses value user-generated content (UGC) and embrace receiving positive and negative customer feedback. Companies can incorporate it into their marketing strategies to realize their full potential.

User comments, reviews, opinions on blog posts or online articles, text submissions, and user-created audio, photos, and videos are some of the many forms of UGC (Naab & Sehl, 2016). UGC can be shared through several platforms, including websites, blogs, and social media platforms like Facebook, Twitter, Instagram, LinkedIn, and YouTube (Ana & Istudor, 2013). Information on products, services, events, and businesses is sometimes given to educate people. Dedeoğlu et al. (2020) assert that it might also be motivated by the desire to sate hedonistic urges.

Technological advancements and the advent of online social networks and platforms have encouraged exchanging travel-related ideas and experiences in written form and more visually attractive media like images and videos. These formats usually have more visual appeal and persuasiveness. This has led to the widespread sharing of tourism-related information via Instagram photographs and YouTube vlogs (Nguyen & Tong, 2022). Since it provides accurate and up-to-date information about popular tourist destinations and practical travel advice, it has flourished as an essential resource in the tourism industry. It lessens their concerns and doubts while assisting future tourists in making decisions. Because of its traits and features, it is an extensively utilized tool.

2.2 Brand Equity

Tourism brand equity alludes to the perceived value of a particular tourism destination or service among prospective tourists. This value encompasses intangible elements, such as a traveller's emotional bond with a specific location, and tangible components, such as its built environment and natural beauty. According to Cervova and Vavrova (2021), if a company projects an image of excellence, reliability, and proficiency, its clients can expect comparable features in both its products and services. As stated by Keller (1993), the conduct being referred to is recognized as customer-based brand equity (CBBE) and characterized as the "differential effect of brand knowledge on consumer response to brand marketing" (p. 2). Consequently, brand equity is acknowledged as an increase in worth conferred upon a product or service when customers possess a positive, robust, and distinguishing perception of the destination; this will ultimately impact how they react towards corporations' advertising strategies. Destination loyalty, destination awareness, destination image and quality are frequently employed when researching customer-based brand equity in tourism (Konečnik & Gartner, 2007).

Destination Awareness - Brand awareness is a significant component regularly used to measure customer-based brand equity for a tourism destination (CBBETD) in the tourism sector, particularly regarding travel destinations (Konečnik & Gartner, 2007; Boo et al., 2009). This dimension reflects how aware and acquainted people are with a good or service (Keller, 1993). In the tourism industry, it is described as a traveller's capacity to recognize and distinguish a place they have heard about before. A traveller's brand awareness grows once they begin learning about a destination (Huerta-Álvarez et al., 2020), and they must strongly prefer one location over competitors (Dedeoğlu et al., 2019). Today, it is crucial to be reachable across the many digital platforms that consumers, mainly tourists, frequently use. The first step in grabbing customers' attention is publishing interesting, pertinent, instructive, and alluring content.

Destination Image - The CBBETD model's image destination is considered its most pertinent and vital dimension. Destination image, as defined by Chiu et al. (2013), is a "set of qualities, attributes, and benefits that visitors have about the destination" (p. 877), which might be crucial for travellers to differentiate one location from another. When positive, this image motivates visitors to visit, return, and suggest the destination to acquaintances (Červová & Vávrová, 2021). According to Ferrer-Rosell and Mariné-Roig (2020), opinions and thoughts can be formed through the corporate image communicated by the tourism company and through sharing opinions by other tourists (e.g., e-word of mouth). The brand positioning must be expressed honestly and truthfully so that the visitor's expectations will be near what is communicated. This CBBETD factor influences a destination's success since those with a positive brand image are more likely to be visited and receive favourable evaluations.

Destination Loyalty - Destination loyalty is another critical component of CBBETD. Destination loyalty in tourism refers to the possibility that visitors will return and recommend a specific site to others (Mechinda et al., 2009). When a visitor enjoys the experience and connects with the place, staying loyal and returning later is natural.

Using all available tools to build and retain brand loyalty in this highly competitive period is crucial. Because of this, a continuous level of quality in tourism-related products or services is required (Lassar et al., 1995). Based on previous travel experiences, the tourist will set expectations that he will then maintain; if the quality of the services declines, the tourist will be dissatisfied on subsequent visits. The tourists' commitment and devotion to the location would decrease, and they might be enticed to hunt for alternatives among the rivals.

Destination Perceived Quality - According to Aaker (1991), perceived destination quality refers to "the customer's perception of the overall quality or superiority of a product or service relative to its intended purpose, relative to alternatives" (p. 85). According to Saeed and Shafique (2019), the construct of perceived quality entails assessing the cost, amenities, and other similar aspects the destination provides. This CBBETD component is relatively easy to determine because it calls for analyzing visitors' perceptions of the goods and services and their experiences while going to the destination (Červová & Vávrová, 2021). A destination's overall quality, which includes its surroundings, natural and cultural attractions, hotel amenities, and activities accessible to tourists, is a significant factor in deciding how satisfied it will be. Tourism organizations must prioritize the standard of their hospitality services to draw tourists and meet their expectations effectively.

2.3 Intention to Visit

The unexpectedness and unpredictability of tourism services set them apart from other products. Therefore, the intention to come is associated with a high-risk investment since visitors still determine their experiences (Chen et al., 2014). According to Albarq (2013), eWOM might influence travellers' perceptions of places and travel plans. As a result, positive feedback or opinions that eWOM receives can affect the consumer's choice and, as a result, the intention to visit. Therefore, potential tourists can trust other travellers' viewpoints and other online information, such as the Firm Generated Content's broadcast of accurate and pertinent information and the opinions of other visitors (UGC and eWOM). The destination's image will be developed and shaped using this data, which can favour travellers' intentions to travel there (Fu et al., 2016). Therefore, the destination image, shaped by cognitive and emotional factors (De La Hoz-Correa & Muñoz-Leiva, 2018) and the destination value and quality (Ranjbarian & Pool, 2015), might affect and predict travellers' intentions. According to de la Hoz-Correa and Muoz-Leiva (2018), this perception is developed through various online and offline information sources, significantly impacting travellers' intent to travel.

2.4 Tourist Destination Online Communication

Nowadays, both socially and economically, tourism is a significant sector. As a result, this industry has more competition, and a more substantial emphasis is placed on the tourism product. As a result, some vacation destinations are increasingly viewed as brands that help countries stand out and compete (Saeed & Shafique, 2019). One of the most significant peculiarities of the tourism industry is that purchasing the tourism product occurs before contact with it. Hence, approaching tourism destinations as brands and implementing promotional techniques becomes increasingly crucial (IPDT, 2023). The primary point of contact for prospective tourists with the tourism product they intend to purchase is increasingly the material others share on social media.

Consequently, advertising is crucial to entice potential tourists and set the place apart from others (IPDT, 2023). Social media and destination promotion are the main driving forces influencing tourist behaviour. The younger generation's predisposition to use social media will only grow, according to Tourism Economics (2019). Hotelmize (Truyols, 2022) figures show that 34% of customers who book a hotel do so after hearing about it from others on social media. Hence, it is essential to comprehend social media in the framework of marketing and communication and use it to promote locations and boost tourism.

2.5 Turismo Centro de Portugal

Global economic growth and social advancement are fueled by tourism. Portugal has always been viewed as a country of considerable interest and focus for various cultures, and it is today accepted as a reliable and well-known tourism destination. The nation's distinct traditions and rich cultural heritage make it intriguing and one of a kind. In addition to its friendliness, gastronomy, and pleasant ambience, many people consider Portugal a preferred vacation spot (Ramos & Costa, 2017). Turismo Centro de Portugal (TCP) is responsible for growing tourism in the Central Region. This organization has garnered several communications honours, enhancing Portugal's position as a top travel destination.

Turismo Centro de Portugal (TCP) has been recognized with various communication accolades for promoting Portuguese tourism. The fast-paced technological advancements within the industry have prompted TCP to prioritize digital channels such as its website and Facebook, Instagram, and Twitter platforms for its latest marketing efforts. In addition, they use a variety of online strategies, namely user-generated content in their social networks. By utilizing these online tools effectively, TCP aims to engage customers by understanding their preferences and fostering stronger relationships.

3. Methodology Approach

A quantitative approach was employed to examine and compare the proposed hypotheses with the observed and collected data. A questionnaire survey was deemed the most suitable research method for this investigation. The survey was conducted among individuals who visited or considered visiting the Central Region of Portugal. The survey's primary objective is to understand how electronic word-of-mouth influences tourists' perceptions of destinations and their intentions to see them. Scales that other authors had already verified were employed to address concerns regarding the accuracy and consistency of the present study. The scales suffered from some adjustments to meet our research's specific needs and objectives. The measurement scale for the four dimensions of destination brand equity was adapted from Boo et al. (2009) study. The scaling used to measure electronic word-of-mouth was derived from the research conducted by Velázquez et al. (2015), while the scale for measuring travel intention was based on the work of Su et al. (2020). All the items on the questionnaire were measured using a 5-point Likert scale ranging from strongly disagree to agree strongly. This questionnaire sample constituted 515 individuals living in Portugal, of whom 69.3% are female and 29.7% are male (Table 1).

Table 1: Sample Characterization

Variable	Items	Frequencies	%
Gender	Male	153	29.7
	Female	357	69.3
	Rather Not Say	5	1.0
Age	≤22	110	21.4
	23-38	299	58.1
	39-54	78	15.1
	55-73	25	4.9
	≥74	3	0.6
Academic Qualifications	Under Primary Education	0	0
	Primary Education	1	0.2
	Lower Secondary Education	10	1.9
	Upper Secondary Education	121	23.5
	Bachelor's Degree	249	48.3
	Master's Degree	127	24.7
	PhD	7	1.4
Professional Status	Employed	255	49.5
	Student	119	23.1
	Unemployed	17	3.3
	Working Student	64	12.4
	Self-Employed	49	9.5
	Retired	7	1.4
	Other	4	0.8

4. Results

The data obtained from the research were evaluated using Smart PLS 3.3.2 software. The reliability and validity of the measurement model were examined to ensure its accuracy and consistency. Afterwards, attention was focused on analyzing the structural model to determine how various constructs are interconnected and thus test for any existing hypotheses. Table 2 presents an overview of metrics that can be used to assess the performance of the measurement model. Results show that all constructs have satisfactory levels of explained variance, reinforcing their relevance in this study (AVE>0.5). The minimum acceptable value for the standardized coefficients of the items is 0.7, according to Hair et al. (2017). Additionally, the composite reliability values ranging from 0.573 to 0.758 demonstrate an acceptable internal consistency among the items within each construct, which aligns with the commonly suggested values in literature (CR > 0.7) for ensuring the robustness and validity of constructs (Hair et al., 2017). The values for Cronbach's Alpha range from 0 to 1 (Cheung et al., 2023), with higher values indicating more excellent reliability (CA > 0.7); therefore, all values are considered acceptable.

Table 2: Measurement Model

Construct	Cronbach's Alpha	Composite Reliability	Average Variance Extracted (AVE)
DA	0.756	0.843	0.573
DI	0.877	0.916	0.733
DL	0.822	0.880	0.648
DPQ	0.845	0.896	0.684
UGC	0.861	0.900	0.644
ITV	0.893	0.926	0.758

Discriminant validity was also assessed using the Fornell and Larcker (1981) criterion, where the square root of the average variance extracted from each construct exceeds its correlations with other latent constructs (Hair et al., 2017). The results in Table 3 indicate a distinction between the constructs, implying discriminant validity.

Table 3: Discriminant Validity - Fornell and Larcker Criterion (1981)

	DA	DI	DL	DPQ	UGC	ITV
DA	0.756					
DI	0.585	0.856				
DL	0.621	0.704	0.805			
DPQ	0.579	0.475	0.605	0.827		
UGC	0.259	0.271	0.271	0.476	0.802	
ITV	0.493	0.271	0.711	0.476	0.374	0.871

As seen in Table 4, three of the five hypotheses formulated were accepted and validated, while the remaining two were not corroborated.

Table 4: Hypothesis Validation - Total Effects

		β	T-Value	P-Value	Result
H1a	User-Generated Content → Destination Awareness	0.109	2.016	0.044	Accepted
H1b	User-Generated Content → Destination Image	0.082	1.658	0.097	Rejected
H1c	User-generated content → Destination Perceived Quality	0.150	2.744	0.006	Accepted
H1d	User-generated content → Destination Loyalty	0.076	1.498	0.134	Rejected
H2	User-Generated Content → Intention to Visit	0.117	3.270	0.001	Accepted

5. Discussion

Concerning Hypothesis 1a, this was supported (p=0.044; p<0.05), validating the literature's assertion that user-generated social media brand communication has a positive impact on brand awareness, as argued by Schivinski and Dabrowski (2015). Additionally, as Dedeoğlu et al. (2020) mentioned, user-generated content on social media platforms incorporating organizations impacts destination awareness. Thus, it can be concluded that user-generated content aids in developing awareness for tourists visiting the central region of Portugal.

The objective of testing this hypothesis (Hypothesis 1b) was to confirm whether user-generated content affects the formation of the destination image. As a result, this variable did not receive validation with a p-value above 0.05 (p=0.097). The lack of validation for this variable could be explained by the potential adaptation of questionnaire items from other cited authors, which may not accurately capture behaviour in the Portuguese context. Nguyen and Tong (2022) also found that passive exposure to travel-related user-generated content did not significantly impact the destination image.

Hypothesis 1c has been confirmed (p=0.006; p<0.01), indicating that user-created content affects brand equity by influencing the perceived quality of the destination, in line with prior research findings in the literature (Schivinski & Dabrowski, 2015; Stojanovic et al., 2022). Schivinski and Dabrowski (2015) suggest that content created by users positively impacts the perceived quality of brands. Similarly, Stojanovic et al. (2022) found that user-generated content positively influences tourist behaviour, highlighting its significance in enhancing the perceived quality and value of destinations. Therefore, it can be deduced that content produced by fellow tourists shapes respondents' perceptions of the quality of the Portuguese central region.

The results indicate that the p-value for Hypothesis 1d is more significant than 0.05 (p=0.134), which means it did not reach statistical significance and cannot be considered conclusive evidence. Therefore, the content created by fellow tourists on social networks could be more extensive in establishing destination loyalty among respondents. There is a notorious gap in this correlation in the tourism sector. Hermaren and Achyar (2018) found no significant connection between brand loyalty and user-generated content in the cosmetics sector. This contradicts the conclusions drawn by Schivinski and Dabrowski (2015), who identified a significant correlation between user-created content and brand loyalty. The inability to confirm this hypothesis might stem from the unimpressive user-generated content related to central Portugal or a need for sufficient information to form a favourable impression among tourists.

Finally, the validation of Hypothesis 2 (p=0.000; p<0.01) enables us to assert that user-generated content significantly influences tourists' willingness to visit, corroborating earlier research results (Latif et al., 2020; Nguyen & Tong, 2022). Latif et al. (2020) state that exposure to travel-related content on Facebook can inspire people's interest in visiting the corresponding destination. Nguyen and Tong (2022) investigated the impact of user-generated content on individuals' preferences for selecting a specific travel destination. The results indicated that having access to such content significantly increased the intention to choose and the eagerness to visit a particular travel location.

6. Final Considerations

Academic research in the field has increasingly emphasized digital content marketing. Nevertheless, more studies must focus on user-generated content and its connection to brand equity dimensions and intention to visit. This study, therefore, aims to understand whether tourists' brand equity is influenced by user-generated content and, in turn, whether this influences tourists' intention to visit.

The findings indicate that the perceptions tourists hold about a destination are influenced by user-generated content, particularly regarding awareness and perceived quality. Additionally, user-generated content has demonstrated an impact on tourists' intention to visit, highlighting the significance of fellow travellers' opinions in attracting potential tourists, irrespective of the medium used (such as text, video, or images).

The findings of this research provide valuable recommendations for marketing experts and tourism destination managers. In the current landscape, tourism brands must prioritize social media as a central element of their marketing approach. Social media platforms and online resources can benefit businesses, enhancing visibility and establishing a solid brand identity. Effectively leveraging these channels allows organizations to capitalize on opportunities to promote themselves in the competitive tourism industry. Marketers must devise compelling methods to encourage tourists to generate and share content featuring appealing landscapes and elements. This approach will not only enhance the brand value of the destination but also captivate the attention and desire of potential visitors to explore the area.

The sociodemographic attributes of the participants posed a potential constraint in validating specific hypotheses. The study sample primarily comprised individuals aged 22 to 38 and mainly resided in districts such as Viseu, Aveiro, and Coimbra in central Portugal. This could be seen as a geographic limitation. To mitigate these constraints, applying the models to more diverse samples encompassing participants across all age brackets and from different geographical locations nationally and internationally is recommended. Furthermore, in future research, it is advisable to implement this study in various national and international settings, as the current research is limited to the Central region of Portugal.

Acknowledgements

This work is funded by National Funds through the FCT—Foundation for Science and Technology, I.P., within the scope of the project Refª UIDB/05583/2020. Furthermore, we would like to thank the Research Centre in Digital Services (CISeD) and the Polytechnic of Viseu for their support.

References

Aaker, D. A. (1991). *Managing brand equity*. New York, Free Press

Albarq, A. N. (2013). Measuring the impacts of online Word-of-Mouth on tourists' attitude and intentions to visit Jordan: an Empirical study. *International Business Research*, 7(1). https://doi.org/10.5539/ibr.v7n1p14

Ana, M., & Istudor, L. (2013). The role of social Media and User-Generated-Content in millennials' travel behavior. *Management Dynamics in the Knowledge Economy Journal*, 7(1), 87–104. https://doi.org/10.25019/mdke/7.1.05

Boo, S., Busser, J. A., & Baloğlu, Ş. (2009). A model of customer-based brand equity and its application to multiple destinations. *Tourism Management*, 30(2), 219–231. https://doi.org/10.1016/j.tourman.2008.06.003

Červová, L., & Vávrová, J. (2021). Customer-Based brand equity for a tourism destination: the case of Croatia. *Economies*, 9(4), 178. https://doi.org/10.3390/economies9040178

Chen, Y., Shang, R., & Li, M. (2014). The effects of perceived relevance of travel blogs' content on the behavioral intention to visit a tourist destination. *Computers in Human Behavior*, 30, 787–799. https://doi.org/10.1016/j.chb.2013.05.019

Cheong, H. J., & Morrison, M. (2008). Consumers' reliance on product information and recommendations found in UGC. *Journal of Interactive Advertising*, 8(2), 38–49. https://doi.org/10.1080/15252019.2008.10722141

Cheung, G. W., Cooper-Thomas, H. D., Lau, R. S., & Wang, L. C. (2023). Reporting reliability, convergent and discriminant validity with structural equation modeling: A review and best-practice recommendations. *Asia Pacific Journal of Management*. https://doi.org/10.1007/s10490-023-09871-y

Chiu, Y. H., Lee, W., & Chen, T. (2013). Environmentally Responsible Behavior in Ecotourism: Exploring the role of destination image and value perception. *Asia Pacific Journal of Tourism Research*, 19(8), 876–889. https://doi.org/10.1080/10941665.2013.818048

De La Hoz-Correa, A., & Muñoz-Leiva, F. (2018). The role of information sources and image on the intention to visit a medical tourism destination: a cross-cultural analysis. *Journal of Travel & Tourism Marketing*, 36(2), 204–219. https://doi.org/10.1080/10548408.2018.1507865

Dedeoğlu, B. B., Taheri, B., Okumuş, F., & Gannon, M. (2020). Understanding consumers' importance to social media sharing (ISMS): Scale development and validation. *Tourism Management*, 76, 103954. https://doi.org/10.1016/j.tourman.2019.103954

Dedeoğlu, B. B., Van Niekerk, M., KüçükergiN, K. G., De Martino, M., & Okumuş, F. (2019a). Effect of social media sharing on destination brand awareness and destination quality. *Journal of Vacation Marketing*, 26(1), 33–56. https://doi.org/10.1177/1356766719858644

Dedeoğlu, B. B., Van Niekerk, M., KüçükergiN, K. G., De Martino, M., & Okumuş, F. (2019b). Effect of social media sharing on destination brand awareness and destination quality. *Journal of Vacation Marketing*, 26(1), 33–56. https://doi.org/10.1177/1356766719858644

Ferrer-Rosell, B., & Mariné-Roig, E. (2020). Projected versus perceived destination image. *Tourism Analysis*, 25(2), 227–237. https://doi.org/10.3727/108354220x15758301241747

Fornell, C., & Larcker, D. F. (1981). Evaluating Structural Equation Models with Unobservable Variables and Measurement Error. *Journal of Marketing Research*, 18(1), 39–50. https://doi.org/10.1177/002224378101800104

Fu, H., Ye, B. H., & Xiang, J. (2016). Reality TV, audience travel intentions, and destination image. *Tourism Management*, pp. 55, 37–48. https://doi.org/10.1016/j.tourman.2016.01.009

Hair, J. F., Hult, G. T. M., Ringle, C. M., & Sarstedt, M. (2015). *A primer on partial least squares structural equation modeling (PLS-SEM)*. http://ci.nii.ac.jp/ncid/BB15179462

Hermaren, V., & Achyar, A. (2018). The effect of firm created content and user generated content evaluation on customer-based brand equity. *Inobis*, 2(1), 86–100. https://doi.org/10.31842/jurnal-inobis.v2i1.63

Huerta-Álvarez, R., Cambra-Fierro, J., & Blasco, M. F. (2020). The interplay between social media communication, brand equity and brand engagement in tourist destinations: An analysis in an emerging economy. *Journal of Destination Marketing and Management*, 16, 100413. https://doi.org/10.1016/j.jdmm.2020.100413

Ipdt. (2023, April 4). As redes sociais e o poder da imagem em turismo | IPDT. *IPDT - Turismo e Consultoria*. https://www.ipdt.pt/redes-sociais-poder-imagem-turismo/

Keller, K. L. (1993). Conceptualizing, measuring, and managing Customer-Based Brand Equity. *Journal of Marketing*, 57(1), 1. https://doi.org/10.2307/1252054

Konečnik, M., & Gartner, W. C. (2007). Customer-based brand equity for a destination. *Annals of Tourism Research*, 34(2), 400–421. https://doi.org/10.1016/j.annals.2006.10.005

Lassar, W. M., Mittal, B., & Sharma, A. (1995). Measuring customer-based brand equity. *Journal of Consumer Marketing*, 12(4), 11–19. https://doi.org/10.1108/07363769510095270

Mechinda, P., Serirat, S., & Gulid, N. (2009). Examining tourists' attitudinal and behavioural loyalty: Comparison between domestic and international tourists. *Journal of Vacation Marketing*, 15(2), 129–148. https://doi.org/10.1177/1356766708100820

Naab, T. K., & Sehl, A. (2016). Studies of user-generated content: A systematic review. *Journalism: Theory, Practice & Criticism*, *18*(10), 1256–1273. https://doi.org/10.1177/1464884916673557

Nguyen, T. T. T., & Tong, S. (2022). The impact of user-generated content on intention to select a travel destination. *Journal of Marketing Analytics*, *11*(3), 443–457. https://doi.org/10.1057/s41270-022-00174-7

Ramos, D., & Costa, C. (2017). TURISMO: TENDÊNCIAS DE EVOLUÇÃO. *PRACS: Revista Eletrônica De Humanidades Do Curso De Ciências Sociais Da UNIFAP*, *10*(1), 21. https://doi.org/10.18468/pracs.2017v10n1.p21-33

Ranjbarian, B., & Pool, J. K. (2015). The impact of perceived quality and value on tourists' satisfaction and intention to revisit Nowshahr City of Iran. *Journal of Quality Assurance in Hospitality & Tourism*, *16*(1), 103–117. https://doi.org/10.1080/1528008x.2015.966295

Saeed, M., & Shafique, I. (2019). Customer-based brand equity and destination visit behaviour in the tourism industry: the contingent role of social media. *Quality & Quantity*, *54*(5–6), 1491–1512. https://doi.org/10.1007/s11135-019-00898-2

Sawaftah, D., Aljarah, A., & Lahuerta-Otero, E. (2021). Power Brand Defense Up, My Friend! Stimulating Brand Defense through Digital Content Marketing. *Sustainability*, *13*(18), 10266. https://doi.org/10.3390/su131810266

Schivinski, B., & Dąbrowski, D. (2015). The impact of brand communication on brand equity through Facebook. *Journal of Research in Interactive Marketing*, *9*(1), 31–53. https://doi.org/10.1108/jrim-02-2014-0007

Stojanović, I., Andreu, L., & Pérez, R. C. (2022). Social media communication and destination brand equity. *Journal of Hospitality and Tourism Technology*, *13*(4), 650–666. https://doi.org/10.1108/jhtt-11-2020-0302

Su, L., Gong, Q., & Huang, Y. (2020). How do destination social responsibility strategies affect tourists' intention to visit? An attribution theory perspective. *Journal of Retailing and Consumer Services*, *54*, 102023. https://doi.org/10.1016/j.jretconser.2019.102023

Timoshenko, A., & Hauser, J. R. (2019). Identifying Customer Needs from User-Generated Content. *Marketing Science*, *38*(1), 1–20. https://doi.org/10.1287/mksc.2018.1123

Tirunillai, S., & Tellis, G. J. (2012). Does chatter really matter? Dynamics of User-Generated content and stock performance. *Marketing Science*, *31*(2), 198–215. https://doi.org/10.1287/mksc.1110.0682

Tourism Economics (2019), https://s3.amazonaws.com/tourism-economics/craft/Case-Studies-Docs/TE-Impact-of-Online-Content-on-Portugal-Tourism.pdf, last accessed 2023/4/26

Truyols, M. (2022, July 13). *Positive and negative effects of Social Media on the Tourism industry*. Mize. https://www.hotelmize.com/blog/positive-and-negative-effects-of-social-media-on-the-tourism-industry/

Velázquez, B. M., Blasco, M. F., & Saura, I. G. (2015). ICT adoption in hotels and electronic word-of-mouth. *Academia*, *28*(2), 227–250. https://doi.org/10.1108/arla-10-2013-0164

Yang, M., Ren, Y., & Adomavičius, G. (2019). Understanding User-Generated content and Customer engagement on Facebook business pages. *Information Systems Research*, *30*(3), 839–855. https://doi.org/10.1287/isre.2019.0834

Effective Elements of Climate Change Videos on the YouTube Platform

Zeinab Shahbazi and Slawomir Nowaczyk

Center for Applied Intelligent Systems Research, Halmstad University Sweden

Zeinab.shahbazi@hh.se (corresponding author)
Slawomir.nowaczyk@hh.se

Abstract: In an era where visual communication is important, understanding the key components that make climate change videos effective is essential for improving awareness and driving meaningful actions. This research presents an overview of YouTube's educational content on climate change, aiming to identify elements that contribute to the effectiveness of these videos. We used a questionnaire targeting bachelor's and master's students to learn about their preferences regarding the available videos and their beliefs concerning the use of YouTube as an educational platform. A curated list of videos was used to explore how students perceive their influence on personal interest and engagement in climate change. Accordingly, each student watched three videos related to climate change and provided information concerning their impressions. By reviewing various attributes of the videos related to climate change, such as the content structure, engagement, and similar, we extracted the essential characteristics that are associated with more positive reactions to these videos as significant educational tools.

Keywords: YouTube platform, Climate changes, Content-based analysis

1. Introduction

Climate change is widely recognized as a major problem for our society. According to the Fourth National Climate Assessment report, the world's climate will keep changing in the next century, and how much it changes depends on the gases people release into the air. The impacts of climate change include more extreme weather, problems with water and food, harm to animals and plants, higher temperatures, and risks to human health. It is important to involve the public more to help deal with climate change through better education, especially for younger people who will experience the effects of today's decisions. In the modern landscape of digital communication, YouTube has emerged as a potent platform for disseminating information and shaping public discourse. With climate change standing as one of the most pressing global challenges, the need to understand how this critical topic is shown and received on YouTube becomes essential. This study presents a comprehensive exploration, employing content-based analysis techniques to explore the user engagement dynamics with climate change content. Unlike traditional research approaches, our focus extends the content itself to examine user preferences, reactions, and the educational prospects offered by YouTube in the area of climate change awareness. As climate-related issues become increasingly connected with community concerns, examining the complexity of user interactions on this popular platform becomes not only relevant but crucial for informed and effective communication strategies. The details in this study promise to enrich our understanding of how YouTube can serve as a climate change awareness and education.

2. Literature Review

While most people express a collective concern for environmental protection and addressing climate change, there exists a notable division regarding the noticed factors underlying these environmental challenges within the public. This division assumes significance considering the extensive behavioral and policy changes required to effectively address climate change. Many people believe that few are doing things about climate change because they see it as something far away and happening in the future.

Wolf, J. and Moser, S.C., (2011), Shahbazi, Z. and Byun, Y.C., (2021) presents that social media platforms have become widely popular channels for accessing information on subjects like science on a global scale. With over 2 billion users spanning diverse levels of science reading skills and age groups, YouTube stands out as one of the most frequently visited websites, offering easily accessible information. Despite existing studies exploring the connection between social media, public awareness, and engagement with climate change, there is a notable gap in comprehensive research concerning the nature of climate change-related information available on YouTube. Social media platforms offer an avenue for certain segments of the public to express opinions and actively participate in discussions about climate change. In comparison to presented work, they pointout on a gap in comprehensive research specifically regarding the climate change-related content on YouTube, emphasizing the potential for public engagement and discussion on social media platform.

Feygina et al. (2020) discovered that promoting climate change through public media channels enhances public engagement. Cody et al. (2015) employed sentiment analysis to assess responses to climate change news, events, and natural disasters shared on Twitter. Uldam, J. and Askanius, T. (2013) delved into YouTube comments related to issues on climate conferences, aiming to grasp viewers' attitudes toward politics and political involvement. Shapiro, M.A. and Park, H.W. (2018) utilized network structures to compare discussion networks within videos, identifying co-comments across various video discussions. These works are focusing on various objectives such as assessing public engagement with climate changes and comparing the discussion network within videos and in comparison with the presented study it differs from using the educational platform to identify the effectiveness of these videos.

Lorenzoni, I., Nicholson-Cole, S. and Whitmarsh, L. (2007) presented active public participation plays a crucial role in addressing the challenges posed by climate change. Effectively altering individual behavior can contribute positively to climate change reduction efforts. The connection between individuals' thoughts, emotions, and subsequent actions regarding climate change is clear. Involvement in climate change is showing an assessment involving cognitive (thoughts), emotional (feelings), and behavioral (actions) elements. In comparison, we incorporate user sentiments recorded in the questionnaire, and respondents assign ratings to the videos based on these sentiments.

The study presented by Meza, X.V., Shapiro, M. and Park, H. (2018) investigates public responses to the trailer of Before the Flood, a climate change documentary released in October 2016. Using semantic analysis, the research explores emotions related to climate change. A comparison of sentiment in comments on videos from previous studies is made with comments on the Before the Flood trailer. The study identifies key influencers in the comment network, analyzes their discourse, and reveals a heightened politicization of comments, influenced by the ongoing U.S. electoral campaign. Despite a decrease in the use of scientific terms, sentiment towards climate change remains stable. This research contributes to the intersection of webometrics and environmental psychology, demonstrating its utility in analyzing media, especially when targeting a global audience. In comparison with the proposed research work, Meza, X.V., Shapiro, M. and Park, H. (2018), Shahbazi, Z. and Byun, Y.C., (2022) mostly focus on sentiment analysis techniques to extract the emotions based on comments and it differs with exploring the user engagement dynamics with climate changes contents.

The study proposed by Duran-Becerra, B. et al. (2020) looks at the most popular YouTube videos about climate change. They searched for the top 100 videos on YouTube using the term climate change. Videos in languages other than English or those deemed irrelevant were not included. The researchers used a fact sheet from NASA to create categories for the video content, and then they coded the videos based on these categories. The goal is to understand what kind of content people are watching the most on YouTube when it comes to climate change.

The study presented by Effrosynidis, D., Sylaios, G. and Arampatzis, A. (2022) investigates how information about global warming and climate change is shared on the internet, focusing on YouTube videos. The researchers analyzed the top 10 most popular videos on this topic, examining how the science of climate change is presented in these videos.

The study proposed by Shapiro, M.A. and Park, H.W. (2015) established the narrative of each video and then analyzed public responses and engagement through comments. The findings reveal that, regardless of the video's content, comments mostly revolved around the science of climate change, often discussing the topic in general rather than specific videos. Without moderators, YouTube users added their thoughts to these popular videos, emphasizing evidence of weak, strong, or politicized science.

The research proposed by Allgaier, J. et sl. (2019) explores the content of climate-related videos on YouTube, focusing on whether they align with or challenge scientific consensus views. The study analyzed 200 videos using ten search terms related to climate science, climate change, and climate engineering. The findings reveal that a majority of the videos (107 out of 200) support worldviews opposing scientific consensus, including denial of anthropogenic climate change and propagation of conspiracy theories. Surprisingly, videos supporting the scientific mainstream view received only slightly more views than those opposing it. The research emphasizes the need to understand strategically distorted communications about climate issues online and critically analyze them.

3. Methodology

In this section, we describe the detailed process we employed for the content-based analysis of climate change videos on the YouTube educational platform. Figure 1 illustrates the proposed methodology details.

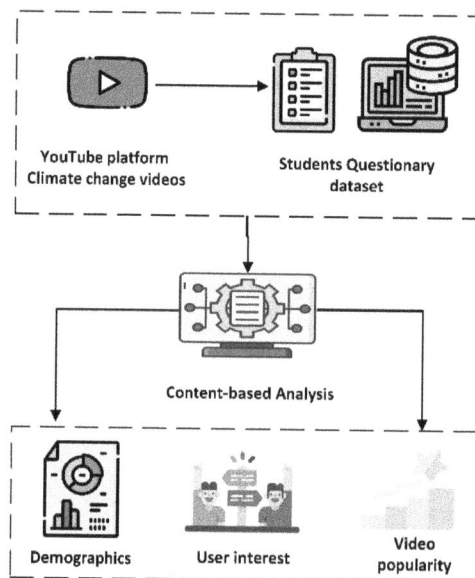

Figure 1: Content-Based Analysis Flowchart

In the first step, we selected 12 videos related to climate change from the YouTube platform and randomly distributed three videos among 60 students from bachelor's and master's university levels. Table 1 shows the list of videos that students watched in this process and Table 2 show the list of majors that students contributed to this questionnaire.

Table 1: List of videos

#	Videos Title
1	What Greta Thunberg does not understand about climate change | Jordan Peterson
2	Climate Scientist Answers Earth Questions From Twitter | Tech Support | WIRED
3	Is It Too Late To Stop Climate Change? Well, it's Complicated.
4	| MOTHER NATURE'S RAGE | Effects of climate change in Kenya's coast region
5	Climate Science: What You Need To Know
6	What the Hockey Stick missed about climate change
7	Climate Change Explained Simply
8	Discussing The Impact Of Climate Change: NASA's New Project | Symone
9	Climate Change – We are the PROBLEM & the SOLUTION (Animated Infographic)
10	Jordan Peterson criticizes climate change | Lex Fridman Podcast Clips
11	When The World Gets 1℃ Hotter | Climate Change: The Facts | BBC Earth
12	Famine propelled by conflict and climate change threatens millions in Somalia

Table 2: List of majors

#	Majors
1	AI and Data Science
2	Computer Engineering
3	Computer Science
4	Development Engineering
5	Master in Embedded System
6	Master in IT
7	Information Technology

In the next step, we prepared a questionnaire form that contains three sections, as follows:

- Section one includes six questions concerning the responder's demographics.
- ection two includes 13 questions related to the specific climate change video that describe the student's engagement and perceptions.
- Section three includes the six questions related to perceptions toward YouTube use in the learning process. Table 3 shows the details of the questionnaire used in this study.

Table 3: Shows the questionnaire details

Demographics	Gender
	Age
	University
	What do you study
	Are you an undergraduate or postgraduate student
	Year of study
Video engagement perceptions	The video helped me understand the topic of climate change better.
	The topic was well-explained in the video.
	The video was easy to learn from.
	I found the video educationally useful.
	The topic of the video was easy to understand.
	I found the video relevant to the topic of climate change.
	The video keeps my attention.
	I think that I was fully focused on the content of the video.
	I felt engaged to the video I just saw.
	I found the video enjoyable.
	I found the video interesting.
	I found the video concise.
	The video uses conversational language.
General perceptions toward YouTube use in the learning process.	The Use of YouTube can enhance the learning process.
	I would like to have YouTube incorporated in my classes.
	The videos can enhance my learning/understanding of course content.
	The videos can create a more exciting learning environment.
	YouTube can make classes more interesting.
	The use of YouTube as a learning tool can engage me to the content of the course.

The questionnaire file for each video was filled separately, and in total, we have 180 responses from 60 students who shared their answers for the above-defined three sections. Based on the collected information, we have performed a content-based analysis to evaluate user's interest and the impact in terms of climate change videos and their interest in using YouTube as an educational and learning platform.

3.1 Content-Based Analysis

In this study, a content-based analysis was conducted to explore user engagement with climate change videos on YouTube. The research involved gathering and analyzing 180 responses from university students who participated in a questionnaire focused on their preferences and perceptions regarding these videos. The study not only showcased diverse user preferences but also detailed broader interests related to integrating YouTube as an educational tool. The findings highlighted the dynamics of user interaction with climate change content, emphasizing YouTube's potential as a valuable platform for educational purposes.

3.2 Demographics

Initiating this process involves inquiries related to demographics, with Halmstad University bachelor's and master's students being the primary focus. This questionnaire section aims to gather data on participants' ages, academic majors, genders, and years of study. The significance of these inquiries lies in clarifying the differences in students' interest in climate change videos. The design intends to provide an understanding of the prevalent sentiments and preferences among different student subgroups.

3.3 User Interest

In this phase, each student actively interacts with three specifically assigned videos, providing valuable subjective insights and evaluations regarding the content that they watch. Students share their perspectives on the videos, conducting a detailed analysis of their interest levels and understanding the presented material. Furthermore, they express their emotional responses to the climate change-related content and critically assess whether the videos effectively encourage thoughts on the topic. Essential to this comprehensive procedure, students assign ratings to the videos, capturing their level of interest and engagement with the presented content. This approach aims to show the different responses of the students, contributing to a comprehensive understanding of the impact and effectiveness of the selected climate change videos.

3.4 Video Popularity

Examining the collective responses from students related to their interest in the watched videos, a comprehensive dataset of 180 responses was collected. Through content-based analysis, we reviewed data to disclose valuable insights. This analytical process allowed us to recognize the high-ranked videos among the 12 options. The video rankings were based on the users' evaluations of their individual levels of interest in the content presented. This approach provides an understanding of the preferences and engagement levels of the students, clarifying the most impactful climate change video in the context of the study.

4. Results

In this section, we explore the details of our analysis regarding YouTube videos on climate change. The first step of our methodology involves an in-depth examination of individual videos focusing on the differences between male and female viewers. The objective is to recognize any gender-based variations in the viewership of each specific video. Table 4 provides detailed insights into the viewership statistics for each video.

Table 4: Video-Specific Watched Records Based on Gender

Videos	Participants	
	Male	**Female**
Video 1	11.82%	3.44%
Video 2	4.30%	11.49%
Video 3	10.75%	5.74%
Video 4	10.75%	6.89%
Video 5	9.67%	8.04%
Video 6	8.60%	5.74%
Video 7	4.30%	13.79%
Video 8	6.45%	10.34%

Videos	Participants	
	Male	**Female**
Video 9	9.67%	9.19%
Video 10	8.60%	9.19%
Video 11	6.45%	8.04%
Video 12	8.60%	8.04%

Following the information presented in Table 4, Figure 2 illustrates the demographic distribution based on gender among participants. The collected data indicates that 51.67% of individuals expressing interest in participating in our questionnaire identified as male, while 48.33% identified as female.

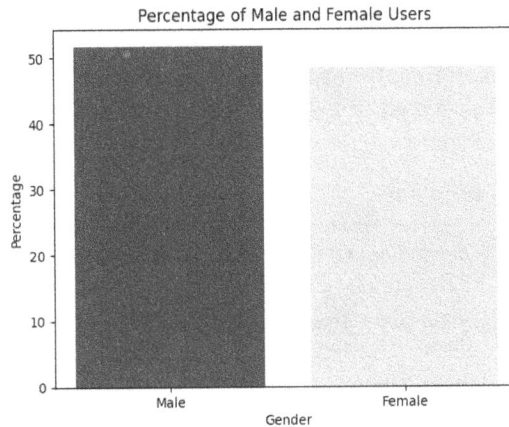

Figure 2: Participants' gender details.

Considering the 180 collected responses, the videos were randomly assigned to students, as detailed in Table 4, presenting the count of views each video received. Subsequently, we computed the average rating for each video by considering the responses to 14 questions posed to students regarding their perception of the watched videos. These questions aimed to measure the level of interest and understandability of the videos. The rating scale ranged from 1 to 5, with "strongly agree" assigned a value of 5, "agree" = 4, "undecided" = 3, "disagree" = 2, and "strongly disagree" = 1. We assigned the questionnaire to 108 students, where, in an ideal world, each video would be evaluated by 27 students. However, we only got responses from 60 students. This means that not every video was watched by the same number of students. The responses collected are summarized in Table 5. The main reason for the differences between the watch counts is the fact that not all the students replied to the questionnaire.

Table 5: Students' rating results

Videos	Watched Count	Average Rating
Video 9	17	3.85
Video 4	16	3.84
Video 7	16	3.84
Video 10	16	3.98
Video 5	16	3.81
Video12	15	3.53
Video 3	15	3.98
Video 8	15	3.33
Video 2	14	3.75
Video 1	14	3.46
Video 11	13	3.86
Video 6	13	3.18

Moreover, the further analysis in this study delved into the reports of different age groups and their interest in the climate change videos they watched. Table 6, presented below, provides a detailed breakdown of the age groups and their average ratings, offering valuable insights into how various demographic factors may influence viewer engagement with climate change content on YouTube.

Table 6: Average rating based on the age group

Age Group	Most Watched Video	Average Rating
0-20	| MOTHER NATURE'S RAGE | Effects of climate change in Kenya's coast region	3.9846
21-30	Climate Change Explained Simply	3.9835
31-40	When The World Gets 1C Hotter | Climate Change: The Facts | BBC Earth	3.8698
41-50	What Greta Thunberg does not understand about climate change | Jordan Peterson	3.8506

Table 7 presents a breakdown of participants' majors and their corresponding average ratings assigned to the climate change videos. This analysis aimed to explore potential variations in viewer engagement based on academic backgrounds and fields of study.

Table 7: Average rating based on the majors

Majors	Most Watched Video	Average Rating
AI and Data Science	What Greta Thunberg does not understand about climate change | Jordan Peterson	3.85
Computer Engineering	When The World Gets 1C Hotter | Climate Change: The Facts | BBC Earth	3.86
Computer Science	What the Hockey Stick missed about climate change	3.53
Development Engineering	Climate Scientist Answers Earth Questions From Twitter | Tech Support | WIRED	3.84
Master in Embedded System	Discussing The Impact Of Climate Change: NASA's New Project | Symone	3.33
Master in IT	| MOTHER NATURE'S RAGE | Effects of climate change in Kenya's coast region	3.98
Information Technology	Climate Change Explained Simply	3.98

Following the examination of user interest in climate change videos, we proceed to assess user preferences regarding the utilization of YouTube as an educational tool within classroom settings. Conducting a real-time analysis, we quantify the average rating derived from students' responses to the incorporation of YouTube, as detailed in Table 8.

Table 8: User rating of YouTube usage as an educational platform

Questions	Average Rating
C1	4.16
C2	4.24
C3	4.16
C4	4.36
C5	4.32
C6	4.37

5. Conclusion

Our analysis presented user engagement with climate change videos on YouTube, revealing detailed dynamics. The study, based on student responses, assessed user interest, preferences, and video ratings. It identified impactful videos, considering gender distribution. Additionally, we explored YouTube's role in education, evaluating its efficacy and user perceptions. The research emphasizes the need for climate change education videos, particularly for youth. Overall, our findings underscore the multifaceted aspects of user interaction with YouTube content, prompting further exploration of its effectiveness in climate change education.

6. Discussion

The findings of this study shed light on the effectiveness of YouTube's educational content in raising awareness about climate change and driving meaningful actions. One significant aspect revealed by this study is the importance of content structure in engaging viewers and fostering interest in climate change topics. Videos that effectively organized their content and presented information in a clear and concise manner tended to elicit more positive reactions from viewers. Additionally, aspects such as visual appeal, narrative coherence, and relevance of the content to viewers' interests emerged as influential factors in enhancing engagement with climate change videos. Furthermore, our research highlights the role of YouTube as a powerful platform for disseminating information and shaping public discourse on climate change. The accessibility and reach of YouTube enable it to serve as an effective medium for delivering educational content to a wide audience. By understanding how climate change topics are presented and received on YouTube, stakeholders can better leverage this platform to promote awareness and education about climate-related issues.

Despite the valuable insights gained from this study, several limitations should be acknowledged. The study's focus on bachelor's and master's students may limit the generalizability of the findings to broader populations. Future research could explore the perceptions and preferences of a more diverse demographic to provide a more comprehensive understanding of user engagement with climate change videos on YouTube. Finally, the study's focus on user perceptions and reactions to climate change videos may overlook other factors influencing engagement, such as algorithmic recommendations, social interactions, and cultural contexts. Future research could explore these factors to provide a more nuanced understanding of user dynamics on YouTube in the context of climate change awareness and education.

Acknowledgement

This work was carried out with from the European Union under Erasmus+ programme, grant agreement No 2022-1-SE01-KA220-HED-000087275, project BTheChange (Be The Change: Innovative Higher Education for Environmental Sustainability)

References

Allgaier, J., 2019. Science and environmental communication on YouTube: strategically distorted communications in online videos on climate change and climate engineering. Frontiers in communication, p.36.

Cody, E.M., Reagan, A.J., Mitchell, L., Dodds, P.S. and Danforth, C.M., 2015. Climate change sentiment on Twitter: An unsolicited public opinion poll. PloS one, 10(8), p.e0136092.

Duran-Becerra, B., Hillyer, G.C., Cosgrove, A. and Basch, C.H., 2020. Climate change on YouTube: A potential platform for youth learning. Health Promotion Perspectives, 10(3), p.282.

Effrosynidis, D., Sylaios, G. and Arampatzis, A., 2022. Exploring climate change on Twitter using seven aspects: Stance, sentiment, aggressiveness, temperature, gender, topics, and disasters. Plos one, 17(9), p.e0274213.

Feygina, I., Myers, T., Placky, B., Sublette, S., Souza, T., Toohey-Morales, J. and Maibach, E., 2020. Localized climate reporting by TV weathercasters enhances public understanding of climate change as a local problem: Evidence from a randomized controlled experiment. Bulletin of the American Meteorological Society, 101(7), pp.E1092-E1100.

Lorenzoni, I., Nicholson-Cole, S. and Whitmarsh, L., 2007. Barriers perceived to engaging with climate change among the UK public and their policy implications. Global environmental change, 17(3-4), pp.445-459.

Meza, X.V., Shapiro, M. and Park, H., 2018. Climate change emotions on YouTube: The case of before the flood. Journal of the Korean Data Analysis Society, 20(4), pp.1697-1708.

Shahbazi, Z. and Byun, Y.C., 2021, December. Twitter Sentiment Analysis Using Natural Language Processing and Machine Learning Techniques. In Proc. KIIT Conf (Vol. 6, pp. 42-44).

Shahbazi, Z. and Byun, Y.C., 2022. NLP-Based Digital Forensic Analysis for Online Social Network Based on System Security. International Journal of Environmental Research and Public Health, 19(12), p.7027.

Shapiro, M.A. and Park, H.W., 2018. Climate change and YouTube: Deliberation potential in post-video discussions. Environmental Communication, 12(1), pp.115-131.

Shapiro, M.A. and Park, H.W., 2015. More than entertainment: YouTube and public responses to the science of global warming and climate change. Social Science Information, 54(1), pp.115-145.

Uldam, J. and Askanius, T., 2013. Online civic cultures? Debating climate change activism on YouTube. International Journal of Communication, 7, p.20.

Wolf, J. and Moser, S.C., 2011. Individual understandings, perceptions, and engagement with climate change: insights from in-depth studies across the world. Wiley Interdisciplinary Reviews: Climate Change, 2(4), pp.547-569.

The Influence of Social Networks on the Purchasing Behavior of Wine Consumers in Portugal

Eulália Silva[1], Paula Oliveira[1], Manuel Sousa Pereira[1] and Álvaro Cairrão[2]
[1]Polytechnic Institute of Viana do Castelo, Portugal
[2]Applied Management Research Unit (UNIAG) Polytechnic Institute of Viana do Castelo, Portugal

eulaliasabino@ipvc.pt
pcristinaoliveira@esce.ipvc.pt
msousa.manuel@gmail.com
acairrao@esce.ipvc.pt

Abstract: The present study was developed to understand the consumer's perception of purchasing wine online, verify whether Social Networks are a good source of information about wine, identify the main sources of information that consumers use to search, and finally assess the importance of Social Networks for SMEs in the wine sector. As a methodological approach, we implemented qualitative and quantitative research, including an in-depth interview with a marketing professional from a company in the wine sector, providing valuable insights into how they manage their brands and the challenges faced by the company in the digital scenario. We also prepared an online questionnaire survey, which investigated the purchasing and consumption behavior of buyers and consumers of Portuguese wines. The conclusions of this study presented significant practical implications for companies in the wine sector in Portugal. Therefore, we also see that these companies will be able to add efficiency to their digital marketing strategies, promoting their products in a more targeted and engaging way. In a complementary way, by recognizing the crucial role of Social Networks, companies will be able to establish a stronger and more authentic digital presence, building solid relationships with consumers.

Keywords: Social networks, Consumer behavior, Wine sector, Social media marketing

1. Introduction

Companies are increasingly using the Internet for commercial activities. With the ability to expand geographic borders by bringing buyers and sellers together, the Internet also allows small companies to compete with industry giants. In fact, the Internet has transformed marketing with its instant yet personalized reach to a global audience.

When analyzing the wine sector in Portugal, the Wine Digital Engagement Index 2019 found that it is a sector with a lot of potential for development in the digital world. Despite the efforts of some producers to keep up with digital trends, there is still a great lack of knowledge on the part of SMEs about how to attract consumers who do not go to traditional stores, but who, instead, research, exchange opinions and buy products online.

Wine has played an important role in society since the earliest times of civilization. It is believed that the first vine was cultivated in the Iberian Peninsula around 2000 years before Christ, by the Tartessians, one of the oldest people on this Peninsula (Instituto da Vinha e do Vinho, 2014).

Consumers are regularly faced with different purchasing decisions, and these decisions are not all made in the same way, some are more complex, require greater effort from the consumer and others are more routine decisions, where the effort required is less (Barber et al., 2009).

In this context, this research aims to demonstrate the importance of Social Networks for the wine consumer, taking as its research question the starting question: "What influence can Social Networks have on the purchasing and consumption behavior of the wine consumer in Portugal?

The general objective is to understand the consumer's perception of purchasing wine online and the specific objectives are: to identify the factors that influence the purchase of wine online; check whether Social Networks are a good source of information and persuasion about wine; identify the main touchpoints that consumers use to research wines; evaluate the importance of Social Networks for an SME in the wine sector.

Based on the objectives outlined in this study, and mentioned previously, the following hypotheses were defined:

H1: Wine buyers/consumers, when choosing a wine brand, are more influenced by wine websites and blogs than by Social Networks;

H2: Social media is not a good source of information about wine;

H3: A friend's recommendation has more influence than Social Networks when purchasing wine;

H4: The Social Networks most used by wine consumers/buyers are Facebook, Instagram and WhatsApp, and the communication strategies with the most impact are stories/reels.

2. Theoretical Framework

2.1 Online Social Networks

Consumers interact with each other and the way in which consumers share information about products, as well as purchasing and consuming those same products, has changed significantly (Skiera, 2010). Social media is one of the most popular activities in today's online world, becoming a massive social phenomenon (Laudon & Traver, 2013). (Recuero et al., 2015) reveal the importance of studying networks when they say that understanding the world through networks has become of great importance as it involves billions of people around the world.

In this context, Social Networks offer great opportunities for all companies, from the smallest and most recent to the oldest and most traditional, to have a presence on Social Networks, as the more connected an organization is on the network, the greater the benefits that can be obtained with it. the use of Web 2.0 tools, especially for small businesses, which use this convenient and low-cost tool for the main purpose of exposure (Gamboa & Gonçalves, 2014).

According to (Kempe et al., 2005) Social Networks are manifestations of relationships and interactions between individuals in each group and play an important role as a means of disseminating information, ideas, and influence. Social Network sites are a type of virtual community (Murray & Weller, 2007). A virtual community consists of a group of people who communicate online. Social Networks are, therefore, a collection of actors (individuals) and their connections. In cyberspace, these networks are complex due to the creation of a new social space, the virtual space (Recuero, 2007).

According to data from the statistics report (Digital, 2023) regarding the adoption of digital media and Social Networks, the Portuguese have become increasingly accustomed to modernization in recent years. According to the same source, Portugal has around 10.26 million inhabitants, of which 8.73 million are Internet users (85.1%) and 8.05 million are active users of Social Networks (78.5% of the population). In this sense, wine consumers increasingly depend on information obtained via the Internet from wine influencers, producers or regular customers sharing their experiences to improve their understanding of wines (Pérez-Rodríguez et al., 2022). Leigon (2011) states that social media platforms encourage wine consumption, allowing users to exchange knowledge and encourage others to try different wines.

2.2 The Importance of Social Media for the Business Development of SMEs

Social media offers a unique method of marketing communication (Eagleman, 2013). By managing user-generated content, companies can predict their customers' purchasing behavior more accurately, increase brand post popularity, attract new customers, raise awareness, increase sales, and build loyalty (Castronovo & Huang, 2012)

The role of social media in business, particularly commerce, has become increasingly significant in recent years. This is evident in the growing number of individuals who use Social Networks to purchase products and/or services and share their experience with other consumers/clients or friends during and after their consumption/use. Therefore, it is no surprise that social media is considered the most important innovative medium (Hunjet et al., 2019). Thus, small family wineries have employed a variety of innovative approaches to remain economically sustainable in the very competitive tourism market (Baggio & Valeri, 2020; Karagiannis & Metaxas, 2020; Valeri & Katsoni, 2021). Examples of this are success in wine tourism and regions and wineries that regularly use "collaborative marketing techniques" (wine trails, wine festivals) to grow (Berghoef & Dodds, 2016).

2.3 Wine Consumer Behavior

The wine sector has adjusted to and is interested in sustainability issues (environmental, social, economic and institutional), and has invested in the development of programs and dissemination of sustainable practices and their dissemination as important marketing tools for the differentiation and acceptance of products. and brands on the market (Sillani et al., 2017).

In recent literature on wines, one of the issues of great interest is knowledge about the behavior of young consumers. This is not only because they represent an important target market, but also because of their ability to create trends and enhance impact on the wine market in the future (Castellini & Samoggia, 2018). This indicates that it is essential to delve deeper into the effect of age on wine consumption decisions, resulting from the influence of biological processes throughout a person's life cycle. However, it is not just age that can be a determining factor in the behavior of young consumers in relation to older ones, as the effects of the period, time or context in which an individual lives can also determine consumption patterns (Rodriguez et al. 2021). In other words, wine tourism, as part of the tourism industry, is information intensive; therefore, it is essential to understand changes in technologies, such as the adoption of social media (Valeri & Baggio, 2020). Social media tools allow companies to reach current and potential customers effectively and budget wisely (Kallmuenzer et al., 2018).

Regarding purchasing wine online, wine is among the most popular alcoholic beverages ordered online (Kohli, 2022). We can see that, although in 2009, it represented only 1% of global sales in the off-trade channel, in 2019, the share increased to 7% (approximately 2 billion bottles). Furthermore, in 2021, online alcohol sales grew 42% compared to the previous year.

According to Wine Intelligence (2021), influencers and social media platforms are gaining relevance in the world of wine, a trend that will certainly increase in the coming years. Since the beginning of the pandemic, the sector's investment in digitalizing business and promoting products through digital channels has been notable. Wine Intelligence states that friends, colleagues and family are the main influencers when choosing labels. This study carried out by the same entity, analyzes countries such as China, the United States and the United Kingdom, which helps to understand the extent to which campaigns with influencers and social media can help strengthen brands and boost sales.

In Portugal, according to Multidados (2023), in the inmarket'22 study, it states that the consumption of wine by the Portuguese increased again as the percentage of consumers who claim to consume wine every day increased by 1.6% and despite the context, with 84.3% of consumers stating that the frequency of consumption will continue in 2023. Combining this data with the increase in purchases through the online channel (90% increase in sales – SAPO, 2021), it is clear the importance of companies in the wine sector having an active marketing strategy that also encompasses digital aspects.

3. Methodology

For a more comprehensive understanding, in this study, triangulation of methods was used as a research strategy. The choice of methodology for this project is based on the use of a qualitative method with the data collection technique – In-Depth Interview – where good practices and recommendations are respected, through an interview guide, explaining the objective of the study to the interviewee. In addition, and in relation to the quantitative method, a Questionnaire Survey was carried out among wine consumers.

3.1 Questionnaire Survey

To achieve the objectives proposed in this investigation, a questionnaire created using the Google Forms tool was developed and implemented, shared on social networks, (Facebook, Instagram and WhatsApp), through the contacts of its authors, to wine consumers and buyers in Portugal, in a convenience sample, from April to June 2023.

In order to achieve a more representative sample, we defined the following as the main research criteria: the characterization of respondents according to gender, age, income and location; the identification of the consumer or buyer; frequency of purchase and the most used social networks, as well as their influence on the choice of wine and purchase decision. When preparing the questionnaire, a 5-point Likert scale was used, ranging from 1 (totally disagree) to 5 (totally agree). The questionnaire is divided into 4 sections: profile of the respondent, purchasing and consumption behavior, people's relationship with social networks and wine and socio-demographic data. The data was statistically analyzed by SPPS, with a pre-test on the questionnaire before sharing. The questionnaire received 131 responses, only 111 of which were correct and complete, as 20 respondents responded that they do not buy or consume wine.

3.2 In-Depth Interview

The purpose of the in-depth (semi-structured) interview was to obtain the perceptions of a specialist in marketing management regarding this topic. Therefore, we interviewed the person responsible for the company (PROVAM, 2023) (a company made up of 10 winegrowers from the Monção and Melgaço Sub-Region) who represent a variety of relevant wine brands on the market. This choice was made after a detailed analysis of the brand's social media and digital performance. Furthermore, the company is immediately available to participate in this investigation.

Contact was established via email with the company, which promptly agreed to participate in the investigation. The interview took place remotely with the company's Marketing Manager, Francisca Danho, via the Zoom platform and followed the defined interview guide. It is worth noting that the interview was recorded, with the consent of PROVAM's marketing manager.

In the transition from interview to writing, we sought to respect, within limits, the specific characteristics of oral transcriptions. However, some specific aspects of the spoken language were corrected, such as word repetition, possible inaccuracies in gender and/or number agreement and redundant repetitions of omitted words. The formal treatment of conversations was also standardized.

There was a concern to write different questions on the subject of study, with an interview guide with 24 questions seeking to obtain information, to answer the research question and hypotheses and in a way to contribute positively to this investigation. The structure allows us to highlight different types of questions, focusing on the profile of the wine consumer in Portugal, the positioning of the brand through Social Networks, digital marketing and communication strategies, the importance of managing Social Networks, frequency of publications, type of content they publish most, the advantages of using Social Networks, the main problems and difficulties in managing Social Networks, strategies for maintaining relationships with customers, how to measure campaign results and customer loyalty through Social Networks .

4. Analysis of Results

4.1 Sample Characterization

Having obtained 111 valid respondents who responded that they buy and/or consume wine, the sample was studied and the results were analyzed. As can be seen, table 2 represents the sociodemographic characterization of the sample. The predominance of females is 66.7% compared to males, 33.3%, and it can be seen that we have a sample of a wine consumer/buyer who is mostly female.

Depending on the age variable, it varies between 19 and 65 years old, since alcohol consumption in Portugal is only permitted for people over 18 years old. Therefore, respondents between 19 and 29 years of age stand out with the highest response percentage, with 31.53%; then respondents between 30 and 39 years of age with 28.82% of the responses, which indicates that the majority of respondents we will deal with are between 19 and 29 years of age.

Regarding the area of residence, the northern region is the region where most of the respondents live (72.1%), followed by the districts of central Portugal (19.8%), south (6.30%) and Islands (1.80%), respectively.

Regarding profession, the highest percentage was found to be wine buyers who are specialists in intellectual and scientific activities (21.4%), followed by consumers who are technicians and with intermediate level professions (18.8%). Soon after, there are respondents who are unemployed (11.6%), workers in personal services, protection and security and salespeople (8.9%), unskilled workers (6.3%) and responses, retired people (5.4%) and the unemployed (1.9%).

Regarding the household's monthly net income, the category of €1001 to €2000 per month presents a greater number of responses (28.8%), followed by the category of those earning less than €760 (25.2%). The lowest percentage focuses on income above €3000 (5.4%). This means that we are dealing with a wine buyer with a monthly net income between €1001 and €2000.

Table 1: Sociodemographic characterization of the sample

Sex	n	%
Masculine	37	33,30%
Feminine	74	66,70%
Others	0	0,00%
Residence zone		
North	80	72,10%

Center	22	19,80%
South	7	6,30%
Islands	2	1,80%
Monthly income		
< 760 euros	28	25,20%
761 euros - 1000 euros	26	23,40%
1001 euros - 2000 euros	32	28,80%
2001 euros - 3000 euros	19	17,10%
> 3000 euros	6	5,40%
Profession		
Unemployed	13	11,60%
Specialists in intellectual and scientific activities	24	21,40%
Intermediate level technicians and professions	21	18,80%
Skilled workers in industry, construction and craftsmen	3	2,70%
Personal, safety and security service workers and salespeople	10	8,90%
Unskilled workers	7	6,30%
Others	34	30,40%

Source: Own preparation

4.2 Analysis and Discussion of the Survey Results

In terms of wine purchasing and consumption behavior, the vast majority (82.9%) of respondents responded that they are wine lovers. Regarding the type of wine that consumers usually buy, red wine (24.7%) and white wine (23%) are the most popular among consumers. Subsequently, Rosé wine (17.9%), sparkling wine (14.5%), Port wine (8.5%) and liqueurs (6.0%) have slightly lower percentages. Still according to the data collected, recommendations from friends are particularly influential when choosing wine. For 33.5% of respondents, friends are the best sources of information about wine brands.

Wine consumption for (36.9%) of respondents is done weekly. Next, respondents prefer to drink wine monthly (26.1%), fortnightly (12.6%) and every day (9.9%). Therefore, according to the sample, the frequency of wine consumption occurs weekly.

4.3 Analysis and Discussion of the Results of the In-Depth Interview

The most used Social Networks are: Instagram and Facebook. According to the manager, Francisca Danho, LinkedIn is on "standby". Instagram and Facebook are the platforms where most content is shared. YouTube will be the next bet with the aim of launching promotional and institutional videos for the new bottles that come with the new label. Twitter, on the other hand, will be something to think about in the long term. PROVAM does not have defined communication and marketing strategies. The marketing manager is responsible for creating content and communicating the company on social media. This company works in partnership with a communications agency to create content for publications.

4.4 Statistical Analysis

To carry out Pearson's correlation analyzes and the Student's t-test, it was necessary to test some assumptions so that the tests were reliable. One of these assumptions is the normal distribution of variable responses. To test it, the Kolmogorov-Smirnov test was used. If it indicates that the variables do not have a normal distribution, it is necessary to resort to the bootstrapping technique that corrects this non-normality of the data and so we can use the tests with confidence in their results (Field, 2009).

The results of the Kolmogorov-Smirnov test indicated that none of the variables investigated presented a normal distribution, as can be seen in Table 2. Therefore, the Pearson correlation and Student's t-test analyzes used the Bootstrap technique to correct non-normality.

Table 2: Kolmogorov-Smirnov test

	The Kolmogorov-Smirnov test		
	Statistic	Degrees of freedom	p-value
Google	0,247	110	< 0,001
Social media	0,243	110	< 0,001
Websites	0,251	110	< 0,001
Youtube	0,168	110	< 0,001
Social Networks Good Sources	0,165	110	< 0,001
Interact with Companies	0,185	110	< 0,001
Social Networks Influence Purchases	0,19	110	< 0,001
Age	0,095	110	0,016

Source: Own preparation

With regard to Pearson correlation analyses, Table 3 presents the correlation coefficients found.

Table 3: Pearson Correlation

Variables		Average	Standard deviation	1	2	3	4	5	6	7
1. Google		3,4	1,23							
2. Social media		3,33	1,27	0,48**						
3. Websites		3,61	1,28	0,31**	0,41**					
4. Youtube		3,03	1,36	0,50**	0,64**	0,53**				
5. Social Networks Good Sources		3,25	1,27	0,14	0,52**	0,32**	0,41**			
6. Interact with Companies		2,92	1,3	0,28**	0,53**	0,28**	0,29**	0,56**		
7. Social Networks Influence Purchases		2,42	1,25	0,16	0,41**	0,25*	0,38**	0,68**	0,56**	
8. Age		36,9	11,6	-0,22**	-0,23**	0,13	-0,19*	-0,16	-0,07	-0,16

Source: Own preparation

Finally, no difference was found between men (M = 2.59; SD = 1.32) and women (M = 3.08; SD = 1.27) in the levels of interaction with companies t(109) = 1 .87 p = 0.063, which suggests that both have similar levels of interaction with companies. These results were confirmed with Bootstrap analyzes 95%CI = -0.027 − 1.00. Graph 27 graphically presents the test results.

4.5 Validation of Hypotheses by triangulation of methods

H1: Wine buyers/consumers, when choosing a wine brand, are more influenced by wine websites and blogs than by Social Networks.

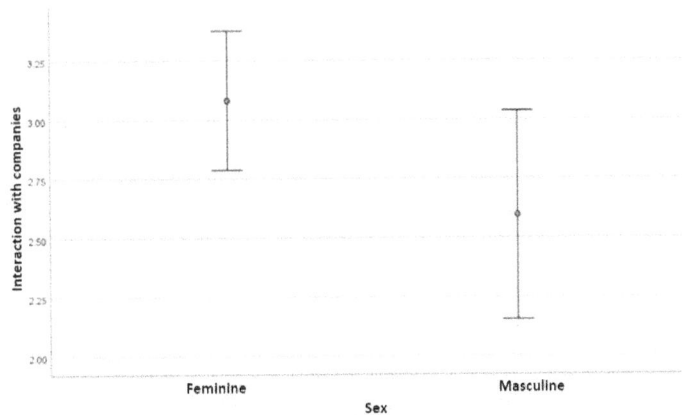

Figure 1: Bar graph and error between gender for levels of interaction with companies. Source: Own preparation

The hypothesis is validated in the quantitative study and not validated in the qualitative study. According to information collected, respondents consider websites and blogs about wine to be a much more interesting source (33%), however, search engines (20%) and Social Networks (20%) are an interesting source. According to the marketing manager, wine buyers/consumers can be influenced, both by wine websites and blogs, and also by Social Networks, when they are directed at the wine consumer.

H2: Social media is not a good source of information about wine

It was partially validated by the qualitative study and validated by the quantitative study, since 41.4% of respondents agree that Social Networks are a good source of information about wine. However, 54% of respondents, after consulting Social Networks, did not decide to purchase wine. According to the PROVAM manager, Social Networks do not always offer the best education like other things on the internet. When looking for information on the Internet, it is necessary to search and consult elsewhere, however, they are a great source of communication for sharing, advice on wines, wine tourism spaces.

H3: A friend's recommendation has more influence than Social Networks on wine purchases

It was validated in the quantitative study, showing that for 79.3% of consumers, a friend's recommendation has much more weight when purchasing wine. Personal recommendations from friends are generally considered more reliable and relevant. Friends who recommend wine often do so based on their own direct experience. This can add weight to the recommendation because the person has had real experience with the product. This hypothesis was also validated by the qualitative study, as the interviewee highlighted that recommendations from friends are much more influential than Social Networks. If a friend, acquaintance or family member recommends something, people will be more aware of the flavor, feeling more confident in purchasing the product.

H4: The Social Networks most used by wine consumers/buyers are Facebook, Instagram and WhatsApp, and the communication strategies with the most impact are stories/reels

This hypothesis was validated with a quantitative study and partially validated by in-depth interviews. Respondents use Social Media a lot. Instagram is the social network with the most followers (28.3%), followed by Facebook (21.5%) and WhatsApp (22.8%). The content formats that respondents most prefer are images (29.4%) and Stories (28.4%). However, content in video format (19.8%) and Reel (17.3%) also attracts respondents. According to the qualitative study, the company has used more images in its publications to show work involving wine tourism, one of its businesses that includes public visits to wineries and vineyards. In addition, they publish award-winning wines, international highlights, celebrations and events they attend. They are posting more images, however, they are currently doing some reels because they noticed that they are getting more engagement.

5. Conclusions

It was found that Social Networks are playing an important role in disseminating information, recommendations and product reviews, as (Pérez-Rodríguez et al., 2022) states, wine consumers increasingly depend on information obtained through Internet, from wine influencers, producers or regular customers, sharing their experiences to improve their understanding of wines.

However, they still do not have a great influence on the purchase of wine, according to the quantitative data collected, only 18% of respondents agree or completely agree that Social Networks can influence the purchase of wine. Quality and price are the most important factors when choosing wine, frequency of consumption is more weekly and supermarkets are distribution channels where the buyer/consumer prefers to buy wine.

Wine websites and blogs proved to be a much more interesting source (33%) compared to Social Networks (20%), search engines (22%) and YouTube (18%), as mentioned (Kallmuenzer et al ., 2018), social media tools allow companies to reach current and potential customers effectively and wisely.

In short, PROVAM still does not recognize the importance of Social Networks, observed by the lack of a clear digital strategy and the prioritization of other areas of the business, however, due to part of its consumers being other companies, they do not perceive the immediate value of Social Networks for the wine sector.

There are several reasons why SMEs in the wine industry may not be able to exploit the potential of Social Media in the most effective way: Lack of knowledge, as some SMEs may not be fully familiar with the benefits and opportunities that Social Media offers. offer, or may not understand how to use them effectively for your business.

From the analysis of the studies carried out, it was found that social networks are very important, however, when making decisions, wine buyers and consumers do not attribute the greatest importance to them, compared to other points of contact. Based on the findings of the qualitative study, we assume that many Portuguese SMEs work with scarce human and financial resources. They don't hire a community manager to manage social networks. The BCG study (2021) states that Portuguese companies are still in an embryonic phase in the digital area, this could probably be one of the reasons: scarcity of resources.

5.1 Limitations and Recommendations

It is considered that the objectives proposed for the study were achieved, however, throughout the investigation there were limitations that are important to mention. One of the limitations of the study was the small number of respondents, corresponding to a relatively small sample and not representative of the universe of online consumers. Another study framework could enable stronger statistical validation of the data collection instrument, as well as a more statistically robust analysis of results.

For future research, a more in-depth qualitative study is suggested, and following the Delphi method, in-depth interviews, or even a focus group, are recommended with a heterogeneous group of experts in the wine field, e.g. : oenologists, marketers, community managers, directors of companies in the sector, professionals responsible for wine associations (for example, Instituto do Vinho e da Vinha, ViniPortugal, Associação de Municípios Portugueses do Vinho, among others), who, due to their vision and professional experience will contribute to a better understanding and provide more knowledge about the influence of digital marketing on wine purchasing and consumption behavior in Portugal.

References

Abecacis, M., Pereira, P., Ferreira, J., Bicacro, E. (2021). The Path to a Bionic Portugal: The digital maturity of Portugal's business fabric. Boston Consulting Group (BCG). In partnership with: Google and Nova School of Business and Economics. https://www.bcg.com/road-to-bionic-portugal

Almeida, C. M., Afonso, C. M., Serra, M., & Antonio, N. (2023). Analysis of Portugal´s Wine Certifying Entities' Social Networks as Communication Channels. In Measuring Consumer Behavior in Hospitality for EKohli, S. (2022). Online Alcohol Sales Booming In The U.S. Through These

Baggio, R., & Valeri, M. (2020). Network science and sustainable performance of family businesses in tourism. Journal of Family Business Journal. https://doi.org/10.1108/JFBM-06-2020-0048

Barber, N., Dodd, T., & Kolyesnikova, N. (2009). Gender differences in information search: implications for retailing. Journal of Consumer Marketing 26 (6), pp. 415-426.

Berghoef, N., & Dodds, R. (2016). Potential for sustainability eco-labeling in Ontario's wine industry. International Journal of Wine Business Research, 23, 298–317. https://doi.org/10.1108/17511061111186488

Castellini, A., & Samoggia, A. (2018). . Millennial consumers' wine consumption and purchasing habits and attitude towards wine innovation. . Wine Economics and Policy.

Castronovo, C., & Huang, L. (2012). Social Media in an Alternative Marketing Communication Model. Journal of Marketing Development & Competitiveness, pp. 117-136.

DataReportal. (2023). Digital 2023. https://datareportal.com

Eagleman, A. N. (2013). Acceptance, motivations, and usage of social media as a marketing communications tool amongst employees of sport national governing bodies. Sport Management Review, 488-497.

Esteves, E. (2010). Statistical Analysis in Food Science. In R.M.S. Cruz (Ed.) Practical Food and Research (pp. 403-446). New York: USA: Nova Science Publishers Inc.

Ferreira, M. F. (2023). Emergence and evolution of e-commerce among Portuguese wine manufacturers: a multiple case study (Doctoral dissertation).

Field, A. (2009). Discovering statistics using IBM SPSS statistics.

Gamboa, A. M., & Gonçalves, H. M. (2014). Customer loyalty through social networks: Lessons from Zara on Facebook. Business Horizons, pp. 709-717.

Hunjet, A., Kozina, G., & Vuković, D. (2019). Consumer of the digital age. Ekonomska misao i praksa, Vol. 28, pp. 639-654.

Kallmuenzer, A., Nikolakis, W., Peters, M., & Zanon, J. (2018). Trade-offs between dimensions of sustainability: Exploratory evidence from family firms in rural tourism regions. Journal of Sustainable Tourism, 26(7), 1204–1221. https://doi.org/10.1080/09669582.2017.1374962

Karagiannis, D., & Metaxas, T. (2020). Sustainable wine tourism development: Case studies from the Greek region of peloponnese. Sustainability, 12, 5223. https://doi.org/10.3390/su12125223

Kempe, D., Kleinberg, J. &., & Tardos, É. (2005). Influential Nodes in a Diffusion Model for Social Networks. Lecture Notes in Computer Science. Lecture Notes in Computer Science, pp. 1127-1138.

Kohli, S. (2022). Online Alcohol Sales Booming In The U.S. Through These Marketplaces. https://futuredrinksexpo.com/en/blog/online-alcohol-salesbooming-in-the-u-s-through-these-marketplaces-419.htm

Laudon, K. C., & Traver, C. G. (2013). E-commerce: business, technology, society (9th ed.). Pearson.

Leigon, B. (2011). Grape/Wine Marketing with new media and return of the boomer. Practical Winery & Vineyard Journal, (Winter)

Marketeer (2023) o consumo de vinho vai manter-se em 2023. https://www.marketeer.sapo.pt

Moya, K. V., & Lucas, M. R. (2021). Portuguese organic wine consumer behavior. Journal of Rural Economics and Sociology, 59, e238888.

Murray, K., & Weller, R. (2007). Social Networking Goes Abroad. International Educato, 56-59.

O'Reilly, T. (2005). What Is Web 2.0 Design Patterns and Business Models for the Next Generation of Software. Obtido de O'Reilly: https://www.oreilly.com/pub/a/web2/archive/what-is-web-20.html

Obermayer, N., Kővári, E., Leinonen, J., Bak, G., & Valeri, M. (2022). How social media practices shape family business performance: the wine industry case study. European Management Journal, 40(3), 360-371.

Pérez-Rodríguez, G., Baptista, J. P., Igrejas, G., Fdez-Riverola, F., & Lourenço, A. (2022). Use Social Media Knowledge for Exploring the Portuguese Wine Industry: Following Talks and Perceptions? Scientific Programming, 2022, e2912770. https://doi.org/10.1155/2022/2912770

PROVAM. (2023). Alvarinho with soul. https://www.provam.com/

Recuero, R. (2007). Typology of Brazilian Social Networks on Fotolog.com. pp. 1-20. Retrieved from https://www.e-compos.org.br/e-compos/article/view/155/156

Recuero, R., Bastos, M., & Zago, G. (2015). Network Analysis for Social Media. Porto Alegre: Sulina.

Rodriguez, M., Rodriguez, M., & Fernandez, V. (2021). Wine consumption preferences among generations X and Y: an analysis of variability. British food journal, 3557 - 3575. doi:DOI: 10.1108/BFJ-12-2020-1156

Sillani, S., Miccoli, A., & Nassivera, F. (2017). Different preferences for wine communication. Wine Economics and Policy, 6(1), 28-39.

Skiera, B. &.-T. (2010). The Impact of New Media on Customer Relationships. Journal of Service Research.

Valeri, M., & Baggio, R. (2020). Social network analysis: Organizational implications in tourism management. International Journal of Organizational Analysis. https://doi.org/10.1108/IJOA-12-2019-1971

Valeri, M., & Baggio, R. (2020a). Social network analysis: Organizational implications in tourism management. International Journal of Organizational Analysis. https://doi. org/10.1108/IJOA-12-2019-1971

Wine intelligence (2021) Does social media impact wine choice? https://www.wineintelligence.com

Customer Engagement in Educational S-Commerce Communities: An Empirical Study

Jiajun Wang and Hok-Yin Lai

Department of Computer Science, Hong Kong Baptist University, China

23439262@life.hkbu.edu.hk
jeanlai@comp.hkbu.edu.hk

Abstract: Many previous scholars have investigated user behavior on social media from multiple perspectives over the last decade. Studies have shown that people today regularly join online communities to find necessary information. Notably, we found that there are a large number of education-related online communities and community members in Hong Kong. In these communities, the majority of posts pertain to interest class enrolment, extracurricular tutorial class enrolment, organizing outdoor activity and parents-child campaign. So, what makes some posts more popular and appealing in this kind of communities? What motivates the interactive behaviour between posters and users? Nevertheless, there are few studies focusing on user behaviors in education-related communities. Therefore, this research aims to examine the impact of post content features in educational online community on customer engagement in online community related to education. Considering the trend of digital transformation in education after Covid-19, we also consider variables such as online vs. offline teaching and the availability of trial classes as potential influencing factors. Consequently, we have incorporated these variables into our research model. The research model employed in this research adopted the S-O-R (stimuli-organism-response) model, utilizing user trust as a mediating variable. This study adopts a quantitative approach and collects data in the form of a questionnaire. The questionnaires will be filled by active participators in education-related online communities on Facebook platform and some parents offline. The questionnaires gathered will be analyzed through PLS-SEM (structural equation modelling) utilizing smartpls. This research can bring value to the evolution of social media platforms. Developers can refine their algorithms for pushing posts based on the findings. In addition, the questionnaire can assist online community managers and users fast-track identification of trustworthy posts. Finally, posters are able to adjust the content of their posts based on the outcome derived from the analysis to improve the quality and attractiveness of their posts.

Keywords: Social media, Online communities, Customer engagement, Recommendation intention, S-O-R Model, PLS-SEM

1. Introduction

In recent years, the normalization of social media usage has indisputably provided users with an abundance of convenient information and news through various platforms. Particularly noteworthy is the increased reliance on the robust information storage and retrieval capabilities of social media platforms, a trend intensified by the sudden outbreak and subsequent resolution of COVID-19. This dependence is exemplified by the active engagement in online virtual communities (Shen et al, 2019). Consequently, to leverage the rapid dissemination and real-time nature of social media, traditional e-commerce is gradually transitioning to social commerce (s-commerce) using virtual communities as a medium to explore new business opportunities. The potential of s-commerce is evidenced by its projected valuation of 84.2 billion USD by 2024, anticipated to contribute 7.8% to the overall U.S. retail e-commerce sales. Despite the promising prospects of s-commerce supported by extensive data and literature, this transformation faces numerous challenges. For instance, certain features of e-commerce platforms, such as detailed product descriptions, personalized consulting services, and sophisticated recommendation systems, are not inherently present in virtual communities. Conversely, virtual communities possess unique charms, including close social relationships among members and real-time user interactions. Identifying the key factors influencing community customers' willingness to engage in s-commerce, and achieving a seamless transition from e-commerce to s-commerce, are critical questions.

Prior research in the realm of s-commerce has primarily focused on brand and shopping communities (Olbrich and Holsing, 2011; Kaur et al, 2020; Xi and Hamari, 2020), with limited studies on education-related online communities. Therefore, this article empirically investigates the factors influencing customer engagement and recommendation in educational s-commerce communities, delving into the current status of s-commerce transformation in the education sector. Educational social commerce communities, primarily revolving around educational information, offer insights into interest activities, tutoring, parenting activities, and children's education topics, as illustrated. A search on Facebook using keywords like "interest classes", "children's courses", and "homework tutoring" reveals the existence of over a hundred related communities with memberships exceeding 50k, as shown in. Moreover, an average of 200 posts per day within these communities indicates a high demand and significant influence on the Facebook platform.

Given that investigating customer intentions and engagement is crucial for the development of social commerce (Liang et al, 2011; Zhang et al, 2014), it is essential to comprehend the factors driving customer engagement.

The impact of environmental factors on consumer behaviors, including website characteristics, platform atmosphere, and interactive experience, has been extensively studied in e-commerce communities (Parboteeah, Valacich, and Wells, 2009). This article explored how post-related features, typically informational quality, poster credibility, and post vividness, influence customer engagement. In general, this article proposes the following questions:

Q1: How do the informational quality, poster credibility, and post vividness impact customer engagement in educational s-commerce communities?

Q2: Whether post trust is used as a mediator variable between post features and customer engagement.

The remainder of the article is organized as follows: Section 2 reviews existing literature around the theoretical background of this study. Section 3 presents the research model and hypotheses based on these theories. Section 4 discusses the methodology of the study, followed by findings and discussion in Section 5. Section 6 concludes the article and propose some limitations of this study.

2. Related Work

2.1 S-O-R Model

The Stimulus-Organism-Response (S-O-R) framework, originally introduced by Mehrabian and Russell (1974) in environmental psychology, suggests that specific environmental elements trigger cognitive and emotional responses in individuals, thereby influencing their behaviors. This model has been widely embraced in various academic fields. For example, Eroglu, Machleit, and Davis (2003) employed the S-O-R framework to investigate interactions, illustrating how atmospheric cues in online shopping websites affect consumers' states, then shaping their buying decisions. Anne Mollen and Hugh Wilson (2009) employed this model to explore the connection between website attributes and customer purchase intention.

Over the past decade, numerous scholars have extended the S-O-R model to study consumer and customer behavior (Islam and Rahman, 2017), affirming its suitability for researching customer behavior.

In a Stimulus-Organism-Response (S-O-R) model, the stimulus (S) is defined as an environmental element that triggers the person, influencing their internal organismic conditions (Eroglu, Machleit, & Davis, 2001). Previous research has identified a diverse range of stimuli in the S-O-R framework, including social support (Zhang et al, 2014), flow (Gao and Bai, 2014), feelings (Vieira, 2013; Kim and Johnson, 2016), and interaction. This research centers on post characteristics that have a notable influence on customers' intentions to engage in educational information communities.

The organism (O) symbolizes a intermediary stage that connect the S and R, facilitating this interaction. This middle state includes customers' emotional well-being, such as mood, emotions, and mindset, in response to environmental cues. Users transform these external stimuli into valuable information to support decision processes. Thus, in this essay, I categorize the intermediary states into post trust.

The response (R) represents customers' approach or avoidance behaviors, as outlined by Sautter, Hyman, and Lukosius (2004). Approach behaviors encompass favorable reactions from community members, such as likes, comments, and shares. Hence, customer engagement is defined as the response (R) for this research.

2.2 Educational S-Commerce Community

Social media encompasses a suite of computer-mediated applications, established on the ideological and technological bedrock of Web 2.0. It empowers individuals to create and disseminate their content, encompassing information, ideas, thoughts, and knowledge, within networks and online communities (Kaplan and Haenlein, 2010). Social commerce communities serve as an innovative virtual platform facilitating interactions and communications between businesses and customers, rooted in various social media platforms. For example, Wang et al. (2020) emphasized the role of social support in boosting consumer engagement within social commerce communities, while Molinillo et al. (2020) identified specific community factors that drive consumer engagement.

While existing research has predominantly concentrated on brand-centric s-commerce communities, conversely, this study focuses on educational s-commerce communities. In these communities, various businesses, including individual vendors jand educational institutions, can showcase their tutoring classes, activities, or other education-related products through posts, with users interacting through the platform. Meanwhile, when purchasing educational products, consumers consider factors like the instructor's reputation and course quality (Ma, Sharif, & Khong, 2022), indicating higher standards for educational services. Consequently, this study delves into customer behavior within these specialized educational communities, given the unique attributes of education-related offerings.

3.   Research Model and Hypothesis

This paper utilizes the Stimulus-Organism-Response (S-O-R) model, initially introduced by Mehrabian and Russell in 1974, as the core framework for assessing the factors that impact customers' inclination to engage and advocate. In this model, three post features argument quality, source credibility and post vividness are as the stimulus (S). Post trust is conceptualized as the organism (O), while customer engagement willingness is designated as the response (R), thereby forming the research model of this study. The research model is depicted in Figure 1.

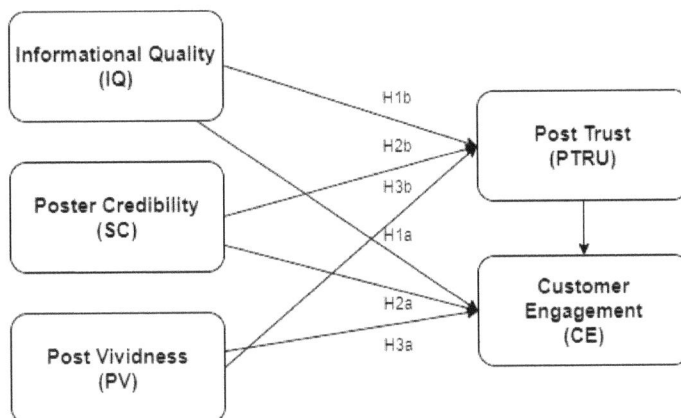

Figure 1: Research Model

3.1   Post Features

Numerous scholarly studies have highlighted that customers' attitudes and behaviors in online communities are influenced by various attributes of posts, such as informational quality, poster credibility and post vividness. Consequently, this paper formulates hypotheses regarding the correlation between these attributes and customer trust.

3.1.1   Influence of informational quality on customer engagement

Petty, Brinol and Priester (2009) defined an argument as a piece of information relevant to assessing the true merits of a position. In this study, the information quality is a comprehensive construct evaluating by the logic, completeness and argument of a post. Lots of previous articles have implies that viewers prefer to believe in the information that is logically presented and well-argued. Meanwhile, Customers heavily rely on informational quality to form attitudes towards messages, especially when uncertain about a blog's credibility. Thus, we hypothesize a link between argument quality and trust in a post.

H1a: Informational quality of posts positively affects customer engagement.

H1b: Informational quality of posts has an indirect impact on customer engagement through post trust.

3.1.2   Influence of poster credibility on customer engagement

Historically, poster credibility has been assessed based on expertise and trustworthiness, indicating the poster's level of knowledge and perceived sincerity, respectively. Pornpitakpan (2004) expanded this concept by adding source likeability as a component. Studies have shown positive associations between poster credibility and factors such as brand community loyalty (Syn and Kim, 2013), health community engagement (McLaughlin, 2016), and advertisement credibility (Morris, Choi, and Ju, 2016). Based on these findings, we propose hypotheses relevant to educational counseling communities.

H2a: Poster credibility of posts positively affects post trust.

H2b: Poster credibility of posts has an indirect impact on customer engagement through post trust.

3.1.3   Influence of post vividness on customer engagement

Vividness refers to how a medium engages individuals' senses, including breadth (the range of senses involved) and depth (the intensity of sensory involvement) (Steuer, Biocca, and Levy, 1995). For instance, video ads are always considered more vivid than image ads and texts ads because they stimulate both visual and auditory senses. Research has demonstrated that vividness captures attention in TV and online ads and boosts click-through rates for banner ads. In the context of brand community posts on Facebook, vivid posts tend to attract more attention than less vivid ones. Therefore, This article proposes the following hypotheses:

H3a: Post vividness positively affects post trust.

H3b: Post vividness has an indirect impact on customer engagement through post trust.

4.   Methodology

In order to obtain data, a questionnaire was designed. The measurement scales used for each constructs were all adapted from previous relevant studies. Based on the survey objects of this paper, all the questionnaires are filled by residents living in Hong Kong. After data collecting, twenty number of questionnaires were excluded because of incompleteness and vague answers. Finally, 314 questionnaires are employed for future analysis.

Table 1 displays the basic information of respondents, such as gender, age, and education level. Most part of respondents fell within the 27-40 age range, constituting approximately 71.34% of the sample, which aligns well with the research theme. Around 50% of the participants held a bachelor's degree.

Table 1: Descriptive analysis

		Frequency	Percentage
Gender	Male	121	38.54%
	Female	193	61.46%
Age range	20~26 years old	8	2.55%
	27~40 years old	224	71.34%
	41~60 years old	76	24.20%
	More than 60 years old	6	1.91%
Education level	Below bachelor	144	45.86%
	Bachelor	144	45.86%
	Master or higher	26	8.28%

Table 2: Direct Effect Testing and Mediating Effect Testing

Hypothesis	Path	Path coefficient(PC)	T	P	Results
H1a	IQ -> CE	0.085	1.396	0.163	Unsupported
H2a	PC -> CE	0.089	1.558	0.119	Unsupported
H3a	PV -> CE	0.138	2.296	0.022	Supported
H1b	IQ -> PTRU -> CE	0.012	1.308	0.191	Unsupported
H2b	PC -> PTRU -> CE	0.003	0.414	0.679	Unsupported
H3b	PV -> PTRU -> CE	0.014	1.319	0.187	Unsupported

5.   Findings and Discussion

We presented the results of the evaluation of the structural model in Table 2, where the path coefficients (PC) were measured and significant paths were indicated with asterisks in the P-value column. The significance tests for all paths were based on the bootstrap resampling procedure. It can be observed that H3a were supported, while H1a, H2a, H1b, H2b and H3b were not supported. Firstly, among the variables developed based on three characteristic attributes of educational information community posts, it was confirmed that only post vividness (PC = 0.138, T = 2.296) significantly influenced customer engagement directly. However, argument quality (PC = 0.085, T = 1.396) and source credibility (PC = 0.089, T = 1.558) did not have a significant impact on customer engagement. Secondly, The indirect path through Post Trust all have very low path coefficient (PC = 0.012, PC = 0.003 and PC = 0.014) and not significant p-value, indicating that this indirect effect is not statistically significant.

6. Conclusion and Limitations

This study offers several theoretical advancements. While many factors influencing customer decision-making have been validated in brand, information sharing and health communities, there has been a scarcity of research in educational s-commerce communities. Drawing from the S-O-R model, this paper introduced three independent variables related to post features to investigate their effects on consumer engagement in community activities. Particularly, the significance of post vividness in influencing consumer engagement was established, enhancing the scholarly understanding within the realm of social commerce. The other relationships, whether direct or mediated, do not reach statistical significance, suggesting that Argument Quality and Source Credibility may not be as important for Customer Engagement as the vividness of the posts in the context studied. This could imply that, for this particular dataset and within the model tested, the clarity, imagery, and emotional appeal conveyed in posts (PV) are more influential on CE than the logical soundness of arguments (IQ) or the perceived trustworthiness of the source (PC).

References

Eroglu, S. A., Machleit, K. A., & Davis, L. M. (2001) "Atmospheric qualities of online retailing: A conceptual model and implications", Journal of Business research, Vol 54, No.2, pp.177-184.

Eroglu, S. A., Machleit, K. A., & Davis, L. M. (2003) "Empirical testing of a model of online store atmospherics and shopper responses", Psychology & marketing, Vol 20, No.2, pp.139-150.

Gao, L., & Bai, X. (2014) "Online consumer behaviour and its relationship to website atmospheric induced flow: Insights into online travel agencies in China", Journal of Retailing and Consumer Services, Vol 21, No.4, pp.653-665.

Islam, J. U., & Rahman, Z. (2017) "The impact of online brand community characteristics on customer engagement: An application of Stimulus-Organism-Response paradigm", Telematics and Informatics, Vol 34, No.4, pp.96-109.

Kaplan, A. M., & Haenlein, M. (2010) "Users of the world, unite! The challenges and opportunities of Social Media", Business horizons, Vol 53, No.1, pp.59-68.

Kaur, H., Paruthi, M., Islam, J., & Hollebeek, L. D. (2020) "The role of brand community identification and reward on consumer brand engagement and brand loyalty in virtual brand communities", Telematics and Informatics, Vol 46, pp.101-321.

Kim, A. J., & Johnson, K. K. (2016) "Power of consumers using social media: Examining the influences of brand-related user-generated content on Facebook" Computers in human behavior, Vol 58, pp.98-108.

Liang, T. P., Ho, Y. T., Li, Y. W., & Turban, E. (2011) "What drives social commerce: The role of social support and relationship quality", International journal of electronic commerce, pp. 69-90.

McLaughlin, C. (2016) "Source credibility and Consumers' responses to marketer involvement in Facebook brand communities: What causes consumers to engage?", Journal of Interactive Advertising, Vol 16, No.2, pp.101-116.

Ma, L., Sharif, S. P., & Khong, K. W. (2022) "What factors drive the purchase of paid online courses? A systematic literature review", Journal of Marketing for Higher Education, pp.1-24.

Mehrabian, A., & Russell, J. A. (1974) "An approach to environmental psychology", the MIT Press.

Molinillo, S., Anaya-Sánchez, R., & Liebana-Cabanillas, F. (2020) "Analyzing the effect of social support and community factors on customer engagement and its impact on loyalty behaviors toward social commerce websites", Computers in Human Behavior, Vol 108, pp.105-980.

Mollen, A., & Wilson, H. (2010) "Engagement, telepresence and interactivity in online consumer experience: Reconciling scholastic and managerial perspectives", Journal of business research, Vol 63, No.9-10, pp.919-925.

Morris, J. D., Choi, Y., & Ju, I. (2016) "Are social marketing and advertising communications (SMACs) meaningful?: A survey of Facebook user emotional responses, source credibility, personal relevance, and perceived intrusiveness", Journal of Current Issues & Research in Advertising, Vol 37, No.2, pp.165-182.

Olbrich, R., & Holsing, C. (2011) "Modeling consumer purchasing behavior in social shopping communities with clickstream data", International Journal of Electronic Commerce, pp.15-40.

Parboteeah, D. V., Valacich, J. S., & Wells, J. D. (2009) "The influence of website characteristics on a consumer's urge to buy impulsively. Information systems research", Vol 20, No. 1, pp.60-78.

Petty, R. E., Brinol, P., & Priester, J. R. (2009) "Mass media attitude change: Implications of the elaboration likelihood model of persuasion", In Media effects, pp. 141-180.

Pornpitakpan, C. (2004) "The effect of celebrity endorsers' perceived credibility on product purchase intention: The case of Singaporeans", Journal of international consumer marketing, Vol 16, No.2, pp.55-74.

Sautter, P., Hyman, M. R., & Lukosius, V. (2004) "E-tail atmospherics: A critique of the literature and model extension", J. Electron. Commer. Res., Vol 5, No.1, pp.14-24.

Shen, X. L., Li, Y. J., Sun, Y., Chen, Z., & Wang, F. (2019) "Understanding the role of technology attractiveness in promoting social commerce engagement: Moderating effect of personal interest", Information & Management, Vol 56, No.2, pp.294-305.

264

Proceedings of the 11th European Conference on Social Media , ECSM 2024

Steuer, J., Biocca, F., & Levy, M. R. (1995) "Defining virtual reality: Dimensions determining telepresence", Communication in the age of virtual reality, Vol 33, pp.37-39.

Syn, S. Y., & Kim, S. U. (2013) "The impact of source credibility on young adults' Health information activities on facebook: Preliminary findings", Proceedings of the American Society for Information Science and Technology, Vol 50, No.1, pp.1-4.

Vieira, V. A. (2013) "Stimuli–organism-response framework: A meta-analytic review in the store environment", Journal of Business research, Vol 66, No.9, pp.1420-1426.

Wang, Y., Wang, J., Yao, T., Li, M., & Wang, X. (2020) "How does social support promote consumers' engagement in the social commerce community? The mediating effect of consumer involvement", Information Processing & Management, Vol 57, No.5, pp.102-272.

Xi, N., & Hamari, J. (2020) "Does gamification affect brand engagement and equity? A study in online brand communities", Journal of Business Research, Vol 109, pp.449-460.

Zhang, H., Lu, Y., Gupta, S., & Zhao, L. (2014) "What motivates customers to participate in social commerce? The impact of technological environments and virtual customer experiences", Information & Management, Vol 51, No.8, pp.1017-1030.

Zhang, H., Lu, Y., Gupta, S., & Zhao, L. (2014) "What motivates customers to participate in social commerce? The impact of technological environments and virtual customer experiences", Information & Management, Vol 51, No.8, pp.1017-1030.

Privacy and Personal Information Protection by Social Media Companies in an AI era

Murdoch Watney

University of Johannesburg, South Africa

mwatney@uj.ac.za

Abstract: Social media platforms have become vast and powerful tools for connecting, communicating, sharing content, conducting business, and disseminating news and information. The history and evolution of social media illustrates not only the digital society's ever-growing dependence on social media, but also the downside to this reliance, namely the challenges of protecting a social media user's privacy and personal information. As technological advancement such as artificial intelligence (AI) grow and impacts on the way data, not only personal but also product and service data, is collected, the spotlight is increasingly focusing on the difficulties in privacy and data protection in an AI-era. The discussion focusses on the misconduct by social media companies in respect of privacy and personal information and the lessons learnt from the way in which social media companies have dealt with social media users' information. Since self-regulation by a social media company does not provide adequate safeguards that privacy and personal information will be protected, limitations to the collection, use, access, and storage of personal information must be imposed by means of legislation. To ensure compliance, non-compliance must be linked to a penalty and enforced by a government. Privacy and data protection regulations were formulated in a pre-AI era, and at that stage, the implications of the rapid evolution of AI on privacy and data protection were not foreseen. To ensure digital trust in an AI era, the legal consequences of misconduct of social media companies must be explored. Social media users must have control of their own data and social media companies must be clear about the kind of data a company will collect on its users, and for what purposes. The lessons learnt from past misconduct is also indicative of whether personal data protection legislation is flexible enough to provide for AI or whether specific legislation must be implemented as society enters the AI era. As the Fourth Industrial Revolution takes shape and AI gains prominence, the data legal landscape is evolving with compliance and enforcement being key to protecting privacy and data, addressing legal uncertainty, and ensuring trust.

Keywords: Social media, Social media privacy and personal data protection, Data protection legislation, Legal consequences of social media companies' misconduct in respect of privacy and personal data protection, Impact of AI on social media privacy and personal information protection

1. Introduction

Billions of users populate major social networks including Facebook, Instagram, TikTok, Snapchat, YouTube, LinkedIn, and dating apps like Grindr and Tinder. The discussion focuses on the cybersecurity and privacy lessons learnt from social media companies' misconduct in respect of privacy and personal data protection and the relevance of these lessons in an AI era.

Social media refers to websites or applications that support content sharing, user interaction and the exchange of messages within a collaborative framework. Key to social media is sharable content and social interaction. While many platforms support uploading content, social media enables greater engagement and collaboration between users (Streets, 2023). The violation of privacy and personal data protection is a cyberthreat that must be mitigated by means of cybersecurity. Cybersecurity is the protection of internet-connected systems such as hardware, software, and data from cyberthreats.

The major social media platforms are Instagram, Facebook, WhatsApp, TikTok, Twitter, LinkedIn, Pinterest, YouTube, and Snapchat, with Facebook being the largest social media platform. As of July 2023, there were 5,19 billion internet users worldwide and of these 4,88 billion were social media users (Rivera, 2023). Facebook's monthly active users (MAU) in April 2023 totalled 2,989 billion making it the most used social media platform in the world with YouTube coming at a close second with 2,5 billion MAU. Meanwhile, WhatsApp and Instagram landed third at 2 billion MAU (Rivera, 2023). Although the extraordinary growth of social media is welcomed, it has given platforms exceptional access and influence into the lives of users. An immense amount of data is created on these platforms with the consequence that social media companies are able to harvest sensitive data about individuals' activities, interests, personal characteristics, political views, purchasing habits, and online behaviour. Personal data held by social media platforms is also vulnerable to being accessed and misused by third parties, including law enforcement agencies (Electronic Privacy Information Centre, 2024). The discussion focuses on the conduct of social media companies and not on a data breach by a third party.

The history and evolution of social media as discussed at paragraph 2 hereafter lays the groundwork in explaining why privacy and personal data protection within the social media digital environment has become contentious and will continue to be so as AI advances and impacts on all industries. At paragraph 3 the relevance of protecting privacy and personal data by means of laws are explained. The lessons learnt from the misconduct by social media companies in respect of privacy and personal information protection are explored at paragraph 4. In 2023, AI truly entered our daily lives. At paragraph 5 the impact of AI on social media is discussed by identifying possible risks of AI use by social media companies and whether specific AI legislation should be implemented.

2. Overview of the History and Evolution of Social Media in an Electronic Medium

Lile (2023) opines that the origin of social media remains under debate. The discussion focuses on social media within an electronic medium and within this context it could be argued that social media was invented when the first social networking website, Six Degrees, was launched in 1997. The Six Degrees founder, Andrew Weinreich, is known as the father of social networking (Lile, 2023). Weinreich named the first website for social media after the "six degrees of separation" theory, which proposes that everyone in the world is connected to everyone else by no more than six degrees of separation. Although Six Degrees did not last long as its own social networking site and expired in 2001, the idea of an inter-active, inter-connective and collaborative platform set the stage for social media's rapid evolution to come.

Social media began as a desktop or laptop experience but due to technological advancement, such as the expansion of cellular services, social media moved to mobile phones and tablets. The expansion of the capabilities of cellular phones turned it into "smartphones"; and soon high-speed wireless internet became more readily available in homes, businesses, and public spaces. With the advent of social media apps that could run on smartphones, end users could take their communities with them wherever they went. Social media evolved from connecting friends to businesses that took advantage of this new consumer mobility by serving their customers new, simpler methods of interacting by means of social media — and therefore new ways of buying goods and services.

Facebook (now Meta) began to place advertisements on its platform as early as 2006. Twitter (now X) enabled ads in 2010. LinkedIn, Instagram, Pinterest, Snapchat, and TikTok all have attempted to monetize their services through various forms of sponsored advertising. In addition to placing ads on social media platforms, companies discovered the potential utility of cultivating an active, engaged social media presence (Lile, 2023). Whereas social media advertising must be paid for, the act of creating and sharing informative or entertaining content on Meta, Instagram, and other platforms is an attempt by brands to grow an audience organically, in other words, without paying for it directly.

The evolution also shows today's world runs on personalization. It has permeated everyday life, from grocery shopping to reading the news (Mahanakrishnan, 2023). Businesses use every single piece of information they can find about their users to deliver seamless, intuitive solutions. To provide relevant products, services, and information to the users, personal data is stored and processed at multiple levels. Initially social media users found the personalised service convenient, but it soon became apparent that without laws in place that the personal information may be misused, and this resulted in users' mistrust in social media as was seen with the 2018 Cambridge Analytica scandal. At paragraph 4 social media companies' misconduct is discussed.

Social media revolves around information and therefore, the phrase 'data is the new oil' explains the relevance of data (Mahanakrishnan, 2023). This phrase is even more apt now with the advancement and expansion of AI. Data is the lifeblood of AI development. Without data, the algorithms and models that power AI would be unable to learn from past experiences. AI, at its core, leverages machine learning algorithms to process data, facilitate autonomous decision-making, and adapt to changes without explicit human instruction. Technology has pervaded almost every industry, from healthcare to fashion, finance to agriculture, and beyond. As AI technology continues to expand across these industries, it creates a labyrinth of privacy and data protection concerns, thereby challenging traditional norms of personal data protection (Sher and Benchloauch, 2023). Social media users' privacy and personal information must be protected by means of laws and the relevance of protection by means of laws will be explained hereafter at paragraph 3.

3. Understanding the Legal Relevance of Social Media Privacy and Data Protection Regulation

3.1 Difference Between Privacy and Data Protection

It is important to understand the difference between privacy and personal data protection. Digwatch (2023) explains that privacy and data protection are two interconnected internet governance issues. Privacy must be scrutinised within the context of personal data protection. Privacy is a fundamental human right and data protection law is the legal mechanism that guards the right to privacy. Privacy is usually defined as the right of any citizen to control their own personal information and to decide whether to disclose information or not. Personal data is any information that can be used to, directly or indirectly, identify a human. Personal data usually comprises name, gender, email address, location information, IP addresses, web cookie information, and biometric data.

3.2 United Nations' Recognition of Digital Privacy

The right to privacy is not only recognised in the Universal Declaration of Human Rights but also in the International Covenant on Civil and Political Rights (ICCPR), and in many other international and regional human rights conventions.

As discussed at paragraph 2, social media has evolved since 1997 and will continue to evolve as technology advances. Technological advancements impact on privacy and data protection as huge amounts of data and not only personal data, is collected, accessed, and stored electronically. The appointment of the first United Nations (UN) Special Rapporteur on the Right to Privacy in the Digital Age in July 2015 is a clear indication that the UN considers privacy important as a global digital policy. The UN recognises the necessity to address privacy rights issues on national and global levels.

3.3 EU and Global Impact of European Union (EU) GDPR

The EU has taken the lead in protecting privacy and personal data and keeping abreast of technological changes. The General Data Protection Regulation (GDPR) was passed in 2016 after the EU decided to update its existing set of data protection laws that were created in 1998. A 160-page document of 99 articles of law was released. As of May 2018, it is mandated that all relevant organizations be compliant with these laws. The GDPR ensures that all personal data is collected by means of a secure and legal process, with proper consent from the users. It places more power at the user's end and extra responsibility at the business end and this approach enhances the user's digital trust. The GDPR is considered the toughest in the world as far as data privacy, collection, and protection of personal information are concerned (Mahanakrishan, 2023; Wolford, 2023).

What makes the EU GDPR relevant on a global level is that the GDPR – although not issued by the UN – has set an universal standard for personal data protection and many countries have implemented personal data processing protection legislation similar to the GDPR. In 2023, 18 countries outside of the EU has GDPR-like data protection laws (Zafar, 2023). The South African data protection legislation, Protection of Personal Information Act 4 of 2013 (POPIA) which came into operation in July 2022, is based on the GDPR albeit with some differences.

GDPR, which focuses on data security and data privacy, applies to all people residing in EU member states. Although the United Kingdom (UK) departed from the EU as of January 2021, the GDPR was enacted before its withdrawal and is therefore considered a valid UK law. However, the UK will have a domestic data protection shift in 2024. The Data Protection (Fundamental Rights and Freedoms) (Amendment) Regulations (SI) (2023) will amend the UK data protection legislation to refer to rights derived from UK law, rather than retained EU law rights. Provided it is approved by parliament, the SI will come into force at the start of 2024.

All businesses that operate within the EU must be GDPR-compliant. Any company that does not primarily operate in the EU, but still has a part of its user base in the EU needs to comply with this set of laws as well. This means that a South African business will have to comply with the GDPR.

An overview of the provisions of the GDPR is relevant to all countries that have business relations with residents of the EU member countries. The GDPR provides that processing of personal data of a data subject refers to data collection, data storage, data sharing, organizing, analysing, structuring, and deleting. The processing must be done in accordance with seven protection and accountability principles. A data subject is the person whose data is being processed. They are the 'users' — consumers or visitors to a product or a website. A data subject must give consent before any of their personal data is collected or processed. Certain prerequisites must be complied with for the consent requirement to be compliant with the GDPR, such as using clear, plain language and explaining how data is going to be used, why and by whom. Users also have the right to revoke this consent at any time. The data controller is a person, organization, or authority that determines the specifics of data processing. This includes what data is to be collected, who the data subjects are, and how it will be used. The controller also decides how this can be achieved. This is usually a business; for example, a retail chain that wants to provide targeted ads to shoppers. The data controller works alone or with other controllers. The data processer is the third party who does the actual processing based on the input provided by the controller.

Compliance is ensured by means of accountability. Both controllers and processors are liable to fines if they fall short of GDPR standards. At paragraph 5 the GDPR will be compared to the EU AI Act.

4. Lessons Learnt From Misconduct by Social Media Companies

The discussion hereafter shows that the misconduct by social media companies have had legal consequences and the legal consequences are also relevant in respect of the impact of AI on social media discussed at paragraph 5.

- Self-regulation of privacy and personal information does not provide adequate protection

In 2018, Facebook acknowledged that it had allowed Cambridge Analytica, a political data mining firm, to access personal information of 87 million Facebook users without the consent of the users. The Cambridge Analytica had far reaching consequences (Harbath and Fernekes, 2023). It focused the attention on various issues, such as the importance of digital trust in the use of AI, the role of social media companies in respect of allowing third party access to information without the consent of the users, the ineffectiveness of self-regulation by social media companies and the role of political adverts.

- Resources: ensuring social media compliance with data protection regulations require resources

In 2020 Germany complained that the Ireland Data Protection Board (DPB) was slow to impose heavy fines on social media companies for non-compliance with the GDPR (Kolbie, 2020). Meta and Google have their European headquarters in Ireland and in terms of the "one stop shop" model, the Ireland DPB is tasked with the investigation into misuse. Ireland DPB has shown a commitment in enforcing compliance of the provisions of the GDPR by imposing heavy fines for non-compliance. In May 2023, the Irish Data Protection Commission (DPC) imposed the largest ever fine of €1,2 billion on Meta, (formerly known as Facebook) the owner of social media platforms such as Instagram and WhatsApp. The fine was issued for the transfer of personal data of European users to the United States (US) without adequate protection. Meta indicated that they plan to appeal the decision (Wessing et al, 2023). Of the top 20 GDPR fines recorded, seven were imposed on Meta or Meta-owned companies. For example, in September 2022, the Data Protection Committee (DPC) levied a fine of €405 million on the company for violating the terms of processing the data of child users on Instagram. Instagram allowed teenagers aged 13-17 to create business accounts on the platform, which made their contact information, such as phone numbers and email addresses, publicly available.

In 2020 Kobie (2020) identified lack of resources such as adequate staff and funding as a key issue in the delay of Ireland DPB for finalising data security and privacy investigations. In 2023, Zafar (2023) reiterated that that the EU's executive arm is severely stretched for resources, funds, expertise, and time. He surmises that this is a huge problem, especially in circumstances in which the EU has to defend its decisions when companies inevitably litigate their penalisation.

The South African Office of Information Regulator (IR) has been criticised for taking a long time in finalising data breaches and it has been alleged that this can be contributed to lack of resources, such as funding, and knowledgeable investigators (Mzekandaba, 2023). If the EU is experiencing resource issues, how much bigger will the issue be in a developing country such as South Africa. A further concern is that if the investigations into personal information misuse by a social media company pose challenges, then the protection of data in the AI era will be even more burdensome.

- Transfer of information between countries: social media companies must ensure adequate protection of social media user's personal information in the transfer of information

The transfer of personal data between countries has been a contentious issue. It must be regulated to provide safeguards for the use, access and storage of personal information. In 2023, the EU and the UK adopted adequacy decisions in relation to data transfers to the United States (US) where importing organisations are signed up to the EU-US Data Privacy Framework (DPF) and UK Data Bridge. US companies will be able to join the EU-US DPF by committing to comply with a detailed set of privacy obligations, for instance the requirement to delete personal data when it is no longer necessary for the purpose for which it was collected, and to ensure continuity of protection when personal data is shared with third parties (European Commission, 2023). Wessing et al (2023) opine that the transfer of personal data between the EU and US may remain contentious in 2024 and that the DPF may be challenged in the European Court of Justice (Wessing et al, 2023).

- Social media companies use of behavioural advertising

Behavioral advertising is a technique used by online advertisers to present targeted ads to consumers by collecting information about their browsing behavior.

In 2023, the European Data Protection Board (2023) issued an instruction to the data regulator of Ireland to impose a permanent ban on Meta for the processing of personal information for behavioural advertising without specific consent from users. Under GDPR, social media users in the EU must give specific consent before they are presented with personalised advertisements.

- Social media companies must provide assurance that sensitive social media users' information will not be accessed by a third party

At the end of 2023 social media lawmakers in the US, EU and Canada have escalated efforts to restrict access to TikTok, the massively popular short-form video app that is owned by the Chinese company, ByteDance, citing security threats. Lawmakers and regulators in the West have increasingly expressed concern that TikTok and its parent company, ByteDance, may put sensitive user data, such as location information, into the hands of the Chinese government. They have pointed to laws that allow the Chinese government to secretly demand data from Chinese companies and citizens for intelligence-gathering operations (Porter, 2023). The 2018 Cambridge Analytica illustrated the importance of ensuring digital trust in social media.

5. AI and Social Media

5.1 Risks of Social Media Companies Usage of AI Technology

Social media companies are already using generative AI technology. Tshabalala (2023) indicates that AI is changing the social media landscape in the following ways:

- The use of content curation: Social media platforms, such as Facebook and Instagram use AI algorithms to curate content that is most relevant to their users. The algorithms consider factors, such as engagement, behaviour, and interests, to deliver personalised content to users. This has led to an increase in engagement and a more personalised social media experience for users.
- Personalisation: AI algorithms can analyse user data, behaviour, and interests to deliver personalised content, product recommendations, and advertisements.
- Chatbots usage: Chatbots can automate customer service, answer frequently asked questions, and provide real-time support to customers.
- Predictive Analytics: Predictive analytics can analyse social media user behaviour and provide insights into preferences and behaviour. This information can be used to create targeted marketing campaigns, improve customer service, and optimise social media content.

One of the most prominent risks associated with AI in social media is privacy. AI algorithms can analyse vast amounts of user data to create detailed profiles, track user behaviour, and predict their preferences. AI's privacy dilemma rests on a handful of key issues. Firstly, the technology's insatiable appetite for extensive personal data to feed its machine-learning algorithms has raised serious concerns about data storage, usage, and access. Moreover, AI's remarkable capacity to analyse data and make complex analyses amplifies privacy concerns. The technology's potential to infer sensitive information, such as a person's location, preferences, and habits, poses risks of unauthorized data dissemination (Sher and Benchloauch, 2023).

5.2 Regulating AI Technology

Self-regulation in the development and use of AI may not be successful and AI may need to be regulated.

At the end of 2023 the European Commission reached a political agreement in respect of the Artificial Intelligence Act (Wessing et al, 2023). The EU is the first body globally to enforce binding rules on AI, and the EU hopes this will help it become the world's go-to tech regulator (Heikklilä, 2023). By becoming the first to formalise rules around AI, the EU retains its first-mover advantage. Much like the GDPR, the AI Act could become a global standard (see paragraph 2). Companies elsewhere that want to do business in the world's second-largest economy will have to comply with the law (Heikklilä, 2023).

A characteristic feature of the AI Act is its so-called "risk-based" approach, which has also become known as the pyramid structure of the AI Act. AI systems will be classified according to the degree of risk they pose to the safety of individuals or fundamental rights (Knibbeler and Zadeh; 2023). Legislators agreed on the unacceptable risk category, which means systems that will be banned. The systems falling under that classification include those that manipulate human behaviour affecting free will, social scoring, and "certain elements of predictive policing" (Heikklilä, 2023). Emotion-recognition technology in the workplace and school systems will also be prohibited (Heikklilä, 2023). Remote biometric identification in public will be banned with specific exemptions for law enforcement, such as preventing human trafficking, fighting terrorism or finding a missing person.

The AI Act provides for 6 principles that AI systems should follow, namely (Pinto, 2023):

- Human agency and oversight;
- Technical robustness and safety;
- Privacy and data governance and for purposes of our discussion, AI system providers and developers should be designing AI systems with data privacy and data protection in mind. The datasets used to train AI systems should be properly governed;
- Transparency: AI systems should be transparent. AI providers should provide clear information about the system's capabilities and limitations, as well as the data sources used to train it;
- Diversity, non-discrimination, and fairness; and
- Social and environmental well-being.

The regulation imposes legally binding rules requiring tech companies to notify people when they are interacting with a chatbot, or with biometric categorization or emotion recognition systems. It will also require them to label deepfakes and AI-generated content, and design systems in such a way that AI-generated media can be detected. The Act will also require all organizations that offer essential services, such as insurance and banking, to conduct an impact assessment on how using AI systems will affect people's fundamental rights. The AI Act will set up a new European AI Office to coordinate compliance, implementation, and enforcement.

It should be noted that the AI Act differs from the GDPR (Knibbeler and Zadeh, 2023). The AI Act applies to providers, users, importers, and distributors of AI systems in the EU market, regardless of their location. On the other hand, the GDPR applies to controllers and processors processing personal data in the EU or offering goods/services to EU data subjects. The AI Act focuses on AI as a product, and even though the AI Act seeks to implement a "human-centric approach", the AI Act regulates AI rather through the concept of product regulation (Knibbeler and Zadeh, 2023). The GDPR plays a dominant role in the processing of personal information, whereas the protection of product or service data may be regulated by other legislation such as the AI Act or the Data Act of 2023 (Wessing, 2023). For example, developing a large language model such as ChatGPT requires the gathering of vast bodies of text through a process called web scraping. These datasets ingest details scraped from open online sources such as social media profiles. The information may be in the public domain but the gathering must still comply with personal data protection such as the GDPR (McLellan, 2023).

Other countries may consider AI legislation in 2024. The US has been discussing such an Act (Ryan-Mosley et al, 2024). The UK has indicated that it is not considering AI regulation at present. China has had a piecemeal approach to AI regulation by releasing individual pieces of legislation every time a new AI product became prominent, for example one set of legislation for deepfake and one for generative AI. China did indicate in 2023 that an AI law was on its agenda. The African Union is working on an AI strategy and likewise African countries such as Rwanda, Nigeria and South Africa are also working on an AI strategy (Ryan-Mosley et al, 2024). The South African Information Regulator could issue a code of conduct in respect of the use of AI for personal information processing in terms of POPIA (De Wet and Fourie, 2023).

6. Conclusion

As society moves forward, it must ensure that the pursuit of technological advancement does not come at the cost of privacy and personal data protection. Sher and Benchloauch (2023) opine that the dialogue on the impact of AI on data privacy is ongoing and complex, necessitating sustained engagement from policymakers, technology developers, and the public to ensure a firm commitment to safeguarding the fundamental rights of individuals. Technological development must be embraced, but AI development cannot go unchecked, and in this regard, the EU AI Act is welcomed. Compliance and enforcement will be key in ensuring digital trust and safeguarding the protection of privacy and personal information by social media companies in an AI era, but this will not be an easy task for governments especially if the relevant resources are not available.

References

Data Protection Amendment Regulations. (2023); [online] https://www.gov.uk/government/publications/the-data-protection-fundamental-rights-and-freedoms-amendment-regulations-2023.

De Wet, PR. and Fourie, J. (2023) "South Africa: AI and data privacy regulations – the complexities of AI technologies and processing personal information", [online], https://vdt.co.za/popia/south-africa-ai-and-data-privacy-regulations-the-complexities-of-ai-technologies-and-processingpersonal-information/.

Digwatch (2023) "Privacy and data protection"; [online]; https://dig.watch/topics/privacy-and-data-protection.

European Commission. (2023) "Data protection: European Commission adopts new adequacy decision for safe and trusted EU-US data flows"; [online]; https://ec.europa.eu/commission/presscorner/detail/en/ip_23_3721.

European Data Protection Board (2023); [online]; https://edpb.europa.eu/news/news/2023/edpb-publishes-urgent-binding-decision-regarding-meta_en.

Electronic Privacy Information Center. (2024) "Social Media Privacy"; [online]; https://epic.org/issues/consumer-privacy/social-media-privacy/.

Harbath, K., and Fernekes, C. (2023) "History of the Cambridge Analytica Controversy"; [online]; https://bipartisanpolicy.org/blog/cambridge-analytica-controversy/.

Heikklilä M. (2023) "Five things you need to know about the EU's new AI Act"; [online]; https://www.technologyreview.com/2023/12/11/1084942/five-things-you-need-to-know-about-the-eus-new-ai-act/.

Knibbeler, D. and Zadeh, S. (2023) "International: The interplay between the AI Act and the GDPR"; [online]; https://www.dataguidance.com/opinion/international-interplay-between-ai-act-and-gdpr.

Kobie (2020) "Germany says GDPR could collapse as Ireland dallies on big fines"; [online]; https://www.wired.co.uk/article/gdpr-fines-google-facebook.

Lile, S. (2023) "Complete history of social media"; [online]; https://smallbiztrends.com/2023/08/history-of-social-media.html.

Mahanakrishnan, R. (2023) "What is the GDPR and why is it important?" [online]; https://www.spiceworks.com/it-security/security-general/articles/what-is-gdpr/.

McLellan, L. (2023) "What does artificial intelligence mean for data privacy"; [online]; https://www.omfif.org/2023/08/what-does-artificial-intelligence-mean-for-data-privacy/.

Mzekandaba, S. (2023) "Information watchdog sees data breaches notifications double", [online], https://www.itweb.co.za/content/j5alrMQAJOQMpYQk.

Pinto, T. (2023) "AI principles"; [online]; https://artificialintelligenceact.com/ai-principles/.

Porter, J. (2023) "Tiktok ban: all the news on attempts to ban the video platform"; [online]; https://www.theverge.com/23651507/tiktok-ban-us-news.

Rivera, M. (2023) "30 Social Media Statistics Marketers and Creators Need to Know for 2024"; [online]; https://www.clearvoice.com/resources/social-media-statistics/.

Ryan-Mosley et al. (2024) "What's next for AI regulation in 2024?"; [online]; https://www.technologyreview.com/2024/01/05/1086203/whats-next-ai-regulation-2024/.

Sher, G., and Benchloauch, A. (2023) "The privacy paradox with AI", [online], https://www.reuters.com/legal/legalindustry/privacy-paradox-with-ai-2023-10-31/.

Streets, M. (2023) "The history and evolution of social media explained"; [online]; https://www.techtarget.com/whatis/feature/The-history-and-evolution-of-social-media-explained.

Tshabalala, A. (2023) "The impact of AI on the future of social media"; [online}; https://www.linkedin.com/pulse/revolutionising-social-media-impact-ai-future-adelaide.

Wessing, T. et al. (2023) "Where will the data flow in 2024"; [online]; https://www.lexology.com/library/detail.aspx?g=c24195a9-20d6-4a1c-8226-bcfc168431c6.

Wolford, B. (2023) "What is GDPR, the EU's new data protection law?"' [online]; https://gdpr.eu/what-is-gdpr/.

Zafar, F. (2023) "Countries with GDPR-like Data Privacy Laws"; (2023); [online]; https://finance.yahoo.com/news/18-countries-gdpr-data-privacy-121428321.html.

Integration of Successful Customer Engagement for SMEs on Social Media

Malte Wattenberg

Bielefeld University of Applied Sciences and Arts, Germany

malte.wattenberg@hsbi.de

Abstract: Customer engagement (CE) is a widely known and accepted conceptual approach to describing the engagement and interactions of social media users with brand pages. Research activities focus on the influencing factors and effects of CE on various platforms, above all, Facebook. The focus is mainly on the corporate presence of large corporations or specific industries. Pages of small and medium-sized companies (SMEs), as the backbone of the global economy, are rarely the starting point for research. Therefore, the question arises as to how SMEs need to design their social media communication to generate a high level of customer engagement on social media. Consequently, this study aims to expand previous research findings on successful CE in relation to SMEs and derive recommendations for action. For this purpose, Facebook users and company representatives were interviewed using semi-structured qualitative interviews. The in-depth evaluation of the interview data was carried out using a qualitative content analysis based on a deductive-inductive coding procedure. As a result, six categories with various sub-categories that constituted relevant influencing factors for the participants and promoted engagement were identified. These are Management, the structure of the presence, general aspects of use, motives, content, reaction, and finally, process and background knowledge. Users expect a website to provide information, entertainment, added value, a personal connection, and the opportunity to communicate. SMEs already have extensive expertise in social media marketing but perceive topic acquisition and a lack of resources as a challenge. They all emphasise the relevance of images, product and company-related topics, and an authentic, informal, understandable communication style with humour. Posts should also appear regularly, be up-to-date and short, and have correct spelling and emojis. Finally, questions, prompts and links are engagement drivers. The added value of this study lies in the deepening of the CE concept in relation to the research gap on SMEs. In addition, the results are discussed regarding their practical implications for SMEs to successfully design their presence on social media.

Keywords: Social media, Facebook, Customer engagement, SME, User interaction, Business communication

1. Introduction

1.1 Theoretical Background

The use of Facebook reaches new highs from year to year. It is the largest social network, with over 3 billion monthly and 2 billion daily users. Companies have long recognised this relevance. According to Hootsuite, 91% of all companies use Facebook for marketing communications (McLachlan, 2024), including around 80 million SMEs (Ayling, 2023).

According to the EU definition, SMEs are companies with up to 500 employees (EU, n.d.). In addition to the quantitative definition, SMEs also differ qualitatively from large companies: They have a comparably limited number of products, technologies, know-how, resources, less developed management systems, a more unsystematic and informal management style and management positions that are either held by the company founders and/or their relatives (van Hoorn, 1979). SMEs often operate regionally, are firmly integrated into the community, and, in addition to their proximity to customers, have a high level of knowledge of local markets and distribution channels (Prashantham and Birkinshaw, 2008). Overall, SMEs are considered a decisive factor for economic development (Kumar, 2017), accounting for more than 95% of all companies globally (Ayyagari et al., 2011).

Customer engagement (CE) is a conceptual approach to characterise the engagement and interactions of social media users with company websites. CE is defined as *"a psychological state that occurs by virtue of interactive, cocreative customer experiences with a focal agent/object (e.g., a brand) in focal service relationships. [...] It is a multidimensional concept subject to a context- and/or stakeholder-specific expression of relevant cognitive, emotional and/or behavioral dimensions."* Brodie et al. (2011, p. 260). In this context, the uses and gratification theory (UGT) is often cited as the basis of CE. This theory states that mass media use is based on fulfilling needs through gratifications (Katz, 1974). The validity for social media was also verified (Dolan et al., 2016).

Many research papers examine the influencing factors, effects and various forms of CE on different platforms. On Facebook, for example, de Vries (2012) found that visual and interactive posts increase the number of likes and questions lead to more comments. Rohm et al. (2013) use the UGT to show that entertainment, product information, incentives, and promotions are the primary motivators for engagement.

The studies mainly focus on the corporate presence of large corporations or specific sectors, which means that despite their high relevance, there is a particular research gap in relation to SMEs. So, what factors are crucial for SMEs to shape their communication on social media and promote interactions successfully?

1.2 Research Question and Structure

The research questions are as follows:

RQ 1: *"How is social media strategically and organizationally integrated in SMEs, and according to which conventions do SMEs create Facebook posts?"*

RQ 2: *"How and why do users use Facebook pages of SMEs, and according to which criteria do they consume and react to Facebook posts of SMEs?"*

The aim is to reveal undiscovered knowledge by posing an open question to the object of research to derive potential success factors of the CE.

The article is divided into four chapters. First, the method is explained before the results are presented. In the last chapter, the results are discussed, and recommendations for action are given.

2. Method

2.1 Survey Method and Sampling

The study includes two qualitative surveys in the form of guideline-based expert interviews (Gläser and Laudel, 2009). The decision favouring this approach is based on the view that gaining insights from individual perspectives is conducive to answering the research questions.

The target groups were company representatives from SMEs and users of company pages on Facebook to determine their motivations and everyday social usage practices. Criteria for selecting SMEs and their representatives were regular postings, consistently noticeable interaction on the pages, and several types of posts and stylistic devices.

The individuals were approached via the author's contacts. Particular emphasis was placed on addressing the interviewees in their role as function holders and the interviewer's role as co-expert. Attention was also paid to contrasting sectors, age groups, and gender.

The following table 1 provides an overview of the sample.

Table 1: Distribution of the sample

Company representatives				Individuals		
Abbr.	Sex, Age	Company	No. of empl.	Abbr.	Sex, Age	Occupation
C. 1	M, 53; M, 57	Car centre	≤ 9	I. 1	F, 25	Fire protect. eng. student
C. 2	M, 47	Art museum	10 - 49	I. 2	F, 30	Trainee teacher
C. 3	M, 36	Regional savings bank	50 - 249	I. 3	F, 28	Psychotherapist
C. 4	M, 47; F, 29	Regional savings bank	250 - 1,000	I. 4	F, 49	Real estate agent
C. 5	M, 35	IT service provider	50 - 249	I. 5	M, 29	PhD student
C. 6	F, 33; F, 21	Dance school	≤ 9	I. 6	M, 52	Photographer
C. 7	F, 46	Construction company	≤ 9	I. 7	F, 32	Food technologist
C. 8	F, 43; M, 56	Bakery	10 - 49	I. 8	F, 32	Certified public accountant

2.2 Interview Guidelines

The starting points for developing the guidelines are a contextualising literature search, logical considerations, and the researcher's prior knowledge.

The guidelines were constructed according to Helfferich's SPSS criteria (2005). Under the acronym SPSS (translated from German: collect, check, sort, subsume), Helfferich (2005) suggests first collecting a large number of questions, checking their relevance to the research questions, sorting them thematically and then subsuming them into thematic blocks.

As a rule, open questions were used as question types. A test interview was conducted to check the guidelines' handling, length, and comprehensibility.

The resulting questionnaire for the survey of company representatives is divided into three subject areas with a total of 15 key questions.

First, the reasons for using Facebook were asked. We also asked about the organisational anchoring of social media in the company, the time required, and the presence's objective. In addition, we asked about the range of topics covered, content challenges, the type of posts, and the language style. Questions were also asked about the influence of specific post characteristics and linguistic elements on interaction. Finally, one question was dedicated to the criteria used to respond to fan reactions and other framework conditions.

The guideline for the interviews with users of company pages on Facebook contains four subject areas with a total of 17 key questions.

This includes questions about the frequency of use and the activities of the people, as well as the motivation to visit and follow company pages. Questions about when and how often companies should show activity on their page were also asked. Furthermore, the type, topics, language style, and other linguistic elements of posts users prefer were examined. Users' activity and forms of interaction on company pages were also addressed, and the motivation to like, comment or share posts was questioned. Finally, the role of questions and encouragement for interaction was addressed.

2.3 Realization and Evaluation

A total of 16 interviews were conducted and digitally recorded with the interviewees' consent.

The total interview duration was 9.5 hours, with an average of 37 minutes per interview. Audio recordings were then transcribed and anonymised by the researcher based on the recommendations of Kuckartz and Rädiker (2023).

The transcripts are evaluated using qualitative content analysis with the aim of systematising and interpreting the material in a systematic manner. In detail, this involves structuring qualitative content analysis as a primary method using thematic categories (Kuckartz and Rädiker, 2023). The procedure was carried out with deductive-inductive category building (Schreier, 2012).

The specific steps involved are as follows:

1. Derivation of main categories and individual subcategories from the guidelines.
2. Creation of a coding guide, including anchor examples.
3. Coding of the transcribed interviews using existing and inductive categories.
4. Checking the validity of the category system by the author after a time interval of several weeks (intra-coder agreement).
5. Evaluation concerning the research questions and systematic description of the categories (Kuckartz and Rädiker, 2023).

The author used the MAXQDA analytical software for this study.

3. Results

The 16 interviews contain 1,139 coded sequences with a 3-level category system.

3.1 Management

This category covers all topics on the part of company representatives that deal with planning and managing people, processes and resources.

3.1.1 Knowledge and skills

The company representatives surveyed showed extensive background knowledge of social media marketing. For example, they know the number of Facebook users and the minimum age for an account. The focus, the role of influencers, legal requirements such as declarations of consent for photos, the options for buying fans and how the algorithm works were also discussed. Overall, there is agreement on the dynamic nature of the processes and the constant adaptation to evolving standards and trends on Facebook.

3.1.2 Organisation and strategy

Interviewees report that the development of the website took place in the early years of Facebook due to the growth in users at the time and existing Facebook groups. In most cases, the Facebook presence was initially seen as a field for experimentation and was then continuously expanded.

Responsibility for the content is mainly in the hands of the company director and family members or an employee on a confidential basis. Trainees are often also included in the responsibility.

Interviewees also commented on topic acquisition and management, which relate to the process of identifying, selecting and procuring topics or content as well as support processes. Topics are identified, for example, through brainstorming or through spontaneous observation of activities within the company. Employees also have the opportunity to suggest topics actively and are specifically asked. The relevance of editorial plans, on the other hand, is controversial. The assessment of whether a topic is posted or not depends on the image material, topicality, urgency and variety.

In addition, respondents highlight the importance of a consistent corporate design (CD) for brand recognition. Other activities include paid contributions, links in emails and on the company website, references in invoices, at events and in print media.

With regard to the amount of time required to manage the website, the respondents made it clear that the time investment varies greatly. This ranges from one hour per week to one to three hours per day.

Overall, the interviewees encounter various restrictions and challenges, mainly due to limited human and financial resources and a lack of time. Further difficulties arise from image selection, post-processing work, and tax or competition-related problems.

The main objective of the respondents is to use the page as a marketing communication tool. The website is considered a free opportunity to reach a broad target group, present itself as a modern and socially responsible company, enter into dialogue with customers, and thus manage its public image. Long-term customer loyalty and the provision of information and entertainment are also emphasised.

Target groups are primarily all existing customers of the companies as well as new customers or non-followers. However, respondents mainly refer to different age groups or special company-relevant target groups, such as women, when naming customer groups more specifically.

The number of likes, comments, shares, impressions and the number of fans are key metrics, with impressions being the most important. Apart from this, participants emphasise the resonance of their presence beyond social media, especially the personal approach in the offline area. The metrics are measured via Insights, which is integrated into Facebook. The majority of respondents regularly check the latest key figures.

Finally, most respondents stated that they question their strategy and situation, e.g., regarding the resources available, their knowledge, the objective and target group, and the influence of certain content aspects and topics.

3.2 Usage

This category is based on the statements of the surveyed users of company pages on Facebook.

Scrolling through the newsfeed and actively visiting pages are the most common types of use across the board.

Some differences and similarities can be identified regarding the intensity of use. The vast majority of respondents state that they use Facebook daily. The number of visits varies from once to several times a day. Overall, usage is generally not tied to a specific pattern with a high variance in usage duration. Some participants only spend a short time on Facebook per session, e.g. a few minutes, while others spend more extended periods of up to 1-2 hours.

In terms of liking, commenting on and sharing posts, a high level of passivity is evident among users. Liking posts is the most common form of interaction overall, followed by occasional comments. The reason for this is, for example, reluctance to engage in discussions due to potentially inappropriate comments from other users. Shares are only rarely made.

3.3 Motivation of Users

This category collects statements from users that provide information about the reasons why they use company pages.

Various interviewees reported using company pages on Facebook to satisfy their need for specific information. They also read customer reviews or opinions, for example, in the form of comments.

In addition, there is the desire for entertainment with content that is not strictly related to the product and provides a specific variety.

Furthermore, the expectation of added value is emphasised, which can be expressed in offers or high-quality articles with valuable information.

The personal connection and interests are also a motivating factor. For instance, several interviewees stated that they follow their employer on Facebook or companies active in the same industry. Furthermore, they associate a personal interest or hobby with the published content, or it is about local companies with which the interviewees identify. Overall, the decision to interact with posts is therefore based on the individual perception of the relevance of the content.

Furthermore, the motivation for interaction is often based on a need to communicate. This is primarily expressed in the desire to give feedback to companies. Users also interact if they share the same opinion or want to involve other users by tagging them.

Finally, interviewees emphasise the relevance of advertisements and Facebook's suggestions.

3.4 Structure

This category summarises statements from both respondent groups that relate to the structure and functionality of the entire company page.

The importance of a structured layout for user-friendliness is emphasised. Users also stress the importance of clarity, a clear structure of information and the recognisable seriousness of the site. Above all, this means providing contact information, including a legal notice, telephone number, and email address. Furthermore, respondents expect information on the company's range of services and opening hours.

3.5 Content

This chapter summarises all statements made by interview participants from both groups about the content of a Facebook page.

3.5.1 Vividness

The company experts surveyed described texts as outdated and that nobody reads them. Users also mention that text is often skipped over or that reading it is even seen as a burden.

Respondents agree that image content conveys information best and is conducive to user response. Images are a mandatory requirement for a post and should also be unique, have recognition value, and be compelling.

Concerning videos, some users express a preference for videos over other types. Other users surveyed stated that they quickly skip videos. This can be due to situation dependency or videos that are too long.

Finally, the majority of users point out that they favour a balanced combination of post types. For example, users perceive the combination of text and images as appealing and a way to reach readers better.

3.5.2 Topic

With regard to the topic, company representatives speak of various sales promotion measures such as offers, competitions, and events such as trade fairs, donation handovers, or competitions. For users, price-related means such as discounts, coupons or special offers are particularly relevant. They also include quizzes, surveys, events, and competitions.

The product or service reference of the information is also relevant, e.g. through in-depth explanations of how a product works or how the service is provided. In addition, there is further information on the range of new products. For users, the presentation of new products, collections, and product tests are also relevant.

In addition, the corporate reference of the topics is addressed, such as a view behind the scenes of the company, reports on awards and prizes received, donation activities, extraordinary events, as well as ongoing projects or the presentation of everyday working life or staff attendance. For users, a presentation of the people involved is also relevant, as well as annual reports, information on gender distribution, home office use or social commitment.

Finally, the topic of market and society also receives attention from company representatives. These include recurring events such as sports championships, vacations, public holidays and theme days, but also industry-related seasonal aspects or socially critical topics such as gender diversity.

3.5.3 Communication style

This section covers all statements dealing with the characteristics, techniques, and approaches companies use to convey their messages and shape communication.

Above all, both groups of respondents consider an authentic communication style relevant. The aim is neither to be perceived as contrived nor to conform to typical clichés. Instead, an authentic communication style should be perceived as approachable, realistic, appreciative, and credible. For users, on the other hand, aspects such as an industry-standard writing style, honesty, consistency, and reflection of the corporate culture constitute a high level of authenticity.

A certain degree of informality in the communication style should also be the norm. According to the company representatives surveyed, this is characterised by a relaxed tone. Texts should also be neutral and friendly. On the other hand, users emphasise the importance of a casual and everyday communication style. Yet, they favour a more formal communication style for demanding topics and companies that want to convey a profound impression, depending on the customer types and target groups.

The company representatives also emphasised that the communication style should express a strong connection with the users. Above all, a post must address the reader personally, express closeness, and be at eye level. They make sure to express appreciation, modesty, and gratitude.

Comprehensibility is also a key element. Users make it clear that getting a quick overview of the content is essential, e.g., through keywords, images, and brief postings. Companies should avoid using technical terms, as not all users may understand them. On the other hand, posts from the tech sector, for example, should not do without them entirely. Company representatives, on the other hand, try to avoid technical terms.

As a final component of a communication style, respondents reflect the need for humorous content, e.g. through funny sayings or amusing interactions, storytelling, exciting content, teasers, and exaggeration. In addition, users also report that they are motivated to interact with posts if they are associated with a specific emotional experience.

3.5.4 Interaction impulse

Especially in connection with competitions, requests to follow the page and comment on the post are seen as a very successful tool by the company respondents. However, interviewees also mention that no requests are posted in principle or outside competitions to avoid negative feedback. Most users state that they follow encouragement, especially in connection with competitions.

Furthermore, interviewees see questions as an effective means of increasing interaction, but not all respondents use them equally actively. For example, reluctance is reported in light of negative feedback or no response. On the other hand, users note that questions tend to positively affect their response behaviour.

Companies also place links to provide the reader with more information. Users emphasise the usefulness of these links in order to obtain further information on a topic. In addition, links increase the degree of self-determination and, thus, the users' sense of autonomy. All respondents see hashtags as an optional addition to posts.

3.5.5 Linguistic aspect

The handling of a greeting formula in the posts varies among the respondents. Some company experts integrate the greeting and the farewell, while others only use the greeting or do without it. Accordingly, users state that a greeting formula is not interesting to them.

The same applies to the labelling of the author: relevance and usefulness are questioned, especially as the circle of moderators is small.

The next aspect mentioned is the use of correct spelling. In addition, spelling mistakes are also corrected when they are recognised later. Users surveyed regularly notice spelling and grammatical errors and perceive them as highly unprofessional.

Several companies use emojis to convey emotions and express humour in their posts. Users perceive emojis as a fun and refreshing element. However, companies should integrate them again depending on their general communication style.

3.5.6 Characteristic

Company experts agree on the required frequency of posts, which should be two to three posts per week. There is no consensus among users regarding a minimum, optimum or maximum number of posts in a defined period. The range extends from one post per month to one post per day. Posting too frequently can also be perceived as spam.

The most promising time to publish a post is after 4 pm, as people read posts online after work. Lunch breaks are also a favourable time. There is disagreement about the day of the week, especially concerning the weekend. Some companies cite these days as particularly successful; others do not.

It is crucial to post up-to-date content, e.g. to remind users of your presence.

Also, posts should be kept short. Although both respondent groups could not name a specific number of characters, they were in favour of avoiding automatic shortening by Facebook, including the display of the *"Show more"* button.

3.6 Contact and Reaction

This category subsumes statements relating to the contact between users and companies as well as companies' reactions.

Users indicate that they prefer to make contact via messenger or email rather than by telephone. They appreciate having a personal contact person. The company representatives surveyed reported that they always respond to users' questions and react to comments, for example, by posting their comments or clicking the "Like" button.

Regarding response time, all company experts surveyed ensure that comments are responded to immediately. They do not rely on business hours across the board and also use the weekend for feedback. However, users do not expect a fast response time to the same extent. Most report that they generally want companies to respond to their inquiries within 24 hours to two days.

3.7 Process and Background Knowledge

The last category is purely inductive and includes all user statements that indicate an understanding of the underlying processes, background, and motives of corporate communication on Facebook.

It turns out that respondents have an overall understanding of many relevant aspects. For example, respondents know that companies publish Facebook pages to achieve specific goals, such as generating reach, improving their image and maximising profits. It is also assumed that companies receive a large number of inquiries and have other tasks to perform, which can lead to longer response times. In addition, respondents are familiar with the basic workings of the Facebook algorithm, which serves content to a larger audience based on the number of interactions.

4. Discussion

4.1 Interpretation

The overall assessment shows an undoubted degree of professionalisation of social media integration in SMEs. Company representatives have actively engaged with the topic and endeavour to expand their knowledge. However, it also became clear that there are limits to a sophisticated social media strategy. This can be seen, for example, in the definition of target groups, partly due to the scarcity of resources typically required by SMEs.

Furthermore, the high level of utilisation confirms the figures from market research. The predominantly passive usage behaviour also corresponds to the social media literature, and the primary motivators correspond to the gratifications sought by the UGT: information, entertainment, rewards, identity formation and social interaction.

The analysis also shows the relevance of a clear structure for a Facebook page and a wide range of options for customising the content of posts. These are perceived similarly by both company experts and users. This shows that the conventions of social media use as a communication tool have reached a significant maturity level. Nevertheless, differences are evident among the interviewees, e.g., the tone of address. At this point, there appears to be a need for further negotiation as well as a high degree of dependence on the sector and target group. Furthermore, company experts from SMEs appear to be reluctant to make extensive use of certain means, such as requests and questions. This may be related to the possible consequences of uncontrolled negative feedback (shitstorm). Finally, the anxiety is also reflected in the desire to respond to feedback immediately, while users only expect this after an appropriate and longer processing time.

4.2 Recommendations for Action

It is advisable for companies to define clear responsibilities and processes and to gain a high level of knowledge of social media communication and the industry and target group. This enables companies to guarantee an authentic style of communication. Successful topic acquisition also appears to be crucial for a successful presence. Companies can ensure this by involving employees, for example. Contributions must fulfil the user's motivation to visit the site. This means providing specific information and entertaining content, as well as clearly emphasising the added value of the post. Discussions should be allowed to satisfy the visitors' need to communicate. Thematically, this can be achieved primarily through product and company-related topics. In addition, there are elements of sales promotion, humour, emotional content, regular, short, up-to-date and understandable postings, emojis, and interactive elements. The use of greetings does not appear to be necessary, but the use of correct spelling certainly is. The best time to post is after work and at least once a week. The combination of images and videos with text is a particularly suitable format. Furthermore, companies should fill out the structural content of the site, especially contact addresses, and respond to user enquiries within one to two days. Finally, companies should make the necessary time resources available to support the page and the strategy should be continuously evaluated based on performance measurement.

4.3 Limitations and Outlook

The following limitation of the study can be identified: To ensure reliability, ideally at least two people should code the material and compare the results (Stamann et al., 2016). This inter-coder reliability could not be realised for the present study, but sufficient intra-coder reliability could be ensured instead.

Overall, the present study clarified the research questions regarding the integration of Facebook in SMEs, the conventions of content creation by SMEs and users' expectations of SMEs' Facebook pages, as well as the reasons why they react to posts. Future studies can quantitatively analyse and deepen these aspects. Likewise, a transfer to other platforms can be carried out.

Acknowledgements

Many thanks to my supervisors Prof. Dr. Karola Pitsch, University of Duisburg-Essen, and Prof. Dr.-Ing. Hans Brandt-Pook, Bielefeld University of Applied Sciences and Arts, for accompanying my doctoral thesis, as part of which this article was written. Many thanks also to the interviewed study participants.

References

Ayyagari, M., Demirgüç-Kunt, A. and Maksimovic, V. (2011). "Small vs. young firms across the world: contribution to employment, job creation, and growth", *World Bank Policy Research Working Papers*, (5631).

Ayling, J. (2023). "59 Facebook Statistics Every Marketer Should Know in 2023", [online], https://xperiencify.com/facebook-statistics/.

Brodie, R.J., Hollebeek, L.D., Jurić, B. and Ilić, A. (2011) "Customer Engagement", *Journal of Service Research*, 14(3), pp 252–271. https://doi.org/10.1177/1094670511411703.

de Vries, L., Gensler, S. and Leeflang, P.S. (2012) „Popularity of Brand Posts on Brand Fan Pages: An Investigation of the Effects of Social Media Marketing", *Journal of Interactive Marketing*, 26(2), pp 83–91. https://doi.org/10.1016/j.intmar.2012.01.003.

Dolan, R., Conduit, J., Fahy, J. and Goodman, S. (2016) "Social media engagement behaviour: a uses and gratifications perspective", *Journal of Strategic Marketing*, 24(3-4), pp 261–277. https://doi.org/10.1080/0965254X.2015.1095222.

European Commission. (n.d.) "SME definition - Internal Market, Industry, Entrepreneurship and SMEs", [online], https://ec.europa.eu/growth/smes/sme-definition_en.

Gläser, J. and Laudel, G. (2009) *Experteninterviews und qualitative Inhaltsanalyse [Expert interviews and qualitative content analysis]*, (3rd rev. ed.), VS Verlag für Sozialwissenschaften, Wiesbaden.

Helfferich, C. (2005) *Die Qualität qualitativer Daten: Manual für die Durchführung qualitativer Interviews [The quality of qualitative data: Manual for conducting qualitative interviews]*, 2nd ed., VS Verlag für Sozialwissenschaften, Wiesbaden.

Katz, E., Blumler, J.G. and Gurevitch, M. (1974) "Utilization of Mass Communication by the individual" In Blumler J.G. (Eds.), *The uses of mass communications: Current perspectives on gratifications research,* pp 19–32. Sage Publications, Beverly Hills.

Kuckartz, U. and Rädiker, S. (2023) *Qualitative Content Analysis. Methods, Practice & Using Software*: Sage Publications, London & Thousand Oaks.

Kumar, R. (2017) "Targeted SME Financing and Employment Effects: What Do We Know and What Can We Do Differently?" *Jobs Working Paper*, (3), [online], https://openknowledge.worldbank.org/handle/10986/27477.

McLachlan, S. (2024) "45 Facebook Statistics Marketers Need to Know in 2024", In *Hootsuite*, [online], https://blog.hootsuite.com/facebook-statistics/.

Prashantham, S. and Birkinshaw, J. (2008) "Dancing with Gorillas: How Small Companies Can Partner Effectively with MNCs", *California Management Review*, 51(1), pp 6–23. https://doi.org/10.2307/41166466.

Rohm, A., D. Kaltcheva, V. and Milne, G. (2013) "A mixed-method approach to examining brand-consumer interactions driven by social media", *Journal of Research in Interactive Marketing*, 7(4), pp 295–311. https://doi.org/10.1108/JRIM-01-2013-0009.

Schreier, M. (2012) *Qualitative content analysis in practice*, Sage Publications, Los Angeles, London, New Delhi, Singapore, Washington DC.

Stamann, C., Janssen, M. and Schreier, M. (2016) „Qualitative Inhaltsanalyse – Versuch einer Begriffsbestimmung und Systematisierung [Qualitative content analysis - an attempt of definition and systematization]", *Forum Qualitative Sozialforschung*, 17(3), Artikel 16, [online], http://nbn-resolving.de/urn:nbn:de:0114-fqs1603166.

Van Hoorn, T. (1979) "Strategic planning in small and medium-sized companies", *Long Range Planning*, 12(2), pp 84–91. https://doi.org/10.1016/0024-6301(79)90076-1.

Hope on YouTube: Mixed Methodology Bridges Mental Health YouTubers and Viewers' Perspectives

Stavroula Ziavras and Katerina Diamantaki

Deree – The American College of Greece, Aghia Paraskeui, Greece

s.ziavras@acg.edu
kdiamantaki@acg.edu

Abstract: The need for accessible therapeutic solutions has been highlighted by the observed youth mental health crisis and the COVID-19 pandemic. Seeking solutions involves a varied pathway, blending traditional therapist-client interactions with everyday aspects, like social media, particularly YouTube, which is used for informal counseling and as an entry point to formal mental healthcare. YouTube mental health content viewers value autopathographies (APs) for interest and mental health professional (MHP) content for information validity, both recently increasing. Hope, a non-specific factor fostering therapeutic change and building the therapist-client relationship, is crucial in the complex pathway to change. Unfortunately, this intricate pathway is often overlooked in psychological and media communication research. Additionally, relevant literature lacks guidance on effectively leveraging social media for user mental health. This study explores hope levels for therapeutic change in APs and MHP content viewers, focusing on the content's role in informal online counseling. Through a mixed methods approach, viewer hope is gauged through direct viewer surveys and indirectly through YouTube content creator interviews. Additionally, the viewer's perception of YouTubers within the informal counselor-client relationship is assessed, influencing counseling effectiveness. Findings indicate that YouTube's APs and MHP content can increase the possibility for therapeutic change for high-hope viewers in formal and informal counseling, underscoring the crucial role of the YouTuber-viewer relationship in informal online counseling. YouTube emerges as a valuable addition to an individual's mental health toolkit.

Keywords: YouTube,Hope, Hope for change, Mental health, Therapeutic relationship

1. Introduction

The advent of social media (SM) magnified online social interactivity, with platforms like YouTube forming hubs for public communication. This includes health communication (Auxier and Anderson, 2021), which is unsurprising with the ongoing young mental health (MH) crisis (Enos, 2020). Among the plethora of health communication research, MH communication on SM has also been explored and even saw a renewed research interest (Alonzo and Popescu, 2021; Latha et al., 2020) during the COVID-19 pandemic, which increased demand in MH services (Vindegaard and Benros, 2020). People seeking MH solutions follow an intricate pathway to therapeutic change that includes the formal counseling setting (Larsen et al., 2007) but also informal counseling solutions (Llewelyn, 1984), such as using YouTube for MH communication (Johnson et al., 2021). *Autopathographies* (APs) and *mental health professional* (MHP) content on YouTube stand out in this context for their well sought-out user benefits of interest (Oliphant, 2013) and credibility (Foster, 2013), respectively. Moreover, an element that leads to therapeutic change is hope (Snyder, 1995). When assessed, it can build the counselor-client relationship and augment client well-being (Bartholomew, Scheel and Cole, 2015).

Despite all this, there is insufficient guidance for users to leverage SM for their MH and a lack of research on both online counseling via SM and the complex pathway towards therapeutic change.

This prosocial study addresses these gaps by exploring how viewers' hope and the YouTuber-viewer relationship can benefit the viewer's MH and overall wellness. Snyder's (2002) popular hope theory guides the application of both quantitative and qualitative research methods, facilitating efficient data triangulation and enabling the generalization of findings. The following research questions and hypotheses are investigated:

- RQ1: What are the levels of hope for change of viewers of mental health AP and MHP content on YouTube?
- H1: Viewers of both YouTube AP and MHP content perceive the respective YouTubers as high in expertness and trustworthiness.

2. Literature Review

2.1 Mental health communication on YouTube

YouTube's importance as a MH information disseminator and educator becomes clear through its rising amount of content (Madathil et al., 2015) and its popularity as a MH communication platform (Giustini et al.,

2018), especially in younger users (Oliphant, 2013) due to its visual and anonymity affordances (Naslund et al., 2016; O'Reilly et al., 2018). MH communication benefits of the platform involve psychoeducational dissemination to diverse age groups, overcoming related stigma, (Godwin, Khan and Yellowlees, 2017; Shu and Woo, 2020), and changing negative MH portrayals from mainstream media by enabling users to share APs, meaning personal MH stories (Ellis, 2012).

APs foster social discourse, helping the narrator and peers and giving valuable insights to medical professionals and the layperson (Ellis, 2012), and offer social and peer support (Foster, 2013). Platform metrics (i.e., likes, views, comment count) evince greater engagement with APs compared to MHP content, and a deeper involvement with personal stories over just informational content (Oliphant, 2013; O'Reilly et al., 2018). User engagement with user-generated and self-disclosure content varies by platform but typically enhances social connectedness, support, and psychological well-being (Balani and De Choudhury, 2015; Blair and Abdullah, 2018).

Despite lower preference, MHP content addresses health professionals' concerns on peer-to-peer misinformation (Rupert et al., 2014), which can adversely impact the healthcare of SM users (Madathil et al., 2015), and users' value for authentic and reliable health information (Foster, 2013; O'Reilly et al., 2018). To combat health misinformation, along with promoting health and supporting users, Park and Goering (2016) suggested an active participation of health professionals on YouTube. MHPs heeded this call, as their clear preference for YouTube was shown by Wardi-Zonna, Hardy and Hardy (2020).

It is concluded that MH APs offer value to YouTube users based on interest levels, and MHP content offers value based on reliability levels. For this, this study utilizes these two types of YouTube MH content to explore its research questions.

2.2 Online Counseling and Social Media

Evolving online communication in the early 2000s made it possible to connect with people with no access to psychotherapists. The psychology field took note of this and initiated studies on cybertherapy. Suler defines cybertherapy as "any psychotherapeutic environment created by computers and designed, facilitated, or prescribed by a mental health professional" (2004, para. 1), which aligns with the dynamic nature of online environments. This broad definition contains online counseling, a popular variant in studies on online psychotherapeutic practices and services (Nagarajan and Yuvaraj, 2019; Speyer and Zack, 2003).

Counseling differs from psychotherapy in that the former can be offered by non-professionals but the latter only by professionals. Regardless, most standard definitions of counseling consider only the perspective of the counselor, without acknowledging that, despite diverse theories and practices, a shared element is that counseling requires the individual seeking help to wish or intend for counseling to occur (McLeod, 2003). A definition that matches others used but also incorporates a user-centric perspective is to undergo psychological therapy, either in-person or online, provided by a healer – professional or peer(s) – trained in a socially approved manner to administer such therapy (Frank and Frank, 1993, p. 2). The online element was added to the definition.

Indeed, scientific literature on online counseling bifurcates into formal and informal forms, where a clinician (Creaner, 2020; Speyer and Zack, 2003) or peer(s) (Johnson et al., 2021; Tan, 2008) is present, respectively. While it is evident that MHPs utilize SM as a tool to communicate, educate, treat (Frankish, Ryan and Harris, 2012), and converse about MH-related issues (Wardi-Zonna, Hardy and Hardy, 2020), research on online counseling via SM is lacking despite the heightened demand created by the pandemic for MH services (Vindegaard and Benros, 2020). Moreover, most existing research sees online counseling as intertwined with the therapeutic bond between therapist and client (Creaner, 2020; Osborn et al., 2014). This myopic view excludes MHPs that discuss MH issues with users on SM like YouTube. Challenging this view, a qualitative analysis of vlogs including YouTube (Johnson et al., 2021), concluded that YouTube content is utilized by some users as informal online counseling and can be a gateway to formal counseling.

Based on the aforementioned, in this study the term "informal online counseling" is stretched to encompass YouTube MHP content. Thus, the two types of YouTube MH content utilized, namely APs and MHP content, are explored in the context of such content being perceived by users as informal online counseling.

2.3 Hope and Informal Online Counseling

The therapist's and patient's perceptions of psychological therapy diverge (Llewelyn, 1984). This obfuscated process involves a complex pathway in individuals seeking therapeutic solutions, but this has been overlooked in both psychological therapy research tackling online counseling (Rochlen et al., 2004) and media communication research tackling MH information dissemination via new media (Giustini et al., 2018). This pathway includes the therapeutic interaction, a dynamic and reciprocal process (Larsen, Edey and Lemay, 2007), as an incentive for change, but also situations that occur in other parts of individuals' lives (Llewelyn, 1984). One such part could be SM, as these networks are often utilized as a form of informal counseling and a gateway to seeking formal counseling (Johnson et al., 2021). Hope is highlighted in psychological therapy research as an important non-specific factor to psychological therapy (Llewelyn, 1984) that can lead to client change in therapy (Snyder, 1995), and assessing hope can build the therapist-patient therapeutic relationship, improving patients' psychological well-being (Bartholomew, Scheel and Cole, 2015).

Hope, a complex concept, has prompted various definitions, mainly categorized as unidimensional or multidimensional. Nuanced as it may be, the multidimensional perspective remains insufficiently investigated (Larsen et al., 2020). Abiding to a more unidimensional view but, still, well-articulated is one of the most influential hope models in psychology, as well as most widely used hope theory by far, Snyder's (2000; 2002) hope theory, which fits both a client and general population setting (Larsen et al., 2020; Redlich-Amirav et al., 2018). Based on Snyder's hope theory, hope is "the perceived capability to derive pathways to desired goals, and motivate oneself via agency thinking to use those pathways" (2002, p. 249). In summary, hope is threefold: *pathways*, *agency*, and *goals*.

The following question emerges.

RQ1: What are the levels of hope for change of viewers of mental health AP and MHP content on YouTube?

2.4 Perception of Therapist

As aforementioned, assessing hope benefits the therapist-client relationship (Bartholomew, Scheel, and Cole, 2015), which is crucial in the therapeutic process, accounting for 30% of therapeutic change (Thomas, 2006). It was also concluded that seeking solutions involves both therapeutic interaction (Larsen, Edey, and Lemay, 2007) and SM usage (Johnson et al., 2021) as an incentive for change. Clients' perception of the counselor's behavior is vital in the effectiveness of counseling outcome (Barak and LaCrosse, 1975) and this is assumed true also in informal online counseling. In this study, the YouTuber is the therapist, the viewer is the client, and the viewer's perception of the YouTuber is assessed.

Counselors' social influence on clients is determined by three key attributes: attractiveness, expertness, and trustworthiness. The counselor's influence on the client can be amplified when seen as credible and attractive. The CRF-S (see Methodology) measures these attributes and at least two of them together, expertness and trustworthiness, are linked to counselor credibility (Barak and LaCrosse, 1975; Strong, 1968).

Expertness is the perception of a communicator as a source of sound statements. This perception is determined by objective evidence of specialized training (i.e., diplomas, certificates, titles), behavioural evidence (i.e., rational and knowledgeable arguments, confidence in presentation), and reputation as an expert (Strong, 1968, p. 216). Perceived *trustworthiness* is related to four factors: the communicator's reputation for honesty, their social role (e.g., physician), their openness and sincerity, and perceived lack of motivation for personal gain (p. 218). *Attractiveness* is the client's perception of the communicator as likeable to them, compatible with them, and similar to them in background, opinions, etc. (p. 219).

A hypothesis occurs:

H1: Viewers of both YouTube AP and MHP content perceive the respective YouTubers as high in expertness and trustworthiness.

3. Methodology

Surveys and semi-structured interviews were used to assess hope for change in YouTube MH viewers. Informed consent was provided by all participants. This study was approved by the Institutional Review Board at the authors' affiliated university.

3.1 Participants, Procedure, and Measures

3.1.1 Interviews

Seven YouTubers (3 MHP, 4 AP; see Table 1), chosen through purposive sampling, that fit the criteria (see Table 2) accepted the email invitation to participate in the study. The semi-structured interviews were conducted via Zoom with the guidance of an interview guide. Data were transcribed verbatim with the help of Google's Live Transcribe app.

Table 1: Interviewees overview

Interviewee code	Type of YouTube content	Professional occupation (MHPs only)/ Channel's main MH focus (APs only)
P1	MHP	Psychotherapist
P2	MHP	Clinical psychologist
P3	MHP	Behavioural scientist and psychology researcher
P4	AP	Depression
P5	AP	Narcissism
P6	AP	Dissociative identity disorder
P7	AP	Dissociative disorders

Table 2: Inclusion criteria based on MH content creator type

Criteria	MHP	AP	Specifications
Be an active YouTube creator	Yes	Yes	Upload at least 1 video/ 3 months
Have at least 100 subscribers	Yes	Yes	First subscriber count milestone
Uploaded content focus primarily on MH	Yes	Yes	-
Primary channel focus on MH content through the lens of a non-mental health professional with personal experience with a MH issue	No	Yes	-
Be a licensed MHP at time of informed consent	Yes	No	-

3.1.2 Survey

Purposive sampling guaranteed the participation of viewers of the YouTuber interviewees. The survey link was shared under the YouTubers' videos and among their official fan communities on Facebook and Reddit. A total of 129 participants (38% 25-34 years-old; 83.7% female) were asked to rate their hope for change via the Hope for Change Through Counseling Scale (HCCS), which utilizes the most widely used hope theory by Snyder (2000; 2002). HCCS is a 19-item 8-point Likert scale adapted from Bartholomew, Scheel and Cole (2015; 1 = Definitely False, 2 = Mostly False, 3 = Somewhat False, 4 = Slightly False, 5 = Slightly True, 6 = Somewhat True, 7 = Mostly True, 8 = Definitely True; α = .96) and comprises three subscales, namely pathways (α = .91), agency (α = .93), and goals (α = .84). A brief definition of counseling was included in the instructions to avoid possible misconceptions by the participants. The definition, with the added online dimension, was based on what Frank and Frank (1993, p. 2) defined as psychotherapy. In their definition, they mention that the healer does not need be a professional, and a peer(s) could fill the role. The author did not specify this in the provided definition and, instead, left it open to each participant's interpretation. The original instructions were simplified to minimize word count, so as not to tire the participants. Participants' perception of the YouTuber they watch was measured via the Counselor Rating Form-Short version (CRF-S) by Corrigan and Schmidt (1983; α = .99), a 12-adjective bipolar scale. CRF-S is a revised version of the Counselor Rating Form (CRF) by Barak and LaCrosse (1975) and was shortened to decrease the length of the subscales while maintaining their reliability, reduce the minimum educational level necessary for reliable word comprehension, and assist greater use of the full 7-point range scale when rating each item (Epperson and Pecnik, 1985). The respondents were asked to rate their perceptions of the YouTuber associated with the channel where they encountered the survey link by using a 7-point scale (1 = not very and 7 = very). Three separate 4-item subscale scores derived from summing the items, namely trustworthiness (α = .93), expertness (α = .97), and attractiveness (α = .97). Sub- scale scores can range from 4 to 28. An initial specification on viewer type (MHP vs AP) and demographics were also requested.

4. Results

4.1 Thematic analysis

Generally, the transcribed interview data was analyzed via grounded theory and thematic analysis. In applying grounded theory, key principles, such as its iterative nature and constant comparison, guided both data gathering and analysis. Iterative analysis informed subsequent data collection cycles, while constant comparison refined theoretical constructs emerging from data analysis (Lingard, Albert and Levinson, 2008). During data transcription, components like the iterative nature were already employed, involving repeated listening for enhanced data comprehension and the emergence of key themes before thematic analysis commenced (Allan, 2018). Within the grounded theory framework, the researcher followed the six thematic analysis phases as described by Braun and Clarke (2006):

1. Familiarizing yourself with your data: Data will be transcribed and then read and re-read while taking notes of initial ideas.
2. Generating initial codes: Interesting characteristics of the data will be systematically coded across the dataset, arranging data according to code relevance.
3. Searching for themes: Codes will be assembled into potential themes, amassing all data that is relevant to each potential theme.
4. Reviewing themes: Two levels of theme reviewing will be followed. In level 1, the emerging themes will be inspected to ensure fit with the coded extracts. In level 2, the emerging themes will be inspected to ensure fit with the entire data set. Through this two-level process, a thematic "map" of the analysis will be produced.
5. Defining and naming themes: Continuous analysis will refine the features of each theme and the general derived story. Each theme will eventually arrive at a clear definition and name.
6. Producing the report: At this final opportunity for analysis, expressive, powerful extract examples will be selected. The selected extracts will be put through final analysis to relate back to the literature and the research questions, generating a scholarly report.

The thematic analysis process is not linear but rather recursive, and phases were revisited as needed.

Specifically, a holistic extraction of the theme "YouTubers' perceptions of viewers' hope connected to YouTube channel" via theoretical/deductive thematic analysis (Braun and Clarke, 2006) was done guided by Snyder's (2002) hope theory. The process involved scanning for hope indicators (revealed pathways, goals, and/or agency) and inhibitors (factors impeding pathways, goals, or agency). Both indicators and inhibitors pertained to viewers' ability or hindrance in deriving pathways that led to desired goals and engaging in self-motivation via agency thinking to use those pathways, as perceived by the YouTuber. Additional instruction that aided the extraction process was taken from Hanna's (2002) counselor implicit/ viewer implicit approach to therapy, as it fit well the circumstances of the current study where statements of hope without a direct discussion of hope were examined. This approach suggests that "The gift of hope is the gift of a desirable future. Thus, hope building is done through any approach that can make the future more tolerable" (p. 265). Thus, statements that fit this mentality were deemed relevant during the extraction process.

Pathways, goals, and agency sub-themes were present in all interviewees' statements. Hope indicators surpassed hope inhibitors in both number and strength (see Figures 1 and 2), indicating a high presence of hope in viewers of both MHP and AP MH content on YouTube. Indicative quotes that match sub-themes are the hope indicator (pathway) "So, I think people know who I am by watching my videos, um, I don't think I'm a particularly [raise brows] good therapist, I just think that people...because of that comfort of knowing who this is, they do reach out for either mental health advice or wanting to be a therapist..." by P2 that matches the sub-theme "Initiate contact with YouTuber" and the hope inhibitor (goal) "Um, I definitely get [nod] a lot of people asking for mental health advice [nod], um, which some of them I will definitely, like, turn down because, you know, I'm not [shake head], like, a clinical professional. Um, sometimes I will get people being, like, 'I'm in a crisis right now and I need support', and I'm not trained for crisis [shake head]." by P6 that matches the sub-theme "YouTuber did not offer support".

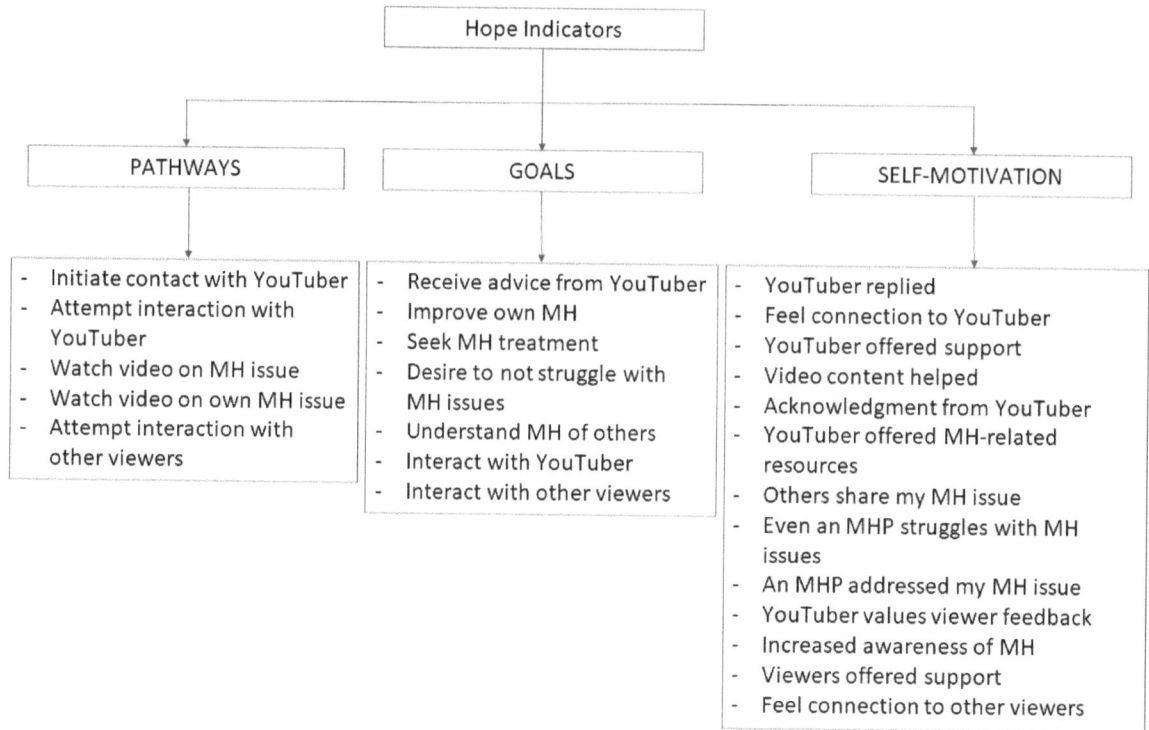

Figure 1: Hope indicator sub-themes in descending strength

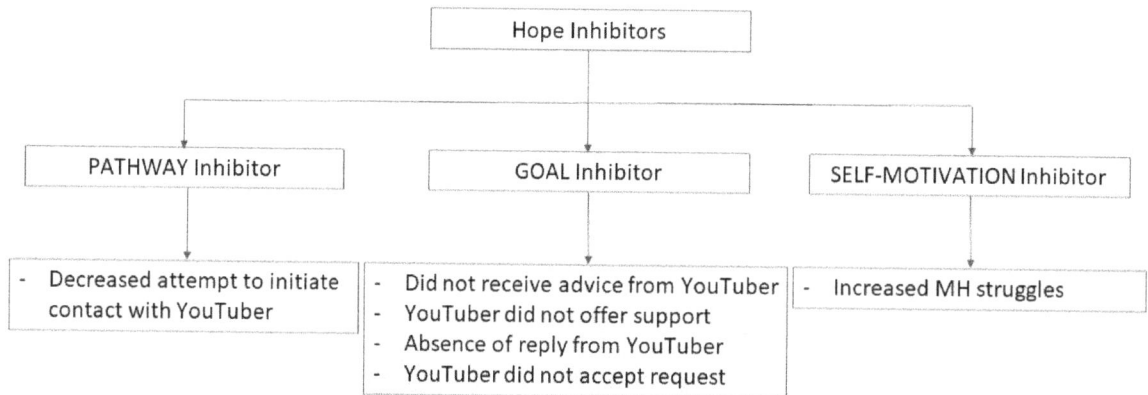

Figure 2: Hope inhibitor sub-themes in descending strength

4.2 Survey Data Analysis

4.2.1 RQ1: What are the levels of hope for change of viewers of mental health AP and MHP content on YouTube?

The HCCS scale and its subscales were computed (see Table 3), revealing overall positive responses. Mean scores for the total scale (M = 6.32, SD = 1.26), pathways (M = 6.49, SD = 1.28), agency (M = 6.24, SD = 1.50), and goal identification (M = 6.17, SD = 1.29) exceeded 6.00 on an 8-point Likert scale, indicating hope for change in MH viewers. The mode for the complete scale was 6.58, and for pathways and agency it was 8.00, indicating most assigned the highest hope scores to those subscales.

Individual group analyses demonstrated similar positive findings (see Table 3). In the MHP group (n = 111), mean scores for the total scale (M = 6.31, SD = 1.26), pathways (M = 6.49, SD = 1.26), agency (M = 6.24, SD = 1.51), and goal identification (M = 6.14, SD = 1.29) surpassed 6.00. The mode for the complete scale was 7.00, and for agency it was 8.00, indicating that most assigned the highest hope scores to this subscale. In the AP group (n = 18), mean scores for the total scale (M = 6.36, SD = 1.34), pathways (M = 6.51, SD = 1.45), agency (M = 6.24, SD = 1.49), and goal identification (M = 6.33, SD = 1.30) also exceeded 6.00. The mode for the pathways subscale was 8.00, indicating most assigned the highest hope scores to this subscale.

Minor score variations, likely due to sample size differences (MHP: n = 111, AP: n = 18), did not significantly impact results.

An independent t-test (see Table 3) compared hope for change levels in counseling between MHP viewers (M = 6.31, SD = 1.26) and AP viewers (M = 6.36, SD = 1.34). The Levene's test was not significant (F = .01, p = .913), indicating equal variances, t(127) = -.175, p = .861.

Table3: Descriptive statistics and t-tests for scales and sub-scales

Measures		Viewer type	Mean		SD		t	df	p
Hope for change	Pathways	MHP	6.49	6.49	1.26	1.28			
		AP	6.51		1.45				
	Agency	MHP	6.24	6.24	1.51	1.50			-
		AP	6.24		1.49				
	Goal	MHP	6.14	6.17	1.29	1.29			
		AP	6.33		1.30				
	Total	MHP	6.31	6.32	1.26	1.26	0.18	127	0.86
		AP	6.36		1.34		-	-	-
Perception of counselor	Trustworthiness	MHP	24.00		5.69		0.43	127	0.67
		AP	24.61		4.46		-	-	-
	Expertness	MHP	24.06		5.57		1.55	127	0.12
		AP	21.83		6.17		-	-	-
	Attractiveness	MHP	23.86		5.66		0.77	127	0.44
		AP	24.94		4.21		-	-	-

4.2.2 *H1: Viewers of both YouTube AP and MHP content perceive the respective YouTubers as high in expertness and trustworthiness.*

Three independent t-tests (see Table 3) explored the impact of viewer type on trustworthiness, expertness, and attractiveness scores in the context of informal MH counseling.

For trustworthiness, MHP viewers (M = 6.00, SD = 1.42) versus AP viewers (M = 6.15, SD = 1.11), the Levene's test was not significant (F = 2.23, p > .137), indicating equal variances t(127) = -.434, p = .665.

For expertness, MHP viewers (M = 6.01, SD = 1.39) versus AP viewers (M = 5.46, SD = 1.54), the Levene's test was not significant (F = .54, p = .465), indicating equal variances t(127) = 1.55, p = .123.

For attractiveness, MHP viewers (M = 5.97, SD = 1.41) versus AP viewers (M = 6.24, SD = 1.05), the Levene's test was not significant (F = 2.83, p = .095), indicating equal variances t(127) = -.774, p = .440.

Subscale scores (Table 3) were calculated to assess YouTuber perceptions within each viewer group. A score of 16 indicates a neutral perception. For the trustworthiness subscale, scores exceeded 16 in both MHP viewers (M = 24.00, SD = 5.69) and AP viewers (M = 24.61, SD = 4.46). For the expertness subscale, scores exceeded 16 in both MHP viewers (M = 24.06, SD = 5.57) and AP viewers (M = 21.83, SD = 6.17). For the attractiveness subscale, scores exceeded 16 in both MHP viewers (M = 23.86, SD = 5.66) and AP viewers (M = 24.94, SD = 4.21).

Overall, perceptions were positive in both viewer groups. Subscale standard deviations were slightly high, possibly due to mean scores leaning toward the scale's extreme right limit, resulting in variance concentrated to the left. This may stem from the scale's nature and the study sample, as participants assess their perception of YouTubers they actively watch.

5. Discussion

The HCCS scale and thematic analysis incorporated Snyder's (2002) hope theory, maximizing data triangulation and findings generalization. Thematic analysis and HCCS scores support the presence of hope for change in both MH viewer types, with scores showing no statistically significant difference in hope levels between the two types. Since SM like YouTube can function as a gateway to formal therapy (Johnson et al., 2021), the increased hope levels could facilitate change in that formal context. Interestingly, high levels of hope could be connected to help-seeking intentions from informal sources (McDermott et al., 2017). Individuals with high hope can devise multiple routes to their goals (Rand and Cheavens, 2009), a point supported by hope sub-themes from thematic analysis. Moreover, individuals may prefer informal sources for one issue and formal for another (Ciarrochi and Deane, 2001). Thus, the role of YouTube MH content is highly relevant both as a gateway to formal counseling, but also as informal online counseling, given preferences for informal over formal support or help (Jorm, Christensen and Griffiths, 2005). Since attitude toward a behaviour and intention to perform said behaviour are positively correlated (Ajzen, 1991), further research could explore connections and predictions of help-seeking attitude and hope levels based on MH YouTube content type.

High hope levels imply a high possibility for therapeutic change (Frank and Frank, 1993; Snyder, 1995) from the viewers, and a possible therapeutic relationship (Bartholomew, Scheel and Cole, 2015) between YouTuber and viewer. This relationship is vital for the therapeutic process (Thomas, 2006) and counseling outcome effectiveness hinges on the client's perception of the counselor's behaviour (Barak and LaCrosse, 1975). This is assumed to be true for informal online counseling as well. MH viewers' perception of YouTubers scored very high on the CRF-S scale, with no statistically significant difference between viewer types. Combined with positive hope results, this underscores the importance of the viewer-YouTuber relationship in MH content watching as informal online counseling. The high CRF-S score on the expertness and trustworthiness subscales indicates MH viewers find both MHP and AP YouTubers credible.

Overall findings suggest that MHP and AP content on YouTube can have a positive effect on the viewer's MH, both as a gateway to formal counseling and as a standalone source of informal online counseling.

This study has limitations. The small sample size (n = 129) reduces result generalizability. The significant size difference between MHP (111 participants) and AP (18 participants) viewers may impact statistical comparisons. Consideration of scales is crucial; the HCCS's validity has been criticized (Redlich-Amirav et al., 2018), and Snyder's (2000; 2002) hope theory, though widely used, faces critiques for being overly unidimensional (Larsen et al., 2020). The CRF-S struggles to encourage broader use of the lower end of its 7-point rating scale (Epperson and Pecnik, 1985).

The interviewee sample was small (3 MHP, 4 AP YouTubers). Further studies are needed to validate this study's thematic analysis of hope levels in MHP and AP YouTube viewers. Thematic analysis, a descriptive method, may miss some context within interview transcriptions. However, integrating theory related to the survey's variables aids thematic analysis by providing a clearer framework, enhancing reproducibility.

6. Conclusion

This study explored the levels of hope for therapeutic change in YouTube viewers of AP and MHP content, in the context of such content being utilized as informal online counseling. The viewer's perception of the YouTubers, in the context of an informal counselor-client relationship, was also assessed, as this contributes to the effectiveness of counseling. Key findings suggest that APs and MHP content on YouTube can increase the possibility for therapeutic change in high-hope viewers in both formal and informal counseling settings and that the YouTuber-viewer relationship is vital in the informal online counseling context. Overall, YouTube can be a useful tool in an individual's MH toolkit.

References

Ajzen, I. (1991) "The Theory of Planned Behavior", *Organizational Behavior and Human Decision Processes*, Vol. 50, No. 2, pp 179–211.

Allan, T. (2018) "Semi-structured interviews and thematic analysis of qualitative data.", [online], *Medium*, https://medium.com/designhealthfacility/semi-structured-interviews-and-thematic-analysis-of-qualitative-data-7ad1857e228d.

Alonzo, D. and Popescu, M. (2021) "Utilizing Social Media Platforms to Promote Mental Health Awareness and Help Seeking in Underserved Communities During the COVID-19 Pandemic", *Journal of Education and Health Promotion*, Vol. 10, No. 1, p 156.

Auxier, B. and Anderson, M. (2021) "Social Media Use in 2021", [online], Pew Research Center, https://www.pewresearch.org/internet/2021/04/07/social-media-use-in-2021/.

Balani, S. and De Choudhury, M. (2015) "Detecting and Characterizing Mental Health Related Self-Disclosure in Social Media" in *Proceedings of the 33rd Annual ACM Conference Extended Abstracts on Human Factors in Computing Systems*, April, pp 1373–1378.

Barak, A. and LaCrosse, M. B. (1975) "Multidimensional Perception of Counselor Behavior", *Journal of Counseling Psychology*, Vol 22, No. 6, pp 471–476.

Bartholomew, T.T., Scheel, M.J. and Cole, B.P. (2015) "Development and Validation of the Hope for Change Through Counseling Scale", *The Counseling Psychologist*, Vol. 43, No. 5, pp 671–702.

Blair, J. and Abdullah, S. (2018) "Supporting Constructive Mental Health Discourse in Social Media" in Proceedings of the *12th EAI International Conference on Pervasive Computing Technologies for Healthcare*, May, pp 299–303.

Braun, V. and Clarke, V. (2006) "Using Thematic Analysis in Psychology", *Qualitative Research in Psychology*, Vol. 3, No. 2, pp 77–101.

Ciarrochi, J.V. and Deane, F.P. (2001) "Emotional Competence and Willingness to Seek Help from Professional and Nonprofessional Sources", *British Journal of Guidance & Counselling*, Vol. 29, No. 2), pp 233–246.

Corrigan, J.D. and Schmidt, L.D. (1983) "Development and Validation of Revisions in the Counselor Rating Form", *Journal of Counseling Psychology*, Vol. 30, No. 1, pp 64–75.

Creaner, M. (2020) 'The Role of Social Media in Counselling and Psychotherapy' in Tribe, R. & Morrissey, J. (eds.) *The Handbook of Professional, Ethical and Research Practice for Psychologists, Counsellors, Psychotherapists and Psychiatrists*, 3rd edn., Routledge, London, pp 117–128.

Ellis, K. (2012) 'New Media as a Powerful Ally in the Representation of Mental Illness: YouTube, Resistance, and Change' in Rubin L.C. (ed.) *Mental Illness in Popular Media: Essays on the Representation of Disorders*, McFarland & Company, pp. 184–201.

Enos, G. (2020) "Millennials, Generation Z Targeted in New Mental Health Initiative", *Mental Health Weekly*, Vol. 30, No. 39, pp 1–5.

Epperson, D.L. and Pecnik, J.A. (1985) "Counselor Rating Form—Short Version: Further Validation and Comparison to the Long Form", *Journal of Counseling Psychology*, Vol. 32, No. 1, p 143.

Foster, C.B. (2013) "Mental Health on Youtube: Exploring the Potential of Interactive Media to Change Knowledge, Attitudes and Behaviors About Mental Health", Ph.D. Thesis, University of South Carolina, https://scholarcommons.sc.edu/etd/2346.

Frank, J.D. and Frank, J.B. (1993) *Persuasion and Healing: A Comparative Study of Psychotherapy*, 3rd edn., The Johns Hopkins University Press.

Frankish, K., Ryan, C. and Harris, A. (2012) "Psychiatry and Online Social Media: Potential, Pitfalls and Ethical Guidelines for Psychiatrists and Trainees", *Australasian Psychiatry*, Vol. 20, No. 3, pp 181–187.

Giustini, D. et al. (2018) "Effective Uses of Social Media in Public Health and Medicine: A Systematic Review of Systematic Reviews", *Online Journal of Public Health Informatics*, Vol. 10, No. 2.

Godwin, H.T., Khan, M. and Yellowlees, P. (2017) "The Educational Potential of YouTube", *Academic Psychiatry*, Vol. 41, No. 6, pp 823–827.

Hanna, F.J. (2002) 'Therapy with Difficult Clients: Using the Precursors Model to Awaken Change' in Hannah, F.J. (ed.) *Building Hope for Change*, American Psychological Association, Washington, DC, pp 265–273.

Johnson, K.F. et al. (2021) "What YouTube Narratives Reveal About Online Support, Counseling Entrance, and How Black Americans Manage Depression Symptomatology", *Informatics for Health and Social Care*, Vol. 46, No. 1, pp 84–99.

Jorm, A.F., Christensen, H. and Griffiths, K.M. (2005) "The Impact of beyondblue: The National Depression Initiative on the Australian Public's Recognition of Depression and Beliefs About Treatments", *Australian & New Zealand Journal of Psychiatry*, Vol. 39, No. 4, pp 248–254.

Larsen, D.J. et al. (2020) "Multidimensional Hope in Counseling and Psychotherapy Scale", *Journal of Psychotherapy Integration*, Vol. 30, No. 3, pp 407–422.

Larsen, D., Edey, W., & Lemay, L. (2007) "Understanding the Role of Hope in Counselling: Exploring the Intentional Uses of Hope", *Counselling Psychology Quarterly*, Vol. 20, No. 4, pp 401–416.

Latha, K. et al. (2020) "Effective Use of Social Media Platforms for Promotion of Mental Health Awareness", *Journal of Education and Health Promotion*, Vol. 9, p. 124.

Lingard, L., Albert, M., and Levinson, W. (2008). Grounded theory, mixed methods, and action research. *BMJ*, p. 337.

Llewelyn, S. P. (1984) "The Experience of Patients and Therapists in Psychological Therapy", Ph.D. Thesis, University of Sheffield, http://etheses.whiterose.ac.uk/2986/1/DX079442.pdf.

Madathil, K.C. et al. (2015) "Healthcare Information on YouTube: A Systematic Review", *Health Informatics Journal*, Vol. 21, No. 3, pp 173–194.

McDermott, R.C. et al. (2017) "Hope for Help-Seeking: A Positive Psychology Perspective of Psychological Help-Seeking Intentions", *The Counseling Psychologist*, Vol. 45, No. 2, pp 237–265.

McLeod, J. (2003), *An Introduction to Counselling*, 3rd edn., Open University Press.

Nagarajan, M., and Yuvaraj, S. (2021) "Mental Health Counsellors' Perceptions on Use of Technology in Counselling", *Current Psychology*, Vol. 40, pp 1760–1766.

Naslund, J.A. et al. (2016) "The Future of Mental Health Care: Peer-to-Peer Support and Social Media", *Epidemiology and Psychiatric Sciences*, Vol. 25, No. 2, pp 113–122.

O'Reilly, M. et al. (2018) "Potential of Social Media in Promoting Mental Health in Adolescents", *Health Promotion International*, Vol. 34, No. 5, pp 981–991.

Oliphant, T. (2013) "User Engagement with Mental Health Videos on YouTube", *Journal of the Canadian Health Libraries Association*, Vol. 34, No. 3, pp 153–158.

Osborn, D.S. et al. (2014) "Technology-Savvy Career Counselling", *Canadian Psychology*, Vol. 55, No. 4, pp 258–265.

Park, D.Y. and Goering, E.M. (2016) "The Health-Related Uses and Gratifications of YouTube: Motive, Cognitive Involvement, Online Activity, and Sense of Empowerment", *Journal of Consumer Health on the Internet*, Vol. 20, No. 1–2, pp 52–70.

Rand, K.L. and Cheavens, S. (2009) 'Hope Theory' in Snyder, C.R. & Lopez, S.J. (eds.), *Oxford Handbook of Positive Psychology*, Oxford Press, pp 323–334.

Redlich-Amirav, D. et al. (2018) "Psychometric Properties of Hope Scales: A Systematic Review", *International Journal of Clinical Practice*, Vol. 72, No. 7, e13213.

Rochlen, A.B., Beretvas, S.N. and Zack, J.S. (2004) "The Online and Face-to-Face Counseling Attitudes Scales: A Validation Study", *Measurement and Evaluation in Counseling and Development*, Vol. 37, No. 2, pp 95–111.

Rupert, D.J. et al. (2014) "Perceived Healthcare Provider Reactions to Patient and Caregiver Use of Online Health Communities", *Patient Education and Counseling*, Vol. 96, No. 3, pp 320–326.

Shu, S. and Woo, B.K.P. (2020) "The Roles of YouTube and WhatsApp in Dementia Education for the Older Chinese American Population: Longitudinal Analysis", *JMIR Aging*, Vol. 3, No. 1, e18179.

Snyder, C.R. (1995) "Conceptualizing, Measuring, and Nurturing Hope", *Journal of Counseling & Development*, Vol. 73, No. 3, pp 355–360.

Snyder, C.R. (2000) "The Past and Possible Futures of Hope", *Journal of Social and Clinical Psychology*, Vol. 19, No. 1, pp 11–28.

Snyder, C.R. (2002) "Hope Theory: Rainbows in the Mind", *Psychological Inquiry*, Vol. 13, No. 4, pp 249–275.

Speyer, C. and Zack, J. (2003) "Online Counselling: Beyond the Pros and Cons", *Psychologica*, Vol. 23, No. 2, pp 11–14.

Strong, S.R. (1968) "Counseling: An Interpersonal Influence Process", *Journal of Counseling Psychology*, Vol. 15, No. 3, pp 215.

Suler, J.R. (2004) "Psychotherapy in Cyberspace: A Five Dimensional Model of Online and Computer-Mediated Psychotherapy", [online], *True Center Publishing*, http://truecenterpublishing.com/psycyber/therapy.html.

Tan, L. (2008) "Psychotherapy 2.0: MySpace® Blogging as Self–Therapy", *American Journal of Psychotherapy*, Vol. 62, No. 2, pp 143–163.

Thomas, M.L. (2006) "The Contributing Factors of Change in a Therapeutic Process", *Contemporary Family Therapy*, Vol. 28, No. 2, pp 201–210.

Vindegaard, N. and Benros, M. E. (2020) "COVID-19 Pandemic and Mental Health Consequences: Systematic Review of the Current Evidence", *Brain, Behavior, and Immunity*, Vol. 89, pp 531–542.

Wardi-Zonna, K., Hardy, J.L. and Hardy, R.M. (2020) "Mental Health Professionals and the Use of Social Media: Navigating Ethical challenges", *Journal of Social Work Values and Ethics*, Vol. 17, No. 2, pp 68–77.

PhD Research Papers

Professional Versus Personal Identities of Young Health Communicators: The Social Media Connection

Souad El Mghari[1], Merete Kolberg Tennfjord[1] and Ragnhild Eg[2]
[1]Kristiania College University, Oslo, Norway
[2]Nofima, Norway

Souad.elmghari@kristiania.no
meretekolberg.tennfjord@kristiania.no
Ragnhild.Eg@Nofima.no

Abstract: The proliferation of social media in the 21st century has redefined health communication, facilitating a participatory culture where individuals play a pivotal role in shaping health-related behaviors. Social networking sites have also become platforms for individuals to express their identity through self-perception and expression. This project thus investigates the relationship between social media and preventive health experts' professional and personal identities. The study will pay particular attention to exploring how health experts and communicators balance their sense of self in their online interactions. Therefore, this project aims to unravel the ambiguity of health communicators' online roles, making social media a safer space for them and their audiences. These individuals carry the responsibility of preserving the health and safety of others, founded in their promotion of health advice, professional guidance, and personal lifestyle demonstrations. The study targets students and experts in nutrition, mental health, and fitness and exercise based in Norway. The scope of the project is restricted to Instagram due to the platform's visual and adaptive affordances for self-expression. The research project is thus divided into three studies: The first study will apply the survey method to explore how content consumed by health students from selected universities and colleges in Norway may impact the formation of their professional identity. The second study will use interviews and content analysis to investigate the impact of the content posted and consumed by a select number of preventive health students in forming their ideal professional and personal identities. These students should be active on Instagram and have garnered over 1000 followers. Lastly, the third study will rely on a combination of interviews and content analysis to research online strategies applied by nutrition, mental health, and exercise and fitness experts to express their professional and personal identities. These individuals will be required to have over 4000 followers on Instagram.

Keywords: Social media, Instagram, Professional identity, Personal identity, Opinion leaders, Health

1. Introduction

The 21st century has seen social media emerge as a key arena for health promotion and communication, with scholars noting its role in shaping a participatory culture (Stark et al., 2022). Consequently, individual health decisions are no longer solely based on a doctor's advice but are often informed by individuals who are considered trustworthy (Dubois et al., 2020). In the context of social networking sites (SNS), these individuals are often referred to as "opinion leaders." This shift in roles comes with a moral responsibility of those health opinion leaders towards their online community, peers, and themselves.

Scholars say that social media has served as a means of identity expression (Andrews et al., 2017). This is meaningful since the significant debate in the research of self-presentation in social media is whether online self-expression is an idealized version of individuals' selves or merely an extension of images drawn in real-life contexts (SOLMAZ, 2017).

There is a noticeable gap in research concerning how individuals creating health-related content on social media perceive and shape their professional and personal identities. By identity, we refer to an individual's traits, attitudes, self-representations, and social roles. More precisely, there is a lack of investigation into the duality of identity and social media.

Considering this gap, our project aims to address the following critical research questions:

- What role does social media content play in shaping the ideal professional identity of students in preventive health fields?
- Which social media strategies are employed by health opinion leaders to express their professional and personal identities?

By exploring these questions, we aim to contribute to a nuanced understanding of the intricate relationship between social media, health promotion, and the construction of professional and personal identities of health opinion leaders. The study will focus on three pervasive topics within preventive health fields: nutrition, mental health, and fitness and exercise.

2. Health Opinion Leaders on Social Media

The development of internet technology has spawned a large number of opinion leaders (Luqiu et al., 2019), constituting worldwide experts in their fields (Savolainen, 2021), such as health. Their followers consider them knowledgeable educators who provide helpful advice (Lynn-Sze and Kamaruddin, 2021). However insightful, available studies tend to address health opinion leaders from the lens of their audience rather than from the content creator's point of view.

3. Identity Through Ervin Goffman

For Goffman, identity is not a natural or genetic state but a series of idealized performances that people present, which are unconscious and conscious (Hurley, 2019). And the mediated nature of social media platforms offers a virtual space for individuals to perform who they are (Bouvier, 2012), and to carefully create an image for themselves (VanBogart, 2014). Goffman has thus proposed an analysis of interpersonal interaction and how individuals perform to project a desirable image.

4. Professional Identity and Social Media

According to Davis (2012), online media technologies play a central part in enabling a multiplicity of identity representations. One of those representations is the professional self. Professional identity represents who you are and how you act as an individual and in groups within the confines of a particular profession (Fredriksson and Johansson, 2014). Wiik (2010) regards it as a social construct that affects how a professional might present themselves and how they might conform to certain behaviours and values. In turn, this leads others to acknowledge and trust in their behaviours as professionals. Thus, this professional identity might be what garners an opinion leader's credibility in online health promotion.

5. Personal Identity and Social Media

Personal identity refers to self-categories that define the individual as unique (Turner, 1999). O'Neil et al. (2022) suggest that personal identity is a somewhat neglected base of identity relative to social roles and identities. Thus, in the context of social media and their affordances related to self-representation, we believe that exploring the personal identity of health opinion leaders would contribute valuable insight into the distinct experiences of an individual (Peter J. Burke 2009). This investigation could further shed light on why some content creators succeed in garnering an extensive following compared to others. For instance, sharing individual values might make opinion leaders more relatable to an audience than the professional identity could achieve alone.

6. Algorithms and Identity

Social media algorithms have often been linked to identity work, such as personal values, self-perceived identity, and identity development (Karizat et al., 2021). They have been defined as computational models for transforming data into personalized content that populates a user's social feeds (Bucher, 2020). According to Bishop (2019), content creators benefit from understanding how algorithms can aid visibility, thus gaining more public attention. This idea is referred to as "Algorithm gossip" and emphasizes the role of perceived affordances of social media platforms in self-presentation choices.

7. Instagram Affordances

Studies into opinion leadership on visually-driven SNS are scarce (Casaló et al., 2020). Instagram offers numerous affordances, including its technical functions such as pinning a post; its conceptual symbolism through linguistic and visual signaling of identities, e.g. sharing images of food; and through aesthetic manipulation of image, identity, and self-presentation. Therefore, the multimodal affordances of Instagram enable users to draw upon social semiotic resources of identity, shifting representations as ideational, idealized, and imaginative affordances (Hurley, 2019).

8. Methodology

Since the impact of online self-presentation on visual platforms and how it influences individuals' self-perceived identities remains an underexplored area, we have opted for Instagram as the focal SNS of our project. Furthermore, most self-presentation research has been so far concentrated on Facebook (SOLMAZ, 2017). In the context of Norway, whose 84.7% of the population is active on social media (We are Social and Meltwater), Instagram comes second after Facebook as the most used platform (Statcounter).

For our research, we have opted for a mixed methods approach. The quantitative data will be administered as a survey targeting preventive health students in Norway. The qualitative data will offer an in-depth understanding of how health opinion leaders express their identities on social networks.

To examine the impact of Instagram content, we will employ content analysis of posts created, curated, and consumed on health opinion leaders' pages. The selection criteria are established prior to the selection process:

- The opinion leader is a student or professional of nutrition, psychology, or exercise and fitness.
- The opinion leader is an active Instagram user with a minimum following on Instagram of 1000 (for students) and 4000 (for established professionals).

In addition to the content analysis, the study will use semi-structured interviews to discuss self-presentation strategies applied by opinion leaders on Instagram. The interviews will take the forms of "a trace interview" and "a scroll back interview."

9. Conclusion

The transformative role of social media in health promotion is a research-worthy topic. Individuals deemed reliable, known as "opinion leaders," significantly influence health attitudes and behaviors. While ethical concerns in this area have been extensively researched, a significant gap exists in understanding how these leaders perceive and shape their identities on social media. Through a nuanced investigation, we hypothesize that the self-presentation processes occur outside the individual's awareness and thus might carry a much more significant impact than we currently assume.

References

andrews, J. C., Boardman, M., Brock, S., Buckler, A. S., Jordan, K. & Nkuyubwatsi, B. 2017. Digital Identity and Social Media. *Journal of Interactive Media in Education*.

Bishop, S. 2019. Managing visibility on YouTube through algorithmic gossip. *New media & society*, 21, 2589-2606.

Bouvier, G. 2012. How Facebook users select identity categories for self-presentation. *Journal of Multicultural Discourses*, 7, 37-57.

Bucher, T. 2020. Nothing to disconnect from? Being singular plural in an age of machine learning. *Media, Culture & Society*, 42, 610-617.

Casaló, L. V., Flavián, C. & Ibáñez-Sánchez, S. 2020. Influencers on Instagram: Antecedents and consequences of opinion leadership. *Journal of business research*, 117, 510-519.

Davis, K. 2012. Tensions of identity in a networked era: Young people's perspectives on the risks and rewards of online self-expression. *new media & society*, 14, 634-651.

Dubois, E., Minaeian, S., Paquet-Labelle, A. & Beaudry, S. 2020. Who to trust on social media: How opinion leaders and seekers avoid disinformation and echo chambers. *Social media+ society*, 6, 2056305120913993.

Fredriksson, M. & Johansson, B. 2014. The dynamics of professional identity: Why journalists view journalists working with PR as a threat to journalism. *Journalism Practice*, 8, 585-595.

Hurley, Z. 2019. Imagined affordances of Instagram and the fantastical authenticity of female Gulf-Arab social media influencers. *Social Media+ Society*, 5, 2056305118819241.

Karizat, N., Delmonaco, D., Eslami, M. & Andalibi, N. 2021. Algorithmic folk theories and identity: How TikTok users co-produce Knowledge of identity and engage in algorithmic resistance. *Proceedings of the ACM on Human-Computer Interaction*, 5, 1-44.

Luqiu, L. R., Schmierbach, M. & Ng, Y.-L. 2019. Willingness to follow opinion leaders: A case study of Chinese Weibo. *Computers in Human behavior*, 101, 42-50.

Lynn-Sze, J. C. & Kamaruddin, A. 2021. Online opinion leaders in the health promotion digital era. *Jurnal Komunikasi: Malaysian Journal of Communication*, 37, 295-309.

O'neil, I., Ucbasaran, D. & York, J. G. 2022. The evolution of founder identity as an authenticity work process. *Journal of business venturing*, 37, 106031.

Peter J. Burke , J. E. S. 2009. *identity theory*.

Savolainen, R. 2021. Expert power as a constituent of opinion leadership: a conceptual analysis.

Solmaz, O. 2017. The presentation of self in social networking sites: An introduction, theory and the current state of the scholarship. *Yeni Medya Elektronik Dergisi*, 5, 49-59.

Stark, A. L., Geukes, C. & Dockweiler, C. 2022. Digital health promotion and prevention in settings: scoping review. *Journal of Medical Internet Research*, 24, e21063.

Turner, J. C. Some current issues in research on social identity and self-categorization theories. 1999.

Vanbogart, S. M. 2014. *Establishing credibility online through impression management*, Gonzaga University.

Wiik, J. 2010. Journalism in transition. The professional identity of Swedish journalists. *rapport nr.: Göteborgsstudier i journalistik och masskommunikation 59*.

Swipe, Watch, Buy: Unraveling the Power of Product Placement in Short Videos on Youth Impulse Purchasing

Sinh Duc Hoang[1], Dao Anh Kim[2], Truong Phi Hung[2] and Nguyet Minh Pham[1]
[1]International University, National University of Vietnam, Vietnam
[2]Faculty of Management and Economics, Tomas Bata University in Zlin, The Czech Republic

hdsinh@hcmiu.edu.vn
kim@utb.cz
ptruong@utb.cz
ngtminhpham@gmail.com

Abstract: Drawing from the Stimulus-Organism-Response (S-O-R) model, this research aims to assess the dynamic impact of short-video product placement on the impulse buying behavior of young consumers. A structured survey was administered to a sample of 328 young consumers, aged between 18 and 30, who regularly engage with short video content on platforms like TikTok, Instagram, and Reels. The findings reveal that product relevance significantly enhances enjoyment, thereby improving engagement with narratives that incorporate product placements seamlessly. Emotional appeal in content markedly increases this enjoyment, underlining the effectiveness of emotionally resonant narratives and visuals. The study further demonstrates that a robust product-influencer fit amplifies the authenticity of the advertising message, leading to greater content enjoyment for viewers. Crucially, it confirms that the perceived enjoyment derived from engaging with short videos has a positive correlation with impulse buying behavior among young consumers. These insights underscore the importance of emotional and experiential elements in short-video content, shaping the purchasing decisions of younger audiences. This research contributes to the understanding of effective marketing strategies in the evolving digital realm, emphasizing the necessity for content creators and advertisers to prioritize narrative integration, emotional connectivity, and authenticity of influencer endorsements to effectively captivate and influence the youth market.

Keywords: Product placement, Short video, Impulse buying, Young consumer, Stimulus-Organism-Response

1. Introduction

The increasing prominence of short-video advertisements on social media platforms, especially TikTok, is revolutionizing the global marketing landscape, marking a significant shift in the mobile internet advertising sector (van der Bend et al., 2023). This trend is propelled by the platforms' extensive reach and inherently engaging content, which resonates with the fast-paced content consumption preferences of contemporary audiences worldwide. Short-video advertisements have become a leading marketing strategy globally, effectively blending entertainment with product promotion (Wang et al., 2023). Influencers and short-video bloggers across various cultures and regions are adeptly capitalizing on this trend, integrating product endorsements into their content to create a more authentic and immersive viewer experience (Ong et al., 2022). This fusion of entertainment and advertising underscores the need for short-video platforms to innovate and develop new e-commerce models. Such models are essential for creating a self-sustaining business ecosystem that attracts and retains top-tier internet celebrities, ensuring a consistent supply of engaging content for global audiences and a dynamic advertising medium for brands. This paradigm shift in digital marketing strategies positions short-video platforms at the forefront of the advertising industry in the mobile internet era, representing a significant evolution in how brands interact with consumers worldwide (Yin et al., 2024).

In the realm of modern social media platforms such as Douyin, Reels, and TikTok, a significant number of online influencers are effectively engaging audiences through the use of humorous and plot-driven short videos, a method that adeptly captures viewer attention (Wang, 2020). These influencers employ a strategic approach by incorporating products into their video narratives, subtly directing their substantial follower base's attention towards these products and fostering a propensity for purchase. This technique of product placement, historically utilized in films, television, and variety shows, is now being innovatively applied to the short-video format (Wang & Chen, 2019). Unlike traditional short-video advertisements that explicitly market products, these narrative-driven placements are more engaging and less intrusive, offering a refined viewer experience. Furthermore, when compared to the more overt product endorsements on older social platforms like Instagram, Facebook, these story-centric product placements in short videos are perceived as less aggressive in their marketing intent. The subtlety of this approach, coupled with its entertainment value, presents a compelling and innovative model for advertising in the dynamic world of short video content, striking a balance between commercial promotion and creative storytelling (Allal-Chérif et al., 2024).

The recent research by (Olayemi, 2022) reveals that the daily routines of the youth demographic, specifically those aged 16 to 24, are significantly influenced by social media, with a staggering 90% of them engaging with these platforms every day and averaging over three hours of usage time. This extensive interaction with social media, particularly platforms like TikTok, has profound implications for their consumer behavior patterns. Notably, there is an emergent propensity for impulse purchasing among young users, influenced by the content they encounter in short videos on TikTok (Zhang et al., 2023). The immediacy, visual appeal, and influencer-driven content of these videos are identified as primary catalysts for impulsive buying decisions. Allal-Chérif et al., 2024) highlights that the persuasive influence of TikTok content creators, coupled with the platform's algorithmically tailored content feeds, significantly elevates the propensity for impulse purchases among this demographic. Brüns & Meißner (2023) further elucidate that the platform's algorithm enhances the relevance and persuasive power of product placements, thereby intensifying their impact. Thus, the pervasive engagement of youth with social media, especially in the context of short video content, is not merely shaping their media consumption habits but is also markedly influencing their purchasing decisions.

Despite the burgeoning trend of marketing through short-video platforms, this approach is still in its nascent stages, with significant challenges in capturing and sustaining audience engagement through product placement (van der Bend et al., 2023). It is crucial for these advertisements to not only capture the attention of viewers but also to persuade them, fostering a deeper interest and inclination towards purchasing the featured products. To acquire a more comprehensive understanding of how viewers perceive and interact with these short-video product placements, and to identify the critical factors influencing their decision-making processes, a detailed empirical research study has been conducted. This study aims to bridge the gap in understanding impulse buying among young consumers in response to product placements in short videos, providing insights into effective marketing strategies in this evolving digital landscape.

2. Literature Review

Product relevance, within the sphere of short video product placement advertising, refers to the degree of alignment between the featured product and the narrative of the video(Deng & Xie, 2022). For product placements to be effective, the products must be interwoven into the storyline seamlessly, so that their presence feels natural and pertinent to the unfolding plot. This congruence ensures that the viewer perceives the product as an organic element of the scenario, which in turn enhances the viewer's receptiveness to the advertising message. When the intrinsic attributes of the product resonate with the context of the plot, the product placement is seen as appropriate and is more likely to be well-received by the audience. Conversely, a mismatch between the product and the plot can lead to viewer dissonance, diminishing the credibility of the placement and potentially resulting in an adverse reaction to both the product and the advertisement itself.

Emotional appeal, in the field of marketing and consumer behavior, refers to the capacity of content to establish a deep emotional connection with the audience (Mogaji et al., 2018). The connection is established by strategically employing narratives, visuals, music, and messaging that strongly resonate with the emotions, principles, and aspirations of the viewers. The emotional appeal is crucial in capturing and maintaining the attention of young consumers who watch short videos on platforms such as TikTok. TikTok content, characterized by its rapid pace and visually captivating nature, effectively elicits a wide array of emotions, including joy, humor, empathy, and inspiration, through its personal and relatable storytelling. These emotions not only stimulate involvement but also shape the viewers' attitudes and behaviors towards the content and any related products or messages. The effectiveness of short videos on TikTok for young consumers, who are primarily motivated by entertainment and emotional experiences, depends greatly on their capacity to elicit emotional responses, thus generating a memorable and influential viewer experience.

The concept of product-influencer fit is defined on the congruence between a product's characteristics and the personal brand of the endorsing influencer (Rayasam & Khattri, 2022). The optimal alignment between a product and an influencer occurs when there is a harmonious relationship between the influencer's well-established image, encompassing their lifestyle and the characteristics of their audience, and the fundamental nature and attributes of the product being promoted. For example, a well-known influencer who is known for promoting a fitness-focused lifestyle would effortlessly promote products related to health. The combination of these factors enhances the genuineness of the endorsement, thereby bolstering the trust and approval of the audience. Conversely, if there is a discrepancy between the influencer's image and the product, it can result in a lack of connection with the audience, which may diminish the effectiveness of the advertisement and potentially harm the reputation of both the product and the influencer. The influencer's portrayal in the story serves as a crucial representative for the product, and their compatibility greatly influences audience perceptions of both the advertisement and the product. When elements are in harmonious alignment, it makes it easier for the audience to accept the message. On the other hand, a stark contrast can disrupt the flow of communication and have a negative impact on how the audience perceives the message.

Perceived enjoyment, in the context of online shopping, is defined as the extent to which a consumer finds pleasure and satisfaction in the shopping experience, independent of the instrumental outcomes of the activity (Ashfaq et al., 2019). This concept, rooted in the intrinsic motivation theory, posits that the enjoyment derived from an activity itself, rather than any external rewards it may bring, can be a powerful motivator for consumer behavior. In online shopping environments, perceived enjoyment is characterized by feelings of fun, pleasure, and entertainment experienced during the browsing and purchasing process. It is a critical factor influencing consumer attitudes towards online shopping, their intention to revisit e-commerce platforms, and their overall satisfaction with the online shopping experience. Perceived enjoyment has been recognized as a significant determinant of online consumer behavior, affecting both the decision to engage in online shopping and the impulse buying behavior (Chan et al., 2022).

The Stimulus-Organism-Response (SOR) model is a psychological framework that explains how individuals react to external stimuli. In this model, a stimulus triggers an internal change within the organism, leading to a behavioral response (Murray & Häubl, 2007). The 'Organism' is the individual's internal processing, encompassing emotional, cognitive, and attitudinal mechanisms, which mediate between the stimulus and the response.

Based on the Stimulus-Organism-Response (SOR) model, the presence of product placement in short videos is identified as a notable stimulus for young consumers (Kim et al., 2021). Primary stimuli in this context include factors such as the product's relevance to the viewer's interests, the emotional impact of the content, and the alignment between the influencer and the product. These factors are intentionally crafted to stimulate the cognitive and emotional processes of young viewers. The organism in this model, specifically the consumer's internal state, is exemplified by perceived enjoyment, which is a combination of entertainment and interest sparked by the video content. The state of enjoyment plays a crucial role by acting as a mediator between external stimuli and the resulting behavioral response (Hoang et al., 2023). The resulting reaction is frequently marked by impulsive purchasing, where the immediate gratification obtained from the captivating viewing experience leads to a spontaneous decision to buy. The motivation behind this behavior is primarily derived from the emotional satisfaction gained from acquiring a product that is associated with enjoyable and captivating content, rather than being driven by the product's practical necessity. Based on the arguments presented above, the following hypotheses are proposed:

H1: Product relevance has a positive effect on perceived enjoyment of young consumer.

H2: Emotional appeal has a positive effect on perceived enjoyment of young consumer

H3: Product Influencer Fit has a positive effect on perceived enjoyment of young consumer

Impulse buying behavior refers to the spontaneous, unplanned decision to purchase a product or service, made just before a purchase (Pradhan, 2018). This behavior is characterized by an immediate, powerful urge to buy something instantly, often triggered by external factors such as advertising, store layout, or promotions, as well as internal states like emotions or mood. In the context of young consumers, impulse buying tends to be more prevalent due to their higher susceptibility to emotional and social influences. Young shoppers, often driven by a desire for instant gratification and influenced by trends and peer behaviors, are more likely to make purchases on a whim. This tendency is further amplified in the digital age, where social media platforms and online shopping provide constant exposure to tempting products and easy, one-click purchasing options. The combination of these factors means that impulse buying among young consumers can be both a frequent and emotionally charged behavior, significantly influenced by the evolving dynamics of modern consumer culture.

Perceived enjoyment in watching short videos plays a pivotal role in driving impulse purchases among young consumers (Siew Chein Teo et al., 2023). This phenomenon can be attributed to the immersive and emotionally engaging nature of short video content, which heightens the viewers' emotional state and lowers their decision-making guard. When young viewers find enjoyment in a video, particularly on platforms like TikTok or Instagram, it creates a positive emotional connection with the content and, by extension, any products featured within it. This heightened emotional state can lead to impulsive decision-making, as the pleasure derived from the video experience translates into a spontaneous desire to purchase related products. The immediacy and ease of online shopping further facilitate this impulse buying behavior. Young consumers, already inclined towards instant gratification and influenced by digital trends, find it easy to act on these impulses, often with just a few clicks.

Thus, the perceived enjoyment of short videos acts as a catalyst, converting the momentary emotional high and the associated desire for a similar experience into an immediate purchase decision.

H4: Perceived enjoyment has a positive effect on impulse buying of young consumer.

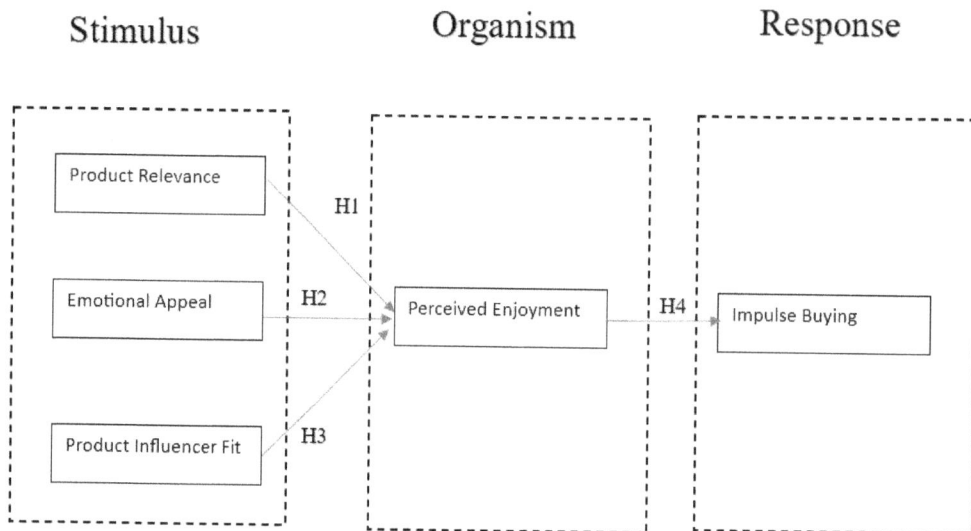

Figure 1: The conceptual framework

3. Methodology

For the empirical aspect of this study, data was gathered using a structured survey. This survey was organized into two sections. The initial section introduced the research scenario to respondents, laying out various measures for each variable under consideration. It prompted participants to think back to their most recent encounter with product placement in a short video advertisement before responding to the subsequent questions. The latter section of the survey was designed to gather demographic information of the individuals. The survey items were carefully crafted, drawing inspiration from established scales and adapting them to the unique context of short video advertising. These items were subject to extensive theoretical scrutiny and validation in line with the objectives of the research, ensuring a high level of academic rigor. The finalized set of survey items can be found detailed in Table 1.

Table 1: Construct measurement

Construct	Items	Sources
Product relevance	PR1: I believe the product featured in the short video closely aligns with the storyline	(Davis et al., 1989)
	PR2: I perceive a strong connection between the product shown in the short video and the depicted scene.	
	PR3: I feel that the product in the short video is well-suited to the characters involved in the narrative.	
Emotional Appeal	EA1: The short video is fun	(Phua & Kim, 2018)
	EA2: The short video is humorous	
	EA3: The short video is amusing	
Product Influencer Fit	PI1: I believe that the influencer is appropriate for promoting the products featured in the short video's storyline.	(Till & Busler, 2000)
	PI2: I feel that there is a good fit between the influencer and the product being advertised.	
Perceived Enjoyment	PE1: The short video evoked a sense of enjoyment in the shopping experience for me	(Meng et al., 2021)
	PE2: I experienced a sense of excitement during the product introductions	

Construct	Items	Sources
	PE3: The captivating nature of the short video content was fascinating to me.	
	PE4: Viewing short videos on social media platforms causes time to pass quickly, making me forget all my concerns.	
Impulse Buying	IB1: I frequently notice that I give in to impulsive purchasing habits while watching short video on social media platform	(X. Zhang et al., 2023)
	IB2: While watching short video on social media platform, I made a spontaneous purchase without thoroughly thinking through and assessing the product.	
	IB3: Some products had previously gone unnoticed by me, but after watching the short video again, I ended up making impulsive purchases of them.	
	IB4: After discovering the product in short video, I suddenly became aware of my need for a specific product, leading me to buy it impulsively	

In this research, a 5-point Likert scale was utilized for quantitative measurement, with the scale ranging from 1 (strongly disagree) to 5 (strongly agree). The survey was disseminated through both online and offline mediums across various age demographics. Participants who completed the survey were offered a nominal compensation as a token of appreciation. The duration for collecting responses spanned from January 12, 2023, to February 12, 2023. Within this one-month period, a total of 562 responses were gathered. However, after removing responses that were either invalid or from individuals who had not encountered product placement ads in short videos, or those outside the 18-30 age range, the final count of valid questionnaires stood at 328.

Table 2 presents the fundamental statistics of the sample population. The data indicates a relatively balanced distribution between male and female participants. The majority of respondents have an undergraduate level of education. A significant portion of the participants reported using short video apps for more than 2 hours a day.

Table 2: Demographic of participants

Variables	Items	Frequency	%
Gender	Male	161	49.08
	Female	167	50.92
Level of education	High school	46	14.02
	Undergraduate	156	47.56
	Postgraduate	126	48.42
Daily engagement with short video app	Below 30 min	67	20.42
	30 min – 1 hour	73	22.25
	1-2 hours	87	26.52
	More than 2 hours	101	30.81

4. Result

In this research, the Partial Least Squares (PLS) method from SmartPLS 3.3 was applied to assess the measurement model's reliability and validity. The reliability of the model was assessed using Cronbach's Alpha (α) and Composite Reliability (CR) values, while its overall validity was determined by the Average Variance Extracted (AVE) value. Discriminant validity was assessed by comparing the square root of the average variance extracted (AVE) with the absolute correlation coefficients between the variable in question and other variables. The model's reliability, overall validity, and discriminant validity are presented in Tables 3 and 4.

According to Table 3, the model demonstrates strong reliability, as evidenced by all item outer loadings exceeding 0.8, CR values surpassing 0.8, and α values ranging from 0.744 to 0.915. The average extracted (AVE) values for all variables, ranging from 0.654 to 0.816, indicate strong overall validity. Table 4 demonstrates the model's strong ability to distinguish between variables, as indicated by the correlation coefficients between variables (values below the diagonal line in columns) being smaller than the square root of each variable's AVE value (values on the diagonal line).

Table 3 Consistency reliability and Convergent validity

Constructs and Relevant Indicators		Convergent validity		Internal consistency reliability		
		Loadings ≥0.70	AVE >0.50	Composite Reliability	Cronbach's Alpha	Rho_A
Product Relevance (PR)	PR1	0.860	0.654	0.848	0.744	0.848
	PR2	0.891				
	PR3	0.856				
Emotional Appeal (EA)	EA1	0.824	0.732	0.891	0.818	0.836
	EA2	0.883				
	EA3	0.858				
Product Influencer Fit (PI)	PI1	0.898	0.816	0.899	0.774	0.776
	PI2	0.909				
Perceived Enjoyment (PE)	PE1	0.868	0.748	0.922	0.887	0.889
	PE2	0.821				
	PE3	0.881				
	PE4	0.889				
Impulse Buying (IB)	IB1	0.884	0.798	0.940	0.915	0.917
	IB2	0.844				
	IB3	0.883				
	IB4	0.959				

Table 4: Discriminant validity

	EA	IB	PE	PI	PR
EA	0.855				
IB	0.478	0.893			
PE	0.443	0.564	0.865		
PI	0.425	0.515	0.479	0.903	
PR	0.448	0.546	0.597	0.671	0.809

The estimated model based on the result is shown in Figure 2

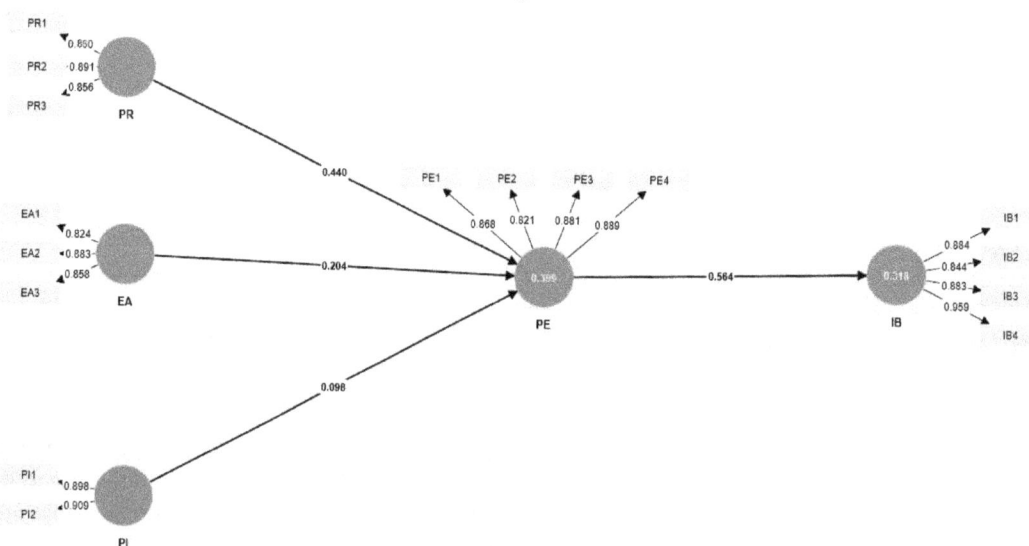

Figure 2: The estimated model

The bootstrapping method will serve as the basis for conducting significance testing in order to assess the extent to which predictors have a substantial impact on target constructs in conceptual models (Hair et al., 2017). This study employs the bootstrapping method, utilizing 5,000 samples at a significance level of 5%, as recommended by Hair et al. (2017), with the assistance of SmartPLS. The findings are succinctly presented in the Table 5

Table 5: Summary of hypothesis testing

	Original sample (O)	Sample mean (M)	Standard deviation (STDEV)	T statistics (|O/STDEV|)	P values
EA -> PE	0.204	0.206	0.062	3.305	0.001
PE -> IB	0.564	0.566	0.049	11.621	0.000
PI -> PE	0.098	0.098	0.070	5.451	0.001
PR -> PE	0.440	0.441	0.051	8.666	0.000

5. Discussion

The findings provide evidence in support of H1, which suggests that the relevance of a product has a positive impact on the perceived enjoyment of young consumers in short video advertising. This finding aligns with established theories in marketing, advertising psychology, and consumer behavior, suggesting that when products are seamlessly integrated into narratives that resonate with the intended audience, it greatly enhances the viewer's enjoyment of the content (Hewei, 2022). It emphasizes that young consumers experience greater enjoyment and fulfillment from brief video content when product placements are seamlessly integrated into the storyline. This observation highlights the importance of having relevant advertising content, particularly in the context of the ever-changing preferences and consumption habits of young consumers. This confirmation suggests that young viewers are more likely to be interested in and value content that demonstrates genuineness and relatability. In such content, product placements are seamlessly incorporated, enhancing the plot instead of interrupting it.

The validation of H2 indicates that the inclusion of emotional appeal in short video advertisements greatly amplifies the perceived pleasure of young consumers, in accordance with contemporary consumer psychology and digital marketing theories. This supports the notion that content that contains a significant amount of emotional elements has a stronger impact on its audience, particularly among younger viewers. The endorsement of H2 suggests an increased inclination among young consumers to appreciate and interact with content that successfully elicits emotional reactions. This trend can be attributed to the significant impact of emotions on the formation of attitudes and the process of decision-making. The utilization of emotionally charged narratives, compelling visuals, and evocative music proves to be a vital element in captivating the young audience, thus enhancing their overall content enjoyment. This highlights the crucial significance of emotional appeal in crafting content that not only captures the attention but also deeply engages young viewers (Akpinar & Berger, 2017).

The findings strongly support H3, which highlights the important influence of product-influencer fit on the perceived enjoyment of young consumers in short video advertising. This emphasizes that the alignment between a product's attributes and the influencer's personal brand is crucial in enhancing the audience's viewing experience. This validation demonstrates that young viewers experience higher levels of enjoyment when the attributes of a product closely align with the influencer's image and lifestyle. This congruency enhances the authenticity and relatability of the advertising message. The seamless alignment between the influencer's image and the endorsed product amplifies the authenticity of the endorsement, thus increasing the audience's involvement and satisfaction with the content (Tian et al., 2022).

The support for H4 confirms that perceived enjoyment from engaging with short video content on platforms like TikTok or Instagram positively influences the impulse buying behavior of young consumers, aligning with key concepts in consumer psychology and behavioral economics (Pradhan, 2018). This validation emphasizes the essential importance of emotional and experiential factors in the digital domain. In this context, the pleasure and emotional involvement offered by such content play a significant role in driving impulsive buying decisions. The captivating quality of these videos engrosses the viewers and elicits instant emotional satisfaction, resulting in impulsive urges to buy the products showcased or linked to the content. This discovery emphasizes the powerful impact of engaging brief video content on shaping the purchasing behaviors of young consumers in the current digital environment.

6. Conclusion

This study has explored the intricate dynamics of short-video product placement and its influence on impulse buying behavior among young consumers, guided by the Stimulus-Organism-Response (S-O-R) model. Our findings shed light on the significant role of product relevance, emotional appeal, and product-influencer fit in enhancing perceived enjoyment, which in turn fosters impulse purchasing among the youth demographic. By seamlessly integrating product placements within engaging narratives that resonate on an emotional level, advertisers and content creators can significantly amplify viewer engagement and spur on-the-spot purchasing decisions.

The evidence suggests that young consumers are not merely passive recipients of advertising content; rather, they are actively engaged by content that is relevant, emotionally resonant, and authentic. This engagement is crucial in a digital age where attention is fragmented and competition for viewer interest is fierce. The study underscores the necessity for marketers to craft strategies that align with the interests and emotional landscapes of their target audience, leveraging the persuasive power of influencers who share a genuine connection with the products they endorse.

Moreover, the positive correlation between perceived enjoyment and impulse buying behavior highlights the importance of creating enjoyable and immersive viewing experiences. In the realm of digital marketing, where the line between entertainment and advertising is increasingly blurred, the ability to entertain becomes as crucial as the ability to persuade.

Implications for Practice

For practitioners, these insights underscore the need to invest in content that not only showcases products but does so in a way that is engaging, emotionally appealing, and authentic. Marketers should prioritize collaborations with influencers whose personal brand aligns with their product values, ensuring a natural and credible integration of product placements into content that captivates and resonates with young audiences.

Future Research Directions

While this study offers valuable insights into the effectiveness of product placement in short videos, future research could explore the long-term impact of such marketing strategies on brand loyalty and consumer behavior. Additionally, investigating the differential impact of various types of emotional appeal and narrative styles across diverse cultural contexts could further enrich our understanding of global consumer behavior in the digital age.

References

Akpinar, E., & Berger, J. (2017). Valuable Virality. *Journal of Marketing Research*, *54*(2), 318–330. https://doi.org/10.1509/jmr.13.0350

Allal-Chérif, O., Puertas, R., & Carracedo, P. (2024). Intelligent influencer marketing: how AI-powered virtual influencers outperform human influencers. *Technological Forecasting and Social Change, 200*, 123113. https://doi.org/10.1016/j.techfore.2023.123113

Ashfaq, M., Yun, J., Waheed, A., Khan, M. S., & Farrukh, M. (2019). Customers' Expectation, Satisfaction, and Repurchase Intention of Used Products Online: Empirical Evidence From China. *SAGE Open, 9*(2), 215824401984621. https://doi.org/10.1177/2158244019846212

Brüns, J. D., & Meißner, M. (2023). Show me that you are advertising: Visual salience of products attenuates detrimental effects of persuasion knowledge activation in influencer advertising. *Computers in Human Behavior, 148*, 107891. https://doi.org/10.1016/j.chb.2023.107891

Chan, X. Y., Rahman, M. K., Mamun, A. Al, A. Salameh, A., Wan Hussain, W. M. H., & Alam, S. S. (2022). Predicting the Intention and Adoption of Mobile Shopping During the COVID-19 Lockdown in Malaysia. *SAGE Open, 12*(2), 215824402210950. https://doi.org/10.1177/21582440221095012

Davis, F. D., Bagozzi, R. P., & Warshaw, P. R. (1989). User Acceptance of Computer Technology: A Comparison of Two Theoretical Models. *Management Science, 35*(8), 982–1003. https://doi.org/10.1287/mnsc.35.8.982

Deng, Z., & Xie, B. (2022). Analysis of Audiences' Attitudes towards Product Placement in Short Videos Based on Appraisal Theory: A Case Study of the Bilibili Platform. *International Journal of Social Science Studies, 10*(4), 83. https://doi.org/10.11114/ijsss.v10i4.5633

Hair, J., Hollingsworth, C. L., Randolph, A. B., & Chong, A. Y. L. (2017). An updated and expanded assessment of PLS-SEM in information systems research. *Industrial Management and Data Systems, 117*(3), 442–458. https://doi.org/10.1108/IMDS-04-2016-0130

Hewei, T. (2022). Factors affecting clothing purchase intention in mobile short video app: Mediation of perceived value and immersion experience. *PLOS ONE, 17*(9), e0273968. https://doi.org/10.1371/journal.pone.0273968

Hoang, S. D., Dey, S. K., Pham, T. P., & Tučková, Z. (2023). Harnessing the power of virtual reality: Enhancing telepresence and inspiring sustainable travel intentions in the tourism industry. *Technology in Society*, 102378. https://doi.org/10.1016/j.techsoc.2023.102378

Jesse P Ong, I., John V Teñoso, D., Nicholas G. Valmonte, M., & E. Etrata, J. A. (2022). Influencer Marketing in the Digital Age: The Response to Authentic Creator Content. *Millennium Journal of Humanities and Social Sciences*, 15–28. https://doi.org/10.47340/mjhss.v3i2.2.2022

Kim, J.-H., Kim, M., Park, M., & Yoo, J. (2021). How interactivity and vividness influence consumer virtual reality shopping experience: the mediating role of telepresence. *Journal of Research in Interactive Marketing*, 15(3), 502–525. https://doi.org/10.1108/JRIM-07-2020-0148

Meng, L. (Monroe), Duan, S., Zhao, Y., Lü, K., & Chen, S. (2021). The impact of online celebrity in livestreaming E-commerce on purchase intention from the perspective of emotional contagion. *Journal of Retailing and Consumer Services*, 63, 102733. https://doi.org/10.1016/j.jretconser.2021.102733

Mogaji, E., Czarnecka, B., & Danbury, A. (2018). Emotional appeals in UK business-to-business financial services advertisements. *International Journal of Bank Marketing*, 36(1), 208–227. https://doi.org/10.1108/IJBM-09-2016-0127

Murray, K. B., & Häubl, G. (2007). Explaining Cognitive Lock-In: The Role of Skill-Based Habits of Use in Consumer Choice. *Journal of Consumer Research*, 34(1), 77–88. https://doi.org/10.1086/513048

Olayemi, O. M. (2022). Perceived Influence of Social Media Usage Among Youth: A Survey. *Open Journal for Information Technology*, 5(2), 41–54. https://doi.org/10.32591/coas.ojit.0502.01041o

Phua, J., & Kim, J. (Jay). (2018). Starring in your own Snapchat advertisement: Influence of self-brand congruity, self-referencing and perceived humor on brand attitude and purchase intention of advertised brands. *Telematics and Informatics*, 35(5), 1524–1533. https://doi.org/10.1016/j.tele.2018.03.020

Pradhan, V. (2018). Study on Impulsive Buying Behavior among Consumers in Supermarket in Kathmandu Valley. *Journal of Business and Social Sciences Research*, 1(2), 215. https://doi.org/10.3126/jbssr.v1i2.20926

Rayasam, L. S., & Khattri, V. (2022). Social Media Influencer Endorsement. *International Journal of Online Marketing*, 12(1), 1–14. https://doi.org/10.4018/IJOM.299403

Siew Chein Teo, Wan Ying Tee, & Tze Wei Liew. (2023). EXPLORING THE TIKTOK INFLUENCES ON CONSUMER IMPULSIVE PURCHASE BEHAVIOUR. *International Journal of Business and Society*, 24(1), 39–55. https://doi.org/10.33736/ijbs.5600.2023

Tian, K., Xuan, W., Hao, L., Wei, W., Li, D., & Zhu, L. (2022). Exploring youth consumer behavior in the context of mobile short video advertising using an extended stimulus–organization–response model. *Frontiers in Psychology*, 13. https://doi.org/10.3389/fpsyg.2022.933542

Till, B. D., & Busler, M. (2000). The Match-Up Hypothesis: Physical Attractiveness, Expertise, and the Role of Fit on Brand Attitude, Purchase Intent and Brand Beliefs. *Journal of Advertising*, 29(3), 1–13. https://doi.org/10.1080/00913367.2000.10673613

van der Bend, D. L. M., Gijsman, N., Bucher, T., Shrewsbury, V. A., van Trijp, H., & van Kleef, E. (2023). Can I @handle it? The effects of sponsorship disclosure in TikTok influencer marketing videos with different product integration levels on adolescents' persuasion knowledge and brand outcomes. *Computers in Human Behavior*, 144, 107723. https://doi.org/10.1016/j.chb.2023.107723

Wang, Y. (2020). Humor and camera view on mobile short-form video apps influence user experience and technology-adoption intent, an example of TikTok (DouYin). *Computers in Human Behavior*, 110, 106373. https://doi.org/10.1016/j.chb.2020.106373

Wang, Y., & Chen, H. (2019). The influence of dialogic engagement and prominence on visual product placement in virtual reality videos. *Journal of Business Research*, 100, 493–502. https://doi.org/10.1016/j.jbusres.2019.01.018

Wang, Y., Mohamed Salim, N. A., Subri, S., Zhang, X., & Zhu, M. (2023). The Features of TikTok Viral Video Advertising: A Systematic Review. *2023 International Conference on Informatics, Multimedia, Cyber and Informations System (ICIMCIS)*, 267–272. https://doi.org/10.1109/ICIMCIS60089.2023.10349038

Yin, X., Li, J., Si, H., & Wu, P. (2024). Attention marketing in fragmented entertainment: How advertising embedding influences purchase decision in short-form video apps. *Journal of Retailing and Consumer Services*, 76, 103572. https://doi.org/10.1016/j.jretconser.2023.103572

Zhang, W., Zhang, W., & Daim, T. U. (2023). Investigating consumer purchase intention in online social media marketing: A case study of Tiktok. *Technology in Society*, 74, 102289. https://doi.org/10.1016/j.techsoc.2023.102289

Zhang, X., Cheng, X., & Huang, X. (2023). "Oh, My God, Buy It!" Investigating Impulse Buying Behavior in Live Streaming Commerce. *International Journal of Human–Computer Interaction*, 39(12), 2436–2449. https://doi.org/10.1080/10447318.2022.2076773

A Comprehensive Bibliometric Study of Product Placement with an Ethical Emphasis

Anh Dao Kim[1], Sinh Duc Hoang[2], Truong Phi Hung[1] and Dieu Hue Nguyen[2]
[1]Faculty of Management and Economics, Tomas Bata University in Zlín, The Czech Republic
[2]International University, National University of Vietnam, Vietnam

kim@utb.cz
hdsinh@hcmiu.edu.vn
ptruong@utb.cz
nguyendieuhue1511@gmail.com

Abstract: Product placement, also known as brand placement, has become a practice, in forms of media such as movies, music, games, cartoons and even social media. By increasing brand visibility and creating a sense of credibility for consumers it offers an avenue for advertising that doesn't feel like marketing. In this research study we have utilized methodologies to analyze the framework of the research field and the specific issue at hand by employing VoSViewer software. Our analysis focuses on a sample of 409 documents published between 1995 and 2023. The objective is to provide indicators including publication trends, citation patterns, notable authors, influential journals, and significant keywords. Additionally, we explore the reach of product placement research by examining its dispersion. This study contributes to both understanding and practical knowledge about product placements impact on consumer behavior brand management practices and social media platforms. Lastly. Importantly we emphasize the considerations that should be considered when implementing product placement as a marketing strategy, for any company.

Keywords: Product placement, Brand placement, Ethical, Bibliometric

1. Introduction

According to Davtyan and Cunningham (2017), the effectiveness of television ads is decreasing because of several factors, including the persistent increase in the amount of ad clutter, the segmentation of the media, the development of gadgets that allow viewers to skip advertisements, and the continuing increase in the cost of television commercials. The field of marketing has undergone changes due to advancements. Social media has replaced media channels ushering in an era of communication and brand engagement. Moreover, the advent of novel digital media, such as social media platforms, has impacted conventional media by giving rise to online platforms and social media (Alzubi, 2022). In response to the age businesses have adapted their strategies to leverage the opportunities it presents. Digital marketing has emerged as a versatile approach that aims to engage a consumer population. Digital marketing relies on tools and platforms to acquire and retain clients effectively. By utilizing digital channels organizations can tailor their messages for demographics resulting in a personalized and engaging brand experience. Companies are fully harnessing the potential of marketing by integrating their brands into different aspects of consumers lives.

An interesting and attention-grabbing strategy that has been gaining popularity is known as product placement or brand placement. This technique involves incorporating brands into forms of media like movies, music, games, cartoons, and social media. The purpose of product placement is to increase brand visibility and establish a connection with consumers that goes beyond advertising methods. By integrating into mainstream culture, it provides an opportunity to connect with people in an organic and immersive way without relying solely on marketing tactics.

In this study we dive into the framework of the emerging field of product placement using methods and the VoSViewer software to build upon research. We thoroughly examine a collection of 409 documents published between 1995 and 2023 to uncover publication patterns, citation trends, influential authors and journals as significant keywords related to product placement. Additionally, we explore how research on product placement is geographically distributed, shedding light on its reach.

The main objective of this research is to deepen our understanding of how product placement impacts consumer behavior, brand management and the vast landscape of media through more than analysis. As the study progresses it becomes evident that while product placement offers promising marketing opportunities ethical considerations must take precedence in its implementation. The report advocates for an approach that encourages businesses to consider the ethical implications of product placement, as an integral part of their overall marketing strategies.

2. Literature Review

2.1 Product Placement Literature Review

Recent technological advancements have had an impact on marketing strategies leading organizations to adapt and adopt approaches to stay competitive (Hair, 2014). Moreover, as the media continues to evolve traditional advertising methods are gradually losing their effectiveness. To tackle this challenge product placement has emerged as a marketing technique that utilizes advertising platforms. Product placement, alternatively known as brand integration involves incorporating branded items or identifiers into media content with objectives in mind (Wiles & Danielova 2009). This could encompass placement in films, TV shows, music videos or video games to capture the attention of consumers and shape their attitudes and behaviors towards the promoted product (Cokki et al., 2023). Despite being more costly compared to advertising methods, product placement has proven effective in establishing positive associations with program attributes enhancing memory retention and building meaningful connections. Given these advantages it offers marketers (Yao & Huang 2017) product placement has become an option, for businesses seeking cost promotional strategies.

Product placement is regarded as a strategy that influences consumers purchase intentions by showcasing advertisements in locations that attract customers attention (Advincula et al., 2021). In a study conducted by Melati and Abdurachman in 2021 the primary aim of this platform is to assist publishers in generating profits. Additionally, it serves as a platform where marketers can promote their products through books. Moreover, product placement is acknowledged as an advertising strategy, in music videos. Is widely utilized in campaigns (Piazzolla et al., 2021). Product placement is renowned for its ability to influence people's perception of brands thus gaining endorsements and maximizing the advantages of featuring products on listing sites (Boeing et al., 2013).

2.2 Bibliometric

2.2.1 Bibliometric analysis

The term "bibliometric analysis" refers to a technique used for reviewing and analyzing a collection of books, in a field of study. When studying the development of knowledge over time it is important to recognize the contributions made by researchers and identify areas where significant advancements have taken place (Hossain, 2020). By adopting this approach researchers can gain insights from studies that focus on the theories related to a research issue. Also suggest avenues for exploration (Ellili, 2022). Ellili is credited with developing this approach. Ahmad et al. (2019) state that bibliometric analysis offers methods to examine research outcomes and quantify efforts in tracking the evolution of knowledge across sectors over time. Academics, such as Winkowska and colleagues (2019) also utilize this method to create representations that illustrate connections and overlaps between areas of study.

Bibliometric analysis has gained recognition for its effectiveness in classifying materials showcasing networks of research contributions and mapping studies within literature fields (Gzahli et al., 2022). This additional aspect has garnered admiration among researchers. They find analysis as a tool for examining research data, especially citations and information found in journals and publications (Ananda & Nandiyanto 2022). It is widely acknowledged for enhancing the quality of research (Ragadhita & Nandiyanto 2021). Researchers have been using analysis to help marketers identify areas and emerging trends, in different fields of study (Chen et al., 2022).

2.2.2 Bibliometric analysis in digital marketing

In the field of marketing bibliometric analysis involves the study and representation of published research papers. This approach assists researchers in exploring research networks identifying patterns and systematically evaluating advancements in marketing research. As mentioned by Amiri et al. (2023) this method provides insights into both the quantity and quality of research networks that focus on marketing subjects.

Researchers employing this methodology analyze publications, authors, and research paths to develop an understanding of the marketing landscape (Pham et al., 2022; Wani, 2023). Furthermore, bibliometric analysis aids in identifying emerging trends and potential opportunities within the realm of marketing for enterprises (SMEs) (Amiri et al., 2023). It also facilitates the exploration of topics of interest and visualization of collaboration networks within the field (Inan, 2023; Sharma et al., 2022). This method empowers us to examine publishing patterns, citation networks and keyword trends to gain insights into marketing resources. Such studies hold value in assessing the importance and impact of marketing research endeavors (Amiri et al., 2023; Gao et al.,

2021; Pham et al., 2022). Jain et al. (2021) emphasized the effectiveness of this method in enhancing our comprehension of the patterns and trends found in publications regarding this matter. Thus, it empowers us to pinpoint areas for investigation and develop a research plan for studies.

3. Method

In order to find scholarly material that was pertinent to the topic at hand, a search was carried out using the phrase "product placement." There are a total of 8639 documents. In the following stage, we will determine the period that spans from 1995 to 2023 and restrict it to two distinct subject areas, namely business management & accounting, and social science. In a consistent manner, we are specifically focused on documenting different sorts of articles (1075) and conference papers (124). We are choosing a filter by 28 key word (product placement, advertising, marketing, commerce, brand placement, television, decision-making, advertising, social media, Internet, content analysis, placement, branding, movies, brand recall, promotion, brands, advertising effectiveness, purchase intention, product placement, brand attitude, purchasing, influencer marketing, consumer behavior, advertising, and promotion, in-game advertising, customer satisfaction, brand awareness). The countries, affiliations, countries, and sorts of sources that we do not disclose are not specified. The non-English article was eliminated from this study. This is because publications written in English have the potential to assist in the compilation of an exhaustive list of all pertinent academic resources, include journals with a high influence, and offer a wide variety of research. After applying filters to the data collection, about 439 documents were discovered. On the other hand, we go through and thoroughly examine 439 papers to eliminate those that are not relevant. In the end, we discovered 408 documents that were pertinent to the scope and purpose of our project.

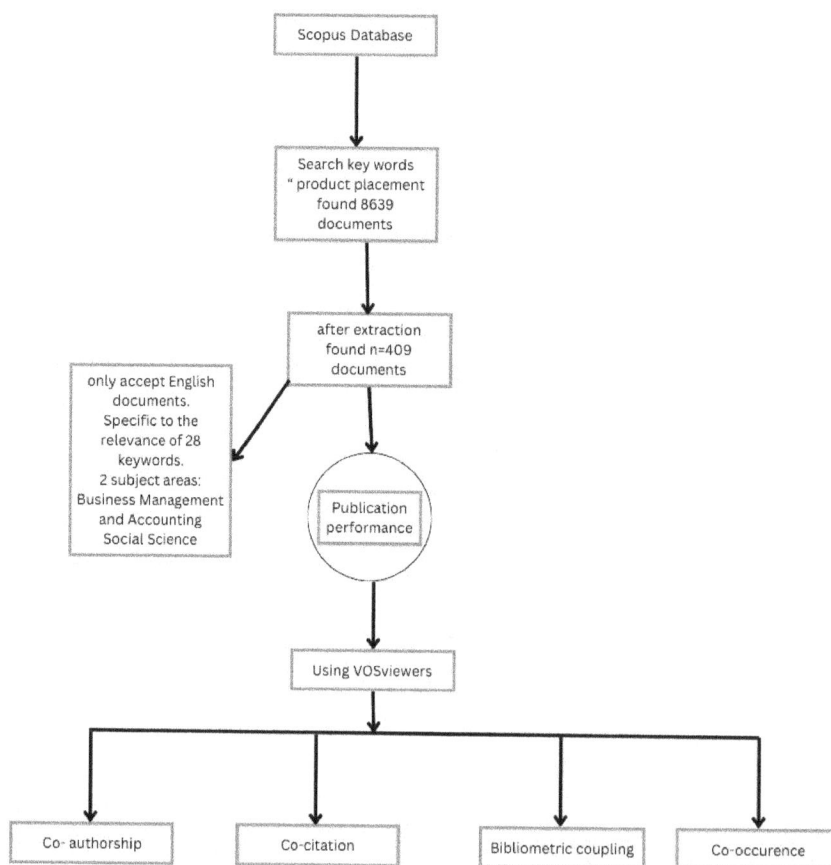

Figure1: Research design

4. Results

4.1 Publication Performance

Between the years 1995 and 2023, a total of 409 research articles were published through various institutions. Since the initial research on product placement was conducted in the late 1990s, we decided to focus on the years 1995–203 as our time frame. A substantial rise in the amount of research conducted on product placement can be traced back to the years 1995–2016. On the other hand, after the year 2016, it appears that the topic has become slightly less prevalent (Figure 2).

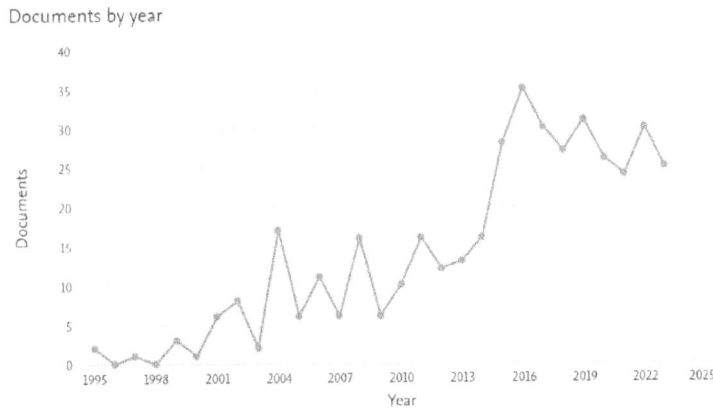

Figure 2: Publications by years (Scopus Data Base)

The Scopus database contains a wide variety of document formats, including but not limited to articles, conference papers, conference reviews, book chapters, and article reviews. Articles are the most common sort of document that are produced, accounting for 78.7% of all documents, as seen in figure 3. When it comes to bibliometrics, we only concentrate on the types of articles and conference papers because these types of papers frequently provide unique contributions to the body of academic and scientific knowledge.

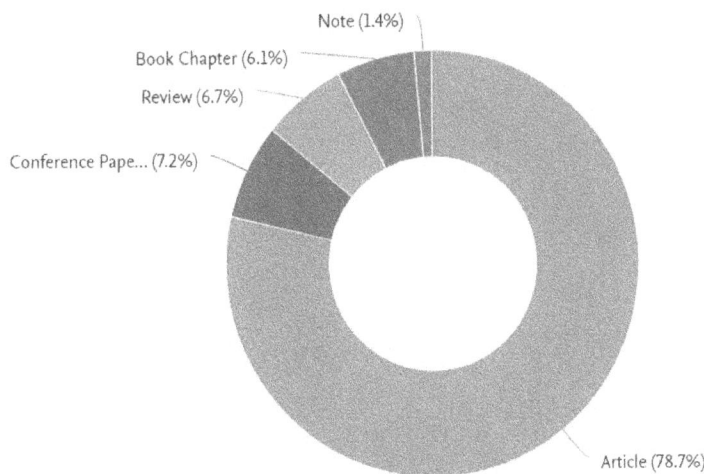

Figure 3: Documents by type (Scopus Data Base)

The percentage of research conducted in each subject area is displayed in the figure below. It is the field of business management that accounts for 37.5% of all work, with the social sciences coming in second with 25.3% of all labor. Some of the fields that do not have a significant amount of study focus on product placement include medicine (6.2%), economics, econometrics, and finance (5.1%), computer science (4.9%), and arts and humanities (4.5%). In a nutshell, there are just two subject areas that we concentrate on in our bibliometric study. These subject areas are business management and social sciences.

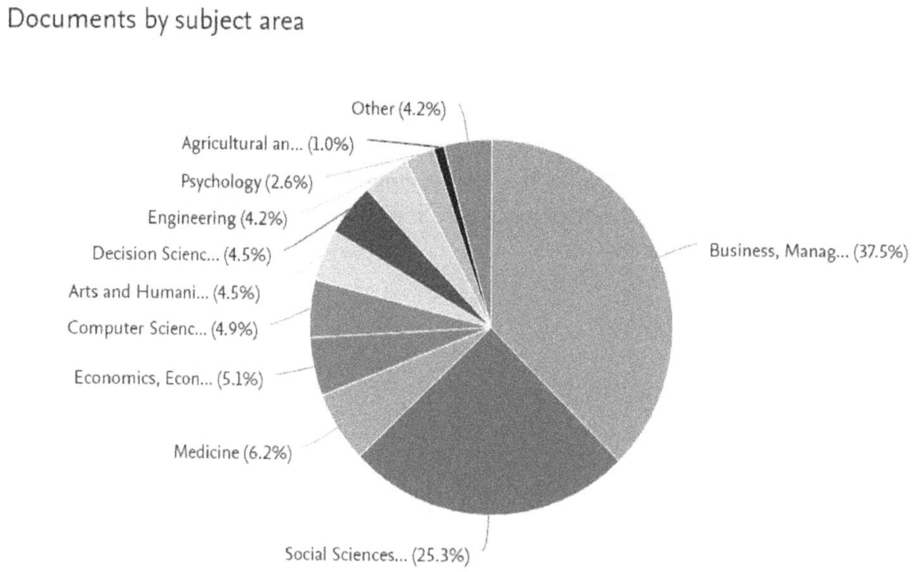

Documents by subject area

Figure 4: Documents by subject area (Scopus Data Base)

4.2 Core Clusters of Intellectual Property

According to Zhang et al. (2013), co-authorship plays a particularly important role in the process of constructing and enhancing professional networks both within and between academic institutions, fields of study, and geographical locations. Researchers could communicate their discoveries with a more extensive audience through the process of co-authorship, which in turn increases the exposure and influence of their work (Hammad et al., 2021).

Of the 63 countries that contributed to the literature, 25 of them produced at least five papers; 22 of these countries are related to one another. Each node in the network represents a different nation, and the connection between two nodes indicates the degree to which the writer collaborated on the project (Leung & Bai 2017).

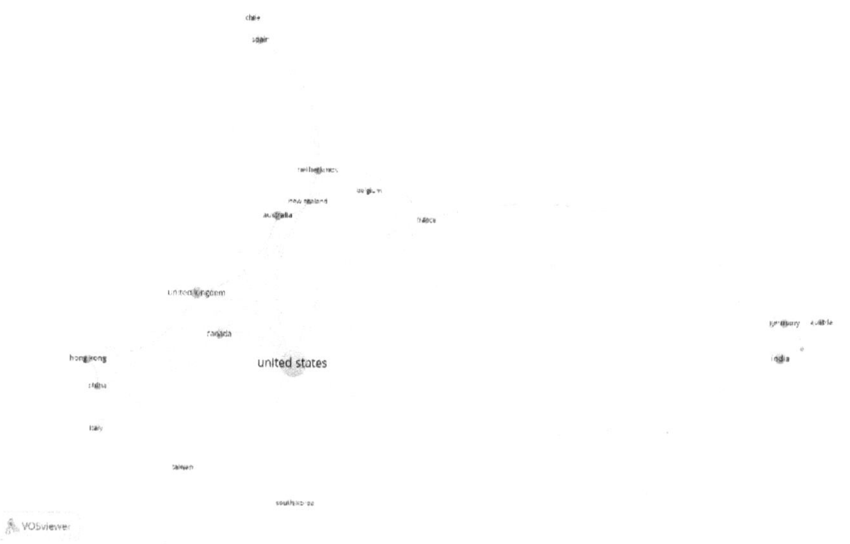

Figure 5: Visualized co-authorship network by countries.

Among the 741 organizations, the minimum number of documents that can be associated with each organization is two, and the maximum number of organizations that can be included in a single document is 25. A calculation will be made to determine the overall strength of the co-authorship relationships with other organizations for each of the seventeen participating organizations. Those organizations that have the highest total link strength will be chosen for this selection. The total number of organizations that will be chosen is seventeen. As a consequence of this, there is a slight connection between Texas Tech University, the Public Health School, and the Business School (about 2.00). Most of the organizations do not link with one another. The three organizations that are used to bind strength together are not included in the document that has received the most citations from the organization.

Figure 6: Visualized co-authorship network by organization.

In order to simplify the author-citation network, the authors with the highest number of citations are illustrated. According to the analysis, a total of 170 authors out of 18,040 had achieved a minimum of 20 citations per author based on the co-citation analysis. Every node inside the network symbolizes an author, while the edge connecting two nodes signifies the co-citation association between the authors.

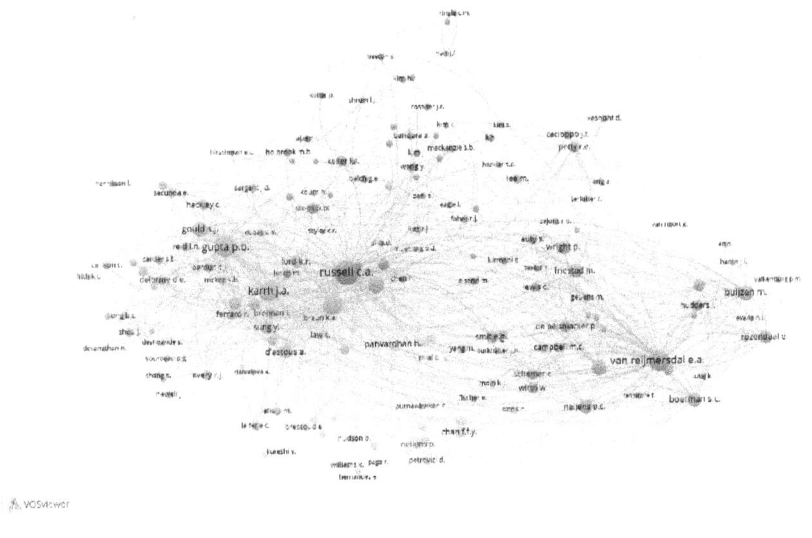

Figure 7: Visualized co-citation network by authors.

Authors who have made important contributions to the overall body of literature are included in the table that follows. Chan (39.83), Lowe, Petrovici, and Redondo are the top three authors who have the highest level of total link strength. The United States of America, the United Kingdom, and Hong Kong were the countries that had the greatest impact on the situation. In addition to that, the investigation revealed that the Journal of Promotion Management, the International Journal of Advertising, and the Journal of Marketing Communications were the publications that had the greatest impact on the most recent collection of research.

Table 1: Top 10 authors for bibliometric coupling based on numbers of links

Author	Documents	Citations	Total Link Strength
Chan F.F	3	24	39.83
Chan;Lowe;Petrovici	2	40	39.21
Redondo	3	90	29.00
Srivastava	3	32	17.50
Chen	3	16	15.21
Kaur; Sharma; Bakshi	2	3	15.05
Spielvogel	2	28	13.93
Uribe; Fuentes	2	13	12.00
Kramolis	2	1	2.67
Lubbers; Adams	2	13	0.00

Table 2: Top 10 countries for bibliometric coupling based on numbers link

Country	Documents	Citations	Total Link Strength
United States	155	3505	1684.32
United Kingdom	31	684	953.09
Hong Kong	17	124	806.60
Canada	21	852	607.08
China	12	68	443.78
France	11	208	408.63
Germany	16	174	321.32
Spain	16	266	301.38
India	26	239	251.34
Netherlands	13	400	250.99

Table 3: Top 10 journals for bibliometric coupling based on numbers of links

Source	Documents	Citations	Total Link Strength
Journal of promotion management	39	563	293.94
International journal of advertising	19	430	257.55
Journal of marketing communications	13	273	155.18
European journal of marketing	7	276	153.13
Journal of product and brand management	4	53	98.32
Journal of international consumer management	8	181	75.27
Marketing intelligence and planning	4	33	68.00
Journal of brand and management	4	55	54.58
Business Horizons	4	107	29.95
Marketing Science	4	44	14.00

According to Müller and Mancuso (2008), co-occurrence analysis is a useful technique for obtaining significant insights from huge datasets, recognizing implicit connections among entities, and assisting with tasks like content analysis, pattern identification, and feature extraction. Out of the 2130 terms examined 110 were discovered to occur five times as, per the studies. This matrix shows the frequency of keywords in the dataset and their interconnections. The notion of product placement is associated with research topics. In the domain of product placement related high frequency keywords include advertising (represented by a node) marketing (represented by a green node) and decision making (represented by a red node). These relationships exemplify how these concepts are interconnected.

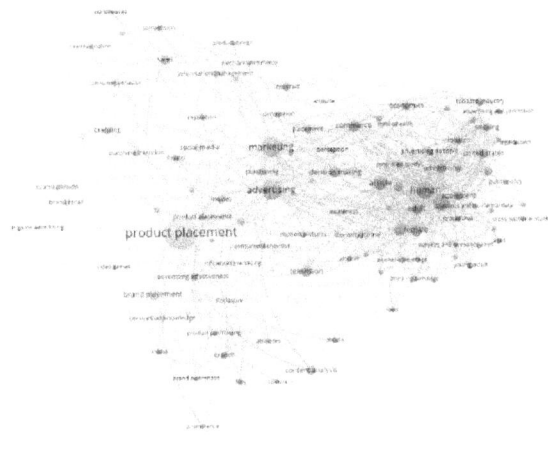

Figure 8: Visualized co-occurrences network all keywords

4.3 Content Analysis of Thematic Cluster

In a study conducted by Cobo et al. (2011) they mentioned that when it comes to research thematic cluster content analysis involves mapping and performance assessment to measure a study area, its subfields (clusters) and how it has evolved over time. This analysis also utilizes methods, like co analysis, co citation network evaluation and thematic analysis to identify potential themes within research areas (Shroff et al., 2022). Moreover, in the field of bibliometrics the clustering methodology relies on a normalized term co matrix and a similarity metric that quantifies the connection between terms or author networks (Kokol et al., 2018).

We were able to identify three groups of decision-making processes that're equally prevalent in small businesses. To do this we used form analysis which involved examining how sectors of advertising use product placement on media and television through measures like co-occurrence, co citation and bibliometric coupling. Our findings can be categorized into two clusters; (1) product placement in television shows and movies; and (2) product placement, on social media platforms.

Cluster 1: Product placement on television and movies

This section explores the study of how product placement's incorporated into movies and advertising for a brand of product or service. It is evident that there has been an increase in the occurrence of product placements (PP), in television broadcasts as embedded brands are now being given importance alongside traditional commercials (Newell, Blevins and Bugeja 2009). Balasubramanian & Gistri (2021) explain the impact of media and ad priming on recall in movie placements. Results show that both media priming and ad priming enhance recall for subtle placements, while no difference exists for prominent placements. (Natarajan et al., 2021) focus on the study about brand placement in reality show in India. The finding shows that product placement in realism produces superior results compared to other media platforms. This study from Chan (2019) investigates the correlation between product placement techniques and product qualities. Consumers searched more frequently for products utilizing product placement marketing compared to products without marketing using the product placement method, as indicated by the findings. (Sánchez-Olmos & Castelló-Martínez, 2020) investigates the utilization of product placement in music, revealing that Adidas, Nike, and Chevrolet are the most prominently featured companies in adopting product placement. Srivastava (2020) found that including the brand name in the movie song positively influences brand personality, equity, customer attitude, and purchase intention. Naderer et al. (2017a) found that at least one instance of brand placement occurred in 64.4% of children's movies released between 1991 and 2015. Comedies and US films exhibited a greater frequency of placements, but animation and movies featuring nature or fantasy settings had a lower frequency. Naderer et al. (2017 b) demonstrated that product placement consistently influences cognitive and conative brand outcomes, regardless of participants' age or prior knowledge about the movie.

Cluster 2: Product placement on social media

The expansion of social marketing is also occurring because of the growth of the internet. Spielvogel et al. (2020) conduct a study on the disclosure policies of the European Union regarding product placement. This research adds to the existing body of knowledge on blog advertising and native advertising. It assists in highlighting the disparity between legal practice and empirical research about the execution of product placement disclosure on media platforms. Consumer materialism influences the acceptability of product placement on social networking sites, with materialism partially mediating the relationship between usage frequency and product placement acceptance. (Wijesundara & Kumara, 2022). Koo's study discovered that product placements on YouTube significantly influence the likelihood of making a purchase. Factors such as the relevance of the product to the content of the YouTuber, the perceived trustworthiness of the YouTuber, and the favorability of the community surrounding the YouTuber determine this effect (Koo, 2023).

5.   Ethical Consideration

Marketers employ product placement, a strategic advertising technique known as "hidden marketing." Nevertheless, the primary focus of this matter remains the necessity for marketers to exercise caution and deliberation prior to promoting the product. Research has indicated that ethical concerns regarding product placement can differ depending on the type of product. There tends to be greater concerns expressed when it comes to ethically controversial products like alcohol, guns, and tobacco (McKechnie & Zhou, 2003; Gupta & Gould, 1997; Kim & McClung, 2010). Some people disapprove of these products because they include 'subliminal' promotional impacts and may use misleading methods, which can influence purchasing decisions without conscious awareness (Gupta & Gould, 1997). Researchers generally agree that children are particularly sensitive to product placement. According to Avery and Ferraro (2000), this is because they have not yet developed sensitivity to this kind of subtle advertising tactic. According to Gupta et al. (2000) and Gunter et al. (2005), it is generally considered that children do not become aware of the commercial motivation behind conventional advertising until they are approximately ten years old. In 1991, the Federal Communications Commission (FCT) was examining whether the practice of featuring cigarette placements in televised movies should necessitate the inclusion of a health advisory. As a result, the tobacco industry stopped engaging in the product placement of cigarettes in movies.

The ethical concerns related to product placement are complex. Influenced by factors, including the product category, the subtle nature of the placement and customer beliefs. To ensure that product placements meet standards and do not unduly influence consumers it is important for lawmakers and marketers to understand these issues.

6.   Implication

Analyzing data on product placement offers insights for scholars, practitioners, and policymakers. The main objective is to identify contributors, track research trends and provide guidance for investigations. This study presents an analysis of product placement in industries such as music, movies, games, and social media. It contributes significantly to understanding of product placement studies. Furthermore, these findings support the development of curricula, open opportunities for international collaboration. Ultimately, this research addresses considerations that help marketers understand consumer behavior from a standpoint so that they can adapt their marketing strategies accordingly.

7.   Conclusion

In conclusion this study was carried out by analyzing a total of 409 papers obtained from the Scopus database focusing on a topic from 1995 to 2023. By conducting an analysis on product placement, we gained insights into the changing research landscape in this dynamic field. Through an examination of publishing patterns, influential authors, and thematic shifts over time we have deepened our understanding of activity surrounding product placement. The identification of authors, institutions and journals also fosters collaboration. Cultivates a sense of community in academic research. Moreover, this research sheds light on the dimensions of product placement contributing to both knowledge and societal values.

Acknowledgements

The authors would like to thank **doc. Ing. Michal Pilík, Ph.D.** for his guidance.

This work is supported by the Internal Grant Agency of FaME, Tomas Bata University in Zlín no.IGA/FaME/2023/008

References

Alzubi, A. M. (2022). Impact of new digital media on conventional media and visual communication in Jordan. Journal of Engineering, Technology, and Applied Science, 4(3), 105-113. https://doi.org/10.36079/lamintang.jetas-0403.383

Avery, R. J., & Feraro, R. (2000). Verisimilitude or advertising? brand appearances on prime-time television. *Journal of Consumer Affairs,* 34(2), 217–244. https://doi.org/10.1111/j.1745-6606.2000.tb00092

Ahmad, P., Dummer, P. M. H., Chaudhry, A., Rashid, U., Saif, S., & Asif, J. A. (2019). A bibliometric study of the top 100 most-cited randomized controlled trials, systematic reviews and meta-analyses published in endodontic journals. International Endodontic Journal, 52(9), 1297-1316. https://doi.org/10.1111/iej.13131

Ananda, R. K. and Nandiyanto, A. B. D. (2022). Bibliometric analysis of publication on protein nanoparticle using Vos viewer. DIPONEGORO MEDICAL JOURNAL (Jurnal Kedokteran Diponegoro), 11(6). https://doi.org/10.14710/dmj.v11i6.35942

Amiri, A. M., Kushwaha, B. P., & Singh, R. K. (2023). Visualisation of global research trends and future research directions of digital marketing in small and medium enterprises using bibliometric analysis. Journal of Small Business and Enterprise Development, 30(3), 621-641. https://doi.org/10.1108/jsbed-04-2022-0206

Boeing, R., Urdan, A. T., & Gentry, J. W. (2013). I saw it in the movies, but does that matter? product placement in a cross cultural study between Brazil and the USA. Revista Brasileira de Marketing, 12(2), 1–28. https://doi.org/10.5585/remark.v12i2.2507

Balasubramanian, S. K., & Gistri, G. (2021). Priming movie product placements: New Insights from a cross-national case study. *International Journal of Advertising,* 41(6), 1064–1094. https://doi.org/10.1080/02650487.2021.1930349

Chan, F. F. (2019). Mapping between placement strategies and placed product attributes in television programs. *Journal of Marketing Communications,* 26(7), 780–798. https://doi.org/10.1080/13527266.2019.1570965

Davtyan, D., & Cunningham, I. (2017). An investigation of brand placement effects on brand attitudes and purchase intentions: Brand placements versus TV commercials. *Journal of Business Research,* 70, 160–167. https://doi.org/10.1016/j.jbusres.2016.08.023

Ellili, N. O. D. (2022). Bibliometric analysis and systematic review of environmental, social, and governance disclosure papers: current topics and recommendations for future research. Environmental Research Communications, 4(9), 092001. https://doi.org/10.1088/2515-7620/ac8b67

Gupta, P. B., & Gould, S. J. (1997). Consumers' perceptions of the ethics and acceptability of product placements in movies: Product category and individual differences. *Journal of Current Issues & Research in Advertising,* 19(1), 37–50. https://doi.org/10.1080/10641734.1997.10505056

Gunter, , B., Oates, C., & Blades, M. (2005). *Apa PsycNet.* American Psychological Association. https://psycnet.apa.org/record/2004-18513-000

Gao, P., Meng, F., Mata, M. N., Martins, J. M., Iqbal, S., Correia, A. B.,& Farrukh, M. (2021). Trends and future research in electronic marketing: a bibliometric analysis of twenty years. Journal of Theoretical and Applied Electronic Commerce Research, 16(5), 1667-1679. https://doi.org/10.3390/jtaer16050094

Gupta, P. B., Balasubramanian, S. K., & Klassen, M. L. (2000). Viewers' evaluations of product placements in movies: Public policy issues and managerial implications. *Journal of Current Issues & Research in Advertising,* 22(2), 41–52. https://doi.org/10.1080/10641734.2000.10505107

Gzahli, N., Mutalib, H. A., & Noor, A. M. (2022). Bibliometric analysis of cash waqf. Jurnal Intelek, 17(2), 63-73. https://doi.org/10.24191/ji.v17i2.18032

Hossain, M. (2020). Current status of global research on novel coronavirus disease (covid-19): a bibliometric analysis and knowledge mapping. F1000Research, 9, 374. https://doi.org/10.12688/f1000research.23690.1

Hair Jr, J., Sarstedt, M., Hopkins, L., & G. Kuppelwieser, V. (2014). Partial least squares structural equation modeling (PLS-SEM). European Business Review, 26(2), 106–121. https://doi.org/10.1108/ebr-10-2013-0128

Hammad, M. A., Elgazzar, S., Obrecht, M., & Sternad, M. (2021). Compatibility about the concept of energy hub: A strict and visual review. *International Journal of Energy Sector Management,* 16(1), 1–20. https://doi.org/10.1108/ijesm-06-2020-0022

Inan, U. S. E. (2023). Evaluation of digital marketing from a bibliometric analysis perspective. Socialist Series in Social Science, 4, 45-58. https://doi.org/10.20319/socv4.4558

Jain, D., Dash, M. K., & Thakur, K. (2021). Development of research agenda on demonetization based on bibliometric visualization. International Journal of Emerging Markets, 17(10), 2584-2604. https://doi.org/10.1108/ijoem-12-2019-1085

Koo, W. (2023). Ways to implement effective product placement on YouTube. *International Journal of E-Business Research,* 19(1), 1–15. https://doi.org/10.4018/ijebr.320232

Leung, X. Y., Sun, J., & Bai, B. (2017). Bibliometrics of social media research: A co-citation and co-word analysis. *International Journal of Hospitality Management,* 66, 35–45. https://doi.org/10.1016/j.ijhm.2017.06.012

Matić, I., & Sunjka, N. (2022). A bibliometric analysis of the Global Value Chains Research Field. *Management,* 27(2), 221–245. https://doi.org/10.30924/mjcmi.27.2.12

Müller, H., & Mancuso, F. (2008). Identification and analysis of co-occurrence networks with net cutter. *PLoS ONE,* 3(9). https://doi.org/10.1371/journal.pone.0003178

Melati, A.S., & Abdurachman, E. (2021). Product Placement Execution Factors and Individual Differences Effect on Purchase Intention Through Consumer's Attitude in Indonesia. International Journal of Organizational Business Excellence.

Natarajan, Thamaraiselvan, Jayapal, J., & Gangadharan, N. (2021). The television cult: Prevalence of brand placements in an Indian reality show. *Journal of Promotion Management,* 27(7), 971–997. https://doi.org/10.1080/10496491.2021.1888176

Newell, J., Blevins, J. L., & Bugeja, M. (2009). Tragedies of the Broadcast Commons: Consumer Perspectives on the ethics of product placement and video news releases. *Journal of Mass Media Ethics,* 24(4), 201–219. https://doi.org/10.1080/08900520903321025

Naderer, B., Matthes, J., & Spielvogel, I. (2017a). How brands appear in children's movies. A systematic content analysis of the past 25 Years. *International Journal of Advertising,* 38(2), 237–257. https://doi.org/10.1080/02650487.2017.1410000

Naderer, B., Matthes, J., & Zeller, P. (2017b). Placing snacks in children's movies: Cognitive, evaluative, and CONATIVE effects of product placements with character product interaction. *International Journal of Advertising, 37*(6), 852–870. https://doi.org/10.1080/02650487.2017.1348034

Piazzolla, S., García Medina, I., & Navarro-Beltrán, M. (2021). Brand Placement in music videos: Effectiveness in UK, Spain and Italy. INDEX COMUNICACION, 11(2), 135–163. https://doi.org/10.33732/ixc/11/02brandp

Pham, X. L., Nguyen, P. M., & Truong, G. N. T. (2022). A co-word and co-citation analysis of digital marketing research. International Journal of Service Science, Management, Engineering, and Technology, 13(1), 1-20. https://doi.org/10.4018/ijssmet.304817

Rothenberg, R. (1991, May 31). *Critics seek F.T.C. Action On Products as movie stars*. The New York Times. https://www.nytimes.com/1991/05/31/business/the-media-business-critics-seek-ftc-action-on-products-as-movie-stars.html

Ragadhita, R. and Nandiyanto, A. B. D. (2021). Computational bibliometric analysis on publication of techno-economic education. Indonesian Journal of Multidiciplinary Research, 2(1), 213-222. https://doi.org/10.17509/ijomr.v2i1.43180

Spielvogel, I., Naderer, B., & Matthes, J. (2020). Disclosing product placement in audiovisual media services: A practical and scientific perspective on the implementation of disclosures across the European Union. *International Journal of Advertising, 40*(1), 5–25. https://doi.org/10.1080/02650487.2020.1781478

Sánchez-Olmos, C., & Castelló-Martínez, A. (2020). Brand Placement in music videos: Artists, Brands and products appearances in the Billboard Hot 100 from 2003 to 2016. *Journal of Promotion Management, 26*(6), 874–892. https://doi.org/10.1080/10496491.2020.1745986

Srivastava, R. (2020). Brand placement in a movie song and its impact on brand equity. *Journal of Promotion Management, 26*(2), 233–252. https://doi.org/10.1080/10496491.2019.1699627

Sharma, P., Saha, S., & Balaji, M. (2022). Retrospective view and thematic analysis of business-to-business relationships through bibliometric analysis. Journal of Business-to-Business Marketing, 29(1), 19-42. https://doi.org/10.1080/1051712x.2022.2039478

Wijesundara, T., & Kumara, S. (2022). Acceptance of product placement in social networking sites: The mediating role of materialism. *Global Knowledge, Memory and Communication, 72*(6/7), 612–627. https://doi.org/10.1108/gkmc-04-2021-0073

Wiles, M. A., & Danielova, A. (2009). The worth of product placement in successful films: An event study analysis. Journal of Marketing, 73(4), 44–63. https://doi.org/10.1509/jmkg.73.4.44

Winkowska, J., Szpilko, D., & Pejić, S. (2019). Smart city concept in the light of the literature review. Engineering Management in Production and Services, 11(2), 70-86. https://doi.org/10.2478/emj-2019-0012

Wani, N. S. (2023). Sustainable marketing in line with sdgs: an extensive bibliometric analysis. International Journal of Research and Review, 10(1), 315-323. https://doi.org/10.52403/ijrr.20230134

Zhang, C., Yu, Q., Fan, Q., & Duan, Z. (2013). Research collaboration in Health Management Research Communities. *BMC Medical Informatics and Decision Making, 13*(1). https://doi.org/10.1186/1472-6947-13-52

Revealing Hybrid Threats: Vulnerability Exploitation in Romania's Social Media Landscape

Georgiana-Daniela Lupulescu

National Defense University "Carol I", Bucharest, Romania

geo.lupulescu@yahoo.co.uk

Abstract: Taking a deep look into hybrid operations characteristics, an important and omnipresent one is targeting vulnerabilities mode of action. As the global landscape evolves and challenges national security like never before, understanding the mechanisms state and non-state entities use to exploit vulnerabilities becomes paramount. By examining the contemporary geopolitical contexts, this article sheds light on the multifaceted strategies deployed by various actors through social media platforms to undermine the resilience of the Romanian state. Due to its geographical location, Romania is not only a major pillar for regional security but also has an important strategic role in maintaining security in both NATO and UE. Exploiting Romania's security weaknesses may be the way hybrid actors pursue their geopolitical interests, ideological aims, and regional power struggles. At the beginning of the study, a short framework will be presented for the concept of vulnerabilities within a state, focusing on the security weaknesses that emerge from several domains, such as economic, political, technological, and in particular social susceptibilities, and how they manifest in social media. Following, the article will include methods and tactics used in social media, by various types of actors, considering the use of cyber-attacks, disinformation campaigns, covert influence, or economic coercion for a clearer image of the target-attack binomial. Furthermore, a short analysis of Romania's exposure to hybrid threats will be provided. Starting from the research hypothesis that Romania's geopolitical and geographical location is the key factor in establishing its vulnerability degree to hybrid threats manifestation, the main question that emerges is how to minimize its vulnerabilities. The methodology that will be used in conducting this research includes a short literature review of the concept of vulnerabilities within a state, as well as weaknesses exploitation through social media, followed by the case study analysis where we will be focusing on some of Romania's vulnerabilities within social media. Through this comprehensive examination, this article underscores the significance of recognizing and addressing vulnerabilities within a state, particularly in the context of evolving global challenges and threats to national security. It emphasizes the strategic importance of Romania in maintaining regional and international security. The article serves as a wake-up call to the potential dangers posed by hybrid actors who exploit these vulnerabilities using social media platforms, urging Romania and its allies to take proactive measures to bolster their defense and resilience against these multifaceted threats.

Keywords: Vulnerability, Disinformation, Resilience, Security weaknesses, Social media

1. Introduction

Hybrid operations seem to be omnipresent in the current global environment. Even if we talk about the continuous existence of hybrid threats or the outbreak of a conflict, there are certainly elements of hybrid operations included. The hybrid term does not have a very long history as Frank Hoffman first defined it (2007) at the beginning of the 2000s from the necessity of naming the change in terms of actors involved, instruments used, and of course the combination of all that we previously knew, or, as Treverton et. al. said: "they differ from previous conflict more in degree than in kind" (Treverton, et al., 2018).

Many authors have tried defining hybrid threat, hybrid war, or hybrid operations, each of them coming with a new point of view, not as much different from other authors'. For example, Hoffman (2007), Bilal (2021), or the experts from Both the European Parliament and the Council (2016) focused on the fusion of regular and irregular warfare taking into account the methods, instruments of power, and actors involved. At the same time, some authors focus on the vulnerability-targeting characteristic of hybrid operations, as a way of achieving strategic goals. This is supported also by Cullen and Reichborn-Kjennerud who emphasize the not-so-new character, but also the shift in terms of synchronization of the instruments of power and the "exploitation of creativity, ambiguity, non-linearity, and the cognitive elements of warfare" (Cullen & Reichborn-Kjennerud, 2017).

In the hybrid operations discussion, one important aspect seems to be that it exceeds borders, so there are many casualties beyond the attacked state. This is of utmost importance when preparing for or facing threats. It shows us that we need to be united and work together, but it also means that the battlefield has changed. Nowadays a website or a social media platform may be a promising environment for hybrid actors to initiate actions from the hybrid operations spectrum.

This article sheds light on the strategic importance of the geopolitical role of Romania in maintaining regional security. The geographical position at the eastern border of both NATO and EU, Romania has and will always have a crucial role for the stability and security of the alliances. Besides the measures taken for military defense such as the multinational bases or the anti-missile shield, there is a tremendous need for actions against hybrid threats or even a possible hybrid operation.

Vulnerability is the key element of hybrid operations targets. When assessing the risk to security, posed by hybrid operations, one should not only look at the possible threats or actors with the means and intent to do that but also at the weaknesses in its own political, military, economic, social, informational, and infrastructure (PMESII) domains. The vulnerabilities within a state could determine the capacity to face and counteract hybrid threats, but not all the weak points need to be exploited, that only happens if it helps the greater goal of hybrid actors. Focusing on Romania's vulnerabilities, I will emphasize those from the PMESII domains that could be exploited through social media platforms. Moreover, the hybrid operations tools used against Romania and its allies using social media platforms as a dissemination channel must be named, acknowledged, and counteracted as fast and as efficiently as possible.

My research will outline some of the methods, tactics, and tools used by hybrid actors in the online environment and a few recommendations to reinforce our resilience in various ways, diminishing our vulnerabilities or strengthening our defense.

1.1 Framework of Vulnerabilities

The national security level within a state is defined by its risk-vulnerability-threat triad. The concept of vulnerability in the acceptance of The National Defense Strategy of Romania for the 2020-2024 period is defined as: "functional-systemic/structural deficiencies that can be exploited or can contribute to the materialization of threats or risks, weakening the state's ability to reduce the impact of events with the potential to seriously affect the normal functioning of its institutions, the life and physical integrity of citizens and the organization of human communities, as well as the capacity to protect, defend and promote national security values, interests, and objectives" (Administrația Prezidențială, 2020). The concept of vulnerabilities within a state is a complex and multifaceted domain, encompassing various dimensions that can be exploited by external actors for strategic, ideological, or geopolitical purposes. Understanding these vulnerabilities is essential for devising effective strategies to fortify a nation's resilience against hybrid threats.

One very important characteristic of hybrid actions is that often they target vulnerabilities from different domains at the same time, achieving a synergic effect. Rarely the main goal will be to create social division, for example. Certainly, there will be some hidden objectives such as diminishing the trust in government institutions or manipulating the population's perception and so being more susceptible to believe and act like they are told by various actors. The affirmation is supported by Petrescu, who sees the hybrid threat as a holistic one, and not as a sum of threats (Petrescu, 2019), which means that usually there is a main strategic goal, the resources and instruments are used innovatively and unpredictably, and the PMESII domains may be subject to attack, all at the same time. Understanding the interplay of the vulnerabilities is crucial for assessing a state's overall susceptibility to hybrid threats. It is important to recognize that the vulnerabilities are often interconnected, and exploitation in one domain may have cascading effects across others.

Simultaneously, while a system may exhibit vulnerabilities, it doesn't automatically render itself susceptible to targeting. The critical factor lies in the existence of a strategic objective that a hybrid actor seeks to attain. Moreover, the pivotal element is the discernible intent to orchestrate a hybrid operation. In essence, the mere presence of vulnerabilities does not precipitate targeting; it is the alignment with a larger strategic purpose and a deliberate intent that sets the stage for potential hybrid engagement.

In this research paper, it is imperative to underscore that our focus diverges from the prevalent discourse on vulnerabilities within networks, informational systems, and computers—subjects extensively covered in the existing literature. We intentionally navigate away from the well-trodden path of cyber-related vulnerabilities, recognizing that the mere existence of such weaknesses does not inherently imply susceptibility to hybrid operations. Instead, our emphasis lies on discerning and elucidating the strategic motives and intentions that drive hybrid actors, acknowledging that vulnerability exploitation in the digital realm does not automatically translate into, or exclusively predicate, the orchestration of a hybrid operation. By delving into this nuanced perspective, we contribute a distinct angle to the broader discourse on security and hybrid threats, enriching the understanding of the multifaceted dynamics involved.

Some of these vulnerabilities within a state, that could be exploited by hybrid actors for each of the PMESII domains are presented in the figure below, with the specification that usually these are mixed and interconnected and the hybrid actors exploit more than one vulnerability at a time.

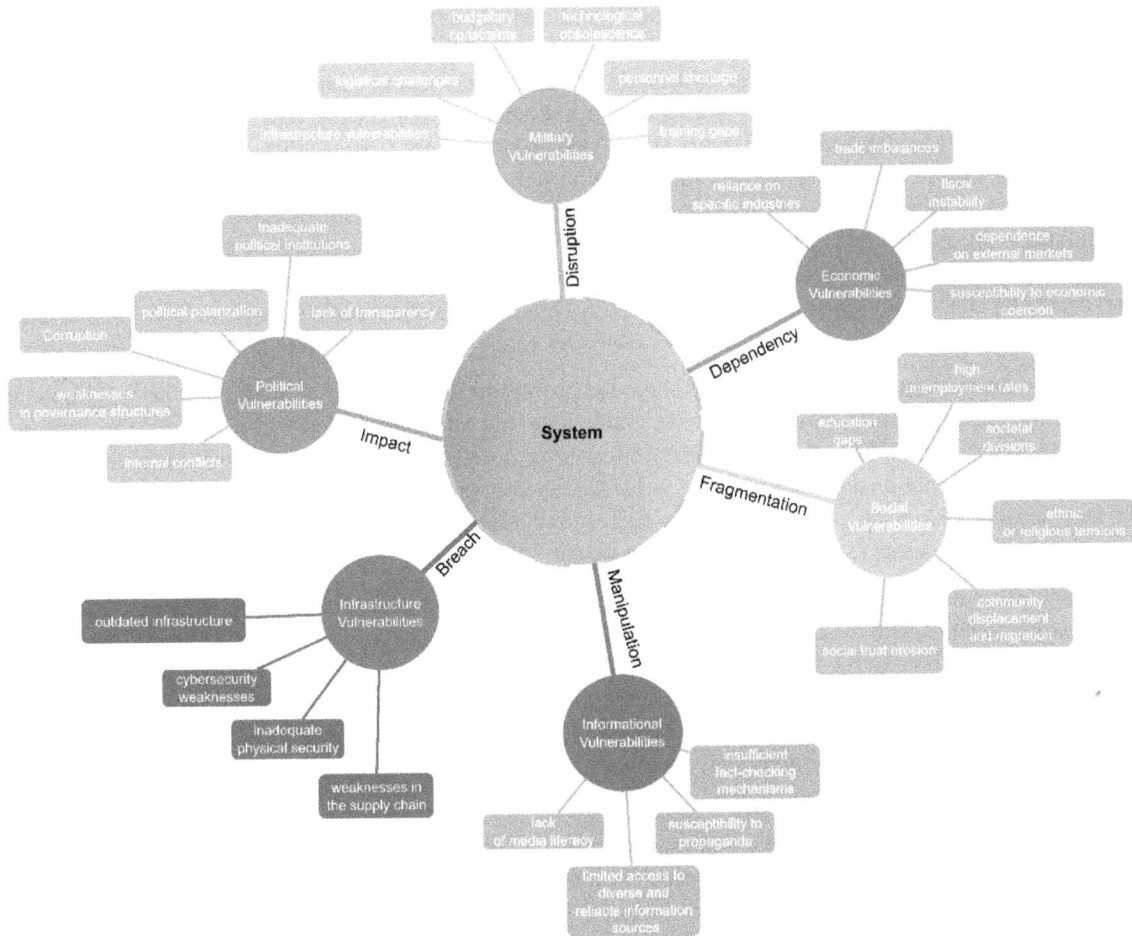

Figure 1: Vulnerabilities in the PMESII domains

As we may see in the figure above, any disorder, any weakness or any other factor that negatively impact the well being of a system or its proper functioning, may constitute into a vulnerability exploitable by hybrid actors. Let's take for example the training gaps in the military domain. Besides its evident harmful impact in terms of inappropriate use of equipment, high injury or mortality rates, and minimum chances of winning a battle, training gaps may be exploited by hybrid actors in various ways. Such an example could be the annexation of Crimea in 2014. The Ukrainian military had undergone significant restructuring and downsizing following the dissolution of the Soviet Union. This restructuring resulted in gaps in training, equipment, and readiness, particularly in areas such as cyber defense, intelligence gathering, and unconventional warfare.

Russian hybrid actors exploited these gaps by launching a sophisticated cyber warfare campaign against Ukrainian military and government infrastructure, disrupting communications, intelligence gathering, and command and control systems. Additionally, Russian propaganda efforts spread disinformation to sow confusion and undermine morale among Ukrainian military personnel.

Furthermore, the Ukrainian military's training and preparedness for unconventional warfare and irregular tactics were not adequately developed, leaving them ill-prepared to counter the hybrid tactics employed by Russian-backed forces, including irregular troops and local separatist militias. Or, as Renz (2016) said: „Ukraine did not have corresponding capabilities and did not even attempt to put up a military resistance". Since then, they adopted reforms across various levels, encompassing tactical and strategic measures, which incorporate both political initiatives such as enhancing transparency, combating corruption, and ensuring civilian oversight of the military, as well as military-focused reforms like modernizing equipment, restructuring command and control, and enhancing professionalism (Bowen, 2022).

The manifestation of vulnerabilities in social media represents a complex and dynamic challenge in today's interconnected digital landscape. Social media platforms, while serving as powerful tools for communication and information sharing, also become breeding grounds for various vulnerabilities that can have wide-ranging consequences. The big change with everyone using social media a lot is how quickly things get shared in real time, and nearly everyone can do it. It means news and updates can spread instantly, breaking down borders and letting people from anywhere connect. People create and share a ton of content, letting anyone have a say in global discussions. Social media makes information go viral fast, shaping public talk and sparking movements in no time. But it also brings challenges like figuring out if what you see is true. With constant access to social media, individuals can express themselves, share their stories, and support different causes. This makes everyone's voice matter, challenging the usual power structures. However, there's also the downside of non-stop connection, leading to an overload of information. Steingartner et. al. also stipulate that "although lies and manipulations in public information space are not a novelty, the quantity and speed of spreading misinformation, especially through social networks and mobile communication applications present an unprecedented challenge." (Steingartner, et al., 2022) Thus, while social media's real-time sharing and broad access bring new opportunities, they also bring new issues that we need to navigate in this digital age.

Unlike other types of vulnerabilities, such as the ones presented above, in social media platforms, people are the weak link and most of the tools used aim to manipulate and influence people's perceptions, thoughts, and opinions (Bruning, et al., 2020). Both state and non-state actors use social media platforms for spreading false and misleading information and the enormous success of their operations is due to very efficient algorithms that take into account all individuals' characteristics such as sex, race, age, ethnicity, culture, religion, preferences, etc. sharing specific messages that impact a certain target.

Vulnerabilities within social media must be viewed from two distinct perspectives, one regarding the system security vulnerabilities, and the other from a social perspective. Even though the first has great influence on the second we will refer only to the social vulnerabilities emerging through social media. For example, CSO's online website provides 15 cases of data breaches from the past few years involving the exposure or selling of users' personal information (Hill & Swinhoe, 2022). As we may see, even great companies, like Yahoo, Facebook, or LinkedIn could be and were vulnerable. Every vulnerability could eventually become the point of entry for those with malicious intent, such as hybrid actors.

The vulnerabilities presented in the figure below could also be considered as threats as they require a malicious actor to initiate and exploit the weaknesses caused especially by the lack of security education and culture, but also by the absence of robust cybersecurity measures. These vulnerabilities not only expose potential points of entry for malicious actors but also highlight the critical role that the human factor plays in exacerbating the overall threat landscape. Additionally, the inadequacy of cybersecurity measures further amplifies the risk, creating an environment where vulnerabilities can be easily exploited. It underscores the importance of comprehensive security strategies that encompass both technological safeguards and an emphasis on fostering a security-conscious culture among users and stakeholders.

Furthermore, Al Hasib (2009) also views the weaknesses exploitable through social media as threats, which he divides into:

- Privacy-related threats which include digital dossier of personal information, face recognition, content-based image retrieval, image tagging and cross-profiling, and difficulty of complete account deletion;
- SNS Variants of Traditional Network and Information Security Threats which include: spamming, cross-site scripting, viruses and worms, and SNS (social networking service) aggregators;
- Identity-related threats: phishing, information leakage, and profile squatting through identity theft;
- Social threats: stalking or corporate espionage.

At the same time, according to Amanda Hetler (2023) six of the most common social media privacy issues are:

- Data mining for identity theft;
- Privacy setting loopholes;
- Location settings;
- Harassment and cyberbullying;
- False information;
- Malware and viruses.

We provide another list of possible threats/exploitable vulnerabilities through social media. These are just a few examples of instruments that hostile actors could use to obtain something, either money or some other material goods, or another kind of strategic advantage like influencing elections (Berghel, 2018).

VULNERABILITIES WITHIN SOCIAL MEDIA PLATFORMS

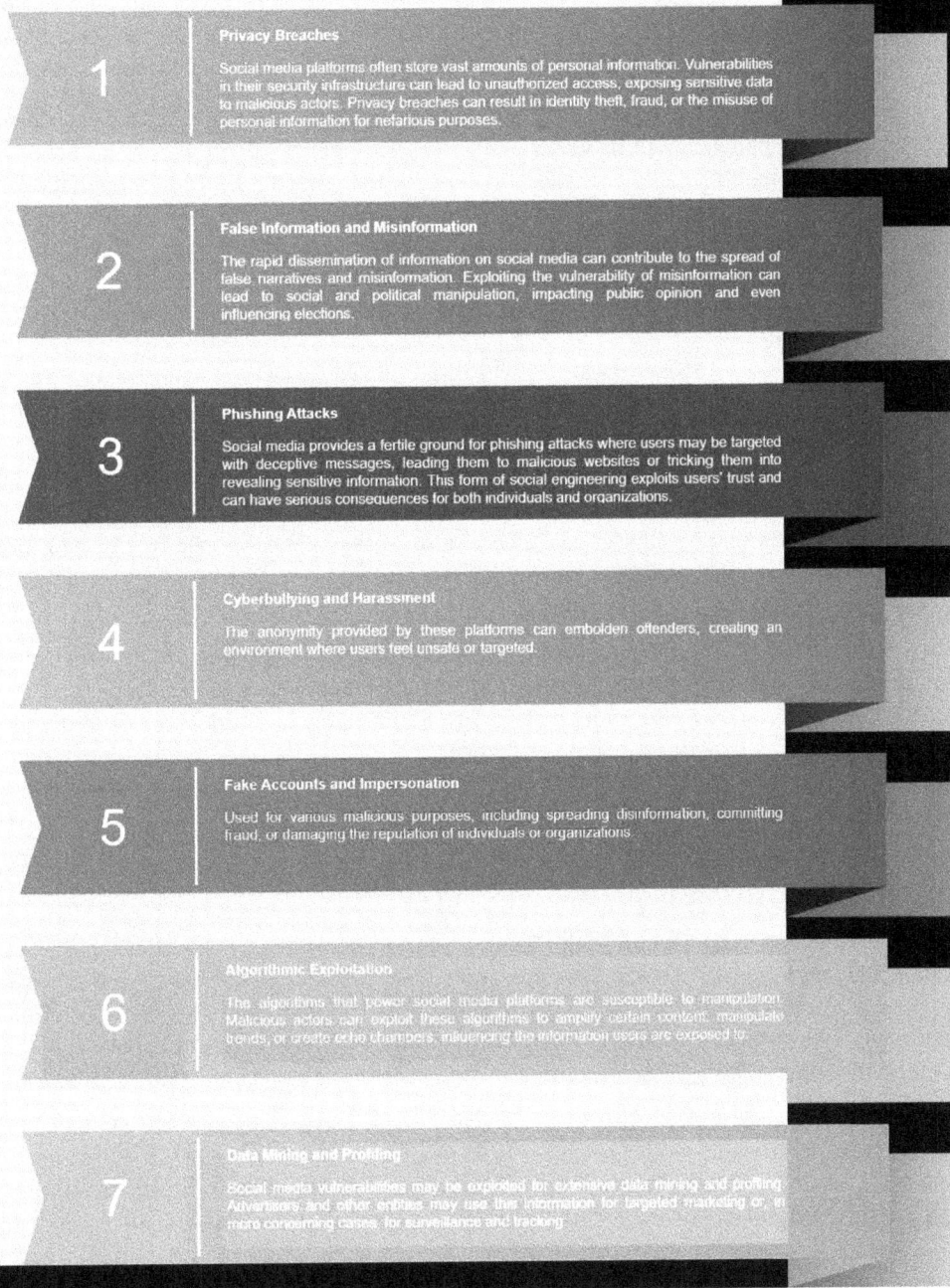

1 Privacy Breaches
Social media platforms often store vast amounts of personal information. Vulnerabilities in their security infrastructure can lead to unauthorized access, exposing sensitive data to malicious actors. Privacy breaches can result in identity theft, fraud, or the misuse of personal information for nefarious purposes.

2 False Information and Misinformation
The rapid dissemination of information on social media can contribute to the spread of false narratives and misinformation. Exploiting the vulnerability of misinformation can lead to social and political manipulation, impacting public opinion and even influencing elections.

3 Phishing Attacks
Social media provides a fertile ground for phishing attacks where users may be targeted with deceptive messages, leading them to malicious websites or tricking them into revealing sensitive information. This form of social engineering exploits users' trust and can have serious consequences for both individuals and organizations.

4 Cyberbullying and Harassment
The anonymity provided by these platforms can embolden offenders, creating an environment where users feel unsafe or targeted.

5 Fake Accounts and Impersonation
Used for various malicious purposes, including spreading disinformation, committing fraud, or damaging the reputation of individuals or organizations.

6 Algorithmic Exploitation
The algorithms that power social media platforms are susceptible to manipulation. Malicious actors can exploit these algorithms to amplify certain content, manipulate trends, or create echo chambers, influencing the information users are exposed to.

7 Data Mining and Profiling
Social media vulnerabilities may be exploited for extensive data mining and profiling. Advertisers and other entities may use this information for targeted marketing or, in more concerning cases, for surveillance and tracking.

Figure 2: Vulnerabilities within social media platforms

Addressing these manifestations of vulnerabilities in social media requires a multi-faceted approach involving technological advancements, robust security measures, user education, and policy frameworks. As social media continues to play a pivotal role in modern communication, understanding and mitigating these vulnerabilities are crucial for fostering a safer and more secure digital environment.

2. Social Media as a Battlefield

In the digital age, social media has evolved into a complex battlefield where ideas, narratives, and influences clash on a global scale. There are plenty of examples, one being the influence of social media in the elections (Davis & Taras, 2022). Far from being mere platforms for social interaction, these networks have become strategic arenas for individuals, groups, and nations to shape public opinion, influence political landscapes, and advance their agendas. Hybrid actors make no exception as the use of propaganda and disinformation has increased on social media platforms. Besides the evident advantage of low cost-high impact, the use of social media platforms provides the hybrid actors the anonymity, ambiguity, and deniability they desire.

Hybrid actors, state, non-state, or a combination of those, including proxy, auxiliary, surrogate, and affiliated forces (Rauta, 2019) employ all the instruments, both conventional and unconventional blending forces, means, purposes, and targets in pursuing a strategic goal. They often present the following characteristics:

- Combination of resources, capabilities, and strategies of both state and non-state entities, leveraging the strengths of both sectors;
- They operate across multiple domains, including military, economic, political, informational, and cyber. They seamlessly integrate these domains to achieve their objectives, making it challenging for traditional military and defense structures to respond effectively;
- They involve asymmetric tactics, where unconventional methods are used to exploit the weaknesses of more conventionally organized opponents. This can include guerrilla warfare, insurgency, and cyber-attacks;
- Hybrid actors often operate in a gray zone, deliberately maintaining ambiguity about their involvement in certain activities. This allows them to deny responsibility, making it difficult for adversaries to respond decisively;
- They manipulate information to shape perceptions, influence public opinion, and create confusion. This includes the use of propaganda, disinformation, and cyber operations to control the narrative;
- They can quickly adjust their tactics and strategies in response to changing circumstances, taking advantage of emerging opportunities or adapting to countermeasures employed by adversaries.

Hybrid actors represent a dynamic and evolving challenge in the contemporary geopolitical landscape. Understanding their characteristics and tactics is essential for developing comprehensive strategies to address the complex nature of hybrid warfare. According to Giannopoulos et. al. "the activity behind Hybrid Threats is undertaken particularly by actors with more or less authoritarian or totalitarian views of power" (Giannopoulos, et al., 2021), and this relates to what we emphasized before, the fact that on one hand, they utilize specific instruments and tools, difficult to anticipate or to counteract by the attacked state and, on the other hand, they manage to disguise their goals and even their identities.

There are plenty of examples of hybrid actors who engaged in hybrid operations within social media but we will remember just a few of them.

First of all, we have to take a look at the Russian Interference in the U.S. elections, particularly during the 2016 presidential campaign, which has been the subject of extensive investigation and scrutiny. The interference involved a combination of social media manipulation, hacking, and the dissemination of disinformation. Furthermore, the Annual Threat Assessment of the US Intelligence Community shows that Russia continued with the influence operations against elections, the most recent one being in the 2022 U.S. midterm elections (2023).

The second state actor to consider is China, which has been accused of conducting influence operations on social media platforms to shape global narratives in its favor. This includes the use of state-controlled media outlets, paid trolls, and coordinated campaigns to spread positive information about China and counter-narratives perceived as unfavorable to the Chinese government. Lots of studies have been conducted regarding Chinese influence but according to Diamond and Schell, "China has not sought to interfere in a national election in the United States or to sow confusion or inflame polarization in our democratic discourse the way Russia has done" (Diamond & Schell, 2019);

Third, Iranian disinformation campaigns must be taken into account as they are aimed at advancing Iranian geopolitical interests, including the creation of fake accounts and the dissemination of misleading content to influence public opinion on issues such as regional conflicts, international relations, and a more evident one, COVID-19. Iran has conducted a massive disinformation campaign about COVID-19, telling lies about the gravity and consequences and bringing as proof false health reports and accusations against other countries (Dubowitz & Ghasseminejad, 2020).

And last, extremist groups, which are considered to be non-state hybrid actors, such as ISIS, have used social media for recruitment and propaganda purposes. These hybrid operations involve disseminating extremist ideologies, recruiting sympathizers, and coordinating activities. Platforms like Twitter and YouTube have faced challenges in combating the spread of such content. A study that analysed 100 Facebook pages and 50 Twitter user accounts has shown that groups like ISIS use social media for recruitment and propaganda, using violent videos and hate speech (Awan, 2017).

Social media, once envisioned as a tool for connecting people and sharing ideas, has transformed into a multifaceted battlefield where information warfare is waged. Understanding the methods and tactics employed in this digital arena is crucial for users to navigate the landscape critically and for policymakers to develop effective strategies to mitigate the negative impacts on society. As social media continues to evolve, the challenge lies in finding a balance between preserving freedom of expression and protecting the public from manipulation and disinformation.

3. Romania's Strategic Vulnerabilities

Romania's geographical location at the crossroads of Europe, along with its membership in NATO and the EU, positions it as a key player in regional security, trade, and cooperation. The country's historical and contemporary importance reflects its multifaceted role in shaping the dynamics of Eastern and Southeastern Europe. Romania is situated at the northern entrance to the Balkan Peninsula, serving as a gateway between Central Europe and the Balkans. Its geographical position has historically made it a bridge between different cultural, economic, and political influences in the region. Moreover, the Carpathian Mountain and the Black Sea access increase its strategic importance for both NATO and the EU's defense against any Eastern interference.

Although both NATO and EU recognize and value Romania's strategic geopolitical locations, some authors believe that Romania does not take full advantage of it and that its great location and a great variety of natural resources are not fully reflected in the country's economy and people's wellbeing (Banea, 2016). Furthermore, Moga and Bureiko argue that even though Romania aspires to a greater status (Administrația Prezidențială, 2020), "the country has so far only displayed a 'small power' behavior" (Moga & Bureiko, 2022).

Furthermore, Banea emphasizes the fact that it is the population's consciousness and education that influence and even determine the position on the global scale (Banea, 2016). This perspective delves into how the collective mindset and educational levels of a society can significantly impact its ability to navigate the complexities of the international arena. There is a huge difference between a well-informed population about global issues, which possesses a nuanced understanding of cultural differences, and demonstrates a high level of social consciousness, and a population that is not interested in geopolitics, security, or the global market. While high levels of consciousness and education empower the state to actively engage in global affairs and contribute positively, a country where the population is not actively involved, faces challenges that may impact its diplomatic, economic, and cultural standing on the international stage. This underscores the critical importance of investing in education and fostering a collective consciousness that enables nations to navigate and thrive in an interconnected world.

At the same time, we must take a look at Romania from the other point of view, the one where its current status was given by its membership in the NATO and EU. Some authors seem to believe that its strategic importance has increased due to the new roles given by the alliances (Moga & Bureiko, 2022).

So, the question remains. Is Romania important in the international security arena due to its geographical position and its internal capabilities or due to its membership in NATO and the EU? We believe that Romania's importance in the international security arena is a result of the intricate interplay between its geographical position, internal capabilities, and memberships in NATO and the EU. A comprehensive understanding of these dynamics is crucial for addressing vulnerabilities and ensuring the nation's continued role as a key player in regional and global security efforts. Continuous efforts to strengthen both internal capacities and international collaborations will contribute to Romania's resilience and effectiveness in the evolving landscape of international security.

We have identified four major pillars which can be viewed on one hand as potential vulnerabilities, and on the other hand as key solutions for strengthening Romania's national security and increasing its role, especially in the regional security framework.

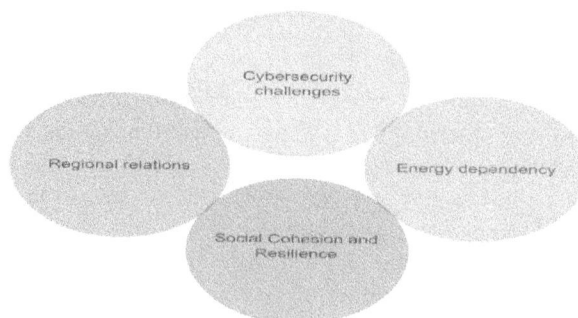

Figure 3: Security pillars

Given the interconnected nature of the modern world, Romania faces cybersecurity challenges that require ongoing attention. Strengthening capabilities to protect against cyber threats is essential for safeguarding national security. While there are lots of threats that could manifest in social media, such as disinformation campaigns, phishing and social engineering, spread of malicious software, identity theft, or manipulation of public perception, besides cyber-attacks, enhancing cybersecurity measures plays a fundamental role. Moreover, robust cybersecurity measures are essential for safeguarding critical infrastructure, including energy grids, transportation systems, and communication networks. Cybersecurity has become an important topic for researchers worldwide as there is plenty of scientific research on networks, security vulnerabilities, threat detection and mitigation strategies, encryption technologies, risk assessment methodologies, incident response protocols, and the development of advanced cybersecurity tools and frameworks. Researchers are actively exploring innovative approaches to address the evolving landscape of cyber threats, ranging from sophisticated cyberattacks to emerging challenges in areas such as the Internet of Things (IoT), artificial intelligence (AI), and cloud computing security. This wealth of research is crucial for enhancing the resilience of digital ecosystems, protecting sensitive data, and fortifying the global cybersecurity infrastructure against constantly evolving cyber risks (Schiappa, et al., 2019), (Sabottke, et al., 2015), (Ozkaya, 2018), (Walter, 2023).

Romania has initiated measures to strengthen its cybersecurity posture, Hackout.ro is just one small example. They started a series of Hackout Talks, as they call them, where specialists from the cyber security field give presentations to raise public awareness of the risks and threats in the online space. Moreover, the Hackout team publishes a series of articles, with the same goal, education and public awareness (Harvat, et al., 2023).

The second pillar, which is both a potential vulnerability and a source of enhancing Romania's security is the energy field and the fact that Romania, despite its energy resources, is still dependent on external energy sources. Diversifying energy sources and ensuring resilience against disruptions may bring huge contributions to national security. A study about the security incidents caused by interruption of electricity supply was conducted by the, besides other specific conclusions, they stipulate that there is a tendency to integrate the communication field among essential services for the functioning of societies as a whole (National Authority for Administration and Regulation in Communications, 2021).

Another important pillar is represented by the regional relations. Romania's President, Klaus Iohannis argues that: "the development of Strategic Partnerships and other bilateral relations, the promotion of the strategic relevance of the Black Sea, the projection of Romania's profile as a factor of stability and the promotion of EU values in the region, as well as the support of political, economic and security interests in areas of interest for our country will be concrete benchmarks of Romania's foreign policy actions" (Iohannis, 2023). Thus, actively managing and fostering positive relations with neighbouring countries can mitigate potential vulnerabilities and contribute to regional stability.

The last pillar, social cohesion and resilience, especially in Romania's case, may have needed to be analysed in a much larger paper as it seems to be the universal answer to all our challenges posed especially by hybrid threats. Romania faces social media challenges that impact its social cohesion and resilience. Despite these challenges, Romania's historical resilience and shared cultural identity contribute to its ability to counteract divisive influences. Fostering digital literacy, promoting media literacy, and enhancing cybersecurity measures are crucial steps for Romania to strengthen social cohesion in the digital age and build resilience against the negative impacts of social media challenges. Moreover, The Social Alternatives Association has conducted a study named *Fake News – Fake Reality: Social Resilience through Critical Thinking* with the main purpose of establishing the first anti-fake news coalition in Central and Eastern Europe (The Social Alternatives Association, 2023).

A similar study on state vulnerabilities within social media was conducted by Faruk Hadžić (2020) in Bosnia and Hertzegovina. Among his conclusions was the imperious need of a broader national security strategy with a great focus on cybersecurity and the increase of vulnerabilities in the cyber domain. Moreover, the appearance of new types of crimes due to social media development entails competent law enforcement institutions, well-trained and equipped, and which act under precise and thorough regulations.

4. Conclusions

The research emphasizes the interconnected and multifaceted nature of vulnerabilities within a state, acknowledging that hybrid actors exploit diverse domains simultaneously. The holistic approach aligns with the idea that hybrid threats often have a main strategic goal, employing innovative and unpredictable methods across various domains. Recognizing the interconnectedness of vulnerabilities is crucial for assessing a state's susceptibility to hybrid threats. The presence of vulnerabilities alone does not precipitate targeting; it is the alignment with a larger strategic purpose and deliberate intent that sets the stage for potential hybrid engagement.

In the context of social media, vulnerabilities take on a unique dimension, often exploiting the human factor. The vulnerabilities identified, including misinformation and manipulation, underscore the challenges posed by the rapid spread of information in real-time. Social media platforms become arenas for influencing perceptions, leveraging efficient algorithms to target specific demographics. Addressing these vulnerabilities requires technological advancements and a comprehensive approach involving user education, policy frameworks, and robust cybersecurity measures. The interplay of human factors, technological safeguards, and security-conscious culture is essential in mitigating the risks associated with social media vulnerabilities.

Romania's global importance results from its strategic location, internal capabilities, and NATO-EU memberships. Balancing geopolitical advantages and alliances is crucial for sustained regional and global influence and strengthening internal capacities and international collaborations is pivotal for resilience. For that, Romania could focus its efforts on four key pillars for national security: robust cybersecurity, diversified energy sources, positive regional relations, and social cohesion and resilience. Initiatives like Hackout.ro showcase proactive steps in cybersecurity, while strategic efforts in energy and regional partnerships contribute to overall security.

References

Administrația Prezidențială, 2020. Strategia Națională de Apărare a țării pentru perioada 2020-2024, București: s.n.
Al Hasib, A., 2009. Threats of Online Social Networks. IJCSNS International Journal of Computer Science and Network Security, 9(11), pp. 288-293.
Awan, I., 2017. Cyber-extremism: Isis and the power of social media. Society, 54(2), pp. 138-149.
Banea, C. B., 2016. Romania: Geographical and Geopolitical Position. Annals of the University of Oradea, Economic Science Series, 25(2).
Berghel, H., 2018. Malice domestic: The Cambridge analytica dystopia. Computer, 51(05), pp. 84-89.
Bilal, A., 2021. Hybrid Warfare – New Threats, Complexity, and 'Trust' as the Antidote. NATO Review, 30 November.
Bowen, A. S., 2022. Ukrainian Armed Forces, s.l.: Congressional Research Service.
Bruning, P. F., Alge, B. J. & Lin, H.-C., 2020. Social networks and social media: Understanding and managing influence vulnerability in a connected society. Business Horizons, Volume 63, pp. 749-761.
Cullen, P. J. & Reichborn-Kjennerud, E., 2017. MCDC Countering Hybrid Warfare Project: Understanding Hybrid Warfare, s.l.: s.n.
Davis, R. & Taras, D., 2022. Electoral Campaigns, Media, and the New World of Digital Politics. In: s.l.:Ann Arbor> University of Michigan Press, pp. 1-22.
Diamond, L. & Schell, O. eds., 2019. China's influence and American interests: Promoting constructive vigilance. s.l.:Hoover Press.
Dubowitz, M. & Ghasseminejad, S., 2020. Iran's COVID-19 disinformation campaign. CTC Sentinel. United States Military Academy.
European Commission, 2016. Joint Framework on countering hybrid threats - a European Union response, Brussels: s.n.
Giannopoulos, G., Smith, H. & Theocharidou, M., 2021. The lanscape of hybrid threats: A conceptual model. Luxembourg: Publications Office of the European Union.
Hadžić, F., 2020. The Influence of Social Media on Threats to Identity, Stability and National Security; Institutional Inefficiency and Vulnerability of B&H. Defendology, Issue 45-46, pp. 67-109.
Harvat, A., Puiu, G., Pitiş, D. & Galea, V., 2023. HACKOUT. Cyber Attacks Portal. [Online] Available at: https://hackout.ro [Accessed 28 December 2023].
Hetler, A., 2023. 6 common social media privacy issues. [Online] Available at: https://www.techtarget.com/whatis/feature/6-common-social-media-privacy-issues [Accessed 28 02 2024].

Hill, M. & Swinhoe, D., 2022. The 15 biggest data breaches of the 21st century. [Online] Available at: https://www.csoonline.com/article/534628/the-biggest-data-breaches-of-the-21st-century.html [Accessed 28 02 2024].

Hoffman, F., 2007. Conflict in the 21st century: The Rise of Hybrid Wars. Arlington(Virginia): Potomac Institute for Policy Studies.

Iohannis, K., 2023. Commitments. Foreign policy. [Online] Available at: https://www.presidency.ro/en/commitments/foreign-policy[Accessed 28 December 2023].

Moga, T. L. & Bureiko, N., 2022. Ambitions yet unrealized: Romania's status and perceptions from the immediate eastern neighbourhood. Southeast European and Black Sea Studies.

National Authority for Administration and Regulation in Communications, 2021. Study on incidents of security caused by interruption of supply electricity, s.l.: s.n.

Office of the Director of National Intelligence, 2023. Annual Threat Assessment of the US Intelligence Community, s.l.: s.n.

Ozkaya, E., 2018. Cybersecurity Challenges in Social Media, s.l.: s.n.

Petrescu, D.-L., 2019. The Hybrid Threat - Action and Counteraction. Bucharest, "Carol I" National Defence University.

Rauta, V., 2019. Towards a typology of non-state actors in „Hybrid Warfare": Proxy, auxiliary, surrogate and affiliated forces. Cambridge Review of International Affairs.

Renz, B., 2016. Russia and 'hybrid warfare'. Contemporary Politics.

Sabottke, C., Suciu, O. & Dumitraș, T., 2015. Vulnerability Disclosure in the Age of Social Media: Exploiting Twitter for Predicting Real-World Exploits. Washington, D.C., s.n.

Schiappa, M., Chantry, G. & Garibay, I., 2019. Cyber Security in a Complex Community: A Social Media Analysis on Common Vulnerabilities and Exposures. s.l., s.n.

Steingartner, W., Možnik, D. & Galinec, D., 2022. Disinformation Campaigns and Resilience in Hybrid Threats Conceptual Model. Poprad, 2022 IEEE 16th International Scientific Conference on Informatics (Informatics), pp. 287-292.

The Social Alternatives Association, 2023. Social Alternatives. [Online] Available at: https://www.alternativesociale.ro/fake-news-fake-reality-2/[Accessed 19 December 2023].

Treverton, G. F. et al., 2018. Addressing Hybrid Threats. s.l.:Swedish Defence University.

Walter, A. T., 2023. Cyber Security and Social Madia. In: S. N. Romaniuk, M. S. Catino & C. A. Martin, eds. The Handbook of Homeland Security. s.l.:CRC Press, pp. 187-196.

Hoaxes in Social Media: Can Game-Based Learning Beat Them?

Vajk Pomichal

University of Ss. Cyril and Methodius in Trnava, Slovakia

pomichal1@ucm.sk

Abstract: In the digital era, people, especially younger generations, are increasingly turning to social media as their primary news source. Reports show a significant increase in the use of online social media networks and an increasing amount of false information spreading on these platforms. False information can have severe consequences, as seen in the recent US presidential elections, the Brexit vote, and the COVID-19 pandemic response. False news can lead to radicalization, fear, and anti-social behavior both online and in real life. Addressing false information involves more than just labeling or filtering it on social media platforms. Cognitive biases like confirmation bias or the echo chamber effect can lead to distrust of such labels. The most effective solution is prevention through education, emphasizing critical thinking skills. It is therefore important to encourage students to think critically to be as resistant as possible to the influence of hoaxes. Given that frontal education does not appear to be an effective approach to developing critical thinking, other alternatives need to be sought. Game-based learning is gaining prominence as an effective educational approach. It offers advantages like increased student motivation, a secure environment for experimentation, and the development of crucial skills, including critical thinking. Several meta-analyses showed that games can improve critical thinking, but the effect depends on factors like game genre, mechanics, instructional approaches, learner demographics, and cultural nuances. Our work is dedicated to the qualitative analysis of games enhancing critical thinking, especially in the context of building immunity towards online false information. Our primary aim is to thoroughly examine these games and their game mechanics and comprehensively assess their advantages and disadvantages within the formal educational context. We systematically playtested selected games based on criteria related to usability in classrooms. We found, that most of these games are strongly story based, typically putting the player in the role of a hoax-monger or alternatively in the role of a fact-checker. The games offer easily understandable game mechanics to support fast onboarding, and therefore offer an effective educational tool to discuss and learn more about the risks of increasing amounts of false information in online space.

Keywords: Education, False information, Game-based learning, Gaming, Hoaxes in social media, Teaching

1. Introduction

In the onine era, there is a shift in news consumption, with younger generations favoring social media over traditional outlets (Flintham et al., 2018). The Media Use in the European Union – Report (Commission and for Communication, 2023) highlights a significant increase in online social media usage, rising from 33% in 2010 to 67% in 2023. Daily usage among those aged 15 to 24 is at 79%, with 93% using social media at least once a week. The same report notes that 69% of respondents frequently encounter news they believe distorts reality or is false.

False news can be defined as information that is created to resemble conventional news but contains false or misleading information (Lazer et al., 2018). The spread of false information can harm both society and individuals in various ways. Prominent instances of this impact include the notable cases of the latest US presidential elections (Gunther, Beck and Nisbet, 2018), the Brexit vote (Höller, 2021), affecting the political scene in other countries (Reichel et al., 2020; Cantarella, Fraccaroli and Volpe, 2023), reducing interest in COVID-19 vaccination (Carrion-Alvarez and Tijerina-Salina, 2020; Montagni et al., 2021). In addition, increased radicalization and spread of fear result in aggressive and anti-social behavior both online and offline (Roberts-Ingleson and McCann, 2023).

Addressing false information goes beyond labelling or filtering on social media platforms, as cognitive biases and distrust complicate this approach (Clayton et al., 2020). Labelling content as true or false is time-consuming and sensitive, with potential errors undermining trust (Kemp, Loaiza and Wahlheim, 2022). Social media developers may resist implementation due to cost and misalignment with their business model. The most effective solution involves prevention through education, emphasizing the development of critical thinking skills (Levy and Ross, 2021).

Conventional educational methods, such as traditional frontal education in classrooms, often fall short of equipping students with the essential skills demanded by the 21st century, including critical thinking skills (Lavi, Tal and Dori, 2021). Consequently, alternative pedagogical approaches are gaining prominence, with game-based learning emerging as an effective solution (Plass, Homer and Kinzer, 2015).

Game-based learning (GBL) uses various games to fulfill educational objectives. This approach offers several key advantages, notably heightened student motivation and engagement in assigned tasks (Anastasiadis, Lampropoulos and Siakas, 2018). Moreover, it provides a secure environment within games where experimentation is encouraged, failure is not punitive but rather an opportunity for learning and improvement(Anastasiadis, Lampropoulos and Siakas, 2018). Additionally, game-based learning empowers educators to shift a portion of the educational process from teacher-led instruction to student interaction with the game itself (Hanghøj, 2013).

Game-based learning can effectively impart knowledge across a spectrum of subjects, spanning traditional disciplines like mathematics(Ramli, Maat and Khalid, 2023), programming (Papadakis and Kalogiannakis, 2019), and history (Scholz, Komornicka and Moore, 2021), while also developing crucial skills such as teamwork and communication (Martín-Hernández et al., 2021), and critical thinking (Mao et al., 2022).

One approach actively used in GBL aimed at developing critical thinking skills includes the inoculation theory (Roozenbeek and van der Linden, 2018). This theory is based on the biological metaphor of inoculation: an organism is exposed to bacteria or viruses in safe amounts so that later when encountering a real disease, it knows how to respond effectively. This works similarly in games where players can be exposed to the threat of false information in a safe environment so that they can later recognize it in real life. Experiments conducted with existing games suggest that games can be a powerful tool for developing critical thinking skills and thus building immunity towards false information (Roozenbeek and van der Linden, 2019; Basol, Roozenbeek and Linden, 2020).

The increasing prevalence of false information on social media platforms and its potential impact on individuals' critical thinking skills prompted this study. Recognizing the challenges in addressing misinformation through traditional means, the researchers explored the potential of game-based learning as an innovative approach to enhance critical thinking skills and build resilience against false information.

2. Methods

Our work is dedicated to the qualitative analysis of games enhancing critical thinking, with a strong focus on the ability to recognize false information. Our primary aim is to thoroughly examine these games and their game mechanics and conduct a comprehensive assessment of their potential within the formal educational context. Therefore, we can formulate the following research questions:

- RQ1: How can these games be used in a formal education context?
- RQ2: What game mechanics do these games use to teach about false information?

2.1 Game Selection

Initially, we searched for games centered on the theme of false information or misinformation. Given that such games are typically free-to-play web-based games, we opted not to explore conventional platforms like Steam or the Google Play Store. Instead, we conducted a targeted web search using the key phrases "fake news game" and "misinformation game," examining the search results to handpick the relevant digital and tabletop games.

In the screening process, we identified 19 game projects. We excluded those that: a) did not directly tackle false information, such as the Interland game aimed at lower primary school children, focusing on general Internet safety; b) addressed false information only through gamified quizzes lacking a deeper game context, like Fakey, a news labeling simulation. After these exclusions, we identified 11 digital and 2 tabletop game projects (see Table 1).

2.2 Examined Criteria

We played the selected games and analyzed them based on the following criteria:

- Platform – on which platform is the game available, this can affect the accessibility of the game in the classroom.
- Pricing – whether the game is free to play, or requires financial investment, which can greatly reduce its accessibility in formal education.
- Number of players – how many players can play the game simultaneously. Determines also, whether the game is single- or multi-player.
- Recommended age – for which age category is the game suitable.
- Average playtime – approximately how long it takes to finish a round or a full game.
- Key features – this broader criterion describes the most important game mechanics of the game. Gives a general explanation of the game's core loop and describes how the game teaches about false information.

- Preparation and equipment needed – what is needed to use the game in the classroom., including technical equipment and preparation needed before the game can be played, such as explaining the rules.

These criteria should help us to identify the key advantages and disadvantages of these games in the formal educational context and determine their usability. The main constraints in general are the pricing, the relatively short duration of classes (typically 45 to 60 minutes), the number of players, and the accessible equipment. Besides these, the teacher needs to understand the game and actively participate in directing the students during playtime, which requires further preparation based on the type and complexity of the game (Hanghøj, 2013).

3. Results

The results obtained from the observed games are shown in Appendix A – Table 1. The table was filled out based on our playtesting of the games (in duration of one or two play sessions per game) and based on available information about the games online (such as the recommended age group).

3.1 Accessibility of the Games

The results show that digital games are predominantly available as browser-based games, except for Cranky Uncle, which has a mobile app, and Escape the Fake, which uses a mobile app and augmented reality. Browser-based games are a good choice for educational games because they are platform-independent and easily accessible on a variety of devices, including mobile and tablet devices, if the webpage is responsive. A possible drawback is that they require a permanent internet connection, but this is ensured in most schools in Europe.

The accessibility of these games is also supported by the fact that they are free to play, as most of the projects were created on academic campuses or at the initiative of non-profit organizations. A standout of these are the tabletop games Lamboozled! and Follow Me, which need to cover printing costs and are therefore charged (in both cases with a price of around 20€ per copy). The authors of Follow Me offer an alternative solution and the possibility to download the game materials as a print-and-play version.

Another common characteristic of digital games is that they are designed for a single player. The exception is Escape the Fake, which offers an escape room experience using augmented reality for a group of players. The advantages of making a single-player game for designers are more control over the flow of the game and easier technical implementation. On the other hand, the possibility of interaction between players can increase the players' engagement in the game because the game also creates a social experience. Thus, in this respect, tabletop games have a certain advantage until the abstinence of a digital game created for multiplayer in the theme of fake information.

3.2 Usability in Formal Education

The primary target audience for these games is teenagers around the age of 14-15. This can be explained by the fact that by this age, children are usually mature enough to deal with more serious topics(Shehata and Amnå, 2017), including politics and democratic principles (as depicted in the games Harmony Square or Libertas Veritas), or illegal migration (as in the game Troll Factory), or the complex motivations behind the creation and dissemination of fake information (as in the games Bad News and Fake it to make it). However, it appears that children are getting exposed to social media and, therefore, to fake information at an increasingly young age, which makes it appropriate to target games with this theme at even younger generations, as the game Fake News Detective does.

It turns out that these games were created with a consideration for use in formal education. They are designed to be short enough to be used effectively within a typical lesson, lasting around 10 to 25 minutes. They also contain simple game mechanics, where the player mostly just reads the text and selects an action from the available choices, which makes the onboarding process easier, and players can start to play without a long explanation or a difficult tutorial. An exception is Fake It to Make It, which has a relatively long game time and a complex simulation of the spread of fake news and the economics of web portals, for this reason, it requires a longer play time, and there is a greater risk that students will stop enjoying the game before they reach the desired level of understanding of the spread of false information. Another limitation for more complex games is the restricted class duration in schools, which does not provide opportunities for longer play sessions. A special case are tabletop games that require an explanation of the rules before playing. In this respect, the Follow Me game has a slight disadvantage due to the higher complexity of the rules, but both tabletop games studied try to simplify the process of learning the rules by using freely available video tutorials that can be watched before playing.

Most of the games do not require much preparation and a lot of tools, just an internet connection and a computer or mobile phone. In the case of tabletop games, it is, of course, necessary to have a sufficient number of copies of these games. Only Escape Fake requires more precise room preparation, printing and hanging the posters according to the freely available instructions. More preparation may be required for the post-play debriefing about the topic of false information and prevention, which has the potential to increase the educational effect of the gameplay; for this purpose, several of the games (for example, Harmony Square, Follow Me, Lamboozled!) offer a freely available methodological guide and sample lessons to assist in the preparation and implementation of the debriefing.

Based on these findings, we can state that the answer to RQ1 is that most of these games are well prepared for implementation in formal education, especially in lessons such as media education or civic education. They are of adequate length and offer enough methodological materials to ensure that their use does not pose an excessive workload for the teacher.

3.3 Key Game Mechanics

In terms of game mechanics, we also find commonalities between the games studied. Most of them are story-based and focus on decision-making between 2-3 offered actions that affect player statistics (for example, credibility or popularity), with the player's main goal being to have these statistics as good as possible at the end of the game; 6 of the 13 games studied work in this way. The Choose Your Own Fake News game is even simpler, it uses only a story with several decisions for the player without any stats, and the player's goal is only to achieve a "good" ending to the story. Other games use game mechanics representing the process of debunking fake news, such as collecting evidence and verifying the article's author (in the case of Lamboozled!, Post Facto, and partially in the game Follow Me!).

Another interesting game in terms of choice of mechanics is Fake News Detective, which is an explorative adventure game where the player discovers a large headquarters of a disinformation portal to find the main director. The player progresses by solving simple puzzles and playing mini-games where they guess the truthfulness of the depicted articles, the educational component is less pronounced in this game, but due to the appealing graphics and elements of adventure, it is suitable for the younger generations. Unique in this respect is the game Escape Fake, which functions as an escape room in augmented reality where players solve various puzzles related to media, fake news, and social networks to meet the game's goal and save the world.

3.4 Story

Most of these games rely heavily on stories. A recurring motive is to put the player in the role of a disinformation spreader with different goals: From arguing within the family (Cranky Uncle) to gaining wealth and popularity (Bad News, Fake It to Make It, Troll Factory), staying in power (Libertas Veritas) to destroying an existing democratic regime (Harmony Square). This makes it easier for the player to understand the motives behind the spread of false information and teaches the most common techniques of creating and spreading hoaxes, building resilience to false information in real life as well, as applying the inoculation theory.

Another group of games puts the player in the role of a fact-checker (Fake News Detective, Post Facto, Lamboozled!, Escape Fake), who tries to uncover hoaxes by using established techniques such as verifying the author of the article, searching for other sources, examining the stylistics of the text and the way the facts are presented and the emotions evoked. These games playfully teach players these important techniques and increase the expectation of using fact-checking in real life as well.

The third group of games puts the player in the position of a person who is not a professional fact-checker, but who can be greatly influenced by the impact of these reports. In the case of the Follow Me game, the player is an influencer on a social network trying to gain popularity, and in the case of the Troubled Times scenario on NewsGamer, the player is put in the role of the chief director of a TV channel trying to maintain popularity, support from the state, and a professional reputation at the same time. In the case of these games, players can experience the negative impact of false information in the safe environment of the game, which again can reinforce their alertness subsequently in real-life situations.

Based on these findings, we can state that the answer to RQ2 is that the key mechanics of these games are predominantly story-based decision-making, embedding the player in the roles of various stakeholders in the creation and dissemination or debunking of false information, and simulating the process of fact-checking through in-game actions.

3.5 Discussion

Existing studies that address game-based learning in the context of fake news predominantly work with quantitative data and look at the impact on the ability to recognize fake information. In this way, the effectiveness of games Bad News (Basol, Roozenbeek and Linden, 2020), Harmony Square (Roozenbeek and van der Linden, 2020) or Crancky Uncle (Cook et al., 2023) has been demonstrated.

In the other hand, a qualitative analysis of Bad News and similar games suggests, that these games by themselves are not as effective and has questionable long term effect (Barabas, 2023), the article however states, that even if the games themselves cannot offer the ultimate solution, they definitely can play a role in the fight against hoaxes. Another qualitative research of games Bad News, Harmony Square and Fake It To Make It made similar finding to our results: their players enjoyed the storylines of games and disliked the complexity of the game Fake It To Make It (Berg, Loewen-Colón and Saridaki, 2021).

4. Conclusion

The current era is marked by an increasing amount of false information being spread, especially online on social networks. This news can seriously threaten both the individual (e.g. bad advice on healthy lifestyles) and society (e.g. influencing public opinion and elections). Young people are extremely exposed to hoaxes as their primary source of information is often social media. Solutions such as news labeling or fact-checking are costly but limited in their effectiveness, so the best solution is prevention and the associated development of critical thinking. Traditional frontal education in schools often fails to develop the skills needed to build resilience to false information effectively enough, so alternative ways of teaching are becoming more popular, including game-based learning, which allows students to learn playfully in a safe environment.

This work aimed to map the available games aimed at educating about false information, to compare their key mechanics and other parameters that influence their usability within the learning process. We identified and analyzed 11 digital and 2 tabletop games.

We found most of these games to be well implementable in the learning process due to their shorter playing time and easy-to-understand mechanics, which primarily involves story-based decision-making and roleplay (most often in the role of a "bad" hoax-maker or "good" fact-checker) and game mechanics simulating the fact-checking process. At the same time, some of the games offer sample lessons and a methodology guide for teachers to facilitate the use of games in the classroom.

A potential limitation of this study lies in the influence of researcher bias, as the effectiveness of games in developing critical thinking skills may be influenced by the researcher/s perspectives and preferences in selecting or designing the gaming scenarios

In future work, we intend to test these games with students and teachers from schools to validate our assumptions and gain a more accurate, data-supported picture of the usefulness of these games in formal education and their effectiveness in building resilience to false information.

Acknowledgement

The paper was elaborated thanks to support and funding provided by the Scientific Grant Agency of the Ministry of Education, Science, Research and Sport of the Slovak Republic and the Slovak Academy of Sciences, specifically thanks to financial resources available within the grant project VEGA No. 1/0489/23 entitled "Innovative Model of Monetization of Digital Games in the Sphere of Creative Industries".

References

Anastasiadis, T., Lampropoulos, G. And Siakas, K. (2018) Digital game-based learning and serious games in education. International Journal of Advances in Scientific Research and Engineering, 4(12), pp. 139–144.

Barabas, R. (2023) What's the News About Bad News? A Review of Bad News Games as a Tool to Teach Media Literacy. Libri, 73(4), pp. 283–292.

Basol, M., Roozenbeek, J. and Linden, S. van der (2020) Good News about Bad News: Gamified Inoculation Boosts Confidence and Cognitive Immunity Against Fake News. Journal of Cognition, 3(1), [Online] Available from: doi.org/10.5334/JOC.91 [Accessed 20/10/2021].

Berg, B., Loewen-Colón, J. and Saridaki, M. (2021) Spreading Learning through Fake News Games. gamevironments, (#15), [Online] Available from: doi.org/10.48783/GAMEVIRON.V15I15.157 [Accessed 10/02/2024].

Cantarella, M., Fraccaroli, N. and Volpe, R. (2023) Does fake news affect voting behaviour? Research Policy, 52(1), p. 104628.

Carrion-Alvarez, D. and Tijerina-Salina, P.X. (2020) Fake news in COVID-19: A perspective. Health Promotion Perspectives, 10(4), p. 290.

Clayton, K. et al. (2020) Real Solutions for Fake News? Measuring the Effectiveness of General Warnings and Fact-Check Tags in Reducing Belief in False Stories on Social Media. Political Behavior, 42(4), pp. 1073–1095.

Commission, E. and for Communication, D.-G. (2023) Media use in the European Union – Report. European Commission.

Cook, J. et al. (2023) The cranky uncle game—combining humor and gamification to build student resilience against climate misinformation. Environmental Education Research, 29(4), pp. 607–623.

Flintham, M. et al. (2018) Falling for fake news: Investigating the consumption of news via social media. Conference on Human Factors in Computing Systems - Proceedings, 2018-April, [Online] Available from: doi.org/10.1145/3173574.3173950 [Accessed 10/01/2022].

Gunther, R., Beck, P.A. and Nisbet, E.C. (2018) Fake news did have a significant impact on the vote in the 2016 election: Original full-length version with methodological appendix. Unpublished manuscript, Ohio State University, Columbus, OH.

Hanghøj, T. (2013) Game-Based Teaching: Practices, Roles, and Pedagogies. https://services.igi-global.com/resolvedoi/resolve.aspx?doi=10.4018/978-1-4666-3950-8.ch005, pp. 81–101.

Höller, M. (2021) The human component in social media and fake news: the performance of UK opinion leaders on Twitter during the Brexit campaign. https://doi.org/10.1080/13825577.2021.1918842, 25(1), pp. 80–95.

Kemp, P.L., Loaiza, V.M. and Wahlheim, C.N. (2022) Fake news reminders and veracity labels differentially benefit memory and belief accuracy for news headlines. Scientific Reports 2022 12:1, 12(1), pp. 1–13.

Lavi, R., Tal, M. and Dori, Y.J. (2021) Perceptions of STEM alumni and students on developing 21st century skills through methods of teaching and learning. Studies in Educational Evaluation, 70, p. 101002.

Lazer, D.M.J. et al. (2018) The science of fake news: Addressing fake news requires a multidisciplinary effort. Science, 359(6380), pp. 1094–1096.

Levy, N. and Ross, R.M. (2021) The cognitive science of fake news. The Routledge Handbook of Political Epistemology, pp. 181–191.

Mao, W. et al. (2022) Effects of Game-Based Learning on Students' Critical Thinking: A Meta-Analysis. Journal of Educational Computing Research, 59(8), pp. 1682–1708.

Martín-Hernández, P. et al. (2021) Fostering University Students' Engagement in Teamwork and Innovation Behaviors through Game-Based Learning (GBL). Sustainability 2021, Vol. 13, Page 13573, 13(24), p. 13573.

Montagni, I. et al. (2021) Acceptance of a Covid-19 vaccine is associated with ability to detect fake news and health literacy. Journal of Public Health (United Kingdom), 43(4), pp. 695–702.

Papadakis, S. and Kalogiannakis, M. (2019) Evaluating the effectiveness of a game-based learning approach in modifying students' behavioural outcomes and competence, in an introductory programming course. A case study in Greece. International Journal of Teaching and Case Studies, 10(3), p. 235.

Plass, J.L., Homer, B.D. and Kinzer, C.K. (2015) Foundations of Game-Based Learning. Educational Psychologist, 50(4), pp. 258–283.

Ramli, I.S.M., Maat, S.M. and Khalid, F. (2023) Learning mathematics in the new norms caused by digital game-based learning and learning analytics. Pegem Journal of Education and Instruction, 13(1), pp. 168–176.

Reichel, J. et al. (2020) Can Fake News Evoke a Positive/Negative Affect (Emotion). In: 13th International Scientific Conference on Distance Learning in Applied Informatics (DIVAI). pp. 563–572.

Roberts-Ingleson, E.M. and McCann, W.S. (2023) The Link between Misinformation and Radicalisation. Perspectives on Terrorism, 17(1), pp. 36–49.

Roozenbeek, J. and van der Linden, S. (2020) Breaking Harmony Square: A game that "inoculates" against political misinformation. The Harvard Kennedy School Misinformation Review.

Roozenbeek, J. and van der Linden, S. (2019) Fake news game confers psychological resistance against online misinformation. Palgrave Communications 2019 5:1, 5(1), pp. 1–10.

Roozenbeek, J. and van der Linden, S. (2018) The fake news game: actively inoculating against the risk of misinformation. Article in Journal of Risk Research, [Online] Available from: doi.org/10.1080/13669877.2018.1443491 [Accessed 15/11/2021].

Scholz, K.W., Komornicka, J.N. and Moore, A. (2021) Gamifying History: Designing and Implementing a Game-Based Learning Course Design Framework. Teaching and Learning Inquiry, 9(1), pp. 99–116.

Shehata, A. and Amnå, E. (2017) The Development of Political Interest Among Adolescents: A Communication Mediation Approach Using Five Waves of Panel Data. https://doi.org/10.1177/0093650217714360, 46(8), pp. 1055–1077.

Appendix A – Results Table

Table 1: Summary of the parameters of the studied games

Game title	Key features	Other information	
Bad News[1]	A narrative game centered on player-character dialogue, driven by decisions impacting stats like credibility and followers. Players take on the role of a 'disinformation and fake news tycoon,' striving to build a social media following inspired by X (formerly Twitter) through the spread of hoaxes	Platform	Web, (mobile friendly)
		No. of players	1
		Playtime (min)	10-15
		Pricing	Free
		Age group	14+
		Preparation & Equipment	computer/mobile, internet access
Choose Your Own Fake News[2]	A nonlinear storytelling game driven by simple player decisions. Choose from three characters and make decisions related to online false information.	Platform	web
		No. of players	1
		Playtime (min)	5-10
		Pricing	Free
		Age group	10+
		Preparation & Equipment	computer, internet access
Cranky Uncle[3]	A linear dialogue-driven game immerses the player in discussions with a 'cranky uncle,' teaching denial techniques like cherry-picking or conspiracy theories. The game features short lessons followed by multiple-choice questions. Players can retry incorrect answers or proceed upon finding the right one, providing a more engaging context than traditional quiz games like Factitious.	Platform	Web, mobile
		No. of players	1
		Playtime (min)	15-20
		Pricing	Free
		Age group	14+
		Preparation & Equipment	computer/mobile app, internet access
Escape Fake[4]	An augmented reality escape room game, where the players need to solve different puzzles related to false information to save the world. The content of the game is accessible through the camera of the mobile phone in combination with printed-out posters.	Platform	Mobile (AR)
		No. of players	1-6
		Playtime (min)	45-60
		Pricing	Free
		Age group	12-16
		Preparation & Equipment	mobile app, internet access, printed posters, an empty room with enough space
Fake It to Make It[5]	A complex game where players assume the role of a hoax spreader, aiming to earn money. The game offers significant freedom with various article options on different topics. Players manage their news portal's	Platform	Web (mobile friendly)
		No. of players	1

---

[1] Avaliable at: https://www.getbadnews.com/

[2] Available at: https://chooseyourownfakenews.com/

[3] Available at: https://crankyuncle.com/

[4] Available at: https://escapefake.org/

[5] Available at: https://www.fakeittomakeitgame.com/

Game title	Key features	Other information	
	economy, including domain costs, hosting, and monetization. To maximize visibility, players select and share articles among groups on social media. The game delves into a detailed model of spreading misinformation, requiring a longer playtime and may not be ideal for casual players.	Playtime (min)	45-60
		Pricing	Free
		Age group	15+
		Preparation & Equipment	computer/mobile, internet access
Fake News Detective[6]	A charming top-down adventure game emphasizes exploration as players take on the role of a detective searching for the head of a misinformation portal. The game includes mini-games where players label real-life inspired articles as true or false.	Platform	Web
		No. of players	1
		Playtime (min)	15-20
		Pricing	Free
		Age group	10-14
		Preparation & Equipment	computer, internet access
Follow me[7]	A card game, that puts the player in the role of an influencer on a fictitious social media platform. Players are trying to gain followers by sharing articles and increasing the credibility of their page. Besides that, they are trying to slow down other players by fact-checking their articles and searching for hoaxes.	Platform	Tabletop
		No. of players	2-4
		Playtime (min)	25-45
		Pricing	26.99€ or print&play
		Age group	10+
		Preparation & Equipment	hard copies of the game, explaining the rules, creating groups
Harmony Square[8]	Non-linear storytelling game based on a dialogue between the player and a fictitious character, driven by the player's decisions, decisions affecting stats such as credibility or following. The player takes the role of the 'Chief Disinformation Officer,' attempting to disrupt peace in the fictional Harmony Square by spreading hoaxes.	Platform	Web (mobile friendly)
		No. of players	1
		Playtime (min)	15-20
		Pricing	Free
		Age group	15+
		Preparation & Equipment	computer/mobile, internet access
Lamboozled![9]	A card game where players aim to build evidence for a randomly selected article using cards for actions like checking sources, authors, and related facts. The game, set in a politically neutral fictional world ruled by lambs, simulates real-life fact-checking processes.	Platform	Tabletop
		No. of players	2-6
		Playtime (min)	20-25
		Pricing	19.95$
		Age group	11+
		Preparation & Equipment	hard copies of the game, explaining the rules, creating groups
	A non-linear storytelling game in which players assume the role of the 'Minister of Integrity' in a dictatorial regime. The player makes decisions to control public opinion,	Platform	Web (mobile friendly)
		No. of players	1

---

[6] Available at: https://fakenewsdetective.com/

[7] Available at: https://www.gamifactory.eu/en/follow-me

[8] Available at: https://harmonysquare.game/en

[9] Available at: https://www.tcpress.com/lamboozled

Game title	Key features	Other information	
Libertas Veritas[10]	appease the 'Glorious Leader,' and manage limited time for actions.	Playtime (min)	10-20
		Pricing	Free
		Age group	15+
		Preparation & Equipment	computer/mobile, internet access
Newsgamer.com – Troubled Times[11]	A non-linear storytelling game where player decisions impact three stats: revenue, government support, and professional reputation. Players take on the role of a chief editor of a news channel, making content decisions to maintain all three stats above a defined level by the end of the game.	Platform	Web (mobile friendly)
		No. of players	1
		Playtime (min)	10-15
		Pricing	Free
		Age group	15+
		Preparation & Equipment	computer/mobile, internet access
Post Facto[12]	In this game, players identify and report suspicious flags in real-world articles to a bot, using a simple interface. The game provides various red flags for different parts of the article, like 'typos' or 'missing sources,' along with additional information such as maps or database records, guiding players through the fact-checking process	Platform	web
		No. of players	1
		Playtime (min)	10-15
		Pricing	Free
		Age group	15+
		Preparation & Equipment	computer, internet access
Troll Factory[13]	A non-linear storytelling game centers on player-character dialogue with a fictitious character, the 'boss.' Players, in the role of a troll seeking online visibility, make choices from several answers in dialogue. The game addresses real-life issues and example articles, including topics like illegal migration.	Platform	Web (mobile friendly)
		No. of players	1
		Playtime (min)	10-15
		Pricing	Free
		Age group	15+
		Preparation & Equipment	computer/mobile, internet access

---

[10]Available at: https://apps.deakin.edu.au/library/dlm/twine/MisinformationGame.html

[11]Available at: https://news-gamer.com/stories

[12]Available at: https://www.postfactogame.com/

[13]Available at: https://trollfactory.yle.fi/

From Passion to Pay Check: The Cyclical Practices of Influencer Brand Building

Emrah Solak

University of Sussex, Brighton, UK

E.Solak@sussex.ac.uk

Abstract: The escalating influence of social media influencers on consumer behaviour continues to captivate the interest of marketing professionals and academic scholars alike. Current literature examines mainly source characteristics, psychological dynamics, and content attributes that explain influencer marketing but there is scanty understanding the mechanisms by which influencers ascend to prominence. This qualitative study introduces the *Four E Framework of Influencer Brand Building*, explaining the cyclical practices by which social media users transform into person-brands within social media ecosystem. The framework comprises four pivotal practices: Exploration, where influencers identify and refine marketable personas; Exploitation, involving the acquisition of tangible and intangible compensation for their digital labour; Evaluation, a critical assessment of brand sustainability and content success; and Extension, during which influencers expand their brand presence across various platforms, adopt alternative personas, or venture into consumer goods to enhance profitability and reduce risks. This model challenges conventional perceptions of influencers as mere marketing tools by repositioning them as central figures in branding literature. The research draws on data collected from influencers and talent managers, providing robust insights into the strategic and operational aspects of influencer brand building. This not only bridges a significant gap in existing academic discourse but also furnishes influencers and marketing professionals with actionable strategies to enhance their brand-building endeavours.

Keywords: Social media, Influencer marketing, Influencers, Self branding

1. Introduction

Social media influencers are one of the driving forces of the spread of social media (Lorenz, 2023), which has fundamentally changed the way individuals obtain and share information (Kietzmann et al., 2011). They are individuals who have amassed a significant following on platforms such as Instagram, YouTube, and TikTok, and leverage their online presence to shape opinions, inspire trends, and influence consumer behaviour (Jin and Muqaddam, 2019; Jun and Yi, 2020). Influencers demonstrate remarkable proficiency in targeting niche audiences (Vrontis et al., 2021), a critical aspect for achieving effectiveness in digital marketing amidst the saturation of online advertising spaces (Hou, 2018). Consumers voluntarily seek their advice for decision making and utilise influencers' content for their own identity projects (Scholz, 2021). While the influencer economy exceeded $20B in 2023 (Dencheva, 2024), being an influencer is increasingly coming to the fore as a lucrative and legitimate career path, especially for generation Z and millennials (Liu, 2023). However -to the best of the authors' knowledge- there is no academic understanding on how this "highly branded social media stars" (Abidin 2018, p. 71) are branded on social media. This study aims to fill this gap by contributing social media marketing and individual branding literature by examining influencers as person-brands (Fournier and Eckhardt, 2019) and attempting to reveal their brand building strategies.

2. Literature Review

The importance of internet technologies in individual branding efforts has been recognized since the first debate in this field (Peters, 1997). Today, the emergence of social media platforms has revolutionized individual branding by providing a cost-effective and efficient means to promote individual brands to a wide audience (Gorbatov, Khapova and Lysova, 2018). This growing trend of branding practices of individuals has also attracted academic attention, leading to an increase in scholarly publications on individual brands, particularly in the fields of marketing, communication, and business administration (Levesque and Pons, 2020). While some studies contribute to a generic understanding of individual brands by defining concepts such as personal brand (Gorbatov et al., 2021), human brand (Thomson, 2006), and person-brand (Fournier and Eckhardt, 2019), other research streams examine individual branding within specialized professions, including politicians (e.g., French and Smith, 2010), CEOs (e.g., Cottan-Nir, 2019), athletes (e.g., Park et al., 2019), and even academics (e.g., Close et al., 2014).

Unlike other individual brands, influencers exist free of gatekeepers and initial financial investment as they are originally ordinary internet users (Abidin, 2015). Thus, they represent a new and unique domain in the field of individual branding which has been extensively studied based on the ground-breaking conceptualizations of Keller (1993) and Aaker (1996). Although these conceptualizations provide a useful framework for many individual brands (Osorio, Centeno, & Cambra-Fierro, 2020), the understanding centres on the one-way communication model of the pre-internet era. However, influencers go beyond using social media as a merely marketing tool, they build and manage their brands purely on social media platforms. Therefore, a study that aims to explore new methods for understanding the branding processes of influencers is timely and rewarding. In fact, Keller (2002) emphasizes developing internet technologies and communication methods and indicates "as branding is applied in more and more different settings, brand theory and best practice guidelines need to be refined to reflect the unique realities of those settings" (p. 171).

Consequently, this research strives to understand how influencers build their individual brands. The study considers influencers as person brands (Fournier and Eckhardt, 2019) and defines the influencer as *a person brand embedded physical or virtual persona that has revealed on digital platform(s) and acquired a sizable audience, regularly produces contents with the aim of shaping their audience perceptions and receives through brand collaborations, licencing and/or subscriptions/views compensation through these contents.* This conceptualisation pioneers to understanding of influencers as brands. Based on the definition, the current study attempts to contribute to the understanding on social media and branding by revealing influencers' branding strategies and practices, while offering a useful framework for (potential) influencers and social media and marketing professionals.

3. Research Method

This study draws on qualitative paradigm and utilises semi-structured interviews to understand brand building practices of influencers. Through theoretical sampling, data from interviews with 16 influencers with audiences ranging from 5000 to 1.5 million and 11 talent managers who provide management and consultancy services to influencers were analysed through reflexive thematic analysis (Braun and Clarke, 2022). Due to the subjective nature of the qualitative paradigm, this study does not claim that its result is only and definitive representation of reality and truth, but that it is one of the multiple.

4. Results

The key finding from the analytical review of data reveals a cyclical practice, here referred to as *Four E Framework of Influencer Brand Building.* This framework depicts the transformation of social media users into person brands, marking the beginning of the person-brand continuum (Osorio, Centeno, & Cambra-Fierro, 2020) for influencers. In the *exploration* process, influencers try to attract the attention of target audiences and stand out in the intensifying social media environment by discovering their marketable identities and the algorithmic functioning of social media platforms through consistent and continuous content production. Subsequently, through the *exploitation* process, influencers receive compensation (tangible or otherwise) for their digital efforts, fostering symbiotic relationships between platforms, marketing professionals and audiences. The increasing reach, commercial relationships, and potential risks of influencers necessitate examining the impact of their social media practices on their brands. During the *evaluation* process, influencers regularly assess both the immediate and enduring success of their brands, while also trying to identify trends and potential opportunities with the data they obtain from platforms and online sources. *Extension* is the fourth process by which influencers seek to diversify their brand presence across various platforms and/or through alternative identities and even consumer products, thus reducing risks and increasing profitability. The extension process results in a return to the exploration process, where the new identity or platform begins to be discovered, thus continuing the brand-building cycle. In rare cases, some influencers choose not to pursue the final process of brand extension, while others continually adapt and evolve their content production to align with new platforms and identities, reinvesting in the cyclical nature of the process. Figure 1 provides the illustration of the cyclical framework.

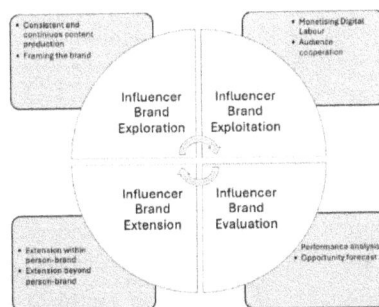

Figure 1: Four E Framework of Influencer Brand Building

4.1 Influencer Brand Exploration

Influencers begin the brand-building process by discovering the value of their online identities to audiences, digital platforms, and marketing professionals. This process consists of two components: consistent and continuous content production and framing the brand. These interconnected steps facilitate the initial shaping of the person brand, a process characterized by learning, experimentation, and amateur collaboration.

Content production is the cornerstone of the influencer brand building process that influencers devote to developing their audience, expanding their reach, building a loyal community. They start creating content without the explicit intention of becoming an influencer, to express their creativity, for enjoyment, or to connect with people who share similar interests. Deliberate focus on a specific niche marks the birth of the journey from being ordinary social media users to emerging as influential figures in their specific niche. Consistency not only builds trust among their audiences, but also synergizes with the algorithms of social media platforms. These platforms increase influencer visibility among users with similar interests by categorizing and promoting their content within the niche through 'explore' or 'for you' pages. Continuity in content production solidifies the influencer's niche position as platforms prioritize and reward continuous content, thus giving influencers a competitive advantage in their field. Participant 7's experiences illustrate the relationship between influencers' motivation and consistency and continuity in content production:

> *"It actually didn't start with the agenda that I have to become an influencer; it just happened. I began by taking pictures with my parents' phone, as I didn't have my own at that time. I'm a very creative person and wanted a medium that could allow my creativity to flow that's the first driver. As I started growing, there were followers, who motivated me to put more and more content out there because they liked it so much. So, the interaction and the kind of reach I got became another driver for me to work even better. And later on, I've collaborated with brands and monetized my content, which is now another driver too, but I never thought about it initially."*

Framing the brand represents the second component of the influencer brand exploration process. Once they reach nano-influencer status, influencers are faced with strategic decisions necessary for their brand-building efforts. In this step, critical decisions are made as they try to establish a balance between their online and offline identities by determining the primary platform for creating content, which aspects of their social identity to include in their content and to what extent. While the primary platform is often determined to be the platform influencers enjoy most as users, the erosion of anonymity in the Web 2.0 era forces influencers to carefully navigate their digital identities. This careful management of identities allows them to navigate audience expectations and protect themselves from personality conflicts. Additionally, this frame serves as the primary defence against online threats such as bullying or trolling. Participant 4 explains:

> *"I run the account, but really, it's all about my dog. I just wanted to connect with other dog lovers, but it turned into something bigger. Now, you'll see me in videos too but I only share stuff about my dog. None of my followers know my personal biz. Sharing my whole life could probably get me more followers – I've seen others do it, sharing all sorts of personal stuff, and it works. That's not for me. I don't want people talk about me, I like keeping things on the down-low, just me and my dog's adventures for anyone who's into it. It is safe."*

Influencer brand exploration process unfolds the strategic essence and inherent motivations behind influencers' initial forays into building their person-brand within social media ecosystem. This process is characterized by a shift from intrinsic motivations to acknowledging the potential for professional growth and financial sustainability. The transition from passion-driven content creation to strategic brand positioning represents a culmination of the influencer's journey through the exploration process. During this process, influencers truly grasp the significance of their digital labour, not just as a medium for personal expression but as a potential value within the social media economy. Realisation of their value leads them to second process, influencer brand exploitation.

4.2 Influencer Brand Exploitation

Influencer brand exploitation process marks a pivotal stage in the influencer brand building process, transitioning influencers from mere content creators to commercially minded digital entrepreneurs. During this phase, influencers navigate the delicate balance between maintaining their authentic, amateur spirit and adopting strategic business acumen; and their digital labour starts to yield tangible rewards in the form of financial compensation and enhanced social recognition. Influencer brand exploitation process consists of two intertwined components: first influencers engage in brand and audience collaborations, and leverage platform mechanisms to generate income; and second a deepened audience cooperation, transforming followers into active participants in the content creation process. This process demonstrates how influencers cultivate a sustainable digital presence that resonates with audiences and attracts the attention of marketing professionals.

Monetising digital labour signifies the culmination of the influencer brand exploration process. With widened reach and solidified engagement with followers, influencers begin to recognize the value of branded identities. This realization often comes as platforms, audiences, or marketing professionals initiate collaborations, signalling the influencers' valuable position within the digital ecosystem. At this stage, influencers start receiving not only direct financial rewards but also gifts or trial products as compensation for their digital efforts. Although they are initially uncertain about fairness of the compensation, this stage symbolizes a material acknowledgment of their brand's worth and prompts influencers to contemplate a career as content producers legitimately. This step thus serves as a pivotal point, empowering influencers to redefine their digital endeavours as viable careers, grounded in a community that values their contributions, platforms that acknowledges their digital assets and marketing professionals accept them as a partner brand. Participant 11 describes the moment when their digital labour first became monetized as:

> "When I hit about 5000 followers, a brand reached out to me. I'd been gifted things before, but this was the first time anyone said, 'what do you charge for a post?' And I was like 'I have no idea'. I thought only celebrities, got paid to post. I had no clue that was a genuine career that someone like me could have. So, I just did a quick Google and there was this sort of 10 pounds per 1,000 followers. I was like '50 pounds', and they said 'yes'. I was like, 'what!'"

A distinctive feature of influencer brands is the active and decisive role that the audience plays in brand creations. Audience cooperation represents the second component of the influencer branding building process and is a key element in influencer branding efforts, encompassing both audience-collaborated content production and audience advocacy. These two components highlight the dynamic interaction between influencers and their followers, where content is not only produced by the influencer but is also deeply influenced by audience interactions, feedback, and demands. Audience collaborative content production emphasises to a shift towards a more participatory form of content creation, where messages, comments, and other forms of audience engagement directly shape the content, allowing it to resonate more deeply with the audience's expectations and interests. At the same time, audience advocacy emerges as a critical protection mechanism that mobilizes community support to counter online negativity, from bullying and trolling to combating fake accounts. Participant 11 states:

> "I ask them regularly what they want to see. They always ask for tutorials. So, they're looking for instruction and guidance from me. If I get a lot of questions or DMs of the same kind of things, I create a content bank of questions that I create content around."

Participant 11's another anecdote exemplifies audience advocacy:

> "When someone is criticizing my skill or my knowledge that I really struggle. That's when my audience do tend to sort of jump in on my behalf because they know me. They've watched all my content. They know that I am capable, yeah, that's when the audience have my back and keep me motivated to create more."

In the influencer brand exploitation process, influencers navigate the intricate balance between authenticity and commercialization, embodying a transition from content creators to digital entrepreneurs. By harmoniously blending their unique identities with strategic business practices, influencers utilise diverse monetisation opportunities while increasing the likelihood of engagement by benefiting from their sizeable audience. Therefore, influencer brand exploitation marks a critical juncture in the influencer brand-building journey, delineating a path where strategic acumen and genuine engagement converge to realize the full potential of influencer brands. While this process makes performance measurements of influencer brands mandatory with their expanding audience and increasing collaborations, it also initiates the search for new opportunities for sustainable growing efforts.

4.3 Influencer Brand Evaluation

To evaluate their brand, influencers need some quantitative and qualitative investigations to improve the direction of their brands and capture new opportunities. This process consists of two components: performance analysis and opportunity forecast.

Performance analysis provides influencers with practical insights to shape their content strategies, audience engagement, and collaborations. As platforms reward accounts that produce regular content, influencers find that they experience increases in views and engagement once they get into a certain content-producing routine. Here, the first metric that stands out is the number of views. Participant 22 shares:

"Story views are key for me. Honestly, the number of followers doesn't really matter, not like story views do. You might have tons of followers who hit 'follow' five years ago and aren't active anymore. So, in reality, the number of followers doesn't contribute to either my earnings or my engagement."

Next, engagement is when your audience interact with the content you share and starts talking about it. This may mean going beyond just seeing the shared content, commenting on it, or sending messages to the influencer and asking questions about the content. When influencers discover the ones that provide the most interaction among these strategies, these strategies emerge as their way of engaging. A pet influencer, Participant 2 shares:

"People really follow us because we produce content that's both easy to understand and educational... But we truly hit our stride when I stepped back and let my dog to the 'talking'... Because when I'm the one talking, people still watch the stories, but when it seems like my dog is the one 'narrating', not only do the views spike, but the real engagement explodes..."

Beside performance analysis, it is also important to examine qualitative metrics for opportunity forecast. By taking advantage of the analytical tools provided by social media platforms, influencers quickly update their content in line with prevailing trends and innovative features, thus being ready to take advantage of opportunities that may arise in the future. Here, social media listening is vital for influencers. Participant 19 explains:

"Stepping out to see what the wider world beyond my followers likes always brings something new to the table... Whether it's joining forums, checking out different hashtags, or just seeing what's buzzing outside my usual space, I'm all about soaking up what's out there... Keeping tabs on what other influencers are doing, especially those in different niches or with varied audiences, is super eye-opening too..."

Trend tracking is stated as another qualitative metric, which includes the use of digital tools, identifying trends and making content stand out in search engines. With data from platforms, creators examine the tastes of their audiences in detail and shape their content accordingly. Participant 23 describes the effective use of these tools:

"There's Google Trends, my go-to for catching the vibe on the latest searches... BuzzSumo is another gem for figuring out what content's firing up on social and the web... Tools like Brandwatch and Mention are my eyes and ears in the digital sphere, perfect for eavesdropping on what folks are chatting about or how my brand's stacking up against the competition..."

It is also important that to be compatible with search intent of audiences. Adapting to search intent requires constant research and content renewal. Creators align their content with consumer trends and provide variety to strength the relevance of the content and their position in the market. Participant 10 explains:

"The magic word in our content creation process is what we call search intent. If someone's Googling protein powder, they're probably looking to buy, and that's why Google shows you products straight up. AI gets this, it figures out what people really want from their searches... We're constantly digging into this, aiming to match our content with what people are searching for in a way that satisfies them."

4.4 Influencer Brand Extension

At the culmination of the influencer branding process, influencer brand extension represents the final practices that signifies the strategic diversification of the influencer brand and marks the transition from established brand presence to expansive growth opportunities. Two basic paths emerge in this process: extension within and beyond the person brand. The first involves a push into new identities and/or platforms, allowing influencers to broaden their reach and engage with their audiences in multifaceted ways. This may include revealing new social identities that complement the influencer's brand core or expanding their online identity across social media platforms to capture broader audiences. The second path, extending beyond the person brand, delves into consumer goods and translates brand equity into physical products. This not only serves to solidify the influencer's brand in the physical world, but also opens up new revenue streams.

Extension within person- brand embodies influencers' strategic endeavours to enhance and utilise their brand through new social identities and the transition of their existing audiences to new platforms. By transcending the confines of their previously established brand boundaries, influencers not only deepen their rapport with audiences by presenting new facets of their social identity but also amplify their online visibility. This extension into new platforms is not merely about broadening reach; it's a calculated move to harness unique engagement opportunities and tap into distinct community cultures. Simultaneously, the venture into new identities allows influencers to introduce their audience to diverse aspects of their persona, adding new attributes to their brand and reaching new audience segments. Participant 10 describes:

"I decide to start my new YouTube channel because people interested in fitness generally want to change their lives. It's not about being more muscular but feeling better. I observed a significant demand from the youth, not just in fitness but also in other areas of life, leading me to start the project aimed at young people and entrepreneurs who are dissatisfied with their current situation and seek improvement. This initiative proved successful, creating its own unique perception. I produce content with guests on this channel, enriching my personal brand significantly. It fostered a deeper emotional connection with people who see fitness as a tool for personal transformation."

Extension beyond the person brand represents a decisive shift for influencers as they venture into the broader ecosystem of product offerings, transcending the frontier of social media. The significance of this phase lies not only in its potential to diversify income streams but also in its potential to set the influencer brand in the physical marketplace. Engaging in product extension, influencers create consumer goods that resonate with their branded identity and audience's lifestyle, offering a physical connection to their digital narratives. While some influencers opt for self-production, leveraging their brand's uniqueness, others resort to contract manufacturing practices, minimizing upfront investment and focusing on marketing practices. Participant 14's experience expanding their brand into consumer products reveals the process:

"I launched my own merchandise related to my videos. It is not going as expected but it's OK. I partnered with a company that didn't require an upfront investment, like a great opportunity to test the waters. While the financial outcome was not as I hoped, the venture taught me about experimentation and resilience in business. It's all about embracing the journey of trial and error, understanding that extending into consumer goods opens up new possibilities."

The culmination of these extension strategies illustrates a comprehensive brand evolution from digital content to a multifaceted brand presence across both digital and physical domains. Despite the potential risks and initial setbacks, extension into consumer goods opens up new avenues for success and audience connection. This blend of digital presence and tangible product offerings serves to reinforce the influencer brand, making it more robust against the volatile nature of social media platforms and digital trends. By extending within person brand, influencers adeptly navigate the digital landscape to unveil new facets of their identity and venture into new platforms. Influencers who extend to new platforms and/or identities recommence the *Four E Framework of Influencer Brand Building* cycle by entering the exploration process again, producing regular content in their new areas, positioning their brands, seizing collaboration opportunities, and measuring their performance.

5. Discussion and Conclusion

The Four E Framework, comprising *exploration, exploitation, evaluation,* and *extension* practices embodies a cyclical process foundational to the influencer brand building efforts. Unlike linear models, this framework acknowledges the fluidity and ongoing nature of brand building on social media platforms, where influencers continuously cycle through these practices, adapting and evolving in response to the dynamic digital ecosystem. Each component is interlinked, with insights and outcomes from one practice informing and shaping the strategies applied in others. This cyclical process ensures that influencers can remain agile, responsive to changes in audience preferences, platform algorithms, and market trends.

The Four E Framework introduces a novel perspective to the existing literature on individual branding, particularly within the context of social media and influencer marketing. Grounded in empirical findings of experiences shared by influencers and talent managers, this framework illuminates the intricacies of the influencer marketing ecosystem. In doing so, the Four E Framework significantly contributes to a deeper understanding of digital marketing, enriching the body of knowledge with robust insights into the complexities and strategies of social media branding.

The Four E Framework also serves as a versatile tool for a broad spectrum of stakeholders within social media ecosystem. For emerging influencers, it provides a structured approach to navigating the complexities of brand development, offering a roadmap that emphasizes adaptability and strategic growth. Marketing professionals can leverage the framework to better understand the influencer branding process, facilitating more effective collaboration and partnership strategies that align with each practice of brand building. By catering to the unique needs and perspectives of each group, the Four E Framework stands as a promising source in the evolving domain of social media and influencer marketing.

Acknowledgement

I would like to express my gratitude for the scholarship provided by the Republic of Türkiye Ministry of National Education and extend my deepest thanks to Professor Michael Beverland and Dr. Achilleas Boukis for their invaluable guidance and steadfast support throughout this project.

References

Aaker, D. (1996) *Building strong brands,* The free Press, London.

Abidin, C. (2015) "Communicative intimacies: influencers and perceived interconnectedness", *Journal of Gender, New Media, and Technology*, Vol 8, pp 1–16.

Abidin, C. (2018) *Internet Celebrity: Understanding Fame Online*, Emerald Publishing Limited, Bingley.

Braun and Clarke, V. (2022) *Thematic Analysis: A Practical Guide*, SAGE Publications, London.

Close, A.G., Moulard, J.G. and Monroe, K.B. (2011) "Establishing human brands: determinants of placement success for first faculty positions in marketing", *Journal of the Academy of Marketing Science*, Vol 39, No.6, pp 922–941.

Cottan-Nir, O. (2019) "Toward a Conceptual Model for Determining CEO Brand Equity", *Corporate reputation review,* Vol 22, No. 4, pp 121–133.

Dencheva, V. (2024) "Global Influencer Market Size 2024", [online], Statista, www.statista.com/statistics/1092819/global-influencer-market-size

Fournier, S. and Eckhardt, G. M. (2019) "Putting the Person Back in Person-Brands: Understanding and Managing the Two-Bodied Brand", *Journal of Marketing Research*, Vol 56, No. 4, pp 602–619.

Freberg et al (2011) "Who are the social media influencers? A study of public perceptions of personality", *Public relations review*, Vol 37, No. 1, pp 90–92.

French, A. and Smith, G. (2010) "Measuring political brand equity: a consumer-oriented approach", *European Journal of Marketing*, Vol 44, No. 3/4, pp. 460–477.

Gorbatov, S., Khapova, S.N. and Lysova, E.I. (2018) "Personal Branding: Interdisciplinary Systematic Review and Research Agenda," *Frontiers in Psychology*, Vol 9, pp 2238–2238.

Gorbatov et al (2021) "Personal brand equity: Scale development and validation," *Personnel Psychology*, Vol 74, No. 3, pp. 505–542.

Hou, M. (2018) "Social Media Celebrity and The Institutionalization of YouTube", *Convergence*, Vol 3, No. 25, pp 534-553.

Jin, S.V. and Muqaddam, A. (2019) "Product placement 2.0: Do Brands Need Influencers, or Do Influencers Need Brands?", *Journal of Brand Management*, Vol 26, No. 5, pp 522–537.

Jun, S. and Yi, J. (2020) "What makes followers loyal? The role of influencer interactivity in building influencer brand equity", Journal of Product & Brand Management, Vol 29, No. 6, pp 803–814.

Keller, K. L. (1993) "Conceptualizing, measuring, and managing customer-based brand equity", Journal of Marketing, Vol 57, No. 1, pp 1-22.

Keller, K.L. (2002) 'Branding and brand equity' in Weitz, B.A. and Wensley, R. (eds) (2002) *Handbook of Marketing*. London: SAGE. pp. 151-172.

Kietzmann et al (2011) "Social media? Get serious! Understanding the functional building blocks of social media", *Business Horizons*, Vol 54 No. 3, pp 241-251.

Levesque, N. and Pons, F. (2020) "The Human Brand: A systematic literature review and research agenda", *Journal of Customer Behaviour*, Vol 19, No. 2, pp.143-174.

Liu, J. (2023) "More than half of Gen Zs think they 'can easily make a career in influencing,' says branding expert", [online], CNBC, www.cnbc.com/2023/09/20/more-than-half-of-gen-zers-think-they-can-easily-make-a-career-in-influencing.html

Lorenz, T. (2023) *Extremely online: The untold story of fame, influence and power on the internet.* WH Allen, London.

Osorio, M.L., Centeno, E. and Cambra-Fierro, J. (2020) "A thematic exploration of human brands: literature review and agenda for future research" *Journal of Product & Brand Management*, Vol 29, No. 6, pp 695–714.

Park et al (2019) "Athletes' brand equity, spectator satisfaction, and behavioural intentions", *Asia Pacific Journal of Marketing and Logistics*, Vol 31, No. 2, pp 541–558.

Peters, T. (1997) "The brand called you", *Fast Company*, Vol 10, No. 10, pp 83-90.

Scholz, J. (2021) "How Consumers Consume Social Media Influence", *Journal of Advertising*, Vol 50, No. 5, pp 510–527.

Thomson, M. (2006) "Human Brands: Investigating Antecedents to Consumers' Strong Attachments to Celebrities", *Journal of Marketing*, Vol 70, No. 3, pp 104–119.

Vrontis et al (2021) "Social media influencer marketing: A systematic review, integrative framework and future research agenda", *International Journal of Consumer Studies*, Vol 45, No. 4, 617–644.

Fandom in Action: Online Mobilisation of Thai Youth in the 2020-2021 Anti-Government Protests

Ploykamol Suwantawit

Department of Communication and Media, University of Liverpool, UK

P.Suwantawit@liverpool.ac.uk

Abstract: The convergence of social media with political communication and the emergence of celebrity politics have significantly altered the landscape of political participation, particularly among the younger generation. Yet, comprehensive research on online political fandom remains limited despite its critical intersection with politics and digital media. This study addresses this gap, focusing on the in-depth case study of the 2020-2021 Thai anti-government protest. It scrutinises how tech-savvy Thai youth, propelled by political fandom surrounding Thanathorn Juangroongruangkit, a Future Forward Party opposition leader, harnessed social media and pre-existing online networks to organise these anti-government protests. Despite lacking a formal hierarchy, their organisational prowess, especially in information dissemination, highlights the intricate interplay of political fandom, social media, and youth mobilisation. By employing a trace interview method and conducting semi-structured interviews, the study explores how political fans transitioned from online engagement to active protest participation. The evidence contributes to a nuanced understanding of how fandom culture shapes their political judgment and behaviour. Participants in this study are political fans who publicly engage with politics on social media and participate in large-scale protests offline. They were recruited through a two-step process: first, the Twitter API identified users with high engagement in political fandom and anti-government hashtags. Then, a snowball sampling method extended the participant pool based on referrals from initial interviewees. A thematic analysis was conducted on the interview transcripts. The initial findings indicate that the influence of charismatic political figures, the empowerment of the fan community, and the belief that online political expression is ineffective draw participants toward offline participation. The resemblance between the political fandom of Thanathorn Juangroongruangkit and the more mainstream popular fandoms highlights the importance of considering the role of popular culture influences in shaping people's political behaviours, particularly in contemporary digital communication technologies. In conclusion, this study aims to uncover the intricate relationship between political fandoms, social media, and offline activism and to emphasise the pervasive influence of popular culture on political behaviours in the digital age.

Keywords: Political fandom, Social media, Youth mobilisation, Thai protest, Hashtag activism

1. Introduction

In the early months of 2020, a series of youth-led protests swept through various universities and campuses across Thailand. These demonstrations were primarily sparked by the dissolution of the Future Forward political party, which had gained significant support among the younger generation due to its charismatic leader, Thanathorn Juangroongruangkit, and its effective online campaigning (Chattharakul, 2019). This move results in many of its supporters feeling marginalised in an attempt to express their opposition to the perceived politically motivated decision to disband the beloved party (Phoborisut, 2020). However, the protests soon evolved to encompass broader democratic themes and demands beyond the party's dissolution, such as the dissolution of the parliament, revision of the constitution, cessation of all forms of harassment against peaceful protestors, and amendment of the *lèse-majesté* law (McCargo, 2021). The youth-led protests were notable for their immediate and decentralised nature, involving individuals who assemble rapidly in a public space, perform a brief act, and then disperse. Furthermore, the lack of a hierarchical leadership structure indicated a leaderless movement. The protests were organised spontaneously using Twitter, resulting in impromptu gatherings with specific hashtags (Sinpeng, 2021). Following the initial event, many protests have arisen nationwide, with Twitter serving as a fundamental mechanism for organising and mobilising activism. The youth-led protests mark a substantial shift in Thai politics and digital landscapes.

Given that the protest movement was mobilised around anti-government and anti-establishment themes, it is essential to understand the factors that first drew protestors to participate. Many protestors who joined the anti-government protests were political fans of Thanathorn, namely *Fah* (BCC Thai, 2020*)*. It is crucial to comprehend the intersection of politics, digital media, and fandom to better understand youth political participation in the digital age, as Dean (2017) recommended that researchers examine this relationship to better understand how people participate in politics today. Furthermore, many studies have suggested that emotions and affective factors also have an impact on individuals' public participation, in addition to rationality (Hinck and Hardin, 2023). To highlight this argument, this study draws on political fans around Thanathorn and the 2020-2021 Thai anti-government protests, examining how political fans transitioned from online engagement to active protest participation and uncovering the influence of popular culture on political behaviours.

2. Literature Review

2.1 Youth Protest Participation in the Digital Era

Social media has become the primary mode of political communication among young people despite the concern that youth have become apolitical. Major global political and social movements in recent years, such as Black Lives Matter, the Arab Spring, and the Umbrella Movement, are driven by youth and social media. The advanced features and possibilities of popular platforms, such as Facebook and Twitter, have made it easy for activists and youth to mobilise and coordinate political activities (Chan et al, 2016; Lane et al, 2017; Zhu et al, 2019). With a platform that is easily accessible and information that can be disseminated quickly, social media has become a crucial instrument for political participation among the younger generation (Skoric and Poor, 2013). Additionally. the advent of social media has transformed the nature of political participation. Instead of engaging with politics through traditional practices like voting or joining a political party membership, individuals can participate in politics via online petitions, networking, and digital activism (Loader et al, 2014). Essentially, social media has introduced a novel form of political participation characterised by personalised and expressive online engagement (Livingstone et al, 2005).

Numerous studies have shown that online activism can encourage individuals to participate in political activities offline (Boulianne, 2015). By utilising social media platforms, people are exposed to political news and information (Gil de Zúñiga et al, 2014), can share their opinions and information (Boyd, 2010), engage in political discussion (Yamamoto et al., 2013), consume user-generated content (Östman, 2012), and join online communities (Ito et al, 2009). This fosters the development of authentic relationships, provides access to information about social movements, and allows individuals to align themselves with a particular cause (Gilbert and Karahalios, 2009; Dalton et al, 2009). Ultimately, these factors motivate and empower individuals, leading them to become involved in traditional forms of political participation and protest in the physical world (Chen et al, 2017; Valenzuela, 2013). However, there is a debate going on about whether online activism has a significant impact on offline activism or not. Some argue that it only occurs in specific cases or to a limited extent, while others believe it leads to significant political participation. Aldrich et al. (2016) discovered that social media does indeed play a role in youth political participation, but traditional methods, such as direct contact from parties, are still more effective in mobilising people. In some cases, social media can increase offline activism in specific events, such as attending offline events promoted on online platforms (Veccari et al, 2015), and have a minimal effect on specific events, such as elections (Boulianne, 2015). These studies showed that different factors might influence offline activism, and the outcomes could vary by event.

Besides social media, youth's political participation is shaped by the experience gained through networks and communities (Loader et al, 2014). Wray-Lake (2019) suggested that young people develop political awareness by connecting with communities and seizing opportunities in their daily lives. With the prevalence of social media, it has become a platform for young people not only to socialise but also engage in political activities. This shift towards using social media in political activism underlies how social media creates a novel form of political participation. It further underscores the significance of communication as a means of uniting individuals, especially among young people, in social movements and protests, as opposed to conventional hierarchical structures to organise and preserve collective identity (Bennett and Segerberg, 2011).

2.2 Political Fandom

The context of fandom has been originally studied by fan scholars; nevertheless, the intersection of fandom and politics has garnered significant attention among researchers in the political science field due to the rise of digital media and celebrity politics (Sandvoss, 2013; Dean and Andrews, 2021). Social media has revolutionised the relationship between politicians and people in a more personalised, private, and intimate way (Wilson, 2011; Bennett and Iyergar, 2008; Stanyer, 2013). This has resulted in blurring the lines between traditional politics and politics as a form of entertainment, making politics more accessible and engaging for all (Sandvoss, 2013). Furthermore, politicians have used entertainment-driven strategies to improve their public image and popularity, turning politics into a show business where politicians are celebrities, and people are consumers (Street, 2004; Scammell, 2007). To this point, the integration of fan practices has expanded from the entertainment business to politics, suggesting that fan practices have become a part of daily life (Sandvoss, 2005; Hills, 2017). Political fandom results from this shift, underscoring the transformative way people participate and communicate in politics (Erikson, 2008; Sandvoss, 2012; Lee and Moon, 2021).

The use of social media in political communication has led to the formation of virtual communities, where individuals with similar beliefs congregate to form communities, including fandom. In fan studies, fandom is defined as "the regular, emotionally involved consumption of a given popular narrative or text" (Sandvoss, 2005, p. 8). Given that political fandom shares a resemblance with fandoms of popular culture, fandom can provide a better understanding of expressive political behaviours (van Zoonen, 2004; Dean, 2017).

This study thus refers to political fandom as "the emotional investment in and active support for political figures, parties, or ideologies" (Le Clue, 2023, p. 3). Individuals' political activism is driven by the emotions associated with a political entity rather than affiliation with a particular political ideology or party (Sandvoss, 2012). This definition emphasises the role of fandom in shaping political participation and good citizenship nowadays (Hinck and Hardin, 2023) and how the form of political engagement has changed (Hinck, 2019). However, political fandom can be understood and studied in two ways: (1) political *fandom* as fans of popular culture who leverage their fandom to participate in political activities or *fans-as-citizens*, and (2) *political fandom* as political activists who harness fandom or fan behaviours to mobilise citizens or *citizens-as-fans* (Reinhard et al., 2022). Accordingly, *Fah* is examined from the perspective of *citizens-as-fans*.

It is worth noting that using the term *fan* to describe political supporters and activists has become more common in recent years (Sandvoss et al, 2017). Fandom has become a common mode of activity in our daily lives, including political participation and communication (Hinck and Davisson, 2020). Through interviews with political fans, I examine the processes of political participation in fandom to understand how they decide to participate in anti-government protests and how fan communities amplify their political activism. To do this, the context of the *Fah* fandom is discussed.

2.3 Defining Fah

During the Chula-Thammasat Traditional Football Match held in February 2019, a male student recorded himself calling out to Thanathorn, "Fah Rak Pho!" (Fah loves daddy). The video, which lasted eight seconds, quickly went viral on Twitter under the hashtag #FahRakPho. It is important to note that the phrase "Fah Rak Pho!" originates from a famous Thai soap opera, Dok Som See Thong, in which *Fah*, the main female character, is romantically involved with an older businessman whom she affectionately calls "Pho" (Daddy), or a sugar daddy. This incident sparked conversations about Thanathorn's public image and whether his fans viewed him as a charming older man or a sugar daddy (McCargo and Chattharakul, 2020). The hashtag became more viral at the end of that day when Thanathorn tweeted, "I went to #TUCUBALL73 today. Many people said "#FahRakPho" to me. I do not understand it much. But thank you for all the cheer. Do not forget to vote #FutureForward". Not long after, he created a new hashtag, #PhoKorRakFah (Daddy also loves Fah), to respond to his supporters. These tweets gained a hundred of thousands of retweets (Figure 1). Thanathorn became "the darlings of Thai voters" (McCargo and Chattharakul, 2020, p. 49), and *Fah* became a term for his political fandom.

The emergence of *Fah* was a clear indication of Thanathorn's growing popularity and the desire for a heroic figure in Thai society, particularly amongst the younger generation (Chattharakul, 2019). *Fah* played a crucial role in assisting Thanathorn and the party in promoting their campaigns by sharing user-generated content under #FahRakPho and Future Forward hashtags. Consequently, the party officially formed *Futurista*, a group of party supporters and volunteers, after witnessing the enthusiasm of *Fah* and other followers (McCargo and Chattharakul, 2020). In turn, the party organised various events to keep its supporters, including *Fah*, engaged and connected with the party. For instance, the party used contemporary places for party gatherings, changed the seating plan from a traditional speech on-stage to a circular one, and introduced its brand merchandise for the supporters to purchase and display their allegiance (Jiajanpong et al, 2022). Their high engagement with the party and effective use of social media resulted in the remarkable success of Future Forward in the 2019 general election in late March. Despite being a relatively new entrant in the political arena, the party secured third place in the election (Sinpeng, 2019; Chattharakul, 2019; Ricks, 2019).

Figure 1: Thanathorn acknowledged #FahRakPho

In addition, McCargo and Chattharakul (2020) made interesting observations about *Fah*'s high engagement and passion closely resembling fandoms of popular culture, especially K-pop fandom. Numerous fan art and drawings were circulated among *Fah*, displaying unwavering support for Thanathorn. Furthermore, several works of fan fiction were published, often centring around the bromance relationship between Thanathorn and Piyabutr, a party secretary-general. South Korean popular culture has significantly impacted Thailand, with its influence observable in various aspects of Thai society. K-pop, in particular, has gained a massive following among Thai fans, who engage in fan practices and social media activities. This trend is most evident on Twitter, where K-pop fandom is among the most active Twitter users and always dominates conversations and hashtags (Smutradontri and Gadavanij, 2020). The community of fans and social movements thus have become closely linked on Thai Twitter. Unquestionably, *Fah*'s user-generated content and behaviours demonstrate a significant confluence with the K-pop fandom, indicating that *Fah* leveraged K-pop fan practices to engage with Thanathorn and the party.

3. Methodology

An interview method was utilised in the study to understand how political fans of Thanathorn participate in offline anti-government protests, drawing inspiration from interview-based approaches employed by many researchers. To gain insight into fandom behaviours that may not be consciously recognised by participants, Parikh (2012) suggested that in-depth interviews are necessary, making this approach effective for exploring the interplay between politics and fandom. Additionally, the study deployed a trace interview method (Dubois and Ford, 2015), in which participants were presented with the visualisation of their digital traces throughout the interview process.

Participants were recruited through a two-step process. Firstly, I utilised Twitter API to identify users with high engagement (i.e., the users who have the most retweets and likes counts) in political fandom (e.g., #FahRakPho and #PhoRakFah) and anti-government hashtags (e.g., #WhatsHappeningInThailand, #DeadlinetoEndDictatorship and #FreeYOUTH). Participants were sent an invitation message to take part in an online survey. The survey uses JISC Online Surveys to check that participants meet the eligibility criteria. At the end of the survey, participants interested in an in-depth interview were asked to express their interest. The survey was aimed at people aged between 21 and 30 years who were self-identified fans of Thanathorn Juangroongruangkit and participated in anti-government protests. The interviews were conducted over Zoom. Following the interviews, participants were asked to refer other political fans to the researcher, which resulted in the use of a snowball sampling method in the recruitment process. This approach ensured a diverse representation of deeply engaged political fans. In total, 18 semi-structured interviews were conducted in this study.

NVivo was employed to conduct a thematic analysis of the transcripts. The analytical process began with creating a list of potential themes based on the interviews. Then, a thorough examination of the transcripts was undertaken, during which NVivo was used to code the identified themes systematically. Following the initial coding, I refined the themes by merging similar and eliminating redundant ones. This iterative refinement aimed to enhance the identified themes' clarity and coherence. Lastly, a comprehensive review of the transcripts was conducted to adjust the codes based on the refined thematic framework (Braun and Clarke, 2006).

4. Preliminary Findings

4.1 'A Loss of Hope': The Role of Emotions in Political Decision

After having interviews with political fans, it becomes evident that their emotions and affection for Thanathorn influenced their decision to participate in protests. Participants frequently mentioned how *relatable* and *authentic* Thanathorn appeared to them, with some emphasising his *difference* and *freshness* compared to other politicians. This magnetic pull of charismatic political figures significantly shapes participants' inclination towards offline participation. The appeal of dynamic leaders who effectively capture the collective imagination can catalyse individuals to transcend their online presence and take concrete steps in the physical realm. This charisma fosters trust and mobilises a diverse group of politically active individuals who rally behind the leader's vision, believing that substantial change demands direct, tangible efforts. This is evident in the case of Thanathorn, where participants viewed him as their representative and someone who *spoke for them*. Consequently, when he was banned from politics, it was akin to a loss of hope, underscoring the profound personal connection participants established with him, leading his supporters to increased mobilisation.

4.2 Fan Communities: A Novel Space of Political Activism

The cohesive *fan* community is a robust driving force that propels individuals towards direct offline involvement. The shared bond among political fans generates unity, encouraging collective action that surpasses virtual boundaries. This communal dynamic becomes a crucible for exchanging ideas, strategies, and mobilisation endeavours, spurring participants towards more tangible forms of political activism. Additionally, the *fan* community provides *emotional* support, strengthening participants' dedication to their shared political objectives. Many express that participating in protests feels like socialising with friends, as everyone shares common goals. This camaraderie fosters an inclusive atmosphere, rendering political participation a socially fulfilling experience. Engaging in discussions and exchanging thoughts about the government with fellow protesters further cements their commitment to the cause.

4.3 Online Participation is not Enough

The prevailing belief that online political expression carries limited efficacy and is inherently futile plays a pivotal role in steering participants towards offline engagement. Participants discern that effecting meaningful political change requires more than virtual advocacy—it demands a physical, palpable presence in spaces of political significance. This realisation propels individuals to venture beyond pixels and screens, prompting them to participate actively in large-scale protests and other offline political engagements. While some participants even assume leadership roles within the rally, organising and guiding the demonstrations, others channel their dedication into becoming vital medical volunteers, providing essential aid and care to fellow protesters. These diverse roles within the offline movement exemplify how participants translate their online enthusiasm into tangible, impactful contributions on the ground.

Table 1: Themes of Interview Transcripts

Themes	Descriptions	Interview Examples
Formation of Political Fan Identity	Participants refer to their affection for Thanathorn or self-identify his political fan	"[The reason why I support Thanathorn] is about emotion. He comes across as sincere, honest, and unafraid…It is easy to connect with him because of his character and communication style." (Participant 3) "I think that Thanathorn, as a person, exhibits strong

Themes	Descriptions	Interview Examples
		leadership qualities... This is something I really admire about Thanathorn and his party." (Participant 17)
Evolution into Protest Participation	Participants describe their increase in political awareness and political participation due to Thanathorn's empowerment	"Being a fan of Thanathorn has significantly impacted on me... His words inspire me and urge me to fight more than ever." (Participant 1) "I typically did not follow political news, but I was well aware of the current political climate in the country... I have begun to realise its significance lately because of Thanathorn's influence." (Participant 11)
Fan Communities Empowerment	Participants describe that they joined the protests via political fandom communities	"...when *Fah* was formed, people started using hashtags to share political information about what was happening in Thailand, and I became more politically aware from that point onward." (Participant 2)
Emotional Support	Participants describe that they joined the protests due to collective power or empowerment among political fandom	"When I joined the protests, I immediately felt a connection with other protesters because of my age group. We used the same language, which created a sense of camaraderie and friendship." (Participant 8) "Going to protests is like going for fun" implies that attending a protest is not merely a recreational activity. Rather, it provides a sense of rejuvenation." (Participant 18)
Offline Participation	Participants refer to their role in the protests (e.g., a medical volunteer, a protest facilitator, a protest leader, and a security guard)	"I attended every protest and was always a volunteer because I wanted to use my potential [as a medical student] to help the protest movement." (Participant 12)
Offline Mobilisation Necessity	Participants describe that they prefer offline mobilisation	"Going out on streets for sure because those in power don't care what we have said on social media... To successfully pressure them, we must go out on the street." (Participant 13)

5. Conclusion

This study aims to uncover the intricate relationship between *political* fandom, social media and offline activism. The initial finding provides further evidence that emotions and affective factors significantly impact political participation, as shown by Thanathorn's strong influence on *Fah*'s decisions. Second, the empowerment of the *fan* community suggests that Twitter has become a pivotal platform for mobilising protests and disseminating information among protestors. On Twitter, *Fah*'s fandom offers a platform for inexperienced young people to participate in political discussions and develop awareness through fan practices, a more familiar form of engagement. Thirdly, although social media helps anti-government movements organise and mobilise successful protests across the country, participants believe traditional forms of activism are necessary. Many participants got involved in protests by being medical volunteers or protest facilitators, suggesting that online activism can spill over into real-world effects.

Furthermore, the juxtaposition of *Fah* with prevalent mainstream popular fandoms, especially K-pop fandom, underscores the substantial influence exerted by popular culture on political conduct, particularly within the contemporary digital milieu and is seemingly particularly pronounced within Thai political culture. By embracing K-pop fan practices, many *Fahs* use fan practices, such as fan art, to express their political activism. In conclusion, this study demonstrates the necessity of understanding the fandom culture that underlines political actions and participation and digital media on youth political participation.

It is important to note that this study has some limitations. For instance, gender, socioeconomic status, geographical location, and education level can influence an individual's political participation. During the recruitment process, it was observed that a majority of the participants were female, with only six male interviewees. Future research should consider these demographic factors and aim to recruit a more diverse group, including more men. However, the findings are believed to have practical implications for political actors, such as politicians, political parties, and social movements. For example, a charismatic leader and fan practice are likely to attract individuals to participate in political activism.

References

Aldrich, J. H. et al. (2016) "Getting out the vote in the social media era: Are digital tools changing the extent, nature and impact of party contacting in elections?", Party Politics, Vol 22, No. 2, pp. 165–178.

BBC Thai. (2020). "แฟลชม็อบนักเรียน-นักศึกษา ประกายไฟในกระทะ หรือ เพลิงลามทุ่ง", [online], https://www.bbc.com/thai/thailand-51640629.

Bennett, W.L. and Iyengar, S. (2008) "A new era of minimal effects? The changing foundations of political communication", *Journal of Communication*, Vol. 58, No. 4, pp. 707–731.

Bennett, W.L., & Segerberg, A. (2011). "Digital media and the personalization of collective action: Social technology and the organization of protests against the global economic crisis", *Information, Communication & Society*, Vol. 14, pp. 770-799.

Boulianne, S. (2015) "Social media use and participation: a meta-analysis of current research", *Information, Communication & Society*, Vol. 18, No. 5, pp. 524–538.

Bruan, V. and Clarke, V. (2006) "Using thematic analysis in psychology", Qualitative Research in Psychology, Vol 3, No. 4, pp. 77–101.

Chan, M., Chen, H.T. and Lee, F.L.F. (2017) "Examining the roles of mobile and social media in political participation: A cross-national analysis of three Asian societies using a communication mediation approach", *New Media and Society*, Vol. 19, No. 12, pp. 2003–2021.

Chattharakul, A. (2019) "Social Media: Hashtag #Futurista", *Contemporary Southeast Asia*, Vol. 41. No. 2, pp. 170–175.

Chen, H.T., Chan, M. and Lee, F.L.F. (2016) "Social media use and democratic engagement: a comparative study of Hong Kong, Taiwan, and China", *Chinese Journal of Communication*, Vol. 9. No. 4, pp. 348–366.

Dalton, R.J., Sickle, A.V., and Weldon, S. (2009). "The individual-institutional nexus of protest behaviour", *British Journal of Political Science*, Vol. 40, pp. 51—73.

Dean, J. (2017) "Politicising fandom", *British Journal of Politics and International Relations*, Vol. 19, No. 2, pp. 408–424.

Dean, J. and Andrews, P. (2021) "Celebritization from Below: Celebrity, Fandom, and Anti-Fandom in British Politics", *New Political Science*, Vol. 43, No. 3, pp. 320–338.

Dubois, E. and Ford, H. (2015) "Trace Interviews: An Actor-Centered Approach", *International Journal of Communication*, Vol. 9, pp. 2067–2091.

Erikson, E. (2008) ""Hillary is my Friend": MySpace and Political Fandom", *Rocky Mountain Communication Review*, Vol. 4, No. 2, pp. 3–16.

Gil de Zúñiga, H., Molyneux, L. and Zheng, P. (2014) "Social media, political expression, and political participation: Panel analysis of lagged and concurrent relationships", *Journal of Communication*, Vol. 64, No. 4, pp. 612–634.

Gilbert, E., and Karahalios, K. (2009) "Predicting tie strength with social media", Paper read at the 27th annual SIGCHI conference on Human Factors in Computing Systems, New York, United States.

Hills, M. (2017) "Always-on fandom, waiting and bingeing: Psychoanalysis as an engagement with fans' "infraordinary" experiences". *The Routledge Companion to Media Fandom*. Routledge, pp. 18–26.

Hinck, A. (2019) *Politics for the Love of Fandom: Fan-Based Citizenship in a Digital World,* Baton Rouge, Louisiana State University Press.

Hinck, A. and Davisson, A. (2020) "Fandom and politics", *Transformative Works and Cultures*, p. 32.

Hinck, A. and Hardin, C. (2023) "Civic culture in the Supernatural fandom: Misha Collins, Destiel, and the 2020 US presidential election", *Convergence*, Vol. 29, No. 6, pp. 1486–1501.

Ito M. *et al.* (2009) *Hanging Out, Messing Around, and Geeking Out: Kids Living and Learning with New Media*, Cambridge, MA, The MIT Press.

Jiajanpong, A., Sheoychitra, P. and Kayunrawat, W. (2022) "The Political Parties' Communication during the 2019 General Election in Thailand", *European Journal of Military Studies*, Vol. 12, No. 4, pp.1773-1782.

Kahne, J., Lee, N.J. and Feezell, J.T. (2013) "The Civic and Political Significance of Online Participatory Cultures among Youth Transitioning to Adulthood", *Journal of Information Technology and Politics*, Vol. 10, No. 1, pp. 1–20.

Lane, D.S. *et al.* (2017) "From online disagreement to offline action: How diverse motivations for using social media can increase political information sharing and catalyze offline political participation", *Social Media and Society*, Vol. 3, No. 3, 1–14.

Le Clue, N. (2023) "The new normal: Online political fandom and the co-opting of morals", *Convergence*, pp. 1–11.

Lee, S. and Moon, W.K. (2021) "New public segmentation for political public relations using political fandom: Understanding relationships between individual politicians and fans", *Public Relations Review*, Vol. 47, No. 4, pp. 1–12.

Livingstone, S., Bober, M. and Helsper, E.J. (2005) "Active participation or just more information?: Young people's take-up of opportunities to act and interact on the Internet", *Information, Communication & Society*, Vol. 8, No. 3, pp. 287–314.

Loader, B.D., Vromen, A. and Xenos, M.A. (2014) *The Networked Young Citizen: Social Media, Political Participation and Civic Engagement*, Routledge.

McCargo, D. (2021) "Disruptors' dilemma? Thailand's 2020 Gen Z protests", *Critical Asian Studies*, Vol. 53, No. 2, pp. 175–191.

McCargo, D. and Chattharakul, A. (2020) *Future Forward: The Rise and Fall of a Thai Political Party*, Copenhagen, Nordic Institute of Asian Studies.

Östman, J. (2012) "Information, expression, participation: How involvement in user-generated content relates to democratic engagement among young people", *New Media & Society*, Vol. 14, No. 6, pp. 1004–1021.

Parikh, K. H. (2012) "Political fandom in the age of social media: Case study of Barack Obama's 2008 presidential campaign" (Unpublished MSc thesis), London School of Economics and Political Science, London.

Phoborisut, P. (2020) "The 2020 Student Uprising in Thailand: A Dynamic Network of Dissent", *ISEAS Yusof Ishak's Perspective*, Vol. 129, pp. 1–10.

Reinhard, C.D., Stanley, D. and Howell, L. (2022) "Fans of Q: The Stakes of QAnon's Functioning as Political Fandom", *American Behavioral Scientist*, Vol. 66, No. 8, pp. 1152–1172.

Ricks, J.I. (2019) "Thailand's 2019 vote: The general's election", *Pacific Affairs*, Vol. 92, No. 3, pp. 443–457.

Sandvoss, C. (2005) *Fans: The Mirror of Consumption*. Malden, MA, Polity Press.

Sandvoss, C. (2012) "Enthusiasm, trust and its erosion in mediated politics: On fans of Obama and the Liberal Democrats", *European Journal of Communication*, Vol. 27, No. 1, pp. 68–81.

Sandvoss, C. (2013) "Toward an understanding of political enthusiasm as media fandom: Blogging, fan productivity and affect in American politics", *Participations Journal of Audience & Reception Studies*, Vol. 10, No. 1, pp. 252–296.

Sandvoss, C., Gray, J. and Harrington, C.L. (2017) "Introduction: Why Still Study Fans?", *Fandom: Identities and Communities in a Mediated World*, New York, New York University Press.

Scammell, M. (2007) "Political brands and consumer citizens: The rebranding of Tony Blair", *Annals of the American Academy of Political and Social Science*, Vol. 611, No. 1, pp. 176–192.

Sinpeng, A. (2021) "Hashtag activism: social media and the #FreeYouth protests in Thailand", *Critical Asian Studies*, Vol. 53, No. 2), pp. 192–205.

Skoric, M.M. and Poor, N. (2013) "Youth Engagement in Singapore: The Interplay of Social and Traditional Media", *Journal of Broadcasting and Electronic Media*, Vol. 57, No. 2, pp. 187–204.

Smutradontri, P. and Gadavanij, S. (2020) "Fandom and identity construction: an analysis of Thai fans' engagement with Twitter", *Humanities and Social Sciences Communications*, Vol. 7, No. 1, pp. 1–13.

Stanyer, J. (2013). *Intimate Politics: Publicity, Privacy and the Personal Lives of Politicians in Media Saturated Democracies*, Cambridge, Polity.

Street, J. (2004) "Celebrity Politicians: Popular Culture and Political Representation", *The British Journal of Politics and International Relations*, Vol. 6, No. 4, pp. 435–452.

Valenzuela, S. (2013) "Unpacking the Use of Social Media for Protest Behavior: The Roles of Information, Opinion Expression, and Activism", *American Behavioral Scientist*, Vol. 57. No. 7, pp. 920–942.

Van Zoonen, L. (2004) "Imagining the Fan Democracy", *European Journal of Communication*, pp. 39–52.

Vaccari, C. et al. (2015) "Political Expression and Action on Social Media: Exploring the Relationship Between Lower- and Higher-Threshold Political Activities Among Twitter Users in Italy", *Journal of Computer-Mediated Communication*, Vol 20, No 2, pp. 221–239.

Wilson, J. (2011) "Playing with politics: Political fans and Twitter faking in post-broadcast democracy", *Convergence*, Vol. 17, No. 4, pp. 445–461.

Wray-Lake, L. (2019) "How Do Young People Become Politically Engaged?", *Child Development Perspectives*, Vol. 13, No. 2, pp. 127–132.

Zhu, J. *et al.* (2018) "Previous civic experience and Asian adolescents' expected participation in legal protest: mediating role of self-efficacy and interest", *Asia Pacific Journal of Education*, Vol. 38, No. 3, pp. 414–431.

Masters Research Papers

Research on the Influence of Video Content Features on User Behaviour

Zhiqi Pu

School of Economics and Management, China University of Petroleum, Qingdao, China

zhiqipu@gmail.com

Abstract: Research on user engagement behaviours within User-Generated Content (*UGC*) video platforms is notably scarce, despite previous studies predominantly focusing on user-level information. This study contends that enriched video information holds significant value. Its objective is to provide a profound understanding of the influence mechanisms of video content features on user engagement behaviours within *UGC* video platforms. Combining exploratory and quantitative methodologies, the research introduces a highly detailed framework for video content features, covering both cognitive and emotional dimensions. The framework encompasses content richness at the video level and emotional features at the user level. Addressing user behaviours, the study encompasses liking, sharing, saving, and tipping, representing users' varied contributions to the platform. The triggers for user behaviours often originate from diverse motivational intentions. The research focuses on a dual perspective, blending user and video viewpoints when examining video content features. Utilizing linear regression equations grounded in social identity theory and emotional support theory, the study explains the role of video content features in triggering user engagement behaviours. Age and gender serve as moderator variables, exploring behavioural disparities between male and female users and across different age groups. Findings indicate that factors triggering user likes and shares primarily stem from the level of interaction in the comment section, while tipping contributions and video saves are influenced by emotional support during viewing. The study also reveals that sadness enhances user participation intentions, while positive emotions in video characters or commenters diminish user engagement intentions. Lastly, the research adopts web crawling through legally accessible interfaces as the primary data collection method, encompassing 435 videos from 25 food category video authors.

Keywords: User engagement behaviours, Linear regression, Video content features, Social identification theory, Emotional support theory

1. Introduction

1.1 Background

Since the era of the pandemic, with the gradual penetration of the video trend into people's lives, the pan-video market is considered to have enormous development potential. In 2023, the short video platform TikTok surpassed Instagram and Facebook in annual downloads, ranking first globally, with over 1 billion users. However, platforms thriving on the pan-video trend face two major challenges. Firstly, the growth rate of traffic slows down due to the competition for existing users. After the pandemic era, the number of users in the pan-video market tends to saturate, and new user acquisition is slow, especially for platforms focusing on content creation by professional users (*PUGC*). *PUGC* content requires the use of relevant video production tools for arranging and editing videos, demanding higher standards compared to the user-generated content (*UGC*) model of short videos, making it challenging to achieve conversion between users and creators. Attracting more users and transforming them into video creators to enrich the content ecosystem becomes a key strategic focus for platform development. Secondly, enhancing user engagement on social media and cultivating highly sticky users is crucial. In 2023, different types of video platforms have displayed a clear development pattern. The inter-competition among video platforms no longer revolves around capturing user usage duration but shifts towards improving user engagement on social media and cultivating users with high stickiness and a sense of identity. Short video platforms grasp users' fragmented time, enhancing engagement through brand live streaming, video accounts, etc., relying on high user penetration rates. Meanwhile, long video platforms have developed a stable consumer base of highly sticky users, concentrated mainly in popular categories. Addressing the issues of user growth and retention, existing research partly explores the impact of video content on consumers' repurchase intentions through consumer behaviour, identifying key factors that convert casual consumers into highly sticky users. Another portion of research focuses on exploring video reputation and users' psychological experiences to derive various factors that enhance social media engagement. However, fewer studies delve into the exploration of the impact of the physical and emotional dimensions of video content itself on social media engagement, Yan Lin et al (2021) consider the potential for broadcaster sentiment, audience sentiment and audience activity to influence each other, but the goal of the study was limited to tips. Moreover, existing research on user social media engagement analysis often adopts a macro perspective using survey questionnaires, lacking granularity in studying individual videos.

1.2   Definition of Research Topics

With the thriving development of social media platforms, Yoshinobu T et al (1993) and Alan H et al (2005) have pointed out that in the Z era, video platforms integrate features of traditional social media and entertainment platforms, demonstrating the ambiguity and multidimensionality of user engagement. Therefore, social media engagement is widely used to explain various aspects of user psychological and behavioural motivations. Jenny Van D et al (2010) demonstrated that user social media engagement can have profound impacts on platforms, such as loyalty, satisfaction, and commitment. Hence, scholars and industry have paid extensive attention to monitoring, measuring, and explaining user social media engagement. Scholars have proposed various concepts and indicators. The definition of social media engagement varies significantly under different concepts due to the diverse nature of the engaging entities. Some scholars, such as Laurence D et al (2016), believe it can be categorized into customer engagement, brand engagement, and online engagement based on the distinction of engaging entities. Another group of scholars categorizes it into behavioural, emotional, and cognitive dimensions based on engagement dimensions. Therefore, there is still no unified definition of social media engagement, but the academic community generally agrees that the engaging entities are individuals or consumers.

1.3   Research Question and Structure

Building upon the preceding discussion, subsequent research questions have been posed: Do different video content features encourage or inhibit users' willingness to engage in actions such as liking, tipping, saving, and sharing? Furthermore, is the motivation behind these actions dominated by social identity theory or emotional support theory? Therefore, this study will be divided into three sub-questions.

Firstly, what is the impact of cognitive features in videos on user behaviours, and what theoretical underpinning governs the influence of rich details about characters and scenes on motivational factors?

Next, what differences exist in the impact of interactive features in the comment section and bullet screen area on user behaviours, and what motivational theories drive user engagement in interactions?

Lastly, what is the role of emotional features in influencing user behaviours, and are there differences in the impact of character emotions in videos compared to emotional expressions in the user comment section?

In the next chapter, a literature review will evaluate the theories employed in this study and previous research on video content features. Following this, the methods and results employed in this study will be presented. Finally, a summary will conclude the research.

2.   State of Research

2.1   User Behaviour Motivation

Theories commonly used to explain user behavioural motivations on social media include Social identity theory and Emotional support theory. Social identity theory, a psychological perspective on motivation and behaviour, refers to an individual perceiving themselves as a member of a group, involving cognitive, emotional, and evaluative components (Dominic A et al, 2006). Cognitive identity reflects the overlap between an individual's self-image and perceived images of others in the group, emotional identity expresses the individual's sense of belonging to the group, and evaluative identity is the individual's perception of their importance within the group. Shih-Chih C et al (2019) highlighted that users in social communities categorize others based on their classification in the online community, either belonging to the same group or another. Limited research exists on the behavioural motivations of social media users (such as liking, tipping and sharing) under the Social identity theory, with most focusing on knowledge sharing and seeking in online communities. Scholars have analyzed the characteristics of the Douyin short video community and its impact on users' intentions for continuous contribution, finding a significant positive correlation between community identity and users' intentions for continuous contribution in *UGC* short video communities. The second theory, Emotional support theory, is a common type of social support closely associated with emotional needs (Ariel S et al, 2020). Users lacking emotional support in the real world often seek it on social media, increasing their willingness to participate (Julia B et al, 2019). Xiaoyu X et al (2019) pointed out that emotional support simultaneously affects users' hedonism, enhances their social presence, motivates them to watch live broadcasts, become loyal fans of the broadcaster, and subsequently engage in consumption behaviour. Additionally, some scholars have found that emotional support enhances viewers' social presence to a certain extent (Donghee Yvette W et al, 2018). However, frequent information interaction weakens this effect of emotional support (Jiada C et al, 2022). Jooyoung L et al (2023) suggested that compared to seeking informational support, supporters of emotional support reveal more self-information, corresponding to fewer comments. Sanghyun K et al (2013) proposed that people can influence and convey emotions to each other through language, behaviour, facial expressions, etc. Thus, in a live-streaming context, the emotions of the host may have a contagious effect, affecting users' cognition and behaviours.

2.2 Video Content Characteristics

Video content characteristics can be classified into cognitive and emotional dimensions. Cognitive features, related to the lower-level physical aspects of video content, are extracted through video summarization, where most state-of-the-art methods focus on analyzing static frames to generate descriptive summaries. Analysis of frames at different scales can extract various essential features, such as different time sliders and sketch representations (HongAn W et al, 2013). Color, a simple yet effective cognitive feature, is commonly used in research on the impact mechanisms of video content on user social media engagement. Besides the widely used RGB components, other cognitive features include hue, saturation, and brightness (Yilin W et al, 2021). Scholars have also studied *UGC* type videos, with Yilin W and colleagues pointing out that the quality of *UGC* videos is determined by CP, CT, and DT (video compression, video content, video distortion). They established a model called TippingVQ to evaluate CT scores by building multippingle granularity content tags and video features. Cognitive features used in TippingVQ include video content (evaluated using tags at various granularity levels), video distortion, compression levels during video uploading, and the average frame quality (William H et al, 2021). In a study on the impact of YouTube videos on user engagement, the contrast of video thumbnails and cognitive features of video categories were found to be the most significant factors influencing video popularity (Shan L et al, 2023). Regarding emotional features, Alan H et al (2005) explored content analysis on the emotional aspects of videos. They used Russell and Mehrabian's definition of emotion, which involves the expected intensity or type of emotion users anticipate while watching a video (James A R et al, 1977). Russell and Mehrabian identified three fundamental dimensions of video emotion: Valence, Arousal, and Control. Valence represents the continuum of emotional states from positive emotions like pleasure and excitement to negative emotions like anger and frustration. Arousal indicates the intensity of Valence, while Control is used to differentiate highly similar valences, such as excitement and happiness. Finally, Shan Lu et al (2023) proposed a variable screening method for component response regression, using deep learning to extract features from multi-modal data of short videos.

3. Methodology

This study conducted a regression analysis of user engagement behaviours on social media platforms based on the user motivation theories outlined above (Figure 1). The data were collected from *Bilibili*, a Chinese social media platform, focusing on videos from creators with over one hundred thousand followers to ensure rich information on user engagement behaviour. Videos were selected from non-holiday periods to exclude the influence of external factors such as seasons. Each individual video was taken as the unit of analysis, and a five-layer high-granularity video content feature framework was constructed for the original videos. This framework included features from both user and video perspectives, incorporating interactive and emotional features. The study integrated and innovatively expanded existing research methods. To measure text sentiment accurately, a personally improved dictionary for network language was employed. Additionally, deep learning techniques were utilized to extract character details and emotional features. From the perspectives of age and gender, moderator variables were introduced, and regression equations were developed for the four user behaviours: liking, tipping, sharing, and saving. The explanatory variables in the regression equation were derived from cognitive and emotional features, with a separation of interactive features (Figure 2).

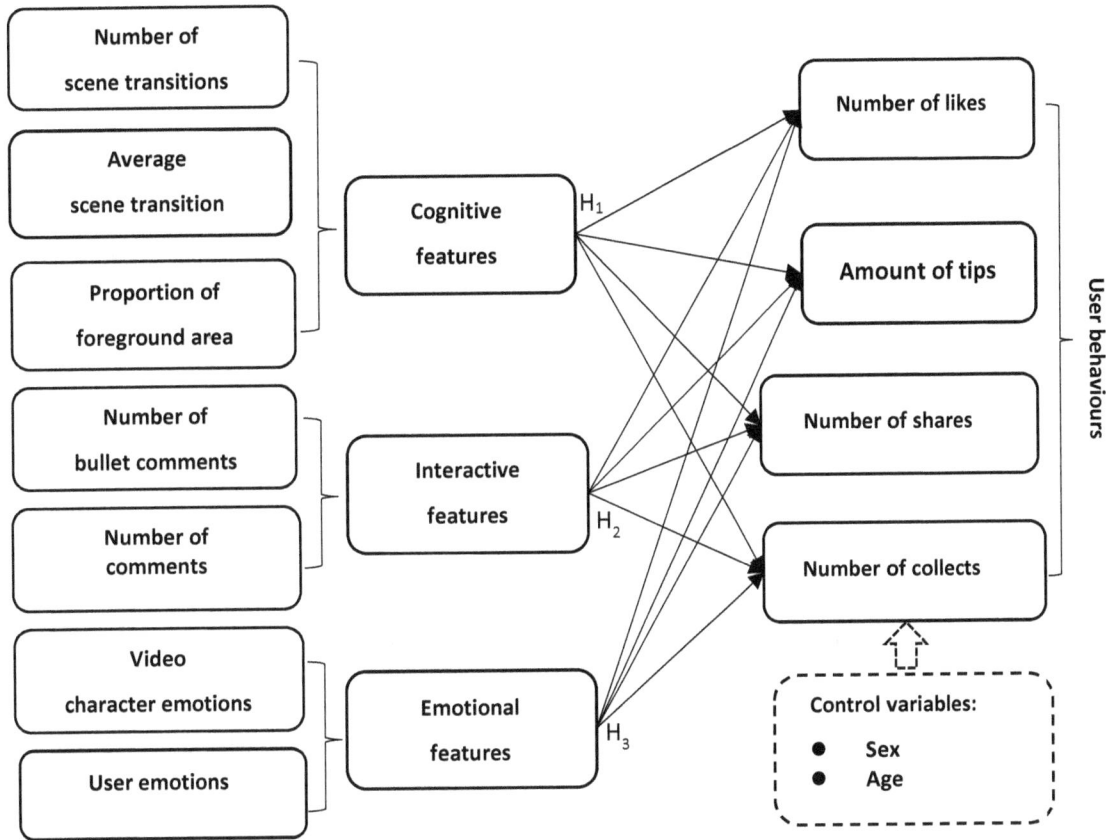

Figure 1: Framework of user behaviours regression equation

Specifically, the interaction features were represented by the number of comments in the comment section and the quantity of bullet comments in the bullet comments section. The comment count not only tallied the headline comments under each subtopic but also calculated collapsed comments across all topics. To extract emotional features from user comments, individual video comments and bullet comments *JSON* files were extracted and integrated into a *TXT* file for analysis. In preprocessing, short texts with fewer than 10 characters in a single line were removed. Subsequently, excessive spaces, consecutive punctuation, and special symbols like emoticons were eliminated. Segmentation was achieved using the CWN Chinese thesaurus and a synonym table based on popular Chinese internet terms. The processed text was then evaluated for sentiment using a pre-labeled sentiment lexicon. For the emotional expressions of characters in the video, *PySceneDetect* was employed to isolate keyframes. These keyframes were transformed into high-dimensional vectors, which were then input into the *FER* model to extract facial expressions of individuals in the video. Simultaneously, Fairface was used to determine the age and gender of individuals in the keyframes.

Video content feature framework		
User behaviour variables	Number of likes, saves, tips, shares	
Interactive feature variable	Number of bullet comments, comments	
Cognitive variables	video richness	Number of scene transitions
	video detail	Average scene transition time
	video attraction	Foreground area proportion, Character proportion duration
	video visual experience	Hue, Brightness, Contrast
Emotional variables	video character emotions	Neutral, Happy, Sad, Angry
	user emotions / general	Positive emotions of the user, Negative emotions of the user
	single	Single positive emotion, Single negative emotion
Moderator	Gender, age	

Figure 2: Video content feature framework in Bilibili context

4. Results

4.1 User Behaviours Dimension Classification

As explained in the preceding chapters, this study employed regression equations to identify significant video content feature variables influencing four user behaviours, summarizing motivational intentions under different user behaviours. Firstly, the research results revealed that the four user behaviours could be categorized into two dimensions based on Social identity theory and Emotional support theory. Liking and sharing were primarily driven by social identification, considering users watching videos as a group with similar interests across different times and spaces. This enhanced user integration into video interactions and fostered a sense of social identity. Accordingly, users are inclined to like and share videos that aligned with their interests or represented their community viewpoints, reinforcing their self-identity based on social identity theory. Simultaneously, the behaviours of tipping and saving were mainly driven by emotionally supporting. Tipping and saving more reflected users' emotional support for video content. The emotional support theory posits that users seek content that satisfies their emotional needs in videos. Once these needs are met, emotional support triggers specific user behaviours. Tipping, as a "substantial" contribution, is primarily influenced by this theory. Users invest their limited virtual tipping, signifying their acknowledgment of the emotional value provided by the video content. The results for saving indicate that the motivation to save is primarily derived from emotional support. Triggering saving behaviour requires a higher level of emotional support from the video compared to tipping.

4.2 Hypothetical Test

In the subsequent paragraphs, this study summarizes key findings regarding the research questions posed earlier (Figure 3). In terms of cognitive features, scene transition frequency has the most pronounced promoting effect on user tipping behaviour. This suggests that a richer variety of scenes in videos gains user approval, thus encouraging tipping rewards. Similarly, cognitive feature variables that have a promoting effect on giving tips include foreground area ratio and average scene transition time. According to the attention focus hypothesis in visual attractiveness theory, a larger area ratio of the foreground area and sufficient dwell time in individual scenes help users concentrate their attention on specific visual elements, ignoring other irrelevant elements, referred to as "visual attractors." Correspondingly, variables that have an inhibitory effect on user tipping include brightness, saturation, video duration, and the proportion of time characters are off-screen. An increase in brightness or saturation leads to color distortion, gradually reducing the user's viewing experience and inhibiting tipping behaviour. The increase in video duration slightly weakens user attention, affecting tipping behaviour. Users also tend to focus their attention on food or the cooking process rather than the characters in the video, validating the promoting effect of the foreground area ratio observed in the previous variables. Simultaneously, variables that have a promoting effect on user liking include brightness and scene transition frequency. However, the impact of scene transitions on promoting liking is relatively limited. The study suggests that rapid changes in scene frequency may shift user attention to the comments or bullet chat area, indirectly affecting liking behaviour. This characteristic is also reflected in the brightness variable; excessive brightness can similarly shift user attention to the comments and bullet comment areas, indirectly promoting liking. Variables that have an inhibitory effect on user liking include video duration, foreground area ratio, proportion of time characters are off-screen, and saturation in video physical features. The study argues that excessively long videos and characters being off-screen for too long reduce user willingness to watch and focus, thus inhibiting liking behaviour. When the foreground area ratio is larger, users focus more on the video content itself than on the comments, weakening their willingness to like. At a higher level, concerning saving and sharing, video duration significantly inhibits saving behaviour. Based on this, the study suggests that not only the content presented in the video but also the way it is presented influences user behaviours. Excessively long videos seem to divert user attention since social identity-based liking behaviour is also inhibited, indicating that longer video duration decreases the overall attractiveness of the video to users. This leads to users ending their viewing or participation earlier, resulting in an overall decrease in willingness. This decrease is reflected in saving, where the emotional support effect generated by the video content is diminished. For sharing, only the hue in physical features has a weak inhibitory effect on sharing, while other cognitive feature variables have no significant impact on it.

Subsequently, the research results regarding interactive features indicate that the interaction level in the comments section and bullet comment area significantly and positively promotes user liking and tipping at a lower level. On one hand, this suggests that intense interaction in the comments and bullet comment areas among users in a shared viewing context directly enhances individual identification with the group, triggering liking behaviour. On the other hand, users derive emotional support from posting and replying to comments, especially when their comments receive numerous likes and replies, leading to emotional satisfaction and subsequently triggering tipping behaviour. When the dependent variable is the number of saves, the results show that the quantity of bullet chat messages in the video remains a key factor in users generating emotional support. The number of bullet comment messages largely determines the intensity of emotional support, thereby promoting user saving or tipping. Simultaneously, the regression results indicate that the number of comments, as a key factor expressing a sense of identification among users, has a certain impact on tipping but no influence on saving. This suggests that the motivation for saving is more dominated by emotional aspects compared to the motivation for tipping, and it is less connected to the sense of identification formed among user groups. When the dependent variable is the number of shares, the number of comments is a key factor influencing user sharing behaviour, while the quantity of bullet comments does not significantly affect sharing behaviour. This indicates that the quantity of bullet comments and the number of comments have different degrees of social identity effects simultaneously.

Continuing with the research results on emotional features, at the level of tipping and liking, users demonstrate emotional support for sad emotions of video characters, thereby promoting tipping behaviour. However, an increase in angry emotions in video characters reduces users' emotional support and inhibits tipping. At the same time, as the number of positive comments increases, users' willingness to liking and tipping decreases. According to the Social identity theory, this study suggests that when users see that most comments are positive, they may feel a certain social identity pressure. This pressure comes from a desire to fit into the group or avoid conflicting with mainstream opinions. In such situations, users may reduce their willingness to like and giving tips to avoid too much inconsistency with other users and maintain social identity.

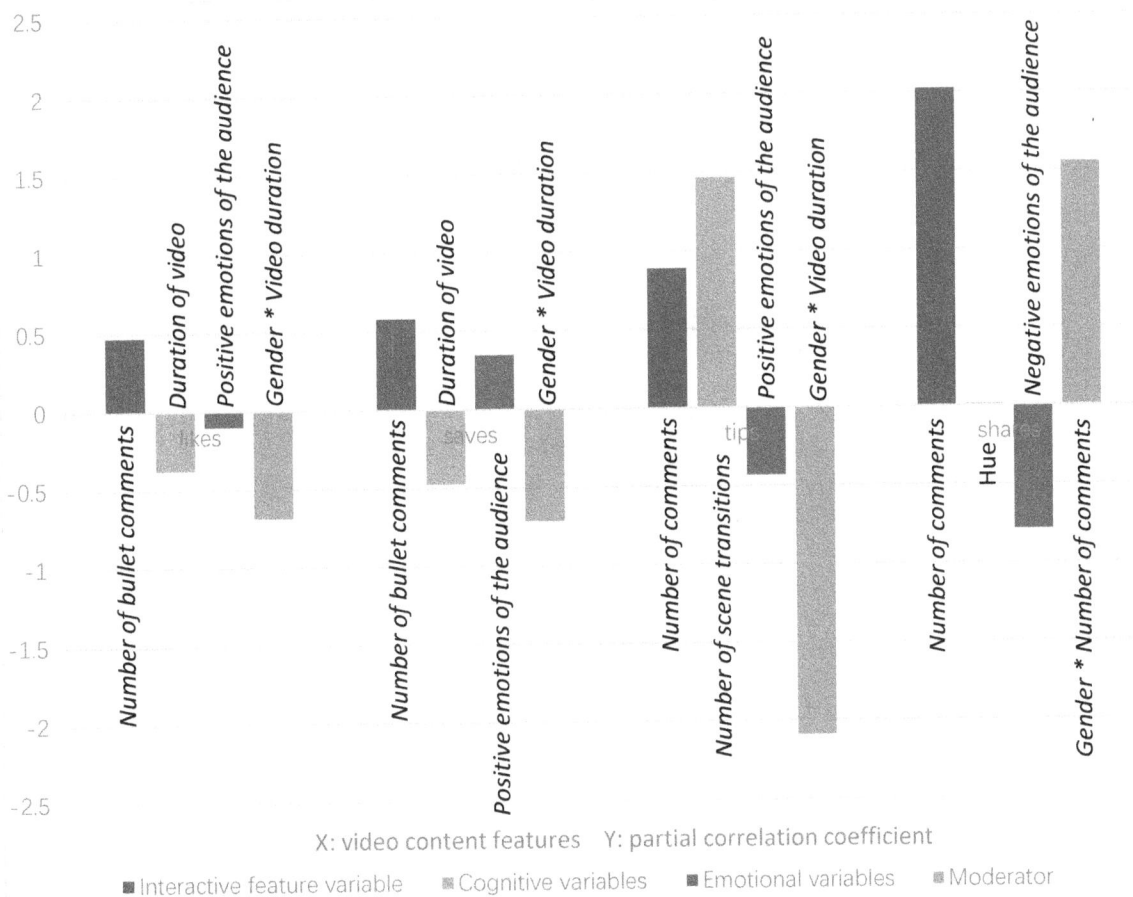

Figure 3: Regression results of video content features on user behaviours

At the level of saving and sharing, this study found opposite effects of angry emotion ratio and user positive emotion ratio in the emotional variables on user tipping and saving. More appearances of angry emotions in video characters and positive emotions in user comments inhibit users tipping. Conversely, these two emotions promote users' willingness to save. Furthermore, users' saving behaviour is influenced by a single negative emotion in the comments, meaning that when there are strongly expressed emotional comments in the comments section, users are more inclined to save the video.

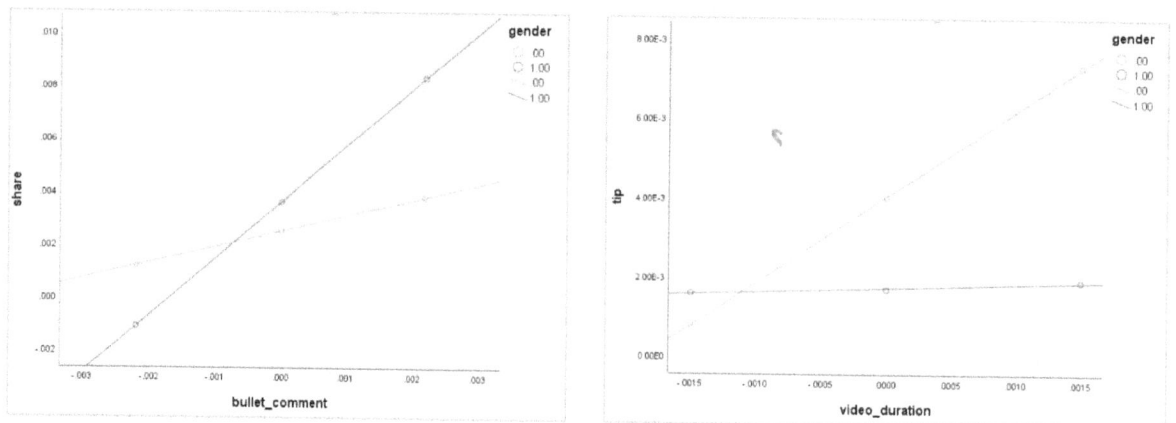

Figure 4: Effect of moderating variable (gender) on sharing and tipping

In the context of moderator variables, the study's findings indicate a significant moderating effect of gender in the influence of video duration on user behaviours. When the user transitions from male to female, the willingness to refrain from actions such as tipping, saving, and liking weakens with the increasing video duration, with tipping showing the most significant decline. Simultaneously, gender's moderating effect on user sharing behaviour is notably pronounced. Female users, in comparison to their male counterparts, tend to favor saving videos as the level of interaction in the video's comment section increases. Furthermore, the study observes that women are more inclined to discontinue liking and tipping as the number of scene transitions in the video rises, with the magnitude of this difference gradually diminishing with an increase in the frequency of scene transitions (Figure 4). Regarding age, older users exhibit a decreasing willingness to like and saving videos as the number of comments and bullet comments increases. This impact tends to diminish with a higher accumulation of comments and bullet comments.

5. Conclusion

In the context of *UGC* videos, this study identifies distinct influencing factors and motivational intentions for user engagement behaviours such as liking, tipping, saving, and sharing. Notably, a rich variety of scene transitions emerges as a primary factor driving users to contribute tips, indicating a preference for emotionally supportive and content-acknowledging scenarios. Additionally, the level of interaction in the video's comment section stimulates tipping behaviour to some extent. Significantly, the study reveals that videos evoking sadness emotions positively influence tipping, while extreme brightness or color distortion during production inhibits tipping. Inaugurally, it's observed that an increase in positive emotional comments in the comment section correlates with a decrease in users' willingness to tip, with negative comments showing no significant impact. In terms of gender and age, female users are more likely to refrain from tipping as video duration increases, and older users may abandon tipping with excessive scene transitions or excessive interaction in the comment section. Social identity emerges as a primary motivational factor for liking behaviour, with the bullet comment section being the strongest contributor, followed closely by the regular comment section. Cognitive factors such as scene transition frequency have a minimal impact on users' tipping intentions. Similarly, extreme brightness, color distortion, and an increase in foreground area proportion inhibit liking behaviour. Emotionally, an increase in the number of positive comments in the comment section suppresses users' willingness to like. In the context of gender and age, female users are more inclined to like as video duration increases, while older users tend to abandon liking with prolonged video duration. Saving and sharing, representing deeper dimensions of user behaviours, show nuanced differences. Saving behaviour primarily stems from emotional support, an extension of tipping behaviour. Sharing behaviour, on the other hand, is an extension of liking, aiming to expand group identity into individual social circles. Emotionally, anger emotions in videos inhibit tipping but encourage saving. Additionally, higher average negative emotions in the comment section strengthen users' motivation to save video. Finally, in the comparative analysis between sharing and liking, it's observed that bullet comment quantity significantly influences liking but has no impact on sharing. Regarding emotional features, anger in videos and excessively negative emotions in the comment section inhibit sharing behaviour.

References

Abrams, D., & Hogg, M. A. (2006). Social identifications: A social psychology of intergroup relations and group processes. Routledge.

Brailovskaia, J., Rohmann, E., Bierhoff, H.-W., Schillack, H., & Margraf, J. (2019). The relationship between daily stress, social support and Facebook addiction disorder. Psychiatry Research, 276, 167–174.

Chen, J., & Liao, J. (2022). Antecedents of viewers' live streaming watching: A perspective of social presence theory. Frontiers in Psychology, 13, 839629.

Chen, S.-C., & Lin, C.-P. (2019). Understanding the effect of social media marketing activities: The mediation of social identification, perceived value, and satisfaction. Technological Forecasting and Social Change, 140, 22–32.

Kang K, Lu J, Guo L, et al. The dynamic effect of interactivity on customer engagement behavior through tie strength: Evidence from live streaming commerce platforms[J]. International Journal of Information Management, 2021, 56: 102251.

Lin Y, Yao D, Chen X. Happiness begets money: Emotion and engagement in live streaming[J]. Journal of Marketing Research, 2021, 58(3): 417-438.

Lu S, Yu M, Wang H. What matters for short videos' user engagement: A multiblock model with variable screening[J]. Expert Systems with Applications, 2023, 218: 119542.

Dessart, L., Veloutsou, C., & Morgan-Thomas, A. (2016). Capturing consumer engagement: Duality, dimensionality and measurement. Journal of Marketing Management, 32(5-6), 399–426.

Hanjalic, A., & Xu, L.-Q. (2005). Affective video content representation and modeling. IEEE Transactions on Multimedia, 7(1), 143–154.

Hoiles, W., Aprem, A., & Krishnamurthy, V. (2017). Engagement and popularity dynamics of YouTube videos and sensitivity to meta-data. IEEE Transactions on Knowledge and Data Engineering, 29(7), 1426–1437.

Hu, M., Zhang, M., & Wang, Y. (2017). Why do audiences choose to keep watching on live video streaming platforms? An explanation of dual identification framework. Computers in Human Behaviour, 75, 594–606.

Kim, S., & Park, H. (2013). Effects of various characteristics of social commerce (s-commerce) on consumers' trust and trust performance. International Journal of Information Management, 33(2), 318–332.

Lee, J., Rajtmajer, S., Srivatsavaya, E., & Wilson, S. (2023). Online self-disclosure, social support, and user engagement during the COVID-19 pandemic. ACM Transactions on Social Computing, 6(3-4), 1–31.

Lu, S., Yu, M., & Wang, H. (2023). What matters for short videos' user engagement: A multiblock model with variable screening. Expert Systems with Applications, 218, 119542.

Russell, J. A., & Mehrabian, A. (1977). Evidence for a three-factor theory of emotions. Journal of Research in Personality, 11(3), 273–294.

Shensa, A., Sidani, J. E., Escobar-Viera, C. G., Switzer, G. E., Primack, B. A., & Choukas-Bradley, S. (2020). Emotional support from social media and face-to-face relationships: Associations with depression risk among young adults. Journal of Affective Disorders, 260, 38–44.

Tonomura, Y., Akutsu, A., Otsuji, K., & Sadakata, T. (1993). Videomap and videospaceicon: Tools for anatomizing video content. In Proceedings of the INTERACT'93 and CHI'93 Conference on Human Factors in Computing Systems (pp. 131–136).

Van Doorn, J., Lemon, K. N., Mittal, V., Nass, S., Pick, D., Pirner, P., & Verhoef, P. C. (2010). Customer engagement behaviour: Theoretical foundations and research directions. Journal of Service Research, 13(3), 253–266.

Wang, H., & Ma, C. (2013). Interactive multi-scale structures for summarizing video content. Science China Information Sciences, 56, 1–12.

Wang, Y., Ke, J., Talebi, H., Yim, J. G., Birkbeck, N., Adsumilli, B., … Yang, F. (2021). Rich features for perceptual quality assessment of UGC videos. In Proceedings of the IEEE/CVF Conference on Computer Vision and Pattern Recognition (pp. 13435–13444).

Wohn, D. Y., Freeman, G., & McLaughlin, C. (2018). Explaining viewers' emotional, instrumental, and financial support provision for live streamers. In Proceedings of the 2018 CHI Conference on Human Factors in Computing Systems (pp. 1–13).

Xu X, Wu J H, Chang Y T, et al. The investigation of hedonic consumption, impulsive consumption and social sharing in e-commerce live-streaming video s[J]. 2019.

Health Misinformation Vs. Facts on Social Media: Co-Occurrence Network Analysis in Bangladesh

Parinda Rahman and Ifeoma Adaji
University of British Columbia, Kelowna, Canada

parinda1@student.ubc.ca
ifeoma.adaji@ubc.ca

Abstract: The increased usage of social media provides a way to disseminate health-related information more quickly. Alternatively, sharing health content on social media poses risks due to unrestricted posting, enabling misinformation to spread. Regional social and cultural contexts influence themes in social media posts, underscoring the importance of understanding content and prevalent misinformation themes. This insight is crucial for tailoring interventions, resource allocation, misinformation detection algorithms, and policy formulation. We conducted word co-occurrence network analysis, creating and analyzing two networks for valid information and misinformation in Bangladesh. The prevalence of misinformation regarding natural ingredients and treatments in Bangladesh underscores the need for targeted efforts to combat health misinformation on social media. For each network, we computed metrics such as betweenness, Katz centrality, out-degree, and degree distribution. Furthermore, we computed the Louvain clustering algorithm to identify word clusters. A comparative analysis of both networks suggested that the context of words used in sentences was important and that both networks contained information about natural remedies or ingredients for health benefits. The misinformation network contained the word *raw turmeric* with the highest bigram frequency of 162. These natural remedies were stated as cures, and there was much misinformation and valid information surrounding common health conditions such as blood pressure. This was depicted through the word *blood* having an outdegree of four and seven in the misinformation and valid information networks, respectively. The valid information network emphasized the beneficial properties of natural ingredients rather than their supposed ability to cure diseases. This study provides insights into the distinctions and parallels between valid health information and misinformation on social media, considering their social and cultural context. It underscores shared semantics and bigram words between them, suggesting that understanding these differences can aid in addressing region-specific challenges.

Keywords: Health, Social media, Misinformation, Social network analysis, Word co-occurrence Network

1. Introduction

Social media serves as a prominent channel for health information dissemination (Chou, Oh and Klein, 2018), utilized by organizations like the World Health Organization (Xiong and Liu, 2014). However, it also poses unprecedented risks as it allows any user to spread health-related information (Cavallo et al., 2014). Misinformation tends to proliferate over social media more than valid scientific information (Vosoughi, Roy and Aral, 2018). In literature, an assertion that is misleading and lacks scientific backing surrounding human health can be referred to as health misinformation (Funk, Salathé and Jansen, 2010). Health misinformation, lacking scientific support, surged during the COVID-19 pandemic, with false cures and rumors circulating widely (Grimes, 2021). Examples include claims of curing COVID-19 with chloroquine, cow urine, alcohol, and hot water (Mackey et al., 2021). Apart from the pandemic, numerous self-proclaimed health experts and practitioners of alternative medicine have promoted unproven medications, concoctions, suggestions, and treatments as means of "boosting" the immune system over social media (Caulfield, 2020). This can lead to harmful outcomes such as deaths from alcohol poisoning from concoctions (Trew, 2020). However, much of the misinformation is motivated by cultural practices, societal stigma about certain diseases, and locally available ingredients (Wang, 2018). While the problem of health misinformation is global, in recent years between 2021 and 2022, Bangladesh has observed a 10.1% rise in its social media user base (Simon, 2021). While much research on this topic focuses on Western countries due to data availability, it's noted that the nature and spread of health misinformation depend heavily on social and cultural contexts (Wang, 2018). Bangladesh's dense population suggests that misinformation could affect many people (Khan et al., 2021).

Past studies have utilized machine learning and deep learning techniques for detecting misinformation (Cabral et al., 2021) but have largely overlooked analyzing themes present in the different contexts between misinformation and valid information. However, customizing algorithms according to regional misinformation contexts could enhance detection and inform targeted policy interventions. In the health misinformation domain, there is little to no literature that analyses the context of misinformation in a specific region or Bangladesh. A recent study focused on COVID-19-related misinformation in India analyzed the themes present and their context using co-occurrence network analysis using bigrams (Naeem, Bhatti and Khan, 2021). However, that work was limited to COVID-19-related misinformation. Co-occurrence network analysis using bigrams encapsulates context by examining the frequency of items appearing together within a defined context and discerning relationships between consecutive word pairs making it suitable for studying health misinformation on social media (Hu, Huang, & Wang, 2018; Nistor & Zadobrischi, 2022).

Addressing this gap, this research aims to conduct a comparative analysis of content between health misinformation and valid information in Bangladesh by exploring bigram co-occurrence network analysis technique. The work aims to investigate what themes of misinformation are prevalent and whether there are differences or similarities with valid information. The work focuses on a comprehensive analysis across diverse health topics as the majority of current literature focuses on a specific disease or on COVID-19 which limits the scope of application. The novel contributions of our work are:

- Curating text data sourced from Facebook through manual scraping.
- Conducting bigram network visualization, community detection, and metric analysis (in-degree, out-degree, centrality measures) on Bangladesh-specific health information.
- Comparing networks of health misinformation and valid information to gain insights.

2. Literature Review

2.1 Health Misinformation on Social Media

The influence of misinformation on social media poses a significant challenge to public health, potentially undermining the efficacy of programs, campaigns, and initiatives designed to promote citizen health, awareness, and well-being (Pulido et al., 2020). Wang et al (2018) conducted a systematic literature review and found that the type of health information shared is often driven by social and cultural contexts. Another study shows the prevalence of misinformation surrounding family planning and contraception in Nigeria due to the lack of awareness about reproductive health and religious teachings (Ankomah, 2011). Sentell et al (2020) identified misinformation surrounding vaping was present in Hawaii due to the misappropriation of native culture. The study underscored the need for customized health interventions targeting specific communities and cultures to counteract the compelling nature of health misinformation online, particularly concerning its impact on youth and the perpetuation of health disparities. These works provide evidence that misinformation is largely dependent on regional social and cultural context.

2.2 Misinformation in South Asia

Previous literature identifies that in Bangladesh, India, and Pakistan, religious beliefs significantly increased vaccine hesitancy (Kanozia and Arya, 2021). Moreover, health practices in this region are guided by many ancient practices of Ayurveda (Haque et al., 2018); thus, a lot of health practices focus on the use of natural ingredients. Ahmed et al (2020) identified that during the COVID-19 pandemic in Bangladesh, preventive measures and beneficial properties of natural ingredients were misrepresented as cures. Moreover, previous studies also suggest that severe societal stigma, a lack of sexual health education, and misinformation surrounding sexual health are prevalent in South Asia (Banik et al., 2023). This work can be used to investigate whether these themes of misinformation are prominent in social media specifically in Bangladesh.

2.3 Network analysis and Co-Occurrence Networks

Previous studies have shown the efficacy of network analysis in understanding the context of health-related misinformation. For instance, one study focused on HPV vaccine misinformation on Instagram, where separate networks for pro and anti-vaccine posts were created, revealing features such as conspiracy theories and unsupported assertions (Massey et al., 2020). Another study during the Zika pandemic examined structural differences between networks disseminating misinformation and accurate information, using metrics like modularity for comparison (Safarnejad et al., 2020). The study compared nine metrics, such as modularity, out-degree, etc., to understand the difference between the two network behaviors. Bigram analysis within network analysis has been widely used to analyze text data. It allows for the examination of lexical structure and semantics, as seen in studies investigating sentiment in political tweets and co-occurring words in tweets discussing vaccine-related blood clots (Fudolig et al., 2022). The majority of these studies focused on a particular health domain such as vaccination or Zika virus, limiting the investigation of other misinformation contexts.

Hence, prior research underscores the significance of cultural and societal contexts in the realm of health-related misinformation. However, despite the prevalence of such misinformation in South Asia, there is a notable absence of studies specifically targeting Bangladesh and comprehensively exploring the contextual nuances across various health domains using network analysis metrics. Existing studies employing co-occurrence analysis tend to concentrate on singular health domains, highlighting the importance and novelty of this work.

3. Methodology

3.1 Data Collection

Due to Facebook not having a publicly available application programming interface (API), automated data collection was not feasible. Bangla text data was manually gathered from publicly accessible Facebook posts by searching using relevant Bangla keywords as no publicly available dataset on health information in Bangladesh existed. The Facebook posts originated between the time frame of 2018 to 2022. The list of keywords used for the data collection was "health", "cure", and "disease". Specific disease-related terms were not considered as keywords for the search rather general words were considered. Facebook, being the most widely used platform for information access in Bangladesh, was chosen as the data source (Al-Zaman, Md Sayeed and Noman, 2021). The collected data was manually classified as false or valid information. The data was translated using Google Translate. To ensure semantic accuracy three native Bengali speakers validated and modified the translations wherever it was required. Data labeling was further validated by a group of Bangladeshi medical specialists proficient in Bengali. English translations of the data were used for the analysis. A total of 3266 credible information posts and 2719 misinformation posts were collected. Figure 1 shows an example data point from the dataset.

Text	Translation
ধুম্রপান, মদ্যপান এবং অন্যান্য ক্ষতিকারক জীবনযাত্রার কারণগুলি ক্যান্সারের ঝুঁকি বাড়াতে পারে না, বরং এটি কেবল দুর্ভাগ্য হতে পারে গবেষণায় দেখা গেছে	Smoking, Drinking and other harmful lifestyle factors does not increase the risk of cancer, rather it simply may be bad luck study finds

Figure 1: Example from the data set of the original Bangla text of the Facebook post and its translation

3.2 Data Preprocessing

Text data segments were concatenated and processed in R using the "tm" library. It was converted to lowercase, and numbers, punctuation, and special characters were also removed. Stop words were removed to retain only significant words. The cleaned text was converted to a data frame, and bigrams were generated separately for valid information and health misinformation using "tidyr". Bigrams with an occurrence frequency of 20 or more were selected for analysis. This criterion was chosen because recurrent bigrams signify the prevalence of word pairs (Evert, 2005). Even after this filtering, over 85% of the total number of bigrams was retained in the network, indicating significant representativeness of the dataset. Following filtration, visualizations were generated using the igraph package in R.

3.3 Data and Network Analysis

For analysis and visualization, two separate directed networks for misinformation and valid information were created, with words representing the nodes and edges indicating connections between two words if they appear one after another in sequence. If a word is pointed toward, it signifies that the word is the second word in the bigram. For example, if in the visualization the word "blood" has a directed edge towards the word "pressure", it is the second word. Edge thickness represents bigram frequency. The following metrics were computed on both networks to gain insights about their content.

3.3.1 Bigram frequency

This metric represents the number of times each bigram occurs in the entire document. Bigrams that occur frequently signify significant and commonly used word pairs in each network, offering insights into the prevalent themes within the dataset.

3.3.2 In- degree

The adjacency matrix's i^{th} row sum equals the in-degree of node i, which represents the total number of connections onto node i (Newman, 2018). In the context of this analysis, the in-degree specifically indicates words that appear as the second word in the bigram pairs within the network.

3.3.3 Out- degree

The entire number of connections originating from node *i* is represented by the out-degree of node *i*, which is the sum of the ith column in the adjacency matrix (Newman, 2018). The out-degree is crucial as it indicates how many other words a particular word connects to within the network.

3.3.4 Betweenness

The betweenness centrality provides information about the flow of information in the network (Newman, 2018). The flow of connector words in the network could be observed to gain insights into the themes and use of language.

3.3.5 Katz Centrality

Katz centrality calculates the relative importance of a node within a directed network by counting the number of immediate neighbors (first-degree nodes) and all other nodes in the network that connect to the node under consideration through these immediate neighbours (Newman, 2018). This measure is crucial in directed networks as it provides insight into the relative importance and influence of words, considering both direct connections and indirect ones.

3.3.6 Louvain Clustering

This community detection method partitions networks into densely connected clusters to optimize modularity, a measure of network division strength. Selected for its speed and availability in open-source libraries, the Louvain algorithm can also detect hierarchical structures within words, revealing prevalent themes (Newman, 2018) and it is widely used for directed networks.

4. Findings

4.1 Basic Network Characteristics

4.1.1 Bigram frequency and network visualization

Table 1 shows the top 5 bigram frequencies in the valid information network and the misinformation network.

Table 1: Top 5 bigram frequencies in the misinformation and the valid information network

Misinformation network			Valid information network		
Word 1	Word 2	Frequency	Word 1	Word 2	Frequency
raw	turmeric	162	blood	pressure	228
black	cumin	128	neem	leaves	125
blood	pressure	108	lemon	juice	121
hot	water	72	blood	sugar	104
leaf	juice	68	heart	disease	76

The misinformation network words from Table 1 highlight that "raw turmeric" and "black cumin" were the most frequently occurring words in the misinformation network, often suggested as remedies for various diseases. Similarly, "leaf juice" and "hot water" indicate the prevalence of natural ingredients as treatments. This aligns with previous findings in India, where garlic and hot water were influential nodes in similar network analyses (Naeem, Bhatti and Khan, 2021). Additionally, the presence of "blood pressure" suggests misinformation surrounding common diseases, consistent with the challenge of misinformation in noncommunicable diseases like hypertension among Bangladeshis (Jafar et al., 2018). The term "blood pressure" appears most frequently in the valid information network. Upon examining the dataset, it was discovered that words like "neem leaves" and "lemon juice" were used to describe the health benefits of these ingredients rather than promoting them as cures, as observed in the misinformation network. Additionally, in the valid information network, words such as "blood," "hair," and "juice" remained popular nodes. Given the presence of medicinal healers utilizing natural ingredients in the country (Rahmatullah et al., 2010; Jahan, 2010), discussions about the beneficial properties of these ingredients are prevalent in the valid information network. Figure 1 shows the misinformation network and Figure 2 shows the communities in the network after using the Louvain algorithm. Due to network disconnection, most communities are small in size, with 24 identified in total, the largest containing 9 nodes. Prominent communities formed around words like "hair," "turmeric," and "blood." Themes within the communities include the presence of natural treatments such as hot water, herbal leaves, spices, and vegetables. Additionally, two communities are associated with sexual health, indicating misinformation in this domain. Notably, common diseases in Bangladesh, such as diabetes, high blood pressure, and high cholesterol (Mostafa et al., 2016), are surrounded by significant misinformation. The word "hair" formed a large cluster, and this is consistent with the findings of Iglesias-Puzas et al (2021) which identified that on social media, the popular discussion area is dermatology, which includes hair. One small community contained the word "Hafez," which refers to a person who knows the Quran by heart and Bangladesh is a Muslim-majority country (Rozario, 2009). This is consistent with the findings of Kanozia and Arya (2021), which state that in South Asia, religion is used to propagate health misinformation.

Figure 1: Visualization of the misinformation network

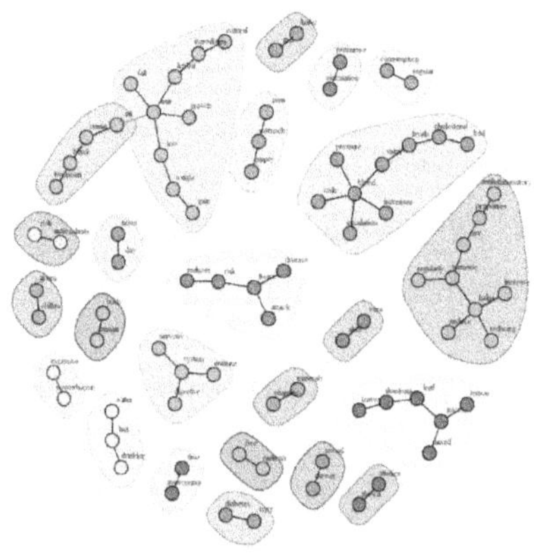

Figure 2: Community detection using the Louvain algorithm for the misinformation network

Figure 3 visualizes the valid information network and Figure 4 illustrates the communities in the valid information network. It can be observed that because the network is disconnected, most of the communities are small in size. There were 34 communities, with the largest containing 14 nodes. The majority of the communities consisted of only 2 nodes, representing disconnected components that form a bigram in the network. The large communities formed around the words "juice" and "helps". "Juice" is connected to many fruits, vegetables, or spices, and its beneficial properties are highlighted, as shown through the use of the word "helps".

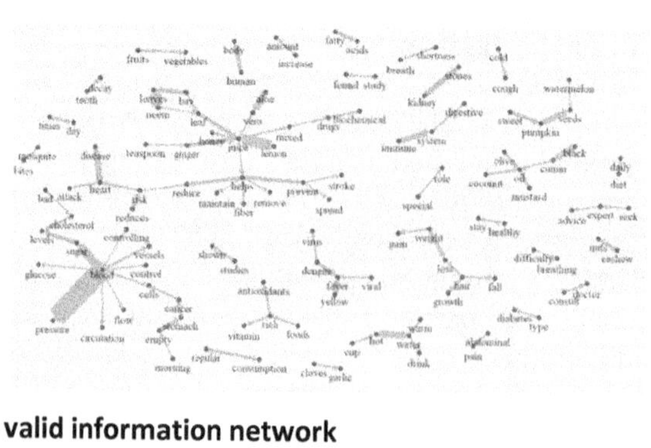

Figure 3: Visualization of the valid information network

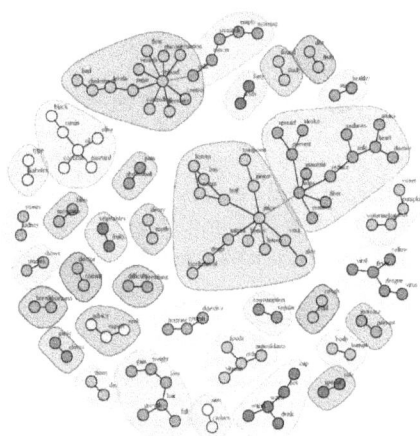

Figure 4: Community detection using the Louvain algorithm for the valid information network

4.2 In-Degree

Table 3 presents the nodes with the highest in-degree for both the misinformation and valid information networks. Nodes with a higher in-degree represent the second word in the bigram. Notably, both networks feature overlapping words such as "system," "juice," and "oil," suggesting similar lexical and semantic usage. However, the contextual meaning of these words varies significantly. This aligns with Garg and Kumar, (2018), which suggests that word co-occurrence networks can be context-dependent, as observed in this paper.

Table 3: Top 5 In-degree of each network

Misinformation Network		Valid Information Network	
Word	Indegree	Word	Indegree
system	3	juice	4
juice	2	oil	4
oil	2	fever	3
levels	2	blood	2
loss	2	helps	2

4.3 Out-Degree

Table 3 lists the top 5 out-degrees of nodes in each network, representing influential nodes that point to the second word in a bigram. Notably, the misinformation network uniquely features words like "herbal" and "thankuni" (Centella Asiatica Plant), indicating the prevalence of natural cures and alternative medicine, consistent with Hossain and Haque (2023), highlighting the false spread of "thankuni" leaves as a COVID-19 cure in Bangladesh. Additionally, "blood" emerges as an influential node in both networks, suggesting the prevalence of discussions surrounding blood-related diseases in social media health discussions. Furthermore, the presence of "hair" in both networks indicates a popular topic in health information, consistent with Iglesias-Puzas et al (2021) identifying dermatology, including hair-related discussions, as a prominent area on social media, often containing misleading cures.

Table 3: Top 5 Out-degree of each network

Misinformation Network		Valid Information Network	
Word	Out degree	Word	Out degree
blood	4	blood	7
hair	4	helps	4
hot	3	hair	3
thankuni	2	heart	2
herbal	2	dengue	2

4.4 Centrality Measures

4.4.1 Betweenness

Words with high bigram frequency as seen in Table 1 were also reported to have a high betweenness score. However, due to numerous structural holes or disconnected components in both networks, it may not fully capture node influence (Hassanzadeh, Khodadust and Zandian, 2012). In the misinformation network, "turmeric" and "raw" had the highest betweenness scores (15 and 12, respectively). Conversely, in the valid information network, "juice" and "helps" scored 104 and 100, respectively. Therefore, this indicates that in Bangladesh "raw turmeric" reported as a cure in the misinformation network. The presence of the word "helps" as an influential node in the valid information network suggests that the benefits of certain substances were highlighted as opposed to stating it as a cure.

4.4.2 Katz centrality

Table 2 displays the Katz centrality scores for each network. Interestingly, both networks exhibit an overlap of nodes with high Katz centrality scores, suggesting that similar words hold influence in both networks. Consequently, distinguishing between the two networks without sentence context proves challenging. For example, the word "oil" and "juice" reported high Katz centrality values. Therefore, no insight could be drawn from the nodes and their Katz centrality score without additional context.

Table 2: Top 5 Katz centrality of each network

Misinformation Network		Valid Information Network	
Word	Katz Centrality	Word	Katz Centrality
system	1.30	juice	1.44
oil	1.22	oil	1.41
levels	1.21	fever	1.30
juice	1.21	mixed	1.25
loss	1.20	helps	1.24

4.5 Comparative Analysis

Results indicate that lexical and semantic features alone are insufficient to differentiate between misinformation and valid information. Contextual understanding is vital, as many nodes share significant metrics across both networks. For example, the word "blood" displays contextual differences: in the valid information network, it has an out-degree of 7, while in the misinformation network, it has an out-degree of 4. While both networks touch upon themes of natural remedies and Ayurveda for health, a notable distinction lies in their portrayal. In the misinformation network, natural remedies are often touted as cures, whereas the valid information network emphasizes their role as preventive measures, as evidenced by terms like "helps" and "reduces." See Figure 5 for the contextual variations of the word "blood."

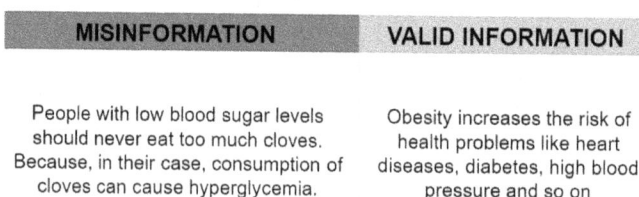

MISINFORMATION	VALID INFORMATION
People with low blood sugar levels should never eat too much cloves. Because, in their case, consumption of cloves can cause hyperglycemia.	Obesity increases the risk of health problems like heart diseases, diabetes, high blood pressure and so on

Figure 5: Varying contexts of the word "blood"

5. Discussion

The findings of this study indicate that discussions on health information in Bangladesh heavily emphasize the use of natural ingredients and treatments. Nodes containing natural ingredients such as "juice" exhibit high out-degree and Katz centrality scores. However, the majority of discussions focus on health benefits as a preventive measure rather than a cure, reflecting the broad nature of the general health information domain and its context-dependency. Consistent with Grimes (2021), "hot water" emerged as a top-occurring bigram in the misinformation network, aligning with its propagation as a cure. Similarities with previous studies on health misinformation in India (Naeem, Bhatti and Khan, 2021) were noted, particularly regarding the prevalence of Ayurvedic practices. However, this study emphasizes the importance of contextual understanding, especially in distinguishing misinformation. Native plants like neem leaves, thankuni leaves, and turmeric, renowned for their medicinal properties in Bengal (Rahmatullah et al., 2010), were prominently featured in the networks. Common diseases in Bangladesh, such as blood pressure and heart diseases, were also key discussion areas in both networks. Despite similarities in lexical usage, the semantic meaning of words differed, posing challenges in misinformation detection without contextual understanding. Clusters formed by the Louvain algorithm revealed misinformation themes related to sexual health, consistent with prior literature (Banik et al., 2023). While one word related to religion was present in the misinformation network, further evidence to elucidate the correlation between religion and misinformation was lacking. Notably, a large cluster centered around the word "hair," aligns with findings on misinformation in dermatology (Iglesias-Puzas et al., 2021). However, the specific relationship between hair-related health information and misinformation in Bangladesh remains unclear. One key limitation of the study is that only one clustering algorithm was used. The study's strength lies in using labeled data validated by health practitioners, enhancing data reliability. Additionally, the comparative analysis between the two networks revealed similar word usage, even in misinformation posts, often employing scientific language for credibility. Focusing on general health information specific to the region provided insights into how cultural and social contexts influence health misinformation. This work has broader implications, potentially aiding in developing region-specific misinformation detection algorithms and informing policymakers on combat strategies, especially in areas like sexual health.

6. Conclusion

In conclusion, the contextuality of co-occurrence network analysis within healthcare is evident, especially in Bangladesh where health misinformation on social media primarily revolves around natural treatments. This study sheds light on the distinctions and overlaps between valid information and misinformation, capturing the social and cultural context of health information dissemination online. It underscores the prevalence of similar semantics and bigram words in both valid information and misinformation. Further research is needed to explore language nuances in these networks, informing policymaking to counter social media misinformation effectively. Additionally, conducting qualitative thematic analysis could validate emerging insights and elucidate misinformation trends in Bangladesh.

References

Ahmed, I., Hasan, M., Akter, R., Sarkar, B.K., Rahman, M., Sarker, M.S. and Samad, M.A. (2020). Behavioral preventive measures and the use of medicines and herbal products among the public in response to COVID-19 in Bangladesh: A cross-sectional study. *PloS one*, 15, p.e0243706.

Ahmed, W., Vidal-Alaball, J. and Vilaseca, Josep M (2022). A social network analysis of Twitter data related to blood clots and vaccines. *International Journal of Environmental Research and Public Health*, 19, p.4584.

Al-Zaman, Md Sayeed and Noman, (2021). Social media news in crisis? Popularity analysis of the top nine Facebook pages of bangladeshi news media. *Journal of Information Science Theory and Practice*, 9, pp.18–32.

Ankomah, A., Anyanti, J. and Oladosu, M., 2011. Myths, misinformation, and communication about family planning and contraceptive use in Nigeria. *Open Access Journal of Contraception*, pp.95-105.

Banik, S., Khan, Jami, H., Sivasubramanian, M., Dhakal, M. and Wilson, E. (2023). Social determinants of sexual health among sexual and gender diverse people in south asia: Lessons learned from india, bangladesh, nepal, and pakistan. Springer, pp.327–352.

Cabral, L., Monteiro, J.M., José, S., Lincoln and Jorge, P. (2021). FakeWhastApp. BR: NLP and machine learning techniques for misinformation detection in brazilian portuguese WhatsApp messages. pp.63–74.

Caulfield, T. (2020). *Pseudoscience and COVID-19-we've had enough already. Nature (Lond.)*.

Cavallo, D.N., Chou, W.-Y.S., McQueen, A., Ramirez, A. and Riley, W.T. (2014). *Cancer prevention and control interventions using social media: user-generated approaches*. AACR.

Chou, W.-Y.S., Oh, A. and Klein, W.M. (2018). Addressing health-related misinformation on social media. *Jama*, 320, pp.2417–2418.

Evert, S., 2005. The statistics of word cooccurrences: word pairs and collocations.

Funk, S., Salathé, M. and Jansen, V.A. (2010). Modelling the influence of human behaviour on the spread of infectious diseases: a review. *Journal of the Royal Society Interface*, 7, pp.1247–1256.

Fudolig, M.I., Alshaabi, T., Arnold, M.V., Danforth, C.M. and Dodds, P.S. (2022). Sentiment and structure in word co-occurrence networks on Twitter. *Applied Network Science*, 7, pp.1–27.

Garg, M. and Kumar, M. (2018). Identifying influential segments from word co-occurrence networks using AHP. *Cognitive Systems Research*, 47, pp.28–41.

Grimes, D.R. (2021). Medical disinformation and the unviable nature of COVID-19 conspiracy theories. *PLoS One*, 16, p.e0245900.

Gurcan, F., Dalveren, Gonca Gokce Menekse, Cagiltay, Nergiz Ercil, Roman, D. and Soylu, A. (2022). Evolution of software testing strategies and trends: Semantic content analysis of software research corpus of the last 40 years. *IEEE Access*, 10, pp.106093–106109.

Haque, M.I., Chowdhury, A.A., Shahjahan, M. and Harun, (2018). Traditional healing practices in rural Bangladesh: a qualitative investigation. *BMC complementary and alternative medicine*, 18, pp.1–15.

Hassanzadeh, M., Khodadust, R. and Zandian, F. (2012). Analysis of co-authorship indicators, betweenness centrality and structural holes of the Iranian nanotechnology researchers in science citation index (1991-2011). *Iranian Journal of Information Processing and Management*, 28, pp.223–249.

Hossain, I. and Haque, A.M. (2023). *A case study on the spread of fake news by social media in the COVID-19 era in bangladesh.*

Hu, J., Huang, R. and Wang, Y. (2018). Geographical visualization of research collaborations of library science in China. *The Electronic Library*, 36, pp.414–429.

Iglesias-Puzas, Á., Conde-Taboada, A., Aranegui-Arteaga, B. and López-Bran, E. (2021). 'Fake news' in dermatology. Results from an observational, cross-sectional study. *International Journal of Dermatology*, 60, pp.358–362.

Jafar, T.H., Gandhi, M., Jehan, I., Naheed, A., Asita, S., H, Shahab, H., Alam, D., Luke, N., Lim, W. and COBRA-BPS Study Group (2018). Determinants of uncontrolled hypertension in rural communities in South Asia—Bangladesh, Pakistan, and Sri Lanka. *American journal of hypertension*, 31, pp.1205–1214.

Kanozia, R. and Arya, R. (2021). 'Fake news', religion, and COVID-19 vaccine hesitancy in India, Pakistan, and Bangladesh. *Media Asia*, 48, pp.313–321.

Mackey, T.K., Purushothaman, V., Haupt, M., Nali, M.C. and Li, J. (2021). Application of unsupervised machine learning to identify and characterise hydroxychloroquine misinformation on Twitter. *The Lancet Digital Health*, 3, pp.e72–e75.

Massey, P.M., Kearney, M.D., Hauer, M.K., Selvan, P., Koku, E. and Leader, A.E. (2020). Dimensions of misinformation about the HPV vaccine on Instagram: Content and network analysis of social media characteristics. *Journal of medical Internet research*, 22, p.e21451.

Mostafa, Z.M., Choudhury, S.R., Ahmed, J., Talukder, M.H. and Rahman, A.S. (2016). Blood glucose and cholesterol levels in adult population of Bangladesh: results from STEPS 2006 survey. *Indian Heart Journal*, 68, pp.52–56.

Naeem, S.B., Bhatti, R. and Khan, A. (2021). An exploration of how fake news is taking over social media and putting public health at risk. *Health Information & Libraries Journal*, 38, pp.143–149.

Newman, M. (2018). *Networks*. Oxford university press.

Nistor, A. and Zadobrischi, E. (2022). The influence of fake news on social media: analysis and verification of web content during the COVID-19 pandemic by advanced machine learning methods and natural language processing. *Sustainability*, 14, p.10466.

Pulido, C.M., Ruiz-Eugenio, L., Redondo-Sama, G. and Villarejo-Carballido, B., 2020. A new application of social impact in social media for overcoming fake news in health. *International journal of environmental research and public health*, 17(7), p.2430.

Rahmatullah, M., Khatun, M.A., Morshed, N., Neogi, Prashanta Kumar, Ahmed, Hossan, Md S, Mahal, M.J. and Jahan, R. (2010). A randomized survey of medicinal plants used by folk medicinal healers of Sylhet Division, Bangladesh. *Advances in Natural and Applied Sciences*, 4, pp.52–62.

Rozario, S. (2009). Allah is the scientist of the scientists: Modern medicine and religious healing among British Bangladeshis. *Culture and religion*, 10, pp.177–199.

Safarnejad, L., Xu, Q., Ge, Y., Krishnan, S., Bagarvathi, A. and Chen, S. (2020). Contrasting misinformation and real-information dissemination network structures on social media during a health emergency. *American journal of public health*, 110, pp.S340–S347.

Sentell, T., Kearney, M., Hazen, A., Dela Cruz, M.R., Yamauchi, J., McHenry, L., Rodericks, B. and Massey, P., 2020. Do you Vape With Aloha?: How culture and place are used to spread misinformation on Instagram. *European Journal of Public Health*, 30(Supplement_5), pp.ckaa165-1005.

Simon, K. (2021). *Digital 2022: Bangladesh. Datareportal*j https://rb. gy/dl37o.

Suryadi, D. and Kim, H. (2019). Automatic identification of product usage contexts from online customer reviews. In: *Cambridge University Press*. pp.2507–2516.

Trew, B. (2020). *Coronavirus: hundreds dead in Iran from drinking methanol amid fake reports it cures disease. Independent.*

Voitalov, I., Der, V., Der, V. and Krioukov, D. (2019). Scale-free networks well done. *Physical Review Research*, 1, p.033034.

Vosoughi, S., Roy, D. and Aral, S. (2018). The spread of true and false news online. *science*, 359, pp.1146–1151.

Wang, Y. (2018). Systematic review on the social mechanism of health misinformation dissemination in the Internet era. *European Journal of Public Health*, 28, pp.cky213-194.

Xiong, F. and Liu, Y. (2014). Opinion formation on social media: an empirical approach. *Chaos: An Interdisciplinary Journal of Nonlinear Science*, 24.

Work in Progress Papers

'It's Just Pictures': The Death of Social Photography as we Know it

Beata Jungselius[1] and Alexandra Weilenmann[2]

[1]School of Business, Economics, and IT, University West, Trollhättan, Sweden

[2]Department of Applied IT, University of Gothenburg, Sweden

beata.jungselius@hv.se

alexandra.weilenmann@gu.se

Abstract: The widespread adoption of smartphones and increased use of social media has changed how people document and share their everyday lives. As social media has evolved over the last decade, so has social photography practice. In this short paper, we discuss this evolution in relation to our work in progress within an ongoing longitudinal qualitative study spanning over ten years. In this project, we have conducted semi-structured interviews with the same group of informants in 2012, 2017 and 2022. This methodological approach has allowed us to examine how social media users reflect on experience, use and practice. In this paper, we highlight how during this last decade there has been a shift in how people document and share their everyday life in social media. More than ever before, social media users of today are able to document and share snapshots of everyday life, keeping friends and memories close and easy to access. However, in the early days of social media, people were more active in terms of their own production of content and posting of pictures, while today, they share less new material. From our analysis, we discuss how our informants report a shift in how they experience social photography, from being a process of editing and sharing photos intensely, to a more passive approach where they describe taking a lot of images, but not sharing them on social media to the same extent as they did before. Based on one representative example from our empirical material, we discuss the implications of the development of social media platforms over this past decade, and how the possibility to edit and share with others 'in the moment' has transformed into something less social over these years. We show how social media photography has evolved from being a practice of editing and sharing memorable content, to being less interactive, and instead involving more individual consumption and reflection, as well as sharing photographs in smaller circles. While the claim that social photography is 'dead' is rather bold, we do believe that there is a trend towards a less social and more individual engagement in social media photography.

Keywords: Social media, Social photography, Longitudinal study, Stimulated recall interviews, Qualitative study, User study

1. Introduction

Social photography, i.e., the practice of documenting and sharing photographs, has been of research interest for decades. Chalfen (1975, 1987) did early and influential work on practices surrounding taking, editing, storing, and sharing photos which still constitute an important theoretical framework for contemporary scholars studying digital and social photo sharing (Shannon, 2022; Simatzkin-Ohana & Frosh, 2022). Within qualitative social media studies, social photography has been of interest especially to researchers interested in specific practices, e.g., networked photography and selfie cultures (Savnal, 2021), as well as activities within specific social networking sites such as Instagram (Barnwell et al., 2023) and Snapchat (Best, 2016). Studying and comparing photo sharing practices on Snapchat and Instagram, Larsen and Kofoed (2016) found a great difference in both aesthetics and message in photos shared on the two platforms. Best (2016) studied motivation behind Snapchat communication and how Snapchat "both extends and intensifies digital photography's shift from memory to communication" (Best, 2016, pg. 2). In recent years, a distinction has been made between active and passive use, where active use is held in contrast to passive use of social media (where the latter refers to "viewing others' social media pages without interacting with the page owner" (Roberts and David, 2023, pg. 240). While intuitively appealing, other scholars have criticized the active use hypothesis (Krause et al., 2023). When reviewing previous research on social media photography, we found that the general focus has mainly been on specific instances, in delimited settings and locations tied to certain platforms and specific practices. In this way previous work has primarily provided us with snapshots of current practices, rather than insights on the development and progression over time. On a related and important note, Miller (2011) highlighted the fact that social media platforms should not be considered static entities. Rather, these platforms can be drawn upon in several different ways, developing into genres of use within different groups and communities while also continuously evolving and changing over time (Miller, 2011). Therefore, within our work, we have aimed to focus on the evolution of cross-platform social media photography during the last decade as experienced by the users themsleves. Building upon previous work and our own rich data corpus of a decade of social media use, we zoom out and approach the evolvement of social photography in contemporary society holistically.

2. Method

The discussion presented in this paper is based on ongoing qualitative longitudinal research (QLR) (Audulv et al., 2023) with the same informants having been interviewed in 2012, 2017 and 2022. In 2012, we started out with an interest in Instagram use, as the then emerging dominant social media and photo sharing platform. Sixteen Instagram users (eleven women and five men between the age of 19 and 38) were recruited and invited to take part in semi-structured in-depth interviews. In 2012, the participants were both asked questions specifically about their social media photography engagements as well as about their social media use in general. In 2017, the same sixteen participants were invited to take part in interviews again. Eleven of them accepted and participated in interviews on their general social media use. In 2022, the same eleven participants as in the 2017 study were interviewed once again. Questions were asked on their social media use as of 2022 and about how their social media activities differed from ten years earlier. At the end of each interview, the participants were shown snippets from previous interviews and asked to comment on their reasonings five and ten years ago, influenced by the stimulated-recall technique (Dempsey, 2010). A more general discussion preceded showing examples from previous interviews. In our work, we have encouraged the participants to reflect upon their past selves and allowed for reflections about changes in both social media practices and life circumstances, while also tying their reasonings to specific, previous statements. The video recorded material as well as the transcribed interviews has been analyzed through thematic analysis (Braun & Clarke, 2006) using NVivo. The data collection has been conducted adhering to the most recent version of AOIR ethical research guidelines available in 2012, 2017 and 2022 respectively.

Table 1: Participant details

Informant	Gender	Age 2012	Occupation 2012	Age 2017	Occupation 2017	Age 2022	Occupation 2022
1	F	19	Shop assistant	24	Student	29	Journalist
2	M	27	Information officer	32	Project manager	37	Business analyst
3	F	27	Home care worker	32	Medical secretary	37	Medical secretary
4	F	26	Student	31	Teacher	36	Planning officer
5	F	29	Journalist	34	Journalist	39	Student
6	F	31	Copywriter	36	Copywriter	41	Copywriter
7	M	28	Group home worker	33	Marketing manager	38	HR specialist
8	F	23	Student	28	Purchaser	33	Purchaser
9	F	29	Marketer	34	Marketer	39	Team manager
10	F	26	Student	31	Social media team leader (on parental leave)	36	Communications manager
11	M	38	Digital producer	43	Strategic digital producer	48	Strategic digital producer

3. Findings and Discussion

For this short paper, we use one representative example from our rich empirical data to illustrate a recognizable theme that have emerged from analysis of how users describe the evolvement in their own social media use over this last decade:

"I have some memory of that when we started this thing many years ago [...] I was an active instagrammer. It was more then of like taking pictures of your everyday life and you were supposed to take pictures of your life and share that, so it wasn't that I posted 20 pictures a day, but it was at least with some frequency. And I remember when we had the follow-up and then it was more of like, yeah, I do post some but maybe rather for myself but not that much for others and maybe that you saved yourself to when you did fun stuff, you were at a festival, you were on vacation, it wasn't a lot of this like basic everyday life. And then now, we are two years into a pandemic, war is burning in Europe and it's just like, I don't post anything. I do a lot of stuff, but that's just pictures saved in my photo album on my phone."

This informant described a shift in how she practices social media photography by relating her current engagement to the previous two interview occasions. She reflected upon how she initially, in 2012, shared everyday life activities very frequently, but in 2017 had become more selective in sharing special moments with less focus on the social and interactional aspects and more on the aim of creating memories for oneself, whereas in 2022 the public sharing on social media platforms were even more selective, and although a lot of images were being taken, very few, if any, were being shared. Despite this trend of posting less actively, somewhat paradoxically, our informants reported still seeing social media as an integrated and intertwined part of their everyday lives, and as a space they spend time in and visit several times a day, and enjoy returning to, to revisit past experiences that appear as memories and highlights.

This leads us to reflect upon how social media photography practices have evolved over time. Miller argued in 2011 that social media platforms are continuously evolving and change over time. In 2016, Larsen and Kofoed (2016) concluded a great difference in both aesthetics and message in photos shared on two platforms and Best suggested an ongoing shift in digital photography," from memory to communication" (Best, 2016, pg. 2). We acknowledge that there might be a great variety in use between both users in general as well as within user groups on different platforms, and that these varieties will also affect the content that these users produce. However, for this short paper, we want to argue that what we are experiencing now is a trend towards a shift, almost opposite to the shift presented by Best in 2016 (Best, 2016). Based on our empirical findings, we argue that we can see a change in the practice of social media photography over this past decade, where the social and interactional aspects of social media photography are no longer as prominent as they initially were. Social media photography has evolved from being a practice of editing, sharing and interacting around memorable events with friends and family, to having become less social, and rather to a greater extent a practice of individual consumption and reflection.

References

Audulv, Å., Westergren, T., Ludvigsen, M. S., Pedersen, M. K., Fegran, L., Hall, E. O. C., Aagaard, H., Robstad, N., & Kneck, Å. (2023). Time and change: a typology for presenting research findings in qualitative longitudinal research. BMC Medical Research Methodology, 23(1). https://doi.org/10.1186/s12874-023-02105-1

Barnwell, A., Neves, B. B., & Ravn, S. (2023). Captured and captioned: Representing family life on Instagram. *New Media & Society*, 25(5), 921-942. https://doi.org/10.1177/14614448211012791

Best, C. M. (2016). 'These snaps are made for talking': Visual communication and instant expression on Snapchat. AoIR Selected Papers of Internet Research. https://journals.uic.edu/ojs/index.php/spir/article/view/8461

Braun, V., & Clarke, V. (2006). Using thematic analysis in psychology. Qualitative Research in Psychology, 3(2), 77–101. https://doi.org/10.1191/1478088706qp063oa

Chalfen, R. (1975). Cinéma Naïveté: A Study of Home Moviemaking as Visual Communication. Studies in Visual Communication, 2(2), 87–103. https://repository.upenn.edu/svc/vol2/iss2/5

Chalfen, R. (1987). Snapshot versions of life. Bowling Green State University Popular Press.

Dempsey, N. P. (2010). Stimulated recall interviews in ethnography. Qualitative Sociology. https://doi.org/10.1007/s11133-010-9157-x

Krause, H. V., große Deters, F., Baumann, A., & Krasnova, H. (2023). Active social media use and its impact on well-being—an experimental study on the effects of posting pictures on Instagram. *Journal of Computer-Mediated Communication*, 28(1), zmac037.

Larsen, M. C., & Kofoed, J. (2016). A snap of intimacy: Investigating photo sharing practices on Snapchat and Instagram. AoIR Selected Papers of Internet Research.

Miller, D. (2011). Tales from Facebook. Polity Press.

Roberts, J. A., & David, M. E. (2023). On the outside looking in: Social media intensity, social connection, and user well-being: The moderating role of passive social media use. *Canadian Journal of Behavioural Science / Revue Canadienne Des Sciences Du Comportement*, 55(3), 240–252. https://doi-org.ezproxy.server.hv.se/10.1037/cbs0000323

Savnal, K. (2021). "It looks better on Instagram": Networked photography and public art in Mumbai. AoIR Selected Papers of Internet Research.

Shannon, C. S. (2022). #Family: Exploring the Display of Family and Family Leisure on Facebook and Instagram. Leisure Sciences, 44(4), 459–475. https://doi.org/10.1080/01490400.2019.1597792

Simatzkin-Ohana, L., & Frosh, P. (2022). From user-generated content to a user-generated aesthetic: Instagram, corporate vernacularization, and the intimate life of brands. Media, Culture & Society, 44(7), 1235–1254. https://doi.org/10.1177/01634437221084107

Interstitial Dialogues: A Phenomenology of News-Comments

MJ O'Leary

Liverpool John Moores University, UK

m.j.oleary@ljmu.ac.uk

Abstract: This paper presents findings from a study that examined the phenomenological detail of the reading process involved in everyday encounters with news microposts. In recent decades, reading the news has become characterised by the micro-texts of social media, but the fine-grained detail of this encounter as a *reading experience* is often overlooked. In a series of reading exercises, long-form news articles and short-form news comments were shown to structure different experiences in terms of meaning and dialogue. These differences were linked to the specific layout of the texts within the website interface. The high volume of negative space surrounding the comments explained the dialogical mode by which the participant-readers made sense of these texts. The findings contribute to understandings of social media as phatic communication and challenge pessimistic accounts that link micro-texts to a decline in critical engagements with the news.

Keywords: Microposts, News comments, Reading experience, Phenomenology, Interface, News layout

1. Introduction

Today, almost half of British and American adults consume news in the form of a social media micropost (Pew Research, 2022; Ofcom, 2023). The micropost is, on average, only 300 characters long, yet it has come to define much public activity online. This paper aims to provide a phenomenological description of the reading process involved in encounters with digital micro-texts. By comparing the experience of reading news-articles with reading user-comments, it attempts to move beyond a concern for the linguistic content of these texts to the experiential structures underpinning our reading of them. The findings reveal how certain material aspects of media texts can enable or constrain experiences of dialogue and meaning while reading them. In recent decades, social media has become an important source of discursive, and often polarising power in society (Törnberg et al, 2016). For this reason, the discourses carried by social media microposts have received much attention (Bouvier, 2016; Papacharissi, 2012). Newspaper user comments are a well-established form of social media and provide a particularly rich source of data for discourse analysis. In an overview, Reimer et al, (2023), highlight the varied themes and linguistic patterns that characterise them, however, there is a growing interest in understanding the micropost beyond its semantic and deliberative aspects (Moores, 2019). In terms of the materiality of the micropost, much research points to a decline in the critical reasoning skills associated with long-form texts. Carr (2010) argues that short texts can only produce 'shallow' emotional reactions while Torppa et al. (2020) find that reading digital 'fragments' scores badly on recall and reflection. Likewise, Hakemulder and Mangen (2024) find the more a user reads short texts on screen, the less likely they are to find existential meaning in them. Nonetheless, collections of microposts (e.g. hashtags), are found to provide vital phatic and affective communication among marginalised groups (Papacharissi, 2014). Taken together, these accounts go some way towards explaining what microposts mean for individuals and for society. However, much remains unspecified about the fine-grained phenomenology of an encounter with the micropost in the digital everyday. Phenomenology is a philosophical method concerned with the ontological structures that undergird the quotidian human-world experience (Husserl, 1970). Phenomenologies of reading reveal the internal structures of the reading process in mid-flow. Wolfgang Iser (1993) identified the virtual gaps, or 'indeterminacies', in narrative detail that prompt heightened meaning-making in the reading experience. In a more material conception of indeterminacies, Genette (1987) identified the role that the negative space surrounding a text plays in conditioning the reading experience. The impact of 'gaps' on digital reading is a central concern in user experience (UX) (Bollini, 2017), but is often overlooked in media and news studies. In this present study, 'gaps' were identified as a central feature of the encounter with microposts via the in-screen layout of the news interface. Website designers aim to offer a 'smooth' user experience in which the interface only registers in the background of user awareness (Bollini, 2017). However, in this paper, the impact of the in-screen layout of microposts is brought into relief. The discussion, therefore, evokes medium theory and questions about the power of technology to determine perception (McLuhan, 1959). However, the position taken in this present study recognises the co-constitutive nature of human agency and technology (Healy, 2020).

2. Interpretative Phenomenology and Reading Case Studies

The findings presented in this paper emerged from a set of reading exercises conducted with participants involved in a wider phenomenological project. The project entailed four participant-case-studies and examined the relationship between media devices and inter/subjectivity in everyday life. The study spanned four years, involved field work in several countries, and was undertaken in English and Spanish. Further information can be seen in Figure 1. As part of this research, ten individual reading exercises were set up to capture the phenomenological elements of 'in-the-thick-of-it' encounters with news microposts. They involved participant and researcher sitting in one of the participants' own everyday settings (at home or at work) and reading newspaper articles and user comments together on one of their usual devices. Each exercise lasted between two and three hours. Situational and embodied data was captured in field notes and the ensuing dialogues were audio-recorded.

The broader project was guided by the principles of an interpretative form of phenomenology. Interpretative phenomenological analysis (IPA; Smith, 2004), is a methodological perspective inspired by the philosophical writings of Husserl (1970), Heidegger (2010) and Gadamer (2013). It requires a focus on the fundamental categories of existence such as *space, time, materiality, and embodiment,* while also accepting the positionality of both researcher and researched, as well as the provisional nature of research findings (Gadamer, 2013). In its empirical mode it therefore pursues something of an anti-method method in its commitment to naturalistic, immersive, and participatory research (Gadamer, 2013). Consequently, the reading exercises in this study were deliberately informal, conversational, and exploratory.

During these exercises we read a selection of news articles and user comments drawn from the participants' own regular news reading habits. 'News' was conceived of broadly as the thematic content within both the news articles and reader commentary published on the newspaper websites. Texts were selected from popular national newspapers in the participants' home countries. The newspapers exist as paper broadsheets as well as websites, and range from the centre left to the centre right in political orientation. It is important to note, however, that the political meaning of these newspapers and their articles are not central to the analysis, where *medium* rather than *press-media* is key. At the same time, however, to allow for some thematic coherence, and to avoid more inflammatory posts, we chose articles discussing the topic of housing (Harlow, 2015). Preliminary examination of the newspapers showed that the news and user comments tended to share some basic tenets of liberal capitalism and a vocabulary of 'civil' debate when discussing housing. Each article ran between 500-2000 words in length and offered at least five reader comments.

Participants/ Social and situational contexts	Maggie	Lola	Alice	Jed
Gender, Sexuality, Family	Cis, heterosexual woman, married, pregnant at time of research	Cis, heterosexual woman, mother of young children, recently divorced	Cis, heterosexual woman, mother of young children on maternity leave at time of research	Cis, heterosexual man, widow, grown-up children
Age	35-55	35-55	35-55	35-55
Ethnicity & Interaction Language	White, Irish (Living in Australia); English	White, Spanish (Living in Spain); Spanish	White, Spanish (Living in Spain); Spanish	White, Irish (Living in Ireland); English
Social Class / Background	Parents in manual labour	Parents in manual labour	Parents in manual labour	Parents small-business owners
Education & Profession	MA - Public Servant (Health)	PhD - Scientist (Chemistry lab)	BA - Secondary School Teacher and fiction writer	MA – Builder and Property Developer
Reading exercise settings, newspaper, and devices	*The Irish Times*, at home, at work office, on laptop	*El País*, at home with young children, on mobile phone	*El País, El Mundo*, at local cafés, at home, mobile phone	*The Irish Times*, at office, on desk top computer

Figure 1: This figure presents the relevant social and setting aspects of the participant-case-studies

Figure 1 illustrates various aspects of the case studies. The participant-case-study approach is recommended in IPA because the huge volume of contextual data required for analysis precludes larger samples (Smith, 2003, p. 54). Participants were recruited through the researcher's own extended personal networks based on the IPA criterion that some minimal shared lifeworld understandings of what *reading microposts means* is required as a starting point for inquiry (Gadamer, 2013). The Jefferson Transcription system was used because it captures subtle verbal, setting and embodied details that go unnoticed in other styles.

3. Finding 1: Microposts and Body Talk

In this study, reading the micropost was an experience of heightened embodied and verbal expression. During the reading exercises, each participant lifted, touched, and moved their devices while reading the comments; they also continuously moved around in their seated or standing positions, and frequently invited the researcher to read and respond to the comments. Likewise, they expressed several emotional responses and several different verbal commentaries while reading them.

> *Maggie is sitting with her feet up on the bed and the laptop in her lap. After reading the news article, she begins eating a biscuit, dropping crumbs on the mouse pad. She brushes the crumbs away and points to the screen about something she 'loves' [a micropost about EU legislation]: "And then I love this kind of detail as well, that goes back to, for example, bits of policy or legislation." She sits up higher on the bed and tilts the laptop towards me to emphasise her point, nodding, chewing, laughing, and pointing.*

> *Fieldnote memo, Melbourne*

The significance of the activity described here is underscored by its comparison to the restrained mode in which each participant had read the preceding news articles. Just moments before reading the comments, each participant read the corresponding news article in almost total silence. Some held their breath, others sighed loudly - each physically constrained their movements until they reached the end of the article. The below fieldnote captures Jed reading news about a housing shortage in Ireland:

> *Jed leans into his computer screen, squints his eyes, holds the mouse lightly, his index finger hovering, holding his breath. He reads quickly and impatiently, appearing to skim along the lines, finally sitting back in his chair, folding his hands in his lap, he swivelled around on his chair and looked at me, waiting for something.*

> *Fieldnotes memo, Cork*

This difference suggests that the readers were enacting a *dialogic* experience while reading the comments, and a *monologic* one while reading the news. Understanding texts is described phenomenologically as a type of dialogue, one involving a sharing of meaning (Gadamer, 2013). Theories of dialogue define it as a mutual, open and polysemic interaction (Wegerif, 2007), while embodiment is that pre-verbal aspect of dialogue that communicates understanding through gesture and kinetic movement (Fletcher, 2014). A monologic encounter is underpinned by one authoritative voice and exclusion of alternative perspectives (Wegerif, 2007). In these terms, Maggie's corporal activity suggests a dialogue in motion, while her comments evince a sense of meaning being shared. The silent and constrained article readings on the other hand, suggest that the readers were being addressed in a uni-directional manner by a journalist-expert who did not invite response.

4. Finding 2: Existential Meaning

Analysis also suggests that reading the microposts was underpinned by an experience of existential meaning, understood as a full sense of meaning and relevance to core values (Gadamer, 2013). This was evident in the many anecdotes, verbalised reasoning, and descriptive and emotional narratives that the participants offered at different points *while* reading comments. Below is the opening sentence of one of many longer anecdotes provided by Lola.

> *Lola Last summer we were visiting J's [husband] best friend in Mallorca. We were talking about the children when she started to say [...] her husband works, and that her husband's colleagues leave the office 'on time', 'they leave work on time!' [...]*

The above anecdote spanned over one whole page of the transcriptions and was offered by Lola in the middle of her reading news comments about the eviction of a family from their home in Madrid. It suggests she is attempting to make-sense of the eviction based on the evictee's income and work-life practices. The emotional excitement and colourful narrative offered here, as well as the many other instances in the transcripts, suggest that the readers were undergoing a full 'sense' of significance and core values while reading the comments. By contrast, as mentioned above, each participant read the news articles in almost complete silence. Moreover, each participant showed signs of struggle when asked for a summary or an opinion of the article, even just after reading it. Below Alice attempts to summarise a news article in *El País* after I had to press her to offer a response:

> Alice   Eh, yeah, it's about [...] it's about evictions, it tells the real-life story of a woman, but it's about evictions. There is a charity to help these people. They also talk about the price of renting, it has completely sky-rocketed in Madrid, and also, em, there is another property bubble forming, because the rent is so high that you just get a mortgage instead. But it also talks about things I don't understand.

But Jed's response perhaps sums up the experience best:

> Jed   To comment on the whole tone of the article, it's blah blah blah.

These quotes suggest that in the absence of a sense of any perceived *existential* meaning, the participants' struggled to translate the news texts into any coherent *discursive* meaning. Since the news articles and comments on housing were selected for their tonal, linguistic, and political similarities, these findings beg the question, What aspects of the texts can account for this difference in reading them?

5.   Finding 3: Interstitial Dialogue

The research analysis suggests that the structure of the digital *interface* played a key role in defining the kind of experience a reader had when reading the news online. The prevalence of short sentences used in microposts, together with the gaps between individual posts, resulted in a higher volume of negative space in the interface. This layout facilitated what I call an *interstitial dialogue* between reader and micropost and was key to the activation of the heightened embodied activity and sense-making in the reading exercises. Much like Iser's (1993) gaps, my interpretation is that the negative space *between* the comments enforced spatial and temporal pauses in the reading process which in turn provided opportunities for reflection and sense-making by the readers. This finding was especially evident in the relationship between the participants' utterances and silences in the audio recordings. Figure 2 is an attempt to visually represent this relationship. The brackets and straight arrows show *when* verbal and embodied expressions occurred during the reading, as well as their corresponding 'spaces'. This *when* was estimated based on the detail in the utterance that suggested which comment it is responding to thematically – the *what* - and is shown by the dash-line arrows. Silences, understood in the context as reading time, are underlined. The 3D rectangles try to bring the taken-for-granted negative space into the foreground to illustrate its relevance to the unfolding dialogue. Linking these different points throughout the transcripts revealed a dialogic 'to and fro' meshwork of arrows in the sections dedicated to the comments, but little to no arrows in the sections related to the news article. Thus, Figure 2 demonstrates the emergence of meaning and dialogue from the interstices between the microposts, rather than from the posts themselves. The low volume of negative space in the long-form article explains the constrained and meaning-less experience in reading it.

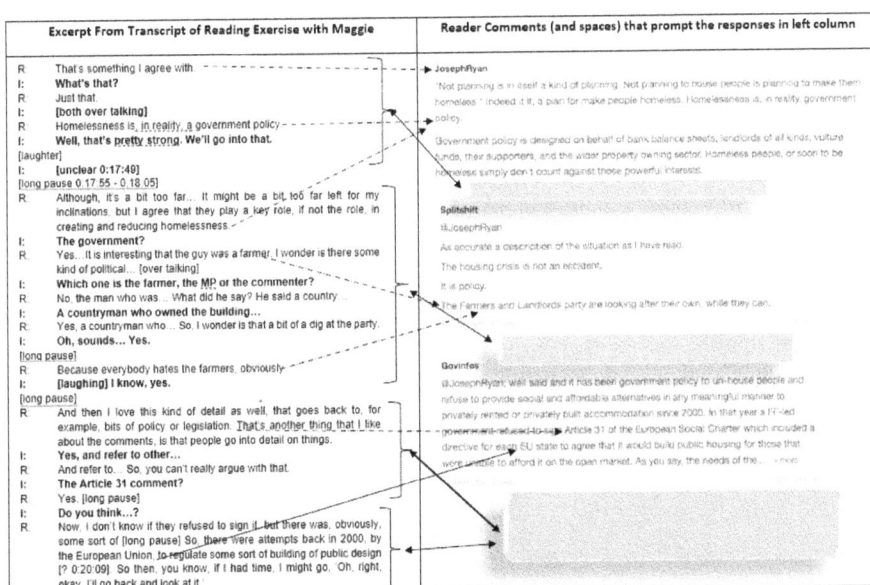

Figure 2: This shows the interrelations between space and participant utterances

6. Discussion – Conclusion

The phenomenological descriptions provided here offer new insight into various claims about the micropost. The embodied dialogue that the participants experienced extends our understanding of 'phatic communication' (Papacharissi, 2014) by showing how connection first manifests as an individual reader's kinetic, emotional, and verbal engagement with the *form* of the micropost, rather than its content or social features. Secondly, the experience of meaningfulness evident in reading the microposts refutes the findings by Hakemulder and Mangen, (2024) that readers of shorter texts are less likely to seek and find existential meaning. By utilising a lens that investigates the experience *subtending* content-level engagement, this study found exactly the opposite case and can hopefully supply new questions for quantitative researchers of digital meaningfulness. Equally, the findings challenge the claim that microposts play a role in the loss of critical reasoning by showing the complexity and nuance in the sense-making that occurs while reading news posts. Finally, the study suggests that official news content may benefit more from a redesign of negative space then from a shift towards more 'sensationalist' content to facilitate a meaningful reading experience.

References

Bollini, L. (2017) "Beautiful interfaces. From user experience to user interface design", *The Design Journal*, Vol 20, Sup1, pp S89-S101.

Carr, N. (2010) *The shallows: How the internet is changing the way we think, read and remember,* Atlantic Books Ltd., London.

Bouvier, G. (2016) *Discourse and social media,* Routledge, London.

Fletcher, N.M. (2014) "Body Talk, Body Taunt-Corporeal Dialogue within a Community of Philosophical Inquiry", *Analytic Teaching and Philosophical Praxis*, Vol 35, No. 1, pp 10-25.

Gadamer, H.G. (2013) *Truth and method,* A&C Black, London.

Genette, G. (1997) *Paratexts: Thresholds of interpretation,* Cambridge University Press, Cambridge.

Hakemulder, F. and Mangen, A. (2024) "Literary Reading on Paper and Screens: Associations Between Reading Habits and Preferences and Experiencing Meaningfulness", *Reading Research Quarterly*, Vol 59, No. 1, pp.57-78.

Healy, P. (2020) "Living with Technology: Human Enhancement or Human Development?", *Cosmos & History*, Vol 16, No. 2, pp 357-369.

Heidegger, M. (2010) *Being and Time,* Suny Press, New York.

Husserl, E. (1970) *The Crisis of European Sciences and Transcendental Phenomenology: An Introduction to Phenomenological Philosophy*, Northwestern University Press, Illinois.

Iser, W. (1993) *The fictive and the imaginary: Charting literary anthropology,* Johns Hopkins University, Baltimore.

Kim, D. H., and Desai, M. (2021) "Are Social Media Worth It for News Media? Explaining News Engagement on Tumblr and Digital Traffic of News Websites", *International Journal on Media Management,* Vol 23, No. 1–2, pp 2–28.

McLuhan, M. (1959) "Myth and mass media", *Daedalus*, Vol 88, No. 2, pp.339-348.

Ofcom (2023) "News Consumption in the UK: 2023", (Online) https://www.ofcom.org.uk/__data/assets/pdf_file/0024/264651/news-consumption-2023.pdf [Accessed 09/04/2024].

Moores, S. (2019) *Media and everyday life in modern society,* Edinburgh University Press, Edinburgh.

Papacharissi, Z. (2014) *Affective Publics: Sentiment, Technology, and Politics,* Oxford Academic, New York.

Pew Research Centre (2023) "Social Media and News Fact Sheet" (Online) https://www.pewresearch.org/journalism/fact-sheet/social-media-and-news-fact-sheet/ [Accessed 09/04/2024].

Reimer, J., Häring, M., Loosen, W., Maalej, W. and Merten, L. (2023) "Content analyses of user comments in journalism: A systematic literature review spanning communication studies and computer science", *Digital Journalism*, Vol 11 No.7, pp 1328-1352.

Smith, J.A. (2004) "Reflecting on the development of interpretative phenomenological analysis and its contribution to qualitative research in psychology", *Qualitative research in psychology*, Vol 1, No. 1, pp 39-54.

Törnberg, A. and Törnberg, P. (2016) "Muslims in social media discourse: Combining topic modelling and critical discourse analysis", *Discourse, Context & Media*, Vol 13, pp 132-142.

Torppa, M., Niemi, P., Vasalampi, K., Lerkkanen, M.K., Tolvanen, A. and Poikkeus, A.M. (2020) "Leisure reading (but not any kind) and reading comprehension support each other—A longitudinal study across grades 1 and 9", *Child development*, Vol 91, No.3, pp.876-900.

Wegerif, R. (2007) *Dialogic Education and Technology,* Springer, New York.

Late Submissions

Deconstructing Digital Rhetoric to Face Geopolitical Challenges: A Social Media Narrative Analysis Framework

Maria-Magdalena Popescu

Carol I National Defense University, Bucharest, Romania

popescu.maria@myunap.net

Abstract: Skyrocketing technological advancement along with changes in environment dynamics allowed people, states and governments to influence each other's diplomacy, security and international relations, using words and images, strings of events, to construct narratives. The rhetoric of power and conflict is distributed in chameleonic volatile environments, targeting members of the society to challenge security status and power balance, while new media instruments feed people's thirst for information to challenge their beliefs into tailoring attitudes and behaviours. Defined by many as a "portrayal of events surrounding change" (Dunford and Jones, 2000) or as "central feature of modern influencing across borders (Wagnsson and Lundström, 2023) in a continuous "battle", (Van Noort, 2017), strategic narratives bear multiple meanings, generated by the versatility of the digital dissemination channels. Understanding these meanings enlighten many directions, like international relations, diplomacy and politics, resulting in risk-free engagement, vulnerability- awareness and controlled decision-making policies, just by using narrative analysis as the appropriate instrument. However, the classical analytical models do not provide enough lenses to grasp all the components generating meaning in a digitally disseminated content and many features are thus ignored, mutilating paramount intelligence otherwise needed to complete the picture. That is why, this paper advances a model framework for a digital narrative analysis that looks at components of the textual narrative backed by the features of the environment, the characteristics of the audience and the dynamics of the dissemination, coupled with more recent social media metrics. To this end, we reviewed literature on Russian formalism (Propp, 1928), (Tomashevsky, 1965) structuralist narratology (Todorov 1969, Genette 1988, Bal 1977), poststructuralism (Chatman,1978) and postclassical narratology (Herman, Fludernik, 1999) to the most recent digitally related approaches (Georgakopoulou, 2020), (Bal, 2021) and then advanced our analysis framework that adds specific traits which social media environments enhance. We thus intend to contribute to the large body of literature with an analytical model, to render a mould of the strategic narratives in the security, defence, politics and international relations.. This paper is part of a larger study, the framework will be piloted in further research, where data will be gathered to validate the model.

Keywords: Strategic narratives, Digital rhetoric, Social media, Resilience, Analysis framework, Geopolitical challenges

1. Background

The ubiquity of handheld devices beyond barriers of age, demographics or geopolitics has transferred dialogues in the online environment, calling this communication 2.0. As a result, any type of human interaction is most frequently unfolded via images and words, while "narrative" and "rhetoric" have become buzz words. These appeal to a myriad of means to coagulate or polarise, to deceive and influence, to change behaviour and shatter confidence in a continuous exchange of information. Dialogues build on language whose syntax is different, shorter and simpler, while lexis is more versatile, changing meaning with every context it inhabits. Visuals are prevalent in front of the words, sounds and multimedia are better message vessels than words, even if this is done implicitly. The message, whose social context index has lowered its relevance in decoding, is able to regenerate itself and change form through user generated content, while control over shared information tends to zero.

Supported by this, international relations unfold differently now, focusing on visibility and transparency in decisions and measures. Governments have turned in favour of extra-linguistic communication with forms that do not replace language, they complete it instead, illuminate it, supplement it (Cohen, 1987), and cultivate foreign public opinion through soft power, through positive attraction and persuasion, to accomplish foreign affair goals through narratives, as a more attractive means, with cooperation rather than force, using the "ability to influence the behaviour of others to get the outcomes you want" (Nye, 2004). They thus develop an interaction at international actors' level, through personalities, organisations and institutions (Mavrodieva, Aleksandrina V., Okky K. Rachman, Vito B. Harahap, and Rajib Shaw, 2019) that meets goals in digital environments.The forms taken by the digital messages, narratives constructed with certain rhetoric, are delivered with a variation of decoding opportunities to allow engagement in digital interactions. (Bjola and Manor, 2024)

Multiplicity of meaning triggers ambiguity, and this sometimes might be a serious factor to impact diplomatic relations. Politicians use rhetoric to gain legitimation or the public acceptance of policy, as "rhetoric influences fundamental elements of grand strategy such as defining national interests, identifying threats, proposing policy options, and mobilising audiences (Goddard and Krebs,2015). Rhetoric is the art of persuading an audience using various language devices. The latter ones are contained in narratives , i.e. in stories that bear meaning and impact the audience as such. Similar to narratives, as vessels of meaning, rhetoric, as a delivering strategy, can also be expressed as speech, text or image.

These are among the most serious reasons why a more complex understanding of the narrative is needed, to ensure a complete apprehension among participants, be they society at large or leaders in international relations, especially since the audience in transmedia is not represented by "readers, players or spectators but invariably fans, a term that suggests fanatic and uncritical devotion to story worlds" (Ryan, 2016)

Secondly, the online environment makes ambiguity prevalent over precision, while ever evolving technologies ubiquitously invade the public sphere, bearing marks on what public engagement was before; openness is more valuable than politeness, emotion is blamed to the detriment of reasoning, discreteness is sold for transparency. All these generate confusion, scaffolded by the characteristics of the online environment where "information overload, visual enhancement, emotional framing, algorithmic-driven engagement" (Bjola, C., Cassidy, J., & Manor, I. 2019) trigger a rise in the number of social movements, with impact on geopolitics, international relations, diplomacy and individuals (Kay, Freely, 2013). People's interaction has changed patterns of communication, styles of interaction, relationships, actions and decisions in the international online environment. As a consequence, diplomatic dynamics may suffer and geopolitics may be translated into a different framework of analysis, threatened by narratives decoded with inappropriate digital keys.

In this context, while large bodies of literature perform critical discourse analysis on international, state or non-state actors` speeches that construct realities or change behaviours through social media, little has been said, yet, about the architecture of information building up strategic narratives, especially when international relations are at stake. The present paper draws on narratology and social media metrics to generate a two tier analytical model for the digital strategic content that impacts power relationships and re-calibrates geopolitics of information. The aim is to bring forth an assessment model that can transfer narrative analysis into the social media environment, where the message should be looked at from a variety of angles, garnering a more complex understanding, especially since current conflicts bear chameleonic changes and challenges, capitalising on words, images and their semiotics.

To meet our goal, we formulated the research question that sets the ground of this paper: What elements should an analytical framework include for a social media narrative analysis to cover all the meaning-generated components in a message, looking at the features of the textual narratology and the metrics of the virtual dissemination environment ?

To answer this question, we reviewed the most representative contributions to textual narratology based on an evolutionary approach. Also, more recent contributions have been called forth, to add the variables brought by the digital characteristics. Integration of the recurrent features and then of the specific digital environment ones resulted in an analytical framework applicable to strategic narratives in social media environments.The use of the resulted model consists in sensible intelligence better revealed, compared to a critical discourse analysis, as a reflection of the concept "good stories are the basis of excellent sociology" (Clegg, 1993) The model will be validated in further research case studies.

2. Textual Narrative Analysis- Narratologists' Evolutionary Linear Approach

While social networks can be used with positive narratives but equally with terror and fear incentives through negative messages, a multi-faceted, multi-strata analysis framework is needed, to let users understand the new form messages take and how an online identity can trigger changes in social behaviour, how it can perform social influence or generate engagement and activism. The analysis should focus on the fluidity of messages that coagulate into narratives, appealing to emotions, to values, to individuals' collective unconsciousness, on the strategies used, by placing targeted individuals in new contexts and giving them new meanings, the meanings intended by the sender. In what follows we will look at textual narrative frameworks and their applicability to online environments.

Considered by most authors as being connected to literary studies, narratives have now become "a type of story that gives meaning to a series of events and occurrences" *(Cobaugh,2019)*. The precursor of this vision was Todorov's *narrative as a universe of representations* (1969), a vision reflective of the social media environments considering its characteristics- fluidity, multimedia content, versatility and volatility of messages brought by the user generated content possibility. Also, *multimedia communication environments* rely heavily on the user-generated -content in conversations, replacing feelings, ideas, attitudes, reactions, metaphors, dialogues, practically a substitute for anything language meant in real interactions.

If authors in the past saw narratives as structures that have *an actor, an action, an intention, a scene, and an instrument* (Burke, 1969), Todorov (1971) adds *equilibrium* (setting and characters presented), *disruption* (sudden outburst that brings imbalance), *recognition* (of the disruption, by the narrator or character, by action), then *resolution* (agent in a quest to restore the equilibrium), and a *new equilibrium* (reached by the character and the plot development) with concluding insight. These elements are useful in analysing the larger frame of a narrative, composed of multiple stories or multiple posts on the same topic, possibly with different meanings, where the action and its evolution can be traced, where the topic is revealed along with the actors involved, through the way they relate to one another and through their position to the topic and to each other.

Focusing on a smaller scale or taking sequences of events that contribute to the whole picture, the narrative content has a *story, plot and pattern* (Forster,1927) ; *story* is similar to what Prince (2003) would later define as 'the set of narrated situations and events in their chronological sequence", where *plot* is defined by the causal connection between events in a story and *pattern* is rendered by the connection between time and recurrent causality. The importance of the effect the plot has upon the *audience* was brought by Friedman (1955) who focuses on *who sees the story, how and with what effect* (i.e.mainly the receiver of the message). For Metz (1974) on the other hand, narrative characteristics add extra elements like music or voice-over, proper to movies, as a precursor of a social media narrative. These aspects complement features designed as important by Labov's model (1972). Actually Labov's vision best describes the live messages, the videos posted in social media and the photos as well, as follows: the *abstract*, seen as summary of the events, anchors the audience's attention and stirs interest, and this is actually the introductory text to any posting in social media; the *orientation* is materialised in the tagging, the check-in and the title of the post; the *complicating action* is composed of events in the narrative, more events in a row, connected in a causal relationship and represented by share of thoughts, statements or actions. The *resolution* is more difficult to be identified in a non-textual narrative, due to the fluidity of the medium (online environment). *Evaluation* of the narrative content can be performed, according to Labov, in several ways, internally (while the story takes place) or externally, after the story is consumed, while an embedded evaluation can be provided by a character in the narrative or indirectly, through another event. Evaluation of the narrative generates another narrative in its turn, as it materialises in comments with text, reactions, i.e. sentiment and also reactions using other posts, photos, GIFs, memes. The value of the story and its real message is always given by the *coda* as Labov calls it, mentioning the connection between the story, the real time and real life events.

If the previous approaches look at the **narrative text,** Genette (1980) considers the **narrator's perspective** and adds more features: *mood* (to show the detailed precision in a narrative and the accuracy of the information conveyed) , *function* (speaks about the narrator who tells the story himself, or interrupts the one who does it and gets involved, showing the source of information, the precision and emotions), *voice* (the narrator as a character or as a presenter), *time* (what happened, what is going to happen or things as happening), *speed* (shows higher or lower intention to the narrative text)and *frequency of events* (seen as the number of times an event occurs in the story or the number of times this is mentioned in the narrative) These elements can be considered in relation to multiple postings and seen as events that create a narrative on a social media wall. In this respect, Genette (1980) mentions three categories :*Singulative narration*, for one or n times narrating what happened once or *n* times (in terms of multiple postings covering the same topic). *Repeating narrative*: Recounting more than once what happened once. *Iterative narrative*: Relating one time what happened several times (in terms of various events coagulated into one significant topic and unique but polyphonic posting) *The order of the narrated event*s is important, since it gives information on the dynamics of the narrative, on the evolution or involution of topic's importance in a story development. This can easily be monitored based on the information gathered from the sharing activity. Placing stories in a narration, in a certain order of events, has an explanatory role as well, stirring curiosity among the targeted individuals.

Beside the narrator's perspective, along with his performance in the story, Bal (1997) advances the important **role of the character** *inside* the narration along with functions he can get, like a helper or an opponent, a sender or a receiver. Bal makes the distinction between a narrative text which tells a story, where a story is a series of related events, connected by causality and an event which is the transition from one state to another, in the story. Herman was yet the one who looked at cognitive sciences, just like Fludernik (1996) who saw narrative as an experience stored emotionally, since its meaning can generate emotions and reactions based on the content inside. Herman (2002) contributes to the vision seeing that humans, both readers and receivers, co-create worlds of stories based on common experiences, about current or future events. In Herman's view, the individual is both a narrator and a subject of the story. Transposing this in the mediatic realm, the speaker's identity arises out of discursive interactions and by looking at narratives through analytical lenses one can draw the identity of the main actors inside, as Thornborrow and Coates (2005) put it. Therefore, our framework will contribute to a deeper understanding of the main actors' identity in their handling of strategic narratives.

What differentiates a strategic narrative from a textual narrative and what overlaps is seen by Miskimmon, O'Loughlin and Roselle (2013) as : "representations of a sequence of *events and identities, a communicative tool* through which political actors—usually elites—attempt to give determined meaning to past, present, and future in order to achieve political objectives. Critically, strategic narratives integrate interests and goals—they articulate end states and suggest how to get there". Events are what the content in social media is mainly focusing on, identities are imagistic, built from the interactions and dialogue, built from the content disseminated. All these communicate about something and communicate to someone, at all times, while their logic allows the sender to accomplish planned goals. This, translated in the fluid social media environment, is completed by Arduser's view (2014) that looks at the characters' position inside a narrative, in relation to each other and to the events, measuring *interactions, relations* and *ties,* to judge dynamics, to see the architecture of social networks beyond the dialogue, exchanged information and sentiment analysis measured in reactions, format used for emotional exchange and metrics of participants and their role in the whole manifestation. These metrics generate adjacent information about the content, more data about the characters and supplementary lenses to understand the implications and the effects the message bears.

3. Digital Narrative Analysis- Narratologists' Multi Perspective Approach

The multi-dimensional analysis model we propose for decoding narratives in social media considers both characteristics taken from the most important textual models (as seen above) and features from the social media analysis perspective. Added to the textual narrative characteristics, we now follow with a literature review on digital environment features. In this respect, Granovetter (1973, 2012), Coser (1975), Burt (1992, 2004), Borgatti & Halgin (2011) concentrate more on the **online imagistic identities** and look at the importance of *ties* and their impact over the posting's itinerary and dissemination force, they look at *social interactions*, with particular focus on the concepts of time, place, person and the context of engagement. Speaking about ties, Haythornthwaite (2002) sees them as the foundation of social networks, as they bear a strong influence upon communicators and help disseminate important exchanges, while weak ties impact communicators in being dependent on protocols established by others. Weak ties are unable to self-sustain due to poor and low frequency exchanges.

Alternatively, Bamberg (2012) looks at narratives from several other perspectives. First of all, stories are seen as components of bigger interactive pictures, the topic narrative, as we would call it, to differentiate.In this context, along characteristics related to the text itself, the social media analysis looks at elements connected to *performance of the actors* in the story, like gestures, posture, facial expression and gaze, to be included, while the actors themselves (mentioned as well), are situated in certain focal places, taking part in certain suggestive events (both of them mentioned). It is important that the analysis nominates these and sets them in relation to one another. Beyond that, the story itself follows the structural linear pattern, considering the plot elements, but the modality of telling is added to this (Georgakopoulou,2007). Going deeper, the author mentions *time* (with a reference to the teller's orientation-present, past or future, especially since there could be more tellers involved in more interactions and possessing various visions to the world) and *place* as well, to be most important in an interaction. Speaking about actors, *identities* are to be analysed from their role and the way they participate, their style of telling. Wortham(2000) and Georgakopoulou (2013) add the importance of *recurring language* to these approaches, along with a selection of *how deeds are presented*, which gives importance to the *actors' social position* and shows the way the social role builds a representative meaning for the interconnected audiences and users.

Later on, Georgakopoulou (2017) completes the analysis framework with a reference to the *content sharing practices* (notifications on *actor's recent activity,* on his *localization and tagging,* assessment of actors' attitude, *activity or emotional state,* and reference to their relationships) as well as to the *rescripting practices* (visual and verbal transformation of already existent stories, to generate new stories, by framing the original to adapt it to a larger different audience. We can mention here the *memes, mashups or parodies*) and *story's distribution* across sites routinely, after the plots have been recontextualized or redefined with various contributors' input. This gives rise to different meaning-making (Georgakopoulou 2014, 2015b) and represents evidence for the fact that moving a topic into a different context triggers its own meaning-making policies. This might be good for the polyphonics of the text but detrimental for the decoding and feedback. (e.g. Perrino 2017; Blommaert and Varis 2015). Another important aspect in what Georgakopoulou, Iversen, Stage, (2020) call is about the *"Numbers and measurements* [which] have also become crucial aspects of the actual stories shared on social media and their mobilisation of users and action" The above mentioned authors state that all these measuring instruments allowed by the digital platforms to seize the communication process are closely concerned with which stories are good to be shared, with how to do that, with how stories appeal to people and how people in the stories make use of the content to present themselves or their lives to others, by counting *how often, for how long, in which order and where communication takes place.* Conversely, other authors speak about the concept of *metricization* (Lupton 2016; Marres 2017) in relation to the interaction and users' behaviour, to the dialogues and activities participants of the narrative unfold, be they audience, authors, narrators or main characters. The indicators discussed so far allow both automatic and manual recording of metrics, but studies have revealed that computational analysis can even identify topics augmented in social media prior to becoming visible and important in mainstream media, from a combination of opinion, fact and emotion "uttered in anticipation of events that had not yet attained recognition through mainstream media (Papacharissi and Oliveira 2012) Numbers are thus important in narrative analysis, metrics in general, to allow us to get a sense of past and present, to identify the flaws and alleviate them, as Hacking (1990) considered.

4. A Social Media Integrated Narrative Analysis Framework

To put it all into a perspective, let us draw the following representation that emerged after the study of the literature in the field and that integrates all the relevant elements.

The model also stemmed from the need to have an instrument that can assess narratives in social media, given the versatility of dissemination channels and the volatility of the messages with user generated content availability. Moreover, with the uprising weaponization of words and images, with the surge in biometric data available in databases, disinformation and cyber-attacks are on the rise. Current analysis allows users to understand actors and their message, their actions and intentions, all characteristics of the environment. Using this model raises awareness among users, allowing them to become resilient in front of adversities. Since these strategies were scarcely disseminated, allowing for the state and non-state actors to use them against individuals,societies and foreign governments, deconstructing these strategies scaffold better understanding against hostile actions.

4.1 Discussion on Functionality

The analysis model developed subsequent to our literature review and discussion consists of four main clusters of information applicable to the textual narrative and four other main clusters applicable to the digital environment. These are events (consisting of the story itself), actors, narrators and characters' identities on the one hand, and social interaction, non-verbal communication, recent activity monitoring, as well as a meta-perspective evaluation of the events, on the other. Each of the clusters can be understood by looking at their discrete elements, as can be seen in Figure 1 and in the description that follows:

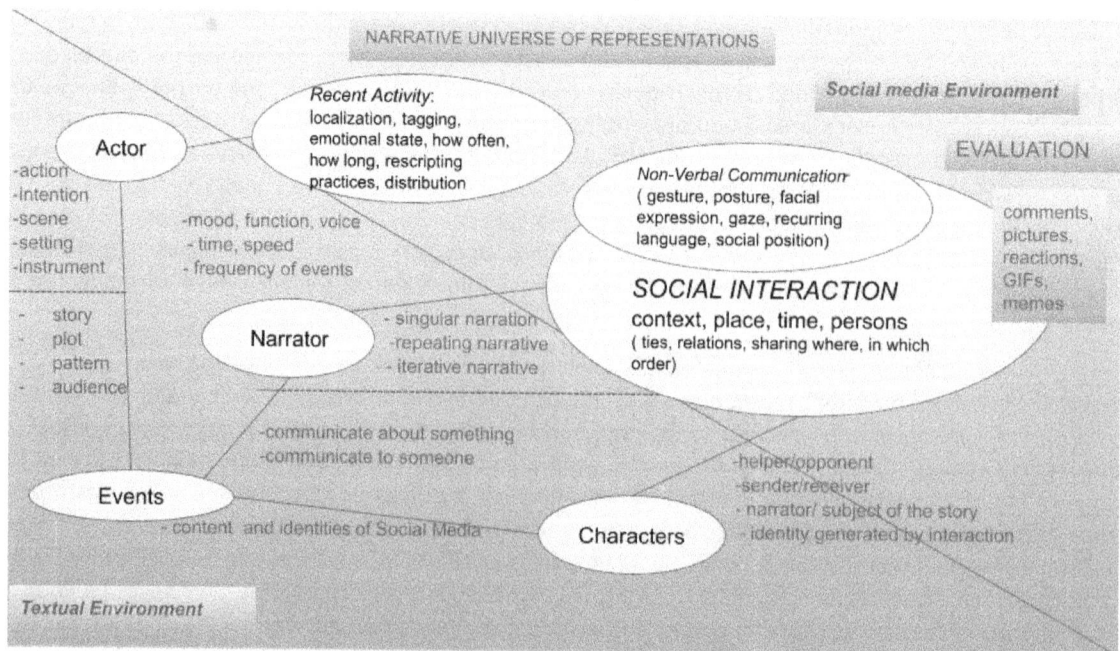

Figure 1: Social media integrated narrative analysis framework - Popescu M.M. (2024)

- **The actor** is usually responsible for the main message of the narrative and for the rhetoric embedded. He has an intention that makes him take action, on a scene and certain setting, while he uses communication (discourse, rhetoric) devices for that purpose. To attain his goal, the actor creates a story that has a certain plot, follows a persuasion pattern. The actor tailors all his message (form and content) to his targeted audience. Behind his story there is always an event that involves other identities, the narrator (s) and the character (s).

- **The narrator** can choose to insist more or less on the narrative he presents (singular/repeating/iterative narration) based on the planned and intended effects but also based on the audience's characteristics. Also, he can choose to just narrate the story or be part of it, presenting something that is developing, that was or will be,or he can just recount someone else's experience. This allows the analysed perspective to be more or less complete or reliable. The frequency of the narrated events and the order in which they are recounted give data for analysis as well.

- **The characters** are those drawing the context of the story, the helpers or the opponents, the senders or the receivers of the narrator's message, the ones who participate in the plot and bring the story back to equilibrium or take the story to another level. Their identity is important in interaction, and it is actually defined by social interaction.

- **Social interaction** concentrates on the narrator and characters defining the context, at a certain time and in a certain place, with certain contributors, yet the third party-contributors to the narration, those that generate comments, posts pictures in return to answer visually, count equally. Thus, the effect of the intended rhetoric and narratives is better seen, through GIFs and memes taken as reactions to the story presented by the narrator and supported by characters. The ties measured through interactions and reactions, through sharings, in which order and to which groups, all facilitate evaluation as well.

- **Non-verbal communication** is here to be seen in relation to the context, the narrator and characters, as all generate evaluation metrics on the quality of social interaction and implicitly on the effects the narration intends on the audience.

- **The recent activity** generates information on the actor's position, his emotional state, his contextual social connections, and from here the suggested framing for the whole story, narration and rhetoric.

- The fourth cluster in each perspective (textual and digital) are self-contained and reflective of all the others mentioned above. Therefore, they are not treated separately as we have included them in the descriptions already performed.

All data is compared to facts in a real-time environment. The research must still consider the difference between the organic, inorganic and viral posts, between the advertising library and the genuine content.

5. Conclusions

In the context of fulminant technological progress corroborated to a continuation of all activities into the digital environment, from communication to entertainment and from international relations and diplomacy to non-kinetic warfare, new assessment tools have to be designed to help us avoid finding ourselves in underestimated contexts that could bear important consequences for society at large. When the most discrete elements that coagulate all actions, be they in real environments or digital arena are the word and the image, constructed in stories, in narratives and delivered following a certain rhetoric, a thorough understanding would reveal data about actors initiating the hostile digital actions (seen today as cognitive or information warfare), about facts and actions, about decisions and plans to unfold. Awareness of all these can contribute to a better resilient attitude members of a society can have. That is why, the current paper comes to present a new model of analysis for a digital narrative, since we all inhabit a digital public sphere, where information is currency, where images have become weapons and where human interaction receives new semiotics.

The new model analyses the strategic narratives in social media, but this paper just advances the theoretical model. Its validation will continue this large study and gather data based on the metrics covered in this framework. The fluidity and evanescence of the digital environment, its volatility, triggered the need for a two sided model, a textual and a digital perspective that, combined, generate information for the general message. The textual angle lends itself to the message, the text per se, with each narrative, from 1 to n in the larger rhetorical discourse, while the Social Media angle is characteristic of the narrator and his characters, with what he does and how he does it in the narratives he builds, but also about what he does in the network where his narratives are, digitally disseminated. Gathering data from a pluralistic perspective allows us to adapt to the new strategies and counteract the new AI driven non-kinetic conflicts, as individuals, as nations and states altogether.

References

Arduser, L.(2014), "Agency in illness narratives: A pluralistic analysis." *Narrative Inquiry* 24, no. 1 : 1-27

Auvinen A. M. (2012) *Social media–the New Power of Political Influence* . Centre for European Studies

Bal, M.(1977). Narratologie (Essais sur la signification narrative dans quatre romans modernes). Paris: Klincksieck.

Bal, M. (1997), Narratology: Introduction to the Theory of Narrative, University of Toronto Press

Bal, M.(2021), Narratology in Practice , University of Toronto Press

Bamberg, M. (2012). Narrative Practice and Identity Navigation. In J. Holstein & J. Gubrium (Eds.), Varieties of Narrative Analysis (pp. 99-125). London: SAGE.

Berman, R. A. (1997) "Narrative theory and narrative development: The Labovian impact" Journal of Narrative and Life History, 7(1-4), 235-244.

Bjola,C.,Cassidy,J.,& Manor,I.(2019).Public diplomacy in the digital age. The Hague Journal of Diplomacy, 14(1-2), 83-101.)

Bjola C and Manor, I (2024), The Oxford Handbook of Digital Diplomacy, OUP

Borgatti, S. & Halgin, D.(2011). On Network Theory. Organization Science.

Burke, K. (1969). A rhetoric of motives. University California Press.

Burt RS.(1992) Structural holes, Cambridge, MA, HArvard University Press

Burt RS, (2004), "Structural holes and good ideas", American. Journal of Sociology, 110:349-399

Chatman, S. (1978). Story and Discourse: Narrative Structure in Fiction and Film. Ithaca: Cornell UP

Clegg, S. (1993). Narrative, power, and social theory. In Narrative and Social Control: Critical Perspectives (pp. 15-46). SAGE Publications

Cobaugh, P. (2019, Narrative warfare, (online) https://medium.com/@paulcobaugh/narrative-warfare-14ab7fa7ef89,

De Fina, A. & Georgakopoulou, A. (2020). "Rethinking Narrative: Tellers, Tales and Identities in Contemporary Worlds". The Cambridge Handbook of Discourse Studies, p. 91-114

De Fina, A. & Perrino, S. (2017). "Storytelling in the Digital Age" Special Issue Narrative Inquiry. Narrative Inquiry. 27. 209-217

Dunford, R. and Jones, D. (2000). Narrative in strategic change. Human relations, 53(9), pp.1207-1226.

Fludernik, M. (1996). Towards a 'Natural' Narratology. London and New York: Routledge

Forster, E. M. (1927). Aspects of the Novel. London: Penguin Books.

Friedman, N. (1955). Forms of the Plot. Journal of General Education. 8: 241-253

Genette, Gérard ([1972] 1980). Narrative Discourse: An Essay in Method. Ithaca: Cornell UP

Genette G. (1988),   Narrative Discourse Revisited. Trans. Jane E. Lewin. Ithaca: Cornell University Press.

Georgakopoulou, A. (2007). Small stories, interaction and identities. Amsterdam: John Benjamins Publishing Company

Georgakopoulou, A. (2013). "Building iterativity into positioning analysis: a practice-based approach to small stories and self." Narrative Inquiry, 23 (1): 89-110.

Georgakopoulou, A. (2014). "Small stories transposition and social media: A micro-perspective on the 'Greek crisis'." Discourse & Society, 25(4), 519–539.

Georgakopoulou, A. (2015). Small Stories Research: Methods – Analysis – Outreach. In A. De Fina, & A. Georgakopoulou (Eds.), The Handbook of Narrative Analysis (pp. 178-193). Hoboken, New Jersey: Wiley Blackwell.

Georgakopoulou, A. (2017). Small stories research: A narrative paradigm for the analysis of social media. The SAGE handbook of social media research methods. London: SAGE, 240-252.

Georgakopoulou, A., Iversen, S., Stage, C, (2020), Quantified Storytelling: A Narrative Analysis of Metrics on Social Media, Springer International Publishing

Goddard,S.and Krebs,R.,(2015), "Rhetoric, Legitimation, and Grand Strategy." *Security Studies* 24, no. 1

Göksu, O. et al, (2021) "Digital Diplomacy: an Evaluation of The Means and Opportunities That Digitalization Brings to Diplomacy" in Digital Siege, Istanbul University Press, 45-67

Granovetter, M. (1973)(2012) " The Strength of Weak Ties". American Journal of Sociology, 78, 1360-1380.

Hacking, I. (1990) The Taming of Chance, Cambridge: Cambridge University

Haythornthwaite, C.(2002) "Strong, Weak, and Latent Ties and the Impact of New Media", The Information Society, 18:5, 385-401

Herman, D.. (Ed), (1999) Narratologies: New Perspectives on Narrative Analysis, Columbus, Ohio State U P

Herman, D., (2002),Story Logic: Problems and Possibilities of Narrative,Lincoln, NE: Univ.of Nebraska Press

Jahn, M.. (2021). Narratology 2.3: A Guide to the Theory of Narrative.English Department, University of Cologne. (online) www.uni-koeln.de/~ame02/pppn.pdf)

Kay S., Freely E. (2013) Social media Heightens Political Risks in Emerging Markets . London, UK

Labov, W. (1972). Language in the inner city Philadelphia: Univ. of Pennsylvania Press

Lupton,D.(2016) "The diverse domains of quantified selves: self-tracking modes and dataveillance", Economy and Society, 45:1, 101-122

Marres, N. (2017). Digital sociology: The reinvention of social research. Polity.

Mavrodieva, A. V., et al. (2019). "Role of Social Media as a Soft Power Tool in Raising Public Awareness and Engagement in Addressing Climate Change" Climate 7, no. 10: 122.

Metz, C. (1974). Language and Cinema, Berlin, Boston: De Gruyter Mouton

Nye, J. (1990) .Bound to Lead: The Changing Nature of American Power; Basic Books: London,UK

Nye, J. (2004) Soft Power: The Means to Success in World Politics; Public Affairs: New York, NY, USA

O'Loughlin, B. & Miskimmon, A. & Roselle, L. (2013). Strategic Narratives: Communication Power and the New World Order. London,Routledge

Papacharissi, Z. & Oliveira, M. (2012). "Affective News and Networks Publics: The Rhythms of News Storytelling on #Egypt". Journal of Communication, Volume 62, Issue 2, April 2012, Pages 266–282

Prince, G.(1973) "Introduction to the study of the narratee". In Jane P. Tompkins (ed.) Reader Response Criticism: From Formalism to Post-Structuralism. Baltimore: Johns Hopkins University Press. 7–25.

Propp, V. (1968). Morphology of the folktale. Svatava Pírková-Jakobsonová, Louis A. Wagner, Alan Dundes (Second edition, revised and edited with a preface by Louis A. Wagner [and a] new introduction by Alan Dundes ed.). Austin.

Radunovic, V. (2022) , "The Geopolitical Internet", in Inter MEDIA, vol 50 issue 2, pg 13-16)

Ryan, M.L. (2016). Transmedia narratology and transmedia storytelling. Artnodes.

Thornborrow, J. & Coates, J. (2005). "The Sociolinguistics of Narrative", Journal of Sociolinguistics 11(1):116-121

Todorov, T. (1971). "The 2 principles of narrative". Diacritics. October 1971 (1): 37–44.

Tomascikova,S.(2009), "Narrative theories and narrative discourse." Bulletin of the Transilvania University of Brasov. Vol. 2 (51) - 2009

Tomashevsky, B. (1965). "Thematics". In L. T. Lemon & M. J. Reis (Eds.), Russian Formalist Criticism: Four Essays (pp. 61–95). University of Nebraska Press.

Van Noort,C., (2017)."Study of strategic narratives:The case of BRICS".Politics and Governance,5(3), pp.121-129.

Varis, P. & Blommaert, J. (2015). "Conviviality and collectives on social media: Virality, memes, and new social structures". Tilburg Papers in Culture Studies, paper 108.

Wagnsson, C. and Lundström, M., (2023). Ringing true? The persuasiveness of Russian strategic narratives. Media, War & Conflict, 16(3), pp.383-400

Wortham,S.(2000)."Interactional positioning and narrative self-construction". Narrative Inquiry, 10 (1):157- 184.

Textism in the Classroom: A Writing Destruction for School Learners in South Africa

Kganathi Shaku

University of South Africa, Pretoria, South Africa

shakukj@unisa.ac.za

Abstract: The rise of the Third Industrial Revolution (3IR) introduced various interactive digital platforms such as computer-mediated communication (CMC). These platforms include social media platforms such as Facebook, WhatsApp, X (formerly known as Twitter), and Instagram. During the exchange of messages, social media users use language distinctively to express their thoughts. Both conventional and non-conventional writing styles manifest. For instance, while others use well-formed language in line with the conventions of a standard language, some use unconventional language, which is termed multiple names such as textism, texteese, and social media language. Since most of the social media users' age profiles match the age group of learners in secondary schools, it became necessary for this study to explore the possible impact of social media on learners' academic writing, particularly in the official indigenous languages of South Africa. This study used a qualitative research approach to explore the impact of social media on learners' writing of the Sepedi language in 10 secondary schools in the Limpopo Province, South Africa. Using focus group interviews and document analysis, the paper discovered that learners' application of writing mechanics such as grammar and punctuation marks are affected by social media. The paper is conceptualised through cultivation theory.

Keywords: Textism, Sepedi language, Social media, Social media effects, Cultivation theory

1. Introduction: Social Media and Language

The technological advancement of the 21st century is centred around the Internet and Internet of Things, which enable the operation of computer-mediated communication (CMC). The CMC facilitates the creation and expansion of social relationships through digital communication platforms such as social media. Social media allows its users to share information (Goldstuck, 2018) and interact either synchronously (having real-time communication with immediate feedback) or asynchronously (posting messages to be attended during the user's spare time). Such social interactions are made possible through social media platforms such as Facebook, WhatsApp, X, Instagram, TikTok, and Snapchat.

Moreover, on social media, language (verbal and non-verbal) is used as a channel through which information and messages are disseminated. According to Datareportal (2023), English is the widely used language on social media worldwide, making it a mutual language between international communities. This makes English to be a dominant language on social media, as compared to other languages. In South Africa, social media users use local languages for communication in addition to English. These local languages include isiZulu, Sepedi, isiNdebele, siSwati, English, isiXhosa, Tshivenda, Sesotho, Afrikaans, Xitsonga, and Setswana (Shaku, 2021).

Researchers such as Crystal (2008), Majola, Pillay, and Hlongwane (2019), and Odey et al. (2014) studied the use of language on social media and reported a distinctive use of language. These studies found that social media users' application of language mechanics differs from the norm. The key findings of the previous studies are that social media is characterised by extensive use of abbreviations, emoticons, shortcuts (word omission), and unconventional grammar. The social media language explained above is termed multiple names such as textism and textese. This paper uses textism to refer to social media language. According to Shortis (2007), textism refers to words written using nonstandard orthography.

Per observation, when social media users send text messages to each other, they often use a special type of register called *textese* (the register that allows the omission of words and the use of *textisms*) (Dyers & Davids, 2015:2; Van Dijk, Van Witteloostuijn, Vasić, Avrutin & Blom, 2016). For instance, social media users usually use English slang language such as *'thanx for reading',* instead of *'thanks for reading'* or *LOL,* as a substitute for *'laughing out loud'*. In comparison, when the Sepedi language (one of the official languages of South Africa) is used on social media, textism also manifests. In such instance, textism appears in the form of unconventional use of grammar and writing style, orthography, and the application of punctuation marks (Shaku, 2021). A case in point, the Sepedi language uses disjunctive orthographic writing (dominated by the writing structure of separating sentential units) (Taljard and Bosch, 2006); however, the orthographic structure of the Sepedi language used on social media is conjunctive (dominated by grouping of sentential units). Therefore, instead of writing *'Sepedi se re: sethokgwa se se tšwago phuti ga se tsebjwe'* (the forest that has a duiker is unknown), one would write *'Sepedi sere: sethokgwa se setšwago phuti gase tsebjwe'*. Furthermore, on social media, punctuation marks are used differently. This appears in a form of extended or exaggerated punctuation marks, and haphazard use of upper and lower cases (Shaku, 2021).

Mittal (2015) and Omar, Miah, and Belmasrour (2014) inform that the kind of language used on social media often has a negative impact on learners' academic writing skills in the classroom. They explain that the continual use of textism negatively affects academic writing mechanics such as punctuation rules, and grammar (morphological and syntactical rules). Their findings reflect the following writing trends in the academic writing of school learners:

- Punctuation errors,
- Capitalisation errors,
- Spelling and typos errors,
- Use of abbreviations (Initialisms) and acronyms; and
- Vowel deletion.

This study explores the impact of social media on secondary school learners' application of writing mechanics in the classroom. It sees a need to explore the impact since the age range of secondary school learners is categorised under people who use social media extensively (Shaku, 2021; Statista, 2023). Since previous analysis of the impact of social media was done only on the English language, this study examines the impact of social media on the writing of the Sepedi language. The Sepedi language is a case of the study as it is the official language in South Africa (National Language Policy Framework of South Africa) and a third largest language spoken in South Africa with 9.7% outside home usage and 10.1% inside-home usage (Statista, 2023). The language is also taught in public schools (South Africa. Department of Education, 2011). The angle taken by this paper is significant as it demonstrates that social media does not only affect the English language, as established by Majola, Pillay and Hlongwane (2019), Marwa and Sabrina (2017), Thubakgale and Chaka (2016), Steyn and Van Greunen (2015), Odey, Essoh and Endong (2014), Risto (2014), Farina and Lyddy (2011), Barasa (2010), and Mphahlele and Mashamaite (2005), but also other languages.

2. Social Media in the 21st Century

According to Al-Tarawneh (2014:1), "social media is the fastest-growing web application in the 21st century. The nature of applications like Wikis, video streaming and applications, and social networks makes it the phenomenon of the century". In South Africa, popular social media platforms include Facebook, YouTube, WhatsApp, Instagram, WeChat, TikTok, Telegram, Snapchat, X, and Linkedin.

The growing trend is that teenagers are the leading participants in social networking platforms, (Al-Tarawneh, 2014). Allison (2013) emphasises a strong association among young people, popular culture, and digital technology. This is explained as a bond brought about by the availability of MP3 players, games, the internet, digital film and television, mobile phones, and apps. Thurairaj, Hoon, Roy and Fong (2015) also note the domination of social media, as they explain that it has become the main form of communication in the 21st century.

CMC makes the world to be a connected village through social media platforms such as Facebook, Twitter, WhatsApp, and LinkedIn. People from different geographical areas, races, educational levels, and ages get connected through social media (Ali, Iqbal, & Iqbal, 2016). Ali et al. (2016) hold that social media plays an important role in people's lives; however, it also affects them positively and negatively. People are exposed to either positive or negative effects of social media as they use it for learning, entertainment, and innovation purposes. More often, language finds itself on the receiving end of social media's negative effects.

The following section presents some of the negative markers of social media observed from school learners' use of language in the classroom.

3. Textism and Writing Mechanics

The studies of McSweeney (2016:109), De Jonge and Kemp (2012), Odey et al. (2014:93), Go´mez-Camacho, Hunt- Go´mez and Valverde- Macías (2017), Lyddy, Farina, Hanney, Farrell and O'Neill (2014, and Verheijen (2013) reveal that, more often, textism appears in the following forms:

- Use of abbreviations and acronyms;
- Words contraction, shortening of words, and vowel omission;
- Capitalisation;

- Spelling and typo errors; and
- Punctuation.

3.1 Abbreviations

The use of abbreviations and acronyms dates to the history of non-formal writing settings (McSweeney, 2016), mostly during notes taking, list-making, and letter writing. With the inception of short messaging services (SMS) and social media in the 1990s, the use of abbreviations and acronyms became widespread and continued even today. When writers use abbreviations, they shorten words or phrases – 'Laughing Out Loud' to 'LOL' (Marwa and Sabrina, 2017). This is closely related to word contraction and vowel omission, presented below.

3.2 Word Contraction and Vowel Omission

Social media users shorten words to form contracted words or omit letters either at the beginning or the end of a word (De Jonge and Kemp, 2012). Odey et al. (2014:93) point out that "vowel deletion is often used for the purposes of brevity. Vowel deletion occurs when the texter create a contracted version of the word(s) he/she intends to use. While the vowels of the intended words are omitted, the consonants are maintained to represent the whole word". The instance of contraction can be seen when a phrase like 'how is it' is written as 'howzit' and 'what is up' is changed to 'whatsup'.

3.3 Capitalisation Errors

In the case of capitalisation errors, words are usually written without appropriate capital letters or with extra capitalisation (Lyddy, Farina, Hanney, Farrell & O'Neill, 2014; Verheijen, 2013). A more noticeable scenario is when social media users use a capital letter in the middle of a sentence or write a whole word, sentence, or paragraph using capital letters (Yi Kay, Jing Kai & Yew Hor, 2014). Thus, even when words are not proper nouns, they are initiated by capital letters in the middle of a sentence. Similarly, proper nouns are initiated by lowercase.

3.4 Punctuating

In addition, punctuation marks are usually disregarded when social media users text; this is because the focus is put on information sharing rather than grammatical aspects (Odey et al., 2014; Lima, Majo, & Nseme, 2017; Sherman & Švelch, 2015). Thus, punctuation marks such as quotation marks, commas, and periods are not prioritised when language is used on social media. Verheijen (2013) and Yi Kay et al. (2014) postulate that punctuation errors on social media do not only involve the punctuation being left out of a sentence but also involve their reduplication (extension). When such happens, their purposes shift from being grammatical markers to emotional markers. In other situations, punctuation marks are replaced by emoticons (Kemp, Wood, & Waldron, 2014).

3.5 Social Media and Education

After the identified control taken by social media and its impact on the use of language, teaching and learning of language becomes vulnerable (Thurairaj et al., 2015). This is evident in the shift from the appropriate use of language, which puts the language grammar (sentence construction, punctuation marks, etc) and orthography at risk. The studies of Singh, Gupta, and Tuteja (2015), Tayebinik and Puteh (2012), and Maryam and Marlia (2012) report that social media affected and continues to affect the youth negatively. The results of such impact include smartphone addiction, poor time management, and poor academic performance. Youth or teenagers (most of whom are still learners/students) spend most of their time participating on social media, which seems to be a daily activity (Datareportal,2023). Nevertheless, Al-Tarawneh (2014) enlightens that social media have both advantages (improving productivity, communication, and injecting fun into the educational system) and disadvantages (addiction, wasting time, and isolation from physical society) in students' lives. Therefore, although authors discovered a shortfall of social media usage by the youth, there is still hope for the potential benefits of social media on youth. Thus, social media could be used to improve youth's lives, benefiting them educationally and socially.

The aim of this paper is to explore the impact of social media on secondary learners' writing of the Sepedi language in the classroom. The focus of this paper is relevant and significant since the engaged literature presented the detriment of social media on the youth.

4. Theoretical Underpinning

One of the assumptions of Gerbner's (1976) cultivation theory is that mass media platforms such as social media often cultivate the minds of their consumers. This paper is conceptualised through Gerbner's theoretical lenses to understand the aftermath of social media language consumption. In the context of this paper, the cultivation theory suggests that the longevity of youth's presence on social media puts them at risk of being affected negatively. Thus, the more they are exposed to textism on social media, the more such kind of language would reflect in their academic writing (Singh, Gupta, & Tuteja, 2015). Making inferences from the study of Tayebinik and Puteh (2012) and Maryam and Marlia (2012), the negative repercussions of social media could be linked to learners' poor academic writing of the Sepedi language, affecting their academic performance. The theory becomes relevant in the context of secondary school learners as Statista (2023) and Datareportal (2023) position them at the centre of social media content consumption. The theory is used to illustrate how school learners' consumption of social media content such as ungrammatical language affects their language in the classroom.

5. Methodology

This paper used qualitative research inquiry to explore the perceptions and experiences of secondary school learners regarding the possible impact of social media on their writing of the Sepedi language in the classroom (Kumar, 2019). The research inquiry allowed me to collect data from secondary schools – the site where learners as participants and consumers of social media are found (Creswell, 2014).

5.1 Research Setting

I collected data from 20 learners in Limpopo Province, South Africa. The learners were randomly selected from two secondary schools. These learners were from Grades 10 and Grade 11 and were taught the Sepedi language as their home language. All learners who participated in the study confirmed that they were active on social media.

5.2 Instruments

I used semi-structured focus group interviews to engage with 20 learners from selected secondary schools. The focus group interviews were guided by the following questions:

- Are you using any social media platform for socialising with your peers after school hours?
- What is your favourite social media platform?
- What do you do most of the time when you have logged into a social media platform?
- Do you follow grammar rules when texting or writing statuses on social media?
- What type of language do your peers or friends use on social media to text or share thoughts? Is it a formal or informal language?
- Do you sometimes use social media language unconsciously when writing in a formal setting like school?
- Do you think your exposure and use of unconventional language on social media might be affecting your writing of Sepedi language in the classroom?

5.3 Data Analysis

I analysed the collected data through thematic analysis – a data analysis strategy that allowed me to categorise learners' responses into similar themes (Given, 2008; Kumar, 2019; Creswell & Creswell, 2018).

6. Results

The results of the paper show that secondary school learners use social media to communicate with friends and family outside of school hours. WhatsApp, Facebook, and X emerged as the mostly used social media platforms., with WhatsApp topping the list. It also appeared that learners use both their home language (Sepedi) and English on social media.

The data also show that learners do not follow grammar rules when texting on social media. However, some of the learners indicated that they use correct grammar on social media. The learners who participated informed that their peers also use informal language (different from the one used in a schooling environment) during communication on social media. Moreover, learners also admitted that social media affects their use of language in the classroom. They indicated that it destroys their minds as they sometimes use textism and forget that they must use formal language in the classroom. Besides the identified negative effects of social media, some learners indicated that they are aware of the impact of social media, and they try to avoid grammatical blunders in the classroom. Ultimately, learners' use of textism in the classroom leads to poor academic performance of the Sepedi language.

7. Discussion of Findings

Grade 10 and Grade 11 learners are affected by social media positively and negatively. Both types of the impacts will be discussed separately.

7.1 Positive Impacts

On a positive note, it has been discovered that learners use social media as a teaching and learning platform. They use it as a channel to share academic information such as question papers and memoranda, and to communicate with their peers about school-related topics. Therefore, social media becomes an instrumental tool that connects learners and enables teaching and learning to continue out of the classroom. Social media has become a convenient tool for information sharing because learners are able to communicate and have instant feedback.

7.2 Negative Impacts

Regarding the negative impact, learners are affected by their imitation of social media language in the classroom. This imitation results from an extensive use of textism (ungrammatical language on social media), which leads to the reproduction of similar language in the classroom. It shows that the regular use of ungrammatical language on social media has an impact on the writing reflexes of learners as texters, and it influences them to use social media language even in the classroom (Odey et al., 2014). Considering this, it has been discovered that learners transfer writing errors such as incorrect use of punctuation marks, sentence structuring (syntax), spelling, and orthography from social media to the classroom. Such writing errors may be intentional or unintentional. They may be intentional because learners assume that teachers will understand their writing. Again, their writing may be unintentional because their minds are accustomed to ungrammatical writing on social media; even if they write ungrammatically, they do not realise it.

The aftermath of using textism in the classroom is realised during the post-classroom assessment. More often, learners become aware of their writing transgressions after teachers have assessed their work and scored them lower. It was also revealed that learners are aware of the impact of social media on their writing of the Sepedi language in the classroom. Although teachers continually make learners aware of acceptable and unacceptable language, learners' language usage does not show improvement. The cultivation theory explains that this is a case because learners are habituated to ungrammatical writing. Consequently, it becomes difficult for them to adjust back to conventional writing. Furthermore, learners' incompetence in the writing of the Sepedi language in the classroom affects their academic performance; this is because teachers deduct marks when learners' written work contains errors. Writing mechanics (such as the use of punctuation marks, syntax, and spelling) are usually allocated between 15 and 20 marks. Therefore, if learners' written work is full of errors, they are at risk of losing the marks. Nonetheless, some learners can distinguish between social media language and classroom language. With such learners, there is no transfer of ungrammatical language from social media to the classroom.

8. Mass Media Cultivation Effects and the Impact of External Factors

The above discussions support Gerbner's (1976) argument that mass media (including social media) can cultivate people's behaviour. Grades 10 and 11 learners agree that their consumption of social media language affects how they write the Sepedi language in the classroom. The learners argued that:

Re fele re šomiša mongwalo wa social media. Re šetše re tlwaetše go ngwala ka mokgwa wo re nyakago, ka hlogong re no re morutiši le yena o tla kwešiša se re se ngwalago. Like ka gore re šomiša social media, ge re ngwala ditaodišo re fele re lebala mantšu a nnete gomme re šomiša ao re a šomišago Facebook. Ke gore menagano ya rena e šetše e tlwaetše. Le English le yona re a e šotekhatha. Ka English essay o kereye re ngwala se mxit, then ga e sharp. (We usually use social media language. We are used to writing as we wish; in our minds, we conclude that a teacher will understand what we wrote. Because of the use social media, when we write essays, we often forget the correct words and we opt for what we use on Facebook. This is because our minds are already accustomed to social media language. In the English subject, we also use shortcuts. In English essays, we often write as if we are writing on Mxit and this is not correct).

The above excerpt shows that the more learners remain active on social media, the more their language in the classroom gets affected. Nonetheless, to some learners the notion of social media cultivation is not the case because they have writing consciousness; thus, when they are on social media, they use textism, but in the classroom they write well without distractions.

9. Conclusion and Limitation

The introduction of social media lead to textism – a writing style used on different social media platforms. Textism is not reduced to English as an international language; other languages such as South African languages also adjusted to textism. This led to a distinct usage of writing mechanics; therefore, one can draw a clear line between unconventional language used on social media and conventional language used in official settings such as the schooling environment.

Social media users' prolonged usage of textism cultivates their minds. Ultimately, some social media users transfer textism from social media to the schooling environment. This is because their minds are accustomed to using textism, hence the conscious and unconscious use in the official setting. As a result, the quality of language written by learners declines and their academic performance drops down.

This paper explored the impact of social media on Grades 10 and 11 learners' application of writing mechanics in the classroom. Many studies showed that there is an existing impact (positive and negative) of social media on the English language (how it is used in official settings such as schooling). This study informs that other world languages such as Sepedi are not immune to the effects of social media. Therefore, it is necessary for researchers to further explore the relationship between language and social media. Research needs to look at how social media becomes a destruction to social elements like language learning and how it aids as a tool through which people learn and share important information. However, the above-mentioned findings cannot be generalised because the study does not represent all the secondary schools and learners in South Africa. Moreover, the focus was only on the Sepedi language and its learners.

References

Ali, A ., Iqbal, A. and Iqbal, K. (2016) "Effects of social media on youth: A case study in the University of Sargodha", *International Journal of Advanced Research*, Vol. 4, No. 11, pp 69-73.

Allison, S. (2013). "Youth and the (potential) power of social media". *Youth Studies Australia*, Vol. 32, No. 3, pp 69-73.

Al-Tarawneh, H.A. (2014) "The influence of social networks on students' performance", *Journal of Emerging Trends in Computing and Information Sciences*, Vol. 5, No.3, pp 200-205.

Barasa, S.N. (2010) *Language, Mobile Phones and Internet: A Study of SMS Texting, Email, IM and SNS Chats in Computer Mediated-Communication (CMC) in Kenya.* Utrecht: LOT.

Creswell, J.W. (2014) *Research Design: Qualitative, quantitative, and mixed approaches* (4th ed). Thousand Oaks, CA: SAGE Publications.

Creswell, J.W., and Creswell, J.D. (2018) *Research design: Qualitative, quantitative, and mixed approaches* (5th ed). Los Angeles, London, New Delhi, Singapore, Washington DC, and Melbourne: SAGE Publications.

Crystal, D. (2008) "Texting". *English Language Teaching Journal*, Vol. 62, No. 1, pp 77 – 83.

Datareportal, *Digital 2023 Global Digital Overview.* (2023) Retrieved April, 2023, from https://datareportal.com/.

De Jonge, S., and Kemp, N. (2012) "Text-message abbreviations and language skills in high school and university students", *Journal of Research in Reading,* Vol. 35, No. 1, pp 49-68.

Dyers, C., and Davids, G. (2015). "Post-modern 'languagers': the effects of texting by university students on three South African languages", *Southern African Linguistics and Applied Language Studies, 33*(1), 21-30.

Farina, F., and Lyddy, F. (2011) "The language of text messaging: "Linguistic ruin" or Resource?", *The Irish Psychologist,* Vol 37, No. 6, pp 145-149.

Gerbner, G., and Gross, L. (1976) "Living with television: The violence profile", *Journal of Communication*, Vol. 26, No. 2, pp 172–199.

Given, L.M. (2008) *The SAGE encyclopaedia of qualitative research methods.* Vol 1 and 2. Los Angeles, London, New Delhi, and Singapore: SAGE Publications.

Go´mez'-Camacho, A, Hunt- Go´mez', C.I. and Valverde- Macías, A. (2017) "Textisms, texting, and spelling in Spanish", *Lingua Vol. 201*, pp 92-101, https://www.sciencedirect.com/science/article/pii/S0024384117301675?via%3Dihub.

Goldstuck., A. SA Social Media Landscape. (2018). Retrieved June 2023, from https://website.ornico.co.za.

Kemp, P., Wood, C. and Waldron, S. (2014) "Do I know it's wrong: children's and adults' use of unconventional grammar in text messaging?", *Reading and Writing: An Interdisciplinary Journal,* Vol. 27, No. 9, pp 1585-1602.

Kumar, R. (2019) *Research methodology: A step-by-step guide for beginners* (5th ed). Los Angeles, London, New Delhi, Singapore, Washington DC and Melbourne: SAGE Publications.

Lima, B.K.L.T., Majo, M.P. and Nseme, S.N. (2017) "Implications of text messaging on students' language skills: The case of the University of Buea", *European Journal of English Language and Literature Studies*, Vol. 5, No. 2, pp 1-14.

Lyddy, F., Farina, F., Hanney, J., Farrell, L. and O'Neill, N.K. (2014) "An Analysis of language in University students' text messages", *Journal of Computer-Mediated Communication*, Vol. 19, No. 3, pp 546-561.

Majola, N., Pillay, P., and Hlongwane, M. (2019) "The Relationship between Texting and Language Development amongst Intermediate Phase Learners in Uthungulu District in Kwazulu-Natal, South Africa", *African Renaissance*, Vol. 16, No. 1, pp 27-40.

Marwa, B. and Sabrina, B.D.A. (2017) *The impact of social media on students' academic writing in the Department of English at Tlemcen University* (Unpublished master's degree in Language Studies). University of Tlemcen: Democratic and Popular Republic of Algeria.

McSweeney, M.A. (2016) *Literacies of bilingual youth: A profile of bilingual academic, social, and TXT literacies* (Doctor of Philosophy). The City University of New York.

Mittal, R. (2015) "Is texting really hurting our literacy skills: How to overcome its effects", *IOSR Journal of Humanities and Social Science*, Vol. 20, No. 10, pp 1-5.

Mphahlele, M.L. and Mashamaite, K. (2005) "The impact of Short Message Service (SMS) Language on Language Proficiency of Learners and the SMS Dictionaries: A Challenge for Educators and Lexicographers", in Isaías, P., Borg, C., Kommers, P. and Bonanno, P. (eds) *Proceedings of the IADIS International Conference on Mobile Learning* 2005. IADIS Press, Portugal, pp 161–168, IADIS International Conference on Mobile Learning 2005, Qawra, Malta, 1/01/05.

Odey, V.E., Essoh, N.E.G. and Endong, F.P.C. (2014) "Effects of SMS texting on the writing skills of university students in Nigeria: Case of the College of Education Akamkpa", *International Journal of Linguistics and Communication*, Vol. 2, No. 3, pp 83-96.

Omar, A., Miah, M. and Belmasrour, R. (2014) "Effect of technology on writing", *International Journal of Science and Applied Information Technology*, Vol. 3, No. 2, pp 59-70.

Republic of South Africa, (2003). *Department of Arts and Culture: National Language Policy Framework*. Pretoria: Government Printer.

Risto, A. (2014) *The impact of texting and social media on students' academic writing skills* (Doctor of Philosophy in Education). Tennessee State University: Nashville, Tennessee.

Shaku, K. J. (2021). *The impact of social media on the writing of Sepedi in secondary schools*. Ph.D. Thesis. University of South Africa. Available at https://uir.unisa.ac.za/handle/10500/29176 (Doctoral dissertation).

Sherman, T. and Švelch, J (2015) "Grammar Nazis never sleep" Facebook humour and the management of standard written language", *Lang Policy*, Vol. 14., No. 4, pp 315-334.

Shortis, T. (2007). Gr8 txtpectations. English Drama Media.

Singh, S., Gupta, D. and Tuteja, R. (2015) A study of text messaging affects teen literacy and language. XVI Annual Conference Proceedings January, 2015. Retrieved December 2020, from https://www.internationalconference.in/XVI_AIC/TS5C-PDF/17Sima_Singh.pdf.

South Africa. Department of Basic Education. (2011) *Curriculum and Assessment Policy Statement. Sepedi Home Language: Grades 10 – 12*. Pretoria: Government Printing.

Statista, Global social network penetration rate 2023, by region. (2023) Retrieved April 2023, from https://www.statista.com/.

Steyn, J. and Van Greunen, D. (2015) *ICTs for inclusive communities in developing societies*. Newcastle upon Tyne: Cambridge Scholars Publishing.

Taljard, E. and Bosch, S.E. (2006) "A Comparison of Approaches to Word Class Tagging: Disjunctively vs Conjunctively Written Bantu Languages", *Nordic Journal of African Studies*, Vol. 15, No. 4, pp 428 – 442.

Tayebinik, M. and Puteh, M. (2012) "Txt Msg N English language literacy", *Procedia-Social and Behavioural Sciences*, Vol. 66, pp 97-105. Available at SSRN: https://ssrn.com/abstract=2276844.

Thubakgale, K. and Chaka, C. (2016) "Possible effects of text messaging on Grade 11 EFAL learners' written work", *Language Matters,* Vol. 47, No. 2, pp 223-245.

Thurairaj, S., Hoon, E.P., Roy, S.S. and Fong, P.W. (2015) "Reflections of students' language Usage in Social Networking Sites: Making or Marring Academic English", *The Electronic Journal of e-Learning*, Vol. 13, No. 4, pp 302-316.

Van Dijk, C.N., Van Witteloostuijn, M., Vasić, N., Avrutin, S. and Blom, E. (2016) The Influence of Texting Language on Grammar and Executive Functions in Primary School Children. *PLOS ONE, 11*(3): e0152409. https://doi.org/10.1371/journal.pone.0152409.

Van Dijk, T.A. (1998) *Ideology: A multidisciplinary study*. London: SAGE Publication.

Verheijen, L. (2013) "The effects of text messaging and instant messaging on literacy", *English Studies*, Vol. 94, No. 5, pp 582-602.

Yi Kay, C., Jing Kai, F. and Yew Hor, W. (2014) *The impact of social network on English proficiency among students in University Tunku Abdul Rahman (UTAR) Sungai Long, Malaysia* (Bachelor of Economics) Universiti Tunku Abdul Rahman.

Current Leading Social Media Platforms Used by Marketers and its Benefits

Lenka Labudová

University of Ss. Cyril and Methodius in Trnava, Faculty of Mass Media Communication, Slovakia

lenka.labudova@ucm.sk

Abstract: In 2024, focusing on social media in marketing is paramount due to its unparalleled reach, influence, and ability to engage diverse audiences. With consumers increasingly reliant on digital platforms for information and interaction, leveraging social media ensures brands remain visible, relevant, and competitive in an ever-evolving marketplace. This paper provides an analysis of the rapidly evolving landscape of social media marketing, with a focus on discerning trends, data preferences, and strategic platform utilization among marketers worldwide. The research draws upon extensive data collected from diverse industries, aiming to illuminate the shifting strategies employed by marketers to amplify their impact on various social media platforms. Examining trends, as indicated by marketers', constitutes a significant aspect of this study. Furthermore, the paper delves into the types of marketing data deemed indispensable by global marketing decision-makers, categorizing them based on their perceived importance. Additionally, the paper explores the domains where enhancing marketing data quality is believed to yield the most substantial benefits according to decision-makers in marketing roles across the globe. Moreover, the research endeavors to uncover the social media platforms perceived to offer the highest return on investment (ROI) by marketers, as well as identifying the platforms considered most critical for their marketing endeavors. We also analyze the leading social media platforms preferred by marketers and outline the primary benefits attributed to the utilization of social media for marketing purposes. The findings of this comprehensive analysis offer invaluable insights for marketers, empowering them to refine their strategies, allocate resources more effectively, and harness the full potential of social media platforms. By providing an overview of emerging trends, data preferences, and platform utilization strategies, this paper serves as a strategic roadmap for marketers navigating the ever-evolving digital landscape, facilitating the optimization of marketing outcomes and business success.

Keywords: Social media, Marketing, Marketers, Social media trends

1. Literature Background

Bartoloni and Ancillai (2023) claim that social media profoundly affected the dynamics of interactions between companies and customers. Studies have increasingly focused on how firms effectively use social media in their marketing strategies. However, the literature appears highly fragmented. Scholars have tended to investigate individual facets of social media marketing (SMM) behaviours, adopting a narrow perspective on their antecedents and outcomes. The other authors (Sutrisno et al, 2023) see that social media has evolved beyond being merely a tool for social interaction; it has become an integral part of corporate business strategies. This shift has given rise to a dynamic, competitive, and constantly changing business environment. Strengthening online reputation, consumer data analysis, product innovation, online reputation risk management, internal transformation, team collaboration, and fostering an innovative culture are key elements in the concept of optimizing business management strategies in the social media era. If we take look at challenges, Tarigan et al (2023) understand that companies in today's social media era are faced with a number of challenges that are dynamic and multifaceted. These challenges involve fast-changing trend fluctuations, significant shifts in consumer behaviour influenced by intensified interactions on social media platforms, and mounting competitive pressures. The other important information is that (Ohara, 2023) the success of a company now depends not only on the quality of the products or services offered, but also on the extent to which they are able to explore the potential of social media to build and strengthen brand image, establish effective communication with customers, and gain a competitive advantage in a changing market. In the current digital era, social media platforms have become the hub of communication, information sharing, and networking. The evolution of social media has redefined the way people connect and interact, making it an essential tool for individuals and organizations to showcase their skills, products, and services. The 21st century skills are a set of competencies that are essential for success in the present-day world. These skills include critical thinking, communication, collaboration, creativity, and digital literacy. When aligned with social media, these skills have the potential to compound growth for individuals and organizations, says Vangani et al (2023). Zhang et al, (2023) see five major trends in the current social media industry in this form- 1) content is king, and that content is moving to visual; 2) artificial intelligence is key to competitive advantage; 3) network effects still matter, but business model innovation can overcome that barrier; 4) the need to broaden revenue sources; and 5) the strive for the everything app. In this changing environment, social media companies need to adapt and innovate their business models proactively to stay ahead. More than half of the global population now uses social media, says Behrend et al, (2024), this technological ubiquity has transformed the way that individuals communicate and engage with the world around them, and consequently has had drastic effects on modern work. In the 20 years since early social media platforms such as LinkedIn and Myspace were first launched, much research on the consequences of social media has been conducted in the fields of organizational psychology and organizational behavior. Content forms the backbone of social media platforms, with studies indicating that ease of content creation leads to prolonged user engagement. The importance of content extends to its fit across various platforms and its ethical usage, leading researchers like Bashar et al. (2024) to explore optimal content strategies that enhance peer-to-peer interactions and effective corporate responses to consumer content. Building on these content strategies, Wayan, S., M. et al. (2023) highlight advanced social media marketing tactics such as the use of video content, influencer collaborations, and immersive technologies like augmented and virtual reality. These methods not only engage but also retain audience interest through dynamic and responsive content strategies. Such marketing innovations are essential for businesses like those described by Setiawan, A. et al. (2024), who utilize social media to forge robust brand identities and cultivate relationships with potential customers across platforms like Facebook and Instagram. These interactions are pivotal in reinforcing brand values and deepening customer connections.

To optimize these interactions, organizations apply various market research techniques and analytics tools, as noted by Udyakar & Choudhary (2024). This approach enables businesses to personalize content effectively, aligning closely with individual consumer preferences and behaviors, thereby enhancing engagement and ensuring marketing messages resonate deeply with their target audience.

The discourse around social media's impact on business strategies underscores its transformative role in customer-company interactions. Bartoloni and Ancillai (2023) note the significant influence of social media on these dynamics, highlighting a fragmented literature landscape focused narrowly on specific behaviors within social media marketing (SMM). Meanwhile, Sutrisno et al. (2023) argue that social media has evolved into a vital component of corporate strategies, adapting businesses to a dynamic and competitive environment. This includes optimizing elements such as online reputation and innovation, as companies face multifaceted challenges like rapidly changing trends and consumer behaviors as per Tarigan et al. (2023). Ohara (2023) stresses the importance of leveraging social media to enhance brand image and competitive positioning in the market. These shifts reflect broader social media trends towards visual content, artificial intelligence, and innovative business models as essential for staying competitive in the industry (Zhang et al., 2023). Lastly, the integration of 21st-century skills with social media is seen as crucial for organizational and individual growth, highlighting the enduring importance of adaptive strategies in the face of global social media ubiquity (Behrend et al., 2024).

2. Methodology

The aim of the present paper is to determine the current state of social platforms, specifically in the area of use by ordinary users and marketers, based on data from respondents. Emphasis is also placed on the RIO of social platforms and the benefits of social media. The data is drawn from Statista https://www.statista.com/. In the first part of the paper, we focus on current views and knowledge in the field of social networking and its role in the marketing and everyday world. This is followed by a brief methodology of the paper and the statement of the research questions. We then look at specific survey results, which we describe and outline possible future developments in the area under study.

Research questions set for the purpose of these paper are these –

Is Facebook still the most used social platform by ordinary users in the world?

Is Facebook still the most used social platform in the world by marketers?

Determining if Facebook is still the primary choice for marketers worldwide is vital to evaluate its effectiveness in reaching target demographics and achieving marketing objectives. It underscores the platform's viability as a tool for promotional activities, consumer engagement, and advertising reach. It also provides a benchmark against which the utility of emerging platforms can be measured.

Are the most used social platforms in the world also the networks that have a high ROI?

Investigating the correlation between platform usage and return on investment (ROI) is essential for justifying marketing spend and strategy. It aids in discerning whether high user engagement translates into tangible business benefits, such as increased sales or improved brand awareness.

What are the biggest benefits of using social platforms by marketers?

Understanding the primary benefits of social media platforms for marketers is fundamental to comprehending why these tools remain integral to modern marketing strategies. It helps delineate the specific advantages, such as targeted advertising, customer interaction, and direct feedback mechanisms, that make social media an indispensable resource for marketers aiming to optimize their outreach and influence.

3. Results

The landscape of social networking as of January 2024 reveals a diverse ecosystem dominated by several major platforms. Facebook maintains its position as the largest platform worldwide, boasting 3.049 billion monthly active users, while YouTube follows closely with 2.491 billion users, emphasizing its role as the premier video-sharing platform. WhatsApp and Instagram, both owned by Facebook, each boast 2 billion monthly active users, showcasing the social media giant's multifaceted reach. TikTok has surged in popularity with 1.562 billion users, particularly among younger demographics, owing to its short-form video content and algorithm-driven discovery. WeChat continues to dominate in China, with 1.336 billion users, offering a comprehensive array of services beyond messaging. Facebook Messenger remains a popular messaging platform globally with 0.979 billion users. Other notable platforms include Telegram, Snapchat, and Kuaishou, each attracting significant user bases with distinct features and target audiences. Meanwhile, Twitter, Sina Weibo, QQ, and Pinterest round out the list with varying degrees of monthly active users, contributing to the rich tapestry of global social networking. These platforms serve as vital channels for communication, content creation, and community-building, reflecting the evolving nature of digital interaction in the modern age. Release date of this study is from January 2024, data is worldwide, survey time period is January 2024.

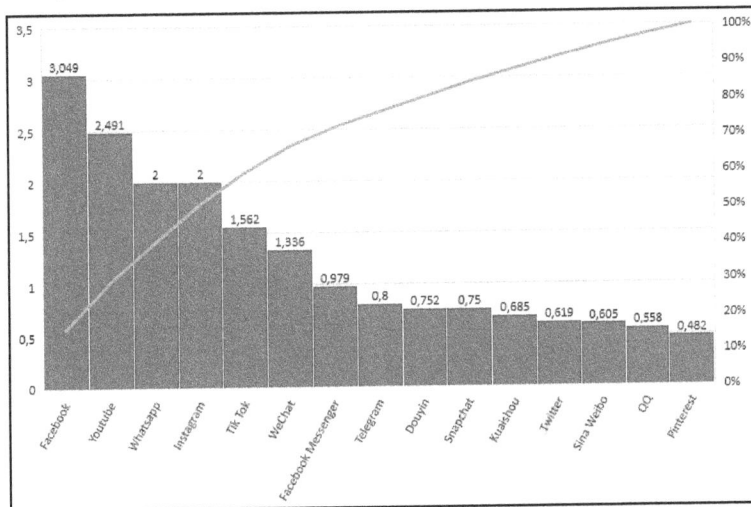

Figure 1: Most popular social networks worldwide as of January 2024, ranked by number of monthly active users (in billions)

Source: Own processing based on https://www.statista.com/statistics/272014/global-social-networks-ranked-by-number-of-users/

The dataset comprises the number of global social media users from 2017 to 2027, measured in billions (Internet users who use a social network site via any device at least once per month), It reveals a consistent upward trend in usership over the specified timeframe. Starting at 2.73 billion users in 2017, there is a noticeable increase each subsequent year. By 2027, the number of social media users reaches 5.85 billion, indicating substantial growth over the decade. This steady expansion suggests a widespread adoption of social media platforms worldwide. The data underscores the pervasive influence and importance of social media in contemporary society. Survey time period of this study is 2017 – 2022, region is worldwide.

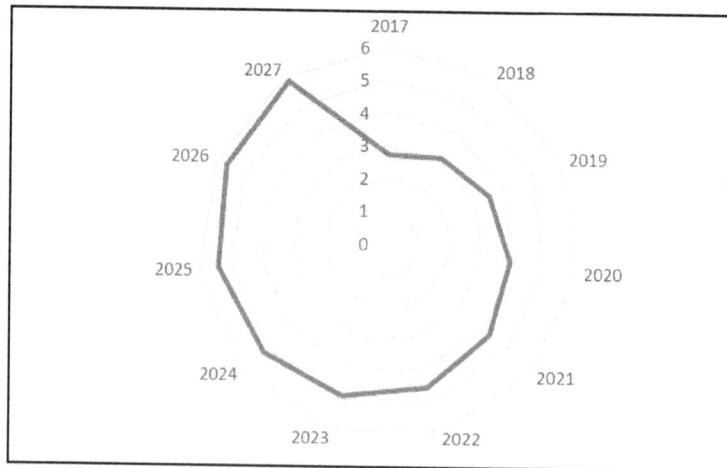

Figure 2: Number of social media users worldwide from 2017 - 2027 (in billions)

Source: Own processing based on https://www.statista.com/statistics/278414/number-of-worldwide-social-network-users/

As of September 2023, marketers (among global marketers from across B2B and B2C companies) worldwide identified Facebook and Instagram as the social media platforms with the highest return on investment (ROI), both yielding an ROI of 29%. Following closely behind, YouTube and TikTok boasted ROIs of 26% and 24%, respectively. LinkedIn and X (formerly Twitter) shared an ROI of 16%, indicating significant returns for marketers utilizing these platforms. Snapchat and Pinterest exhibited lower ROIs of 6%, while Twitch trailed slightly behind at 5%. Meanwhile, Tumblr recorded the lowest ROI among the listed platforms, with only 2%. These findings highlight the effectiveness of Facebook-owned platforms, as well as the growing influence of video-centric platforms like YouTube and TikTok in generating returns for marketers. Number of respondents of this study represent 1460 wordwide, survey time period is September 2023.

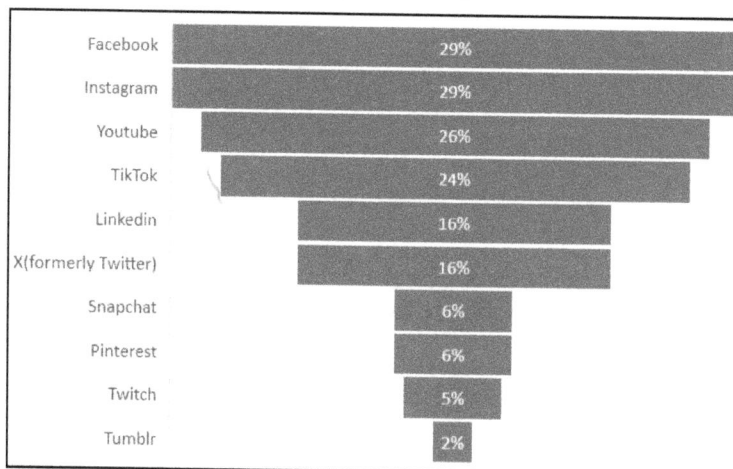

Figure 3: Social media platforms with the largest return on investment (ROI) accordint to marketers worldwide as of September 2023

Source: Own processing based on https://www.statista.com/statistics/1284484/social-media-platforms-highest-return-on-investment/

The data presents the leading social media platforms utilized by marketers worldwide as of January 2023 (63% of marketers work in B2C, 37% in B2B), measured by the percentage of marketers who employ each platform in their strategies. Facebook emerges as the dominant platform, with a substantial 89% of marketers incorporating it into their marketing efforts. Following closely behind is Instagram, with 80% of marketers leveraging its features for promotional purposes. LinkedIn ranks third in usage among marketers, with 64% utilizing the professional networking platform to engage with their target audience. YouTube and Twitter also exhibit significant adoption rates, with 54% and 44% of marketers utilizing these platforms, respectively. TikTok, a relatively newer entrant into the social media landscape, demonstrates a notable presence among marketers, with 26% incorporating it into their marketing strategies. Number of respondents of this study is 2133 worldwide, survey time period is January 2023.

Table 1: Leading social media platforms used by marketers worldwide as of January 2023

Social media platform	Usage by marketers in %
Facebook	89%
Instagram	80%
Linkedin	64%
Youtube	54%
Twitter	44%
TikTok	26%

Source: Own processing based on https://www.statista.com/statistics/259379/social-media-platforms-used-by-marketers-worldwide/

The data outlines the primary benefits of utilizing social media for marketing purposes worldwide, as of January 2023 (63% of marketers work in B2C, 37% in B2B.), expressed as percentages representing the prevalence of each benefit among marketers (multiple answers were possible). The most prominent benefit identified is "Increased exposure," with a substantial 86% of marketers acknowledging the platform's effectiveness in enhancing brand visibility and reach. Following closely behind is "Increased traffic," cited by 76% of marketers, indicating social media's role in driving users to websites or other digital properties. "Generated leads" emerge as another significant benefit, with 64% of marketers recognizing social media's capacity to generate potential customers or clients. Additionally, "Developed loyal fans" is noted by 56% of marketers, highlighting social media's ability to cultivate a dedicated following and foster brand loyalty. "Improved sales" rounds out the list, acknowledged by 55% of marketers, indicating the platform's contribution to driving conversions and boosting revenue. Release date of this study was June 2023, number of respondents represent 2133 worldwide.

Table 2: Leading benefits of using social media for marketing purposes worldwide as of January 2023

The benefits	
Increased exposure	86%
Increased traffic	76%
Generated leads	64%
Developed loyal fans	56%
Improved sales	55%

Source: Own processing based on https://www.statista.com/statistics/188447/influence-of-global-social-media-marketing-usage-on-businesses/

The data presents planned changes in the use of selected social media platforms for marketing purposes worldwide, as reported by marketers (63% of marketers work in B2C, 37% in B2B), with percentages indicating the proportion of respondents intending to increase, maintain, decrease, or abstain from utilizing each platform.

For Facebook, 53% of marketers express intentions to increase their usage for marketing purposes, indicating a notable inclination towards leveraging the platform's capabilities for brand promotion. A substantial 32% plan to maintain their current level of utilization, reflecting the platform's enduring relevance in marketing strategies. Conversely, only 5% of marketers anticipate decreasing their use of Facebook, suggesting a prevailing confidence in its efficacy. Meanwhile, 10% of marketers have no immediate plans to utilize Facebook for marketing.

Similar trends are observed for Instagram and YouTube, with 66% and 65% of marketers respectively intending to increase their usage, highlighting the platforms' growing importance in marketing strategies. Both platforms also exhibit low percentages of marketers planning to decrease their usage (3% for Instagram and 2% for YouTube), indicating a strong preference for maintaining or enhancing their presence. However, 10% of marketers for both platforms report no plans to utilize them for marketing purposes.

LinkedIn shows a slightly different pattern, with 48% of marketers intending to increase their usage, indicative of its importance for professional networking and B2B marketing. A notable proportion (22%) of marketers have no immediate plans to utilize LinkedIn, suggesting potential areas for growth or untapped opportunities within the platform.

Twitter displays lower rates of planned increases in usage compared to other platforms, with only 22% of marketers intending to do so. Additionally, 9% of marketers plan to decrease their usage of Twitter, possibly reflecting evolving preferences or challenges associated with the platform's effectiveness in certain marketing contexts. A significant portion (40%) of marketers report no plans to utilize Twitter for marketing, indicating a perceived mismatch between its capabilities and their marketing objectives.

TikTok emerges as a platform with notable potential for growth, with 43% of marketers planning to increase their usage, underscoring its rising prominence in marketing strategies. However, a sizable proportion (45%) of marketers report no plans to utilize TikTok for marketing, suggesting varying levels of readiness or apprehension regarding its suitability for their brand or target audience. Survey time period is January 2023 with 2133 respondents worldwide

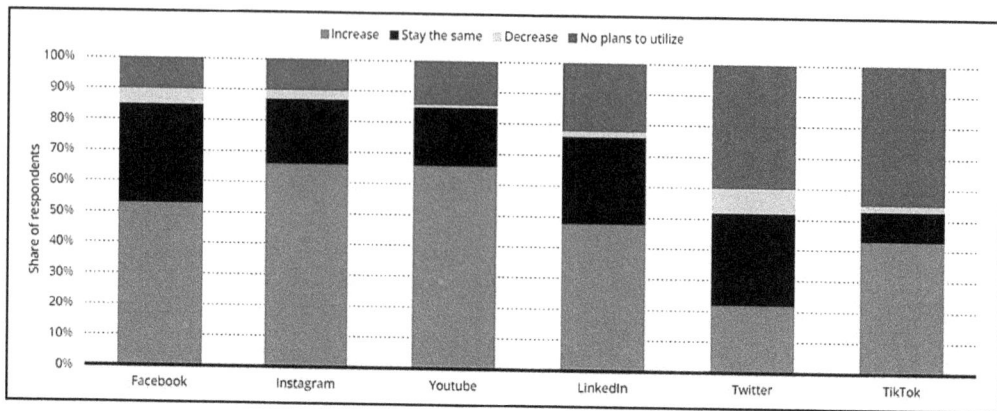

Figure 4: Planned changes in use of selected social media for marketing purposes worldwide as of January 2023 (in percentage)

Source: Own processing based on https://www.statista.com/statistics/258974/future-use-of-social-media-among-marketers-worldwide-by-platform/

The global landscape of social media in January 2024 shows a diverse ecosystem led by major platforms such as Facebook, with 3.049 billion monthly active users, and YouTube at 2.491 billion. Instagram and WhatsApp also hold significant shares with 2 billion users each. TikTok has rapidly grown to 1.562 billion users, popular among the youth for its short-form videos. WeChat dominates in China with 1.336 billion users, and Facebook Messenger has 0.979 billion users globally. Other platforms like Telegram, Snapchat, and Kuaishou have substantial user bases with unique features. The data from 2017 to 2027 indicates a consistent increase in social media users worldwide, forecasting 5.85 billion by 2027. Marketers find Facebook and Instagram to offer the highest ROI, significantly impacting marketing strategies. The primary benefits of using social media for marketing include increased exposure, traffic, leads, loyalty, and sales. Current trends show a growing inclination among marketers to enhance their use of these platforms to capitalize on their vast potential for brand promotion and audience engagement.

4. In Conclusion

The analysis of data reveals dynamic trends in the utilization of social media platforms for marketing purposes worldwide.Facebook and Instagram emerge as the dominant platforms, offering marketers unparalleled opportunities for increased exposure and engagement. YouTube and LinkedIn also command significant usage among marketers, emphasizing the importance of video content and professional networking in contemporary marketing strategies. Meanwhile, Twitter exhibits lower rates of planned increases in usage, potentially indicating shifting preferences or challenges in maximizing its effectiveness for marketing.

The benefits of using social media for marketing purposes are rich, with increased exposure, traffic, lead generation, and the development of loyal fan bases cited as primary advantages. These findings underscore the multifaceted benefits that social media platforms offer marketers in enhancing brand visibility, driving engagement, and ultimately, contributing to business growth.

Looking ahead, the data suggests several noteworthy trends and potential future assumptions. The continued dominance of Facebook-owned platforms, the growing influence of video-centric platforms such as TikTok and

YouTube, and the rise of professional networking platforms like LinkedIn are expected to shape the landscape of social media marketing. Additionally, the emergence of newer platforms and technologies may offer new opportunities for marketers to connect with their target audiences in innovative ways.

The data highlights the indispensable role of social media platforms in modern marketing strategies. With the majority of marketers planning to increase their usage of key platforms such as Facebook, Instagram, and YouTube, it is evident that social media will remain a cornerstone of marketing efforts across industries. The ability to harness the benefits of increased exposure, traffic, and lead generation underscores the significance of social media as a powerful tool for driving business growth and cultivating brand loyalty.

As technology continues to evolve and consumer behaviors evolve in tandem, marketers must remain adaptable and proactive in leveraging emerging trends and platforms to stay ahead of the curve. By understanding current trends, anticipating future developments, and aligning strategies with evolving consumer preferences, businesses can maximize the potential of social media platforms to achieve their marketing objectives and thrive in an increasingly digital-centric landscape.

The analysis of data pertaining to the usage of social media platforms by both ordinary users and marketers, as well as the associated return on investment (ROI) and perceived benefits, offers valuable insights into the future landscape of marketing on social media platforms.

For future marketing on social media platforms, several possible key implications emerge:

Continued Importance of Facebook. Despite the emergence of new platforms and shifts in user preferences, Facebook remains a cornerstone of social media marketing. Its enduring popularity among both ordinary users and marketers, coupled with its high ROI, suggests that Facebook will continue to play a pivotal role in marketing strategies.

Rise of Visual Platforms. Platforms such as Instagram and TikTok, which prioritize visual content, have seen significant growth and are favored by marketers for their high ROI. This trend underscores the increasing importance of visual storytelling and short-form video content in capturing audience attention and driving engagement.

Integration of Marketing Strategies. The alignment between the most used social platforms and those with high ROI indicates a convergence between user engagement and marketing effectiveness. Marketers are likely to prioritize platforms that offer both a large user base and strong returns on investment, leading to a more integrated approach to social media marketing.

Focus on Benefits. The identified benefits of using social platforms for marketing, including increased exposure, traffic, leads, loyal fans, and sales, underscore the multifaceted advantages that social media offers for businesses. Future marketing strategies are likely to continue leveraging these benefits to enhance brand visibility, drive engagement, and ultimately, achieve business objectives.

Research questions set for the purpose of the paper were as we mentioned in methodology, and are answered below.

Is Facebook still the most used social platform by ordinary users in the world?

According to the data provided, Facebook maintains its position as one of the most widely used social media platforms, with consistently high monthly active user counts. While other platforms such as Instagram and TikTok have seen significant growth, Facebook remains a dominant force in the social media landscape.

Is Facebook still the most used social platform in the world by marketers?

Yes, Facebook continues to be one of the most utilized social platforms by marketers, as indicated by the high percentage of marketers planning to increase their usage of the platform for marketing purposes. Instagram, another platform owned by Facebook, also ranks high among marketers, underscoring the continued importance of Facebook-owned properties in marketing strategies.

Are the most used social platforms in the world also the platforms that have a high ROI?

The data indicates that platforms like Facebook, Instagram, and YouTube, which are among the most used social platforms globally, also exhibit high returns on investment (ROI) according to marketers. These platforms consistently rank among the top in terms of planned increases in usage and perceived ROI, suggesting a correlation between platform usage and ROI.

What are the biggest benefits of using social platforms by marketers?

The primary benefits identified by marketers in using social media platforms for marketing purposes include increased exposure, increased traffic, generated leads, developed loyal fans, and improved sales. These benefits underscore the multifaceted advantages that social media offers in enhancing brand visibility, driving engagement, and ultimately, contributing to business growth.

Acknowledgements

This contribution is a partial result of the project Vega no. 1/0304/24 The impact and value of digitization of product marketing communication innovations for generations of ecological users.

References

Bartoloni, S., & Ancillai, C. (2023) "Twenty years of social media marketing: A systematic review, integrative framework, and future research agenda", *International Journal of Management Reviews*, pp. 12 – 30.

Bashar, A., Wasiq, M., Nyagadza, B., & Maziriri, E. T. (2024). "Emerging Trends in Social Media Marketing: A Retrospective Review Using Data Mining and Bibliometric Analysis", *Journal of Contemporary Trends in Marketing*, Vol 10, No 1, pp. 1-26.

Behrend, T. S., Ravid, D. M., & Thapa, S. (2024) "Implications of Social Media for a Changing Work Landscape", *Annual review of organizational psychology and organizational behavior*, Vol 11, pp 337-361.

Kumar, U., & Choudhary, R. A. (2024). "Navigating the Social Media Landscape: Strategies for Effective Marketing Engagement", Mit World Peace University, Faculty of Management, Batch 22-24

Maitri, W. S., Suherlan, S., Prakosos, R. D. Y., Subagja, A. D., & Ausat, A. M. A. (2023). "Recent Trends in Social Media Marketing Strategy", *Jurnal Minfo Polgan*, Vol 12, No. 1, pp. 842-850.

Setiawan, A., Mubarok, A., Efendi, E., & Globalisasi, S. E. (2024). "The Trend of Using Social Media Technology for Business Actors for the Branding Process", Technium Romanian Journal of Applied Sciences and Technology, Vol 20, pp. 42-48.

Statista.com https://www.statista.com/

Sutrisno, S., Purnomo, S. H., & Purba, J. H. V. (2023) "Optimizing Business Management Strategies in the Social Media Era: Facing New Year Challenges with Digital-Based Excellence", *Journal of Contemporary Administration and Management (ADMAN)*, Vol 1, No. 3, pp 251–257.

Tarigan, I. M., Harahap, K. M. A., Sari, D. M., Sakinah, R. D., & Ausat, A. M. A. (2023) "Understanding Social Media: Benefits of Social Media for Individuals", *Journal Pendidikan Tambusai*, Vol 7, No. 1, pp 2317–2322.

Ohara, M. R. (2023) "The Role of Social Media in Educational Communication Management", *Journal of Contemporary Administration and Management (ADMAN)*, Vol 1, No. 2, pp 70-76.

Vangani, N., Makwana, H., Radia, P., & Nanavati, K. (2023) "Role of 21st Century Skills Aligned with social media for Compounding Growth", *International Journal for Research in Applied Science & Engineering Technology (IJRASET)*, Vol 11, No. 3, pp 107-111.

Zhang, Y., Nguyen, H. W., Jung, Y. H., & Ren, I. Y. (2023) "The social media industry: where is it heading?", *Journal of Business Strategy*, Vol 45, No. 2, pp 81-88.

www.ingramcontent.com/pod-product-compliance
Lightning Source LLC
Chambersburg PA
CBHW082304210326

41598CB00028B/4437